The Lives of
ENOCH POWELL

Patrick Cosgrave

W0007468

Pan Books
in association with The Bodley Head

This one is – and only could be – for Shirley

First published 1989 by The Bodley Head Ltd, London
This edition published 1990 by Pan Books Ltd,
Cavaye Place, London SW10 9PG
in association with the Bodley Head Ltd

9 8 7 6 5 4 3 2 1

ISBN 0 330 31437 8
Printed in England by Clays Ltd, St Ives plc

Contents

List of Illustrations

Cartoons are reproduced by kind permission of: Cummings, courtesy of Express Newspapers, PLC (pages 256, 276, 309, 346, 422), Franklin, courtesy of *The Daily Telegraph* (page 274), Garland, courtesy of Rex Features (page 344), Richard Wilson © *The Times* (page 432)

He nothing common did or mean
Upon that memorable scene
   But with his keener eye
   The axe's edge did try.

Andrew Marvell

Preface

We in our day ought well to guard, as highly to honour, the parent stem of England, and its royal talisman; for we know not what branches yet that wonderful tree will have the power to put forth. The danger is not always violence and force: them we have withstood before and can withstand again. The peril can also be indifference and humbug, which might squander the accumulated wealth of tradition and devalue our sacred symbolism to achieve some cheap compromise or some evanescent purpose.

> – *J. Enoch Powell to the Royal Society of St George,*
> *22 April 1961.*

John Enoch Powell has attracted more attention – supportive and hostile – than any other British politician of our time. He has exercised a greater fascination, for commentators and public alike, than any of his contemporaries. He has done so for a longer period of time than have any of them. And he has done so – this is one of the most singular things about him – without holding more than relatively junior office, and that for brief periods: he served only fifteen months (as Minister of Health) in a Cabinet, that of Harold Macmillan.

His critics (and some of his supporters) believe that all this dates only from April 1968, when his Birmingham speech on immigration created what amounted to a thermonuclear political explosion, and procured his instant dismissal from the Conservative Shadow Cabinet led by Edward Heath. There is undoubtedly

1

some truth in this, and it is proper to remember it. But two other points should be made as well.

First, from the moment of his entry to the House of Commons as Member for Wolverhampton South-West after the general election of 1950 Powell was, and was seen by his colleagues to be, a man apart. He never hesitated to provoke major controversy by taking an independent stand, and he had the unexampled temerity to decline office under Churchill. So, though it is true to say that the Birmingham speech was the one that launched him as a major national politician, he had become a figure of substance long before; and everything he did excited interest, if often of a puzzled or hostile kind.

Second, it is a fact (unpalatable though it may be to his enemies) that Powell has been able to maintain his hold on the public and the media for twenty-one years since the 1968 speech. I have already mentioned that he has been able to do so in spite of holding no office, an achievement without parallel in the British democratic system. Moreover, he has done it without being what the Americans call a 'single-issue politician'. At one point – as he told the Banstead Young Conservative Association on 15 February 1971 – he allowed eight months to elapse without a single public reference to immigration, save for a brief intervention in the House of Commons. He was nonetheless able to hold his public audience with speeches, articles and broadcasts on a variety of topics, contributions to debate equalled neither in their number nor their variety by any other public figure this century.

In 1974, further, he abandoned his main platform, when he declined to stand – for reasons that will be more fully examined later – in the general election of February of that year. He returned to the House in the election of the following October, but as an Ulster Unionist, not a Conservative. From the fastness of his constituency in South Down he continued until 1987 on his buccaneering way. Indeed, during the unsteady period of Labour government between October 1974 and June 1979 (when the Conservatives were returned at Westminster with a comfortable overall majority) he used his exceptional skill as a parliamentarian to secure concessions for Ulster which would hitherto have been unimaginable as coming from a Labour government.

There is one other point to make. After the 1970, and again after the 1974 (February and October) general elections Powell (and his friends) claimed that he had turned the issue on each occasion: on the first in the Conservative favour, on the others for Labour. This claim was judged, by most commentators, to be extravagant. In particular, in the Nuffield[1] studies of both elections – successive editions of which constitute a virtual Bible of psephological and electoral studies – Michael Steed dismissed it. Later research (which I will examine in Chapter Six) by R. W. Johnson and Douglas Schoen[2] demonstrated conclusively that Powell's claim was easy to justify, and that it had something, but only something, to do with immigration. Considering that Powell, in February 1974, was no more than a private citizen, that achievement is exceptional. I shall demonstrate later, moreover, that intelligent collusion between Powell and the private office of Harold Wilson – still Labour leader, and striving to overthrow the verdict of 1970 – made sure that this private citizen's impact on events would be of maximum efficiency.

We are dealing, therefore, with no ordinary man, and no ordinary politician. We are certainly – to repeat the phrase – dealing with no 'single-issue politician'. In a brilliant article in *The Times* on 2 August 1976 Geoffrey Smith, having described Powell's platform manner with the most delicate and effective of artistic brushes, went on to say:

> But his skill in communicating comes also from his readiness to take his audiences seriously. In his eve of poll speech in a neighbouring constituency in 1970 . . . he held the rapt attention of some hundreds of the Conservative faithful, predominantly middle class, many of them housewives, with a disquisition on the virtues of a floating exchange rate.

In my judgement most of his enemies (this is not true of so many of his critics) seek to confine themselves and him to the argument on immigration (where they regard him as self-evidently in the wrong) because they cannot tackle him on the multitude of other subjects to which he addresses his mind. In the following pages I hope to give a fuller account than has been given heretofore of the career of this remarkable man. It is not, I believe, an uncritical account, but I hope that, at every stage, I will buttress argument with evidence.

In writing of so protean a figure as Powell one has to depend on help from a wide variety of individuals (and their writings) in different walks of life. Though he is seen (in this book as elsewhere) principally as a politician, he has been, and is, many other things as well. One fascination of working on the book has been the extent to which it has broadened my own reading. (I have not, however, I must confess, gone to the lengths of viewing again the films of the Marx Brothers, or of Jacques Tâti, all of which delight my subject and about all of which – as one might expect – he displays encyclopaedic knowledge.) Many of those consulted did not wish to be named, so I have followed the practice of naming only a very few. Even from the point of view of research, indeed, it was virtually impossible to make an advance list of those whom it might have been profitable to interview. I will give one among many examples. Just after I had started to write I met, at a publishing party, a former Minister whom I knew slightly. He had cropped up once or twice in the Powell archive, as the recipient of a couple of formal letters. It turned out, however, that he had had many conversations with Powell over the years, and had been an acute observer of Powell's parliamentary performance. The conversation was extremely valuable to me.

Two debts, however, I can specifically record, and am delighted to do so.

There have been a number of books written about Powell, from various angles. The first in the field, *Powell: the man and his thinking*, by T. E. Utley, was written at great speed and appeared in 1968. The pressure of so close a deadline (the book was commissioned after Powell's 1968 immigration speech) did nothing to inhibit Mr. Utley's customary clarity of thought, nor did it impede his invariably elegant prose style. Though so much has occurred since that the book is in many obvious ways out of date, it is still well worth reading.

Peter (as he was invariably called) Utley died suddenly in 1988. He was a man of remarkable parts. Blind from childhood, he nonetheless was one of the most distinguished students of his time at Cambridge. Subsequently, he added lustre to the profession of journalism, at the *Spectator*, *The Daily Telegraph* and, in his last years, *The Times*. He was a scholar of politics, but there was nothing about either his personality or his writing which was dull. Even his shortest articles and reviews were the outer expression of a profound mind. He was a Conservative thinker of some considerable importance and, as such, had no little part to play in the intellectual development which preceded the Thatcher era.

But there was more to Peter Utley than that. He was ever ready with a quip or a joke, even about his own affliction, which would have destroyed most men. There was an extraordinary generosity

4

in his nature: no young writer who came to him for advice or assistance was turned away. The advice was always measured, and never less than wise – as I have good cause to know. His passing was mourned not just by his contemporaries, but by countless younger men and women who had benefited from his counsel, conveyed, more often than not, over a glass or two in the Kings' and Keys public house in Fleet Street. When he died it was as though a whole tradition of scrupulous, analytical and – I dare to say it – gentlemanly political writing had died too.

My second literary debt is to Mr. Andrew Roth, for his *Enoch Powell: Tory Tribune* (1970). Mr. Roth was the first writer to attempt a major objective and factual study of Powell's life and (as one would expect from his other work) he was indefatigable in his search for detailed and often recondite information. His book is an indispensable starting point for any serious work on the subject.

I am also grateful to my old friend and literary collaborator, Lt. Col. George Richey, for preparing me a detailed memo on defence policy and, in general, for his advice and instruction on military matters over the years.

The major debt now falls to be recorded. I first met Enoch Powell in 1966, but fairly briefly. I began to get to know him better in 1970, when I became political editor of the *Spectator*. Over the succeeding years we have seen sometimes a lot and sometimes a little of one another. I have written a number of articles about him, usually without consulting him on content or approach. He has written reviews of two of my books, without mentioning either to me before their appearance.

When I broached the present book to him we had lunch together. He was willing to help on generous terms. He allowed me to use a room in his house – which he called, in suitably academic parlance, a 'search room'. He provided me with ready access to the text of his public speeches and all the published material covering the period of his lifetime.

He, further, gave me two extended interviews for the purposes of this book. The text of these interviews is frequently quoted in the following pages. At the lunch to which I have just referred he said that, if I wished, he would read my manuscript. 'Only if you wish. But I will confine myself to drawing attention to errors of omission or fact. I will make no comment as to value.'

He was, however, better than his word. He has read the text, but on the clear understanding that this did not imply that he had noticed all the errors, or that he agreed with, or accepted the contents of the work. It goes without saying that I am responsible for all the statements and views which it contains. When I say that he was better than his word I mean, not merely that his company was enriching, but that he allowed himself to make remarks about my style, some of which made me blush. 'Before I die,' he once said, 'I will try to cure you of your love for the mixed metaphor.'

I have to say here how grateful I am to Powell, to his wife, Pamela, and to his secretary, Monica Wilson, who looked after me, as well as him, on frequent occasions at 33 South Eaton Place.

The history of the most challenging of post-war British politicians will, undoubtedly, be written in a more considered and informed way in the future. This, however, is my offer, in 1989.

Patrick Cosgrave
January 1989

1
The Man
1912–

The life of nations, no less than that of men, is lived
largely in the imagination. It is what an individual
thinks about his life, much more than the objective
condition in which he lives, which determines whether
he will be happy or unhappy and therefore, in the truest
sense, successful or unsuccessful. The same circumstances in which one man is contented and prosperous,
because he has perhaps sought and desired them or
at least regards them as right and fitting, will make
another man violently unhappy, if he considers them
to be the result of personal failure or unjust treatment.
– *J. Enoch Powell, Trinity College,*
Dublin, 13 November 1964.

John Biffen, then Lord Privy Seal and Leader of the House
of Commons, and one of the most widely respected figures in
British public life, wrote to me on 4 July 1986 in response to
a request I had made to come and talk about Enoch Powell.
He readily acceded, and added, 'The longer I hang around in
politics the more fascinated I am by his integrity and his capacity
to elevate.' Of the same man, however, Mr. Anthony Wedgwood
Benn, in the course of an election speech on 3 June 1970, said,
'The flag of racialism which has been hoisted in Wolverhampton
is beginning to look like the one that fluttered twenty-five years
ago over Dachau and Belsen.' The same evening, in a reply to
Wedgwood Benn's speech (given in response to a BBC reporter), Powell said: 'For myself, in 1939 I voluntarily returned

7

from Australia to this country, to serve as a private soldier against Germany and Nazism. I am the same man today.' The writer George Gale delivered a report on Powell's meeting that evening to the *London Evening Standard*. Its opening sentence read, 'A moment of dignity has occurred in this election.' The National Union of Journalists' chapel at the *Standard* sought to black the copy, on the grounds that so evil a man should not be given friendly coverage. In a later account of the fate of his article (which duly appeared, owing to the determination of the editor, Charles Wintour) Gale wrote[1] that he met ' . . . a degree of hostility towards me from journalist friends and acquaintances surprising in its intensity.' Some time later the *Observer*, in a leading article [2] suggested that the British Press should voluntarily agree not to report any of Powell's utterances. This was, to say the least of it, an unexpected argument to come from a newspaper which has consistently prided itself on its advocacy of free speech and full reporting. But it is indicative of the fear and loathing with which Powell was, at the time, regarded by liberal opinion. It would not have been easy, then, to predict that, by 1987, his articles (often adapted from speeches) would be appearing with great regularity in *The Guardian*.

The source of this intense hostility – expressed by many more than Benn, the *Standard* chapel and the *Observer* – was, of course, the 20 April 1968 Birmingham speech on immigration. I do not, myself, believe that the speech was the most important Powell has ever made, nor his most elegantly turned. Nor was it, by any means, the first time he had addressed himself to that subject. He had spoken more forcefully on the matter a little earlier in the year at Walsall. Further back, on 6 April 1966[3], after the general election defeat, he had told the City of London Young Conservatives that immigration was one of the most important subjects the Conservative Party would have to examine as they sought to regroup intellectually during what would certainly be a prolonged period of Labour government. (The Labour Party had gained a majority of 111 over the Conservatives, and 98 over all parties in the March election.) Some, indeed, would trace the origins of his attitude to immigration back as far as his March 1952 attack on the Royal Titles Bill in the House of Commons. The Bill, among other things, removed the word 'British' from the phrase 'British Commonwealth'.[4] The implication of his speech was that those who did not accept the sovereignty of the Crown could have no part of the Crown. In that speech, therefore, lies the essence of

8

his theory of allegiance, and the consistent justification of his eventual opposition to the entry into this country of peoples owing neither political nor cultural allegiance to it. Asked, when the storm began to blow in 1968, whether he was a racialist he replied:

> What I take racialist to mean is a person who believes in the inherent inferiority of one race of mankind to another, and who acts and speaks in that belief. So the answer to the question of whether I am a racialist is no – unless, perhaps, it is to be a racialist in reverse.[5]

None the less, the 1968 speech, in the context of the time, had an explosive effect. That effect was not merely public and national, but personal. 'I did not anticipate the reaction to it,' Powell says, 'but once that reaction had . . . erupted I realized how significant it all was for me. 1968 was important in that after it I never expected to hold office again. Certainly, to put it another way, I was expected never to hold office again. It meant that all possibilities, rules and circumstances were changed, completely.'[6]

Not everybody saw the matter that way at the time. Once Edward Heath won the general election of 1970, and embarked on what initially seemed to be a bold adventure in radical government, Powell seemed consigned to oblivion: during the 1970 campaign, indeed, Heath had made it publicly clear that Powell would in no circumstances be invited to join his administration. In 1972, however, the brave dreams of radical politics which Heath, in his first Party Conference speech as Prime Minister, gathered under the rubric 'the quiet revolution'[7] were trampled underfoot. From then on Powell embarked on a sustained and – some thought – even demoniac attack on virtually every aspect of government policy. Immigration was only one of the subjects touched upon: essentially the quarrel between the Member for Wolverhampton South-West and the Leader of his Party was the drift of the government towards collectivism – especially as this was enshrined in a compulsory incomes policy – and away from the ideals of free enterprise and the rolling back of the state adumbrated in the Conservative manifesto of 1970. Between them there lay, also, the issue of whether or not the United Kingdom ought to join the Common Market: joining was the major cause of Heath's public life; to Powell it was an inconceivable and unacceptable sacrifice of national sovereignty and national identity.

As the clouds of trouble gathered around the government the conflict between the two men intensified. At the Party Conference of 1973 the Chancellor of the Exchequer, Anthony Barber, described Powell as a 'frustrated fanatic'. In the House of Commons Powell asked acidly (during Prime Minister's question time) whether Heath had taken leave of his senses, in a manner that strongly implied mental imbalance on the part of the Prime Minister.[8] Bitterness abounded. The absolute conviction of Powell's enemies – and of most of those who, from a Socialist or left wing point of view disliked and feared him – was that he was seeking to destroy the government for the sake of personal advancement: there were numerous references to '*Colombey les deux Wolverhampton*'. His friends and admirers, naturally, took a very different view: as the government plunged more and more deeply into the morass of inflation and industrial relations strife he was, to them, a beacon of hope. As 1973 marched towards its gloomy close 'what if' conversations were the staple of talk for Conservatives (and they were increasing in number) disaffected from Heath. What if, in the face of the miners, Ted called a general election, and lost? What if the Party then wanted a new Leader? Then, 'what if' suddenly became embodied in the person of Enoch Powell.

The world of Westminster politics – and of the Press – was increasingly divided, as was the nation, in a fashion and to a depth few could recall. Were Heath to lose an electoral confrontation (and it is fair to say that there were few who thought he would), Powell seemed to be the man who could inherit the Tory purple. To some that was a spectacle – a possibility – which excited deep apprehension. To others it represented a beacon of hope. In due course Heath called a general election, and to the amazement of his enemies and the consternation of his admirers Powell announced, in a brusque letter to his constituency chairman, that he would not be a candidate.

The letter, brief though it was, had been long prepared. A few close friends in the political world – a smaller circle within the much wider one of his admirers – had suspected its existence from the moment – in the autumn of 1973 – when, in the face of further strife in the coal mining industry, rumours of an early general election began to spread. At the time Powell argued publicly that there would be no moral justification for an early appeal by Edward Heath to the country, since he had a perfectly adequate majority in the House of Commons for any measures he chose to take.[9] Whereas the prevailing view in the

Conservative Party was that a thumping Heath victory (which was the general expectation, not merely in the Party, but in the Press and throughout the country) would reinforce the government's authority and thus enable measures to be taken against trade union disruptors of the public weal which could not otherwise be taken, Powell's judgement was that an appeal to the electorate would be a contemptible act of cutting and running. Among the Prime Minister's closest advisers Lord Carrington (suddenly moved by Heath into a particularly hot seat as Secretary of State for Energy) favoured the idea of an early election – the sooner the better, in his view – which would, in essence, take the form of a referendum on the authority of government. William Whitelaw, on the other hand, though he was far less decided than Carrington in his stand, held to some part at least of the Powell argument. Whitelaw believed that governments were elected to govern, and that the people would take a dim view of a Prime Minister who troubled them for their votes at a time when he still enjoyed a plurality in Parliament. He also thought that a British general election could not be fought on one issue alone, and that it was foolish to risk office, however strong the indications were that the ministry would triumph.

It is important to stress that Powell was, at the time, convinced that Heath would gain an increased majority in the event of an election. In this sense he subscribed to the predictive fashion of the day. His critics believed that his attempt to use his popularity and authority to forestall this eventuality was due to a conviction on his part that a Heath re-installed in office, with a magnified authority, would be able further to extend his exclusion from the centre of politics. The reality – the personal reality – was quite different. 'I cannot,' he said, 'stand as a Conservative candidate and ask my electors in Wolverhampton to endorse policies, and particularly a policy, in which I do not believe and, indeed, which I implacably oppose.'

The policy was British membership of the European Economic Community. The irony of the situation as 1973 drew to its close was that one of those most passionate in his attempts to persuade Powell not to renounce his Wolverhampton base, Nicholas Ridley (subsequently a Cabinet Minister in Mrs. Thatcher's ministries), was a devoted pro-European – as the cant phrase went. 'Time after time,' says Ridley, 'we sat there with this great man, and watched him wrestle with his conscience.' Had Powell decided to remain as the Conservative candidate for Wolverhampton South-West, and spoken only on local issues during the campaign then –

people like Ridley believed – he could have a reasonable chance of the leadership after Heath had lost. Were he the Machiavelli of his enemies' perception, that is the course he would have adopted. But he could not do it. Besides, being the man he is, he invariably follows a train of thought to its conclusion. If he regarded membership of the EEC as the paramount issue, if he regarded the Conservative Party as irrevocably committed to membership, and if he saw the Labour Party as offering a chance – albeit a slender one – of withdrawal, he would then, in honour bound, have to advocate a Labour vote in the general election. This is what he did, in a manner and with consequences discussed below.[10]

This protracted episode in Powell's career illustrates one very important aspect of his character. It is his aloneness. A further part of it is that he is perfectly content in being alone. 'I'm not a clubbable man in the conventional sense,' he says, 'yet I love clubs. I love institutions. I loved the Army. I love the House of Commons.' Yet, when he was out of the House in 1974 and I asked him whether he missed it he replied, 'I was certain I would, and deeply. Now I have to pinch myself to remind myself that that was what I expected. For I find I do not miss it at all.' This capacity to be alone, and to be content with being alone, separates him in his nature from almost all other politicians, the practice of whose profession depends upon gregariousness, even if it is a forced gregariousness. He is, as I will show in later chapters, a superb parliamentary tactician and as capable of making deals as the best of them – provided there is not even the slightest possibility that the deal being made infringes his concept of what is fundamental. He can be kind and gracious and charming, especially as a host. But he has a detached – even if, paradoxically, an emotional – capacity to stand outside his own experience and, as it were, weigh it. In an enchanting essay on his work room in his house he wrote:

Two other blocks, left and right of the window, house the collection of books about India which I greedily acquired along with an interpretership in Urdu during the three years of my love affair with that land in 1943-6. It has grown steadily since, and still grows, but more slowly. A tiny bit of the debris of the British Raj, material and emotional, which time has washed up on the beach of history, is there in those volumes, some with the student's eager manuscript notes, some with cockroach tracks over the covers, others with a *munshi*'s *pan* stains on the pages. The dust gathers on them now: nothing is so closed as a closed book – unless it be a closed era.

And he goes on, in a passage of great interest to the student of his personality:

> On reflection, what gives this room of mine its comforting and reassuring character is its very incongruity. The past years, unchangeable in their familiar shapes and now beyond the reach of effort or regret, observe with kindly tolerance the feverish endeavours crammed into the narrow space of the present, with a sort of Housmanic 'lie down, lie down, young yeoman, the sun moves ever west.' The pokiness of the room, only a pace or two in any direction, is part of the secret of its soothing quality, as if the passion for concentration and self-sufficiency which is part of its occupant found a matching mood in the confined and crowded space. I think I never could be at ease in a room with ample vistas and large acres of wall and carpet.[11]

The capacity to be alone was evident from his schooldays. To some extent it may be said that there was a desire to be alone, and he was certainly, as a student at Trinity, Cambridge, abrupt in his reaction to overtures of friendship, even from fellow former pupils of King Edward's school – though he paid his two shillings and sixpence annual subscription to the Old Edwardians' Society he never attended its meetings. Today, however, he points out that he did not, out of any act of will, reject the company of his fellows. 'There was a certain social ignorance, a failure to realize how much one can learn from one's fellow men directly, rather than indirectly through their products and their books.' And 'I didn't know there was anything else to do except work . . . the social life of a college was a social life completely unfamiliar to me – even the sheer mechanics of it, of how to tie a bow-tie, were completely unfamiliar to me.' None the less, he became attached to Trinity as an institution: the theme of attachment to institutions in his life has already been mentioned, and will recur again and again in the following pages. He went, for example, into the Army in 1939 with the conviction that he would almost certainly be killed in the course of the war: before joining up he donated the great bulk of his classical library to his old college. And as late as December 1986 when an address he was delivering to the Cambridge University Conservative Association (an undergraduate body) was disrupted by left wing hooligans he was particularly shocked because it had happened *there*. In the few weeks previously he had had similar problems at Bristol and Cardiff but they, somehow, did not seem to count – though, at the urging of his wife, he reacted to them by cancelling, for the foreseeable future, university engagements. It hurt particularly, however, that for security reasons he was forced to leave 'my own college' by a side exit. There have been many occasions in Powell's later public life when he has been compelled to take evasive action in the face of thuggish manifestations. There is one, however, from an earlier period which the episode at Trinity calls to mind and which is useful, in this introductory chapter, for the purpose of showing the essential character of the man as it remained constant over the years from youth.

In 1962 he was Minister of Health. The then Chancellor of the Exchequer, Selwyn Lloyd, had introduced a pay pause, designed to limit all pay increases to two and a half per cent. Powell, as a free market economist, disagreed – and disagrees to this day – with the whole principle of incomes policy and pay pauses enforced by government, whether by persuasion or statute. None the less, he went along with his Cabinet colleagues. He faced a pay claim by nurses, a profession which, as ever, commanded the almost total sympathy of the populace in its demands for a decent wage. He turned the nurses down, and was faced by an angry demonstration on seeking to leave the House of Commons: he was compelled to leave via the House of Lords instead. But he was implacable. No doubt he was influenced by the doctrine of Cabinet solidarity. But he had his own highly individualistic reasons for his action as well. 'If one claims,' he said, 'to be in a profession as the result of having a vocation, the monetary considerations – considerations of income – cannot be primary in choosing a course of action. A vocation has to be paid for. That is its nature.'[12] In like manner during his years in the House of Commons, Powell always refused to accept increases in remuneration voted to themselves by Members of Parliament between general elections. 'We are the only body in the country with the power to vote an order to allocate to ourselves any stipend we wish.' He accepts that victory in a general election for an individual member sanctions a previously approved pay rise. 'In other words,' said an admiring colleague, 'Enoch is always one pay hike behind the rest of us.' Now, it is not unknown for rich men (Lord Young of Graffham is a recent example) to accept high office without pay; nor for senior ministers (Mrs. Margaret Thatcher is a case in point) to decline increases in their ministerial stipend. But I have not been able to trace any other case of a backbencher refusing a pay rise. Indeed the common (and accurate) complaint of legislators at Westminster is that they are paid far less well comparatively than the members of the United States Congress, or their equivalents in Western Europe. None the less, Powell is austere with himself, as he was austere with the nurses.

Light is cast on this attitude of mind by an article he wrote in 1948.[12] Field-Marshal Slim had just been appointed Chief of the Imperial Staff, in consequence of which he had to resign a position on the railways executive. The pay of a field-marshal in those far-off days was £3,285 a year. Powell pointed out that chairmen, or even directors, of nationalized industries could earn up to £8,000. He went on:

> How is it that the community expects to get such service so cheap? The secret is worth finding out at a time when we are abolishing the voluntary element in one field after another, from hospitals to government, and then scratching our heads and scraping our pockets to produce what are called 'incentives'.

'It is a world,' he continued (which Slim was re-entering)

> in which honour is current coin, service the understood reason for one's being there at all, and comradeship – even at the top – the compensation. The men who belong to a calling – be it priesthood or profession of arms – where they are marked out and in a sense dedicated, will all, from the lowest to the highest, give the community more service for a less tangible return.

Now Powell is a man seriously careful about money. I recall an occasion when I gave lunch to him and an American lawyer who was writing a comparative study of race relations legislation around the world, and who wanted to consult the Member for Wolverhampton South-West. They had little in common: my American guest had been an assistant to Robert Kennedy when he was United States Attorney-General and was an enthusiastic advocate of all the then fashionable so-called positive schemes for ameliorating if not ending racial discrimination. Powell, then as now, believed that such programmes would be not merely ineffective but counter-productive. At the end of the lunch, however, the American was still professing himself eager to learn. From his briefcase Powell produced a volume of his own speeches. He announced that as he had to leave, the best he could do was to proffer the book as a summation of his own thinking. He then asked for thirty shillings – less than what it retailed for, but exactly the price the author would have to pay to his publisher for copies over and above the complimentary ones allowed for in his contract.

I tell the anecdote to illustrate and emphasize the precision with which Powell approaches all financial transactions, however small. Precision, indeed, is evident in his approach to every subject to which he turns his mind. Such a man might have been expected – as many commentators would – to rail against the fact that Slim was ill-paid by comparison with captains of industry. But he did not, because his sense of value transcends his sense of money. That an individual with a more cavalier approach to matters of personal finance should extol the virtues of service and patriotism would come as no surprise: that so careful a man should do so, not merely by way of exhortation, but in his own professional life, is unusual, and merits remark.

Economy was bred into young Jack (as he was familiarly called in childhood and youth) from an early age. His parents were not rich. They were not poor either, and he recalls that he never felt stinted for anything as a child.[13] But there was a necessity as well as a will to practise economy, and the will has remained with him all his life. As an undergraduate, for example, it was not merely the desire to excel that caused him to enter for the Craven scholarship: it was also the fact that victory would add £100 a year to his existing scholarships of £300. In a feat without precedent he won the Craven in his freshman year and thus, as a student, had an income higher than that of the average industrial worker.

Powell would, I believe, consider the recital of such details as these beneath consideration. He spoke to an interviewer once for the *Sunday Times* colour magazine feature *A life in the day of* . . .[14] which encourages its subject to speak about his or her general interests and preoccupations within the framework of quotidian activity. He began with some asperity, questioning the triviality of the whole exercise, and adding, 'Why it should matter at what time the subject gets up each morning, I don't know. However, I wake at 7 a.m. and start the day on a flask of tea prepared the night before.' Soon, however, he had disposed of the framework of detail and gone into reminiscence and speculation. There is a certain paradox here, for no man is more precise in his domestic organization, nor enjoys its detail more. He has said that one of the fascinations of politics is the fact that there is no other profession in which the details of personal experience are an essential part of the evidence for seeking out and defining the wellsprings of action.[15] Particularly in his later speeches there is a constant return to the theme of the reaction between personality and events; between personality and decision.

Moreover – though it is easy to see why such a man reacts with scorn to *purely* trivial gossip about individual idiosyncrasies – the details of the way an individual conducts his life can often be illuminating for the student of his public conduct. The obsessive grimness, for example, with which Curzon examined his household accounts tells much about his approach to the business of the Foreign Office, for they were the same; the largeness of attitude in handling his domestic life of Churchill was reflected in the largeness of his approach to the management of the affairs of the nation; once the rural preoccupation of Grey with Fallodon (and especially with his birds and squirrels) is understood the student has learned a great deal about his clinical and authoritarian handling of government affairs. So it is with Powell. Seeing him, at his own lunch table, explaining to a female guest (and captivating her in the course of doing so) how a particular cheese was made is to see at work in domestic surroundings the same mind that is on display in the remorseless unravelling of some political argument or proposition on the public stage. Indeed, in a way, one sees the characteristic Powell all the more readily, for one is not distracted by having to consider, at the same time as one is considering the man, the political implications of what he is saying: one sees more of the essence.

An important distinction has, however, to be made between the private and the public Powell. When humour appears on public occasions it is invariably a grim humour, as when he observed, during the 1970 general election that, 'A great part of the electorate . . . are just being invited to decide if they prefer the country and the economy, which will be much the same anyhow, to be presided over by a man with a pipe or a man with a boat.'[16] The private humour is quite different. He once gave me some cuttings of a handsome shrub in his garden which I had greatly admired. I explained that I was going to attempt to grow them initially in a new-fangled gel. (He was disappointed that I had not taken the trouble to investigate the constituent elements of the gel.) I said that, if they took, I would bring a pot back to him: 'Ah. You are being the foster parent to my favourite shrub. I warn you. I may call in the social workers to demand an early return.'

Even when he is being gently humorous, however, it is impossible to avoid a sense of the volcanic in Powell's nature. The combination of the almost excessively remorseless logician and the almost excessively (and openly) emotional individual is what produces the dramatic effect that he invariably has on his interlocutors. Subsidiary to these two main characteristics – but important for the functioning of their combination – are other characteristics, principally industry, a hunger for knowledge and a thirst for precision.

Powell is a man of quite phenomenal industry, as his vast output of speeches, articles and books – on a bewildering variety of subjects – readily demonstrates. The voracity for knowledge takes a special form, the form being a desire not merely to know, but to know the *how* and *why* of the subject that has attracted him. 'A child playing with a toy,' he once wrote, 'gets pleasure from how one thing fits with another, finding out how it makes sense . . . So I suppose I am still like a child with a plaything – by turns inquisitive, puzzled, then delighted.'[17] He pursues things that interest him with an awesome efficiency: that is part of his love of precision, though he explains it more simply, saying, 'The essence of efficiency is to do anything that can be done immediately, immediately, or at any rate as soon as it can possibly be done.'

The passion that is so evident in his speeches often conceals from the audience the rigour with which they are organized; and it is therefore frequently only on reading the text that the pattern of the argument, invariably following on from a premise initially stated, can be seen. His critics, even those sympathetic to him,[18] most frequently concentrate on his choice of premise, for it is virtually impossible to fault – in logical terms – its working out.

In his rhetoric, however, the precision of logic is supported by a precision of articulacy. He never, in private or in public, speaks other than in rounded and fully formed sentences, even when answering questions in public, an achievement to which few people whose business requires them to respond to audience inquisition can aspire. (His wife's mother, on being told that Pamela had accepted his proposal of marriage, expressed a certain concern to the effect 'that it would be like going on a life-long university course'. Repetition of this anecdote gives him great delight.) The perfect Powell speech (from the artistic point of view) is on a large subject, involves a personal decision of his own, and is followed by questions. In the Birmingham Bull Ring during the February 1974 general election campaign there was just such an event. The subject was British membership of the EEC. The decision was his advocacy of a vote for Labour in the general election. He dilated on what he saw as the Heath government's chicanery in presenting the issue to Parliament and people and asked whether the electorate could now take the decision on membership back into their own hands:

> I do not believe they can be prevented: for they are now at a general election, provided with a clear, definite and practicable alternative, namely, a fundamental renegotiation directed to regain free access to world food markets and recover or retain the powers of Parliament, a renegotiation to be followed in any event by a specific submission of the outcome to the electorate, a renegotiation protected by an immediate moratorium or stop on all further integration of the UK into the Community. This alternative is offered, as such an alternative must be in our parliamentary democracy, by a political party capable of securing a majority in the House of Commons and sustaining a government.

Both in the body of the speech, and in answer to several friendly questions, he explained why he could not stand as an independent candidate, in spite of many pleas for him to do just that.[19] 'The engine of democracy,' he said, 'is party. You must vote for a party.' By and large his audience was supportive and sympathetic. But there was opposition, and one man cried out, 'Judas.' Powell swung in the direction of the voice. The agony on his face and in his tone I found then, as I find it now, indescribable. 'Judas,' he said, 'was paid. I am sacrificing my whole political life.' Indeed, at that time he believed he was. The impact on his listeners was explosive. They rose, and they cheered; and they cheered.

Mr. Berkeley[20] finds this sort of combination of drama and argument excessive. But his criticism demonstrates his lack of a sense of history: it is only in the age of technology that the draining of the drama out of politics has begun. In earlier ages, it is perfectly true, there were dull and bumbling politicians; but

19

there was a substantial number at almost any given time who gave almost as much attention to the theatrical quality of their public appearances as they did to the intellectual quality of their arguments. Even today there is something of the actor-manager in most politicians; it issues too often, however, in bombast. Powell pays a great deal of attention to his mode of delivery, but the argument comes first. He is slavish in the preparation of a text: 'The curious thing is that the more elaborately a part of the speech is worked on, the more natural it sounds. On the other hand, if a whole slab has written itself, run off the end of the pen, it always sounds wooden when it is delivered.' At his oratorical best a speech has most impact when argument and rhetoric are brought together, as emotion and logic are fused in his personality.

I have quoted Mr. Geoffrey Smith as saying that Powell pays his audience the compliment of taking it seriously in argument.[21] But he also pays it the no less important compliment of taking it seriously technically, even physically. No doubt it is the underlying passion of his nature that provides the most important spring for the controlled energy, and the gestures, one sees in any speech he makes. But the gestures – the turn of his body from side to side, the movement of the head as his eyes seek out segment after segment of the crowd, the use of his hands and arms in a manner that gives appropriate emphasis to a particular passage in the speech, or a particular emphasis in the argument – are all considered, not in any Machiavellian way, but as part of his commitment to giving his all to the people who have come to hear him. It does not matter whether the gathering is an important one – the House of Commons (though his style is, in keeping with his view of the nature of the chamber, much quieter there), the (as in the past) Conservative Party Conference, or a hall in the shadow of the mountains of Mourne. Any group whose invitation he accepts gets the whole Powell: he will have given his full mind to the subject; he will have taken the greatest pains over the text; and he will give to its delivery every possible ounce of physical and oratorical effort. Not for him the tendency of so many politicians to treat some meetings as more important than others; to talk down to those listening, or to patronize intellectually. In a man generally thought to be so arrogant, and who is perhaps surer in himself that he is right on any given issue than is any contemporary, all this demonstrates a remarkable humility. 'I want to give the people a tune to whistle,' he says, but he works exceptionally hard at the quality of the tune.

On the other hand he knows how to use silence as a gesture. In 1956 a number of Members distressed at the British withdrawal from the Suez Canal expected at least some private support from him, though a ministerial resignation was hardly to be hoped for, since he had so vehemently opposed the withdrawal from the Canal Zone which preceded it.[22] They got nothing. In 1963, during the weeks of the government crisis over the conduct of John Profumo, the great part of the Press were satisfied that, though a relatively junior Cabinet Minister, he had the power to bring the government down. It was widely felt that his own high code of moral conduct and his unimpeachable integrity were so generally recognized that his resignation would convince the nation that there was something rotten at the heart of the state (as most media commentators were inclined to believe). He kept silence until the last possible moment and then, with devastating effect, pronounced his support for Harold Macmillan.[23] It was an extraordinary situation in which the Minister of Health, rather than one or more of the holders of the major offices of state, was so generally regarded as an acceptable judge of morality, and the arbiter of the fate of a government. That it was so was due principally to an understanding of what made up his character, but it was also due in some manner to the fashion in which he regulated his silence. Again, after he and Iain Macleod had refused to serve under Alec Douglas-Home in 1963, while Macleod spent a large part of the following year stumping the country propounding his own ideas of Toryism, covered by veiled criticism of the government, Powell went quietly about his duties and sought no great public effect.

Both men had been devoted to Home's rival, R. A. Butler, and having declared themselves so strongly for him, felt they could serve no one else. They were also disgusted by the chicanery with which the Prime Minister, Harold Macmillan, had arranged the succession. But, whereas Macleod was soon in print in the *Spectator* (of which paper he had become editor) in 1964, Powell held his fire on this particular aspect of the history of modern politics until, years later, he reviewed Macmillan's memoirs, also in the *Spectator*.[24] His silences, indeed, can often be as eloquent as his words.

The silences, like the speeches, are usually the product of calculation. By calculation in this sense I mean nothing disreputable. Contrary to general opinion, Powell is not a man who makes up his mind instantly on a given subject. Usually, indeed, he feels the need to acquire a great deal of evidence

– and his retentive mind is extremely efficient at the business of holding and processing it – before he makes a judgement. Thus, in the second of the examples just cited, he certainly needed to go through a Cabinet meeting (which took place a few days before he made his speech in support of Macmillan) before he was certain of the right course of action. Lord Hailsham once described him as possessing 'the best mind in politics, until it's made up.' The assurance with which he pronounces on such a variety of subjects conceals from his listener – or reader – the sheer quantity of dogged hard work and conscientious investigation that precedes every judgement. Many examples of this will appear in the following pages, and they will be concerned with great public issues. But a taste of his view of the acquisition of knowledge, as well as his voracity for it, which I have already mentioned, can be gleaned from a reply to a letter of 1986 the writer of which had asked his advice on the learning of Finnish. Powell replied:

I am afraid that in my opinion an adult learning a new language has no satisfactory alternative to "sweating it out" with the assistance of grammars, dictionaries and textbooks. I conclude this from my own personal experience in attempting to acquire Hebrew during my seventh and eighth decades.

There can be few men or women who, in their seventies, would set out to learn Hebrew (his purpose in doing which being part of his preparation for a major work on the interpretation of the New Testament) and can hardly have ever been – there certainly is not now – an assiduous and senior politician who has done so.[25]

'I am a very slow reader,' he says, 'but I am also, by training, methodical.' He claims to have a poor memory[26] but that has to be whimsy. What he unquestionably has is a formidably organized mind, and a formidably organized life. During his years as an MP, the time he spent in the House of Commons (when not absent on some speaking, broadcasting or social engagement) was divided between the Chamber – where he sat, arms folded, head thrown back, attention to what was going on visible in every lineament – and the Library, reading, annotating, writing. Every moment of time was usefully employed. He did not make use of those facilities for relaxation which quite a substantial number of Members make too much use of. Asked about a former colleague with whom he had once been in close alliance, but with whom he had broken, he replied: 'I believe he is going to pieces. But I

22

cannot say that with certainty. I do not frequent those parts of the House of Commons where gentlemen go to pieces.'

Yet, he is in no sense an anti-social being. He is frequently to be seen at parties, particularly those given by papers he writes for. He entertains, and is entertained, a great deal. He never gives the impression of being in a hurry, or under the pressure of a timetable, and always has time for whoever he is talking to. Yet another example of the order of his mind – as well as of the courtesy with which he handles conversation – comes from a party given by parliamentary journalists for politicians which Powell attended. One of the journalists had brought his girl friend, an Icelandic ballet dancer. She had formed an admiration for Powell, and sought an introduction. Within moments they were immersed in a conversation on opera. As it drew towards its close she asked him whether he had seen a current fashionable production. He replied that he had not been to the opera for many years. She was more than somewhat taken aback for, evidently, he had satisfied her that he knew her world. 'I haven't been,' he replied, 'because I loved it so much that I could not take it in small doses. I was like a drugged man. I could have gone every night. So I stopped going altogether.'

His industry and organization can be further illustrated in the political field by his method as a constituency member. 'He takes a constituency by the throat,' observed an admiring Conservative Central Office agent after having studied the method in Wolverhampton South-West, which Powell represented for so many years. The first step is to open a card index. Everybody on the electoral roll has a card. There is nothing particularly unusual about that, for many members do it. The second step is to visit *every* elector, in whatever area, and of whatever supposed party sympathies. He has more than once expressed surprise at baffled reaction to the third step. It is to make house visits between elections. It is, of course, common practice for candidates of all parties to make symbolic visits to hostile areas in their constituencies during campaigns. But regular and sustained visiting to voters in the intervals between campaigns, especially to non-supporters, is a rarity. Powell's practice aroused puzzlement, even hostility, when the Official Ulster Unionists chose him for Down South, for he immediately made it clear that he considered the Catholic segment of his electorate as being entitled to the full attention of their member, even though only a handful could have been expected to vote for him. In the context of a true understanding of his character, however (and unusual though the Unionists found it, because of past history of the province of Ulster), Powell's attitude to his new responsibilities in County Down should be seen as natural and necessary. It is, even, a door – one of many – that can be passed through, given the acquisition of the key to the lock, on the way into the recesses of his nature.

Mr. Robert Rhodes James has written[27] that 'for much of Powell's career, and certainly until 1966, one of his principal characteristics has been his unpredictability . . .But after 1966 one is increasingly conscious of a change that can only be explained by the fact that he believed that his hour was approaching.' To the contrary. There has been little about Powell's career at any stage that has been unpredictable. The difficulty, over the years, in assessing his conduct, and assessing the reasons for his taking any particular action, arises solely from a failure to appreciate that he is, quite simply, unlike any other politician of our time, not in effect, always, but in character. Whatever is made, by way of analysis or judgement, of the rightness or otherwise of any position he has taken up; whether or not one accepts the critical view that, however rigorous his logic may be on a given issue, it more often than not proceeds from a false premise, the fact of the matter is that he is always, and has always been, true to himself. Thus, for example, his justly celebrated speech on the Hola Camp killings of 1959.[28]

It is the convention of Conservative politics that a minister who resigns (and Powell had earlier resigned as Financial Secretary to the Treasury, along with the Chancellor and the other Treasury Minister over budgetary policy) makes a polite statement of his reasons and composes himself in peace until, perchance, he is recalled to the colours. If he speaks at all in a critical fashion it should be in the area of his previous responsibility, and he should speak in a cautious fashion. Save for Powell there has been no exception to that rule this century; not even in the prosecution of his career by Churchill.

In 1959 Britain governed Kenya. The security forces there had the difficult – and ultimately impossible – task of putting down the Mau-Mau rebellion. A number of suspected – or actual – Mau-Mau activists had been confined for years in the Hola Camp, in perhaps the most arid part of the colony. They had been seen as sullen and recalcitrant. A decision was taken to make them work (although, strictly speaking, this was illegal under Kenyan law – the law of the colony as prescribed in Westminster). Force was used, batons and rifle butts applied.

The Kenya government (the colonial administration) announced that ten men who died had suffered this ultimate fate because they had drunk contaminated water.

For more than a year the Labour Party had been concerned, and had been making much noise about, the treatment of Mau-Mau prisoners. Many Conservatives were uneasy about what had happened – but no more than uneasy. There was sufficient public concern, however, for the government to allow a debate. The government's business managers chose their time: the debate was to begin at 10.30 p.m. on the evening of 27 July 1959. The House was to rise the following day for the summer recess. The government Whips merely wanted to avoid rows, and were prepared to confess to 'administrative error' on the part of the colonial authorities. A Conservative backbencher, John Peel, less worried and less nice in his feelings than most of his colleagues, made a contribution to the debate the tone of which suggested that Hola was a matter of no great moment, and that those who had suffered were 'sub-human'.[29]

At one o'clock in the morning on 28 July Powell rose. 'He was so pale, and so stricken,' said an observer, 'and yet so powerful.'

We cannot say we will have African standards in Africa and Asian standards in Asia and perhaps British standards at home. It has been said – and it is a fact [that it has been said] – that these eleven[30] men were the lowest of the low; 'sub-human' was the word my honourable friend used. So be it. But that cannot be relevant to the acceptance of responsibility for their death . . . In general, I would say that it is a fearful doctrine, which must recoil upon the heads of those who pronounce it, to stand in judgement on a fellow being and to say, 'Because he was such-and-such, therefore the consequences which would otherwise flow from his death shall not flow.

As a result of this totally unexpected intervention, by a former Minister who should have been confining himself (according to the rules) to economic matters, the care of black prisoners in Kenya was taken out of the hands of the colony's Prison Department and, thereafter, closely supervised. This was not all that Powell wanted, but it made a material difference to the health, safety and welfare of many Kenyan subjects of the Crown. Powell would have liked indictment, prosecution and punishment for those involved in the eleven deaths: he could not get that; but he did get what can only be called future justice for subsequent detainees.

'Not understanding Enoch,' Michael Foot once said, 'has been a condition of intelligent parliamentarians since he was first elected.'[31] The point of Powell's intervention in the debate was, of course, its necessity. The Conservative fashion of the day was to say that eleven deaths were irrelevant to the business of government. His view was that eleven deaths when the government was responsible for the individuals concerned was a subject not merely of immediate, but of fundamental, importance. And he made his statement without care for thought of advancement.

Indeed, just a few weeks later, Macmillan invited him to return to government responsibility. He, the Chancellor, Peter Thorneycroft, and Nigel Birch, Chief Secretary to the Treasury,[32] had resigned together.[33] Birch's eyesight was failing; it was impossible to imagine that he could resume office – and, besides, he so detested Macmillan that it was inconceivable that he should take office again in a Macmillan administration. There remained Thorneycroft and Powell available for rehabilitation. Perhaps as a deliberate slight to the senior man, Thorneycroft, Macmillan first offered the opportunity of a comeback to Powell. Powell declined: he would not, he said, accept office until it was offered to Thorneycroft as well.

To most politicians of the day this seemed to be behaviour quixotic to a point of absurdity beyond even that implied by the adjective. This was all the more so in that Powell was no knight-errant type of politician who cared nothing for office. He had never concealed his deep and hungry ambition. Having worked with Iain Macleod in the Conservative Research Department, and having been elected to the House of Commons at the same time as Macleod, he made little secret of his irritation that his friend and contemporary attained office before he did. In spite of that, however, when he was offered a junior ministerial job at the Home Office (with responsibility for Welsh affairs) he turned it down, because it did not suit him. As in later years he puzzled his fellow parliamentarians, so Powell puzzled them then.

But his conduct throughout his career was enigmatic or confusing only by comparison with the conduct of other politicians. 'I am a fellow traveller,' Macleod observed by way of commentary on Powell's policies,[34] 'but sometimes I leave Powell's train a few stations down the line, before it reaches and sometimes crashes into the terminal buffers. I am certainly less logical in my political approach, but I would argue that Powell suffers sometimes from an excess of logic.' Macleod, of course, was speaking of logic in the sense that the vast majority of politicians understand it. To them it has seemed from the beginning incomprehensible that one of their number, a man so ready openly to declare his ambition (another unusual characteristic, for it is not done, how- ever avid one is for advancement, to do other than sidle into the limelight) was so unwilling to compromise for its sake, once he was convinced that a point of principle was involved.

What is further confusing about Powell, and what has created many of the contradictory reactions to him, is the fact that this intense, academic and remote creature has an unparal- leled capacity to excite loyalty and admiration in the hearts of masses of ordinary citizens. That a former university professor and soldier should become a Member of Parliament is nothing special. There was a Conservative professor, Esmond Wright, in the 1966 Parliament, and the number of ex-professional (as opposed to temporary) soldiers, sailors and airmen in the ranks of that Party have been legion. Such people, however, rarely reach the forefront of politics: they simply tend not to have the demagogic – or democratic – abilities to endear themselves to, or dominate, either the electorate or their colleagues. Their training has lain in a different direction, and adjustment is difficult, if not impossible. Moreover, such dons and warriors have rarely, either, been in the front rank of their earlier professions.

Powell is a different case. He was a professor in Australia at twenty-five. He had been elected to a chair at Durham in 1940. This was held open for him for the duration of the war. In 1944 however he resigned it in order to enter politics. He was the only soldier to go from private to brigadier in the whole course of the war. The Conservative Party and the House of Commons thus acquired, in the general election of 1950, a young man who had reached the top in two quite different professions. Moreover, in the years that followed, he did not slough off the characteristics nor the preoccupations of those professions: he has remained academic in his analysis of problems, and military in his approach to the organization of his own life and career, as well as being active in defence circles. And if it is fair to say that his political career has been a failure, in that he has not attained the highest office, nor even office of a seniority appropriate to his talents, he has shown a magician's capacity to enthral the public, beyond the capacity of any post-war politician.

None of this can be explained, except by pointing to it. Powell himself regards it all with a certain amount of humour.

This is because there is a good deal of the fatalist in him. Some time after his dismissal from the Shadow Cabinet I asked him how he had felt in the traumatic weeks that had followed his Birmingham speech in 1968. He replied:

> I felt like a man who had been walking innocently down a street when a tile fell from a roof and hit him on the head. I was stunned for a moment. Then I took thought. I decided to pick up the tile and throw it back. In other words, I determined to make use of the situation, unhappy though it was, in which I found myself. And I was, of course, sustained by the evidence of extraordinary public support for me.

It was the extent and depth of that public support that frightened his critics and enemies – and even the leadership of the Conservative Party – in the late 1960s and early 1970s. In the British system a popular politician is envied; but he is not feared simply because of his popularity. It was the intensity of the support for Powell – especially but not solely on the issue of immigration – that scared other politicians, not to mention reporters, editors, clergymen and what can only be called the establishment. It was their fear of him that led to wild talk about dictatorial ambitions on his part – wild because nobody who had given a moment's thought to the man's nature, attitudes and principles could sustain such ideas. Throughout his career, indeed, Powell has constantly railed against any expansion of the central power of the state, and particularly prescriptive expansion, by which is meant attempts by successive governments to acquire power for themselves without going through every necessary stage in Parliament. Thus, for example, when the first government of Harold Wilson sought to enforce an incomes policy by bullying business (rather than by putting a Bill through Parliament) Powell resigned – at some personal financial cost to himself, which he could ill afford – his sole directorship, because the board of his company decided to co-operate with ministers.

This, then, is the man who has exercised such fascination for politicians, commentators and public alike for so many years, and who has still not lost his capacity to surprise. In his late seventies, moreover, there is no sign of any diminution of his powers or appetites. He has written:

> The notion young people have that the old are settled, staid and comfortable, because nothing shakes them, is quite

mistaken. One is much more likely to question things. One ceases to take anything for granted. Everything on which your gaze lights can conceal a puzzle. Wonderment, I find, is a response which grows more powerful with the years. Perhaps in this respect, as in so many others, I am a lucky man.

2

The Scholar
1920–1939

The autumn leaves that strew the grass,
The flocks of migrant birds,
They are all poems; but alas,
I cannot find the words
> – *J. Enoch Powell*
> First Poems *(XX, London, 1937).*

'I was born,' said Powell, 'at ten o'clock on a Sunday night in a house overlooking a railway cutting in Stechford, Birmingham.' He leant forward and laughed heartily. 'During a thunderstorm.' The date was 16 June 1912. Many years later, in July 1968 in Canada, he told journalists who had flocked to quiz the stormy petrel of British Conservative politics and, in particular, to ask him whether he would leave his party and found his own, 'I was born a Tory.' And he added, 'I have lived a Tory. I will die a Tory.'

The statement, as so often with Powell, sounds exaggerated, or at least extravagant. For while his father Albert was a Liberal of an uncertainly radical hue his mother Ellen (*née* Breese) *was* a Tory; and of the two it was she who was to have by far the greater influence on him. As he later wrote:[1]

> Mother, with longing ever new
> And joy too great for telling,
> I turn again to rest in you
> My earliest dwelling.

As nearly always, therefore, there is a justified (once one has found the key) precision for even his most dramatic remarks. Indeed, the taste for drama which I mentioned in the last chapter as evident in his mature years made an early appearance in his young life.[2]

Most writers on Powell have acknowledged the influence of his mother: they could hardly do otherwise, for he emphasizes it himself with great frequency.

> My childhood is very much my mother . . . She was also my first teacher and I suppose some of my earliest recollections are of my mother putting up the alphabet around the kitchen wall so that I could learn it – and my saying the most elementary lessons to her standing on a chair in the kitchen, while she worked at the stove or at the sink. And, from the very beginning, right up to the Sixth at grammar school, she took a part in my learning, encouraging me and helping me and very much working with me.

None the less, it does not do altogether to dismiss the influence of his father. Powell, in giving personal interviews, does not often advert to him. But that is understandable, principally because, in the field in which he made his first conquests, that of classics – and particularly of Greek – it was his mother who was the driving force. The more private Powell, however, the one who has been more ready to talk about himself in broadcasts and in print as he has grown older, betrays, in many of his tastes, the influence of his father. 'My father was a warm presence, and another boy around the house.' But the long country walks which the adult Powell likes – his pleasure in day-long outings and picnics is often a joy, but sometimes a trial, to his family, especially since he does not care to alter a planned schedule, even if the weather is unfavourable – are a product of Albert's taste. Further, when the time came to join the Army in 1939 young Enoch chose the Royal Warwicks, in the volunteer battalion of which his father had once served.[3] It is, indeed, in Warwick that he will be buried.

So, though his mother is clearly the more evident – and, from the point of view of the way he works and thinks and acts the more significant – influence on his life, his father's role is far from unimportant (as has so often been assumed) when one considers the early formation of his character. Indeed, the two influences came together in one of his most important scholarly achievements, the translation and publication (in collaboration with Stephen Williams) of the book of laws of the Welsh king Hywel the Good, the *Llyfr Blegywryd*. Mrs. Powell had created the circumstances in which her son had the training for which his mind hungered, and the discipline such as was required to teach himself medieval Welsh, without acquiring colloquial skills.[4] But 'My father always made me conscious of my Welsh roots.' Just as today Powell likes to take summer holidays ('The holiday period in the Powell household comes in pieces between February and November.') which involve the thorough exploration of a particular area (in recent years invariably France) so, in his childhood, the Welsh borders, and that part of Shropshire from which his mother came, were the vacation stamping grounds of two schoolteachers and their precocious little only son.

Albert and Ellen were both primary school teachers when they met in 1907. He was thirty-five, she twenty-one. Albert's family came originally from Radnorshire, though he was born in Staffordshire, the son of a general merchant. Ellen was the daughter of a Liverpool policeman, but the family had derived originally from Newport. Their child was born three years after the marriage and he was given as his second name the one by which he is now familiarly known and addressed, in tribute to his paternal grandfather and, in all probability, in part because it was popular in the Primitive Methodist circles from which his family had sprung.[5]

So far as profession was concerned Powell's roots on both sides of his family were overwhelmingly artisan – 'working class', to use an old-fashioned term – his paternal great-grandfather being a coal-miner and another ancestor being a general labourer. What was being instilled into the progeny of both the Breese and the Powell families by the beginning of the twentieth century, however, was not merely the Victorian ideal of hard work and self-improvement, but the concept of the value of education. This meant not just education as an end in itself, but education as a means to advancement.

The turn of the nineteenth century saw the beginning of a remarkable burgeoning of a desire for learning among sections of the working class. It was, perhaps, most noticeable among Welsh coal-mining communities: until recently, indeed, it had its commemoration in the libraries and the tutorial traditions of coal-mining areas of the country, though the memory has been in decline since the advent of more secularly ambitious and more Socialist inclined trade unions. While there were shades of ambition, the impulse for education tended to divide into two strands. There were those families who regarded it as an inbuilt and traditional necessity for their descendants to continue doing the same thing the family had always done, but on better terms, and with more leisure for the finer things of life. But there were also those families who saw the training of the mind as a means whereby their children – and their children's children – could escape from the restrictions of their own lives, and into a new and better world.

From this latter tradition Ellen Powell sprang. But it is important to note that for all her emphasis on thrift and financial independence (as witnessed in my account of her son in the last chapter) there was nothing mercenary about this striving. Had young Jack (as he was called when a child) gone on to develop as a musician (which, at one time he wanted to do, for he was a good clarinetist) he would have been set fair to make a great deal more money than he could expect as a teacher of Greek. Father and mother alike, however, did not encourage his musical bent; and he accepted that the necessary scholarships could not be won if he tried to cultivate music as he was cultivating book learning.

So I put away my instrument, and I have scarcely read a sheet of music since. I did, though, later read Wagner's librettos, and they played an important part in my growing passion for German culture. When I was at Cambridge I listened to music quite a lot. Eventually, though, it passed out of my life, and is left behind as so many things have to be left behind on the way through life.

The particular educational bent that Ellen (who gave up teaching when her son was born) had needs to be defined a little more clearly than simply by the negation of saying that it was not mercenary. In some, and particularly in Welsh, circles it tended to be religious: Biblical and theological studies were greatly in vogue and, as in Catholic Ireland, it was a great triumph to have a son who became a priest, so in Wales it was a great thing to have a minister in the family. Outside the orbit of religion, however, the educational drive moved in the same direction as did, increasingly, that of the upper classes in the nineteenth century – towards the humanities, which were believed to provide not merely a grounding in pure knowledge, but a training for living.

Formally, Powell's parents were Anglican, but Ellen had ceased for some time to have any religious faith. (This did not, however, prevent her from ensuring that her son had a sound Christian training, for she believed that he might want to opt for belief in later life, as, indeed, he did.) She had the same insatiable intellectual curiosity as a child and a young woman as he was to demonstrate at an astonishingly early age. Thus, in order (partly at least) to be able to plumb the depths of the New Testament, she taught herself Greek as a schoolgirl. (Many years later Powell was to write to a middle-aged correspondent, 'I am afraid I have to say that only a thorough knowledge of Greek, which is difficult to acquire in later years, is in my opinion, adequate for critical work on the New Testament.') It followed that, when he exhibited a bent for the classics, he had the exceptional good fortune, in a household such as his, to have a parent eager and able to assist: when he was at grammar school, younger than the other boys in his class, and keen to progress at speed, she got him up early in the morning to give him extra coaching herself.

To the modern parent Powell's childhood might seem something of a hothouse affair. It is often thought, indeed, that the kind of intense drilling to which he was subjected produces revolt in children; and not a few of Powell's enemies have attributed what they see as his warped attitudes and behaviour to his early life. But the fact of the matter is that Ellen Powell found in him the perfect recipient of her own drive and ambition. He loved it all: 'If I could remake it and reconstruct it, I wouldn't know what to do to make it better.' The child was reading Harmsworth's encyclopaedia at four, and he had begun his translation of Herodotus before leaving school. It is evident, therefore, that his mother did not direct him nor dominate him: the eagerness, so to speak, was bred in him, perhaps genetically ordained, and whenever he looked around, seeking knowledge or guidance, his mother was to hand, ready to devote every spare moment to his intellectual development.

There was also the fact that he was an only child, so there were no sibling distractions. With his tastes, however, and his drive, it is scarcely surprising to learn that he was not gregarious, and all his young life he was regarded as a loner, in the same way as, so many years later, he was described as *the* loner in politics.[6] What might be called his intellectual private life was, however, astonishing in its variety. The classics, naturally, predominated. But there were many other subjects as well (evidently often culled from the encyclopaedia) and he was able to astonish his parents at the age of six when, on a visit to Caernarvon Castle, he doffed his cap in a particular room, explaining to them that it was the room in which the first Prince of Wales was born. His later almost obsessive interest in matters German did not begin until he was fifteen, and it was a necessary outgrowth of his classical studies, for most of the important work in those years was being done by German scholars. But his thirst ran to things that by no stretch of the imagination could be regarded as central to his schoolwork. Thus, in a 1959 review of Wilfred Thesiger's *Arabian Sands*[7] he began by saying that he still had in his possession a fat packet of maps which, at the age of nine, 'I meticulously copied from the works of the classical Arabian travellers.' He goes on:

> The haunting and the fascination flowed back like a tide after forty years as I opened the pages of Thesiger's *Arabian Sands*. Here were the old emotions stirred by the dotted lines marking dry water courses, and the photographs of walls and mud domes, the descriptions of evening meals in the desert after dark. In the pouch at the back of the book was a familiar sort of map, brown for desert, white for the rest, with the author's route across both marked in red.

This passage, like so many in his writing, demonstrates his remarkable ability, as a writer, to evoke feeling, particularly feeling about the past. In his political speaking that capacity is also evident, but there it is much harsher; it is more lush; it is evidently designed to impose a view, or counsel a course of action. When, for example, he uses a disquisition on the history of his country (or, more specifically, in recent years, on the history of Ulster), feeling and emotion are important parts of the enforcing of his argument. The matter is simplified in order that it may be the better dramatized. It is only when we get him writing about subjects outside his political concerns of the moment that we can appreciate to the full his skill with the nostalgic forms.

There is, then, a threnodic element in the style: it is the plangency of a lament. And yet, the lament is not wholly sad, for there lurks behind it a love of the experiences he has had. In, for example, a 1960 article[8] (to which I shall return) he opens:

> It was the last building left. Everything else on that side of the street had been demolished by war damage, by slum clearance, but now to make way for one of the great new thoroughfares which were rapidly removing one of the known landmarks from the city where I was born and went to school.
> As a schoolboy I used to make my way along it once or

twice a month in the lunch hour, to rummage in the penny boxes and scan the sixpenny shelves. This particular shop, it was commonly agreed between us of the classical Sixth, had an exceptionally good penny box in those days, and more than one leather-bound volume out of it stands on my shelves today.

All this, however, was for later. When he was six his parents moved house to Woodlands Park Road. The decision was taken not to send the boy to the regular elementary school, but to a private establishment, small in size, and run by Miss Mabel Pane. Miss Pane was a friend of Ellen's and Ellen had (accurately) assessed her as being a teacher with remarkable gifts for drawing out the quality of her small charges. According to Powell himself, 'She was a great teacher.' A female contemporary of his observed, 'Miss Pane was a wonderful woman and her influence is still felt by those of us who were fortunate enough to be taught by her – quiet dignity, a great sense of fair play and wonderful sense of humour were outstanding in her character.'

The redoubtable Miss Pane was herself an example of self-improvement. The area in which the Powells had come to live was a somewhat isolated one from the point of view of bringing up a six year old. Albert, Ellen and Jack moved in 1918. There was no council school for toddlers nearer than Bournville, which was over a mile away. Miss Pane therefore began to hold classes in her own front room. Such was her popularity with parents and children alike that she eventually took over the village hall. Her reputation was justified, for a large number of her pupils first gained scholarships to the King's Norton Secondary School and, later, passed on to King Edward's Grammar School, renowned not only in Birmingham but in the great universities for its emphasis on hard work, competitiveness and scholastic excellence. This was the path that young Powell trod; and it can safely be said that no school in the country would have suited a boy of his nature better than King Edward's.

The ambience in the Powell household had more than a touch of Puritanism: in that sense (in its emphasis on hard work, plain food and serious conversation, and with neither alcohol nor nicotine consumed) it was remarkably like the home of another famous Tory politician, young Margaret Roberts, some years later.[9] The Roberts family in Grantham was much better off than the Powell family in Birmingham, but the Methodist roots were the same, as were the *mores* both venerated. At the time of the move to Woodlands Park Road, King's Norton, Albert Powell was earning fifty shillings a week, and his pay was invariably handed over to his wife, who dealt with the household budget. It was not exactly a princely sum, even then, but it was adequate, and young Jack lacked for nothing that he considered to be important. Economy was, however, enjoined upon him and, as to food, 'My mother used to quote St. Paul: eat what is set before you asking no questions.' He adds that this is what he does to this day, though he evinces a particular liking for such delicacies as bullock's heart and steak and kidney pudding.

Where some, at least, of the income went can be gleaned from an account of a visit to the house by a local girl, a few years older than Jack.[10]

There was such an array of books! I remember there were a number of Jack Londons. I – not an avid reader by any means – was invited to select one, read it and bring it back next week and choose another. This I did, and to prove that I *had* read it he would ask me a lot of questions about it. I was four years older, and it felt terrible if I couldn't answer the questions correctly, or got one book mixed up with another whereupon he would quote chapter and verse for my special benefit. But we were very good friends and sometimes I was invited to tea. On these occasions I do not remember meeting his parents, but I do remember the Bourbon biscuits – I simply adored Bourbon biscuits. We had our tea in the kitchen and then proceeded to the library of course.

Around this time the young Powell (he was eight) organized a local children's debating society. The idea was that at each meeting one child discoursed on a subject that took the fancy and, at the end of half an hour, the others would ask questions. One such occasion that has come down through history was Powell arguing his belief that Bacon, and not Shakespeare, wrote at least *Henry V* and *A Midsummer Night's Dream*, as well as other plays in the Shakespearian canon. He seemed to have forgotten this episode by 1983, when he recalled[11] that his first doubts as to the authorship of the plays were aroused when in 1963, he had been asked to contribute three talks to the BBC World Service's celebration of Shakespeare's quatercentenary:

It so happens that the two most important books of the Western world present endless challenges to the turn of mind that finds acute delight in pitting the intellect against the doubtless ultimately insoluble problems of which they bear the evidence on their faces. I am referring to the collection of Elizabethan and Jacobean plays called 'Shakespeare', and to the library of Christian books called 'the New Testament'.

His conviction is that the plays[12] demonstrate too great a political maturity for the man Shakespeare: 'The maturity of political insight started me looking at dates, dates of performance, dates of publication, dates altogether.' And he goes on to say that he broke off only when he found himself delving into the greater mystery of the evolution of the New Testament. But the origins of his proposition are not to be found in an insight dated 1963, but in the children's gatherings in Woodlands Park Road.

Meanwhile Jack was devoting more and more time to science subjects, excellence in which was required to win the (necessary) scholarship for King Edward's. His secondary school made no particular impression on him. He was not to visit it after leaving for twenty-seven years, when he returned as a Member of Parliament. In due course he procured his scholarship, and went to King Edward's, two years younger than usual, and rather to the chagrin of the King's Norton teaching staff.[13]

Powell was to be immensely happy at his new school, but he got off to a false start, being initially placed – because of his scholarship results – on the science side. For physical exercise he resorted to the school gymnasium. He took no part in the various extra-curricular ball games ('. . . those team games which I have never myself been able to appreciate . . .') nor in the OTC, which comes as a surprise when one considers his subsequent distinguished military career. 'Boys playing at soldiers,' he says, 'never had any appeal for me.' For relaxation he chose to pursue music, his instrument the clarinet. The reason for the choice is itself interesting. He had learned that the clarinet was the only instrument used in both band and orchestra, and the concealed exuberance of his nature inclined him to want to let himself go in a band.

For some time music – into the study as well as the performance of which he, as usual, threw his mind and spirit – threatened to draw him away from his earlier studies. 'He was either at his books,' reports a contemporary, C. F. Evans, 'or he was walking purposively [sic] from A to B with a goal in mind, with either his books or his clarinet under his arm, pale, head rather forward, shoulders slightly stooped.' Or, as the contemporary quoted earlier, recorded: '. . . I can still picture him arriving home – much later than the rest of us because of the long journey from King Edward's – with his dark blue cap with the light blue rings round it pulled well down over his forehead and his bulging satchel under his arm.'

The exclusion of all other interests (the gymnasium was simply a convenient way of keeping fit) save books and music was not, surprisingly enough, something that made his mother altogether happy. Certainly, she had concentrated her enormous industry and her steely will on giving her boy every opportunity to excel at his studies but, as he testifies, she was also anxious that he should play some part in extra-curricular activities. The child turned down all such proposals quite firmly: they simply did not interest him. It followed that the only occasions on which he forgathered with a group of his schoolfellows was when he was playing the clarinet in what one boy who wrote music later called 'that really rather awful school orchestra'.

After a term Powell was moved from science to the classics form, which was, as it happened, somewhat under strength. He was younger than many of his fellows and he had besides, missed two and a half years of Greek. He announced that he would be top of the form within two terms and – with his mother getting him up earlier than usual in the morning for extra coaching – he fulfilled his boast.

It was to take some time before the clarinet was exorcized. At the age of fifteen Powell paused in his consideration of his future. He was becoming increasingly entranced by music. He felt he was a good performer, and he was turning his eyes towards a scholarship at the Royal Academy of Music and, for a brief period, seriously entertained the thought of devoting himself entirely to an artistic life. Debate took place at home and his parents – wisely, one feels – dissuaded him. With a gesture reminiscent of the Duke of Wellington burning his beloved violin upon joining the Army and settling for a military career, Powell immediately abandoned the clarinet. Years later, on being asked why he so rarely listened to music he replied, 'I don't like things which interfere with one's heart strings. It doesn't do to awaken longings that can't be fulfilled.'[14]

The willingness to be alone – the liking of being alone – which his fellow schoolboys saw in the young Powell was reflected, many years later, by an article he wrote for the school magazine, *The*

Old Edwardians' Gazette.[15] Here we find not a single reference to school friends, or outside activities. To a degree that would amount to insufferable toadying in a boy, or a recent graduate, but which is simply striking in a mature man of sixty, he concentrates on the school as an institution, and on his teachers. Thus, on the Headmaster in his time:

> Even in the closing years of his career, Carey Gillson – the fifth headmaster I think in succession to have been a Fellow of Trinity, Cambridge – dominated the school in its entirety, but especially and above all – fortunately for those who belonged to it – the Classical Sixth. Characteristically and wisely he devoted his few teaching hours with us to subjects outside the central prescribed necessity. It was an outline of economics one term, comparative religion or the history of science another, or in a third the Epistles of St. Paul. I have been astonished to discover how many of the memorable sayings and moments of those crucial years in the Sixth occurred in the extra-curricular hours with Carey Gillson. He personified the ideal of the sort of scholarship to which no endeavour or achievement of the human mind could be foreign soil.

It is conceivable, of course, that Powell, writing when he did, and looking back down the years to a vanished time when he was meeting his first serious challenges from high intellects, is reading back into the insubstantial memories of school days something of the characteristics of his own mature personality. But it does not seem likely, for all the evidence we have suggests that King Edward's was just such a school as he describes. That, for example, the boys were required to take part in a parliamentary debate at the end of each year (after exams) would not be thought unusual. But at King Edward's the debate was in Latin.

As his teachers impressed him, so he impressed them. 'Of all my pupils,' observed, D. J. D. Smith, one of the classics masters, 'he always insisted on the highest standards of accuracy and knowledge in those who taught him. Woe betide the careless young master, as I was, who was guilty of a rash statement because, from the back bench of the Upper Sixth would come a voice, "But, sir," followed by a long quotation from an author. He was a pupil from whom I learnt more than most.' He was never to be shy about asserting himself intellectually: at his very first supervision at Trinity (with Walter Hamilton) he corrected his teacher's use of a Greek accent.

The same intellectual self-certainty is to be seen in his decision to be called 'Enoch' – and to subscribe himself 'J. Enoch Powell'. The clarinet having been abandoned, he set himself to become the foremost classical scholar of his time – the equivalent of, or superior to, the legendary A. E. Housman (the manner of whose lyric poetry Powell also later adopted). Just before he left school, having been reading Thucydides, he decided that all the existing editions were inadequate, and resolved to make his own. At the time there was another Powell – by name John Undershell – in the field of classical scholarship. He was half a century older than Powell, and a Fellow of St John's College, Oxford. Since 'I am going to be a classical scholar and writing articles much better than his, I must make sure that there's no confusion between us.' Thus was 'Enoch' born.

And further intellectual delights were coming his way. Learning German was, as I have already mentioned,[16] a natural progression for a youngster anxious to excel in classical studies. ('One was certainly not saying, "Well, if I go to Cambridge, I can get a degree in so-and-so and then I can have a career as a this or that . . ." It was much more than "here is an opportunity, an opportunity to rise . . ." ') Powell himself avers that he took up the language with no more than a very moderate interest. But then the magic casements opened:

The recollection of Nietzsche exemplifies an observation which I believe to be common: that the memory of big experiences in the world of books is flavoured with the tang of the physical setting in which they happened. I shall never be able to dissociate *Ecce Homo* from the old flying boat route to the Antipodes, with the long hours of waiting and sweltering heat in the Gulf and across India and the forbidding aridity of Australia's northern deserts. Or again, the long avenues of thought that have led from Fraser's *Golden Bough* seem to start physically in front of the dining room fireplace of the home where as a boy of fifteen I sat hour after hour absorbing first the one volume abridgement and then the three volume edition. I cannot imagine how different my mental and religious life would have been if the impact of J. G. Fraser had come at another time or not at all. Then, about the same time, there was the detonation of *Sartor Resartus*: I still hear, when I recall the first reading of those intoxicating pages, the gentle hissing of the incandescent gas mantle above the table where homework was done, and the tone of my father's voice saying that I would find Carlyle as great an experience as he had done at the same age.[17]

Albert Powell, therefore – for all that he was less forceful than his wife – was clearly not as intellectually unimportant as he has been represented as being, nor unsupportive of his son's mental precocity.

Young Powell plunged headlong into the German experience 'where I was destined to voyage long after romantic and uncritical enthusiasm had perished forever with the rise of Nazism, and even after realization of the weakness and limitation of the "German soul" had opened the way for still growing appreciation of its Gallic antithesis.' But 'The happiest and most glorious hours of my life with books – confess it I must – have been with German books.' It was, however, characteristic of him that, much as he admired Nietzsche, he wanted to beat him as well. Nietzsche had become a professor at twenty-four. Very well: Powell would do better than that. However, 'much to my chagrin' he was not to become the occupant of a full chair until he was twenty-five.

All of these exciting new preoccupations did not in any way impede his progress at school – 'going through the place like a swathe', as a contemporary put it. The school offered three prizes – for work on Thucydides, Herodotus and Divinity. He won them all. 'I must confess to having been something of a pot hunter. If I saw something by way of a prize in view in any field I was interested in I had to go after it.' Later, at Cambridge, the winning of a pot sometimes had attached to it a certain monetary benefit. 'But I would have gone after them anyway.' The most important pot he acquired at school, however, was a crucial one – a classics scholarship to Trinity, Cambridge. The seventeen-year-old reclusive bird departed the nest of Woodlands Park Road, to flap his wings not merely in the British university most revered at the time by classical scholars the world over, but in the college which was the beating heart of classics in that university, where Housman lectured, and Gow taught, and every classics Fellow was a man of international distinction. Whatever there was – and there was little enough – of a taste for fellowship in Powell's make-up (such as might be represented in his childhood debating society) vanished utterly on the banks of the Cam. A university, he opined later, 'is a hospital in which nearly all cases are incurable . . .' And again, 'I literally worked from half past five in the morning until half past nine at night behind a sported oak, except when I went out to lectures.'[18]

The boy from King's Norton was the reverse of overwhelmed by the assumptions – social and other – of the place in which he found himself, and by a position to which very few youngsters, however able, of his class, could aspire at the time. This was perhaps because his grammar school produced more scholarship boys for Oxford and Cambridge than did any other school, private or state-funded, in the country. The fact remained, however, that boys from state-funded schools were invariably less at ease than their contemporaries from the private sector: this was as true of the brilliant 'Old Edwardians' as it was of the graduates of less famous schools. It is still a legend in Trinity that, when invited by the Master's wife to a dinner she gave each year (this was 1930) for first-year students he declined (albeit politely) on the grounds that he would be too busy working. There was no precedent for such a response: no student had ever turned down such an invitation. 'But I *was* busy. I had so much work to do.'

There is another anecdote about Powell in his first year at Trinity which has been often quoted, but which bears repetition as illustrating the self-sufficiency that he had determined he would enjoy. C. F. Evans had been at King Edward's with Powell, but had preceded him by a year to Trinity. There was a Cambridge 'Old Edwardians' Society which, among other activities, sought to smooth the passage in this new and challenging environment of their junior schoolmates. Evans therefore called on Powell. What happened is best told in his own words:

> I went to ask him to tea, as one used to ask freshmen from the old school, and climbed up the stairs of those garret rooms at Trinity and knocked on the door and Powell said, 'Come in.' I opened the door and I think I'm right in saying that it was in the middle of November and very cold; the room was quite bare except for the College furniture; as I remember it there was no fire, there were no pictures, Powell was sitting in his overcoat with a rug across his knees and he was surrounded by eighteenth-century folios. I said: 'Hello, Powell, would you like to come to tea?' and he said 'No.' I'd never met this response before and so to recover my wits I walked over to his mantelpiece and leant on it and took out a cigarette and he said, 'Would you mind not smoking.' And so I left.

The abruptness of Powell's manner at the time (and quite often since that time) was, and has been, put down to an inherent lack of grace in the man. 'I'm afraid that people often consider me rude – I mean in the conventional and not the accurate sense – when I do not mean to be so. It is a constant difficulty to interpret what other people expect. I confess to finding it just so.'

Almost immediately on his arrival in Cambridge, however, Powell, who could snub others, was outfaced. His tutor[19] was A. S. F. Gow, renowned as a close reader of the classical texts. Gow was a friend of A. E. Housman, noted as a poet in his own right as well as the editor of the Roman poet Manilius. The Housmanic view of classical scholarship was, at the time, in the ascendant. It amounted to an ideal of recension – that is to say, recovery of accurate texts. To men of Housman's and Gow's generation the moving spirit of Greek and Roman times was better interpreted in the visual art of the ancients, rather than in their words. So far as the words were concerned the vital business was to get them right. Not only in his *Manilius*[20] but in dozens of stinging reviews, Housman made clear how little he thought of scholars who paid less attention than he did to precise recension. Housman and Gow were teachers most likely to encourage the intensity of young Powell. But, on his first meeting with Gow, Powell, the most improbably well read of his schoolfellows, the most learned of children in King's Norton, the boy called 'professor' at the age of five, was slapped down. 'Well,' said Gow, 'I must say, for a scholar of the College this reading list [the list Powell was obliged to present, of books he had read in his field] is excessively thin.' 'I still hear,' Powell later recorded,[21] 'the drawling disgust of A. S. F. Gow . . . as he surveyed the gaps in my classical reading.'

I first met Gow towards the end of his life, and it was shortly after I had first met Powell. He told the story of their first meeting more or less exactly as Powell tells it. But he added the obvious (to a Cambridge teacher) rider that he thought the young man from the north needed taking down a peg or two – though he did add that Powell *was* insufficiently acquainted with the work of German scholars in his field. In any event, Powell was to recall Gow with affection. Lamenting his own lack of ability to read fast, and to absorb matter quickly, he concluded his 1962 article by saying, 'Alas, I fear that when I come to submit my reading list in the Elysian Fields, my tutor – there is no escaping him there – will still pronounce it to be "exceedingly thin".'[21]

44

A young man of Powell's diligence, thrust suddenly into a world of pure scholarship, the kind of world for which he had been preparing himself for so long, met with such a rebuke as Gow's, was bound to read ever more intensively, especially since 'I am a painfully slow reader':

> This habit of slow and intensive reading, not gladly missing a footnote or a misprint (and usually officiously proof-correcting, regardless of ownership), was perhaps the foundation of an early and continuing taste for textual criticism; but whatever may be its advantages, and I do not rate them highly, it limits severely the amount of literature a man gets through in his reading life. It also, incidentally, makes the reading of press and periodicals a weariness to the flesh so intolerable that I do as little of it as I can, and far, far less than a politician should.[22]

In my own judgement Powell's account of himself as a slow reader is on a par with his constant references to himself as having a poor memory. In his own estimation he may have those deficiencies but his is a rather special kind of estimation. It is the estimation not merely of his childhood, but of the particular Cambridge stream of educational life which he entered in 1930. To repeat what is a vital theme in the skein of his life,[23] the intensity and the closeness of the reading of texts was then adjudged the essential activity of the student of Greek and Latin. The habit of close reading was already with Powell. Its development – albeit still within the fairly close confines of international classical scholarship – was the contribution Trinity made to his life.

He immured himself in his rooms. He ventured out for his regulation dinners, to the library and, of an evening and for exercise, to walk to Cambridge railway station and back. That walk takes rather more than an hour, assuming one is stepping out briskly and is, as Mr. Roth observes,[24] 'about the least agreeable walk in Cambridge.' 'I simply picked a place to walk to, and back from. The station seemed a good destination.' The beauties of that area of the University called 'the Backs' – because it backs on the older colleges – where the River Cam flows between seemingly endless meadows and gardens, held no attractions for him. There is a curious hiatus here between the child who delighted in his father's instruction in wild life and the joy of walks and the other man who derives so much pleasure from a stroll in wooded land. For all his love of place Powell never seems to me to have enjoyed Cambridge as a place: to him Cambridge was reading, and study.

He also, of course, ventured out to lectures. He has left a memorable picture of his ideal scholar, A. E. Housman, in the *Housman Society Journal* of Summer 1972:

> His face as he read was expressionless, and the effect, especially with the heavy overhanging moustache and bald cranium, was of a voice proceeding from the mouth of one of those masks which the actors wore on the Greek tragic stage. The only movement of the body likely to be observed was a quick prefatory wielding of the window pole to exclude the hated draught from above his rostrum. The lecture having been read – always precisely fifty minutes in length – he donned his mortar board and stalked impassively back to his fastness above the Jesus Lane entrance to the repellent pile of Whetwell's Court . . . The severity of Housman's presentation was the severity not of passionlessness, but of suppressed passion, passion for true poetry and passion for truthfulness.

And Powell goes on, in what I consider to be an exceptionally revealing – and admirable – passage:

> For Housman textual criticism was the exercise of moral self-discipline, a lesson which I was later to endeavour to communicate in my own lecture-room at the University of Sydney . . . No one, I believe, ever heard Housman on Horace, *Epistles* i.7.29, the passage where Bentley[25] by conjecture restored *nitedula* (fieldmouse) in place of the nonsensical *volpecula* (little fox) of the manuscripts, without receiving the moral enlargement of a great sermon.

The fundamental point about the study of the classics in those years was that (apparently) dry work was tackled not merely with assiduity, but with emotion. To take but the easiest of many examples one should point out that anybody working on Greek texts (and the Greek is Powell's first and major love) has to start with Byzantine (roughly, medieval) copies of originals. The teasing out of interpretation, the comparison of notes and texts, and sheer frustration of the business, require not merely ability, but commitment. Commitment involves emotion, unless the student is merely a workhorse. I will record, at this point, my belief that everything Powell has done in politics has been done in a fashion he learned at Trinity.

It was evident, however, that scholarship was not enough for Housman. Apart from his homosexual friendships his nature forced him to find a release – or relief – in poetry. Not merely did he write verse, he sought a theoretical justification of his manner of doing so, especially in his formidable lecture *The name and the nature of poetry*.[26] Like the more brilliant Robert Graves,[27] who defended a very similar metrical practice years later, in his lectures as Oxford's Professor of Poetry, Housman believed that metre should be flat and tight and that, when verse was read aloud, it should be read without expression. Thus, the rolling periods of W. B. Yeats – to take but one example, which can still be heard on old records – were not for him. But nor were the loose free-verse lines of T. S. Eliot, where the stress in any given line is placed wherever the poet (or reader) wants to place it. It was in the Housmanic mode that Powell began to write his own poetry, though he records that 'the correct use of red pepper was the only actual piece of learning I ever imbibed from him in personal intercourse.' This was because, when Powell became a Fellow, and was by way of meeting Housman regularly, the great man was nearing the end of his life. He rarely spoke in the Combination Room, and never about the classics nor poetry, confining himself to discussing food and keeping an eye on the kitchen. His last writings were for the kitchen suggestion book, and consist of such gems as 'jugged hare without redcurrant jelly is not food.'

The fashion in which Powell began and continued merits digression, for it is highly revealing of his character. What characterizes most poetry in English until the twentieth century is the tension it enjoys over prose. The rules of metre require the ordering of stress within a line, and the ordering of rhythm within a poem. In general it may be said that the historically prevailing pattern in English poetry is iambic, an iamb being an unstressed followed by a stressed syllable. In anapaestic verse, however, two unstressed syllables are followed by one which is stressed. The way in which stresses are organized constitutes the music of poetry, and in Powell's case it may well be that the resonance which poetry allowed him to exploit was not merely a vent through which suppressed emotion could pour, but a replacement for the music he had abandoned at fifteen. The great thing for writers like himself and Housman was that poetry was organized emotion.[28]

However, increasingly in the twentieth century, poets began to stress the emotion rather than the organization. Rhythm – as used, say, by Ezra Pound or W. B. Yeats – continued to be important, but the naked display of feeling was even more so. Thus, verse became free – the original phrase describing this practice was French, *vers libre*, which became current in the late nineteenth century – and the placing of stress became the business of the poet himself, who did not respond to any rules of poetical grammar laid down by tradition. This made agreed reading of lines an exceptionally difficult business, for nobody could be sure exactly where the stress – and thus the pitch of emotion – should be laid. Chaucer's hope that no reader should 'thee mismetre for the faute of tongue'[29] became ever more difficult of fulfilment. The danger of free verse became the long and straggling line, with emphasis jumping about all over the place, according to who was reading.

All these difficulties were compounded for a classicist who wanted to write poetry. Greek and Latin verse depends on quantity rather than stress. 'In classical prosody,' writes one of the best scholars of this subject, 'emphasis is subordinate to duration.'[30] The English language is peculiarly resistant to this way of expression, and perhaps only Charles Kingsley in *Andromeda* has succeeded in the use of the classical mode. The problems Powell and Housman faced can be demonstrated by reference to that poem:

Hovering/over the water/he came,//upon/glittering/pinions,
Living, a/wonder out/grown//from the/tight-laced/
fold of his/sandals.

A single stroke above indicates a brief pause, a double stroke a double pause. At its best this practice is cumbersome in English. Neither Housman nor Powell were averse to experiment in their verse, but their essential ambition was to express emotion in compressed – and because compressed explosive – form. Housman, indeed, experimented with catalectic modes, meaning that, where he could, he would drop syllables (or, to speak technically, truncate the line). Both Housman and Powell were in a great poetic tradition, but their main work, of course, lay elsewhere. It is significant, however, that both felt the need to write poetry, and in their poetry one can find, in their purest forms, the various combinations of the characteristics of ordered logic and emotion which inform their prose work, spoken or written.

Powell's first public triumph in Cambridge was his winning of the Craven scholarship (for which, that year, Housman was the senior examiner), an almost unheard of achievement for a freshman. He went on to take the Pemberton, the Members' Latin Essay Prize, the Browne Medal and the Porson Prize (the reward for winning which, a steel engraving of the Greek scholar, hangs above his desk in his room today). Many years later, he was to consider, for a series being run by the *Sunday Times* in which living writers invented dialogues with the great deceased, Porson as a subject, 'but he would probably have been too drunk to carry on a conversation.'[31] Of all these prizes, however, the Craven made most difference to his mode of life: he had £300 from his scholarships; the Craven gave him an extra £100 a year. Like John Buchan in an earlier generation at the other university he became 'rather rich for an undergraduate'. He was able to defray the costs of numerous forays to the continent, to German and Italian libraries in particular, in pursuit of his work. He travelled around his own country for vacation time pleasure as well, but he did so parsimoniously, frequently spending the night on railway platforms, rather than going to the expense of lodgings.

The *Lexicon to Herodotus* is perhaps his most formidable and pure – as it is certainly the most forbidding – contribution to classical scholarship. This extraordinarily meticulous work proceeded in tandem with his translation of the *History*, which he was to persuade the Oxford University Press to bring out in the language of the Authorized Version because 'the simple and flowing language of Herodotus needs least remoulding for modern English ears if presented in the style and cadences rendered familiar by the Bible.'

Powell graduated with the expected first in 1933 and, in recognition of a dissertation on Thucydides, was awarded a fellowship. He had scarcely, it seemed, noticed the rise of Nazism in his (by now beloved) Germany, but in 1934 his world of dreams about what he called 'my spiritual homeland' crumbled around him. On 30 June 1934 Hitler ordered the slaughter of Ernst Roehm and the Brown Shirt leaders, and the naked brutality of his regime became immediately apparent.

I can still remember clearly how I sat for hours in a state of shock, shock which you experience when, around you, you see the debris of a beautiful building in which you have lived for a long time . . . So it had all been illusion, all fantasy, all a self-created myth. Music, philosophy, poetry, science and the language itself – everything was demolished, broken to bits on the cliffs of a monstrous reality. The spiritual homeland had not been a spiritual homeland after all, since nothing can be a homeland, let alone a spiritual homeland, where there is no justice, where justice does not reign. Overnight my spiritual homeland had disappeared and I was left only with my geographical homeland.[32]

With the Roehm killings Powell began his interest in politics – not in domestic, but in foreign politics. (His interest in a domestic political career did not begin until he was in India at the end of the war.) The events of 1934, moreover, convinced him that war with Germany was inevitable, his conviction being that so brutal (and brutalizing) a government would eventually turn its aggression on neighbouring nations, as well as upon its own people. Further, while it would be wrong to say that he was socially familiar with German society, his extensive acquaintance among the ranks of German scholars provided something of a conduit of information and feeling, particularly as some of his connections – and perhaps most notably Paul Maas[33] – were Jews. He resolved that he would join up instantly on the outbreak of war (indeed, he made something of an effort to enlist on the Ethiopian side when that country was invaded by Italy in 1936), and announced his intention to all those universities to which he applied for professorships, beginning immediately after he had acquired his own fellowship. He recalls, indeed, that the Vice Chancellor in Sydney, where he landed his chair, thought him a little odd to expect war.

His perception in 1934 had a further, and more immediate, impact on him. If there was to be a war, and if he was going to fight in it, and if – as he fully expected – he was to be killed, then there was a great deal of work to be done before the conflict began. He redoubled his efforts. It was in 1932 that he encountered the Rendel Harris Papyri in Birmingham. These documentary records (written in Greek) of Egyptian life between about 200 and 400 A.D. had been brought to England many years previously by Dr. James Rendel Harris, Curator of the Rylands Library in Manchester, who encouraged Powell in a project to mount, translate and publish them. All this had been achieved by 1936, a year after Powell had read - in Italian – an outstanding paper on the subject to the International Congress of Papyrology in Florence.

The translation of Herodotus and the *Lexicon* proceeded. In

1936 he discovered (as I have already mentioned) the manuscript of the *Llyfr Blegywryd* in Trinity College Library. He reported on his find in the *Bulletin of the Board of Welsh Studies*, and this report attracted the attention of the Welsh scholar Stephen Williams, who subsequently recorded his amazement that Powell had, unaided, made himself into a highly competent scholar of medieval Welsh. The two men entered into collaboration, and their edition of the book appeared in 1942.

In these pre-war years, reclusive though he was, he made two friendships that were to last. The first was with Edward Curtis, an undergraduate at Clare College. It was a relationship which puzzled their contemporaries, for Curtis was no intellectual. However, friendship blossomed, and years later Curtis was to be best man at Powell's wedding. At this period, between 1933 and 1936, Powell spent a great deal of time in German and Italian libraries, working furiously to 'beat the clock of war', and sustained by the fact that Trinity had agreed to make a grant towards the publication of the *Lexicon*. In Rome he made the acquaintance of Andrew Freeth, a talented artist from Birmingham, whose sketches of the young Powell, not infrequently used to adorn later writings by him, are an invaluable part of the story of his early manhood.

The *Lexicon* was an enormous task, aided though he was by the acquisition in 1935 of a substantial collection of slips of paper (compiled before the First World War by the German scholars Ludwig Kalpers and Fritz Nawak) listing total word usage in Herodotus. Powell developed the Kalpers-Nawak system into a much more elaborate one and his task – the book listed every variation of meaning, and every wrong attribution – was finalized by 1937: the achievement was herculean.

All this time he continued writing poetry, though (as my earlier analysis indicates) his style and mode remained fixed, and were increasingly out of sympathy with developing modernism. There was, moreover, a great deal of scholarship (other than the Papyri and the *Llyfr*) outside the strict scope of his own major research. That he should write in *The Classical Quarterly* in April 1938 on 'The archetype of Thucydides' or on Herodotus (many times) in such journals as *Philologische Wochenschrift* is to be expected, but what are we to make of 'A palimpsest of St Chrysostom' in the *Journal of Theological Studies* in April 1938?

The truth is that the enormous pressure of his main work in no way impeded that intellectual voracity of which I have already made mention. He could not see an intellectual puzzle without tackling it, and without coming to firm conclusions about it. The buckram-bound volumes containing these early works in the classics field now repose in his house (a large part of his original classics library he gave to Trinity when he joined the Army) and the range of his notes and essays (for all that they are written in the clipped shorthand favoured by the classical journals) is quite amazing. I understand that he is less, in the view of other classicists, an original or imaginative thinker, more a scholar of the utmost meticulousness and, of course, industry.

I am not, myself, competent to judge the place of his output in the history of classical scholarship. Reading the dense and tight prose, however, difficult though the subject matter may be, one is struck by one characteristic habit of mind and style which has remained with him into the full maturity of his political career. It has often been remarked that there is a particular methodology to any major Powell speech. He first sets out the view he is about to attack, in tones of mock astonishment. He then expounds on its complexity or, rather, its supposed complexity. He then announces that he has discovered a solution – or an alternative – which is devastatingly simple. In an article entitled 'The sources of Plutarch's Alexander' he addresses himself to the question of whether Alexander the Great's two biographers; Plutarch and Arrian, could have copied from one another. After a rigorous examination of texts, Powell shows – to my mind conclusively – that both writers were using the same source, a compilation biography now lost. In the 1939 *Journal of Hellenic Studies* he writes:

The sources of Plutarch's Alexander have hitherto been a subject passed by without examination in detail, not because examination was superfluous but because the task was considered hopeless on account of its apparent complexity. Our enquiry has shown the fallacy of that appearance and the way in which the biography has to be treated as a historical source; all passages under suspicion of deriving from the spurious letters of Alexander had to be rejected; the rest represents an imperfect and often careless epitome, which may be supplemented from Arrian, of an encyclopaedic Alexandrine biography.

All the tone of later Powell is to be found foreshadowed in that passage.

For all his new-found perception of the threat to European

peace, however, Powell did nothing to throw himself into the battle against appeasement. 'I was, if you like, fatalistic. There was nothing I could do to change the course of events, nor their outcome. I was sure that war would come, and I was content to leave it at that.' There is, however, an interesting report[34] of a lecture he gave to the Classical Association. His subject was 'The War and its aftermath in their influence on Thucydidean studies'. The immediate experience of the war, he wrote,

> . . . left critics more open-minded and less moralistic. Especially significant of this is the change of interpretation of the Melian Dialogue, which is now more commonly regarded as a defence than as a condemnation of Athenian policy. Questions like Imperialism and the command of the sea are now approached in an atmosphere of greater reality, with corresponding advantage of the comprehension of Thucydides.

But

> In contrast with the war itself, post-war politics have exercised a baneful influence in that, consciously or unconsciously, the interpretation of Thucydides has been perverted to partisan ends. In England, for instance, the historian has been represented as a pacifist in the modern style; while in Germany, where the effect of National Socialism on classical studies is particularly lamentable, Thucydides is being systematically interpreted as the unrecognized prophet of Nazi ideology and the Thucydidean Pericles made into a prototype of Hitler.

It is common – every generation does it – to interpret the past in terms of the needs and beliefs of the present. The Whig interpretation of English history – according to which that history demonstrates a linear improvement both in aspiration and achievement over generations – still has influence. It was dominant until Herbert Butterfield destroyed it on scholarly grounds.[35] Even then, in another book,[36] Butterfield himself put forward a similarly normative view of the history of his country. One of Powell's own favourite historians, Jacob Burckhardt, the Swiss historian of the Renaissance – and a man who did more than any other scholar to create Europe-wide interest in that fascinating period of classical revival in Italy – 'consciously or unconsciously' re-arranged his perspective in the light less of the evidence than of his own preoccupations. What is striking about

Powell's lecture on Thucydides is that, at so tender an age, he was clearly alive to the dangers and pitfalls of what is called historicism, precisely that idea of identifying with the past in terms of the present, the character of which I have adumbrated.

It is important, further,[37] to recall that the practice of the day in classical studies – and the sinews of the educational tradition from which Powell himself derived – saw education as improvement, and the classics (given exceptions devoted to pure scholarship such as Housman) as a method of training for public service and government. In 1936 the twenty-four-year-old Mr. Powell of Trinity was able to cut through all this and, in a remarkable piece of historiography,[38] to lay bare with clinical force the use being made of – and the comfort being taken from – the first ancient Greek historian by the elite classes of two of the most gifted nations in the world. For his biographer this moment in 1936 is of immense importance: I have suggested that the method of analysis Powell displayed before the Classical Association demonstrates the presence in the young man of the force of the older politician. But it is the fusion of concerns that is, truly, the vital point to emphasize: to this day Powell uses classical tags in political speeches. But, whereas such adornment of a text by other politicians is, usually, no more or no less than that – an adornment, the use of what Churchill called 'a serviceable quotation'[39] – with Powell it is a part of the fabric of his thought, an expression of the organized unity of his mind.

Nor, after he had been elected to his fellowship, did Powell demonstrate any lack of belief in himself and his abilities. 'Never, I think, having been guilty of underestimating my claims, I didn't consider myself suitable for being a Lecturer or a Reader. So I thought I'd better get a chair. I put in for professorships and quite a number of them went jolly well until they discovered that I was only twenty-three, and then there was a marked coolness.'

The University of Sydney was the only university in the Commonwealth of Australia that funded a chair in Greek although, interestingly, Greek and Latin were widely taught in Australian and New Zealand schools.[40] The Australians were undeterred by the youth of this brilliant applicant – 'Just out of nappies, and as arrogant as hell to boot,' as one of his students, Gough Whitlam, later Prime Minister of Australia, observed – and, at twenty-five, he took up his appointment. 'Nietzsche, much to my chagrin, beat me.'

The journey to Australia brought him first to Darwin, by flying boat. A later essay[41] recalls his early impressions, and I insert it here because of its significance as telling us of certain perceptions of his which were to become significant in his life a decade later. He was trying to sort out his impressions of the great new country in which he found himself resident, so young, and yet so (in academic terms) senior. He noted the unwillingness of Australian governments to countenance immigration from Asia, and remarked:

> Finding herself providentially lacking the elements of racial division, yet able to achieve her national development without creating them, Australia would be worse than foolish if she did not jealously preserve the advantage of an all-white population. There will be problem enough in the assimilation of the 'new Australians' from Europe who have been increasing the population of Australia by immigration at an average rate of 1% a year since the war.

It could be argued that, in 1958, Powell was not perhaps altogether accurately recalling first impressions already more than twenty years old. But surely it cannot be gainsaid, that, at least as early as 1958, he was seized of the dangers of racial division.

On the dreary journey to Australia Powell read Nietzsche and d'Annunzio, and continued with his emendations of Arrian. Mere discomfort has never inhibited his ability to work. Before he had left Cambridge, however, certain reservations had been expressed about how so private and intense a scholar would make out as a teacher. Powell was in no doubt, and he was already seized of a philosophy about the matter which he was to express many years later in an article about the reforms Lord Franks had recommended to the University of Oxford.[42]

> The distinction between learning and teaching is always a more or less false distinction. The double meaning of the word 'doctor', someone who is learned because he teaches and teaches because he is learned, is a constant reminder of the fact. Those who pursue knowledge together will always be found surrounded by people attracted to them by the prospect of being taught . . .

The tradition of classical scholarship in Australia, if not exactly flourishing, was promising. Powell was the fourth Professor of Greek at Sydney, the third successor to Charles Badham, who founded the chair in 1866. Powell recalls having thirty to forty pupils in a class, of which number about a dozen were of honours standard. He set himself a missionary as well as a pedagogic challenge, for he determined on (and succeeded in) visiting every school or institution in Australia and New Zealand which offered a classics course, to spread the missionary word of his inaugural lecture – that the only civilized man was the one who knew Greek.

He threw himself, then, into his work with the organized enthusiasm of which he was so readily capable. He even began to broadcast, being given a regular half-hour slot by the Australian Broadcasting Corporation to descant on 'Antiquity in the News'. In the lecture room, however, his methods were not such as readily to endear him to any but the most dedicated students. He was widely described as a 'textual pervert' (the coinage being popularly attributed to Gough Whitlam) for he brought to the Antipodes that rigorous and even fierce concentration on the business of establishing a purified text that was the be-all and end-all of the Cambridge tradition. The principle is undoubtedly admirable and (as some of the reviewers of the *Lexicon* observed) the gentler (and perhaps more romantic) cultivation of classical culture is impossible without a corpus of clearly authoritative texts – the work of such men as Housman and Powell was to establish, as far as possible, the authority of as many texts as possible. Powell at least gave his attention to far more significant works than did Housman: the latter may be judged the finer scholar – but, then, he devoted his life to scholarly work – but no one could pretend that it is as important to have his *Manilius* as it is to have Powell's guide to the language of Herodotus and Thucydides.

His teaching method was not one for the faint-hearted, nor for a student with only a moderate interest in the subject. He liked to take a Greek text which contained a famous corruption. A victim (one can hardly use any other word) would be selected from his class and asked one question after another. 'The whole idea was to lead the pupil to make his own discovery. We would question him closely, but never reveal our hand. He would be driven from pillar to post until he could see only one way out – the way towards the right reading.'

For a student such as Powell himself had been, and for any boy or girl who was set on becoming a critic of the classical texts, this method (and it has been used in other places on other subjects[43]) is superb. But it is important to emphasize again that it is truly suited only to the exceptionally able, and the exceptionally dedicated. But, then, these were the pupils in whom Powell was most interested: his zeal for the spread of the classics was a zeal directed essentially towards the gifted, and his principles were of the greatest austerity.

Powell's attitude to Australia and Australians (and theirs to him) cannot be very precisely defined. He was certainly greatly attracted by the virginity of the soil, both intellectual and physical, on which he found himself. He rightly praised the Australians for their eagerness and energy in all fields, and derided by comparison the slothful and self-indulgent fellow countrymen he had left behind. 'No one can deny, I am afraid, that a good deal of present-day English writing is very shoddy stuff. With rare exceptions, the newspapers and the wireless tend powerfully to promote vulgarity. By day and by night in our cities the eyes and ears are continually assaulted by objects of bad taste . . .'

None the less, he was homesick. He recalled 'the dull pang I had known and shared in Sydney University . . . the heartache of the exile, the oppressive sense of being remote, from everything that ultimately mattered, from all that gave one birth.'[44] Relations with his colleagues, if not unhappy, were certainly not intimate. His intellectual isolation and the brusqueness of his manners hardly made for friendship. His shyness in teaching female pupils – indeed, his difficulties in establishing relations with women generally – was thought odd. It was no surprise, even if it was a trifle disconcerting, to learn that his arrival in Sydney had not meant his giving up his search for a chair more congenially placed geographically. Of course, there were reasons for this search other than the purely personal: Australia *was* remote for anybody specializing in Powell's line of work, and there was his settled conviction that there would be a war, and that he would have a role in it. In any event, in 1938 he was offered the Chair of Greek and Classical Literature at Durham and in December of that year he returned briefly to England to make arrangements to take up the appointment at the beginning of 1940.[45]

That winter he visited Germany, and, particularly, Königsberg. In 1984, in a speech at Uppingham, he referred to the two periods in his life in which he was 'ashamed of my own country. The first period was the Chamberlainite appeasement era of 1937-39, and I recall to this day my sensation of embarrassment on producing a British passport at the German frontier in December 1938.'[46]

He was on a mission of mercy. In Florence in 1935 he

had met the great German-Jewish classicist, Paul Maas. Maas was interested in all of Powell's work, but their friendship had started with the Rendel Harris Papyri. Powell had come to warn his friend to flee Germany, before the assault on the Jews reached its apogee. Maas was reluctant but, in order to provide him with a means of escape Powell travelled to Berlin and obtained a visa from the British consulate there. In the event Maas made use of the document at the last possible moment, and arrived in England on 31 August 1939.

Back in Australia Powell continued his arduous round, but his preoccupations were turning more and more towards home. In June of 1939 an Englishman, one R. M. Tinkler, was bayoneted to death in Tientsin, in the course of the Sino-Japanese conflict. Powell wrote:

> Murdered, deny who can,
> Here lies an Englishman;
> The steel that through him ran
> Was tempered in Japan.
>
> Who then the murderer?
> England, that would not stir,
> Not though he died for her;
> England, the slumberer.
>
> His cries she would not hear
> Because insensate fear
> Had stopped the mother's ear;
> But now revenge is near,
>
> For while his land forgets
> And bends the knee to threats,
> His vengeful spirit whets
> The German bayonets.

On September 3 war began. Powell was on his way from New Zealand to Australia. He arrived on September 4, resigned, pinned a note announcing his departure (written in Greek) to his lecture room door, and booked a flight home, to take the King's shilling as a private in the Royal Warwickshire Regiment.

3

The Soldier
1940-1945

One can never resolve in the span of a human lifetime
that kind of a revolution [the end of empire] without
the marks being left of a struggle. I confess to you that
for all that I write, for all that I think, for all that I try
to demonstrate to myself and others I shall go to the
grave with a conviction at the back of my mind that
Her Majesty's ships still sweep the oceans of the world
in case there should be any hostile warships which it
might be necessary to sink. That hallucination will be
there when the mind stops.

– J. Enoch Powell, 'The consequences of the general election'
in Swinton College Journal, Summer, 1965.

The reader will recall[1] that, at school, Powell professed something
very like contempt for the OTC (which had a strong tradition
and following at King Edward's), deriding it as 'schoolboy
soldiering'. His attitude was not, however, as simple as that
of the academically inclined pupil who despises (and, perhaps,
fears) the roughness and pugnacity of team games, the aggression
of soldiering and, usually, the spit and polish of even childish military effort. His two Greek historians, Herodotus and Thucydides,
were historians of war, and he made a quixotic effort to join the
Ethiopian fighting against Mussolini. At that time a hint was given
him that there would be a place in the Intelligence Services for
him in the event of European conflict, and with that half-promise
he had to be content. It was, indeed, in Intelligence that he spent
much of his war, and it was there that he gave the distinguished
service which helped him to rise from private to being the

youngest brigadier in the Army, just as he had been the youngest professor in the Commonwealth.

Powell was not however prepared to accept the assumption, very common at the time, that academics *should* go into Intelligence, not only because they had trained minds and would be good at sorting out the mass of information expected to flow from resistance movements on the continent and from the great mass of decoded German material available to the Ultra station at Bletchley Park,[2] but also because (in R. H. S. Crossman's formulation) they, trained to truth, would prove expert at telling the lies propaganda required.[3] Powell wanted to fight. He was quite prepared to believe that he would be killed and, indeed, more than half expected it. But if he were not, he determined that he would end the war as a major-general – an ambition he came within an ace of achieving. To this day, however, he expresses chagrin that he came no nearer action than hearing at the GHQ of 8th Army the boom of advancing German guns.

On returning to Britain in September 1939 he found himself baulked by the 'phoney war'. The army was not accepting recruits without previous military training with the fighting arms. By a lucky chance he heard that the Australian High Commission had intervened on behalf of Australians who, having come home to serve, were on their beam ends when unable to enlist, and had agreed that certified Australians would be accepted straight away in to the lowest rank. Powell obtained such a certificate, and was enlisted at Edgware recruiting office on 20 October with 'the regiment of his choice', the Royal Warwicks. He has claimed ever since to be the only Englishman who got into the British Army by passing himself off as an Australian.[4]

There was, in truth, something particular in Powell's nature that made him relish the thought of starting at the very bottom of the heap. Another man possessed of his vaulting ambition, and even some part of his intelligence, would have – and with perfect justification – used his qualities and the record of what he had done even in so different a field, to enter at least some rungs further up the ladder, and proceed from there. Powell found what many of those who have become close to him over the years consider to be a perverse satisfaction in proving to himself and others that he could get anywhere he wanted from wherever he chose to start and that, indeed, the bottom was the best place for beginning to learn in every detail about an institution which he rapidly came to revere and his love for which has done nothing but wax over the years since 1939.

Of course, there were many other gifted young men in that intake of staggering quality. After Powell had served his apprenticeship and was posted to Aldershot he found himself in the company of such as Hardy Amies, the publisher James MacGibbon, the budding diplomat (and linguist) David Hunt.[5] Later there was Malcolm Muggeridge, who told Andrew Roth,[6] 'I was immediately impressed by him. I remember this strange-looking man who had a rather remarkable moustache – it was almost a soup-strainer moustache . . . I asked him why afterwards, and with his usual honesty he replied that he grew it to convey an impression of Nietzsche. He was an extraordinary young man.'

Even so, Powell stood out from the beginning, as much because of his manner and character as because of his achievements and brilliance. His fellows did not find him unfriendly, and he was a good deal more clubbable than he had been either at Cambridge or in Sydney. In part, of course, this was because Army life did not allow for the kind of seclusion he had granted himself in earlier years. But there was also the fact that his instantly acquired reverence for the Army as an institution, and his realization that comradeship underpinned it, made him, if not softer, at least more approachable.

From the very first moment he threw himself into the history and theory of warfare. His first experience was one of surprise, for he immediately discovered that his professional superiors by no means shared his enthusiasm for the war in Europe. 'The surprise was repeated at the Staff College, in 1941, when I arrived with Clausewitz, Jomini,[7] the textbooks on the American Civil and the Russo-Jap, etc., already devoured in barrackrooms and billets, to discover that the war of nations, *la grande guerre*, was not the passion and the life interest of highly talented and professional instructors.'[8]

The trouble was, of course, that the British was an imperial Army. 'I had come up against a capital fact about the British Army, anxious for "this show" to be over, so as to "get down to some real soldiering again".' And, later in the same article,[8] 'The horror and loathing inspired in retrospect by Passchendaele and the Somme confirmed the nation's instinctive conviction that the continent was no place for the British Army.'

Though he was no stranger to quite intense imperial feelings – particularly as regards India – Powell in 1939 came to war quite unencumbered by colonial distractions, or habits acquired that would inhibit a virtually exclusive military emphasis on Europe. The bulk of what he read was concerned either with continental war, or with wars fought by soldiers who had, essentially, learned from the European model. But, as he says:

> This is Powell the wartime soldier's comment on the pre-war peacetime Army and the institution for which he retains the liveliest affection and admiration. But I wasn't entirely surprised by this because the whole stance of the United Kingdom towards the continent of Europe had seemed to me to ignore the nature of grand warfare from which modern post-Napoleonic Europe derived and I never felt that England, even after the Boer War, had come to terms with the Napoleonic revolution in warfare. At the Staff College it was my jest that the regular officer was uneasy with any formation larger than a brigade. You might possibly push him up to considering a division or even, at the utmost extent, an Army Corps, but the notion that there were such things as armies and groups of armies was abhorrent to him. That was not a world in which he would wish to live. Unfortunately, that was the world with which the United Kingdom was threatened.

As the years have gone by, moreover, this emphasis has been given ever greater stress. The last time he took what might be called an imperialist or colonial stance on matters military was in 1954, when he supported the Conservative rebels against Anthony Eden's plans for withdrawal from the Suez Canal Zone. It is worth noting here that his keen support for Mrs. Thatcher during the war for the Falkland Islands was not part of an imperial argument, for he regarded the Falklands as being in an entirely different category from that of other remnants of empire. His conviction was that:

> The invasion of the Falklands was a threat to our command of the sea which we had to command, and I had previously as it happened, in 1967, designated the Falklands as a position of strategic importance to these islands . . . Putting it another way, if they had been uninhabited the case for the expedition would have been the same, as indeed was the case for recovering South Georgia – 'Rejoice, Rejoice.' I wonder if she noticed there was nobody on South Georgia?

But he did not set out to be merely a theoretical soldier. He was both assiduous and meticulous in the performance of his duties, however humble, showing none of the frequently expressed (and understandable) irritation of other high-powered brains with the menial side of military life. To this day he records in *Who's Who* the occasion on which he placed his foot on the first rung of the awesome ladder of military advancement, when he became a lance-corporal. Of this achievement he has since observed: 'It was really tremendous . . . It was the biggest kick-up I've ever had. Perhaps becoming a Privy Councillor was comparable. But for sheer crossing of a barrier I don't think I've ever known anything otherwise quite like it.'

It is important to stress that, for all his openly declared ambition (he was prone to telling his companions, with very little prompting, that he would be at least a brigadier by the end of the war, and his seemingly naïve self-faith caused not infrequent amusement) Powell was exceptionally happy at every stage of his military life. Perhaps this was because 'the whole institution of the Army, the framework of discipline, the exactitude of rank, the precision of duty, was something almost restful and attractive to me and I took great pride in smartness at drill.' He has, indeed, often proclaimed a natural taste for institutions of any kind, from Trinity to the House of Commons, though I am inclined to think that the attachment to Trinity has become somewhat exaggerated over time: certainly, he wasted no time leaving Cambridge once the Sydney offer was made.

However, this preoccupation with his new existence, and his dedication to the new position of service in which he found himself, did not inhibit pursuit of his other interests. He continued to write poetry. At Warwick, where he was first stationed, he had the River Avon, and its great castle. Within striking distance there was also Kenilworth, with another castle, the one associated with Walter Scott's novel. And, partly to improve his understanding of military cartography, he undertook an intensive study of the Ordnance Survey. Even on a visit to his parents, by this time retired to Seaford, he embarked on a lengthy hike to establish an error in the Survey. It is worth noting, somewhat out of chronology, that this, like his other interests, has never died: he was reviewing, and correcting, the latest Survey in *The Daily Telegraph* as late as 1983. He has complained frequently of his own inability to keep up with his manifold interests – 'I never look into that corner of my room where the classics stand, or the Indian books, without a feeling of regret, or even shame, that I have neglected such good old friends' – but the truth is that every topic or subject that he has taken up has remained with him through his long life's journey. And if, understandably, he is less than perfectly acquainted with the latest literature on any one of them, he still possesses a firm grounding in the essence, and a set of firm and well worked out opinions. A partial exception, which he regrets, is the poetry. 'The Muse simply departed some time after the war. She just went, flew out of the window, if you like. I don't know why these things happen. But that is the way it happened to me.' He thus writes no more verse for publication, though, on their wedding anniversary each year Pamela Powell does receive a dedicatory poem. The truth, perhaps, is that, once he found politics, not merely as a profession, but as an expression of life itself, he poured all the publicly emotional side of his life into its rhetoric, particularly its nationalist rhetoric. A university don, or a soldier, may well choose to state the emotional side of his view of existence in imaginative literature, whether poetry or prose, but a politician who believes so profoundly in the very sanctity of the nation, and the institutions through which it is governed, has other ways of communicating with his fellow countrymen.

What has to be stressed about his early months at Warwick is that, eagerly though he sought promotion, he did so only by the means most obviously available to him – doing every job handed to him punctiliously. (He likes to recall the boyish delight with which he received a compliment from his sergeant that he was the smartest soldier in the company.) It was, indeed, at least partly by accident that, at the beginning of 1940, he was plucked away from his regiment. A brigadier undertaking a tour of inspection asked Powell how he liked kitchen work. Powell replied with a classical Greek quip. The brigadier understood it, and promptly inquired why such a man was on such duties. Shortly afterwards Lance-Corporal Powell was posted to an Arctic barracks at Aldershot for training as an Intelligence officer.

The stay at Aldershot with other cadets hand-picked for linguistic ability produced two experiences, one fairly trivial and even comic, and one indicative of his intellectual omnivorousness. First, he acquired a temporary licence to drive any military vehicle, and very nearly killed both himself and his instructor. Later, he was to attempt the motorcycle, with equivalent lack of success. There is, still later, a delightful account of his driving in North Africa.[9] To this day it is uncomfortable, if not exactly dangerous, to travel as his passenger, particularly since he entertains the conviction that all speedometers are set at five m.p.h. above the actual speed of the car.

It was at this time that he began his acquaintance with Portuguese literature. So improbably widely read did he seem to his fellow trainees (there was no A. S. F. Gow here to criticize the narrowness of his learning) that it became a hobby with many to pick holes in his knowledge. He had to confess, on one occasion, that he was unfamiliar with the work of the late medieval Portuguese epic poet Camoes. The man who teased him on this point got his come-uppance more than a year later in Africa when he repeated his jest. Powell had by then learned Portuguese, and had a finger-tip knowledge of the works of Camoes. In the early 1970s, when he undertook arduous speaking tours not only in Britain, but on the continent, expressing opposition to plans for the United Kingdom to join the Common Market, he spoke fluently in public in three languages. This illustrates again the important point about the retentiveness of his mind. Most people find that fluency – or, at any rate, competence – in a foreign language is a flower that easily withers unless fostered by use. The organization of Powell's mind, however, is such that the passage of time seems scarcely at all to cause a rusting over of knowledge once garnered. It is true, as I have already observed, that those who know these things criticize the stilted character of his use of foreign languages (the French were vastly puzzled by his translation of 'Shadow Cabinet' as '*Cabinet Ombre*'). But it would be a harsh critic (and it would have to be a polyglot) who could withhold admiration from his linguistic achievements. But, then, language is of immense importance to him for in language, he believes, resides the essence of a nation. 'Tell me,' he pronounced once at a party after one of his anti-EEC forays, 'how dare Heath and Wilson go around claiming to be good Europeans? Neither can speak half-decent French. How dares Heath, in particular, to set himself up as something approaching the ideal European citizen? There is no prominent British politician who has a quarter – a tenth – of my knowledge of European culture. *I* am the truest European.' This was not said in any way boastfully: it was merely a statement of what he saw as a fact; and if there was outrage in his tone, it was outrage at the thought of all those who did not recognize the fact as he saw it.

In 1941 he was promoted to captain, and transferred to the general staff of the 9th Armoured division at Guilsborough. Here again he was fortunate. He delighted, in general, his seniors with his diligence. But he particularly pleased his Commanding Officer, Major-General Montagu Burrows. The C.O. even went so far as to invite this beginner to lecture the staff on the likely evolution of the war. Burrows evidently saw that his men were in danger of being disheartened. It was a difficult time. Britain seemed to be on the retreat everywhere. The North African picture was gloomy. The *materiel* required particularly by the armoured divisions was slow to arrive and poor in quality. It would be wrong to say that defeatism had taken hold, but it was certainly in the air. Men naturally looked to their own concerns, and the poverty of their equipment at Guilsborough was under their noses: it was not easy to take a broad strategic view there.

Powell, however, had been learning Russian, and he had begun to look at the overall picture of the war in a way that few of his colleagues could. His thesis – obvious enough in retrospect – was bracingly original for his time.[10] He took the view that Germany would ultimately attack Russia, and that economic and other considerations would draw the United States into the war. 'Once that happens Hitler is finished.' One of those present when Captain Powell produced these novel conclusions – and who had doubted not merely his country's capacity to win, but even her capacity to survive – sketched the effect on Powell's audience. 'It wasn't just what he said. It was the way he put it all. He made his conclusions not merely convincing, but inevitable. You kicked yourself for not seeing it all before. And you felt shamefaced if you had even the tiniest reservation, so overpowering was he as a lecturer.' Many in political audiences in later years would recognize the force of that analysis.

From the moment he re-entered government in 1939 – but with vastly greater power after he had become Prime Minister in 1940 – Churchill sought to broaden the war.[11] What he had seen in the traumatic weeks of the battle of France, when he had to overthrow all his own convictions to the effect that Hitler's offensive in the West would bog down in the stalemate of trench warfare that had marked the 1914-18 conflict, convinced him that the thrust of German power had to be dispersed. Hitler had destroyed Poland in twenty-seven days; he had needed only thirty-six for France.[12] To defend herself the United Kingdom had three principal assets – the English Channel, the Royal Navy, and the Royal Air Force. Her ground strength was severely limited: before Captain Powell had achieved that rank there came the retreat from Dunkirk. Churchill warned the country not to take that retreat as a victory, for wars were not won by retreats. The advantage of Dunkirk lay in the return to this country of the bulk of the British Expeditionary Force, to whom were added reasonably substantial numbers of French soldiers who chose to follow General de Gaulle into exile. The great disadvantage of the Anglo-French defeat, however, was that the BEF had left most of its equipment behind. The island redoubt would have to stand on the defensive for some time before a return to the continent could even come into contemplation. Meanwhile, there were considerable benefits to be gained from President Roosevelt's determination to sanction almost any help short of war. This was until American opinion generally, and Congressional opinion in particular, came round to the idea of the necessity of war: the President was not to know the tragic circumstances in which that opinion would change, after Pearl Harbor.

Even given his straitened circumstances, however, Churchill was determined to do what he could to dissipate German strength. It is now generally accepted by historians[13] that his decision to launch token bombing raids on Berlin was important in causing the *Luftwaffe* to break off its attack on the RAF's fighter stations – which were strategic – and concentrate firepower on London and other cities – which were not. He supported Greece in her stand against Mussolini's Italy. The British action ended in failure. But the failure was ensured only because Hitler diverted crack troops to the Mediterranean front. Churchill encouraged the Free French in their abortive raid on Dakar. All these sideshows (as Lord Allenby had called a similar effort in the Middle East in the First World War) were heavily criticized at the time. But the strategic vision that underlay them was an accurate one. While Churchill's determination to be aggressive on every front risked (as beating followed beating) the kind of demoralization which was beginning to affect the young men to whom Captain Powell spoke, the German effort *was* being spread far and wide.

Part of the spreading was the war in North Africa. Certainly, once the fall of France had assured Germany of practical, if not actual, control over that part of the north of the continent then ruled by France (it continued under the nominal suzerainty of the puppet government of Vichy) Hitler had a direct interest there. Further, Italy had an African colony in Libya, and a conquest – Abyssinia – in the Horn of Africa. Finally, in terms of territory, there were, for the Germans, potentially rich pickings in Egypt, dominated by Britain. Her control over Egypt and Gibraltar meant that Britain could at least seal the Mediterranean Sea (as well as, at this stage of the war, make use of her control of the Mediterranean islands of Malta, Cyprus and Crete). Command of the sea itself was a matter of dispute: for some time the Royal Navy did not care to dispute the ruling of the waves with the Italian Navy, supported as it was by German air power. All these factors dictated the necessity of armed conflict in the desert. The British began brilliantly under General Archibald Wavell, but fell back badly once the Afrika Corps under General Erwin Rommel stiffened the Italians, and rolled back the Allied forces.

The war in these two associated theatres – land in North Africa, and the sea itself – ebbed and flowed, and was ever volatile. To this war Powell was posted in the autumn of 1941, after a war course at the Staff College in Camberley. In that theatre he was to become Secretary to the Joint Intelligence Committee. Perhaps, and most certainly for his biographer, the most important appointment to his staff was Major Michael Strachan (he himself was promoted to Lieutenant-Colonel).[14] In general, though, it may be said that Powell formed around him a brilliant, and tightly-knit group of exceptionally intelligent young men.

It disappointed him, of course, that he could now see no way to find a posting that would involve him in combat. But his superiors had very good reasons for his appointment.

At the time some, but by no means all, in the British military and political hierarchy had begun to appreciate how valuable was the material being received from the 'Ultra' unit based at Bletchley.[15] Briefly, using a decoding machine developed with pre-war Polish know-how, the men and women at Bletchley were able to interpret a vast number of encoded German messages. Certainly in the beginning, but even as the war advanced, Whitehall opinion varied on the importance of the raw material thus provided, and the professional Army, particularly in North Africa, was sceptical.

Powell's mind and training were admirably suited to the processing of evidence, in however unorganized a form: Bletchley Park simply sent on to Cairo, decoded and translated into English, relevant intercepted German messages. Powell's Cairo unit was required to provide all the Services in the theatre with up to the minute assessments of what Rommel was planning, and to anticipate his mood. Starting early each morning Powell provided a succinct briefing for the Chiefs of Staff meeting at nine. He was a notoriously hard taskmaster, and his icy rage was felt by any officer who produced work that was less than perfect.

This is not the place to set down in any detail the history of the North African war, but it is necessary to provide an outline sketch of its character so as to appreciate the context in which Powell was working, and the contribution he was able to make. The essential question for his unit was Rommel's supply – on land, certainly, but particularly by sea. If the Afrika Corps could be denied supplies and reinforcements across the Mediterranean, then nothing could be more certain than his defeat, in spite of his brilliance even when most stretched. And shortly after the arrival of Powell in Cairo one incident, which was deeply to influence his attitude, and the attitude of the British High Command in general, to the importance of Ultra, occurred. This was the affair of the German supply ship, *Ankara*.

The British were pressing Rommel hard. In spite of his straitened resources, however, he was to change the daily pattern of the battle, and even contemplate an attack on Tobruk. The German High Command made prodigious efforts to relieve him: in December a tank-carrying convoy – No. 52 – set out. Two of its ships were sunk by British submarines. The convoy split, one part going to Tripoli, which it successfully reached, the other to Benghazi. At the latter port *Ankara* unloaded twenty-two tanks, with the aid of which Rommel fought two brilliantly successful local actions against forward British forces, engagements in which the British lost sixty tanks. From this ineluctably followed a British withdrawal, and yet another German advance. The defeats essentially stemmed from the fact that Rommel's tank reinforcements were, by many, unexpected. But Ultra had warned of the splitting of the convoy, and reported to North Africa the significance of that event. The material had been virtually ignored, and one of the consequences was the dismissal of Brigadier John Shearer, the intelligence officer responsible for advising the command in the field. Another, and greater, consequence was the immediate and fundamental upgrading of respect for Ultra in the minds of all concerned.

All this was of the greatest importance because of the nature of the desert war, dependent as its development was on a multitude of small-scale battles rather than on major engagements. The achievement of Montgomery at the battle of El Alamein in 1942 was to bring about by intelligent planning (though the original idea was not wholly his) a massive confrontation. His material superiority on the battlefield was so great that he could scarcely lose.

After the events following the docking of *Ankara* it became the prime job of British Intelligence to assess Rommel's future reinforcement capability. This was not an easy task, for it could not be assumed that Hitler would in the future strain every nerve on behalf of his quondam favourite. Germany was too heavily committed in Russia, where the cost of war was proving to be vastly greater than had been anticipated, and German Intelligence knew that there were already voices being raised in Russia and the United States, as well as in Britain, in favour of the opening of a second front in the West. The flow of reinforcements to North Africa was unpredictable, and accurate assessment was becoming ever more difficult.

One episode[16] illustrates a part of the problem. Rommel was informed that he would receive 164 Light Division between July and August 1942 through Greece. The Ultra unit decoded the whole message, and advised Cairo that the division would be arriving four platoons a day. The unlikelihood of using such a method of conveyance puzzled Cairo. For the reinforcement to be significant 164 should arrive all together, mass being of even more critical importance in North Africa than it is generally in war. For a day much thought was devoted to divining the intention and the future. In the middle of the night Powell woke, thought again, and moments later burst into the operations room shouting 'Trains, trains, trains', for he had recalled that the German word for platoon was the same as that for train, and thus that Bletchley had mistranslated. Getting it right was not, at the stage that had been reached, and given the decline in Rommel's forces and the rise in those of the Eighth Army, of the first importance, but it is an apt illustration of the workings of Powell's mind. If the piecing together of information, however plausible, did not form a logical and sensible pattern, then there was something wrong in the interpretation.

The vision of Powell dancing with delight at the correct interpretation of the interception, of a Powell hooting with joy at having caught the omniscient specialists of Bletchley out in a misunderstanding of the German language, was not, certainly, one that would have occurred readily to those who had known him at Cambridge or Sydney. It might not, however, have surprised people who knew the infant who had chosen the clarinet as an instrument of musical expression because it was played both in the orchestra and in the band. The boyishness displayed in his pleasure at correctly interpreting the German word *zug*, however, did not indicate a change of character. A former colleague from Aldershot who paid a social call in Cairo was told that Powell could give him three minutes. He turned on his heel and left, just as a former schoolmate had done in Trinity some years before.[17]

In the middle of 1942 the war in North Africa seemed finely balanced. As Rommel, at the end of June, approached the Alamein defences, orders went out for the burning of official papers in Cairo. American aid – in the form, essentially, of Sherman tanks – was on its way. The question was, would it arrive in time? The answer was that it did and at Alamein Montgomery administered the defeat that Churchill called 'the end of the beginning'.

Like so many on the Allied side, Powell was fascinated by Rommel. He did not keep a portrait of the great adversary on his wall, as Montgomery did, but he did achieve a certain fondness for the elusive enemy commander who seemed to be able to do so much with so little; who disappeared and reappeared again with such devastating effect; who seemed always to have the Eighth Army guessing. None the less, while the regard for Rommel persisted in the minds of many British officers long after the war[18] Powell fairly quickly became disenchanted, and for a very typical reason. A copy of Rommel's textbook *Infantry Attack*[19] fell into Allied hands. The then Commander-in-Chief, General Auchinleck, ordered a translation and Powell – who had, after all, been studying and plotting the German leader's moves and stratagems with an admiring and scholarly devotion – fell upon the task. But 'We were surprised and disappointed to find the contents to be utterly pedestrian and unilluminating. Approached more nearly, he seemed to fade into the featureless type of German professional soldier.' The problem was that Powell – like others of his bent, if not of his ability, on the Intelligence staff – assumed that brilliant action required and indicated brilliant intellect, and brilliance of conceptualization. Powell did not see, in his disappointment, that Rommel in print provided him with nothing like the intellectual challenge of Rommel in the flesh (or, more often, as the Eighth Army had often ruefully to confess, Rommel in the shadow), that the Field-Marshal had many of the attributes of the Nietzschean hero of action, rather than mind. But, of course, as had been the case when he first joined up and found himself so amazed that the professional officers of the British Army did not see the conspectus of military possibility, and of the political future, he was (and remains) perpetually bewildered that other men did not think as hard, and with such rigour, as he did himself.

In the spring of 1943, Operation Torch (the landing of American troops in North Africa) having taken place, the Afrika Corps were finally expelled from their foothold on the continent. Powell had been gazetted MBE for his part in the war effort which he had enjoyed 'enormously'. Over the period from Torch, however, he had acquired a quantity of new intellectual baggage which was greatly to influence his future perceptions in politics, and to dominate his thinking in later life with ever increasing fervour.

It would be putting it too bluntly and simply to say that he found himself almost immediately averse to Americans. Two strands in that aversion can certainly be traced to their origins in this period. But, while one is relatively simple, the other is more important and more complex and, moreover, it reflects an accurate perception of the future of international relations.

Like many of his fellow officers Powell was both amazed and impressed – but also appalled – by the sheer profligacy of the American way of warfare. He has more than once recalled a conversation with an American officer in early 1943. A local German counter-attack had resulted in the capture of fifty American tanks. The British, after two slogging and heartbreaking years of warfare, Powell recalls, 'knew what Rommel could do with a few captured tanks', but the American simply observed, 'Hell, there's plenty more where they came from.'

The open-handed assumption that the possession of unlimited resources guarantees victory is a characteristic American attitude; and it has led the United States to many humiliating defeats. Years later, in a series of articles and speeches on the war in Vietnam,[20] Powell was accurately to predict their ultimate failure in a way that no other Conservative politician could: his perception came from those far-off days in the desert in North Africa. For the moment, however, the dislike, shared by so many, was in large part made up of resentment. It was difficult for the men of the Eighth Army (and their Commonwealth and Free French colleagues) to appreciate that the uncaring juggernaut that they saw pouring its might and treasure into the war was unaffectedly on their side. They had borne the burden and heat of the day. They had been straitened, and had fought off a once seemingly invincible enemy. They had done so by cunning and tenacity. None of this seemed to matter to the Americans, who simply proposed to plough on, with ever increasing mountains of armour, until the enemy was obliterated.

This was offensive to Powell not merely as a nationalist and a British soldier, but as an intelligent man. He had carefully studied the American Civil War, and he had intellectually mixed feelings about it: there had been brilliant moments – like Sherman's march through the West to outflank Lee[21] – but, in essence, it had been a matter of attrition. Powell could appreciate what the Duke of Wellington at Waterloo called a hard pounding, but as a soldier he was more in the manner of Clausewitz, a thinker, and a believer in placing force at the strategic point in a battle, not simply throwing it forward at all points. The difference was understandable, and the arguments on both sides were understandable. The Americans thought simply of the quickest way of doing the job, and they had the force to do it quickly. The British, on the other hand, had a tradition of warfare according to which they were perennially constrained by the limited means available to them. The Empire, after all, had been created with astonishingly slender resources, and had been sustained by an elaborate and exceptionally intelligent bluff (in the military sense). Except in the dreadful carnage of the First World War, Britain had not sought to win by force and weight alone; and the cost of that attempt had sunk deeply into men's natures. Powell, unconsciously, had been more influenced (by 1943) than he realized until years later by the professional British officer's concept of how war should be waged. But there was also, of course, the buried but fundamentally powerful attitude of mind adumbrated in the quotation at the head of this chapter: that what was happening in North Africa from the moment the Americans landed was, quite simply, not right. It was for the politicians at the top, men like Churchill and the minister he sent to North Africa, Harold Macmillan, to be unfeignedly appreciative of the American effort. Below that level feelings smouldered, nowhere more so than in Powell's heart.

From the moment – the moment of his disillusion with his ideal Germany – that Powell began to think about politics in an international way, he also thought in a national way. There is no paradox here, though the terms of any discussion, either of him, or of the millions who considered the future as the war against Hitler advanced towards its close, need to be very sharply defined.

Whereas, today, the word 'international' is taken to have a meaning of communality, even an assumption of moral authority superior to the strivings (from whatever motives) of individual nations, in 1942-3 it had a definition that was more traditional, and more soundly historically based. It meant what it said – the relations between nation states. To be sure, there were idealists – like Jean Monnet, who spent most of the war in the United States devising what has become the European Economic Community – but there were not so many of them. Most practical men certainly looked forward to a better-ordered world when the conflict was over, one in which the prospect of a Nazi Germany would never arise again; but their hopes were not grandiose, unless they were Americans. For, seeing themselves for the second time in a century required to come to the aid of the Old World, the Americans determined not merely that nothing like Nazism should ever happen again, but that, in addition, the geopolitical structure of the world should be changed. The colonial empires would be brought to an end. The subject peoples, particularly in Asia, would be free. While President Roosevelt and his closest advisers were as helpful as they could be – and affectionate – towards the British and Free French effort in Europe, they were implacable in their desire to hasten the end of empires. All this Powell learned in Algiers. Having already found himself 'antipathetic to the American culture – the American style, if you like', he now found more intellectually formidable reasons for dislike and distrust.

As it happens, the British reaction to the Rooseveltian proposition at a high level was more muted, and less strenuous in its opposition than might have been supposed. So far as the East was concerned, empire to Britain meant India. And long before the war considerable strides had been taken down the road to Indian independence. Churchill had once, in the Thirties, opposed enfranchisement for Indians, and the movement of that great territory towards at least substantial independence (in the form of Dominion status). He had resigned from the Conservative front bench on the issue, and fought the India Bill tooth and nail, line by line, in the House of Commons. But in 1943 he knew in his heart that the battle was over. (The Conservatives were later to voice no more than token opposition to Clement Attlee's India Independence Bill in the House of Commons.) He had more pressing matters to attend to, of which the preservation of the Anglo-American Alliance was to him the foremost, and getting his way in the strategy of the war's end-game a substantial part of it.

The strategic differences between Churchill and Roosevelt

were now substantial. They boiled down to this. Russia had been taking terrible losses on the Eastern Front, and was unceasing in her pleas for an Anglo-American landing on the coast of France at an early date. (Stalin's agitation on this matter was vigorously supported in Britain by the left wing of the Labour Party, and by none more vociferously than Michael Foot.) Roosevelt was keen to respond to these appeals. He was, further, sublimely confident that the sheer weight of American power would be sufficient to overcome such coastal defences as the Germans could muster. Churchill demurred, for two reasons. He had – though it would have been impolite to make too much of it – the gravest doubts about the wisdom of throwing however many raw American soldiers against seasoned German troops in an opposed landing. Moreover, for all his affability towards Stalin, he was much more suspicious of the dictator than was the President.

Churchill fought long and hard – and for a considerable period successfully – against the idea of a second front.[22] But he also had a preferred strategy. This was to attack through Italy, destroy Mussolini, drive the German forces back across the mountains, and liberate Eastern Europe before the Russian bear could get its claws on the area.[23] An Italian offensive was eventually launched. The half-heartedness of the Americans was no doubt one of the reasons why it was less successful than it might have been. But the brutal fact of the matter was that Alexander, in overall command of the operation, with the American Patton and the Briton Montgomery under his orders, made such slow progress that the American and British public alike chafed at the bit, and craved for drama in the form of an opposed landing in France. They got their wish on D-Day.

Powell detested the idea of a second front and saw no reason 'why we should contemplate it because of the whinings of the Russians.' Nor was he enamoured of a peninsular strategy such as the Italian. By September 1942, according to his friend Nicholas Hammond, he was convinced that the war in North Africa was to all intents and purposes over, and that the European war itself would, likewise, soon be finished. He thus found it somewhat difficult to take a great deal of interest in the closing phases. Indeed, he more than once went so far as to criticize the Allied doctrine of demanding the unconditional surrender of Germany, suggesting, rather, that it would be better to accept a surrender on terms, to make what was always called in diplomatic circles 'a Bismarckian peace[24] leaving the Nazi regime which had led their people to failure to be dealt with by themselves.'

What has to be understood, however, is the fact that with Powell no observation was – or is – random. In his nature emotion and reason, though occasionally at war with one another, normally march together. In his days as a pure scholar and occasional poet he managed to get the two, fairly successfully, into separate compartments. Once he became a soldier, however, though the poetry continued to get written, emotion and rationality bedded down together in consideration of both nationhood (and empire – though he dislikes being thought of as what is nowadays called an imperialist) and the business of fighting. Since the Guilsborough lectures, moreover, he had taken it upon himself to provide his superiors at regular intervals with an overall appreciation of the war and its progress, as well as of the future which would follow it. He had been beyond the common run of thought in predicting both the entry of the United States into the conflict and the entry – forced or otherwise – of the Soviet Union. Each analysis built on its predecessors. And it was on the basis of constant reasoning – not simply the day to day study of the immediate problem of Rommel and the Afrika Corps – that he advanced by Christmas 1942 to the conclusions that governed his next moves in his own career.

From his perception of a coming war he had concentrated on the threat to the British homeland posed by Germany. During his time in Australia it was that threat, and the prospect of a European war, that most preoccupied him. None the less, in Australia he was living in a part of the Empire. His ceaseless pedagogical journeyings gave him more and more insights into what he was later to call the mystery of the British Empire – the far flung nature of the dominion of a small island off the coast of Europe. It would be wrong to say that the wider lesson of his Australian experience sunk, at that moment, into his nature; but the impression was there in the subconscious to be resurrected when its time came in the desert in 1942.

Whereas the Allied High Command – whatever attention they might from time to time give to the post-war settlement – continued to concentrate on beating Germany until the moment of unconditional surrender, Powell, having made up his own mind on the inevitability of victory, 'or at least the certainty that there could be no defeat', turned his mind outwards. The first proposition he arrived at concerned the difficulty of restoring the pre-war boundaries of the British Empire.

It is important to realize at this point, in view of what was to follow in his career, that his predictions, hopes and fears did not encompass India. The difference between India and the territories with which he was concerned was that India had not been occupied. (Nor, for that matter, had any of Britain's African territories.) Hong Kong, Malaya, Burma and Singapore had, however, all been taken by the Japanese. It was on the recovery of those territories, therefore, that Powell concentrated his attention.

The Pacific War, moreover, was an American war to the extent that the European War – despite the enormous preponderance of American power in what was to amount to an invasion of the continent in 1944 – was not. It was, indeed, the attack on Pearl Harbor that had brought the United States into the conflict, and made it world wide. Powell, as we have seen, disliked American culture. He saw the thrusting nature of American power. And he feared the nature of American ambition. Looking into the future he feared the Axis powers (soon to be defeated anyway) less than he feared the mighty ally. It seemed to him, therefore, that the place to be was now the Far East. Indian considerations counted with him to a very small extent.

He set himself, therefore, to securing a Far Eastern posting. First, though, he had to return to Cairo, and it is to his decision to make the journey back from Algiers overland that we owe certainly the most beautifully written, certainly the most intelligent, and certainly – even above all – the most entertaining portrait of Powell that has so far appeared.[25]

The journey was to take two weeks, which Powell had decided to devote not only to the study of the sites of recent battles, but to their relationship to the battlefields of ancient times. He was also determined to learn to drive properly, and he reckoned that a fortnight in inhospitable territory would be sufficient to educate himself in a field where competence had so far eluded him.

Even he, however, did not propose to undertake the trek alone, so he took Michael Strachan along as his companion and co-driver. Major Strachan was a Scot, in many respects Powell's antithesis, relaxed, amusing, self-confident, and blessed with a humorous eye and pen. For literary purposes Strachan in 1949 dubbed his desert companion 'The Professor'. He also gave a name – 'Pinafore' – to their battered army lorry and another – 'Auntie' – to the box in which Powell stored his papers. Powell, Strachan wrote,

77

was my senior officer, and if he was a singular and in some ways unorthodox lieutenant-colonel, he certainly looked more like a soldier than an absent-minded scholar. He was still in his early thirties,[26] stockily built, with a pale face and brown hair *en brosse*. His eyes were greenish, very penetrating and rather sinister; they indicated something of their owner's intellectual brilliance and something of his force of character.

The beginning of the journey was not auspicious. Strachan took the first turn at the wheel, and Powell was therefore in charge of the travelling kitchen. He was deputed to cook breakfast.

The fire smouldered dejectedly until he teased it with a gill of petrol, and then it sprang up and singed his moustache; and when he assaulted the sausages the tin counter-attacked and cut his finger; the water refused to boil and while he was not looking tipped itself over into the fire. 'Oh the malice – the cursed, diabolical malice of inanimate objects!' muttered the Professor ferociously between clenched teeth. 'Here, let me help,' I said. 'You keep away,' he snarled. 'If they want to be bloody-minded, I'll show them, by God I will,' booting the empty sausage-tin into a cactus bush.

For all the humour, Strachan was the one who immediately saw into the essential character of Powell.

The sausages were cold and flabby, tea-leaves floated on top of a grey, tepid liquid which I tactfully consumed with feigned relish. But the Professor was not deceived and went about shaking his head, muttering, 'Bloody inefficient! Bloody inefficient!', too angry to eat. If he had a failing it was an overbearing intolerance of stupidity and inefficiency. People less acute and less energetic than himself, that is virtually every other human being with whom he came into contact, were very liable to excite his wrath.

Powell was later to acquire very considerable manual and culinary dexterity. But his first attempt to drive 'Pinafore' was not, for Strachan at least, a happy one. He had mastered the theory of driving to perfection, and resented (the by now somewhat worried) Strachan's attempts to instruct him. But (as with his earlier acquaintance with the internal combustion engine) some deficiency of co-ordination prevented the perfectly ordered knowledge in his head from transmitting itself to his hands and feet. He blamed the lorry for his problems and, in particular, the steering. On one occasion they had to turn around on the main road:

> Instead of slowing down he suddenly accelerated, at the same time swaying about in his seat as though wrestling for possession of the wheel. We turned neither to the right nor left, but shot straight on towards a stone wall on the far side. We stopped with a lurch a few inches short of the wall and I found that I had subconsciously pulled the handbrake hard on. 'You see what I mean?' asked the Professor, quite unperturbed. 'Yes, I see,' I replied, wiping the sweat off my hands, determined to be equally composed.

When the manoeuvre was, at length, successfully completed Powell merely cried, 'Done it.' 'What particularly disturbed me,' Strachan comments, 'was that the Professor seemed to have no sense of guilt or danger.'

For both men, however,[27] the journey had a usefulness that went far beyond the provision of comedy. Their lives had lain in very different directions, and it followed that whole areas of knowledge and experience available to one were closed books to the other. They decided, therefore, at Powell's suggestion, that the passenger would lecture the driver of the moment on his own areas of knowledge. Strachan was given the full benefit of Powell's already encyclopaedic knowledge of the classical history of North Africa (and of classical history in general). They stopped at appropriate sites, including Carthage, and the ready availability of such places lent colour, and even drama, to the Professor's homilies.

Strachan had no learning of an equivalent profundity to impart. That, however, was not important, for the things he could teach were things Powell wanted to know about. Strachan records his regularly renewed amazement when, each morning, Powell woke him with his morning tea, and then returned to the task of polishing the brass on his full regimental uniform. Like most other soldiers travelling in the desert Strachan dressed for comfort, in shorts and a bush shirt. Full uniform, however, *was* comfort for Powell. As he explained to his companion, appearances were important for keeping up his morale. But further – the uniform appeared to cause him no discomfort, and he did not suffer from the heat.

What Powell wanted to know, and what Strachan could impart, was information about the *mores* and habits of the upper class. Of all the subjects that Strachan covered the one that took Powell's fancy most was fox-hunting. 'I've made up my mind,' he said on one occasion, 'I shall hunt.'[28] Strachan's lecture periods, however, did not pass without moments of discomfort, and even danger. When Powell was particularly interested in, or amused by, a given point his foot invariably went down on the accelerator. This risky habit more than once led them into semi-collisions with other Allied vehicles and on one occasion he put the lorry into a ditch, where it lay at a fifty-five degree angle.

Towards the end of their hair-raising (if also hilarious) journey Powell asked Strachan if he would pass him fit to drive. As can be imagined the question gave rise to some doubts, even perturbation. Strachan's basic problem was his painfully acquired knowledge that, for quite lengthy periods, Powell would drive, if not brilliantly, then at least safely. Then for no apparent reason he would go erratic, and put them in peril (not that any such occasion seemed to trouble him in the least). Strachan wanted to say that this strange man who had become his friend was competent, but he feared the consequences. He compromised by setting Powell a test. They were approaching Cairo, where the traffic was as notoriously difficult then as it is now. Strachan told him that if he could drive the ungainly 'Pinafore' from the outskirts of the city to GHQ he would pass him fit to drive. Powell applied himself to this task (difficult enough for even a good driver) with unremitting concentration, and succeeded to perfection.

All the justifiably exhausted Strachan wanted now was sleep. Once they had reported in and discharged their various bureaucratic obligations, however, Powell set out on a tour of the bookshops of Cairo, seeking, essentially, those classics on fox-hunting which had been recommended to him. He procured a number, and hauled Strachan, by now weary beyond protest, off to the Gezirah Club for tea. The repast consumed, and the purchases examined and admired, Powell suggested that they should go immediately to the Polo Club, where Strachan could explain the intricacies of the game to him. ' "Presently," I murmured, "presently," and dropped off to sleep in my chair.'

Strachan and Powell were perfect foils to one another. One can only shudder at the disaster such a trip would have been had the Professor's companion been a more ordinary creature, or one less ready to be fascinated by the human comedy of the situation. Of course, they had worked together, and Strachan therefore already had a certain idea of what to expect. But no other likely companion, even if he had survived the journey, could have been expected to leave to posterity a record of such value.

With the purchase of Surtees[29] in Cairo, however, Powell's comedy ended. North Africa now irritated him. He was bored at the prospect of incarceration in an Intelligence unit there or, even worse, by the prospect of being sent along with the armies prepared for the invasion of the Italian peninsula. He was determined to get to the Far East, though it is fair to add that this was not because of his old yearning for combat. 'I no longer expected nor hoped for that. If I could go, I knew it would be in a staff capacity.' The geopolitical struggle of the aftermath of the war which he had foreseen was about to begin, and the theatre that excited his interest was the South East Asian. 'Burma, Burma, Burma,' one of his then colleagues recalls him as saying with what amounted to an obsessive frequency. He sought employment with Orde Wingate's Chindits, who were fighting a brilliant and unorthodox campaign in that territory acquired for the British Empire by Lord Randolph Churchill (his only act of note as Indian Secretary), and it is said that Powell bearded Wingate himself with an appeal to work on his staff, though with no success.[30]

Powell's increasing restlessness was readily known to his superiors. He, of course, could not know that their decision as to his future would mark the whole of the rest of his life, in a way that nothing that had happened to him before had. He was to be given – because of his desire to move, but also by way of happenstance – an interest which for a time consumed him and which, into his eighth decade, still marks him. In the service of that interest he took on another, through which he became the Powell of fact and legend of British politics. He says:

By the end of 1942 it was clear to me that victory in Europe was assured or rather that defeat in Europe was now excluded and that for the survival of the British Empire what was overwhelmingly important was that the Far East – India and the Far East – Burma and the Far East – would be recovered by Britain before they were occupied by the United States. The important theatre therefore was the Far Eastern theatre and in accepting an opportunity to go to India which was offered to me by General Cawthorne of Military Intelligence India I was regarding it as a stepping stone to direct participation which wouldn't necessarily mean other than staff participation in the reconquest of Malaysia, the Dutch East Indies and the Far East.

The biographer should not, perhaps, be intrusive or portentous in seeking to define turning points. None the less, it is his duty to offer a judgement; I believe this is the moment to do so.

Had Powell been given combat duty at an early stage in his military career he might have – as he fully expected – been killed; or he might have been led to a quite different life from the one he has enjoyed. Again, had he been granted his most earnest wish and finished his war in the Far East, his fate would certainly have been different. It is, after all, hard to imagine Burma or Hong Kong taking hold of him in the way India did. He was not the general pro-consular type and, as I will shortly show, had little appetite for imposing over other races an authority which required the exercise of any sort of general suppression, or collective brutality. Thus:

> I do abhor this use of the word 'imperial' with its connotations. I doubt whether the charge of believing in the British mission to rule over palm and pine can ever be authenticated. I've used the term 'inevitability', and I've used it as a qualification for righteousness in terms of the Raj but . . . Dominion founded on force, on compulsion, has never been something which I recognized or still less have been attracted by.

His thoughts, as described above, about the world after the war were hammered out with respect to, essentially, Anglo-American relations. They were thoughts of power, and of competition, between the United Kingdom and the United States. He wanted to be in on the action of what he saw would be a conflict of interest, and not merely a quarrel between old friends. None the less, some hand-scribbled note determined, in August 1943, the outline of a career that has followed an undeviating road since that date.

Reflecting, Powell tends to dismiss such large and general thoughts as these, as applied to himself. He is a man wholly without personal ego – in the sense in which that word now suggests an assertion of personality, or of glorification. He is, certainly, intellectually arrogant – as Michael Strachan saw so clearly a generation ago – but only in a sort of exasperated way, the way in which he complains, sometimes with a somewhat heavy and academic humour, sometimes with the glee of a schoolboy, of the inability of others to see the simple verities of life as defined – and seen – by him.

He rebuked me, once, when I sought to place him (talking about the period 1943 and onwards) in a large historical context. In doing so he was, in my judgement, insufficiently historically minded, as he was certainly un-self-regarding. The fact of the matter remains, historically speaking, that the life of the man who was, from 1968 onwards, to change the face of British politics by force of intellect, force of character, and force of conviction – and by unambitious courage as well – was determined by a decision, not made by him, but made for him in 1943.

The general situation was this. The Commander-in-Chief Middle East, General Auchinleck, was Powell's ultimate boss when he arrived in Cairo. It was he who had commanded the translation of Rommel's infantry manual which Powell provided. Auchinleck, as Mr. Roger Parkinson[31] convincingly argues, was a fighting soldier but not, perhaps, a great Commander-in-Chief. Churchill had already replaced an initially successful commander of the war in North Africa, and had sent him to India. In August 1942, he determined to do the same to Auchinleck. It is impossible to resist quoting Lord Moran's description of how the Auk (as he was always familiarly known) received the news of his replacement by General Alexander:

> I could not hear what the CIGS[32] was saying, nor could I see the expression on Auchinleck's face, but I did not need any help to follow what was happening. Auchinleck sat with his forearms resting on his thighs, his hands hanging down between his knees, his head drooping forward like a flower on a broken stalk. His long, lean limbs were relaxed; the whole attitude expressed grief: the man was completely undone.[33]

Churchill's position in domestic politics was, at the time, a parlous one. In 1940 he had had himself made Minister of Defence, and he had never scrupled to instruct generals in the field on their duties and their tactics. If they did not enjoy his confidence they had to go; and it was right that they had to go. Auchinleck, having made it clear that he would be selective about any future appointment – he had no desire to be relegated, as had happened to Gort, the Commander-in-Chief of the British Expeditionary Force on its retreat to Dunkirk, to such a position as Governor of Gibraltar, and would have preferred retirement – finally agreed to take the command of the Army of India, in India. This was a position he had held, and with great distinction, before.

Auchinleck had one particular brief – to investigate the general state of morale in the Indian Army. At one stage during the war a number of Indians had been captured by the Japanese (who had been contemplating an invasion of the sub-continent) and had succumbed to the charms of the most militant of Indian Nationalist leaders, Subhas Chandra Bose. Whatever was to happen to the global pattern of power once the war was over, it was clearly of considerable interest to the British government to know whether or not the Indian Army had been infected by thoughts of what would have been mutiny; or whether more or less stately negotiations with the Congress Party under the Mahatma Gandhi could continue towards independence.

In his final and ailing years Field-Marshal Auchinleck liked to claim that Powell's appointment was made by him directly. Whatever the case, in August 1943, just before his promotion to full colonel, Powell was posted to India as Secretary to the Joint Intelligence Committee for India and South-East Asia Command. It was not what he had set his heart on; but he was happy to accept the job since it took him half-way towards his real goal. This he never reached.

In the succeeding years Powell has often repeated his wondering account of the way he fell in love with India. The falling was instant, the effect deep and lasting. In four stout boxes in the personal archive, containing his journalism over the years – a formidable collection covering a multitude of subjects – the proportion of articles and reviews devoted to India and Indian history and the history of the British in India is striking, and it has, if anything, increased as the years have gone by, though he claims that his Urdu is now rusty, and that the pace of accumulation of books about India has slowed. None the less, the quality and the range of the output is amazing in a man with so many other preoccupations. It is interesting to note, further, that though he from time to time claims to have loved Australia, there is little expression of love or interest for that country in his writing. There is an occasional review here, an article (on British politics) for an Australian paper there, but no more.

What Powell had learned from Strachan about the conduct

of officers and gentlemen was certainly not knowledge acquired in order to seek comradely membership of some exclusive social club: it was, rather, more like material accumulated by the anthropologist in the course of his study of some odd species. It is true that he continued his practice of dressing formally and immaculately on all occasions,[34] but this was more the expression of an innate character trait than a desire to imitate. Indeed, had it been such a desire he would have demonstrated a quite remarkable insensitivity, for his colleagues took the opportunity to dress down on all possible occasions.

He went out of his way, furthermore, to set himself apart, and even to ridicule the tastes and attitudes of others. Philip Mason, for example,[35] recalls entering the mess in Dehra Dun as a guest and finding Powell alone there. Powell said, 'Will you have a whisky and soda? I have observed that this is what an English gentleman considers suitable after a journey.'

The 'I have observed' gives a perfect flavour of what I have suggested is almost an anthropological attitude, one, moreover, which does not merely apply to the British officer caste in India, but to the human race in general, and to himself. An anecdote given out of chronology illustrates it. On his sixtieth birthday, he came to lunch at the *Spectator*, where I was then deputy editor. He entered our boardroom shaking his head in some wonderment. It emerged that he had travelled to Gower Street by underground. While waiting on the platform for the train he had seen, some distance from him, a small coloured child move somewhat close to the platform's edge. He had started forward in automatic horror to assist, though he was too far away to have been of any use. 'And yet,' he told us, 'I have not noticed any marked increase in philoprogenitiveness on my part. It must be a function of advancing age, whereby our thoughts turn increasingly towards the future of the race.'

What Mason noticed on their first meeting (when Powell called to inspect a document in Mason's care) was 'that he looked *wrong*':

There before me was a figure that a Japanese cartoonist might have drawn if he wished to portray a British officer. His uniform was formally correct – but it was not what people wore. Others in GHQ at that time of year kept as cool as possible; they wore shorts and soft bush shirts of cotton twill with badges of rank in worsted. This man was in starched Khaki drill, with a tunic, long stiffly creased trousers, a collar and tie; he looked as if he were going to a ceremonial parade. His badges of rank were of burnished brass and heraldic antelopes pranced in brazen splendour on the lapels of his tunic. He looked very uncomfortable.[36]

Powell differed (and perhaps sought to differ) in other ways than appearance. He liked, for example, to work in the afternoon, while his fellows sought refuge from the searing heat in sleep. Whereas a light lunch was thought suitable to the climate, Powell's favourite was steak and kidney pudding followed by jam roly-poly. And he sought, against a perfectly understandable and irritated resistance, to impose a sixteen hour working day on those in his office. To all remonstrance a cold and impersonal face was turned.

In his new post in India, he set himself two tasks, to learn Urdu, and to learn to ride a bicycle. The second ambition was neither as inconsequential nor as simple as it sounds: 'I started at the top of Kingsway.[37] I fell off and got on again all the way down Kingsway, but at the end of the road I could ride the bike.' It was not inconsequential, for a bicycle was certainly the most convenient instrument for a task of exploration which he approached with the same thoroughness once visited on the problems of the Ordnance Survey – the acquisition of a thorough knowledge of the countryside around Delhi, with the villagers of which he practised his Urdu. Mr. Napal[38] criticizes him for being over interested in the Muslim side of Indian life, and insufficiently concerned with the Hindi. If anything, the reverse seems to me to be true.[39]

He acquired, for example, a more than passing acquaintance (he passed an examination in the subject) with Devanagri, the oldest living Indian script, which is the medium of both Hindi and Sanskrit. He has told[40] of how, on one of his trips, a young Brahmin drew up beside him and they travelled on together, getting deeper and deeper into conversation. At length Powell was invited to the man's home for a glass of water. His host drank from a brass pot, Powell from earthenware. On leaving he smashed the earthenware mug. 'You see,' said a smiling host to his family, 'he is really a Hindu,' for he had known the rules of caste.

When Powell tells a story like this he does not mean to show off. It is, rather, to give himself an opportunity to exult in a kind of intellectual and spiritual identification. Knowledge, for him, is not for power or for glory: it is a necessary condition of happiness, a source of delight in itself.

None the less, the question must be asked: why did India give him this particularly powerful gratification, more profound, I believe, than any other in his life, even the institutions of the British Army, or of the House of Commons? To his modern detractors – especially since 1968 – it was merely an imperialist lust to dominate, an expression of a former phase of history which such detractors despise and traduce. Such a judgement (if one may call it that) could not survive even a slight impartial reading of his reviews and essays on the subject. Mason thought his attitude to India was a consequence of his reverence for Nietzsche, that is to say, it grew out of a reverence for power (power, in this case, in the guise of the British presence in the sub-continent), but of an exalted order. And many of his friends have expressed to me the opinion that it was an outburst of that pent up romanticism that was always deep within him, but had hitherto found only very limited expression in his poetry. They see it, as one put it, as 'a part of Enoch's past, really. Remember, he was only in his thirties. He was a young man in a strange and magical land. He had no English friends, and he was always curious about things. It was a phase. He grew out of it, and went on to serious work. I shouldn't give it too much attention in your book, if I were you.'

All of this seems to me to be wrong. There were, I believe, two separate fascinations (which came together in a way that we shall shortly see). The first was with India herself: the strangeness certainly attracted him, but so did the complexity, the layer upon layer upon layer of bewilderingly mixed political and cultural histories, and the multiplicity of historical philosophies and achievements. To his avid mind and seeking personality the attraction could not fail to be powerful. By comparison, the resources of Australia had been slender, and the friend I have just quoted had a good point when he observed that Powell had few friends of his own race.

The second fascination was, of course, with Britain in India. He once told me of a journey he had made through Bihar, when in the middle of his passage, 'It struck me almost as a blinding revelation that I was the only Englishman within thirty, forty, maybe fifty or sixty miles, and *that this was a part of the natural order of things*.' The nature of the relationship between the British and Indians at its best was what one can only call one of unbalanced but mutual acceptability. In his reflections over the years since, Powell has many times called it illusory,[41] and the process by which it was maintained one of 'hocus-pocus, a sort of wonderful, gigantic, stunning conjuring trick.' In many book reviews[42] on the lives of the British rulers of India Powell gives consideration to this historically unparalleled relationship between a tiny and a huge country, but of all the Britons who ruled there the one whose views approximate most closely to Powell's own is Curzon.[43] A British Secretary of State for India once complained that Curzon, as Viceroy, regarded himself as representing a foreign power to Westminster, rather than as serving his Sovereign overseas. 'If,' he said in the last year of his viceroyalty, 'I felt that we were not working here for the good of India in obedience to a higher law and a nobler aim, then I would see the link that holds England and India together severed without a sigh.' Powell could not have expressed his own view better. It is a formulation that may be regarded today as patronizing, but that it was sincerely held, and that it partook of a considerable nobility, no fair-minded person could doubt.

> I had detached, in the nineteen-thirties, external from internal politics. I was contemptuous of and hostile to the Baldwin-Chamberlain defence and foreign policy . . . I was disinterested in the issues of British internal policy and in the mechanism of internal policy.

Yet Powell vividly recalls his father saying to him, on more than one occasion, and with relish, 'Perish India.' The quotation came from the nineteenth-century Radical John Bright, and expressed the strong and vociferous opposition to the building of British power in India that was expressed so often in the nineteenth century. Thus, as Powell never ceases to emphasize, to the idea of the British Empire in India as illusory must be added the idea of it as transient and transitory. The pre-eminence of Britain lasted, indeed, a very short time; and widespread acceptance of – and even pride in – it lasted even shorter. Powell believes that only his own generation (or, rather, those members of it who served and took an interest in India) regarded the jewel in the crown as an immutable part of life. The generation before – his father's – bred many sceptics and many who were downright hostile. The post-Second World War generation may, according to temperament, consider it something glorious or something hateful, but in any event it is a part of history almost as remote as the events and circumstances that once led English monarchs to regard themselves as kings of France.

But the illusion through which a mere handful of men with

white skins were able, even for so brief a period, effectively to rule millions with brown skins was a highly potent one. The power of its draught perhaps explains how it was that a man of such a keen analytical and critical intelligence as Powell scarcely at all regulated his conduct and attitude between 1943 and 1946 in the light of the fact that the dominion was coming to an end, and coming to an end, moreover, by agreement between the government in London and the powerful Congress Party in India.

Later in life Powell frequently showed an intellectual – and practical – ruthlessness in abandoning positions 'when the facts repudiated me'. Thus, for example, in 1954 he was among a group of Conservative Members of Parliament[44] who opposed British withdrawal from the Suez Canal Zone. Two years later he was (privately, since as a government Minister he was bound by the rules of responsibility, and did not feel it was a resignation issue) against Sir Anthony Eden's determination to launch an attack on Egypt after the Egyptian nationalization of the Suez Canal. 'The pass had been sold.' It may be that his one exercise in compromise on a major matter,[45] hardly realized by him at the time to be what it was, left him with an inherent distaste for repeating the experiment.

His career in India falls into two parts. The first was doing the job – an increasingly simple military intelligence job – to which he was first appointed, in Delhi. The second brought the two fascinations with India into not merely intellectual or emotional togetherness, but administrative unity as well.

By 1944 it was clear that the war was, to all intents and purposes, over. Germany might fight on for some time in her redoubt of fanaticism; Japan might retreat only inch by inch into the fastnesses of her islands. But the tide of Allied might was now inexorable. Within the circle of that might, however, there were important local problems. The one that most concerns the subject of this book was the future of the Indian Army. That subject was itself a kernel within the nut of a larger, the problem of the political future of India. Whatever political resolution was found the military – and, by extension, the civil – order had to be retained: this was common ground between the British government and Congress. Indeed, it was to examine and, if necessary, re-organize the Army of India that Auchinleck had been returned to the sub-continent in the first place. A Reorganization Committee had to be set up. It required a secretary. Powell's boss, Major-General Walter Cawthorn, recommended him. He secured the post, and was promoted brigadier. He was thirty-two.

Powell once wrote, in a review of two books about Churchill,[46] of how important it was for Churchill's career that he was comparatively young at each critical stage of his life. When he himself became the youngest brigadier in the Army he was not merely young: he was virtually a child, in both military and political terms. But the esteem in which he was held, and the regard that was paid to him, has to be given its due estimation by any honest student of his life. He had never sought to ingratiate himself; he had never played the social game; he had never concealed his views on any subject that had come up. For all that he had most carefully observed the rules of the institution in which he was, he had observed them in his own fashion. The rigour, not only of his intellectual processes, but of his behaviour and demeanour, within willingly accepted constraints, had never been varied. Walking his own path, holding to his own view of what was right, he had none the less travelled a long distance that was not merely geographical from 'a house overlooking a railway cutting in Stechford, Birmingham.'

He outworked his Committee, not, according to Philip Mason,[47] by 'monopolizing the discussion' but 'by getting up very early in the morning and drafting the next chapter'. The job had, for Powell at this stage of his development, two tremendous advantages. First, it brought him up against all the administrative detail of the relationship between his own country and India. Hitherto, for all his absorption in Indian cultural and political history, and for all his musings on the relations between the two countries, there had been two separate subjects in his mind. Second, he was no longer confined in the physical explorations to the environs of Delhi or Dehra Dun (where the Reorganization Committee had placed its headquarters). His job required him to travel, and to travel extensively. What he had examined intensively and in detail around Delhi itself, he could now survey, as it were, panoramically. Of necessity, it had to be something of a Cook's tour; and he was later to refer, derisively, to the folk-saying (among Britons serving in India) that British politicians required merely 'twenty-one days in India' to understand all the problems thereof.[48]

The remorseless tide of information and opinion flowed in; and the remorseless young brigadier digested and presented it. Much of the information thus garnered, and many of the experiences lived through, passed away from his memory. In 1986, however, he had a sharp reminder of himself and his attitudes as a young man.

Powell and his wife were invited through the Indian High Commission in London to lunch with General K. M. Cariappa. A slender ray of light dawned. Cariappa was the first Chief-of-Staff of the Army of independent India, but he had also been a member of the Reorganization Committee. That much Powell remembered. What he did not remember – but what he was reminded of at lunch – was that he and the general had, in the course of the Committee's work, paid a visit to Poona in 1944. Their driver and escort first took them to the Byculla Club. Thereat Powell's bags were unloaded. He gestured to the driver to unload Cariappa's. It was quickly, and *sotto voce*, explained to him that the Indian could not possibly stay at the club. Powell gave instructions for his cases to be reloaded. 'I,' he is remembered as saying, 'will stay where Cariappa is staying.' To this day he tends to romanticism in discussion of the British in India; but no other single act could have so readily marked him out from their general number.

Fourteen years later, in a review of Colin Cross's *The Fall of the British Empire*[49] Powell was to write this:

> The emphasis on India, both in bulk and in content, is wholly right. The key insight into the history of the British Empire, and into the persistent hallucination of the British politician, is to grasp the central importance of the two-hundred-year long link between Britain and India. It was for the sake of India, or rather of the supposed necessities of that link with India, that literally every other possession in the Old World was acquired and maintained . . . So the psychoanalysis through which lies the cure for Britain's sickness has to be twofold: first, we must identify and overcome the mythology of the late Victorian empire; then, we must penetrate to deeper levels and eradicate the fixation with India from our subconscious.

Thus wrote a man who had himself been deeply marked by the experience of his own youth.

The Final Report of the Reorganization Committee is now matter for the historians of the end of Empire.[50] Powell's contributions – confined strictly to its military remit, but with obviously portentous political implications – were two. First came the conclusion that a very long period – twenty-five years was what he had in mind – would be required to prepare militarily for independence. (Powell, it should be mentioned here, accepted the principle accepted by all high-minded British devotees of Indian Empire, that independence would come one day; their equivalent in Africa, on the other hand, generally took the view that there would never be independent black states.) Secondly, and in the interim, he visualized that, as political progress marched steadily on, the Indian Army would require a high proportion – up to a half – of British officers. The climate of the times being what it was, Auchinleck dismissed it. The facts of the situation repudiated Brigadier Powell.

I am not sure that he did not, deep down, expect this conclusion. I am not sure, indeed, that even now he knows himself. Certainly, had his recommendations as to the constitution of the Indian Army officer corps been accepted, it is more than likely that he would have sought a career in the Army of the New India.

What it is interesting to observe of this young man who had first come to love the British Army as an institution, and then had come to refine his regard down to the Army in India, is that he never for a moment considered the possibility of a career in the peacetime British Army. Many might indeed – in spite of those preoccupations about the post-war international balance of power which began to gain roots in his mind in North Africa in 1942 – have expected that the cessation of hostilities would see a return to his first love, the classics.

In December 1938 he had been elected to the chair of Greek and Classical Philology at Durham.[51] As was the case with multitudinous other such appointments, in the academic as in other worlds, the appointment was suspended for the duration of hostilities.

His work in India had, however, brought him ineluctably closer to an entirely different world, that of politics. When, before and during the war, he had considered political situations he had considered them in their international dimensions. It might be put this way. The might and character of the German *Reich* posed a threat which would soon become a reality to the security of Britain. The British government did not see that and its members were, moreover, foolish, vain and decadent. A challenge would none the less sooner or later be posed and Professor Powell, infinitesimal though his contribution might be, would play a part in the response – which, he had no doubt, would be made, under whatever political leadership. Similarly, in 1944, his conclusion was that, the war over, the British Empire would face a challenge from its about-to-be-erstwhile ally, the United States, and again, Colonel Powell would be at hand, to offer what vision and succour and effort one man could.

But the politicians themselves, and the systems they inhabited, were, to him, abstracts, idealizations. The one political entity he seems to have identified was that of the nation; and the nation had to be regarded as a conglomerate of people, culture, tradition, and character. The idealization (a word which has nothing to do with what we commonly call 'ideals', but rather means the projection on to quotidian affairs of a definition of the fundamental nature of those affairs: it derives to a very great extent from German, and, ultimately, Greek philosophy) was all to him. Men and systems meant little, and he had no care for the mundanities of domestic politics. In so far as he considered practicalities, they were military ones. Thus, while not unprepared for the rejection of the Reorganization Committee's Report, he almost certainly would not have made his contribution any other way, whatever the circumstances.

What, however, was he to do? In June 1944, on the day the monsoon broke in Delhi, he made his decision. He realized that he was going to survive (it will be remembered that he had begun his war with a well-formed conviction that he would die in its course), and that he did not want to continue in uniform. He had had his achievements. He would have his gratuity. He wrote to Durham to resign the chair he had never occupied.

> I thought of how Burke had said 160 years earlier that the keys of India were not in Calcutta, not in Delhi, they were in that box – the Despatch Box at the House of Commons. I decided at that time that I must go there.

And so, he went.

4

The Backbencher
1945-1955

There can I believe be no dispute as to what to Britain
has been the central institution which has embodied our
national values, and whose history has been essential to
our perception and acceptance of those values. That
institution is Parliament. Our national experience has
been unique and our national values are unique because
there is no other nation of which the statement I have
just made can be predicated. It cannot be said of the
Congress of the United States any more than of the
representative assemblies which other Western nations
have erected at various stages in their history. From
the common root of the feudal court there grew and
flourished in the special conditions of Britain alone, by
a kind of ecological exception, the institution of Parliament. The British are a parliamentary nation: internally
and externally they are conditioned and defined by that
institution and that historical experience.

            – *J. Enoch Powell*, Hansard, *19 December 1974.*

Powerful – and, indeed, over-mastering – as was the impulse
which caused Powell to throw up the Durham chair, to abandon
what was already a distinguished, and could have been a remarkable military career, and throw his bread upon the uncertain
and often murky waters of domestic British politics, there was
one immediate problem to be faced. It was rather splendidly
mundane in comparison to the vision that had come to him,
the determination he had defined, during the Delhi monsoon.

It was the necessity to earn a living; the necessity of finding a job.

To this necessity was added a conviction and a sense of something he lacked. The conviction was that he was a Conservative, and that he would make his future in that Party. The sense was of his lack of knowledge of domestic British politics, without which knowledge he felt – rightly – that his chances of an early parliamentary candidature were slender. His chosen Party was not then, and was not for many years to come to be, sympathetic to high-faluting academics. He had a further disadvantage: he had never belonged to any Party, and had never as it happened been able to vote in a general election. His sense of nationhood, and of empire, had been developing for more than a decade when he arrived home on 27 February 1946; but they had been developing in isolation or, at the very least, in the very special circumstances of military service. His classical studies and his historical reading had fuelled his imagination and his will.[1] But the fire that now burned was not one at which the powers that were in Conservative constituency associations were likely to want to warm their hands.

He repaired immediately to his parents' retirement home in Seaford. From there he telephoned Conservative Central Office in Smith Square. He was given an interview with Marjorie Maxse, then one of the Party's Vice-Chairmen. Miss Maxse, formidable lady though she was, was later to retail the deep impression Brigadier Powell made upon her, principally because of his certainty and his intensity. It happened that the Tories were looking out for people like him. The Party had suffered a terrible – not least because unexpected – hammering in the general election of the previous year, when the voters had thrown down the great war leader, Winston Churchill, from power and awarded to his hitherto despised Labour rival, Clement Attlee, a House of Commons majority of 146. There was a general feeling abroad, sensed by Churchill, more fully articulated by R. A. Butler,[2] that Toryism had gone intellectually astray. They had been preoccupied, they told themselves, in fighting a war, while Labour had got on with the business of preparing the ammunition for post-war political campaigns. There is something in this, though less than there seemed to be at the time.[3] During the war itself substantial sections of the Party had bitterly suspected, and strongly resisted, the laying of the foundation stones of what has come to be known as the Welfare State. They had done so with no great tactical intelligence. But, if time was to reveal serious practical deficiencies in the architecture of the new social order of equality and massive medical and social provision, supplied by and organized by the state, these weaknesses were not all that evident in 1945. The fact of the matter was that the nation was determined not to go back to the conditions of 1939; and the nation was convinced that the Conservatives wanted to do just that. The people, therefore, bade a polite and affectionate farewell to Churchill, and cocked a snook at his Party.

The Tory leadership saw that an intellectual (and moral) renaissance was required. They had at least the rudiments of the necessary machinery to hand. One of these was the Conservative Political Centre and another the Conservative Research Department (then still divided, as it was to be for some time, into a Parliamentary Secretariat, concerned with providing shadow ministers with material for speeches and debates, and a longer-thinking Policy Unit). It was expected (and rightly expected) that the disbandment of the wartime armed forces would make some able and ambitious young men available for service in these bodies. Miss Maxse saw such a man in Powell, and made appointments for him both at the CPC and at the Research Department. David Clarke, the Director of the CRD, was first to see Powell and, somewhat bewildered though he was by his interviewee's appearance in full brigadier's uniform, was the first to offer him a job. Powell accepted and, a fortnight later, began a new life.

To understand the first few years of that life requires a little understanding of the structure of the organization of the Conservative Party at the time.[4]

The Parliamentary Secretariat of the Conservative Party was originally devised by Neville Chamberlain, simply and sensibly as a means of providing intelligent, but not just routine, briefings on day to day policy (usually to be used in parliamentary debates, but also in the constituencies) for ministers (or shadow ministers) and backbenchers. The Conservative Political Centre was designed to reach a wider audience and, principally, to serve as a counterpart to the much praised Fabian Society, which was widely held to have taken the intellectual high ground in politics on behalf of the Labour Party. At the time of Powell's recruitment, and for many years thereafter (until shortly after the election of Mrs. Margaret Thatcher to the leadership of the Party), the two bodies were separately housed, the CPC in Conservative Central Office in Smith Square, and the CRD[5] in two charming houses in Old Queen Street – a stone's throw from Fabian headquarters in

Dartmouth Street. This physical separation of the CRD from the main headquarters of the Party came to have a significance which was more than functional.

It can be put like this. Whereas the greater number of workers in Central Office planned to make a career in the Party, and the CPC was in possession of a small staff, controlled often by politicians who had outside careers, Old Queen Street had a quite different life. Apart from the secretaries, there were two kinds of functionaries, always called 'officers'. On the one hand there was a group of men (and, later, women) who were understood to be birds of passage. In 1946 most of them were like Powell, youngsters just out of the Armed Services, marking time before embarking on parliamentary careers; in later years these were to be replaced by university graduates, most of whom had ambitions similar to his. Above them, as section head, there were people either doing a retirement job (often former civil servants) or – like their coevals at Central Office – lifetime servants of the Party. The latter preserved the continuity of the Department's administration; the former its intellectual zest.

Until its financial emasculation (and move to Smith Square) under Mrs. Thatcher, the CRD tended to look down, intellectually, on Party Headquarters, just as the Central Office staff tended to regard the inhabitants of 24 and 32 Old Queen Street as effete theorizers. A Research Department officer could spend a year, or longer, without ever darkening the doors of Central Office. The Department's attention was focused in a different direction, the Palace of Westminster, five minutes' brisk walk away. The elected politicians thrown out of office after any general election tend to suffer disorientation. If they have been ministers there is the abrupt – and, in the British system – brutal, loss of privilege and the attentions of the civil service. If they have been merely backbenchers they lose any hope of immediate preferment, or even the simple personal satisfaction of belonging, in however humble a way, to a Party in office, and thus enjoying access to ministers. These problems, suffered by the Party of every overthrown government, were made much worse for the Conservatives in 1945 by the fact that they had been in office (alone or in coalition) for almost thirty years.

The Forties, moreover, was, unlike the present day, not a period of fulltime politicians – at least in the Conservative Party. It followed that background briefings had to be particularly good, for the parliamentarians devoted little of their own time to reading and research. Money, until Lord Woolton became

Chairman of the Party,[6] reshaped its organization, and raised substantial funds, was short. Powell, at the beginning, earned less than twenty pounds a week and – as he told David Clarke he would – had to draw on his savings not merely to live but to finance his new obsession: he had, as he promised Michael Strachan he would, taken up hunting. Apart from a little journalism (which did increase as time went on) he had no other source of income. Of course, there were others in the same boat, and most of these ambitious young men were happy to endure a period of penury in the hope of future political glory; more than most of them, Powell was convinced his opportunity would come early.

There were also, of course, men who enjoyed other privileges than brains. One was Henry Hopkinson, the rich son of a rich father, and for a brief period Powell's boss. He had little difficulty finding a safe seat, and was subsequently a disastrous minister. But the Party's composition was changing, to the benefit of middle (or lower middle) class boys like the trio of Powell, Reginald Maudling and Iain Macleod, who shared rooms in 24/32 Old Queen Street[7] and whose fortunes were subsequently to be entwined to the extent of their sitting in the same Cabinet; these were the representatives of the future. Their chances were enhanced when Lord Woolton became Party Chairman, for one of Woolton's many important reforms was to take steps to encourage just such an intake, in particular by forbidding rich candidates to subsidize their own constituency association, thus making impossible a hitherto common practice, that of buying nominations.

Woolton's provision was a wise one and, indeed, Powell himself was later directly to benefit from it.[8] But those in the new post-war Party intake had one priceless advantage in their relations with senior Opposition leaders over those many bright young things who, in subsequent years, were to take their places in the burgeoning institution of the Research Department. 'We were all grown men,' as Powell says, 'and we had been in the war.' Of course, there was still an immeasurable gulf between them and their political masters. But they had a personal and intellectual self-confidence which stood them in good stead. No departmental officer of, say, my generation would say, as Powell once said, to a shadow minister who had challenged the conclusions in one of his briefs, 'The Research Department has its reasons: let us leave it at that.' The advantage of military experience also served, of course, in the pursuit of parliamentary candidacies, though less for such abrasive characters as Enoch Powell and Edward Heath than for more evidently emollient and charming men. It is an entertaining fact, in view of their subsequent conflicts, that Powell and Heath were rejected by exactly the same number of constituencies before they achieved adoption; the figure was nineteen.

Still, for all these similarities between members of the post-war Tory generation, Powell in Old Queen Street made – as he had done everywhere else he had been – a quite different impact from other men. It was not just that he worked improbably long hours, arriving early and staying late – while Iain Macleod, for example, was wont to slip off early substantially to supplement his exiguous income by playing bridge, at which he reached international standard.[9] It was his method of doing things. 'I was quite startled,' a contemporary of Powell's recalls, 'to arrive one morning at what was, for me, an unusually early hour to find him cleaning up his room. His coat was hanging neatly in a cupboard and he had his sleeves rolled up while he swept the floor. I expressed astonishment and he merely stated that he intended to do the dusting since, in his opinion, the cleaning ladies were lamentably inefficient.' 'He was already a legend,' Iain Macleod said of Powell shortly after his appointment. 'He used to travel from Earl's Court on a workman's ticket at some unearthly hour in the morning and in full hunting kit to revel in a day's hunting.' He continued, indeed, to hunt until his marriage, and to ride until, after a fall in his sixties, one of his daughters persuaded him to give it up.

In general, Powell's office behaviour caused a certain amount of consternation. With, for some time, a small staff, the Conservative Research Department was a busy place, and there were many demands on the time and energy of its officers and secretaries which eased with the passage of time, and the greater flow of money from Lord Woolton's spectacularly successful fund raising efforts. But, even by necessary standards of industry, his activities were phenomenal. Two items in his initial brief were India and defence. The former he held until he insisted on giving it up when the Party decided to offer no serious opposition to the government's legislation on Indian independence. The latter he lost when Clarke found a replacement, for the Director held to the very English view (still in vogue in the Department more than twenty years later) that, when you found a man who was expert on one thing you should give him another to tackle. Powell was thus handed responsibility for housing, rents, local government, and town and country planning. This heavy load, of course, suited him perfectly. He had the energy and ability to master his subjects, and he badly needed to learn about domestic politics: it would hardly do to ask a constituency committee to select him solely on his military and imperial knowledge. 'It was like going back to school,' he said, 'or at least to university. And I loved every moment of it.' The experience was, indeed, not merely to stand him in good stead immediately, but many years later, when his circumstances required him to exercise his mind and his tongue on more or less any subject which came up. The natural bent of his mind, as refined by his training, was (and is) to seek the principle of existence or activity in any area or subject, and to apply that principle to factual material. Such a principle, once learned, is never forgotten, and if it needs to be applied again after a long passage of time, it can be taken down, dusted off, and put to work with effect.

However, as one contemporary without parliamentary ambitions put it, 'They were *all* difficult, especially those two.' By 'those two', he meant Macleod and Powell. The problems the two men presented to their chief (and to the parliamentarians to whom they had to report) were of different kinds. Macleod was puckish, and something of a mischief maker. Powell was grim and demanding, and, if some thought his brusqueness masked shyness, others simply observed a somewhat ferocious and dedicated demeanour, and preferred to give him as wide as possible a berth.

He was not, then, judged to be a tolerant boss (by the secretaries) nor a tolerant colleague. Years later, however, he remembered tolerance as being of the essence in his relationship with David Clarke who had 'a tolerance of nature and easy-going habits which he could combine with responsibility, and which meant that he could allow responsibility to others.' 'Good jockeys,' Powell once said, 'can ride difficult horses.' Clarke was certainly a first-class jockey; and he knew how to handle his horses.

There is, however, a matter of historical dispute, which is important to any study of Powell's career, and which can conveniently be handled here.

I have already said – which is widely known – that the shattered leadership of the Conservative Party in 1945 realized that something had to be done which, while restoring morale in their own ranks, would also enable them to regain the intellectual initiative. Woolton could handle the organization. R. A. Butler was given the task of presiding over the business of re-assessing policy, and given a certain vague suzerainty over the Research Department.[10] In the years that followed – and particularly after the Conservative Party returned to power in the general election of 1951 – the immediate post-war years acquired something of the character of an imagined golden age. The legend grew in lustre through the 1950s and even into the 1960s, not least because of the burgeoning reputations of Powell, Macleod and Maudling, but also because of the refusal of the first two to serve in the government formed by Lord Home in 1963, on the grounds that R. A. Butler had been wrongfully passed over for the leadership of the Party. Macleod and Powell, by their refusal to take office under Home (although both Butler himself and Reginald Maudling did) became almost indelibly, and retrospectively, identified as 'Rab's backroom boys'.

It now seems clear, however,[11] that Butler's reputation for innovation has been very greatly exaggerated, and that the changes made to Party policy between 1945 and 1951 were more cosmetic than substantial. What did make a change, which was of great consequence for the future political history of Britain, was the acquiescence by the Conservatives in the reforms of the Attlee government, particularly in that *mélange* of measures which popularly goes under the title of the 'Welfare State'. Dr. Seldon argues convincingly, however, that what changes were made had little impact on the outcome of the 1951 election.[12]

Of course, it has to be remembered that many of the foundation stones of the Welfare State had been laid during the life of the wartime coalition government; and if the Conservatives had often dragged their feet in the face of change[13] they could not implausibly claim a substantial share in the changes that the Attlee government brought about. What came to be known in the 1950s as 'Butskellism' – to express the supposedly shared beliefs of R. A. Butler and Hugh Gaitskell – had its roots in the social deliberations of the coalition government formed by Churchill in 1940. What was significant in Conservative behaviour after 1945 was the acceptance by Churchill and Butler of the great bulk of Attlee's measures, and their stout resistance to the still larger number of Tory backbenchers who wanted to put the social and economic clock back to 1939.

Powell's work at Old Queen Street was marked less by originality than by his exceptional industry and acuity. To this day, however, he dislikes the tendency to over-identify him with Butler. He points out, perfectly fairly, that it was Butler's practice to let the Research Department get on with its own work, and confine himself to arguing the modernist case in the Shadow Cabinet. To Powell personally Butler was most important as a senior figure who had lent his name as referee in Powell's search for a constituency.

Then, as now, it was the general expectation of the Conservative Party that ambitious young men should prove their mettle by fighting unwinnable seats. Towards the end of 1946 Powell put himself forward for Normanton, a Yorkshire mining constituency, and he was adopted as the Prospective Parliamentary Candidate for the Conservative Party on 11 January 1947. He proved himself (as he was to do again and again in subsequent years) to be a doughty and resourceful campaigner, not at all daunted by the magnitude of the task set him. His campaign style was uncompromising almost to excess: he stood as a foursquare Empire man, and was resolute in spelling out, in a most unpromising area, the distinctive nature of Conservative policy – going, in fact, rather further than leading frontbenchers did at that time. In the event, though – as he certainly expected – he was thoroughly beaten, his Labour rival in the by-election held on 12 February having a majority of 14,827. Despite this there was, none the less, a certain consolation, for he had reduced the 1945 Labour majority by over 8,000, and he had won golden opinions as a tireless worker. Although he was to suffer many disappointments before he did secure a winnable seat he had none the less laid an important plank in his future reputation, having demonstrated to a sceptical North-country audience that his academic tendencies did not prevent him – as one of his constituency committee afterwards approvingly put it – 'rolling up his sleeves and getting his nails dirty.'

1947 was, however, to see the beginning of a far more important development in Powell's life than the fighting of a hopeless seat for, on 3 May 1947, Margaret Pamela Wilson joined the research Department and was appointed as his secretary.

Miss Wilson was the daughter of a colonel in the Indian Army – 'I outranked my future father-in-law,' Powell used later to proclaim with some glee. Pam (as she has always been called) thus came under the supervision of Miss Avis Lewis, head of personnel at the Department, a title which, essentially, gave her charge of the welfare of the secretaries as of right and of the officers by sheer dominating force of personality. 'Avis,' said one of David Clarke's successors as Director, 'was the only one who scared us all.'

Avis Lewis took the view – then and for many years later – that the only suitable husbands for Research Department secretaries were Research Department officers, and that the only suitable wives for those officers were 'my' secretaries. A spinster herself, Avis Lewis was a notorious – or, at least famous – matchmaker. She, also, had an Indian Army background, for her father had served on the sub-continent and she had spent much of her youth there. She is of elfin charm, and it was long rumoured that many young officers had thrown themselves at her feet only to be rejected. She decided (so she told me) that Miss Wilson was the secretary who might be able to persuade Brigadier Powell to smile.

Miss Wilson succeeded, though, somewhat to the chagrin of Avis Lewis, as well as other colleagues amused by what one called 'the slow emergence of civility and humanity in Enoch', they did not marry until 1952, Pamela having in the meantime done a stint working for the Council of Europe in Strasbourg, and Powell himself having forsaken his familial allegiance to teetotalism 'because I told him my father would never allow me to marry a teetotaller.' Before they married, moreover, Pamela was blooded as a candidate's helpmate in a punishing election campaign in 1951.

In the three years between his defeat at Normanton and his victory at Wolverhampton South-West – destined to be his political home for twenty-four years – Powell's schedule became ever more exigent. There was a heavy workload at the Research Department; there was a small, but increasing journalistic practice; and there was the unending and frustrating search for a seat. In 1947, moreover, he took another burden on himself which was to take him twenty years (and the necessary help of a collaborator) to dispose of.

The Labour government intended to nationalize the iron and steel industries, and the Opposition intended to frustrate this ambition by using its inbuilt majority in the House of Lords. The Labour Party found that prospect intolerable: after all, their victory in 1945 had given them a majority of 180 Commons seats over the Conservatives (and 146 over all parties). They were determined not to be denied a piece of legislation which had been clearly set down in their manifesto. In the event, the Tory leaders thought better of outright opposition and, as the then Tory leader in the House of Lords, the fifth Marquis of Salisbury, explained to Dr. Janet Morgan in 1970:[14]

The Conservative Party came to the conclusion that where something was in the Labour Party manifesto we would regard it as approved by the country . . . If they produced something that wasn't in the manifesto, we reserved the right to do what we thought best . . . We passed on Second Reading nearly all the nationalization bills – in the one case of the Iron and Steel Bill we rather went further as we didn't think they'd justified demand. So we put in an amendment not to put it into force until after the election.

This was not, however, good enough for Attlee and eventually – in 1949 – the government legislated to reduce further the power of the House of Lords (as defined in legislation passed in 1911) to hamper the designs of a government enjoying a majority in the Commons.

In the period between the introduction of the Iron and Steel Bill and the government's 1949 success in reducing the Lords' power to delay legislation by nine months, there was a great deal of constitutional discussion, and it fell to Powell to brief his superiors. 'In sketching out a brief outline [of the history of the House of Lords] for my own use I became aware that no history of the House as an institution, as distinct from the history of Parliament, existed.'[15] He took it upon himself to repair the omission. Material and drafts were steadily amassed until 1955, when he joined the Eden government. Work was then suspended until 1958, when he left Harold Macmillan's ministry. It was suspended again when he became Minister of Health in 1960, and when it had already assumed very substantial proportions. He then took two decisions, the first to halt the first part of the work at 1540 – roughly, the end of the truly medieval House – and the other to enlist a co-author, Keith Wallis, a specialist in the history of the fifteenth-century baronies. In 1968 a formidable tome of 671 pages finally saw the light of day.

By any standards – and even allowing for the help given by Wallis, which 'could only be fitly recognized by placing his name on the title-page as joint author' – *The House of Lords in the Middle Ages* is a monumental scholarly achievement, and the circumstances of its composition make the effort entailed all the more staggering.[16] Its eventual completion, so long after the first outline was prepared as a research brief, illustrates the formidable tenacity of Powell's character, and demonstrates that capacity to concentrate however great the pressures on him, of which he is so justly proud. 'I don't know,' he once observed, 'how one acquires – if it *is* acquired – concentration, whether it is at school or university, but it is a valuable attribute.'

The search for a seat eventually met with success, but in circumstances that were not altogether happy. After being turned down so frequently (and being rather put out by the fact that Iain Macleod, having first been adopted for Enfield in 1946, was again adopted in December 1948 for the redrawn constituency of Enfield West) Powell's attention began to turn towards his native West Midlands. He considered an application for Brierley Hill which was vacant, but on reflection thought it too much like Normanton. (He was right: Brierley Hill did not fall to the Conservatives until the runaway general election victory of 1959.)

The situation in Wolverhampton, however, looked more promising. A boundary adjustment was expected which would add large tracts of territory to the old constituency of Wolverhampton West to form a new constituency, Wolverhampton South-West. Wolverhampton West had been held by Labour with a majority of just over 7,000, but circumstances bade fair, once the Boundary Commission had done their work, to be more propitious for whoever gained the Conservative nomination.

There was the rub, for Wolverhampton West already had a candidate, Patrick Stirling, a barrister from London who had gone to live in the constituency. While technically speaking a selection had to be made afresh for the new constituency, it was initially supposed that Stirling would be chosen. Amid a certain degree of acrimony, and a good deal of bitterness on his part, Stirling was dispensed with.

What happened was that social circumstances, and the fact that his background was humble, which had worked against Powell in his search for other nominations, actually helped in Wolverhampton. Stirling was unpopular, not because he was not hard-working and conscientious, but because he was deemed to be upper class. At this period Woolton and his aides were working hard to diversify the social background of Conservative candidates and MPs, while in Wolverhampton a majority of the local Party was coming round to the view that, if the seat was to be won, the task could be performed only by 'one of our own'. Powell was from the area, and he was proud of his origins. He had not lost his West Midlands accent. He could identify with the locals and, perhaps of supreme importance, he was prepared to work virtually full-time (he resigned from the Research Department to do so) at nursing the constituency. What is more he made an extraordinarily good impression at his interview, where his performance was described as 'stunning'. On 17 December 1948 he was adopted. Powell was identified in two ways in his new constituency. First, he was a local man, and for all that he was rightly seen to be a formidable selection, and found it (because of his gruff shyness) by no means an easy task to undertake the massive programme of canvassing (with the object of visiting every house in Wolverhampton South-West) he had set himself, his ability to identify with the area stood him in excellent stead. Second, he was perceived as a robust right-wing imperialist: no supposedly progressive Butlerite strains appeared in his oratorical lineaments as he traversed what was to become virtually his fief from end to end.

Even for a man of his phenomenal industry, however, the burdens were becoming too great, particularly after (at the suggestion of Henry Brooke, later to serve as Home Secretary in Harold Macmillan's administration) he joined the Housing Committee of the London County Council. Having acquired a small and frugally appointed flat in the constituency, he therefore resigned his full-time job at the Research Department in the middle of 1949, though retaining a role as part-time adviser on local government and associated matters. He had become something that was new to the Conservative Party – the full-time candidate. Riding and hunting as a part of his life declined in terms of the amount of time they occupied, but the writing continued in the minuscule flat where, it seemed to visitors, he lived on sausages.

His life was still spartan, but his journalistic practice was growing, particularly for a local paper, the *Birmingham Post*, and the Newcastle *Journal*. His subjects were many and various, from book reviews through foreign policy to the gritty details of domestic affairs. The style was set early, and it has retained its early characteristics ever since. From his more substantial writings Powell brought to his journalism a singular trenchancy, a coldness of manner and a frequently distinctly dismissive attitude to his subjects or, at least, his targets. The view of America, for example, was expressed forcefully in a review of Eisenhower's memoirs for the *Sunday Sun* on 2 January 1949:

The narrative is unpartisan to the extent of being sometimes almost impersonal; the style is unpretentious and even wooden. What human character the book discloses in its author is typically American in that lack of subtlety and of appreciation for the complex and problematic which often makes it appear to the Englishman crude and naïve.

The tone was very different when on 26 June 1949 he reviewed Churchill for the same newspaper:

> The great thing in the book is the mass of minutes from the Prime Minister to the Chiefs of Staff and members of the Cabinet – hundreds in the text and another eight pages in an appendix. They afford us an insight into the methods and mentality which made him the greatest of our war ministers . . . Here, in this simple machine driven from the centre, but checked and guided by the civil ministers and the military chiefs, is the secret. Ultimate authority and initiative, military as well as civil, were concentrated in a single person.

The decisive note of Powell's style – the seeking out of the central point of an argument and the hammering home of it – is already fully present.

But he did not confine himself simply to reviews, and two articles of this pre-parliamentary period are particularly worth mentioning, foreshadowing as they do the preoccupations of later years. Both appeared in the Newcastle *Journal*, on 2 July and 30 July 1949 respectively. The first concerned the future of Korea (war was to break out there in June of the following year), the second the future of the atomic bomb. He was later to be totally silent on the Korean imbroglio in the House of Commons, distrusting the international character of the effort to save South Korea from the North, but in 1949 he was prepared to accept the proposition that Japan was vital to American interests, and Korea vital to Japan's security. However, and characteristically, he put the looming Asian conflict into a world framework, predicting not only a long drawn-out conflict between the United States and the USSR (which was a common enough perception) but stressing that:

> lying off each coast of the Old World is an important group of islands. Off the European coast lie the British Isles. Almost exactly corresponding to them off the opposite, or Asiatic, coast lies another chain of islands, Japan in the centre, Sakhalin to the north and Formosa to the south.

And

> To carry the comparison further both groups of islands have

been the home of a naval empire, which has swayed the destinies of its neighbours on the mainland; for what Britain has been to Europe Japan has been to Asia.

The naval theme which was to become ever more dominant in his military thinking was already present for 'In the world drama of the twentieth century these two island groups are immensely important to the protagonists. They are the keys to the Atlantic and Pacific respectively.

This was strong analytical meat for a small provincial paper; but it was hardly, in its essence, controversial. The article 'The atom bomb may not be used', on the other hand, flew in the face of all conventional wisdom. 'Is it worth it and is it necessary?' Powell asked. 'It will be some years before any nation likely to be our enemy is ready to wage war with atomic bombs . . . Later on, when atom bombs are a stock line in the principal arsenals of the world, the absolute certainty of reprisals reduces the likelihood of their being used, though it cannot, of course, eliminate the possibility.' Though this argument has since become a great deal more elaborate, the anti-nuclear stance is now a standard part of Powell's intellectual repertoire; and it is striking to see how early he deployed it. What remains a mystery is how he managed, in 1965, to secure appointment as Conservative Shadow Minister of Defence.

Again, in contrast to so many other candidates, Powell sought to deploy his partisan arguments within a generalized framework, as when he wrote in the *Birmingham Post* on 26 October 1950:

The Socialist aims at equality (sometimes disguised as equality of opportunity) and sets no limit to the sphere of government. He therefore uses the social services as a deliberate means of equalization and . . . entrusts to the state the responsibility for fulfilling all the individual's needs. The Tory believes that inequality is not only natural and inevitable, but within the framework of a sound society is of infinite value. He sets definite limits to the sphere of government and the responsibilities of the state, and would preserve and strengthen those of the individual and the family.

Powell ran the Socialist scare argument – suggesting that a returned Labour government would go so far as to nationalize even the retail trade – as hard as Churchill (disastrously) had in 1945, and far harder than did the national leadership of his Party. His rhetoric would certainly prove to anybody who attended to it that he was no very close follower of R. A. Butler. But Wolverhampton did not figure very largely in the eye of London, and when he reached the House of Commons the Research Department tag for some time attached itself to him. In any event, the tough electors of Wolverhampton liked not only what he had to say, but how he said it; his assiduous canvassing (dubbed 'Operation Knocker') endeared him to his Party activists. He was as ready as any candidate conceivably could be when the election was called for 23 February 1950.

By the end of 1949 the Attlee administration was exhausted: the Prime Minister himself, for example – not to mention a number of senior ministers – had served in Cabinet since 1940. They had first endured the terrible pressures of war and then undertaken the arduous passage of the great mass of reforming legislation to which they were committed. They were showing the strain. Later, cracks were to appear in the façade of their unity, notably with the resignation of the Minister for Health, Aneurin Bevan, and the President of the Board of Trade, Harold Wilson, in April 1951, on the issue of the implementation of prescription charges in the Health Service. The Tories, on the other hand, were well rested, and they combined the advantages of familiarity, with the great war leader still at their head, and novelty, with a series of new charters – or mini-manifestos – on a variety of subjects.[17]

Still, no Conservative underestimated the size of the task ahead. In 1945 Labour had gained an overall Commons majority of 146. But their advantage over the Conservatives was 182 (if one remembers to exclude the Speaker, D. Clifton Brown, a Conservative, the advantage was 183). In the event, and after a vigorous campaign, the Opposition only just failed: Labour retained a majority of six overall and 17 over the Conservatives.

Such a Parliament could not, given the circumstances, last very long. On 25 October 1951 there was another appeal to the country, and Churchill came home with a majority of 16 overall and 25 over Labour. This was to be the beginning of thirteen years of Conservative rule in which the majority rose first, in 1955, under Anthony Eden, to 58 overall and 67 over Labour and second, in 1959, under Harold Macmillan, to over 100 overall and 107 over Labour.

Powell fought his own campaign in 1950 as he has fought every campaign since – as though he were in danger of losing. And, indeed, in Wolverhampton South-West the precaution was advisable. There was a strong Labour organization in the constituency and the sitting Member, H. D. Hughes, was highly regarded. Again, however encouraging demographic facts look to a candidate in a new seat, one can never be wholly confident of their accuracy. In the event, however, Powell was victorious by 20,239 votes to 19,548, with the Liberal candidate trailing on 4,229. The figure of 691 was not one on which even a less energetic member than Powell could afford to rest. But, over the life of the 1950 Parliament he was helped in the constituency not only by his own efforts but by the retirement of Hughes from politics and the decision of the Liberals not to field a candidate in 1951.

The actual detail of the campaign is not of very great interest, save in the emphasis it offers on Powell as what might be called a technical candidate. In general he held to the Party line of turning back Socialism, abandoning the wartime controls on the economy which were still in force and broadening individual liberty. If there was a difference between his and the national campaign it was rather on emphasis: his oratory on domestic matters was distinctly harsher than the general, and for all that his beloved India (not to mention Pakistan, Burma and Ceylon) had attained independence, the interest and attraction of Empire was still very much to the fore in his speeches and writings. It was to be some time before he came to the conclusion that the loss of India meant the end of Empire. What did, however, give his victory an especially satisfying personal flavour was that his own had been the first election in which he had ever been able to vote; and that he had been elected for a seat in the Black Country, his ancestral heath.

It will be convenient to review here, out of strict chronological sequence, Powell's relations with his constituency between the 1950 and 1951 general elections, and then to discuss his early Parliamentary career as a sequential whole. The general elections were held so closely together that he could hardly be sure of his tenure until he had considerably increased his majority and, besides, an extraordinary (as even his friends and supporters saw it) episode in November 1950 seriously damaged member-constituency relations, and even threatened to put an early end to a Parliamentary career only just begun. The most dramatic shot in what was to be a short but bitter battle came on 13 November when the newspapers reported that the Member for Wolverhampton South-West had decided not to stand at the next general election.

Powell had decided to make a public stand of principle on an issue which he conceived to be of the first importance, though few shared his judgement. Though at this distance in time the matter does appear a trivial one, there can be no doubt that the business showed Powell for the first time displaying those characteristics of utter determination, at whatever cost to himself, when his mind is made up, and a powerful relish for dramatic conduct in any confrontation. In other words we have here our first glimpse of the fully-fledged public personality of Powell which has so often over the years had such an impact on British politics, to an extent, his critics would say, which bedevilled them, which brought issues he favoured to the very forefront of public argument, and which destroyed two governments.

The matter at issue was this. To avoid falling foul of electoral law local political parties are dissolved during general election campaigns. While the 1950 campaign was on, therefore, Powell felt himself perfectly free from any of the customary restraints imposed – usually in a friendly way – by a constituency association on its candidate or member. Powell concluded (as, indeed, most forceful election candidates do, in similar circumstances, conclude) that in this situation he was entitled to become in effect the dictator of the campaign.

He expected from his voluntary workers the same levels of application and industry that he had demanded from his juniors in the Army without, perhaps, fully realizing that free citizens donating their time to a political party will not necessarily hold themselves under the same discipline as serving soldiers. In any event, he was displeased with the efforts being made by his committee in Graisley Ward, descended upon them, and told them in no uncertain terms where they were going wrong. Once the general election was over, and Powell having won the seat, the committee passed a resolution of mild rebuke, arguing that they should receive orders only from the relevant committee of the Constituency Association – although, of course, no such committee was in legal existence at the time.

Powell was furious, though general opinion had it that he was over-reacting, *The Daily Telegraph* of 14 November observing, with the heavy suggestion that he was over-concerned with things as he saw them, that '. . . Mr. Powell has the kind of intellect that burns more fuel than a frail frame can contain.' He would not be content, even, with a unanimous vote of confidence from his constituency executive, the Vice President of which subsequently resigned. What he had to have, he insisted, was the resignation of all the officers of the Graisley Ward committee, and in December he got them. In January 1951, moreover, those officers who had crossed him were not allowed to stand again; there was subsequently a major walk-out from a meeting which Powell was addressing. But his authority was never again challenged, even during the years when he was carrying on a species of bitter siege warfare against a Conservative government.

The 1951 campaign in Wolverhampton was marked by an incident and an emphasis. Pamela Wilson, back at Central Office, offered to go north to be Powell's personal aide in the struggle (a common practice when staff is to spare). The weather was foul, and her train was delayed for a number of hours. On her eventual arrival, the sodden candidate was waiting patiently on the platform, and she began to suspect that there might be more than ordinary politeness in his attitude towards her. Their courtship did not, however, immediately become serious, and they did not marry until the following year. She once observed, indeed – and only half-humorously – that he did not decide to propose until, by accident, he learned that she had at least some competence in Latin. He was present when, years later, she made this remark and, on being questioned as to its truth he laughed and said: 'It may be so. It may well be so.'

The emphasis of the campaign speeches was heavily imperial, far more so than in 1950. He was preoccupied with the attitude of the Persian Prime Minister, Mossadeq, towards British interests and was equally critical of Egypt, arguing, on 11 October:

> . . . there is no reason to suppose that unless there is some change those things will not go on. The alternative is to hold what we have, to stand upon those rights, upon that land and upon that property which still remains to us. At the same time we must make it clear to ourselves and to the world that there will be no more retreat and no more surrender. Make it clear to those who threaten us: 'There is nothing more doing. Good morning!'

His enthusiasm for Empire was, indeed, general, and combined, as it had been for Joseph Chamberlain (much later to be the subject of a biography by Powell) with a view of the needs of domestic policy. Thus, on 17 October:

> Britain in the world outside is in retreat. At home she is strangling her own endeavours. The products of the Empire,

sold abroad for dollars, have been paying for our food. Only the Empire has kept us, since the war, from disaster.

Indeed, Powell went so far, during the campaign, as to advocate Chamberlain's favourite cause, Imperial Preference.

These speeches give rise to a certain problem of chronology. Powell has more than once recorded the shocked reaction which he had to the loss of the Indian Empire,[18] and from his realization of that loss stemmed his ultimate rejection of all the vestiges of the Empire, with rare and specifically justified exceptions, such as the Falkland Islands. His extremely carefully phrased criticism, made between 1965 and 1968, when he was Shadow Defence Minister, of the policy of maintaining a British military presence east of Suez got him into very hot water with Conservative backbenchers. Now, India was lost in 1947, and he recalls, 'one evening, I think in 1947, after separation of India[19] had become a political fact, walking about the streets all night trying to digest it. One's whole world had been altered.' Even in 1987 he speaks with the same feeling when he says: 'I realized in 1946-7 that that [the Empire] had gone by and I had to make my inner peace with it.'

The subsequent torrent of speeches and articles on the subject of the hallucination of Empire[20] make frequent reference to his shock at the loss of India, and it would be easy to assume from their tone and detail that his realization of the death of Empire stemmed from that first reaction to separation. But if that reaction is to be dated to 1947 (and there is every reason to believe it is, not merely because he says so, but because it was in August of that year that India was partitioned, and Powell had already resigned as Secretary to the backbench India committee) then it took a long time for the global significance of the loss of India to sink in, and for him to draw from it the conclusion he has since been at pains to emphasize. For my own part – as I will argue later[21] – the decisive moment was not in 1947, but in 1954, when the best efforts of the Suez Group, of which he was a member, and the deep reservations of Churchill, were not enough to prevent Anthony Eden concluding a treaty with Egypt which involved the withdrawal of British troops from the Suez Canal Base.[22] That withdrawal severed the last military link of consequence and power between Britain and the East. Once it was gone the last shreds of the dream of Empire had gone as well. But the working out of what all this meant, with all its implications for his own political development as an isolation-ist nationalist, took a great deal longer than he sometimes implies.

It has to be remembered [23] that while still in India Powell had come to the military view that, whatever the political constitution of India in the future, there would remain in the ranks of the Indian Army a substantial British officer corps which, had it been created, he says he would almost certainly have joined. It is, in my judgement, certainly this background that influenced the principal elements in his maiden speech in the House on 16 March 1950, only a fortnight after he had taken his seat. The subject was defence, and the principal antagonists Emanuel Shinwell, the Defence Minister, and Churchill, who vied with one another on the question of whether enough was being spent – and spent with sufficient efficiency – on the Armed Forces. Churchill's assumption was that, whatever resources were necessary they could be found. Powell felt himself rather more in sympathy with Labour Members who felt that the economy was already badly overstretched. He had, however, as might be expected, a novel solution. India had gone; but, although:

. . . we have lost the greatest non-European army which the world has ever seen, an army which made possible, as did no other institution in the world, the active and affectionate co-operation of European and non-European,

Still:

If we are an Empire defending the Empire, we must draw far more than we do on the vast reserves of colonial manpower which exist within our Empire. The virtues which enabled British officers and British administrators to create this great army are not dead. The virtues which made the Indian army so great an instrument, although some of them are perhaps peculiar to the martial races of India, are paralleled in other parts of the world. Not only is it not impossible, it is imperative that we should create from the other parts of His Majesty's dominions a replacement for that which we have lost.

This was a truly staggering, not to say far-fetched idea; but it was one the unrealism of which Powell was not to detect for some time. It is an interesting speech none the less, for it shows the way in which his thought was evolving. Though it is impossible, writing about this early period of his political career, to avoid describing him as an imperialist, or, at least, a man of Empire, today he likes neither phrase, because of the connotations of domination which they have had imposed on them over the subsequent years. He was fully aware, while he was in India, of the extremely delicate equipoise which had for so long enabled the British to maintain their position in the sub-continent, and he has certainly never advocated the retention of territory by sheer force, going even so far as to say that he would not resist the sundering of Scotland from the United Kingdom provided that were the demonstrable wish of the Scottish people, for in a nation:

> . . . the sense of unity implies the relationship of parts to a whole. The inhabitants of Coventry and Plymouth accepted the consequences to themselves of Great Britain being at war, because they imagined Coventry and Plymouth only as parts of a whole: if the whole survived and prospered they could be comparatively indifferent to the fate of the parts . . . Whatever degrees of local independence or 'self-government' there may be within a nation, it will not remain a nation unless the parts instinctively subordinate what they imagine to be their separate welfare to the welfare of the whole.[24]

It is because this strain of thinking is so clear and strong in his work from the beginning that I reject utterly a *canard* mentioned by Mr. Utley and Mr. Roth (among others), and once assiduously spread around Cambridge dining tables by R. A. Butler, that Powell had conceived a plan to re-conquer India with ten divisions.[25]

The young (he was thirty-eight when elected, which for the time was considered young) backbencher such as Powell is fortunate if he comes to the House of Commons from such a background as the Conservative Research Department. He will not – like, say, a new entrant from the City, or industry – be confined in his knowledge to one subject. He will probably have a good grasp of several. Moreover, he will be up to date with the latest thinking of the Party leadership on policy, and know the inner thoughts and reservations of at least some ministers or shadow ministers on his own special subjects. In addition, of course, Powell had his considerable military and overseas expertise to fall back on. As in earlier periods of his career, he demonstrated an improbable range of expertise and, despite a certain proneness, occasionally to rebellion, more frequently to forthright criticism (after the

Party had returned to government), he was popular with the Whips. It has frequently been said since the days of Joseph Chamberlain[26] that Whips require of backbenchers merely votes, and not voices. But, though this is true in general, every Chief Whip likes to have a small reserve of young backbenchers who can hold their own in debate, and put an official case with force and clarity. Particularly since he was so industrious, Powell was highly regarded, and often encouraged.

Yet it was to be five years from the date of his entry into Parliament before he held office. Iain Macleod, somewhat to Powell's not always concealed irritation (they were good, though guarded, friends, but intense rivals) easily preceded him, becoming Minister of Health on the strength of one stunning onslaught on Aneurin Bevan, who was a particular *bête noire* of Churchill. Though Powell could make quite as dramatic a speech as Macleod at any stage of their careers he did not, in the early years, seem to have the knack (or perhaps the desire) to choose subjects or occasions on which he could make the kind of impact enjoyed by his old colleague. It is important to record here, however, that he was, in November 1952, offered a junior Home Office job, with responsibility for Welsh affairs (he had, after all, drafted the Conservative *Charter for Wales and Monmouthshire*). He turned it down, because he wanted something more in the centre of affairs. This was regarded on high as extravagant, and even eccentric behaviour. For one thing, ambitious young backbenchers did not turn down jobs. For another, Powell regularly marked his concern for Wales by intervening in the annual general debate on the Principality, and regularly restating his pride in his Welsh origins. His interventions raised some hackles among Welsh Members for, then as now, it was rare and resented for Englishmen sitting for English seats to take part in debates which Scottish and Welsh Members considered to be their exclusive preserves.[27]

By speaking for the first time only a fortnight after his arrival – and to some extent defying the convention that a maiden speech should be uncontroversial if not platitudinous – Powell had signified his intention of setting a cracking pace. In June he won a small but significant victory on a matter which affected his constituency by procuring amendments to a Bill governing the activity of the British Electricity Authority. In the same month, with five other backbenchers, he abstained in a vote on the Schuman Plan. The object of the Plan was to integrate the coal and steel industries of Western Europe. The government judged that the conditions for entering talks were too onerous.

The Tories disagreed and put down a critical motion. Powell and his friends declined to support their front bench, so here was (although he was later to sit in a Conservative government, and on an Opposition front bench which supported entry into the EEC) the first glimmering of a suspicion in his mind of entanglement with the countries of the continent. The impulse, however, was pro-imperial rather than anti-European (all the abstainers were later members of the Suez Group, opposing withdrawal from the Canal Zone) but it is none the less biographically interesting.

So multifarious were Powell's activities during his first two parliamentary years that it is difficult to give them a common theme. So far as domestic matters were concerned, however, he found a common focus for his preoccupations in the One Nation Group. The Group was, in essence, founded by two of the 1950 intake, Cuthbert Alport[28] and Angus Maude.[29] Apart from Powell it came to include Iain Macleod, Gilbert Longden, Edward Heath and Robert Carr.[30] The title the Group took to itself was inspired by Disraeli's novel, *Sybil or The Two Nations*, in which the great Victorian Tory leader lamented division within society and pointed to its cure. The Group sought to make realistic for modern times the aspiration for one nation, in terms both of opportunity for individuals and adequate social provision for all. Its first pamphlet (edited by Maude and Macleod) expressed this aspiration in general terms, and was widely taken to mean that the most gifted of the 1950 intake were determined that there should be no backsliding on the still fairly novel Conservative commitment to welfare provision. It is important to note, however, that the Group had nothing to say on overseas policy: in that area its members were sharply divided, and the best way of expressing that division is to point to the fact that, whereas Powell was an Empire man suspicious of Europe, Edward Heath was already seeking the best way of involving his country more closely with European affairs, and had little interest in the problems of Empire.

At the same time the 1945 educational efforts of the Conservative Political Centre – which Powell had so nearly joined in preference to the Research Department – were being redoubled. Apart from its general pamphlets the principal engine of the CPC was what was then (and still is) called the 'two-way movement of ideas'. Groups were formed within constituencies. At regular meetings they received from Central Office a leaflet outlining a paticular policy or problem. The groups discussed these leaflets and returned individual reports, which were then analysed, usually by the Research Department, and passed on into the bloodstream of policy-making. It was all part of improving the political awareness of local Conservative Associations, which Butler and Woolton held to be abysmally low, but it had the further functions of improving the quality of local political debate, and alerting the leadership, in a more systematic fashion than had hitherto been attempted, to local concerns which might have passed beneath notice. In June 1950 Powell took over the chairmanship of the West Midlands CPC, thus presiding over 150 discussion groups.

It is difficult to say what effect all this enthusiasm for education and debate had, and it is fair to say that recent historians like Dr. Anthony Seldon tend to be rather dismissive of it. Intellectual activity, particularly on such a scale, however, should never be underrated, simply because it is so hard to pin down precisely its effect. That there is some effect, however, I do not personally doubt: the convictions of men at the outset of their political careers may be held for all sorts of reasons, and made up of personal and educational experiences. They may become diluted as the political ladder is mounted. They may be abandoned, or adhered to with excessive rigour. But – unless the men are of no quality, which is a condition rarer than supposed in political life – when power is attained something of those early convictions, those early formulations, will remain, like the rich silt on a river bank after the flood (in this case the flood of youthful enthusiasm) has receded. It is rarely possible for the historian successfully to analyse all the elements in the silt, and to decide which ones can be attributed to which action of the flood. But I record here the conviction that there is a connection.

So far as Powell's life is concerned I will give one example. Certainly in the 1960s and the 1970s, he was widely (though not by the discerning) regarded as *the* apostle of an untrammelled free market, in education, health and welfare, as well as in commerce and industry. This was the man who, in the 1950 Parliament, responding to a decision announced by David Hardman, the Parliamentary Under Secretary of Education, to increase the price of school meals from fivepence to sixpence, responded with asperity and emotion by saying that school meals should be free 'as it ensures that the children are in a condition, and in a frame of mind, to benefit from their instruction'.

But there has been no change of mind: there is no paradox. In 1970 Powell sought to define the borderline (on social welfare matters in general, but I quote him on education) in this way:

The fact that the state finances the overwhelming majority of school education, both during the years of compulsory attendance and thereafter, is no reason why the provision and pattern of university education and of technical training at maturer ages ought not to be determined by a variety of forces, among which economic motivation would predominate, and the role of the state would be to supply or safeguard some of the elements which are believed desirable on other than economic grounds and which might otherwise not be maintained. The principle holds good throughout the social services . . .

The juxtaposition of the two speeches illustrates more than a simply biographical point. From 1945 onwards the Conservative Party has engaged in a continuous debate on the matter of where to draw the line between public and private provision in health and welfare. This debate began between 1945 and 1950 and was made necessary by the decision to accept and retain the reforms of the Attlee government in the social field. The difficulty (apart from any matter of conscience) arose from the fact that the Tories had an emotional as well as a hard-headed commitment to the idea of creating national wealth through free enterprise to an extent that was shared by not even the most moderate member of the Labour Party. (Conversely, Labour had an emotional commitment in the other direction – to universal state provision as the most important objective of government.) The argument continues to this day, and it is an interesting footnote to history to record that in 1984 Cuthbert Alport resigned as the Conservative Whip in the House of Lords on the ground that, in his opinion, Mrs. Thatcher had strayed too far towards insisting on the provision of health and welfare services through the market.

It was with this question of the search for an ideal balance between free economic enterprise and the proper role of the state that the One Nation Group struggled. And while today Powell has worked out a formula satisfactory to himself[31] the whole matter was less easy to settle in 1950. Powell and Macleod (at the latter's suggestion) recalling their Research Department collaboration on these matters, set out in 1951 to produce a pamphlet *Social Services: Needs and Means* which appeared the following year. For two men who seemed so to disagree on these matters in later years it is instructive that they had little difficulty in striking at least a rhetorical balance.

None of this took up all of Powell's time, not even his

parliamentary time. He continued his preoccupation with the creation of an Imperial Army, and on 3 July 1950 advanced the idea that British officers serving with the Gurkha Regiment should be exempt from income tax. He spoke in heat at the end of 1950 – not as substantially, but as sceptically critical – against the methods by which the government proposed to raise the reserves for participation in the war in Korea. He opposed the government's Minerals Bill (designed to facilitate the restoration of land ruined by mineral workings) on the grounds that it discriminated between different entrepreneurs. He argued against extra payment for nurses working with tuberculosis patients on the grounds that there was no evidence for the suggestion of contagion. He opposed the Diplomatic Immunities Bill of 1951 on the grounds that it extended to Commonwealth representatives privileges accorded to foreigners though they were subjects of the King. And he beavered away in his constituency.

By the end of 1951, therefore, Powell had established himself as a coming parliamentary politician, eventually, probably, a senior Minister (as James Callaghan was to predict in February 1952). But puzzles hung over his head. That he was formidable, nobody doubted; that he was human, many did. He was never seen in a bar, never observed at a party. He did not smile; he did not socialize. His favourite place was the Chamber; his next favourite the Library. Having collected his correspondence he bore it about with him and, in spare moments, wrote out the answers. He had no small talk, and made little secret of the fact that he despised its practice. Furthermore, however generally his erudition was admired, and however much even his sharpest critics admitted the perfection of his logic (while invariably adding that it was not of the real world, and was based on faulty premises), he found it impossible to make the purpose of his life understood. He has, it must be said, faced this problem throughout his life. He labours to make his meaning and – perhaps on occasion more important – his intention plain. He is a fine, if occasionally archaic, prose stylist. But he was in those early years, as so often later, quite simply misunderstood. And this misunderstanding as often as not grew less out of hostility than out of wonder, out of the question, 'what manner of man has come upon us?' Thus, impressive as he was in his first couple of years as a Member, the very distance he seemed deliberately to set between himself and his fellows meant that they set a further distance. Enoch Powell was judged a maverick, a loner, in Michael Foot's later formulation.[32]

In any event, other things were happening in his life than the parliamentary. Among the less important was the growth – if not exactly the burgeoning – of his journalistic career. He had added the *Spectator*, *Time and Tide*, *Truth*, and *Confluence* as well as, occasionally, national newspapers, to his outlets. The BBC World Service had been delighted to find a speaker who could broadcast for them as readily in Urdu (he had gained his advanced diploma, as promised[33] to himself, in 1947) as in German, and this led to further work for the domestic services of the Corporation. Besides political speeches, and the pamphlet in collaboration just mentioned, he was at work on his history of the House of Lords, had engaged on a popular history, *Biography of a Nation*, with Angus Maude, and was continuing with his poetry. The summer of 1951 was partly taken up with putting together *Dancer's End* (wartime poems) and *Wedding Gift*. The latter volume can best be described as a series of love poems dedicated to a woman he had cared for who had married another man.

Thus Powell the scholar-politician. But there are other things, even in the life of a man with so many facets as Powell, than his scholarship or his politics.

In Sydney he had been not merely an atheist, but an aggressive atheist. He had a good grounding in the texts of Christianity from his mother[34] for all that she had lost her own belief and, naturally, as a classical student and historian he had addressed himself from time to time to the evidential justification it offered specifically for the Godhead of Jesus Christ and, more generally, for belief in God – that is, a belief in monotheism, in a single God in whose image man is made. He could find no such justification in the texts available to him.[35] In so far as he attended to religion it was to consider it brutally, practically, and from a point of view of the interests of the state that would have been applauded by Machiavelli.[36] Thus:

> I am an Anglican atheist. I think nothing of religion, but I think there ought to be an established Church and the King of England ought to be its Head.[37]

So far as it mattered to him, therefore, religion was the handmaiden of a particular national and political order. In that sense, from an early age Powell had been a pagan. The word 'pagan' has, in recent centuries, acquired a connotation of vice. For Powell no vice was intended. He had an intense sense of his nation. He could see no merit in a Christian case, save in that it sustained an order that would preserve the nation. Such was his position at the end of the war.

At some point thereafter there came a great change. It is right to mention here (and this, like any other book about him, is inevitably preoccupied with this fact) that Powell has changed his view on various political issues over the years in circumstances which might allow of an accusation of self-interest;[38] such circumstances saw the public man in public action. The inner man can yield to no such criticisms. Yet, something that happened to the inner man suddenly became vitally important in his early parliamentary years or, perhaps, even earlier; and it had, initially, nothing to do with anything but himself.

Powell had been in churches – and mosques and temples, for that matter – many times, and had studied them with interest. But the interest was academic. Then:

One winter Sunday not long after the war I did something against my will and against my better judgement. I entered a church just before evensong and sat down. For twenty years I had never crossed the threshold of any church except for architectural curiosity, and that rarely.[39] I felt ashamed of what I was doing because I could not give myself a good account of it. So I chose a dark corner, near the door, hoping to escape my own notice. However, ashamed or not, I came again and again, until presently I realized I was caught fast, not by anything external, whether personal or material, but by an inner logic or necessity. Suddenly I found my feet were set on a path where I could turn neither aside nor back.

It is impossible to doubt the genuineness of the feeling which Powell's account conveys. His religious feelings, beliefs, and arguments became an increasingly important part of his life in subsequent years, and I will study them at greater length later.[40] Suffice it to say for the moment that Powell has, particularly in recent years, published a great deal of closely argued work on religion and theology (which are not at all the same thing); that his major work in hand in 1989 is devoted to a study of the textual evaluation of the synoptic gospels, Matthew being at its heart, and – this is not a cheap, but a serious point – that at a time of anguished debate about whether or not there should – or could – be women priests in the Church of England, his views (taking the debate into a larger dimension than has been done so far) commanded publication in the summer edition of *Faith and Worship* (the journal of the Prayer Book Society) and respectful attention on the part of Mr. Clifford Longley, the Religious Correspondent of *The Times* on 3 August 1987.

The new religious concerns were transmuted beyond his own personality into something that could be shared. Powell proposed marriage to Pamela Wilson and was accepted. 'They tell me Enoch's getting married,' said Iain Macleod to his wife, 'I can hardly believe it.'[41] The members of the Conservative Association in Wolverhampton, and particularly its president, Sir Robert Bird, were scarcely less surprised, though, of course, they were pleased, since every constituency likes its Member to have a wife. The many who had noticed a dour man with gifts of a somewhat academic and iron order striding gracelessly about the House of Commons and holding forth in its Chamber in an acerbic and (to more than a few) intolerant way were equally taken aback by his fortune in winning so charming, unaffected, and pleasant a bride.

They were married on 2 January 1952 at Pamela's mother's church in Lancaster Gate, and departed for a honeymoon in Catalonia and Majorca. The initial ceremony was a simple preface to what was to prove to be a marital alliance, not merely loving but formidable. Pamela wore a dress of oyster silk (from the family chest) with a veil of Brussels lace, her bridegroom a hired suit. Their car was an already elderly Austin which, to her terror, he insisted on driving. Like Michael Strachan, Pamela Powell was to learn of the determination and the oddity of her husband's driving.

But they were back from Spain in time for the resumption of the new session of Parliament, to begin housekeeping in his grim little flat in Earl's Court. The supposedly irredeemable bachelor was shown to have his own nesting instinct. He had already adorned the flat with book cases of his own manufacture. He now added such things as Pamela would require, notably cupboards with sliding doors. 'I had not imagined,' R. A. Butler said, many years later, 'that Powell could be a happy man. But he was, because of his lady.' A routine was quickly established. According to it Pamela did duty as Powell's occasional typist in the morning, and attended to the needs of their modest household in the afternoon, when he went to the Commons.

Their circumstances were, if not spartan, at least frugal. Powell's income as a Member of Parliament was £1,000 a year. In his bachelor days he had reckoned that he could save at least £100 of that sum. By eating in the House of Commons – and never outside – he would have to spend only £2 a week on culinary subsistence. Travel between Wolverhampton and London was free, as it remains for all Members of Parliament going to and from their constituencies. The rents for his London and constituency bases were, as he describes them, 'vestigial'. By the time he married, moreover, there was a variable income from journalism, of the written and spoken kind. In 1952 – to anticipate the financial story a trifle – he succeeded Macleod as a director of the London Municipal Society, a local authority version of the Conservative Research Department. This task – an onerous one, involving constant scrutiny of housing in the London area – added £500 a year to his income.

The first Powell child, Susan Mary, was born on 13 January 1954, and her father left the Baptismal ceremony (in the Crypt Chapel in the Palace of Westminster) to answer a Division Bell calling him to vote. Powell set about making more changes to the flat, changes which included the fitting of grooved rails to the steps which led down to the garden, so that Susan's pram could be readily wheeled out to give the baby air.

While married life – and fatherhood – was generally held to have, if not exactly softened Powell, at least made him more approachable, it did not diminish his appetite for work, nor alter anything essential in his character. Some of the quirkiness of personality (endearing to his friends, regarded as evidence of an almost lunatic inhumanity by his enemies) remained, as when just after their honeymoon, having engaged to meet his wife in the central lobby of the House of Commons, he paced about becoming increasingly cross at her lateness, and failed to recognise her sitting in a corner, amused at his evident irritation.

Some of his friends did, however, believe that his marriage had dulled his appetite for office. There was certainly a sense in which he seemed almost to prefer the freedom and isolation of his role as the independent, intellectual backbencher. But when, on 27 March 1952, Macleod was called to speak before him in a debate on the National Health Service and, with the opening words of his attack on Aneurin Bevan, created a national reputation, Powell had reason to believe that luck as well as patronage had passed him by. From Macleod's first paragraph it was clear that his would be the speech of the day. Powell, who had prepared an equally stinging attack on the creator of the National Health Service, put it away and concentrated instead on a rather technical assault on the Labour Party's record.

Both men were to sit on, and do yeoman service for, the

Standing Committee on the Bill, but it was Macleod's speech that won him office. From the first sentence – 'I want to deal closely and with relish with the vulgar, crude and intemperate speech to which the House of Commons has just listened . . .' – it was clear that the Conservatives had found a warrior who could take on one of the greatest parliamentary performers of the time. But it was his quickness of thought on his feet that enabled him to take advantage of a singular piece of good fortune. When preparing his speech he had decided to use the hackneyed remark that a debate on the NHS without Bevan would be like a performance of *Hamlet* without the Prince. As he glanced at his notes, however, he made a change, and the passage came out as 'To have a debate on the National Health Service without the Right Honourable Gentleman would be like putting on *Hamlet* with no one in the part of the First Gravedigger.' The good fortune was that Churchill, who had a legendary dislike of Bevan, was in the Chamber to hear this sally. He did not know Macleod, but immediately asked the Chief Whip, Patrick Buchan-Hepburn, who he was. From that moment Macleod was certain of preferment, though when, a little later, he became Minister of Health, he had to inquire where the Department was located.

The Macleod appointment caused a deterioration in relations between himself and Powell. Powell felt, not unjustly, that he had been more industrious than Macleod, and he certainly had a more organized mind. Their coolness did not, however, last, and it was Powell who repaired the breach. At the end of May Macleod's wife, Eve, fell seriously ill. Macleod later recalled that Powell arrived unannounced one day in his room, laid a key on his desk and said, gruffly, 'There's a room ready for you in my flat. Come and go as you wish.' The old friendship was resumed, and it lasted until 1968.

Whatever his resentment, however, Powell simply redoubled his efforts, and his workload. With Angus Maude he worked on the potted history of Britain (*Biography of a Nation*, which was, in general, ill-received) and the One Nation Group pamphlet, *Change is our Ally*, which was given markedly respectful attention. Through his work at the London Municipal Society he became expert in matters of housing and transport. He was becoming increasingly interested in, and conversant with, economics and, in truth, there were very few subjects on which he had no comment to make, thus first exciting the implicitly critical judgement, 'there is a Powell policy for everything.' In general, his purpose was to push his Party further than it wished to go on liberalizing the economy and deregulating industry; there were, indeed, prolonged verbal tussles between himself and Maude during the preparation of *Change is our Ally*.

Powell had never been less than outspoken, but from 1952 onwards his outspokenness was increasingly that of a rebel. On 9 February 1952, in *Time and Tide*, he took on R. A. Butler on the subject of similarity between Conservative and Labour policy:

> Nevertheless, the statement which the Chancellor of the Exchequer had to present [to Parliament] was not free of embarrassment on two counts: first its very similarity in kind to those in 1947 and 1949 and, second, the contrast between the expansionist and libertarian spirit in which the government entered upon office and the restrictive nature of the first economic measures to be proposed.

Powell, indeed, was rapidly coming to be thought of as the conscience of the Party. In February 1954 he became the conscience of the House as well.

In that month a Select Committee, appointed to review the question of Members' pay, recommended an increase, to which it was known the government was sympathetic. Powell stated his policy:

> Should an actual increase be made, I should regard it as my duty not to accept it as long as this Parliament lasts. I hope to speak against it. Members of Parliament are the only people who can vote themselves an increase out of the public pocket; that is a very responsible position to be in.

He was joined in his opposition to the increase by the bulk of Tory MPs, though, in a free vote on the matter in May, an alliance between the Labour Party and a Conservative minority carried the principle of an increase of £500 over the basic parliamentary salary of £1,000. Given the preponderance of opposition, however, Churchill announced the withdrawal of the proposal. From that day until his defeat at South Down in 1987 Powell held true to his principle. He never accepted an increase in pay without the supervention of a general election, taking the view that a new parliament is elected on new terms.

It seems clear that, during these years, Powell had given up hope of receiving an appointment from the Churchill government, and knew that he would have to wait his chance until, as expected,

Anthony Eden succeeded as Prime Minister. (He knew Eden, though not particularly well, having briefed him on housing policy during his own time at the Research Department.)[42] He did not, however, seek to ingratiate himself with the Foreign Secretary, and his opposition to Eden leads to consideration of the two events of this period in the back bench wilderness which are crucial to an understanding of his views and their evolution.

Eden, despite the reputation he gained because of the invasion of Egypt in 1956 which led to his resignation as Prime Minister, was by nature a conciliatory diplomat. Though they were not strictly speaking his departmental responsibility he worked to encourage links with the emerging independent nations of the Commonwealth; and in 1953 it became known that he was keen to come to an agreement with Egypt which would involve the withdrawal of the 80,000 British troops then stationed in the Suez Canal Zone. Lord Moran[43] records Churchill's distaste for withdrawal: 'I may have to say something in the Suez debate, but I shall put Anthony in front. It's his business. If he likes this policy of scuttle in Egypt he must defend it.' Churchill had already developed doubts about Eden's calibre, and he fought long and hard at least to delay the succession, but on all matters of foreign policy except relations between the West and the Soviet Union he tended to leave the Foreign Secretary to his own devices.

Powell's attitudes on what remained of the Empire – and on the changing Commonwealth – were, from 1951 onwards, mixed. On 6 November 1952, in the *Birmingham Post* he wrote:

No one would suspect that in a period as short as five years the most fundamental changes would have taken place within the Empire – India outside the allegiance of the Crown, Africa thrown into political discord and rent with racial antagonism, the Dominions of the old and the new world seeking new alliances and alignments for themselves to the exclusion of the mother country. To most of the world outside it seems that the British Empire, if it does not already belong to the past, has but a short lease of life. Only here in England, like a nation of Rip van Winkles, do we live in a dream world of undisturbed complacency.

In 1948, as a Research Department officer, he tried to persuade the Tories to vote against the British Nationality Bill of that year.

In another part of the article just quoted he stated his reasons publicly:

> Any Tory will tell you that the Crown is the great link which binds the Empire together in a common loyalty. But the British Nationality Act of 1948 took away allegiance to the Crown as the basis for British citizenship and made it possible for the citizen of a Republic to be a British citizen. Did the Conservative Party vote against this Act? They did not. By legislation of 1949 into 1950 the citizens of the Irish Republic and of the Indian Union were expressly given all the rights and privileges of British subjects, though repudiating the King as their sovereign. Did the Conservative Party protest against this? They did not.

In 1952, at the Commonwealth Prime Ministers' Conference, a number of heads of government of newly independent states had expressed dislike for the Queen's title: 'By the Grace of God of Great Britain, Northern Ireland, and of the British Dominions beyond the Sea Queen, Defender of the Faith.' In deference to their views the government the following year introduced the Royal Titles Bill, and advocated a new style: 'By the Grace of God of the United Kingdom of Great Britain and Northern Ireland, and of her other Realms and Territories Queen, Head of the Commonwealth, Defender of the Faith.' Powell was incensed.

He spoke against the Bill in trenchant terms, and to this day he considers the speech to be 'one of the parliamentary speeches I was most glad to have been able to make.' He had many objections to the Bill, but two were central. The first was the acceptance of the break-up of the old Imperial unity. The second was the abandonment (not only in the title of the Monarch, but for other occasions) of the word 'British' before 'Commonwealth'.

> That unity we are now formally and deliberately giving up, and we are substituting what is, in effect, a fortuitous aggregation of a number of separate entities . . . By recognizing the division of the realm into separate realms, are we not opening the way for the other unity – the last unity of all – that of the person of the Monarch to go the way of the rest?

On the removal of 'British' before 'Commonwealth' he said:

> Why is it then that we are so anxious in the description of our

own Monarch, in a title for use in this country, to eliminate any reference to the seat, the focus and the origin of this vast aggregation of territories? Why is it that this 'teeming womb of Royal Kings', as the dying Gaunt calls it, wishes now to be anonymous?

He was sarcastic as well as emotional. 'I recognize,' he said, 'the Rt. Hon. Member for Walthamstow (Mr. Attlee) as Leader of the Opposition, but that does not make me a member of Her Majesty's Opposition.' But his fiercest resentment was at the fact that the change had been made at the behest of the Commonwealth leaders, for if they had been truly friends they would not have sought it. 'I deny that there is present in that former part of Her Majesty's dominions which have cast off allegiance to her, that minimum, basic recognition of belonging to a great whole which involves the ultimate consequence in certain circumstances of self sacrifice in the interests of the whole.' And:

> However, the underlying evil of this is that we are doing it not for the sake of our friends but for those who are not our friends. We are doing this for the sake of those to whom the very names 'Britain' and 'British' are repugnant. We are doing it for the sake of those who have deliberately cast off their allegiance to a common Monarch.

His critics then and now have taken the view that he greatly exaggerated the importance of the change that was being made. Such critics had (and have) no objection to republics within the Commonwealth, and there was even, once, a suggestion that Japan might be invited to join.[44] But there was no questioning the depth of his feeling on the matter, nor the fact that he saw in this change, considered a trivial matter of good manners by ministers, the true end of the old Empire which he had come into politics to save. He concluded:

> Now I am not under any illusion that my words on this occasion can have any practical effect, but none the less they are not necessarily in vain. We in this House, whether we are the humblest of the backbenchers or the First Lord of the Treasury [Sir Winston Churchill] himself, are in ourselves, in our individual capacities, quite unimportant. We have a meaning in this place only in so far as in our time and generation we represent great principles, great elements in the national life,

great strands in our society and national being. Sometimes, elements which are essential to the life, growth and existence of Britain seem for a time to be cast into shadow, obscured, and even destroyed. Yet in the past they have remained alive – they have survived – they have come to the surface again, and they have been the means of a new flowering, which no one had expected. It is because I believe that, in a sense, for a brief moment I represent and speak for an indispensable element in the British Constitution and in British life that I have spoken. And, I pray, not entirely in vain.

I believe, with Mr. Berkeley, that 'Powell's present view on defence, immigration, the European Economic Community and Ulster can be traced directly back to this point.'[45]

He did not immediately, however, cast off the idea of imperial commitments. In December 1953 he joined a group of forty Tory backbenchers (the Suez Group) who were determined to oppose withdrawal from the Canal Zone. The plan was for the withdrawal of the garrison of 80,000, but the maintenance in place of 4,000 technicians, Britain having the right to reoccupy the base in case of necessity. In the magazine *New Commonwealth* on 4 January 1954 Powell wrote:

Unless the attitude and behaviour of Egypt changes with miraculous completeness and suddenness, this amounts to an agreement for unconditional evacuation; for to imagine that 4,000 technicians will fare better than 80,000 troops or that Egypt will be less ready to repudiate her new agreements than her old, argues an optimism which has no place in foreign relations.

And in *Truth* on 5 March 1954:

Suppose the present Egyptian government (whatever it is) accepts the British terms and we commit ourselves to evacuate the zone, retaining for a limited time only 4,000 engineers with sidearms. And suppose that what happened last week happens again next week. Is it reasonable to suppose that Colonel Nasser or whatever regime succeeds Neguib, or whatever regime succeeds that, will fulfil the terms of the agreement in amity and concord with Britain? Will the Egyptians who are now sniping at 80,000 British troops then become the guardian angels of 4,000 technicians? Will the base and its facilities be open to us at need without prevarication or demur? Will there even be 'liberty and entire security of navigation' of the Suez Canal (to use the words of the 1936 Anglo-Egyptian Treaty)?

This was prophetic for, of course, two years later Nasser nationalized the Canal and precipitated the Suez war.

However, strongly held though his views were – on this as on everything else – Powell did not take a senior part in the struggle which quickly unfolded. On 13 July Churchill himself spoke to the 1922 Committee (which consists of all Conservative backbenchers) in favour of Eden's policy, and Butler supported him on economic grounds. On 14 July Major Harry Legge-Bourke resigned the Conservative Whip. On 27 July agreement was reached with Egypt. The following day the House debated the issue. Powell was not called to speak but, with twenty-six others, voted against the government. He can hardly have been surprised that, in a minor reshuffle of the government on the 27th, nothing was offered to him.

Powell had already given warning – at a CPC Summer School in Oxford on 12 July – that if the agreement with Egypt went through he would regard it as irreversible. The attitudes he then expressed were far more in tune with his *Birmingham Post* article of 6 November 1952, and with his speech on the Royal Titles, than they were with his support of the Suez Group. 'What is surprising,' he said, 'is not that this sovereignty [of Empire] should be dismembered, but that its dismemberment should be so long postponed.' He now took the view that he has ever since maintained – that the essential object of holding the Canal Base was to protect the sea route to India. India gone – and, moreover, transmuted into a republic – the base had ceased to have real use. 'I must confess,' he said much later, 'that I had not seen the vital interconnection between the base and India nor, indeed, the full consequences of the loss of India.' His old Suez Group colleagues were rather taken aback when the House of Commons met again in October, to learn that Powell was no longer one of their number, believing that 'the Egyptian question belongs to the past.'

He resumed his various campaigns on domestic issues, as Eden waited with increasing impatience for Churchill to go. In February 1955 he argued for the restructuring of the railway system, on 15 February on housing in a speech so effective that it attracted wide notice, on a Private Member's Bill on Clean Air (presented by Gerald Nabarro) which he helped to draft, and later in the same month on hanging where, to the astonishment of many of his admirers and constituents, he proved to be for abolition. And in May 1955 he was back on the hustings, for Eden, having finally achieved the succession, wanted a majority of his own. The campaign was uneventful; the Prime Minister increased his parliamentary majority; and Powell his own to 8,420.

But Eden did not take the opportunity he had sought drastically to reconstruct the government. He reshuffled just before the election, and among the junior posts the most interesting appointment was that of Edward Boyle (who was elected in 1950) to be Economic Secretary to the Treasury, while Reginald Maudling became Minister of Supply. Powell's two old roommates at the Research Department therefore now had their feet placed well up the ministerial ladder, but Powell himself was still ignored. He ploughed on undaunted, and in June made a contribution to the Rating and Valuation Bill so effective that the responsible parliamentary Under Secretary, William Deedes, declined to add to it.[46] And, as an indicator of the esteem in which he was increasingly held by other backbenchers, he was, in November elected Vice Chairman of the 1922 Committee.

On 21 November an incident of pleasing symmetry in the history of British politics occurred. It will be remembered that Macleod hoisted himself to office on the strength of an attack on Aneurin Bevan. On 21 November 1955 Bevan launched an attack on the government's housing policy, in particular assailing the reduction in housing subsidies, and suggesting that the Conservatives had as their principal intention the enrichment of builders. Bevan was foolish enough to challenge Powell's argument in favour of more private housing, and was tartly reminded of a Bill he himself had introduced in 1946 providing for just such a reduction. 'Not only that,' said Powell. 'So convinced was the Rt. Hon. Gentleman that these subsidies were of a temporary nature that he actually obliged himself, if he were not able to start reducing them after twelve months, to come to the House with a report explaining why not.' The following month Powell was appointed as Parliamentary Under Secretary to the Department of Housing and Local Government under Duncan Sandys, who had been particularly impressed by his handling of Bevan. Thus it was that two of the most striking figures in the modern history of the Conservative Party both first reached office as the result of jousts with Aneurin Bevan.

Powell's joy was, however, shortlived. After his mother's death in 1953 he and Pamela had bought a house in Wolverhampton, where they installed his father, now in his eighties. This was comfortable for Albert and, of course, it meant that they could see more of him. However, particularly after the appointment, it was decided to spend Christmas in London, and Albert came down to join his son, daughter-in-law, and grandchild in the capital. Pamela's mother came to the family for Christmas dinner, and there could hardly have been a happier gathering. At the weekend, however, Albert, who had been in excellent form, collapsed, and died almost immediately after reaching hospital. He was buried with his wife at Worthing, just as his son was entering on his first ministerial challenge.

5

The Minister
1955-1963

By the end of 1964 we were saying and doing things which were inconsistent with any intelligible view, Socialist or non-Socialist, of the future destiny of this country. Our first task, therefore, is to recognize this among ourselves. In these last few months I personally have been trying to underline the practical implications of the belief that we can best work out the use of our resources by making the choices for ourselves. I am not interested in the working of the market economy from any academic interest in its beauty or consistency. It is intellectually satisfying as is any consistent interpretation of reality. But we are not about that business in politics. I am interested in pushing these debates through as far as they can be pushed, exposing the contradictions of policies like the Incomes and the Regional policies, because if a nation is to have faith in what it is doing it must sense that this can be argued out and stand up to the most rigorous analysis . . . Surely if the use of price, of profit, of market forces in competition are the processes by which a free nation discovers what it alone can give the world, we cannot use these processes effectively if we do so with half our minds looking the other way, in fear that someone will point the finger of scorn at us. Difficult things will have to be done if the habits of this nation – in so far as legislation can change habits – are to become truly and fearlessly competitive.

– *J. Enoch Powell,* ‘*The consequences of the general election*’
in Swinton College Journal, *Summer, 1965.*

When Powell became a Minister[1] his political as well as his personal life necessarily changed. It was not merely that, as the junior to Duncan Sandys, he had to undertake all the most tedious and time-consuming departmental jobs – particularly in answering debates held late at night in the House – but that his freedom of expression was truncated, since he fell victim to the doctrine of collective responsibility, according to which Ministers are supposed invariably to express the view of the government. During the Suez war of 1956, for example, there were not a few who felt that the supposedly high-principled Powell had betrayed his convictions in the interests of long-sought office. This was particularly the case as that unhappy conflict sped to its humiliating close, when a sick Eden, under severe American pressure, saw senior colleagues – and particularly Harold Macmillan – desert him and seek a peace on any terms, had to accept defeat and, shortly thereafter, loss of his office.

All the while Powell remained immersed in his departmental work, making only one speech – generally judged somewhat enigmatic – in his constituency just after the Anglo-French fleet had sailed for Egypt, in which he said that all debate should now be stilled, and all criticism silenced, since British troops were on their way to battle. The general truth of the matter is, however, rather different from what his critics on the right averred. Powell was certainly – as he had told them – no longer of their number. If he had been tempted to rebel it would have been more likely to be on the side of that small, but insistent, group of Tories (which included Edward Boyle and Anthony Nutting, Minister of State at the Foreign Office, both of whom resigned) critical of the whole venture. As it was, he kept his counsel, and saw no great issue of conscience involved. He was more troubled, indeed, by his personal position in a debate on capital punishment on 16 February 1956. There was to be a free vote; but the government was known to favour retention. In such circumstances a free vote is somewhat less than completely free, especially since the numbers were expected to be close, and Ministers are expected to do their duty. In the event Powell abstained.

His arrival in office excited the liveliest interest in the village that is Westminster. In any given Parliament there are two kinds of backbencher, those of whom it is held (by everybody except themselves and their families) that they are unlikely ever to hold office, and those who are fully expected at least to be given a chance. As regards the latter, interest is concentrated on whether they will fulfil their promise, or fall flat on their faces. From very early in his Commons career Powell was undoubtedly expected to hold office, and even those who disliked him felt that successive governments had taken an unconscionably long time to give him an opportunity to show his ministerial paces.

On the other hand, his personality, his seeming intellectual arrogance, his cold ferocity in debate, the incredible range of subjects which he seemed to have no difficulty in 'getting up', and his frank (even naked) ambition ensured that there was an even larger number than usual expecting – and hoping – to see him fail. Their views were well expressed by James Callaghan (though Callaghan did not share the underlying personal resentment of Powell's self-certitude) in a debate on Welsh affairs on 4 February 1952 when he said, 'When the Hon. Gentleman reaches the stage of becoming a Minister – as I am quite sure he will one day – he will see just how far his theorizing falls short of practice.'

That was just the point. Powell was not the only theoretician – or, at any rate, not the only politician who sought to put the policies he propounded in some sort of rational or philosophical form – in the House of Commons, though there were many more on the Labour benches than on the Tory. But he was by far and away the most *complete* logician in the Chamber. He was then, and always has since been (as the quotation at the head of this chapter shows) irritated by attacks on him as being in some way impractical, or deficient in his realization of the practical consequences of putting his ideas into effect. It is, furthermore, only fair to say that no contemporary politician has so constantly insisted on the *irrational* elements in the conduct of his profession. He has examined the distinction between the formulation of ideas and their application to political life many times, but early on he expressed a conclusion from which he has never varied, in an article in the *Birmingham Post* on 23 May 1952 entitled, 'Should economists take charge of politics?':

For the sake of argument, let us admit that economics is a science and therefore has nothing to do with party politics. But the policy of a party, in the economic sphere as much as any other, springs from the ideas which that party exists to embody. When you examine those ideas, you find that they are not derived from economics or concerned with economic ends. Economic policy, like foreign policy, imperial policy, or any other sort of policy, is the application of those fundamental ideas in the economic, external, imperial or whatever other field it may be.

The two essential elements in the administration of domestic policy which make up what has come to be called Powellism are the desire as far as possible to reduce the power of the state and increase the freedom of the individual; and to define and state as exactly as possible where the line should be drawn between the two. (There are, of course, a great many more facets to his thinking, and a great many more origins of his ideas, which I will consider in due course. But I am concerned here with the administration of a spending department which also has very considerable regulatory powers, so these two are the vital considerations.)

When Powell had rejected responsibility for Welsh affairs in the Churchill government it was believed to be because he wanted a Treasury job. The truth was that he considered a Welsh post difficult for an English MP to handle. His aspirations lay in the direction of Transport, for he was playing a vigorous part in supporting the Bill on that subject. The available job went to John Profumo. But, at least so far as domestic policy was concerned, he had made his reputation by speaking and writing on housing, health and welfare. In these areas he had trained himself in the Research Department, and his subsequent pamphlet with Macleod had attracted a good deal of friendly attention. It was understandable, therefore, that, increasingly as his future was discussed among parliamentary colleagues, speculation turned on a post in one of the social ministries. This, in turn, led to concern on the part of a number of Tories – even some who wished him well – about the effect such a man would have in a ministry devoted to social amelioration. Quite apart from conscience, the Conservatives were not, before the 1955 election, at all inclined to feel secure about their electoral position. Apart from the diehard right, the great majority of the parliamentary party was more than content with the 1951 government's decision to accept, and continue to develop, the greater number of the Attlee reforms. Powell, in spite of his membership of the One Nation Group, in spite of his devoted attention to the problems of his poorer constituents, in spite of his frequent parliamentary interventions on behalf of pensioners and the socially unfortunate, had gained a reputation for uncaring coldness. He was to turn out to be a highly efficient Minister, but experience was to show that these worried critics were not wholly wrong, within the framework of the usual in governmental politics. Spending Ministers are constantly engaged, particularly from August of one year to the spring Budget of the next, in tussling with the Treasury over spending allocations. The battle is continuous, and unremitting. Yet, Powell was later to record, specifically of his time as Minister of Health, but implicitly of his time at Housing, 'In my own particular case the question hardly arose: for to the best of my recollection I was never at variance on any departmental issue with either of the two Chancellors of the Exchequer with whom I served.'[2]

However, theory (or ideology) apart, economy at Housing and Local Government, as in all spending departments, was necessary. The irony of the situation was that Sandys and Powell would have to carry out a programme of economies under the eye of the man who had caused many of their problems, Harold Macmillan, who had replaced Butler as Chancellor on 20 December 1955. Macmillan had left Housing and Local Government in October 1954, for a brief stint as Minister of Defence and an even briefer one as Foreign Secretary. As far as Sandys (and later Powell) was concerned, his legacy was not a happy one.

The difficulty arose from a resolution passed at the Conservative Party Conference of 1950 in the face of opposition from the leadership. The resolution called for the building of 300,000 houses a year. It seemed an impossible task, and was accepted by Lord Woolton only because of the massive determination of the Party representatives assembled to secure the commitment and thus outdo Labour in the propaganda battle. Though Macmillan could reasonably – after his wartime period as Minister Resident in North Africa, where his relationship with General Eisenhower had been crucial to the Allied war effort – have expected a more senior post, the vital importance of fulfilling this pledge so publicly and dramatically made was apparent to him. He called to his aid a Birmingham industrialist, Sir Percy Mills, who was known for his ability to get things done, and for his willingness to take a pair of scissors to red tape. By 1955 the target had been achieved.

It had been achieved, however, at very considerable cost, which Powell fully realized, though in the heat of the 1955 general election – on 13 May – he did not find it necessary to draw the attention of the readers of the *Evening News* to the cost, only to the achievement:

From the moment they took over in 1951 the Conservative government proceeded without fuss and violence but also, without avoidable delay, to denationalize house building and restore it to its place among our other industries which worked under the guidance of price and profit to fulfil the basic needs of the people.

This was a trifle disingenuous. The denationalization certainly lifted wartime and Labour government restrictions on private house building, and the building industry was given a tremendous fillip by the greatly expanded programme of council house construction. But, in the first place, the high priority accorded to housing meant the appropriation of excessive quantities of scarce, and often imported material and, in the second, it required imprudent allocations of public money. By October 1954, when the promise of 1950 had at any rate been kept, it was time to move the profligate Macmillan on, and put the ministry about on a different tack.

Moreover, 1955 saw the emergence of more general economic worries. The buoyancy of the late 1950s (artificial and temporary as we can now see) had not arrived; there was uncertainty about the future; and even beyond the ranks of those Conservatives who had little taste for taxation-funded welfare projects, there was a growing feeling that public expenditure was getting out of hand. Butler, in keeping with his past, wanted to preserve as much as possible. In his last speech to the House as Chancellor, on 26 October 1955, he rounded on the critics:

Do those who say that government expenditure could be drastically reduced propose a reversal of policy in education, or a cut in the cost of pensions? Or are we to hold up work on the roads? Perhaps I can answer by saying that in each of these spheres we have to do all we can to meet imperative needs – in the case of education, of a rising school population, in the case of the old, of an increased number of retired persons, and in the case of roads, with a programme which I cannot increase but which is already insufficient to deal with the needs of the country.

However, it is interesting that, in this catalogue (which Mr. Howard[3] calls 'unrepentant') there is no mention of housing, and it may fairly be said – as is so often the case with Butler's speeches – that the tone is stronger than the actual content. But of all the members of Eden's Cabinet it is probably true to say that Butler was the one most concerned with social policy as a particular and defined good; and that he was certainly more intellectually possessed of a conviction that the method of public expenditure would provide solutions to problems.

Macmillan's similar concern was much more loudly trumpeted, particularly after he became Prime Minister, and even more after he retired; but his concern – while certainly real – was generalized. None the less, Eden was convinced that Butler had to go.

It may seem strange that, in the light of Macmillan's conduct as Minister of Housing and Local Government, Eden should have wanted him at the Treasury at a time when restrictions and cheeseparing were clearly needed. There had been rumours that, after the 1951 election, Eden (who had the ear of Churchill in these matters, if rather less influence than he imagined) would have preferred Macmillan to Butler as Chancellor then. It seems more probable, however, that the new Prime Minister – who was distinctly unversed in the details of anything except foreign policy – regarded Macmillan's work at Housing as that of a splendid technician, who would do whatever was required and, moreover, present the resultant policy with more panache than Butler. Certainly, as Eden was to discover to his cost towards the end of the Suez war, Macmillan was particularly adroit at changing front and policy when necessary and, as Butler was twice to discover to *his* cost (in 1957 and 1963) he was especially gifted in the art of political intrigue. It is impossible to say now exactly what kind of economic policy Macmillan would have pursued had he enjoyed a long run at the Treasury: as it was he was there for little more than a year, and his tenure was dominated by the Suez affair.[4]

In any events this was the climate, economic and political, in which Powell first took office. It was an office he was to hold for little more than a year, after which, with the fall of Sir Anthony Eden, he was moved to the Treasury. None the less, he made his mark on the department. In doing this he was helped by two things. The first was that Sandys, who worked quite as hard and meticulously as he did himself, but who was intellectually much slower, was a member of the Cabinet and, both by virtue of his position there and of his personal interest, was much preoccupied by the events which followed the nationalization of the Suez Canal.

The second was the extraordinary, and sometimes – in those days of more decorous parliamentary behaviour than we expect today – it seemed demented opposition aroused in Labour breasts by what the government proposed to do. There were two charges on Sandys and Powell, assisted or obstructed as she judged fit by the Permanent Secretary to the department, Evelyn Sharp, whom Powell judged (as, later, did Richard Crossman) to be the most formidable civil servant he had ever met: to save money, and to repeal and revise Labour legislation in a way that was both economical and congruent with the deregulative instinct of Conservative philosophy. Piquancy was added to the situation by the fact that Bevan would be the main Labour spokesman on these matters, and challenge by the fact that many of his Labour seconds would be men who had come into the House of Commons through the jungle of local government, and could, therefore, be expected to be formidable opponents.

Because Sandys had been at the department for more than a year before he was himself appointed, Powell had been able to observe from the back benches what kind of task they would together have to face. A decision had been made in 1954 to cut back on subsidies for the construction of council houses. It had not been thought prudent to bring this proposal forward before the 1955 general election, but in October Sandys announced that the subsidies were to be progressively abolished and that, further, the government was to legislate to relax rent controls (which, essentially, restricted the charges that could be made by private property owners). On 27 October 1955 Sandys announced his subsidy proposals. There was a tremendous uproar on the Labour benches. A less determined Minister would have been silenced, but Sandys ploughed on, though he was often inaudible. On the face of it, Sandys and Powell were an odd combination and, indeed, over the next year the Minister seemed occasionally to fear that his Parliamentary Under Secretary was inclined to take logic rather too far, and to be over-zealous for combat. The oddity of the combination, however, lay not in any difference over policy, but in difference of background. Sandys was of the Tory purple. He was wealthy. He was the son of an MP. He had done duty in the Diplomatic Service (in the course of which he had acquired fluency in German, which was at least one point in common with his junior). He had fought in Norway in 1940, and was married to Winston Churchill's daughter. And he enjoyed the massive distinction of winning a protracted and bitter argument against Churchill's chief scientific adviser, F. A. Lindemann (later Lord Cherwell) on the question of whether or not the Germans were building long-range rockets at Peenemünde.

He was far less quick than Powell when he was on his feet in the House of Commons – a fact that he recognized by having Powell open the November 1956 debate on the Rent Bill while himself winding up. He and Powell had their differences, spoken and unspoken. Sandys was, in 1947, a founder member of the European Movement, and involved with many other of those European organizations which led to the creation of the European Economic Community, all entanglements which Powell regarded with suspicion. Sandys, though not central to the executive debates on the Suez operation, was wholehearted-ly behind Eden's attack while Powell was convinced of its folly. This, however, was not a subject they talked about. The business of their department was, and from time to time the enthusiasm of the Parliamentary Secretary for thorough-going solutions alarmed the Minister. None the less, it is right to record that when, over the year from the general election of 1979 I saw a good deal of Lord Duncan-Sandys (as he had become) I never heard him speak with anything but the greatest regard and affection (an affection sometimes tinged with wryness) of Powell.

Nothing is more daunting for a new Minister – particularly if he is a first-time Minister – than having to take up his appointment at a time when his department is sponsoring com-plex and much-disputed legislation. In Powell's case, moreover, the Housing Subsidies Bill foreshadowed by Sandys the previous October was being taken in a Committee of the Whole House, that is to say, in the Chamber itself and not in some gratifyingly obscure room upstairs, where a man might reasonably hope to learn the ropes.[5] He had, therefore, cause to bless the fact that he had worked so hard in the years before being given office for, on the substance of the matter in hand, he had little to learn.

But he had a difficulty, which Bevan and his Labour col-leagues were eager to exploit. The Bill was essentially about halving the existing housing subsidy as a prelude to its abolition. The government was, however, prepared to allow increased sub-sidies in certain areas (the most dramatic was in the provision of extra housing in mining areas, to encourage greater availability of miners) where the results of such provision could be expected to be desirable. This apparent (it was no more than that) contra-diction in the legislation left Powell open to Labour attacks that he had been at least partly converted to their own desire for state intervention in housing and to Tory criticism which asserted that the department was being cowardly (in the matter of increased selective provision) where it ought to be courageous. He gave a staunch account of himself, however, even though he was worried about the loose phrasing of the Bill where it concerned selective subsidy. By 1 February, though – the third day of the Committee – he had persuaded Sandys to tighten up the Bill in certain important respects, to the fury of his Labour opponents, one of whom, James McColl, launched a particularly bitter attack on him on 2 February. In a curious way, the Opposition were now satisfied that their fears about the doctrinaire instincts of the new Minister seemed at last to be justified.

The Report stage of the Bill was held on 14 February, the Third Reading the following day (this being the last consideration of the matter before the legislation was sent on to the House of Lords). Most of the steam had gone out of the business by now, though Powell was able to launch a poisoned dart at Bevan on the Third Reading by reminding him of a speech he had made to the Labour Conference in 1950 deploring the fact that private owners of poor housing had to subsidize the construction of superior homes for council tenants. This was then, and ever since has remained, a powerful weapon for Conservatives in their attacks on the Labour Party's devotion to publicly funded housing.

It would be tiresome to go through all the details of Powell's brief career at Housing and Local Government, with the exception of his parliamentary management of legislation, for their place is in administrative history, rather than in biography. So far, however, as his life and career were concerned there are a number of points to be picked out from what was a seminal year for him, and an eventful and tragic one for the nation.

So far as his personal life was concerned, the most important event was the birth, on 17 October, of his second daughter, Jennifer Helen, one of whose godmothers was Barbara Brooke,[6] wife of his old friend Henry Brooke, who had introduced him to the Housing Committee of the London County Council, and who was to succeed Sandys at the Department three months later. The birth of a second child made a house move necessary, and the Powells eventually settled down in what has remained their home ever since, in South Eaton Place. While it was not expensive to purchase it was not in good repair, so Powell the carpenter and handyman was reborn and shelves, cupboards and other amenities – including a completely new floor – made their appearance. Although the days when he engaged on this kind of reconstruction are long gone, there is still, at the end of the basement room where fireproof safes contain many of his files, a board on which is hung, immaculately clean and cared for, a bewildering array of tools. 'For a time, though,' he recalled, 'books were piled higgeldy-piggeldy on the floors. And when the books went up on the shelves they stayed there. The forces of inertia are great, and thirty years has not been enough time to get them into order.' It is rather comforting to find at least one task which has not been handled with his customary awesome efficiency.

Powell had the pleasure of seeing the Clean Air Bill, which he had helped Gerald Nabarro to draft, through its final Commons stages, and this was perhaps the only unalloyed political pleasure he enjoyed that year. It had started as a Private Member's Bill but, as is often the way with these things, had, since it enjoyed general approval, been taken over by the government. There was nothing contentious about the Third Reading, since virtually everybody, on both sides of the House, was pleased with it and plaudits were poured over Powell, not only from Nabarro, but from the Labour side, and from Sandys himself. The Minister pointed out what is not readily grasped when a measure is uncontroversial – that to be good it must incorporate reference to virtually every other piece of statute law remotely concerned with its subject. It had not been necessary for Powell to rely (as most Ministers do) on the parliamentary draftsmen to provide these references since he had, in Sandy's words, 'a profound grasp' of all the measures himself. He enjoyed a similarly popular reception (though it, naturally, did not give as much personal pleasure) in steering the Slum Clearance (Compensation) Bill through the House. This measure – which provided extra compensation for local authorities compelled to buy unfit houses – commanded, again, widespread assent.

But in two respects, or, at least, in two areas, it was the grimmer side of his pre-ministerial reputation that was confirmed. It was his duty as a Minister to receive many local authority deputations. These would have a variety of requests and complaints but would in large numbers be requiring ministerial assent to compulsory purchase orders for property which they intended to put to uses of their own. It seemed that Powell took delight in refusing as many requests, whatever they were for, as he could, and some at least who were turned away from his door later successfully took their cases to Sandys. His brusqueness, indeed, appalled even some of his civil servants, normally in such matters highly protective of a Minister, and his reputation for a hard fierceness of attitude, and for utter inflexibility once his mind was made up, soon exceeded any he had enjoyed at the Research Department.

At the same time his parliamentary reputation, except when he was engaged in battle, regressed. As a backbencher he had always been listened to with impressed attention, if not always with comprehension. As a Minister he seemed to go out of his way to demonstrate his knowledge on the most recondite of subjects, and often at excessive length. His brilliance was far less in evidence than his erudition, and he was sometimes adjudged plain boring.

All this, however, was to change with the Rent Bill, prefigured by Sandys at the Llandudno Party Conference in October 1956 and in Parliament in an adjournment debate by Powell on 6 November, the momentous day on which Eden told the House of the cessation of Anglo-French military action at Suez. The scheduled debate on the Queen's Speech was postponed, and Powell was left with an audience of a handful to discuss rent, while the rest of the House dispersed for excited and excitable conversation on Eden's humiliation.[7]

The Rent Bill was one of those few measures (though they have been far more frequent since the election of Mrs. Margaret Thatcher in 1979) where there is an absolute divide of principle and ideology between government and Opposition. The Labour Party believed absolutely in statutory control of rent. The Tories did not, and argued that rent controls were driving the private landlord out of business.[8] Labour retorted that decontrol of rents encouraged racketeering landlords who let inadequate accommodation for exorbitant sums and so exploited the needy. Still the Tories did not hold as fast to their position as Labour did to theirs, until Powell.

The Conservative policy document of 1949, *The Right Road for Britain*, did concede the retention of rent controls until the virtual elimination of housing need which, of course, the Macmillan building programme was designed to ensure. But Powell wanted nothing of compromise: he had always been in favour of the total elimination of rent controls, and fell eagerly on a Bill favouring just this measure which was available in the Department in outline when he arrived there.

Two days – 21 and 22 November – were allotted for the Second Reading of the Bill. Again, greater events threw their shadow across what was an increasingly acrimonious exchange of views for on the 21st it was announced that the Prime Minister's health had given way, and that he was repairing to the West Indies for a three week rest. Further, it was also announced that the United Nations, which had taken over the policing of the ceasefire on the Canal, would not allow British and French troops to remain, even under the international organization's own flag, a suggestion made by France and Britain as a means of saving at least a little face. These outside happenings meant a thin House for the Second Reading, and it meant also that many Members were distracted.

It was not to fall to Powell to put the Rent Bill through to the Statute Book (that was to be the task of Henry Brooke) but he made the doctrinal position, and his own beliefs, crystal clear in his opening speech. He believed that demand for and supply of homes was now, or shortly would be, in balance (which was a dubious proposition, to say the least), and that therefore the Conservative undertaking of 1949 had been fulfilled. In consequence, the government could safely and honourably proceed to the deregulation of rents. Labour Member after Labour Member went on the attack, and some Conservatives joined in, the principal argument of all the critics being that, allowed a free hand, landlords would exploit tenants and prospective tenants. Powell's belief that, as long as rents were held low landlords would either sell at the market price once a property was vacant or, alternatively, keep it vacant until the market price was satisfactory, thus reducing the housing stock, was derided. There was, though, he said:

> . . . an injustice arising from the fact that there is no relation between the size of the property and its rent. There is the injustice arising from landlords being called upon in many cases, by rent restriction, to subsidize the incomes of tenants who are better off than they are. There is, therefore, a general recognition of the evils which rent control, as we have it, is producing and increasingly producing. There is general recognition that the time is now ripe for that to be dealt with.

It was all to no avail. The Labour Party concentrated not on the injustices Powell saw, but on the injustices they saw – the fact that the improvement in housing conditions brought about by Macmillan was not evenly spread all over the country and the sufferings that the government's provisions would ensure for those sections of the population unable to protect themselves. There was, in fact, a certain amount of merit on both sides and, indeed, the deregulation provisions eventually enacted had nothing like the effect that Powell had hoped for. But, in any event, it was his swansong in the Department of Housing and Local Government.

This is not the place to examine the history of the Suez war.[9] However, there are some points about its origins, character and outcome which are highly relevant to the evolution of British political history, to the future of the Conservative Party and, ultimately, to the career of Enoch Powell.

Even before war broke out the burgeoning crisis which gave it birth was seen in Britain, by Eden and those about him most clearly, but by the wider public as well, as a test for Britain in the Middle East, and as a question of whether or not she could maintain her supposedly powerful position there. This was clear from the first (tangential) act in the drama, the dismissal of Sir John Glubb (Glubb Pasha) from his post as Chief of the Jordanian General Staff and Commander of the Arab Legion. Glubb had held both posts for thirty years. He was (and remained) devoted to Jordan and to the Hashemite family of King Hussein. To sections of the Arab world, however, and particularly to Colonel Gamal Abdel Nasser of Egypt, he represented a detested colonial presence. Under Egyptian pressure the King dismissed him without warning. Eden immediately saw the challenge and from that moment was bent on revenge on Nasser.

In July the United States, irritated by Nasser's flirtations with the Soviet Union, withdrew promised finance for the Aswan high dam, which was vital to Egyptian plans vastly to extend the irrigated areas of the country. In instant response Nasser nationalized the Suez Canal Company, an Anglo-French consortium which administered the Canal, collected dues from passing ships, and paid the shareholders. Western – and particularly British and French – opinion was in uproar. It was argued that the Egyptians could not run the Canal (which was not true) and that Nasser had posed a threat to the international freedom of the sea (which was only partly true and, in any event, concerned only Israel). Even the Labour Party was outraged; Hugh Gaitskell, its leader, and Aneurin Bevan (who was to become the foremost campaigner against Eden) made noises sympathetic to the Prime Minister. Had it been possible for British (or British and French) forces to strike instantly and surgically, a great triumph, applauded throughout the democracies at least, could have been achieved.

But, as Powell had foreseen, the Canal Base having been surrendered, it was not possible to strike instantly. Assembling the requisite force was going to take weeks, and even months. This delay was fatal to the political prospects of any military initiative. The United States was in a presidential election year, and President Eisenhower and his Secretary of State, John Foster Dulles (who had been the instigator of finance for Aswan, and the instigator of its withdrawal, and who behaved in a thoroughly devious and disreputable manner throughout) wanted no trouble anywhere in the world where the United States had an interest. Innumerable diplomatic solutions were canvassed, the most notable of them involving mediation by the Australian Prime Minister, Sir Robert Menzies.

These prevarications had three vital consequences in British politics. They revealed Eden as an irresolute leader who, by failing to give a clear lead to the Armed Forces impeded their preparations and bruised their morale. They allowed time for the nascent pro-Egyptian elements in the Labour Party to make their weight felt, and eventually ensured that the Opposition was totally united against military action. And, finally, they ensured a split in the Conservative Party. From delay came the doom of Eden.

It is certain that the great majority of Conservatives (and the better part of the electorate) favoured action if action could be effective. The most vociferous element favouring action was the now greatly enlarged Suez Group, who rubbed their eyes and suddenly discovered in Eden, the traitor of 1954 who had given away the base, the hero of the hour. There was a much smaller, though not insignificant, number, however, who abhorred the idea of an attack on Egypt, and two Ministers – Boyle and Eden's quondam favourite Anthony Nutting – resigned.[10]

During the period of delay the French came up with a wheeze. Israel was in a state of static war with Egypt and felt herself in constant danger. She was, therefore, a natural ally for Britain and France, and was certainly capable of overcoming the Egyptian defence forces in a swift attack. However, David Ben Gurion, the Israeli Prime Minister, would not act alone (and, in fact, was reluctant to act at all). At a series of secret meetings in France, Britain was represented by the Foreign Secretary, Selwyn Lloyd. Of Lloyd, who had deep reservations about how things were going, General Moshe Dayan observed, 'Britain's foreign minister may well have been a friendly man, pleasant, charming, amiable. If so, he showed near-genius in concealing these virtues. His whole demeanour expressed distaste – for the place,[11] the company, the topic.'[12]

A plan was worked out whereby Israel would strike at Egypt. Britain and France would call on the two powers to separate and would then attack Egypt. On 31 October 1956 Israeli tanks rolled into the Sinai. That night the British and French Air Forces bombed Egyptian airfields. Five days later Anglo-French paratroopers landed at Port Said and the Egyptian garrison surrendered. A slow advance on Suez began.

Very few people doubted that the British and French governments were acting in collusion with Israel, though Eden and Lloyd lied again and again to the House on the subject. These perceived lies were immensely damaging to Eden's moral authority. For long into the future, however, these two – and Harold Macmillan – continued the fiction of no collusion, even after French and Israeli memoirs established the facts beyond doubt. Of course, many in the Conservative Party in particular would have applauded an open alliance with Israel. But such a stroke of *Realpolitik* was impossible because of Eden's hypocritical determination to pose as the chief of a political fire brigade, dousing the flames of war.

In any event the government of the United States – which, quite reasonably, given their earlier attitude, had been denied all knowledge of British and French plans – acted decisively by withdrawing all oil supplies from Britain and denouncing the expedition in no uncertain terms. Sterling was then a reserve currency, that is, one in which other countries were content to hold their wealth, the British government giving assurances as to the stability of its value. There began a run on the pound of horrendous proportions as country after country hurried to get out of sterling. Harold Macmillan, as Chancellor the custodian of the nation's finances, panicked and, on 6 November told the Cabinet that $270 million of Britain's reserves had gone. Having been at the outset the most bellicose of Eden's colleagues he now executed a smart about turn, provoking the bitter comment that he was both first in and first out.

The ceasefire came into effect and Eden shortly afterwards departed to rest at the house of the novelist Ian Fleming in Jamaica. The way in which events had unfolded and were about to unfold had a decisive effect on the political future of the Conservative Party and the nation. About the more general effect – on national morale, national sense of identity and Britain's standing in the world – it is hard to be precise, though it is safe to assert that the effect was very bad, and perhaps catastrophic. About the effect on the Party, and the government, however, it is possible to make unchallengeable statements.

Butler loved, and indeed, cultivated, ambiguity. Nothing pleased him better than to express an opinion in the form of a quip which left an interlocutor bewildered, or at least uncertain, as to his real meaning. He had had the gravest reservations about the handling of the Suez imbroglio from the outset and, though he stoutly defended the government in public outside the House of Commons, he seemed far less committed within. Reginald Maudling later wrote[13] that he gave 'the impression that he was lifting his skirt to avoid the dirt'. He could thus hope neither for support from the right (which had always mistrusted him) nor even from the centre of the Party, stung as they were by the humiliation just endured. He was now, further, placed in a position in which, however effectively he performed, he could not enhance his reputation with the Party, for Eden asked him to look after the government in his absence. This had happened before when Churchill had made a similar request, both himself and Eden being ill, and Butler had performed admirably. Memory of this occasion reassured Eden and, besides, he thought Macmillan would be fully occupied looking after sterling.

On 22 November Butler, accompanied by Macmillan, attended a meeting of the 1922 Committee. Strictly speaking Butler had no need to ask Macmillan to join him, but he seemed to think that the two of them together would have the required effect on the assembled MPs. In the event it was one of the worst decisions he could have made so far as his personal ambitions were concerned (neither he nor Macmillan thought Eden would last long as Prime Minister). He spoke in a manner which, he thought, suited the hour, sombre and serious and brief. Macmillan, on the other hand, spoke for thirty-five minutes, making what amounted to a stirring rallying call. It went down beautifully, and erased all memory of just how quickly he had come to urge a scuttle on Eden. Powell later said:

> One of the most horrible things that I remember in politics was seeing the two of them at that 1922 Committee Meeting – seeing the way in which Harold Macmillan, with all the skill of the old actor-manager, succeeded in false-footing RAB. The sheer devilry of it was disgusting.[14]

In the days that followed Macmillan – while denying he was doing any such thing – began quietly seeing putative supporters. Butler continued with the discharge of government business. Almost everything under his hand had to do with repairing the damage done by the Suez operation, and almost everything he had to do, naturally, further rubbed the consciousness of humiliation into the mind of the nation and that of the Party, to the extent that he became identified with the humiliation. It was a disastrous position to be in.

On 14 December Eden returned from Jamaica. On 7 January 1957 it was announced that for health reasons[15] he would be compelled to resign. On 9 January he did so. On the same day Lord Salisbury and Lord Kilmuir canvassed the Cabinet on their choice of successor; a great majority favoured Macmillan. Edward Heath, the Conservative Chief Whip, was supposed to have undertaken a similar canvass among Members of the House of Commons, though a number of Members – including Powell, who made no secret of his preference for Butler for the succession – have always maintained that they were never polled. On 10 January Salisbury and Kilmuir reported to the Palace, as did Sir Winston Churchill (the Monarch having chosen to exercise her right to consult elder statesmen about her decision). Eden was asked what his opinion was, though it is impossible to be sure whom he recommended: Churchill was certainly for Macmillan. That same day Harold Macmillan was summoned to the Palace and kissed hands on his appointment as Prime Minister.

The choice thus made was to have profound consequences for the nation, as well as for the subject of this biography. Had Butler become Prime Minister he would certainly have promoted Iain Macleod, who was his protégé,[16] and Powell might well have been given ministerial office. Had Butler been Prime Minister, moreover, it is extremely unlikely that the economic policy favoured by Macmillan would have been followed to the extent that it was in 1958: the whole pattern of Powell's career might well have – indeed, almost certainly would have – evolved in a different way. As it was, on 14 January, Powell accepted the post of Financial Secretary to the Treasury (essentially, the Treasury Minister with responsibility for negotiating overall departmental budgets each year) under the new Chancellor Peter Thorneycroft, and with Nigel Birch beside him as Economic Secretary.

'It would be difficult to find in government,' Powell once said, 'three more diverse individuals in personality, temperament and background.' Thorneycroft was an easy-going, friendly man from a wealthy industrial background who had been a soldier and a barrister. First elected to the House in 1938, he had been on the left wing of the Party and had played a part in the creation of the Tory Reform Group,[17] which agitated for social reform. He lost in 1945, but was returned shortly thereafter for Monmouth in a by-election. He was (and is)[18] one of those individuals who, while capable of immensely hard work, manage to convey that they always have time on their hands.

Nigel Birch,[19] who ranked immediately below Powell in the Treasury hierarchy, likewise enjoyed a rich family background. It was also military, his father having been a general. On leaving school Birch went into the City and, still a very young man, parlayed the small fortune he had been left into a very large one, subsequently also marrying money in the person of a banking heiress. He thus had no difficulty in accepting his demotion from the Secretaryship of State for Air, which involved a £3,000 drop in annual salary. Like Powell, he had always wanted a Treasury job, for he believed from his City days in strong currencies and restrained public expenditure. Birch was an acquired taste (and Powell acquired the taste) for he made it clear that his ambition was limited and that he was not totally devoted to a political career; his money gave him total independence, and his humour was acerbic. 'Nigel,' said an admiring colleague, 'had a damn your eyes attitude to everybody, the more senior the better.' He was later to deliver one of the most devastating rebukes a backbencher has ever delivered to his Party leader,[20] and in his later years as failing eyesight declined into total blindness, he bore every misfortune with great cheer.

Butler, meanwhile, continued as Leader of the House and – in spite of heartfelt pleading with Macmillan for the Foreign Office – was appointed Home Secretary.[21] He was thus to some extent shunted to the sidelines of government policy-making and Macmillan had thus taken the first of many steps designed to ensure that he would never become Prime Minister.[22]

From the very outset Macmillan had two things in mind, the restoration of the economy and victory at the next general election. The one, of course, depended upon the other. Neither objective was possible without the reunification of the Conservative Party, and in performing that task Macmillan, in 1957 at the height of his powers, proved himself to be a master. As one example of the balancing act which he set himself to perform he brought Edward Boyle back into government; but he also appointed his own son-in-law, Julian Amery, one of the stoutest supporters of the Suez attack, into office. Slowly, he built up a House of Commons reputation which was to acquire legendary proportions, and he re-established relations with the United States (he had, after all, been close to Eisenhower in the North African campaign) to a point of almost embarrassing intimacy. Having firmly decided that the age of Empire was over he none the less behaved as though it were not, while setting about disembarrassing Britain of her African colonies

152

and turning policy in the direction of the European Economic Community. As Thorneycroft, Powell and Birch were all soon to learn, he was master of doing one thing while seeming to do another; and when he met a difficulty he smiled at it and thereafter ignored it.

However, in spite of all this, and of a multitude of other problems, it was perfectly clear that the government would stand or fall by its handling of the economy and the Treasury was thus, as so often, the central department of state. Initially, Thorneycroft and his junior Ministers had little chance to make their own mark on affairs for, when they took office, general preparations for the 1957 Budget were well in train. When presented on 9 April it therefore bore more the marks of Macmillan's thinking than of anybody else's. Its essence lay in the cutting of taxes, cuts shared between British companies operating overseas, payers of income tax and purchase tax. After the ritual attack on the Chancellor by the Shadow Chancellor, Harold Wilson, Powell (speaking on the third day of the Budget debate) concentrated on two essential points. The first was that the Budget was essentially a liberalizing one, what the Prime Minister had called an opportunity Budget. Wilson had derided it – and was to deride it more and more frequently in the future – for the way it awarded benefits to the better off rather than (though there were some benefits here as well) to the poor and the old. This is part of an age-old Tory-Labour battle, the Tory position being based on the belief that concessions in the higher tax brackets creates more national wealth, and thus makes conditions better for all. Powell's second point was an attack on Labour's liking for a controlled economy, which was anathema to him even more than to his Treasury colleagues, and certainly more than to his Prime Minister. 'We had controls,' he said, 'operated by the Party opposite. A whole armoury of controls – thank heaven more controls than there are today . . . and they were associated with reserves slumping, first, to a convertibility crisis, then to a devaluation crisis and, finally, to a run-away-from-government crisis.'

He proclaimed himself happy with the central thrust of the Budget:

This is not an inflationary Budget. It is a balanced and a prudent Budget which continues the work of the last five years in lightening the real burden of taxation upon this country. Every year, from 1951 onwards the government have taken a progressively smaller proportion of the national income by way of taxation.

From April until 19 July – when the Third Reading of the Finance Bill implementing the Budget proposals was passed by the House of Commons – Powell took on his shoulders the principal burden of seeing the legislation through the jungle of opposition and qualification. As was to be expected, he mastered subjects foreign to him – like tax on cinemas – and was on top in every technical exchange. What he managed to do throughout, whether attracting praise or criticism, was conceal from the House his own reservations about the conduct of economic policy.

He was more popular with Treasury civil servants than he had been with their equivalents at the Department of Housing and Local Government (though he thought the higher ranks not superior to those in his former department). This was partly because, while he came to Housing as a fully-fledged expert, he came to the greatest of the departments of state with a good deal of, but not total, knowledge. He knew he had much to learn, and he spent his early weeks learning, while he was also tackling a major piece of legislation in the House. None the less, as he looked into the future he began to feel – as did Nigel Birch, though not initially Thorneycroft – that all on the horizon was not sunny.

Throughout the year the overall political situation, starting as finely balanced, veered towards possible disaster. There were a number of problems incidental to the central one of managing the economy. Lord Salisbury resigned from the Cabinet because the government decided to release Archbishop Makarios of Cyprus from detention, though this long expected event provoked far less fuss than the Marquis had anticipated. Macmillan having decided to retain for Britain a nuclear capacity, he had to negotiate with the United States for its purchase, which decision and which negotiations involved Powell and his Treasury colleagues in tough budgetary dealing with his old chief Duncan Sandys, by now Minister of Defence. Above all the Rent Act – which came into force in June, but the character of which was known long before – was proving decidedly unpopular: the Conservatives went down badly in the local elections in May, and lost a string of by-elections. The necessary by-election at Warwick and Leamington, Eden's old seat, saw a swing against the Conservatives of twelve per cent; North Lewisham fell to Labour; and in Hornsey a Tory majority of 13,000 fell to 3,000. Further, industrial relations (now

154

under the purview of Iain Macleod as Minister of Labour) were in a seemingly endless state of turmoil. Strikes occurred or were threatened in a variety of industries, the most serious, and the longest since the general strike a generation previously, being in the shipbuilding industry. This was eventually ended in part by a generous settlement, and in part by the promise of a Court of Enquiry into industrial relations, which itself issued in a Council for Prices, Productivity and Incomes, the first gaunt shadow of the complicated incomes policies of succeeding years up to 1979.

The circumstances were, thus, not such as would encourage any government to add to national tribulation by deflating the economy, which would involve a necessary sharp increase in unemployment. In July Macmillan made two very important speeches, one of which was to dog him to the end of his days, but both of which, taken together, offer a guide to his conduct of the crisis which was to arise at the end of the year. First at Bedford, he said:

> Let's be frank about it, most of our people have never had it so good. Go around the country, go to the industrial towns, go to the farms, and you will see a state of prosperity such as we have never had in my lifetime – nor indeed ever in the history of this country.

It is true that he qualified this passage later on, and that he added, 'Our constant concern today is, can prices be steadied while at the same time we maintain full employment in an expanding economy? Can we control inflation? That is the problem of our time.' All this was perfectly true, and expressed as a series of generalities, there was no fault to find with Macmillan's argument. Its tone, however, was insouciant, and the tone was to come back to haunt him when times got worse. Making reference to the Bedford speech he told the House of Commons on 24 July, after repeating his theme of current prosperity:

> Nevertheless, I say this: if the mass of our people ever believed that there was an intention to bring about large scale unemployment they would set their faces – and I think rightly so – against every reasonable and proper measure this or any other government might propose.

This passage is less clear than it seems at first glance. No government sets out to *achieve* unemployment. The test of British governments since the war has to be defined in a different way. The question may be put like this: if certain measures are judged necessary for, say, the stability of the currency or the future of the economy, and if such measures cause unemployment, how much unemployment is tolerable? That question – it might be better to call it a conundrum – had to be faced by every government between 1945 and 1979, when a government was elected which was prepared to take the risk of removing unemployment from the argument.

The stage was now set for a confrontation between the Prime Minister and the Treasury. When he sent Thorneycroft to the Treasury Macmillan accepted that the tightest possible rein had to be kept on public expenditure, and it was for that reason that Powell was appointed as the Chancellor's second in command. However, the Prime Minister's essential instinct always was – in the cant phrase – to go for growth, and he had an almost mystical belief in the virtue of cutting taxes. In general it may be said that Thorneycroft was, on his appointment, in sympathy with that point of view, that Birch was happy as long as the currency was stable, and that Powell was learning his job and found his brief acceptable, if not ideal. But it should never be forgotten that for the 1957 Budget there were two Chancellors, Macmillan and Thorneycroft.

There was a curtain-raiser to the main act of confrontation. Throughout the summer the Bank of England had to spend constantly to sustain the (then fixed) exchange rate of the pound. Indeed, the last act of the Suez affair occurred when the United States insisted on a speeded-up withdrawal from the Canal as a *quid pro quo* for helping to sustain sterling. By 2 August (when the House rose for the summer recess) it emerged that gold and dollar reserves had fallen by $14 million in July. Defending sterling in August was to cost $400 million, and Powell was alone in advocating the adoption of a floating currency.

The situation was in serious danger of getting out of hand. Short of an emergency Budget, which would have required the recall of Parliament, there was one step the government could take. This was sharply to increase Bank Rate (the equivalent of an increase in interest rates today) in order to stem the outward flow of funds. The Governor of the Bank of England, Cameron Cobbold, advocated a two per cent rise, to seven per cent. After protracted discussion this rise was agreed on 19 September. On 23 September Powell – standing in for Thorneycroft, who was in

Washington – received a letter from Harold Wilson, reporting rumours that businessmen who had enjoyed advance notice of the Bank Rate increase had made killings and demanding an inquiry. After prolonged wrangling this request was granted eight weeks later but, diverting though Wilson's escapade was, no malfeasance ever appeared.

The view from inside the Treasury looked increasingly gloomy. Thorneycroft was now as anxious about the state of economic affairs as his junior colleagues had been for some time; the discussion he had had over the Bank Rate had both frightened and fortified him. Macmillan – who later confessed regret at his agreement to raise Bank Rate[23] – was becoming increasingly worried by the Chancellor's evidently deflationary intentions. On 5 October Birch told his constituency of hard times to come. On 8 October Thorneycroft preached the same message at the Mansion House. On the afternoon of 10 October, at the Tory Party Conference at Brighton, Powell – to whom it was a considerable compliment to be chosen as supporting speaker to the Chancellor – hammered home the message, a message he repeated a little later at Newbury. He made the most of Conservative stewardship of the economy and particularly of steadily declining levels of taxation. But the essence of what he had to say sounded less than musical to electoral ears: reduction in government expenditure was essential, and there could be no reduction on the scale required without a real reduction in services. The other Treasury Ministers had said the same thing, but Powell said it more clearly than either, and then returned to London to fight the annual battle with the spending ministries. The Conservatives had fallen ten per cent behind Labour in the opinion polls.

Treasury Ministers are rarely popular with their colleagues, and unpopularity reaches a high pitch when departmental budgets are being negotiated. As those negotiations proceeded, and as the Cabinet met again and again to discuss the demands for retrenchment of an increasingly implacable Chancellor, rumours about the Treasury's intentions spread. Duncan Sandys was particularly incensed. Since he was intent on building a nuclear armoury he thought he should be more leniently treated than his fellows: this hope on his part was greeted with a certain amount of amusement in the Treasury, since Thorneycroft, Birch and Powell were all, for different reasons, intensely sceptical about the necessity or even desirability of Britain obtaining her own nuclear weapon.

In the economic debate in the House on 29 and 30 October Thorneycroft made it clear, albeit in general terms, that when he said retrenchment he meant retrenchment: he intended to hold the current percentage of national income spent by government (about one third) at its present rate in real terms – and that meant serious cuts in all programmes. At this time the three Treasury Ministers were coming even closer together personally, locked in battle as they were, not only with their political colleagues, but with their own civil servants, who were highly dubious about the monetary policy being advocated. Still, they were not in despair: Thorneycroft's obduracy was winning inch after inch of ground in Cabinet and by the Christmas recess a gap of only £250 million separated him from his colleagues. After Christmas rumours began to circulate that Thorneycroft was entirely in thrall to his two juniors and, in Iain Macleod's view, particularly Powell. There was no foundation to these rumours. Certainly, in the time they had served together Thorneycroft had moved towards Birch and Powell, but that was as much because of how he read the facts that crossed his desk as because of their arguments. The fact of the matter was that the trio were by now bound together by hoops of steel.

After Christmas the drama generally heightened, and the pace quickened. The situation was unusual in that the Prime Minister planned to leave for a six week tour of the Commonwealth on 7 January, so the Estimates process had to take less time than in an average year. By 3 January the notional sum dividing the Treasury from the others was £50 million (though, as I shall shortly show, the matter was not quite as simple as that). The choice of area for this remaining cut lay, in Thorneycroft's view, between defence and the social services. Sandys would not accept cuts in his department and the rest of the Cabinet, led by Macleod, felt it too dangerous to cut social services. Thorneycroft made it clear to his Cabinet colleagues that if he did not get his way he would resign, but he was very careful not to include Birch and Powell in his threat for he had, indeed, insisted to the two men that they need not sacrifice themselves for him.

An emergency Cabinet meeting – which only some Members could attend – was held on Sunday 5 January in the evening. Absent Ministers were telephoned for their views. By ten-thirty it was clear that Thorneycroft had lost. At ten-thirty the following morning Macmillan duly received three letters. By eleven Macmillan had appointed Derick Heathcoat Amory, the Minister of Agriculture, as Chancellor. On Tuesday morning,

Macmillan flew off on his tour, telling stunned journalists who besieged him at the airport that it was all 'a little local difficulty'. His insouciance amazed the Press and, for that matter, the public, and it was, indeed, a fine stroke, and a tribute to the Prime Minister that he kept his nerve in an unprecedented situation. His departure further took attention away from the three. More: since the £50 million at issue did seem to be a trivial amount and since, with the partial exception of Birch none of the ex-Ministers wished to create serious trouble for the government, the storm of public interest did not last long. Indeed, its dissipation was assisted when Powell told his constituents on 9 January:

> But one thing I am determined on is that I will say and do nothing in any way which will weaken or embarrass the government. I am determined I will not enter, or allow myself to be drawn, into discussions which might involve matters of Cabinet secrecy being divulged or dragged into public.

This was as plain a declaration as there could be that a resignation on principle was not to be merely the first event in a long sniping match against the government. The question, however, was whether the principle at issue could bear the weight of the sacrifice made for it. Powell's speech on 9 January, being the first made by one of the three, was, naturally, ransacked for clues as to their real purposes. Powell was sensitive to the charge that the resignations were over a 'trivial' sum for 'I do not personally regard £50 million or one per cent of national expenditure as a triviality.'

In explaining the resignations in terms that might be understood clearly by the public and the Press, Powell (and the same applied to Birch and Thorneycroft) faced the major difficulty of their self-denying ordinance against attacks on the Macmillan Cabinet. For, in truth, one of the major reasons for their making £50 million a sticking point was their lack of trust in Macmillan himself, and their conviction that, unrestrained, he would lead the nation down a highly inflationary path. As Thorneycroft said many years later, when inflation was rampant, and public expenditure out of control, 'If only I had won on the £50 million. What would have been relatively easy then, and what would have established a principle of control, requires massive courage now.'[24]

'The issue,' Powell continued in the speech to his constituents on 9 January,

> was whether Mr Thorneycroft felt he had the necessary mini-
> mum support from his colleagues for the policy to which he
> and they were committed. He was forced to the conclusion
> that he had not that support. Neither Mr. Birch nor I could
> avoid coming to the same conclusion.

'We each,' he went on, referring to the three of them,

> looked from a different angle at the economic problems
> of the country and the issues involved in the amount and
> character of the Estimates. In this last six or eight weeks
> no one of us has influenced the other two. We have each
> come to our conclusion, the same conclusion, independently
> and spontaneously.

Powell has never wavered in his conviction – indeed, it has strengthened over the years – that 1958 was 'the great turning point that marked the beginning of the true Macmillan Era' which is to him, in essence, an era of inflation. As it happened, the inflationary signs were far from immediately apparent. It took more than a year before the warnings of Peter Thorneycroft and his departmental colleagues began to show their truth. By then the country was moving towards a general election. That election signalled a great triumph for Macmillan – for he came back with a majority of 100 – after which inflation, panic, dissolution and scandal began to eat at the vitals of the government he led.

Only the most blind of Powell's admirers could have accepted the speech of 9 January as an entirely convincing one, not because it was in any way illogical, but because it was incomplete. In any event, so far as politics were concerned he seemed content to take a breather. He had a number of domestic problems on his hands. In June of 1957 he had received an increase in his ministerial salary. Upon resignation his parliamentary income fell back immediately from £3,250 a year to £1,750. Yet the Powells had just bought their new London house, and they still had the residence in Wolverhampton to keep up. Times were, again, straitened, and it was therefore all the more creditable that, when serious money could have been made from assailing a government he was convinced was doing wrong in the (economic) field he felt he knew best, he took out the material for the history of the House of Lords and 'I began to revise and expand again from the start . . .'

There was, of course, some journalism, and some broadcasting, though it was not, being unsensational, of the more lucrative kind. The BBC World Service welcomed back their Urdu speaker, and he spoke for them also in Italian. Between his resignation and his return to office in July 1960, indeed, it sometimes seemed that Powell – with two exceptions which I will shortly discuss – had resumed his career as scholar and teacher. He broadcast for the BBC on the history of Parliament among other matters and, in the early months of 1958, persuaded the Wolverhampton *Express and Star* to accept from him a series of articles which, so the paper's introduction editorially and proudly announced, 'will be entirely without party political content, and will deal with such subjects as the Estimates, the balance of trade, gold reserves, and other matters affecting the economics of our daily lives.' The articles did, indeed, constitute a scintillating series, which would bear reprinting even today, for the clarity and even the homeliness with which they describe the whole business of preparing a national Budget, and the role of the Treasury in administering it. The articles were embellished by metaphors which came – as has increasingly become his habit – from subjects that interest him, but metaphors which are always used to the point. Thus – to take but one example – in discussing the three ways in which the House of Commons can control the Treasury (approval of estimates; permission to pay out from the Consolidated Fund; and legislation specifying in what way the Fund can be raised) he starts with a piece of religious history:[25]

> Many churches contain an old chest with three locks. The keys to those three locks were held by the parson and the two churchwardens, and they were all different. Only, therefore, by the co-operation of all three could anything be extracted from the parish chest.

It is a characteristic of Powell's political career that, whether by accident or design (and I am very strongly of the opinion that it is not by design but by some strange combination of accident and intuition), he never does what is expected of him. A politician of his ambition and character, who had resigned in the circumstances in which he had resigned, might have been expected to redouble his parliamentary efforts, and to concentrate his efforts in the area in which he had served. He was, indeed, to speak critically of the

Budget of April 1958 but, as Mr. Roth observes,[26] between then and the end of the parliamentary session he made no contribution to the business of Parliament as conducted in the Chamber.

Of course – and this has always been one of Powell's greatest sources of strength – he had other things than politics to attend to. The basic and ordered pattern of his life – reading and writing at home, reading and writing in the Library of the House of Commons, sitting in the Chamber, attending to the constituency – was resumed after resignation and, to adapt a phrase of Churchill's, he had his 'happy family around him' whether in South Eaton Place or Wolverhampton South-West. He had, further, one priceless advantage which he derived from his resignation: even if he was thought puritanical or pedantic he now had a national, and not just a parliamentary, reputation for integrity. Whatever he did he was believed to be his own man.

This reputation was enhanced by two striking parliamentary interventions, one of which was considered to be mildly eccentric (though it was unquestionably deeply felt) and the other of which was electrifying.

The first occasion was on 12 February 1958 when the government introduced a Bill to provide for the creation of life peerages. The proposition was not new, having first been canvassed in the nineteenth century. It was argued, further (by the Attorney General, Sir Reginald Manningham-Buller) that such a provision would enable the Prime Minister of the day to be flexible in his appointments, and obtain the services of able men who did not want to endure the hurly-burly of electioneering without, however, ennobling their heirs. Since the mood of the times was beginning to turn against the creation of new hereditary peerages (though Macmillan never showed any marked inhibitions in this regard), the measure was expected to be uncontroversial, and probably opposed only by the most antediluvian traditionalists and those left wingers who wanted to abolish the Upper House anyway. Powell's attack on its provisions was completely unexpected. As always, he brought to a debate on constitutional matters a passion rarely found in the deliberations of those who like to discuss such matters. His thesis was not merely that the Lords worked very well as it was (though he did make that point) but that tampering with a traditional institution of state was to endanger the fabric of the nation itself. He likened the Upper House to the Monarchy, and argued, as he was to argue on countless occasions in future years, that the unique character of the evolution of British history set this nation apart from all

162

others, and thus rendered mechanical thinking of the kind envisaged all the more dangerous:

> Neither logic nor statute nor theory is the basis of that other institution by which it comes about that a young woman holds sway over countless millions. The authority of this House itself does not, in the last resort, rest upon any logic in the principles upon which we are formed or elected; it rests upon the acceptance by the nation of an institution the history of which cannot be divorced or torn out of the context of the history of the nation itself.

However well argued, and however elegantly turned, the case he presented passed his listeners by. To most of them it was merely another example of Powell's fondness for lost, or at any rate impossibly *recherché*, causes. Nobody present could have imagined that twenty years later Powell would be fighting, and winning, a great battle on House of Lords reform.

The second intervention, however, had an entirely different reception. This was the attack on the colonial administration of Kenya over events at Hola Camp, which I have already described.[27] It was, by any standards, a magnificent piece of oratory, and it did produce some – though not all – of the reforms he demanded. But its significance for his future career, and for his reputation, can hardly be exaggerated. This is not in any sense to demean or diminish the moral grandeur of his stand: no speech he has ever made was conceived with less of an eye on tactics, or with less preconception.

There was, none the less, a chemical mix that there had never been before, even when the House had been at its most attentive and respectful. The elements had never come together in quite the same way before. These elements were, first, a subject of great importance, the significance and nature of which was clear to the audience; second, the (usual) disciplined order of Powell's thought and the precision of his language; and third, his almost incandescent emotion. I do not believe that Powell has ever in his life made a speech which did not contain the second and third of these elements, nor one in which the first was not apparent to him. But for true rapport between audience and speaker the audience must understand the significance too. When Powell sat down in the early hours of the morning of 28 July 1959 he was a major politician, no longer merely one of intriguing if uncertain promise.

If silent for long periods of time until the general election of 1959 in the House, and if engaged intensely both on his scholarly work and on the business of earning a living (apart from his journalism he acquired two directorships after his resignation, worth in all about £1,000 a year), Powell did not neglect extra-parliamentary fora. Essentially, he was trying to do two things. First, he wanted to erect a general, as opposed to a local, justification of what he, with Thorneycroft and Birch, had done. Second, he was trying to construct a general system of philosophical reasoning to underpin Conservatism. Thus, in the spring 1958 issue of *Crossbow* (the journal of the Bow Group, composed of mainly young and articulate Tories):

> Take Conservative 'freedom'. We believe it 'works', and that the doses administered since 1951 have done Britain good. But, so far as I know, no one has mapped its outline and indicated how much yet remains to be filled out. If a market price for goods and services is right and healthy, why is a market price for money wrong and dangerous? Or, put it another way, why does the party which has freed all other markets continue to control the capital market?

He goes on to question the desirability of fixed exchange rates and clearly imply his support for a floating currency (another battle which he was to win fifteen years later). Then:

> Perhaps one should not demand of foreign and Commonwealth affairs the same clear and demonstrable consistency as it is legitimate to seek in financial and economic policy. But I would make bold to trace some of the Conservative Party's most serious internal difficulties, both before and after Suez, to a failure to have explored and exposed the assumptions about Britain's position and future in the world on which a foreign and Commonwealth policy ought to be based.

All this was general, but there could be little doubt that the foundation stones of a formidable intellectual edifice were being laid. The point was made again in the spring 1960 issue of *Crossbow*, where he wrote:

> I would be prepared to go further and contend that a Party and a cause can gain great strength from the readiness with which their actions and policies are related by the public to

some broad, well-understood principle; and to instance 18th century Whiggism, 19th century Liberalism, and 20th century Socialism as cases in point.

However many subjects he discussed, Powell's central concern was economic policy and, within economic policy, the issue of public expenditure. Here, for the whole of his exile from office, he was never able to enjoy that satisfaction which (however fine his feelings), a resigning Minister hopes for: that of seeing the evil which he has predicted come to pass. It is true that Macmillan and Heathcoat Amory were steadily doing what the old Treasury team had all along feared they would do: that is, plunge into inflation. In May Bank Rate was cut to 5.5 per cent. In June a further half per cent was lopped off. Credit restrictions were eased, and bank lending encouraged. At the Party Conference of October 1958 Macmillan enjoyed a singular personal triumph and general election speculation was much in the air. In November capital investment in the nationalized industries was increased, restrictions on hire purchase were lifted, and a whole series of measures making money available for road and school building and house loans were announced. From August the Conservative Party was ahead in the public opinion polls.

In the face of all these developments Thorneycroft was inclined to trim, and welcomed many of the steps the government was taking. Powell, however, continued to hoe his own furrow alone. He did so in the most circumspect of manners. The 1958 and 1959 Budgets were criticized in the House in a highly technical fashion. Even in his journalism he posed questions rather than laying down the law. Thus, in the Wolverhampton *Express and Star* on 16 April 1958:

> The question of aiming to borrow too much or too little raises the whole question of the causes, the prospects and the cure of inflation. There is no dispute that if the government aims to borrow more than people are willing to lend it, the result is the printing of new money to fill the gap. There is also no dispute that in the past year this, to some extent, actually happened.

He remained utterly convinced that, however long it took, the Macmillan bubble would eventually burst. But he had no illusions that the anti-inflationary policies he was recommending in times of unprecedented prosperity would prove immediately popular, even though the electorate in general was willing to assent to the idea that expenditure should be controlled. He put these two points succinctly in an article in *The Daily Telegraph* on 9 July 1958:

I believe that most people, and by no means only the Conservatives, do not wish to mark time but are anxious to see the proportion of the national income which the government collects and spends falling steadily, if not dramatically, to a substantially lower level.

But

Economy is not popular until its fruits ripen and are gathered. Till then it is always unpopular . . . All public expenditure is payment to somebody for goods and services; and that somebody does not like it when the payment stops, even though the same purchasing power is used there or elsewhere by a private agency instead.

It was all to no public avail. At the time it was hard to argue against the delight of a nation enjoying the sweet fruit which was ripening after years of austerity and which believed, further, that the crop would be ever renewing. It was not until disappointment succeeded disappointment in the 1960s and 1970s, when short-lived booms were invariably followed by painful busts, and when inflation seemed to have a killing grip on the throat of the economy, that the people were willing to elect a government pledged to strict economy. Powell, it is fair to say, believed throughout 1958 and 1959 that the electorate should be educated into support for government without inflation. But there were few politicians who believed him. Even Thorneycroft, before his resignation, had declared that he was prepared to lose an election, if that was the price to be paid for putting the economy on the right course: it was obvious that defeat was a consequence much in his mind.

Powell's political journalism was now steadily appearing in specialist magazines, notably *The Stock Exchange Gazette* and *The Banker* and, throughout 1958 and 1959, the reader can sense an increasingly easy command of his various economic and financial subjects. Apart from command of the material, however, what he brought to these and other worthy journals was a capacity for vivid prose. The same capacity can be seen in his historical writing, in the course of which he from time to time drew contemporary parallels. As an illustration of his capacity for vivid writing – allied to the most scrupulous scholarship – one cannot do better than quote from the talks he gave on the BBC Third Programme (as it then was) in October 1958.[28] His subject was 'Bishops and Kings' and, specifically, that grand historical topic of relations between Church and State. Just as he used the language of the Authorized Version for his translation of Herodotus, so he could find a style – this time his own – for transmuting into dramatic glory the dry prose of medieval chroniclers. The point to remember is that he nowhere does the slightest damage to the texts he is using. For example, in his account of the breach between Henry II and Thomas Becket at the Council of Northampton, the chaplains who set down what we have by way of record of what were earth-shattering events and decisions were not present at the main debates. Powell stresses this when he says, 'The King himself, surrounded by the lay and clerical members of his Council, remains out of our view, because out of the view of the two chaplains through whose eyes we are seeing.' As a good scholar should, Powell sticks to what the evidence tells him.

The issue on which the dispute between King and Archbishop turned (though it was far from being the whole matter of their disagreement) was whether Becket had appealed past the King to Rome. Powell (who, incidentally, personally takes the King's side in this dispute) describes the conclusion of the drama, which ended in Becket's flight to France:

As time passed, tension mounted and angry voices could be heard from the upper chamber. Twice deputations came down to the Archbishop. The first consisted of a number of earls and barons who enquired whether in fact he had appealed to Rome over the King's head. On his confirming that he had done so, some of them withdrew in silence while others, in a tone which they took care should be loud enough to be overheard, recalled to one another various brutalities which Norman kings had perpetrated upon contumacious clergy.[29] On the second occasion, the Bishops came down and endeavoured to no purpose to shake the Archbishop's determination. At last a decision was arrived at in the upper room. The prelates, in order not to have part in pronouncing sentence on their Metropolitan, whose appeal to the Pope was already lodged, withdrew and resumed their seats downstairs, and presently the lay barons descended to announce the sentence on the Archbishop.

I have already argued[30] how essential it is to any understanding of Powell's thinking to appreciate the way in which he brings to bear on any contemporary problem a profound view based on national history. Most politicians, at one time or another, use historical reference, sometimes with knowledge, sometimes casually, sometimes cynically. In Powell's time in the House of Commons there were Members who could read Greek and Latin, and Members who could scan verse. Winston Churchill himself wrote a lengthy, sloppy, and unscholarly series of volumes on *The History of the English-Speaking Peoples*. Powell is the only politician of his generation, however, who is a scholar in the fullest and truest sense. It is possible, naturally and even inevitably, to dispute the conclusions a scholar draws from his evidence. It is widely recognized among historians that their predecessors and contemporaries in the field are influenced by their own times in their judgements. Every historian, as Herbert Butterfield[31] showed, sees his subject through the prism of his own time, and there is nothing disreputable about that. So far as Powell is concerned, this is an important point because he has brought to bear on his own time a scholar's interpretation of history. This is so unusual that one is startled to come across this passage in the BBC lectures on 'Bishops and Kings'. He is talking about the charitable services provided by the Church in the Middle Ages, and what happened to them after the Henrician Reformation:

> If you look from this point of view at the current activities of the state, you begin to see the divide everywhere. What we today call the Welfare State can be traced back along an unbroken line of development to the endeavours after the Reformation to replace the functions of the Church in education and in the care for want and suffering. The secular state has grown a whole new organ to meet demands and obey requirements which in the last analysis are moral rather than material. If in consequence we find frictions and conflicts between these and its other functions, if we find the state attempting to harmonize incompatibilities, there is no reason to be surprised.

Finding the origins of the Welfare State in a medieval dispute may seem far-fetched, but it is an idea with a decent pretension.

Another subject with which Powell was peripherally concerned, and which must be mentioned here because of its significance in his later career, was immigration.[32] The problem had not yet assumed anything like the proportions it reached later, nor was it at the forefront of Powell's mind. None the less, there were warning signs – riots in Notting Hill, Nottingham and Dudley. The immigrant population then being – probably – about a quarter of a million, some Conservative Members began to be agitated and one of these, Sir Cyril Osborne, the Member for Louth, sought Powell's aid in raising the matter in the House:

> Sometime in 1958 or 1959 Cyril Osborne approached me. He said something had to be done about immigration, and, knowing my views on the subject, he tried to get me to join in his campaign – to raise it in Parliament and at the 1959 election. Given the situation I didn't believe it was easier to do it by Cyril Osborne's approach and Cyril felt, I think he felt, deserted by me . . . The more *farouche* the more difficult it is to do it. It was a tactical problem. I thought that such a fundamental change in the law of the country was a monkey which was easier caught softly . . . So I thought: I won't make a major speech about it. Someone's bound to ask me a question about it. A Conservative government, if elected, will have to do something about it, to introduce legislation, and I didn't think it was a good idea to push it into the forefront at this time.[33]

Eventually the Conservative government did do something about it, by passing, in 1962, under the aegis of Butler and in the face of fierce Labour opposition, an Act to control Commonwealth immigration. Long before that, however, on 5 December 1958, Osborne had introduced a debate on immigration control: Powell did not take part.

Eventually Macmillan called the general election for 8 October. It was an uneventful affair, for the government started well ahead and stayed well ahead, increasing its majority to 100, as opposed to 58 in 1955. On 21 October the Prime Minister sent for Powell. He wanted, he said, to offer him the Parliamentary Under Secretaryship at the Department of Education. He hastened to add that, although this was a much lower ranking than Powell had hitherto enjoyed, this was not intended as a slight: it was merely that, having resigned in so dramatic a fashion, Powell had to work his passage back. Powell inquired whether Thorneycroft had been offered anything (Birch was now out of the running because of his failing eyesight) and, on being told he had not, declined the invitation. Unlike his previous refusal of office this one was not kept secret, and Powell won golden opinions, from the Press and his colleagues alike, for his principled stand.

He was immediately elected Chairman of the backbench Finance Committee and from this position of enhanced authority his criticism of the government's economic policy took on a sharper tone. He had also become particularly interested in the question of savings, national and private. His was a characteristically anti-interventionist view. In effect, he argued, the government used savings as a loan, to make up shortfalls in its own income. He even managed to find the time to write a slim volume on the subject, replete with illustrations and forcefully restating his essentially capitalist thesis.[34] He also put together a series of his own talks in an enchanting volume entitled *Great Parliamentary Occasions*.

As the year wore on there were signs that Powell's more dire predictions were coming true, as inflation rose and the economy began to slow down. It was still not clear to the public, however, that Macmillan's boom years were moving to their close, and that the government was falling into disarray. Against Heathcoat Amory's wishes, however, Macmillan kept to his own course in the 1960 Budget and not long afterwards the Chancellor retired. But Powell was now to become part of the débâcle: on 27 July he was appointed Minister of Health while Thorneycroft became Minister of Aviation. It was not lost on commentators that Powell's was the more senior position. It did not carry with it, however, a seat in the Cabinet: Powell was not elevated to Cabinet rank until July 1962. None the less, Powell now headed a major ministry with an annual outlay of some £500 million and a number of employees in excess of 400,000. It was, moreover, a ministry constantly in the public eye. The National Health Service was the dearest creation of the Labour Party, and its activities and responsibilities in one way or another affected everybody in the land. Thus, for example, it was the contention of a substantial number of Conservatives that, even if an individual used the private medical sector, paying for his doctor and any hospitalization he required, given that the private patient not only sustained the NHS through his taxes but lightened its burden by paying for treatment, he should get any medicines he needed virtually free – subject, that is, only to the prescription charge in force. Throughout his three and a half years as Minister Powell resisted this change, but less out of conviction than because he knew it was incompatible with retrenchments which he would be advocating.

Powell spent the months intervening between his appointment and the return of Parliament after the summer recess immersing himself in the details of his job. The reception of the new Minister, though mixed, had been broadly favourable. So far as his own attitude to his charge was concerned, it has to be remembered (as a number of Tories were astonished to discover) that he ranked the Health Service with defence as one of those subjects which had been definitively placed in the charge of the state, and were not, therefore, subject to that play of market forces the virtues of which he was constantly espousing. At the outset Labour's senior spokesmen realized this view of his and they were, in any event, fully preoccupied with their own internecine struggle over whether Britain should retain nuclear weapons or not.

Powell's time at the ministry was dominated by four considerations – hospitals, drugs, prescription charges and pay, especially nurses' pay. He did not set out to be controversial and, indeed, was later to record the view that 'If a service is administered by a department of state, neither the personality nor the status of the individual Minister is going to vary very much, or make, in principle, much difference.'[35] None the less, at one time or another, on one issue or another, he was to run seriously foul both of Conservative and of Labour opinion.

The first thing Powell realized was that the National Health Service, only twelve years after its creation, was already in decay. It was over-extended and under-funded. In part this was, as he realized,[36] inevitable. The service was free at the point of use, and such a service generated a theoretically infinite demand. Powell's ambition, assisted by his old friend and Birmingham Member, Edith Pitt, as Parliamentary Secretary, and Bruce Fraser – whom he had known at the Treasury – as his Permanent Secretary, was to bring the administration of the Service into order, and to make one major and lasting contribution. That contribution, he decided, would be the devising and implementation of a major plan for rebuilding the nation's hospitals, almost without exception in decay.

He was, as might have been expected, a furiously active Minister, and his tours of individual health authority areas became legendary. It was his practice to descend on a particular area, during a whirlwind tour to note deficiencies, sharply to rebuke those responsible for them, and quickly to take action to see that these deficiencies were repaired. In general he took the view that there was too great a tendency (as there is in any bureaucratic system) to operate the service for the benefit of those who ran it, rather than for the benefit of the patients. There is, for example, a celebrated story (perfectly true) that in one hospital he found that imminent births were signalled by the clanging of a massive bell, to the irritation and inconvenience of all patients. He saw to it that the bell was replaced by a more discreet electrical alarm system. This, of course, was the kind of detailed work at which he excelled. More important, though, was his grand design for British hospitals, and especially for the mental hospitals, the grimness of which beggared his belief. He estimated that £500 million and ten years would be required to replace the hospital stock, and set matters in train immediately. He did not, however, think it right (or feasible) while raising this massive sum to load increased current expenditure on to the Treasury, and determined both to increase prescription charges and save money where possible. On 17 January 1961 he announced his grand plan at a Press conference, somewhat to the astonishment of those who had expected the principal exponent of the merits of capitalism to set about running the NHS down further. On 9 March 1961 he startled the National Association for Mental Health by announcing that existing mental hospitals would have to come down for, 'A hospital is a shell, a framework, however complex, to contain certain processes, and when the processes are changed or superseded the shell must probably be scrapped and the framework dismantled.' He gained, however, no support from the Association and found there, as he was to find in other areas of his responsibility, a distinct and conservative tendency to resist change, and to take the Minister's expression of his views as personal criticism.

On 25 January 1962 the great hospital plan was unveiled in the form of a government White Paper. It envisaged the spending of £777 million over ten years, throughout the kingdom. There were to be ninety or more completely new hospitals, and everything that was possible would be done to provide them with sufficient staff in the form of doctors and nurses, even if these had to be students and trainees from abroad. It was afterwards to be a charge laid at Powell's door, once he took up the immigration issue in earnest, that he had himself at this time encouraged immigration. He asserted not merely subsequently, but then, that he envisaged most such immigrants as temporary, people whose sojourn in Britain would eventually redound to the advantage of their own countries on their return, and who would be replaced by further immigrants.

In general, among the public, his parliamentary colleagues and the Press, Powell gained golden opinions for the hospital programme. The same was true of his handling of the extraordinarily difficult question of the supply of drugs to the NHS.

On the matter of free drugs for private patients he was adamant, and he particularly excited the wrath of the Conservative Party Conference in October 1960 when, despite the evident interest in the matter of previous speakers, he simply failed to refer to it at all when he summed up. When Parliament re-assembled he replied to questions from the backbench Health Committee, and angered and confused his audience by both saying that the cost of the desired remission (some £3 million) was bearable, but that he would not bear it. Nor would he take the way out that might have won him sympathy – a hint broad enough to be understood clearly that the Cabinet would not permit him.

But the really crucial issue concerning drugs was the matter of their supply and cost. Most of the drugs used by NHS practitioners were supplied by a small number of large companies and these companies, in a virtually monopolistic position, charged heavily for their products (largely, they argued, in order to fund necessary research). They employed, furthermore, exceptionally aggressive selling techniques, and the Department had often hesitated to recommend cheaper drugs for fear that it might be accused of infringing the freedom of individual doctors to prescribe as they wished.

Initially, Powell tackled the problem by regulating the rights of doctors according to a formula devised by a committee headed by Lord Cohen of Birkenhead. After prolonged study, however, he announced, on 17 May 1961, a much more daring measure. He had decided, he told an astonished drug industry, to apply the Patents Act of 1940 to them and their products. The Act, designed essentially for wartime use, enabled the government of the day to use an alternative supplier for any commodity it judged essential in spite of the rights of the patent holder, who would be recompensed either by negotiation or by arbitration. The drug companies were right in their assertion that the Act had not been designed for such a case as theirs, but only one company – Pfizer – took the risk of challenging the Department in the courts: they lost.

Powell's line on the drug companies caused general surprise among those who had not studied or understood his philosophy. The fact of the matter was that monopoly was one of the things he most detested, and it was also the case that he desperately needed to show the Treasury that he was making every effort possible to economize on outlay in order to assist the funding of the hospital plan.

On the other two matters which preoccupied him, however, he

was not destined to enjoy presentational success. He determined to increase prescription charges; and he constantly resisted the wages demands of the nursing profession, first as a matter of economy but later, as the life of the government was drawing to its close, in the service of a determination on the part of the Cabinet to restrain incomes – the first and crudest of many unsuccessful incomes policies. In both matters he was unlucky and high principled. It was perfectly reasonable of him to argue, as he did ceaselessly, that it did not lie in the mouth of the Labour Party to attack him over prescription charges, for it was they who had first introduced them. The fact of the matter was that he was an exceptionally convenient target for a party embroiled in its own quarrels, one against which all sections of the Labour Opposition could unite. In the case of the nurses he necessarily appeared to be harsh with a much-loved profession, and there were ranged against him not only the whole of the Opposition, but many Conservatives as well, and particularly the flamboyant and redoubtable Irene Ward. It was particularly unfortunate for him, moreover, that, while the incomes policy was in force, and while he was still resisting the nurses (whose claim finally went to successful arbitration) a substantial increase in pay (some nine per cent) went to the dockers, who commanded greater industrial muscle.

On the other hand, it had been suggested more than once that he should give way to the nurses before pay restraint was announced. This would have been perfectly understood by a Cabinet which appreciated the immense public hostility to his stand, and the personal difficulties in reputation that it cost him. He would not give way, preferring to stand by general government policy even if other Ministers did not. Then, again, his manner and style of presenting and defending his policies left a good deal to be desired in a situation in which a little hand-wringing would not have come amiss. He preferred to point out that at current pay the numbers and standard of recruits were rising.

Powell attended the Cabinet of 18 October 1960 where he explained his charges to his colleagues, it being necessary to do this since legislation would be required. The news began to leak out that a Minister who had just (under terms recommended by the Pilkington Committee) announced an extra £37.6 million in doctors' pay, and was about to unveil a visionary hospital plan, was none the less about to bump up prescription charges. On 1 February the following year he announced the increases in the House, increases designed to net £65 million a year. The Labour response was more than predictably furious, and large sections of the Press joined in castigation the following day. On 8 February, when the Bill to sanction increases was debated, Powell was pilloried still more savagely, and the Opposition even sought to disrupt proceedings. Eventually, on 2 March, it became necessary to guillotine debate on the Bill – that is, to curtail time for discussion of it by resolution – and, after seven hours of debate, the government had a majority of 82.

At least, during the battle over prescription charges Powell had the comfort provided by the support of a united Party behind him. It was not so in the case of the nurses. In August 1961 the profession entered a pay claim through the machinery of the Whitley Council, the body charged with oversight of their claims. At a meeting on 9 January 1962 the management side met to consider a pay claim that, in some cases, amounted to twenty-five per cent. Powell himself came to this meeting and, brooking no discussion, insisted that the offer should be no more than two and a half per cent. This offer was made and rejected on 13 February. On 12 March, in the House, Powell was left in no doubt of the strength of feeling against himself and the government. Dame Irene Ward was also on the council of the Royal College of Nurses and, for all that she was generally regarded as an amusing eccentric, her dedication to good causes was widely accepted and admired. She turned with force on Powell; he refused to move, and denied that nurses were to suffer more than anybody else during the 'pay pause'. 'Nurses are not singled out for treatment,' he said. 'The nursing situation is not disastrous in view of the fact that the nursing force today is at its highest point ever. I do not for a moment accept that one can have regard to the merits of a claim in complete isolation from the economic situation.'

There were three things about Powell's approach to the subject which gave an edge to the anger deployed against him. The first was that, in spite of being opposed to the pay pause, and having argued against it, he was more zealous than any other Minister in enforcing it, and utterly refused to take up tentative offers to let him make the nurses an exception. The second was the attitude revealed in the quotation just given: if he was satisfied with the number of nurses available (and his figures were frequently disputed) then he saw no need to increase his offer, for demand and supply were in balance. The third was his expression of a recurring theme, not only in this dispute, but generally in his view of life.

This was his view (already mentioned in the case of Field-Marshal Slim)[37] that those who take employment that is not merely a job, but a vocation, should be content with remuneration that might otherwise be regarded as deficient, because of the satisfaction their work afforded. The general view, of course, was quite the other way round.

From 6.30 p.m. on 27 March to 7.20 the following morning the House debated pay in the NHS. Powell was subjected to the most bitter and protracted attack. To the exceptional irritation of his enemies, however, he simply ignored the most strenuous criticisms and ploughed on with his own view of the state of the Service and his own vision for the future. His suit of armour undented, he was still obliged to face demonstrations around the country, but most notably in the House of Commons Lobby itself on 13 April. On that occasion he was compelled to leave Parliament through the House of Lords. On being advised by his Parliamentary Private Secretary that it would be unwise, even, for him to return home by tube (there is a tunnel connecting the Commons with Westminster underground station) he simply walked to South Eaton Place through the rain: Powell was never one of those senior politicians who stood on ceremony, or indulged themselves in the comforts available to them.

The pity of all this, in the view of Powell's supporters, was that it obscured all the things he was doing which were generally considered admirable. He found more money for doctors in difficult practices. He intensified the Department's campaign against smoking.[38] He greatly improved liaison between the hospital authorities and the local health authorities. The Health Visitor system was improved, and he issued a Mothers' Charter, which made life a great deal more comfortable for pregnant women in NHS hospitals.

None the less, the dispute with the nurses substantially dented a reputation that had been waxing to such an extent that prominent people were beginning seriously to think of him as a future Prime Minister. The conviction was growing that, after Macmillan, it might be wise to skip a generation with the new leader or, at least, that if somebody like Butler succeeded Macmillan then the next leader should come from the 1950 intake. The names most generally canvassed had been those of Macleod and Maudling. But Macleod was now Colonial Secretary, and busy enthusiastically disposing of the remaining assets of the British Empire in Africa, thus upsetting the Tory Party, while Maudling seemed

becalmed at the Board of Trade. While few thought of Powell as
an obvious choice as Prime Minister, or as a man possessed of the
gifts usually displayed or the gregarious talents normally thought
indispensable to those seeking that office, there was something
about his flint-like integrity, something about his very *difference*
from other politicians, that made it possible to entertain the idea
of him as the tenant in No. 10 Downing Street. There is always
a yearning in the political world for the ideals of disinterest and
for the spurning of supposedly sordid compromises, and Powell's
character was such that it seemed he might satisfy that yearning.
It was considered more likely, however, that he might, in a
reshuffle that could not long be delayed, become Chancellor of
the Exchequer.

For, in 1962, Powell's troubles over the nurses were quickly
being subsumed by a series of seismic blows inflicted on the
government. The dissatisfaction with Macmillan's ministry arose
from several sources. The electorate no longer had confidence
in the government's economic policy. Selwyn Lloyd, who had
succeeded Heathcoat Amory as Chancellor, had continued with
expansionist policies in the 1961 Budget. In July, however, he
was forced to move towards deflation: he introduced the pay
pause, raised Bank Rate, and increased taxes. While behaving –
as we have seen in the case of the nurses – with perfect loyalty,
in practice Powell was not averse to making his doubts public,
and in Oxford in September he again raised the question of the
usefulness of government intervention, albeit in general terms:

> The level of demand for labour, the fluctuations of trade and
> economic activity are attributed not only to government poli-
> cies generally, but to specific acts of government inside each
> particular country, while all the evidence shows that deeper
> forces are at work. It is doubtful how far governments can
> or do influence and control economic activity and growth
> itself; but delusions of grandeur about the government's role
> as regulator of the economy may easily obscure its duty to
> preserve the honesty and validity of the nation's money.

For whatever reason, however, the clouds louring over the
government were growing darker. The opinion polls were moving
steadily against Macmillan: a National Opinion Poll on 8 January
1962 found more than half the electorate dissatisfied. At the
Blackpool North by-election in March the Conservative majority
was reduced from 15,857 to 973 and there was worse at Orpington,'

Kent, where a Conservative majority of 14,760 was converted into a Liberal plurality of 7,855.

The government was tottering, and Macmillan cast about for ways of regaining the initiative. Negotiations were under way to join the European Economic Community, though it could hardly be said that they were meeting with any great success. Under the charge of Edward Heath these negotiations began (after certain preliminary soundings had been taken by Macmillan himself) in August 1961. They lasted for eighteen months, and ended with a veto imposed by General de Gaulle on British entry.

Powell supported the idea of entry to the EEC, but he did not see the proposed entanglement in anything like the same way that the Prime Minister did. Then, and for several years thereafter, in spite of constantly sniffing for undesirable political ramifications to the application to enter, he saw the EEC essentially as a free-trading area and, as such, he favoured it. In Macmillan's mind, however, lurked far grander ideas of ultimate political union which had nevertheless carefully to be hidden from the public. The problem was to combine uplift – which would give the government itself a new lease of life – with the prospect of material advantage. Macmillan was uncommonly nervous before he launched, on 13 April 1962, the new policy at a by-election in Stockton, the seat he had held before the war. Not one of many drafts seemed satisfactory and the right tone was not hit until, in the train north, scribbling on the backs of British Rail menu cards, his Press Officer, George Hutchinson, finally produced what was required.[39]

But the lift did not come and, in July, Macmillan panicked. On what was immediately dubbed 'the night of the long knives' seven Members of the Cabinet – including the Chancellor of the Exchequer and the Lord Chancellor – were dismissed. Macmillan had long felt that he had been unwise not to bring forward younger men after the 1959 triumph, and he determined to remedy that omission now. The changes that aroused most comment were the granting of a Cabinet place to Powell, the promotion of Reginald Maudling to the Treasury and the appointment of Butler (who gave up the Home Office to Henry Brooke) as First Secretary of State and Deputy Prime Minister (he continued to be responsible for Central African affairs).

This drastic restructuring had the opposite effect to that intended. 'Greater love hath no man than this,' said Jeremy Thorpe, the Liberal Leader, in the House of Commons, 'that he lay down his friends for his life.' It was perfectly clear that'

178

the promotion of Maudling was intended to herald a new burst of expansionism in the economy, and Nigel Birch wrote acidly to *The Times* on 20 July, 'For the second time he has got rid of a Chancellor of the Exchequer who tried to get expenditure under control. Once is more than enough.' But it was the evident nervous brutality of the exercise that shocked, particularly in the case of Selwyn Lloyd. Lloyd was not a particularly popular man, and he had few gifts of camaraderie. But he had given yeoman service to two Prime Ministers. Even Eden (by now Lord Avon) who had been scrupulous never to criticize his successor, observed in a speech on 21 July, 'I feel that Mr. Lloyd has been harshly treated.' When Macmillan rose for his first session of Prime Minister's Questions after the massacre he was greeted in stony silence, and even his admiring biographer, Nigel Fisher, agrees that the reshuffle was a serious mistake.[40]

Powell was naturally disappointed that, even though he was now a Member of the Cabinet, he was not promoted to a more senior department, but he was realist enough to understand that he would not have been the kind of Chancellor Macmillan wanted. He did feel, however, that his work at the Department of Health was more or less finished, and he had a settled conviction that Ministers should not stay too long in the same department. As he wrote later:[41]

> The political head, though he must cope with everything that events throw in his path, can only take personal control and initiative on very few fronts at once. He must select his points of attack and throw all his available weight and attention there. By the time his initiative has attained its objects, even its preliminary objects, it will usually be too late to recommence the same process elsewhere. The essence of a Minister's initiative is to alter what otherwise would have happened – to upset, in a word.

While there were still things to do in the Department – dealing with the emergence of the thalidomide problem, for example, or encouraging the fluoridation of water – it was the general deterioration in the political situation that increasingly occupied Powell's and every other politician's mind. In December the United States cancelled the Skybolt missile project: Britain had been going to buy this weapon as a central part of defence strategy so this was a heavy blow. The hammer blow, however, came in January, when de Gaulle vetoed the application to join the

Common Market which had, increasingly, become the foundation of Macmillan's foreign policy. The fact that the veto had been delivered after a summit between President and Prime Minister at which Macmillan had simply failed to notice the hints given him of French intentions raised further serious doubts about his competence.

There was even worse at home. From 1961 to 1963 the government was bedevilled by a series of security scandals. In January 1961 three spies – Gordon Lonsdale and the husband and wife Kroger team were unveiled. In April George Blake, a Russian agent in the Foreign Office, was arrested (he was later sentenced to forty-two years). In September 1962 William Vassall, a junior official at the Admiralty who none the less had access to important papers through the work he did for the First Lord, T. G. D. Galbraith, was arrested. While Macmillan, not unjustly, complained that it was only when spies were caught that governments suffered from security scares, it was the very number of these unmaskings that excited public disquiet. Moreover, some newspapers hinted at an improper relationship between Galbraith and Vassall, who was a homosexual. The Radcliffe Tribunal was set up to investigate these charges and, while it cleared Galbraith (who, none the less, resigned) in the course of its work, it imprisoned two journalists for six months for refusing to reveal their sources, and Macmillan thereby earned the undying enmity of most of Fleet Street.

The very worst was yet to come. For some time there had been rumours in Westminster and Fleet Street that the private life of the Secretary of State for War, John Profumo, was not at all what would be expected of a happily married family man and Conservative Minister. It appeared that Profumo was in the habit of frequenting the London flat of Stephen Ward, a society osteopath and amateur procurer, and, further, of attending louche parties at Cliveden, the home of Lord Astor. Through Ward, the story went, the Minister had struck up a relationshp with Christine Keeler who, if not as Nigel Birch was to call her 'a professional prostitute', was certainly of easy virtue. Moreover – and more dangerously, given Profumo's position – another of Ward's regular guests was a certain Major Ivanov, the military attaché at the Soviet Embassy.[42] The national newspapers initially handled the matter cautiously, because of their experience over Galbraith but, on 8 March, in his newsheet, *Westminster Confidential*, Andrew Roth printed the story.

Since 14 February the Labour Party had a new Leader,

Harold Wilson, elected after the death of Hugh Gaitskell on 17 January. Guided by George Wigg in security matters Wilson began to explore how the Profumo affair (as it came to be called) could be exploited. On 14 March the *Daily Express* printed photographs of Profumo and Miss Keeler, as broad a hint as they thought they could risk. The next day the *Daily Sketch* carried a story by Miss Mandy Rice-Davies, a friend of Miss Keeler, which mentioned Ivanov and hinted at all sorts of sleazy goings-on in London society. Though Miss Rice-Davies was perfectly willing to do so, the paper was unwilling to risk a libel action by naming Profumo. On 21 March, however, Mrs. Barbara Castle and Richard Crossman both asked in the House for a Select Committee to investigate the relations between Miss Keeler and an unnamed Minister. From then on the Labour Party, in order, they hoped, to avoid charges of prurience, tried to concentrate on Ivanov, justifying their interest in Profumo's affairs on security grounds.

That night a group of Ministers (both of the government Law Officers; the Chief Whip, Martin Redmayne; Macleod; and the Minister without Portfolio, William Deedes) gathered for a meeting with Profumo and his solicitor at No. 11 Downing Street (No. 10 having been in the hands of builders and restorers for some time). Profumo's assurances of innocence were accepted (whether they were really believed is another matter, about which there has been some dispute) and a statement was drafted for Profumo to deliver to the House the following – Friday – morning. Butler, who had just returned from Africa, was summoned by Macmillan to 'hold Profumo's hand'[43] during the statement. What worried Butler most was that Friday morning, when the House is normally almost empty, was an unfortunate time for an important personal statement.

The personal statement is a rare parliamentary occasion. But the rules governing such affairs had one great advantage for Profumo: a Member making a personal statement cannot be questioned. While he admitted meeting both Ward and Miss Keeler he absolutely denied any impropriety and ended, 'I shall not hesitate to issue writs for libel and slander if scandalous allegations are made or repeated outside the House.'[44] But the dam was not to hold. On 27 May Wilson harried the Prime Minister, who agreed to set up an inquiry. This was to be headed by the Lord Chancellor Lord Dilhorne and, although it had not yet been formally established, Dilhorne – formerly Sir Reginald

Manningham-Buller, QC – asked Profumo to come and see him. On 4 June Profumo told his wife that the stories were true and on 5 June he resigned. He immediately applied for the Chiltern Hundreds, which application is a device for MPs who wish to leave their seats immediately to do so, the Hundreds being notionally an office of profit under the Crown and hence incompatible with holding a seat in the House of Commons.

This was a staggering blow to the government. Moreover, when a scandal arising from sleazy sexual behaviour was added to yet more evidence of sheer incompetence, there seemed to hang over Macmillan a distasteful miasma. He had been wrong in his handling of the Vassall business; he had failed to read the signs over the EEC application, and therefore had no serious foreign or economic policy;[45] and, suddenly, there was added to all this his readiness to believe a louche liar. There was, of course, a good deal of hypocrisy on all sides in this. Profumo was – thus the argument ran – driven from public life because he had lied to the House of Commons but[46] Macmillan had himself consistently lied to the House over a far more important matter – collusion with Israel in the 1956 war. None the less, the mood of the times was such – and it was reflected in a number of instant books[47] – that almost anything could be believed of Conservative Ministers. It was said, for example, that Macmillan knew that Profumo had been lying to him at the ministerial meeting on 21 March, and that all the others present knew that too. The consequential belief was that a cover-up had been planned, which had gone wrong. A further crop of rumours then began, most of which related to the supposed sexual proclivities of other Ministers. It was in these seedy circumstances that Powell suddenly became a figure of some importance.

It is not too much to say that, for about five days, Powell held the fate and the future of the government in his hands. Whatever else may have been thought about him in Westminster and Fleet Street, it was accepted that he was wholly incorruptible (*The Times* applied the phrase once used of Robespierre to him – 'sea-green incorruptible' – which carried the connotation of grimness as well as honesty). He had been out of London on a tour of hospitals when Profumo resigned, but on his return refused comment. A whole series of stories was planted in London newspapers by Nigel Birch[48] to the effect that he was contemplating resignation, out of distaste and concern. Powell, however, kept his own counsel, though he moved about with what amounted to a bodyguard of journalists and television cameramen. As events unfolded Powell continued to fulfil the engagements in his diary. On 13 June, for example, he went to lay a foundation stone for a new Centre for the Jewish Blind. Once his job was done he asked the journalists following whether, as he hoped, they would continue to show the same eagerness in their coverage of the plight of the handicapped. But of politics he would say nothing.

Birch's conviction – and, for once the view of this arrogant and isolated, but brilliant man was shared by the majority – was that a Powell resignation over Profumo would bring Macmillan down. The whole business was to be debated in the House of Commons on 17 June, and the Cabinet met on 12 June and 13 June to discuss what the government's attitude should be. (Among their eventual decisions was that to commission Lord Denning to inquire into the whole affair: he produced a report so racy that it became a best seller, though he concluded that there had been no breaches of security arising out of Profumo's indiscretions.) According to Birch's calculations, a Powell resignation would provoke such a flood of Tory abstentions on 17 June as to create the same effect as in the debate on Norway in 1940, when seventy Tory abstainers brought down Neville Chamberlain. In that case he intended to organize a campaign to make Powell Prime Minister.

The Conservative Party was in a state of panic, just as the Press was in a state of feverish excitement. The Labour Party – twenty or so per cent ahead in most opinion polls – could hardly contain their excitement. Powell, meanwhile, in the course of intense questioning in the Cabinet, had come to the conclusion that Macmillan had been no more than gullible in his handling of Profumo. On Saturday 15 June he rose to his feet in Narborough, a small town in Norfolk, and said:

> I will speak out here and now. I am convinced that from the beginning to the end of the affair, and in every aspect of it, the personal honour and integrity of the Prime Minister, Harold Macmillan, are absolutely unsullied. I look to be in my place on Monday to support him.

And he continued with a disquisition on freedom and the Socialist state.

In the event twenty-seven Conservative MPs abstained at the end of the Monday debate but, despite an outstanding performance by Harold Wilson (concentrating on the supposed security aspects of the matter) and a limp one from the Prime

Minister, the government was no longer in danger. Monday, 17 June 1963 will, however, be long remembered for one of the most savage and wounding attacks ever made by one party colleague on another. Nigel Birch, bitterly disappointed with Powell, had his say:

> We know a great deal more now about Profumo than we did at the time of his statement, but we have all known him pretty well for a number of years in this House. I must say he never struck me as a man at all like a cloistered monk; and Miss Keeler was a professional prostitute. There seems to me a certain basic improbability about the proposition that their relationship was purely Platonic. What are whores about? Yet Profumo's word was accepted. It was accepted from a colleague. Would that word have been accepted if Profumo had been a political opponent?

He called for Macmillan's resignation, and ended with the terrible lines from Browning's poem *The Lost Leader*, written when Wordsworth accepted a sinecure job from the government of the day:

> Let him never come back to us
> There will be doubt, hesitation, and pain.
> False praise on our part, the glimmer of twilight,
> Never glad confident morning again.

Imbued in very substantial part by the determination that 'I will not be brought down by that girl', Macmillan embarked on a rallying of the troops, one moment in which was a speech in Wolverhampton South-West on 28 June. None the less, throughout the summer, speculation about his future, conversations about his future, intrigues against his future, ebbed and flowed.[49] Lord Home, the Foreign Secretary, advised him to retire before a general election which could not be delayed longer than October 1964.[50] His own mood changed regularly. The signature of the Test Ban Treaty in Moscow (which had been largely his contriving) and his visit to President Kennedy at the end of June, enlivened him. It was none the less clear that he had lost most of his appetite for holding power.

Meanwhile, something little noticed, but of profound importance, happened. The government's Peerage Bill had been winding its way through the House of Lords. In its original essence it permitted successors to peerages to disclaim their titles and, further, it provided that peers sitting at the moment it received the Royal Assent could do likewise, thus making both categories of individual eligible for seats in the House of Commons. One proviso was that peers currently sitting could not disclaim until the then Parliament was dissolved. On 16 July, however, their Lordships amended the Bill to allow any one of their current number to disclaim immediately or, at any rate, within twelve months of the Bill's passage. This seemed, for those taking part in the debate, an innocuous and commonsense provision. It was not immediately noticed that, were Macmillan to resign in the near future, it would make available two more potential candidates for the succession, Lord Home and Lord Hailsham.

The literature on the months that followed is extensive[51] and I do not propose here to go into all the ramifications of the struggle for the Tory leadership that occurred in October 1963. An outline of events is, however, necessary so that the reasoning behind Powell's eventual decision is clear.

Macmillan was determined that, if he were to go, Butler should not succeed him.[52] He gave opportunities to both Macleod and Maudling to establish themselves as challengers. Macleod, by his liberalization (as it was thought to be then) programme in Africa lost his prospects, and Maudling, too, failed to make a sufficient impact, though he did talk to Butler about his prospects.[53] After the Lords vote of 16 July, however, Macmillan's eye fell first on Quintin Hailsham and, second, on Alec Home.

On Tuesday 8 October 1963 the Cabinet met at 10 a.m. This was to be their last meeting before the Party Conference and most of those present would be leaving for Blackpool that day, the Prime Minister to follow later in the week, for it was then the practice of the Conservative Party that the Leader only turned up for the final rally, on Saturday morning. Macmillan seemed to find it difficult to concentrate on business, and his colleagues noticed that he seemed ill. Just before twelve he was brought a glass of a milky fluid which he sipped. He then told the Cabinet that he would announce a decision about his future intentions at Blackpool and left the room.

That evening Butler, still in London, attended a cocktail party at No. 10, held to celebrate the renovation of the house. In its course Macmillan explained that he was in serious pain and finding it impossible to urinate. An operation, he said, would be necessary, but he thought that, with palliatives, he might still be able to make his speech at Blackpool. Before the end of the party, however – having left it briefly to see his doctors – he told Butler that the operation would have to take place immediately. The following morning Macmillan was visited in hospital by the Foreign Secretary, Alec Home, who argued persuasively that he should now resign. A letter to this effect was drafted by the two men, and Home took it north to Blackpool. By a coincidence that turned out very happily for him, Home was President of the National Union that year, so it fell to him to read out the Prime Minister's message of resignation. Mr. Howard believes[54] – and I agree with him – that Macmillan, uncertain of whether Hailsham could win the leadership, deliberately put Home in a prominent position, intimately engaged in the drama of the resignation, so that he might later be a candidate.

Blackpool immediately became Bedlam, and there was no subject to discuss except the leadership. There were two intensely dramatic events. First, at a highly emotional fringe meeting Hailsham declared that he was disclaiming his peerage and would seek election to the House of Commons. Second, Butler, who had, with difficulty, obtained the agreement of his colleagues to make the speech at the Saturday morning rally, was heckled in the course of his rather dull oration. Home, in the chair in his capacity as President, rose to rebuke the hecklers and received an ovation such as he had never before received in his political life. Early in the day he had told Butler, apparently casually, that he would be seeing his doctor the following week in London. The intimation was clear: there was now another candidate for the succession.

On the surface, at any rate, things were quieter in London. Everybody, of course, had their preferences for the succession, and a handful had hopes of achieving it. Hailsham, however, for all his popularity with the party faithful, seemed unlikely to be an election winner, and Maudling had simply failed to make any serious impression. Soundings were being undertaken of backbench Tory opinion, by the Chief Whip, Martin Redmayne, in the Commons and by Lord St. Aldwyn and Lord Poole in the Lords. In those days there were, of course, no formal electoral procedures for choosing a Conservative Leader; he was supposed to 'emerge'. All findings were, however, reported to Macmillan, in bed in the King Edward VII Hospital for Officers. He remained Prime Minister until he formally gave his resignation to the Queen (who had already been told of his intentions) and advised her as to whom she ought to send for.[55]

Macleod and Powell were solidly for Butler. Macleod, it must be said, had a vested interest in the Butler succession for, as Butler himself later wrote,[56] 'Iain Macleod and I had a secret . . . he always said he hoped that I would be Prime Minister, and he wished himself to succeed me.' Powell had no such plan: he merely believed, but with his usual intensity believed with fervour, that Butler was incomparably the best man. This was the view (although Macmillan lied about that too) of the majority of the Cabinet whose views the Lord Chancellor had purported to sound.

On 17 October, Macleod heard, at breakfast, by a circuitous route, that Home would be invited to form a government that day. He was astonished, not simply by the choice, but by the fact that he, Chairman of the Party and Leader of the House of Commons, had heard not a whisper of this development. After a morning meeting he had a drink with Maudling, and learned that the Chancellor of the Exchequer was likewise ignorant of what was in the wind. A telephone call to the Lord Chancellor, Lord Dilhorne, elicited the information that he and other canvassers were to present their views and reports to Macmillan that afternoon. Macleod and Maudling lunched together. During the afternoon a Fleet Street friend, William Rees-Mogg, telephoned Macleod to tell him that Home had 'emerged' as successor. Macleod arranged to meet Maudling and Powell at his own flat, he having been in close touch with Powell since Blackpool. Other members of the government began to show up as the telephone, in constant use, summoned them.

The meeting broke up late in the afternoon and Macleod and his wife went to a dinner, he having told her that, given the way the succession had been fixed, he could not serve Home. After dinner they adjourned to Powell's house in South Eaton Place. From there both men spoke to Home on the telephone and put it to him that he was an unsuitable candidate, not merely because he was a peer, but because it would appear absurd that the Party could not find a suitable Leader from among its 363 Members in the Commons.

As the evening wore on Maudling, Frederick Erroll (President of the Board of Trade), and Lord Aldington arrived at South Eaton Place. Hailsham spoke on the telephone. Redmayne was informed of the view and he, too, repaired to Powell's house to be told that all of those there were solidly for Butler. The following morning Maudling and Hailsham waited on Butler, who was staying in the St. Ermin's Hotel while his town house was being renovated. They told him that they were of the same mind as Macleod and Powell: if he, Butler, would decline to serve so would they, and Home would be unable to form a government.

Throughout all this Butler made no effort whatsoever to assert his interests. Certainly, if he refused to serve Home he would have himself become Prime Minister. But he remained supine. As Powell later said, 'We handed him a loaded revolver and told him all he had to do was pull the trigger. He asked if it would make a noise and we said, "That is in the nature of guns, RAB." He asked if it would hurt and we said, "That too is in the nature of guns, RAB," and he said, "I don't think I will. D'you mind?" '[57]

Macleod had a slightly different metaphor, saying they had 'put the golden ball in his lap, if he drops it now it's his own fault.'

The previous afternoon Home had seen the Queen and undertaken to make inquiries about forming a government. He then saw Butler and offered him the Foreign Office, which Butler had coveted for years and which he accepted. Since Butler was willing to serve under Home, Maudling and Hailsham saw no bar to their doing so. Macleod and Powell, however, albeit politely, told Home that the manner of his appointment was such that they could not join a government headed by him.[58] So the two old Research Department colleagues marched off into the wilderness which they were to inhabit until Home lost the general election of 1964.

6

The Loner
1963-1970

We must regain, before the die is cast, the view
of those great simplicities in the light of which the
nation's decision ought to be taken. In saying to you,
and through you to the country: 'Vote, and vote Tory',
I have at least one accidental advantage. It is not
such as anyone would go looking for; but having it,
I claim the right to use it. I have no personal gain
to expect from the outcome, other than that of any
other citizen. I am not among those candidates at this
election who can look forward with assurance, or at
least with hope, to retaining or to achieving political
office under the Crown according as the result of the
election inclines one way or the other. Whatever might
have been obscure or undefined about the policies of
the Conservative Party, this at least has been made
crystal clear, over and over again, by the Leader of the
Party, that if there is a Conservative Government after
Thursday, I shall not be a member of it . . . Nor have I
received in the recent past from men who will form a
Conservative Cabinet even the ordinary loyalties and
courtesies that prevail generally between colleagues in
the same cause. Not for them to repudiate attacks upon
me which were unfounded, and which they knew to be
unfounded. Not for them to place upon my words and
arguments the more favourable, or the most obvious,
construction, or even to accept my own assertion of
my own meaning. Not for them to protest when in
the House of Commons language has been used about

189

me, and insults have been cast, the obscenity of which
has lowered the dignity of Parliament itself . . . On
Thursday your vote is about a Britain that, with all
its faults and failings, is still free, and great because it
is free. On Thursday your vote decides whether that
freedom shall survive or not. You dare not entrust it
to any government but a Conservative government.

> – *J. Enoch Powell, Wolverhampton, 16 June 1970.*

Then and since, great puzzlement was and has been expressed,
both by their admirers and by the wider audience of politicians
and commentators, over Macleod's and Powell's refusal to serve
in the government of Sir Alec Douglas-Home, as Lord Home
quickly became. The puzzlement arose, not simply because of
the refusal to serve – that was not unprecedented – but because
Butler himself took the Foreign Office from Home's hands. It
seemed quixotic to a degree to refuse office because a particular man did not become Leader when that man himself found
no difficulty in accepting it. For that reason it is important to
understand the thinking of the two men. Broadly speaking, it
was the same in both cases, but there were significant points
of difference which indicated different policies and different
objectives. Macleod unquestionably felt slighted that he had
not been consulted during the process by which Home emerged
and he had every reason to feel so, since he was both Leader of
the House of Commons and Joint Chairman of the Party: the
exclusion from consultation of a man holding both of these jobs
was tangible evidence that there was a plot afoot. Macleod was
a proud man, and the affront to his dignity alone might have
dictated a refusal.

There was no comparable affront to Powell. The constitution-
alist in him was angered by both Conservative reforms of the
House of Lords. The first occurred in 1958: the legislation enabled
the government of the day to create Life Peers. The second
reform which was passed in 1963 enabled hereditary peers to
disclaim their titles within nine months of succession. The most
notable beneficiary of the second measure was the second
Lord Stansgate, now Tony Benn. Subsequent beneficiaries
included the Earl of Home, Lord Hailsham. Powell was
amazed that Home should *want* to disclaim the earldom of
which he was the fourteenth holder. Like Macleod, he was
appalled at the public impression given that the Party had nobody

in the Commons thought fit to be Prime Minister.[1] Again, like Macleod, he thought it disgraceful that Butler should be passed over for the second time, but he had no such ties of friendship with and personal loyalty to Butler as bound Macleod, who observed later, 'Even if RAB was not going to be loyal to himself, I determined that I would be loyal to him.' Powell's regulation of his own conduct was determined by the fact that he had nailed his colours so firmly to Butler's mast, and told Home so with such definition, that he felt he could not join his government.

But there was another, and perhaps decisive, influence on both of them. That was the fact that there had been a conspiracy, and that conspiracy Powell in particular thought was corrupting. Though they agreed, just after Home kissed hands, that they would refrain from overt criticism, so as not to rock the boat of the new Prime Minister and not further to divide the Party, Macleod's temper snapped in January 1964 when Randolph Churchill's *The Fight for the Tory Leadership*, giving the Macmillan version of events ('the trailer for the screenplay of his memoirs', Macleod called it) was published. Through the good offices of its owner, the Tory backbencher Ian Gilmour, Macleod had become editor of the *Spectator*, and he took more than a page to savage Churchill's little volume. Afterwards Powell, who was to say nothing in any detail until much later (also in the *Spectator*), commented, 'I can confirm the accuracy of Mr. Macleod's narrative on all matters within my knowledge and I agree with his general assessment of these events.'[2]

The kernel of Macleod's case was that Macmillan's statement to the Queen (the details of which had been released to the Press and repeated in a speech by the Chief Whip, Martin Redmayne, on 25 October) about the views of the Cabinet members was false. The statement had said that the Cabinet members were 'overwhelmingly' for Home. But, as Macleod pointed out, that simply could not be true. At a lunch on 18 October five members of the Cabinet agreed that they were for candidates other than Home. Three members were not present – Butler himself was not there; neither was Hailsham (who was for himself or Butler), nor Edward Boyle (who was for Butler). There were half a dozen others but, as Macleod observes, 'Even if there wasn't a single one of these for Butler or Maudling or Hailsham, the figures in the book . . . are simply impossible.' Powell and Macleod, therefore, seeing that Butler was the victim of chicanery, took the most dramatic means available of registering their disapproval.

Out of office, however, Powell and Macleod, though they kept in reasonably close touch, took rather different courses. Macleod had the editorship of the *Spectator* as a platform from which to expound his own vision of Conservatism. This was not at all doctrinaire, for there was little enough that Macleod – who had resisted Amory's fairly serious, and Lloyd's belated, attempts to impose economic discipline – disagreed with the government about. He wanted, certainly, a heavier stress on the social services, but his principal crusade was the building of a classless Conservative Party. His review of Churchill's book had shown rage at the fact that the men who had manoeuvred the succession for Home (those he called 'the magic circle', in a phrase that was to become famous) were all from the same background: when he listed them in his review he added, to make his point, 'Eight of the nine mentioned in the last sentence went to Eton.' Macleod himself went to Fettes, a distinguished Scottish public school, but his own educational background did not free him from an animus more often found in people with fewer advantages than he himself had enjoyed. He was seen over the next year as embarking upon an effort to create a new kind of Tory Party, and to be staking out his claim to its leadership.

These things did not concern Powell. He merely resumed his life as it had been before he became Minister of Health in 1960, a mixture of scholarship and polemic. This time, though, the criticism of intellectual and political fashion was sharper and harsher than it had been before and, while he eschewed attacks on individuals, it was clear that he had little time for the policies which the Home government was pursuing. In previous periods on the backbenches he had shown at least some care for his future prospects and, while he was perfectly willing to rebel, he chose the subject of his rebellions with care: on one occasion, when the creation of the Central African Federation was being discussed (in 1953), he put away a prepared speech, because he felt that he had enough rebellions under way. After 1963, and even during his time as front bench spokesman on transport and then on defence (between 1964 and 1968) he seemed to care less and less about the susceptibilities of his colleagues.

The loners in politics, Michael Foot wrote, in a charming essay on Powell,[3] are:

. . . men and women who preferred to act alone in the last resort, who would always follow their own star or search out their own circuitous destiny, who, for whatever reason, would find the associations of party loyalty too insulting or irksome to bear.

He applied this general definition to Powell:

> Enoch Powell, it seems to me, has always been a loner – no doubt his old leader and eternal enemy, Edward Heath, would concur – but at once the assertion prompts some complicated questionings. He is also the strong upholder of party ties and traditions, the sworn enemy of coalitions in any shape and contrivance. He is, further, as anyone who has ever had any personal dealings with him will testify, the soul of honour and loyalty. No one so far as I know has ever accused him of a personal breach of trust . . .

Mr. Foot's final judgement is not one generally shared by those who have taken occasion to write or comment about Powell. More than a few of his old colleagues in the Conservative Party have been willing over the years to accuse him of deliberate bad faith. These accusations have usually arisen from a partially unconscious confusion of the interests of the Party with the interests of the country. When, for example, Anthony (now Lord) Barber, then Chancellor of the Exchequer, on the evening of the day on which he publicly dubbed Powell a 'frustrated fanatic'[4] called him, in conversation, a 'traitor', he was stating an opinion that he was a traitor to his party, and assuming that the ascription was justified. Barber did not, on this occasion at least, seem to understand that so strong a word can only properly be used of action against one's country, and cannot be taken as serious vilification of a man who happens to disagree on principle at a given moment with that partly accidental and partly self-interested conglomeration of individuals who make up a political party. Mr. Berkeley, who started his book from a moral position profoundly antipathetic to that of Powell, puts the matter altogether more sensibly when he writes:[5]

> Yet I have found it not only simpler, but more often factually correct, to assume political good faith unless the contrary can be directly proved. Powell has, on occasion, been prone to assume bad faith on the part of those who differ from him. To assume this of him, in return, will not necessarily give the seeker after a genuine understanding of his motives a clearer guide.

Before Mr. Foot wrote his essay he had had the experience of working with Powell as a House of Commons colleague on three issues of moment – the proposed reform of the House of Lords when Harold Wilson was Prime Minister, the matter of British entry into the European Economic Community when Edward Heath held that position, and the issue of the price to be paid in terms of the interests and desires of Ulster when James Callaghan was heading a ministry which survived from day to day only in the most parlous of fashions, and only by its willingness to make concessions to the Ulster Unionists, the Liberals and the Nationalists (Scottish and Welsh alike). Throughout these years the most delicate of manoeuvres were required on all sides. The most intricate of negotiations had to be entered into. The most absolute trust of one man in another had to be taken for granted; and nobody found that Powell was other than straightforward. Mr. Foot arrives at his judgement, therefore, out of experience. Mr. Berkeley arrives at his after much thought and reading. The judgement, however, is the same. It is a judgement that says little for the Conservative Party.

From October 1963 onwards it does seem perfectly clear that the Party – at least the Parliamentary Party – lost a good deal of Powell's allegiance, and lost it because of the way in which the succession to Macmillan was decided. The more cruel, the more determined and, even, the more reckless, note in the speeches made between 1963 and the general election of 1964 can be traced to disgust with what had been dishonourable conduct. The line of argument – especially on matters economic – had not changed, but the ferocity of expression could now much more readily be marked. On 28 January 1964 he described the policies of the government as 'hocus pocus'. On 3 April he denounced all attempts at regional planning as futile and attacked the Cabinet for 'cajoling particular firms and industries to establish themselves in places which they would not otherwise have chosen.' In the same speech he ridiculed attempts by the government to reduce unemployment in Scotland, and on 29 July he assaulted with scorn the notion – always popular in Conservative circles – that the activities of trade unions had anything to do with inflation.

Shortly after becoming Prime Minister, Home made an announcement on the date of the general election. Election speculation had reached fever point by the time of the succession. It is not common for parliaments to run the whole of their maximum five-year term, for doing so sharply reduces the room for manoeuvre available to the Prime Minister of the day. It deprives him of the highly considered opportunity of wrong-footing the Opposition, either – through the use of teasing hints about his intentions – forcing them to keep at full financial stretch for long periods in order to be ready, or by picking a moment when the Shadow Cabinet is unready. The ability to choose the date for electoral combat is, by the head of any majority government, a highly prized one. Moreover, Reginald Maudling, the Chancellor of the Exchequer, feared that the economy was overheating and that by the last possible moment – October 1964 – the Labour Party might well be able to make accusations of incompetence stick.

Home, however, thought differently. He dearly wanted, as he put it himself, time to play himself in. He felt, further, that the scandals of recent years, the abrupt departure of Macmillan, and the furious argument that accompanied his own appointment (including two refusals to serve) had left the Conservative Party in a depressed and confused state, and he needed time to lick his troops into shape. But he did accept that constant public discussion of his plans was also damaging, to his as yet uncertain standing and in the financial markets. He decided, therefore, to clear the air, and announced that the government would soldier on to the bitter end. This stilled all the talk, and somewhat steadied the situation, though it had the disadvantage of seeing the greater part of 1964 devoted to a protracted general election campaign, with the attendant dangers of public boredom and frustration.

Nationally the 1964 campaign was a 'backs to the wall' affair for the Prime Minister. Harold Wilson was seen as an exceptionally adroit Opposition leader, Home as a fumbling Prime Minister, unaccustomed, after all his years in the House of Lords, to the rough and tumble of electoral politics and wretchedly ill at ease over the whole range of domestic policy. The Tories did their best, none the less, to make a favourable contrast between their candidate's straightforwardness and dignity and Wilson's supposed wiliness. Certainly, there was a last-minute reluctance to trust Wilson who, as Maudling had feared, devoted most of his time to assaults on Conservative economic management, and particularly to exploiting the balance of payments deficit. Nor was Home's doughty rearguard action entirely in vain: he lost, but he held the Labour majority to a derisory four seats.

Powell's own campaign was interesting, but in the main uneventful. By now he had a headlock on Wolverhampton South-West, and he again recorded a slight increase in his majority. The campaign was notable, however, for the public predominance of immigration as an issue, at least in the Black Country. Powell, though he referred to the subject in his general election address, and had begun to write about it[6] was not, however, deeply involved in the efforts of a number of local Tories to force the issue into the public limelight and on the attention of the Party leadership: he did not, for example, attend a meeting on 23 July 1964 when a group of Northern MPs agreed to act in concert on immigration.[7] He was, none the less, kept well informed of their activities. The way in which the situation was developing was indicated by the fact that the Tories unexpectedly won two Midlands seats. The Shadow Foreign Secretary, Patrick Gordon-Walker, went down to Peter Griffiths in Smethwick and Wyndham Davies took Perry Barr with a majority of 327: both men consistently and intensely campaigned against further immigration. Feelings ran high, and tactics were not always seemly; the new Prime Minister, indeed, referred in the House on 3 November to Griffiths as a 'parliamentary leper'.

In the aftermath of the general election the positions of Macleod and Powell within the Party changed somewhat, as was to be seen the following year when Home stood down. The fact of the matter was that there was a distinct and substantial desire to blame both men for Home's defeat. Had he won – or at least won comfortably – he would have been able to ignore the two of them. Had he lost heavily – as had initially been expected – blame would have been more generally diffused, and while Macleod and Powell would have come in for some of it, most would have fallen on Home himself, and more on those who had chosen him as Leader. The narrowness of the defeat, however, and the admiration he had earned by his fight, meant that it was easy to focus on the most dramatic blow the government he headed had suffered, and that at the outset of his brief term.

But Home needed talent on a now badly shaken opposition front bench, and Powell and Macleod were among the finest debaters in the House of Commons as well as, outside it, being the two best public speakers in the Party. Home immediately invited them both to return, but with the proviso that they had to work their way back, starting on lower rungs of the ladder of preferment than they had occupied a year earlier. Powell's acceptance of the transport shadow portfolio caused general surprise. The question that excited much speculation, however, was why they decided to serve at all, having refused Home in 1963. The explanation both gave was that the objection then had been not to Home personally (Macleod had even told him that, had he been in the Commons, he would have been a strong candidate) but to the method of his emergence. Anyway, it was now plain that the furore raised over the circumstances of his appointment had excited great unease. Although three quarters of backbenchers polled by the *Sunday Times* on 7 January 1965 said they were happy for Home to continue as Leader, substantial sections of the Party had begun the hunt for a new man. Even more importantly – and certainly influenced by the stand Macleod and Powell had made in 1963 – an irresistible determination had arisen to ensure the election of the next Leader by secret ballot among Members of Parliament. The maverick backbencher Humphry Berkeley had long been the foremost intellectual champion of this move and, although he was later to leave the Party altogether,[8] few backbenchers have ever contributed more to changing the political direction of party and country than he: without a vote Edward Heath, the eventual successor, would still probably have beaten Maudling in 1965, but Margaret Thatcher would never have been chosen in 1975. In any event, Home gracefully agreed to set up a committee to study the method of choice. His growing band of supporters wanted him to put himself up under the new rules, whenever they were hammered out, for they were sure that, not least because of a tide of sentiment, he would emerge victorious. However, before the designated polling date of 26 July, he decided not to be a candidate, observing to a friend, no doubt taking account of an alternative suggestion that the new rules should come into effect only when he retired, 'If they want me I will remain Leader. But I don't want it badly enough to fight for it.' With him a political generation passed down from the peaks: the grandees were never again to hold sway in the Conservative Party.

This was all still some way into the future when Powell agreed to take transport as his subject in the new Parliament. But he made an important proviso. The idea had been gaining ground for some time (it was to take hold under Edward Heath and become dominant under Margaret Thatcher) that the members of the Shadow Cabinet should come under strict discipline. The demands of the modern age were so complicated, it was argued, and the difficulty for a man with only the Conservative Research Department behind him in taking on Ministers backed by a powerful civil service was so great that specialization should be the order of the day and the logic of that was – one Shadow, one subject. Powell demurred, and made his demurral clear to

Home who, unlike both of his successors, lacked an authoritarian personality and was ready enough to assent.

This was highly advantageous to Powell. He was determined intellectually to reconstruct the Conservative Party. He thought such a gigantic undertaking would take time, but he was convinced that there *was* time since, unlike a large number of his colleagues, he did not believe there would be an early return to office (and, of course, was proved right in that assumption in 1966). In such circumstances it was a considerable advantage to a man of his inclination, ability and industry to have a voice in the higher councils of the Party while being quite unrestrained in his exposition of new policies in the country. 'As a Tory,' he told Tyne Tees Television in March 1969, 'I have great respect for authority, for traditional instruments of authority. But intellectually speaking there is no such thing as authority. Someone may have the right to tell me to do something, but there cannot be authority for a view. You cannot have anyone else's ideas but your own – at least I can't.'

Powell was quickly, and characteristically, in action and ready, it was clear, to fire and fight on all cylinders and fronts. On 3 November 1964 in the *Financial Times* he attacked the government for its imposition of a fifteen per cent surcharge on imports, which was designed to correct the imbalance of payments. But he was not content with a narrow attack, such as his colleagues were all making. He stated his conviction that the real difficulty lay in the fact that the exchange rate was fixed by fiat of the government of the day and the Bank of England. He wanted to float the pound.[9] Under the fixed system, he argued, imports were cheap and exports hard to sell: the imbalance arising had to be paid for by borrowing or out of the reserves. The following day he was in his place in the House for his first appearance as transport spokesman: the government again came under fire, this time for refusing to continue the closure of unprofitable railway lines. On 13 November he was speaking in Trinity College, Dublin, denouncing the existing concept of the history of the British Empire and, essentially, continuing with the demolition work he had long been about. The economic attacks continued: on 21 November he again attacked Labour's adoption of emergency measures, but, significantly, added the sentence, 'They have adopted, with an attitude that can only be stigmatized as plagiarism, the assertions of their political opponents,' a judgement which was rightly considered by critics and colleagues to be an attack on the conduct of Treasury policy under Lloyd and

Maudling, for he also attacked an increase in Bank Rate and the adoption of an incomes policy. He supported Neil Marten (the MP for Banbury) in proposals to denationalize the state airlines and for good measure stated on 11 December that in making a start on denationalization his own favourite was the telephone service. In December, and again in January 1965, he voted against capital punishment (and in May he was to support a Bill to legalize homosexual conduct between consenting male adults in private).

The industry and the effervescence seemed endless, so much so that I am now giving only a partial list of his activities up to the election for the leadership in 26 July 1965. On 18 December 1964 he attacked a lack of professionalism in the Conservative organization in the country, saying, 'We have tolerated . . . a level of Party organization in the country which no management of a business enterprise would tolerate.' On 26 February, in *The Statist*, he was attacking current policy on the docks. In this he condemned the fact that dockland was nationalized, and called for denationalization:

> The incentive of so operating them as to make a profit for shareholders and to attract from the market new investment for expansion is wholly absent. Without a word of reproach to the respective authorities or their servants, their motives are, by definition, non-commercial.

To this he added an insertion that, in the political climate of opinion at the time, which held trade union practices to be wholly at fault in the decline of the docks, he knew would be intensely provocative:

> Let me not be misheard: I am not blaming or criticizing the workers or their trade unions or their 'unofficial' leaders. Given the legal and economic setting in which they live and work their actions and attitudes are natural, rational and indeed inevitable. Those who created and who maintain that legal and economic setting have no right to expect anything else: they have denied to the employee, as they have denied to the employer, the means and the incentive to use his efforts to best advantage.

On 21 April 1965 in the *Western Mail* he derided the worship of the export effort:

. . . let it be said quite firmly that exports are not in themselves 'a good thing'. They are a means to an end, and that end is importing: the only purpose of exports is to buy imports. (Incidentally overseas investment is only a method of buying imports in advance, and overseas expenditure, on garrisons, for instance, is as much an import as foreign holidays.)

On 6 May, in the *Glasgow Herald* the subject was steel, which the Labour government hoped to nationalize:[10]

Nationalisation used to be commended of yore on political, class-warfare grounds; it was to be an instrument in the transfer of power from one class to another. The criterion was not economic – whether capital and labour would be more productively employed. The criterion was political – whether one set of persons would be able to govern the lives of another set of persons.

On 9 May 1965, in an article in *New Society*, he laid siege to the whole concept of international aid (making it clear that the attack was on government to government aid, and not such voluntary resources as were raised by charities). Though it had many other facets, this argument rested upon two central points: first, that the use by governments of national resources in this way was a cheat upon the electorate; and second, that the assumption behind it was that states could decide better than the market what was the most efficient use of resources, an assertion that he had dismissed throughout his political life.

During all this time, of course, there was his work as transport spokesman, a directorship of the National Discount Company (which he was later to resign on the grounds of the board's co-operation with the government's incomes policies) and a host of other speeches, articles and essays as well as broadcasts, learned and polemical. There were, to take but two examples, a scholarly dissertation on the history of the institution of the Speakership of the House of Commons in the Winter 1964-5 issue of *Parliamentary Affairs*, in which he argued conclusively that there were at least two earlier Speakers than the fourteenth century Mr. Speaker Hungerford, who had generally been accepted as the first to hold the office; and a contribution to the July Festival of Birmingham University, in which he took a learned and strong line against then (and currently) fashionable notions for parliamentary reform, such as increased salaries for Members and a curtailment of the parliamentary timetable.

Colleagues and commentators alike looked upon this veritable plethora of activity with, in some cases, bewilderment, but in others growing irritation and even anger. To an increasing number of newspaper and magazine editors, as well as to radio and TV producers he was, of course, a delight – never late, always concise, and always provocative. The bewilderment arose from awe at his rate of output. But the irritation arose from the fact that almost every speech, however overtly directed against a Labour government, could be read in its parts as an attack on both the Home government and the Shadow Cabinet of which he was a member.

His tactical dilemma was acute. He had no personal base outside his constituency; his following in the House (at least of those who understood what he was saying) was minuscule; and the proliferation of the right wing and free market think tanks which were of such value to Mrs. Thatcher when she became Leader in 1975 did not exist: even the subsequently famous (and influential) Institute of Economic Affairs was in its infancy. Though Powell retained excellent relations with the IEA and its founders, Ralph Harris[11] and Arthur Seldon, and contributed, in 1964, an essay to their volume *The Rebirth of Britain*, they were not yet prominent enough to be of major help to him. Of course, the desire to cover the whole spectrum of politics was one that came out of his personality; it is also necessary to recognize that, given his commitment to re-educating the Party (and the nation) he simply had to be in constant intellectual movement, constantly in the public eye, constantly on the attack. And he was fortunate that he had just the right inclination and just the right qualities for his task.

He faced several difficulties with the Conservative Party. It is not an intellectual organization and, for all his gift for the flashing phrase, Powell is essentially an intellectual. Then, while all but a very few Tories would agree that (certainly on economic matters and such branches of them as nationalization) there was a lot in what he said, they did not want to go all the way with him, for most Tories are unadventurous people. Finally, the Party sets great store by at least declared loyalty to the current Leader (whatever may be going on in private) and it was becoming all too apparent that Powell was not, in the generally understood sense, loyal. None the less, for all these problems, his reputation continued to grow, and he was now mature as a politician in a way he had not been in his previous periods out of office.

For the summer 1965 issue of the *Swinton College Journal* he prepared an article – 'The consequences of the general election' – which was, in effect, a summation of all he had been arguing in the frenetic months since the defeat in October 1964. The opening passages take up what has been a favourite theme of his over the years, and an amplified version of it as it applies to individual Ministers can be found in one of his books.[12] The theme is that continuity of the same party in office inhibits the quality of creative action and that a break with office, whatever gloom it may cause for the moment, in fact offers a splendid opportunity for re-evaluation. This conviction enabled him to argue to the (mainly young) readers of the *Journal* that there were sound historical and logical reasons for making a break with the thirteen years of Tory government from 1951:

> . . . the continuing chain of responsibility which had stretched through without a break from November 1951 to October 1964 was broken. It is a consequence, and a necessary consequence of the principle of collective Cabinet responsibility, that as long as one government of the same party succeeds another, nothing which has been done or said during the whole of the lengthy period can ever explicitly be disavowed or even criticized.

But, of course, in a period as long as thirteen years problems do change, and previous words and commitments become oppressive, a process which 'was immensely accelerated in the last three years before the election'. He goes on to say that only absence from office can enable a party to find a new position, not necessarily a 'novel' position but 'that position which we should wish to occupy and which we should wish to commend to our countrymen whatever was said and done at any particular point in the past.'

He goes on to argue that on several matters of attitude and policy – the British concept of the history of Empire is the most stressed – it is now possible to reconsider what has hitherto been held to be true. He rehearses his argument that the post-war British malaise is due to an entirely incorrect understanding of imperial history and that it can now be shrugged off, because there is no Empire. There are then two highly important passages which show exactly the state of his thinking about the future:

What sort of achievement in the modern world is there for Britain? I can only see one answer myself: it must consist of the exploration and exploitation of what we have in these islands, and what we can make the rest of the world want from us in terms of goods, services and ideas.

But

I confess I am driving blind. I don't know what, if any, would be the practical outcome of thinking and arguing this way. I don't know whether it is in the stars that we shall be able to regain a sense of achievement and self-confidence, a picture of the place of this country in the world which will give us as great a self-respect as we enjoyed in the past. But there are times in the lives of parties and persons when they have to drive blind, leaving the rest to time and other forces.

That was the general statement of the credo evolved by the middle of 1965, a mixture of intellectual daring, of provocation (for political parties are prone indeed to resent proposals which suggest abandoning what they have said and done) and of that fatalism which has always been an important part of Powell's make-up.

On one other important issue, that of immigration – which I will consider more fully later in this chapter and where I will group together in sequence the evolution of the subject so far as it concerns Powell's career – there were changes of stance within the Shadow Cabinet and, later, in Conservative policy. Upon his defeat Home had appointed Powell's old chief, Peter Thorneycroft, as Shadow Home Secretary. There being, after the election, considerable agitation on the backbenches over immigration (some of it, no doubt, unprincipled and influenced by the startling electoral successes of Peter Griffiths and Wyndham Davies, but some of it unquestionably reflecting the honest concern of members who saw – and whose constituents saw – steady change in the composition of whole areas) Thorneycroft took up the cudgels. He urged, with the support of Powell, but against the opposition of both Boyle and Macleod, the adoption of a policy of stern controls on immigration. Very largely under Powell's direct influence, Home himself made a speech along these lines on 3 February in Hampstead. Among other recommendations the Leader of the Opposition advocated assisted repatriation and the vigorous pursuit of illegal immigrants. On 2 March a motion sponsored by Sir Cyril Osborne was debated in the House. Osborne had long wanted draconian immigration curbs, and had advocated as much in the 1958-9 session of Parliament, when Powell declined to help him raise the issue.[13] Under gentle pressure from Thorneycroft the original terms of the motion were somewhat modified, but proposals for the deportation of illegal immigrants remained. In the division 162 Conservative Members, including Powell, voted to support Osborne. Three days later, speaking at the Conservative Central Council, Thorneycroft made a speech in very similar terms, the main emphasis of which was on the desirability of a complete cessation of mass immigration. He delivered the same message to the Conservative Parliamentary Committee on Home Affairs on 15 March and, again, in a parliamentary debate on 23 March which the House debated under the shadow of the proposed Race Relations Bill, designed to place legal curbs on racial discrimination. Thorneycroft opposed the Bill, but he did so – and persuaded his colleagues to agree with him – by way of reasoned amendment, a parliamentary device by which criticism of a proposed measure may be made, without the obligation of outright opposition to it. Throughout May and June policy and rhetoric continued to develop in the direction of further controls. For the most part Powell was content to follow Thorneycroft's lead, but on 21 May he made his strongest speech yet (to the women's branch of his constituency Association). This speech marked an important turning point. Whereas the anti-immigration argument had hitherto been put for the most part by reference to the prospect of increases in residential numbers through fresh immigration, he now pointed to the dangers of the natural increase of those already in Britain.

However, the whole debate – in which evident public concern, and the willingness of some prominent Tory politicians to consider further curbs, had alarmed left and liberal opinion – had yet to attain focus and definition. More urgent for Powell was a practical test at hand. Home having stood down, the election for the new Leader was to take place on 26 July, with a provision for a further ballot a week later if no candidate had a clear majority. Powell had to decide whether he would stand. He had been for some time inclined to do so.

The principal candidates were agreed to be Maudling and Edward Heath, who had emerged from silent obscurity as Macmillan's Chief Whip (it is a parliamentary convention that Whips do not speak in the House of Commons)[14] through his abortive negotiations to join the EEC and a brief period of glory as Home's Secretary of State for Trade, Industry and the Regions. Maudling was emollient in manner and conduct, Heath aggressive and (in a fashionable word of the day) abrasive. So far as these two men were concerned, the parliamentary Party was being offered a choice less of substance than of style, though it is fair to say that, at the time, Heath was more inclined to favour at least a version of the economic policies that Powell was setting out on his political market stall than was Maudling.

It was reasonably certain that one of these two would win: Heath seemed to have more support in the House (and benefited from a high octane campaign waged by his young lieutenant, Peter Walker), while Maudling, if the opinion polls were to be trusted, was the choice of the country. MPs, of course, might well, against their own preference, vote for him for that reason as a potential election winner.

Macleod flirted with a challenge, but only briefly. He was going through one of his periods of poor health at the time, his life, which was sadly truncated in 1970, having constantly been dogged by the pain of an old war wound aggravated by arthritis. He consulted his friends, and the conclusion all came to was that the hostility his African decolonization programme had excited, the continuing reverberations from his refusal to serve Home in 1963, and the unpopularity of his position on immigration and social affairs, would render his vote derisory. He announced that he would not be a candidate.

As had happened before, Macleod and Powell were in similar and yet dissimilar positions. Macleod did not stand because he saw no chance of winning; it was as simple as that. If there had been a prospect of victory, he would have relished a battle. There being none he saw no point in putting down a marker or making a gesture. Powell, like Macleod, did not seriously entertain the thought of becoming Leader at that point. But he did think that he had a certain duty to the ideas he had been so vigorously expounding. It was not quite enough simply to go on in the role of the philosopher-king of his Party when there was a litmus paper test of how much support his views actually enjoyed. Most of his friends – and particularly Nicholas Ridley, the Member for Cirencester and Tewkesbury, who was later to hold middle level office under Edward Heath, to leave the Heath government with acrimony on both sides, and to return to high office under Margaret Thatcher – thought his hardening determination to stand unwise. He had – so their case ran – a position which enjoyed growing respect in both Party and country. He was, to many, an enigma. People puzzled over what sort of political animal he really was, and puzzled over his views. Being enigmatic, and, apparently, above the mundane struggles for personal power which are a large part of day to day politics, was a distinct advantage and one which he should not waste. If he scored badly in an election he would lose advantage. He thought, and decided, none the less, to put the matter to the touch, 'to leave my visiting card', as he put it.

At 2.15 p.m. on Tuesday, 26 July 1965 the result of a poll of 298 Conservative MPs was announced. Heath had garnered 150 votes, Maudling (who had fully expected to win) 133. Powell rounded up fifteen, of whom, after this passage of time, we can identify only nine – John Biffen, John Hay, Bernard Braine, Thomas Galbraith, Edith Pitt (his old friend from West Midlands and Ministry of Health days), Michael Alison, Nicholas Ridley, John Vaughan-Morgan and Harry d'Avigdor Goldsmid. Maudling could have forced a second ballot since Heath had not gained the required fifty per cent plus one of those entitled to vote, that is all Conservative Members of Parliament. Nevertheless he and Powell immediately acknowledged Heath as Leader.

The view of the Press was summed up by Alan Watkins, who wrote in the *Spectator* on 30 July that no longer 'can Powell's speeches be written up as if they represent the views of any significant group within the Conservative Party. No longer can he be described as the Tory equivalent of Aneurin Bevan:[15] for Bevan, despite his distaste for machine politics, never polled as badly as Mr. Powell did on Tuesday . . .' Watkins was later to make amends, after the Conservative Party Conference in October when he wrote, 'Powell is no more than a stimulating theorist. But the reception he evoked at the Tory Conference will not have escaped Mr. Heath. He remains a potential threat to Tory unity.' And, rather more significantly, Macleod had his say as well. Just before the leadership election Powell had produced his first volume of speeches, *A Nation Not Afraid*. Macleod reviewed it in the *Spectator* on 16 July and concluded that 'Powellism is gaining converts every day. Much of our programme when the general election comes will be based on his ideas.'

'Nothing,' Powell says, 'is predictable in politics. There is no profession which is so unpredictable in its twists and turns.'

After 26 July Heath began immediately to make his Shadow Cabinet dispositions. He created the new post of Deputy Leader, for Maudling, and made Macleod Shadow Chancellor. Powell, suddenly in the position of being written off as 'no more than a stimulating theorist' could have expected little, for his evidently thin support meant that Heath had no obligation to conciliate him, or recognize his force. However, when the new Leader saw Powell he simply asked him what position of those available he would prefer. Powell replied quickly 'Defence', and emerged from the meeting as Shadow Secretary of State for Defence. 'I don't know quite why I asked Ted for Defence,' he says now. 'I had always of course, been concerned with the subject. But now, and upon reflection, I think I had been almost subconsciously thinking of it more and more over a period of time before I saw him. He could not have given me greater satisfaction.' It is one of the supreme ironies of modern British political history that of these two men who were later to be locked in mortal political battle for six years, one was first to make the other Prime Minister and then destroy him who had given him such satisfaction immediately after what was widely regarded as a humiliation.

The Powell appointment was regarded as the most surprising of what was pleasurably accepted, by Party and Press alike, as a strikingly imaginative Shadow Cabinet reconstruction. Continuity was preserved in that Sir Alec Douglas-Home became Shadow Foreign Secretary, and intellectual *élan* was demonstrated by the movement upwards of Macleod and Powell. The new Leader was widely welcomed as a man of the future, something of a technocrat, having less of that personal appeal about him than the Tory Party likes in its Leaders,[16] perhaps, but a man of vision none the less, a harbinger of a future of national achievement. For a brief time the leadership was a happy band of brothers.

There were reasons why it all did not, in general, last; and there were also particular reasons related to Powell. That he was at the centre of coming storms was much influenced by his personality, but the storms were general rather than particular. They derived largely from a confusion in the Conservative Party over what it was about (apart simply from holding office), which confusion in turn derived from a post-imperial attitude of mind. Powell had for years been trying to work out the consequence to the sense of national identity of victory in a major war in Europe which was combined with the loss of most of the Empire. He would be the last man to pretend that he had always got the right solution to the problem, for he was discussing himself as much as he was discussing the nation. That discussion, however personally expressed in speeches, was never egotistical, in the sense of being arrogant. Identification mattered to him; but so did accurate appreciation of immanent reality. The way in which he tried, however, not merely to commune with himself in his study ('Daddy's room'),[17] but with every audience to which he spoke, to define problems and seek, if not immediate answers, then, at least, serious ones is, even now, an important part of his character. In July 1965 he was given an opportunity by Edward Heath to state his view on what was becoming so increasingly important to him – how best to defend an island lying off the coast of Europe. He had, in his political as well as his military thinking, retrenched.

Edward Heath was an equally unfamiliar animal to the Conservative Party at the time. Powell could, most certainly, have rallied the dignified infantry of those who would preserve Empire in its tattered shreds behind him, but saw that it *should* not be so. Heath had neither experience of service in the Empire (though he later took a serious and dedicated interest in its residuals) nor any emotional feelings about it. While his book about his travels, amiably guyed by his friend James Prior,[18] and suggesting his internationalism, arrived late in life, and concerned only the country he was in, the fact was that as a child before the war, as an artillery Major during the war, and as the Conservative candidate for Bexley after the war what influenced Heath most was 'sitting on the cliffs and looking over to Calais'.[19]

There is some dispute about the degree to which Heath was willing to allow Powell the kind of latitude he had enjoyed under Home. Certainly, Powell indicated to the new Leader that he intended to go on speaking his mind on as various a range of political topics as before and certainly, at the outset at least, Heath did not attempt to stop him. But it was also the case that Heath intended to take several steps further the process by which, as I have already mentioned,[20] Shadow Cabinet responsibilities were becoming more rigidly compartmentalized. 'Ted as official man', as Powell puts it, intended the Shadow Cabinet, in earlier years, and still in strict theoretical parlance called 'the Leader's Advisory Committee', to be just that, with each front bench speaker concentrating on one government department and one Minister. He had (as he was particularly to show when he became Prime Minister) an intense interest in the machinery of government. He took a rigidly bureaucratic attitude to politics and liked things neatly regimented according to the old housekeeping notion of 'a place for everything and everything in its place.' With one exception – that of the desirability of British membership of the EEC – he possessed no burning conviction about the rightness of one policy rather than another. The procedure he favoured was the exhaustive examination of every option, the choosing of one and, finally, the devotion of immense energy to the administration of that option.

Again, apart from the EEC, there was very little of the intuitive or romantic about him. His attitude to politics was, indeed, as is the case with most politicians, a reflection of his attitude to his personal life. I recall, for example, a meeting in his chambers at Albany convened to discuss his general conduct of that twice weekly gladiatorial combat decorously called 'Questions to the Prime Minister.' When we [21] assembled he was studying a selection of cuff links neatly laid out on his coffee table. He was considering which pair or pairs he should buy, and everybody's advice was sought on the matter. Those who sailed with him – these were the great sailing days which culminated in his remarkable triumph in the Sydney to Hobart Admiral's Cup yacht race – frequently commented on his fanatical, but mechanistic, obsession with detail. He set up a great network of committees, involving the recruitment of an army of experts who were not politicians, to scrutinize every facet of British government, and slowly and laboriously built their conclusions into the programme of what he proudly declared to be 'the best prepared Opposition for government of modern times'.[22] He had an unforced contempt for the Prime Minister, Harold Wilson, whose skill at political manoeuvre was already legendary, for he regarded him as incurably light-minded and frivolous. And finally, in spite of having been a Chief Whip, and one who, in the aftermath of the Suez fiasco, had performed brilliantly, he constantly evinced impatience and irritation with the (to him) inefficient meanderings of parliamentary procedure.

Powell was unlikely to get along very well for very long with such a man. However, at the beginning there were certain points of congruence between them. Most important was the fact that both men were concerned with the re-appraisal of policy over its whole range. They were both concerned with the questioning of encrusted assumptions about national affairs, about British power, about British responsibilities and about the life of the nation. Then, again, both had already arrived at the conclusion that the state should begin to retreat from its expanding control over, and interference with, the individual's conduct of his or her own affairs. Both believed, as Heath was to put it in his speech to the first Party Conference held after the 1970 general election, that there should be 'less government, and of a better quality'. And both had a considerable suspicion of the modern Commonwealth, believing, as Heath put it in that same 1970 speech, that 'The Commonwealth can only thrive . . . if all its members realize that Britain, like themselves, enjoys full independence of action.' Powell would have gone further than Heath in criticism of the Commonwealth, but the emphasis on British independence was wholly palatable to him.

Thus, if the two men were never likely to become close, there was a definite prospect of a fruitful partnership and Heath, after all, had been more than willing to accede to Powell's desire for the defence portfolio since that was one area in which, he was convinced, serious re-examination was required. Powell had two months to prepare for his debut in his new job, at the Party Conference in Brighton, but he did not spend them solely in contemplation of what he was going to say. There was the annual family holiday, the unceasing oratorical round and, in September, first of all in *History Today* and then in the Wolverhampton *Express and Star*, a piece of pure scholarship, 'Riddle of a King's Tomb', in which he set out his conviction that the tomb in the parish church at King's Langley, Hertfordshire, had been designed to hold the mortal remains of Richard II. He clearly did not intend his new responsibility to bear so heavily upon him as to involve the curtailment of his other interests.

Powell prepared his Conference speech with what was, even for him, unusual care. There were two aspects of defence policy where his views were likely to excite controversy – the proper extent of British overseas military responsibilities and the desirability or otherwise of the continued possession by the United Kingdom of an independent nuclear weapon. His sceptical attitude to the retention of British troops in places as far flung as Malaysia and Singapore was fairly widely known; his doubts about the efficacy of the nuclear deterrent much less so. Both were critical issues so far as Conservative sentiment was concerned. The East of Suez (as it was generally called) military capability (and responsibility) was an article of faith with most Tories, who saw in it a worthy and worthwhile continuation of the imperial past. The nuclear deterrent had been an important bone of contention during the 1964 general election campaign, Home vigorously asserting its necessity while Harold

Wilson (whose Labour Party then as now had, if not a majority then at least a substantial number of supporters addicted to the principle of unilateral nuclear disarmament) derided it.[23] Powell decided that at Brighton he would fight on only one front, but he did take the trouble to show his text to the Shadow Foreign Secretary, Alec Douglas-Home, who passed it fit for Party consumption.

Powell began both by expressing his delight with his appointment and referring in a slighting and even flippant fashion to his previous appearances as Health Minister at earlier Conferences. While immensely proud of his time at the Department of Health, Powell never cared much for the ordeal of performing before assemblies of the Party faithful. He observed that it had been 'a number of years since I have had the opportunity to address this conference on any subject more important than the supply of wigs and teeth to foreigners under the NHS . . .' He came immediately to the central core of his argument, the belief that 'Whatever obligations and commitments we have . . . the ultimate reason and the ultimate justification for those commitments is that we hold them to be necessary or advantageous for the defence of the United Kingdom.' He stressed that Britain was above all a European power, 'Therefore an alliance which can successfully defend Western Europe against attack from the East . . . is central to our defence policy.' He committed himself to the policy of an independent nuclear weapon. Then he began to move into dangerous waters.

International trade was essential to the economic life of Britain, he said, but went on to decry the belief that the nexus of British trade was dependent on global military effort for 'Nations, competitors of ours, which depend equally or more on trade, have outstripped our own performance without any military presence in the areas from which their raw materials are derived or in those where their principal markets are situated.'

Step by step he stripped bare the illusions that dominated the minds of the vast majority of his audience. He admitted the dangers posed to Western interests by the existence of the Russian and Chinese 'Empires', dominated as they were by the doctrine of Communism – though he was also careful to say that, Communism being a theory, 'you do not shoot theories with bullets.' But, he went on to argue, the fact of the matter was that the United Kingdom simply no longer possessed the resources necessary to play a significant part in the containment of the two empires. However desirable such containment might, in the abstract, be considered to be 'we should still have to measure the practical effect of British military effort against the size of the resources it demands and the consequences of diverting them from other pressing uses . . .' He mentioned the existence of antagonism between the USSR and China and concluded that the future would be 'fixed by a balance of forces which will itself be Asiatic and African'. The emergence of such a balance, he predicted, might well be hindered rather than helped by Western military intervention, while such intervention would inhibit or at least constrict the essential concentration of effort on the defence of Western Europe, which defence was a vital interest for the security of the United Kingdom itself.

It is often the case that the importance of a speech – even, frequently, its very content – is not apparent at the moment of delivery. Powell had, as ever, shown panache and intensity in his delivery. He captured his audience more by his manner than his matter, and was applauded with enthusiasm. By the following day, however, the message had sunk in.

One MP, Aidan Crawley, formerly of the Labour Party, and an enthusiast for what remained of the old imperial network, went so far as to call for his resignation. Many others made angry and worried representations to Home and Heath. While Home defended Powell to an excited backbench audience, he qualified the Brighton speech to some extent, laying stress on his own acceptance of existing British responsibilities overseas. But the Press, of course – even those parts of it in sympathy with the general Powell thesis – fell with delight on the spectacle of Party division, as it always does. Powell offered a partial restatement of his views in *The Daily Telegraph* on 5 December in an impenetrable review of a book by General Andre Beaufre, who had been the senior French commander at Suez. Here he even went so far as to question excessive reliance on nuclear deterrence, though within the protective penumbra of a call for more conventional resources and particularly for the strengthening of the Territorial Army, always a safe subject with Conservative audiences. None the less, the independence of his views, even where they did not, strictly speaking, differ from those of the leadership generally, excited attention. Thus, for example, the Shadow Cabinet was moving carefully towards what was intended to be a major revision of trade union legislation, one which would remove many of the immunities which the unions had enjoyed since early in the century. There were two reasons for wanting revisionary laws. The first (and to Heath the more important) was based on the belief that over-mighty unions, with their insistence on high wage settlements, were stoking up inflation. The second was the spreading rash of intimidation by shop stewards: this provoked great public unease and was, tactically as well as in principle, an excellent subject to be taken up by an Opposition facing a governing party in thrall to the unions and financially very largely dependent on them. For this second reason Powell could readily go along with the proposals being formulated. The first, however, he derided. Most particularly, in a speech at Streatley on 15 March he stressed that intimidation was the crucial consideration and that the law would have to be changed because the 1906 Act (the essential charter of trade unionism) permitted picketing which was 'intimidation by all means short of personal violence'. What Heath, Macleod and Maudling all resented, however, was the exclusive stress on intimidation. When Angus Maude, the Opposition spokesman on aviation, uttered very similar sentiments in the *Spectator* and *Encounter* in January 1966, Heath instantly dismissed him from the front bench. Though the matter cannot be proved (at least until the publication of Heath's own memoirs) this was widely interpreted as a warning to Powell.

His potential for aggravation was all the more important because of the imminence of a general election. Wilson was finding it extremely difficult to govern with his vestigial majority, and repeatedly gave its size as the excuse for not proceeding with the supposedly more radical elements of Labour policy. One of the government's major commitments, for example, was to nationalize the steel industry. To this plan the Conservative and Liberal parties were implacably opposed. But so were two of the government's own backbenchers, the late Desmond Donnelly and Woodrow (now Lord) Wyatt. The legislation could not, therefore, be proceeded with. Since steel nationalization was a cause inexpressibly close to the hearts of the vast majority of Labour Members and followers, and since the major trade unions were constantly pressing for it, the Prime Minister was continually urged from all sides to go back to the country for a fresh mandate. It was widely (and, as the event showed, correctly) felt that he would get it, but he had to choose his moment with care. The unveiling of Labour's economic plans had caused a serious outflow of sterling and the Tories worked might and main to convince the electorate of the inherent irresponsibility of the Cabinet and to warn of the approaching devaluation of sterling (which came about in 1967). Wilson's line was to insist that his troubles were caused by thirteen years of Conservative misrule: this, however, was a wasting asset, and he could not afford to hang on until it was altogether dissipated. On the other hand, he had to wait long enough for a sufficient head of steam to build up behind the notion that it would be right and proper for the country, having installed him, to give him the tools to finish the job. Another advantage which he enjoyed was that of Heath's inexperience; this advantage would wither in time, but its life was prolonged by his own near-perfect mastery of the House of Commons, and his opponent's woodenness as a communicator.

Powell continued as though oblivious to these considerations. Just as during the last months of the Home leadership he went about his business in his own way, not seeming to care that his shafts struck friend as often and with as much force as they struck foe. While it is true that scorn of incomes policies, voluntary or compulsory, was one thing that united him to Heath, the fact was that the Deputy Leader, Reginald Maudling, had operated such a policy. He was not best pleased when Powell, speaking to the Manchester Statistical Society on 12 January, scorned the notion that an incomes policy was required both to restrain trade unions and to avert the potential damage of their actions to the balance of payments. He attacked, further, the notion that such policies were required to keep unemployment down. There was no necessity, even, to worry about the effect of union action on inflation. He scorned a recent suggestion by Maudling that government should negotiate a wages restraint deal with the unions (a suggestion that made up an important strand of Conservative thinking until the advent of Mrs. Thatcher). Two days later, at Cambourne, he launched a wide-ranging attack on Britain's problems. He attacked the Commonwealth, and the idea (first put forward by India, but topical because of the recent independence of Guyana) that republics could, or should, remain within the organization.

Most interestingly in many respects he struck a pose for himself as the spokesman of ordinary people, something that he was increasingly to do in the years ahead. The thesis was that the British people were becoming more and more disillusioned, and rightly so, with the Commonwealth. The principal reasons for this disillusion were the frequently expressed hostility of Commonwealth countries to Britain, immigration ('a visible menace now for a decade . . .'), the amount of aid Britain gave to

Commonwealth countries, and the fact that British membership inhibited policy towards Rhodesia.

On the subject of Rhodesia he was on tricky, if potentially fruitful, ground. There was a great deal of sentiment for Rhodesia, then under exclusively white government, on the right wing of the Conservative Party. Heath and Home (with, in the House of Lords, Lord Carrington, the Tory Leader there) were to struggle for years to maintain a bipartisan approach to the subject, agreeing with Wilson (and with Commonwealth opinion, which Powell so despised) that independence could not be granted before satisfactory provisions were made for participation in the political process by the black population. Of the various principles laid down, all of which had to be satisfied before independence could be negotiated, the one that came to assume most importance in international opinion went under the convenient acronym NIBMAR – no independence before majority rule. Later in the year, when the Salisbury government led by Ian Smith declared independence unilaterally, the pace hotted up, and successive governments, Labour and Conservative, joined in half-heartedly applied sanctions against Smith. This led to ever fiercer (and well-organized) support for Smith from the right, a support that, to a degree, coalesced around the figure of the ageing Marquis of Salisbury (him who resigned from the Macmillan government over the release of Archbishop Makarios of Cyprus).[24] These men and women began to look with increasing favour on Powell, though it was not until he left the Shadow Cabinet in 1968 that he began openly to advocate recognition of independence without strings. He did so on the typically unsentimental grounds that Britain had no real power to influence the situation anyway, and not in deference to the blood ties which existed with the white community. In 1966, however, his principal argument, at Cambourne and elsewhere, was the unacceptability of the proposition that to deal with Smith would break up the Commonwealth: this he held to be an unacceptable limitation on Britain's independent right to make her own foreign policy.

On 28 January, in Birmingham, he was back in Maudling and Macleod territory, arguing that concern for the balance of payments was the result of an 'hallucination'. Maudling, who had more than once complained to Heath about Powell's transgression of the supposed rules of Shadow Cabinet solidarity, now renewed the complaint, this time supported by Macleod. Heath decided to stay his hand: he had, apparently, no desire to provoke a confrontation with Powell when a general election was, clearly, close. He even, on 11 March 1966, uttered some wan words in praise of Powell for the fashion in which he stimulated debate.

As might be expected, moreover, Powell was, at least in terms of industry, doing a meticulous job with the defence portfolio. On the whole he was successful in shading, if not entirely concealing, his reservations about the independent deterrent. Here he was helped by the government's decision to cut spending on conventional defence and, in particular, to cancel the development of the low level strike aircraft TSR2 and cut the Territorial Army budget to the bone. In such circumstances it was easy to guy the failure of Ministers to keep their promise to absorb British warheads in an Atlantic Nuclear Force and deplore their neglect of conventional defence capability. The first shots of the New Year on these subjects he fired at Harrow on 24 January. But on 17 February, in *The Listener*, replying to a diptych of talks by Lord Chalfont, Labour's Minister for Disarmament and formerly a regular soldier, and *The Times* defence correspondent Alun Gwynne-Jones, he began to outline the shape of his non-nuclear hypothesis. Essentially he was concerned to stress the possibility of a conventional war between nuclear powers in which nuclear weapons were not used, but he was equally anxious to make the point that the strongest power in the world, the United States, embedded in the quagmire of Vietnam, could not, for various reasons of inhibition, extricate herself by the use of nuclear armaments:

I admit that in each individual case it is possible by special pleading to explain why the existence of nuclear weapons neither prevented the conflict from breaking into violence nor yet caused it to escalate into the nuclear dimension. Nevertheless, looking at the picture as a whole, it becomes increasingly difficult to sustain with any conviction propositions which have been widely, if not dogmatically, held to be self-evident at various times during the last twenty years. There was the proposition, so memorably enshrined in the opening of the British Defence White Paper of 1958, that 'the world today is poised between the hope of total peace and the fear of total war', in other words that there could be no war that was not total, that is nuclear.

He pointed out that the so-called 'tripwire' strategy of the 1958 White Paper (according to which a conventional Soviet incursion into Western Europe would trigger a nuclear response) had been abandoned as unbelievable, and he doubted that, even before Russia's possession of nuclear weapons, the fact that the Western allies had them had been the crucial factor deterring a move in the European Central Region:

> Perhaps after all in 1949-50 the Alliance halted Russian penetration of Western Europe simply because the Russians then concluded that further forcible advance involved the risk of war with the United States and Britain and did not sufficiently like the look of it.

Even this relatively tentative questioning of nuclear strategy was heady stuff coming from a Conservative spokesman, for the Party generally took the independent deterrent to be not merely the symbol but the very stuff of national virility. However, Powell's almost philosophical balancing of hypotheses was well above the heads of most of those who would have been outraged at an unequivocal statement of his views. He was on much safer ground when, on 25 February 1966, he launched a full-blooded attack on the Defence Estimates (which included a projection of expenditure to 1970). The essential thesis was that the projection was 'another triumph in the art of optical illusion', the point being that, given the retrenchment forced on the government in 1964, the commitment to fixed spending would prove impossible to attain. Privately, Powell was the reverse of unhappy at some parts of the policy of the Secretary of State for Defence, Denis Healey, notably the abandonment of the British position in Aden. But for the defence debate of 7-8 March he was compelled by his colleagues (the speech was discussed carefully in the Shadow Cabinet) to attack the withdrawal from Aden, not greatly to his comfort.

There was, however, another aspect of his handling of his brief up to and during the election campaign which ended on 31 March, which caused increasing disquiet among his colleagues and excited vehement Labour opposition. This was the emergence of his latent and deep suspicion of the United States. He had already turned a deaf ear to suggestions that he visit America, itself regarded as extraordinary conduct for a Conservative Shadow Minister of Defence.[25] In the defence debate on 15 February, indeed, he attacked Healey's recent frequent visits across the Atlantic, finding it '. . . rather curious that the Secretary for Defence has to go to the United States twice within three weeks in order to see if it is O.K. before decisions are taken and announced [to the House of Commons] . . .' Here, of course, it was constitutional impropriety as much as excessive dependence on the Americans which outraged him, and he was reflecting not only his own feelings but those of his Leader. Heath, with his intense European concerns, knew that France was suspicious of the so-called special relationship between Britain and the USA and was more than willing to end the tradition of cosy amiability that had in general (with the exception of Eden) marked relationships between post-war Presidents and Prime Ministers. After 1970, indeed, relations between London and Washington were to be at their coolest since Suez.

It was an aspect of those relations which put Powell on front pages during the election campaign, the only occasion on which he was to achieve prominence. This was in spite of the fact that his industry was, even by his standards, exceptional, extending outside his constituency to sometimes as many as eight speeches a day. There was not, understandably, a great deal of variation in this prodigious output, and to make matters manageable, he chose a central theme, the value of sterling, with only a few diversions into non-economic subjects. Sound money had ever been a fundamental preoccupation of his and, indeed, all his assaults on the economic policies of the government had centred around the necessity of correctly valuing the currency, the solidity of the value of which could only, in his view, be achieved through the operation of a free market in which government was neither interfering with industry nor tinkering with the exchange rate. Still, important as this central theme undoubtedly was, it was not the stuff of exciting debate on the hustings.

The trouble was that the campaign of 1966 was irretrievably a dull one, and nothing even the most talented of orators did could for long distract attention from the spectacle of the fortunes of the two actors at the centre of a dull three-week drama – the cocky, but sober-sided Wilson asking for a majority with which he could govern, and the helpless and flat-footed Heath (who was, however, to redeem his reputation with a television broadcast of great dignity and certainty in the closing days, even when he knew in his bones that he had lost) whose agony attracted comment that often verged on the sadistic. Nobody doubted that the electorate would give Wilson his mandate, and commentators and public alike had yet to see such extraordinary reversals of fortune as occurred in June 1970 and February 1974. It was, quite simply, impossible to make a continuing impact on events from a secondary position.

It was, however, possible to make a singular dramatic splash. This Powell did on 27 March. At Falkirk he voiced 'an apprehension which is better voiced now than when it will be too late'. He feared, he went on, 'that there were contingency plans to send British troops to Vietnam. The American administration have made no secret of desiring this, for reasons which are understandable from their point of view . . .' But:

> . . . it would be intolerable if such a step on Britain's part, with all the large and unforeseeable consequences which would ensue, were to come about as part of a package deal arising from pressure on sterling, or a bout of short term insolvency. If any such step is even remotely in contemplation, the Prime Minister ought to confirm or deny it now . . .

And he concluded:

> Under the Labour government in the last eighteen months Britain has behaved, perfectly clearly and perfectly recognizably, as an American satellite.

The following day, after the speech had excited outrage (through Denis Healey) from the Labour Party and after it was disowned by Heath ('Mr. Powell was speaking on his own behalf'), Powell insisted that he had not made an accusation, merely asked a question about a possibility.

It is now clear, from evidence recently made available to me, that the contemporary public analysis of, and comment on, Powell's speech did not tell anything like the whole truth of its origins. It should be understood that differences had been arising for some time between the Leader of the Party and his front bench spokesman on defence. For example, Heath had asked each Shadow Minister to submit proposals, written at length, for inclusion in the election manifesto; but also, in their entirety, for separate publication as pamphlets by the Conservative Political Centre. 'It was,' says Powell, 'all grinding policy, in the months running up to the general election.' Shortly before publication of the pamphlet on defence was due, Powell was informed by Conservative Central Office, and not by Heath, that it would not appear. Upon his inquiring whether his work was to be wasted on the direct instruction of the Leader he was told that this was not the case.

On 25 March Powell was again telephoned from Central Office.

He was informed of a rumour that the government was contemplating the sending of a nominal British contingent to support the United States in Vietnam. Powell inquired whether this rumour was well founded. He was advised that it was. The suggestion was then made to him that, as the official Conservative defence spokesman, he should speak out on the subject. He asked whether he would be doing so at the wish of the Leader of the Party and was told that that was so. Powell was, therefore, naturally taken aback when Heath subsequently disowned the Falkirk speech as an individual act of independence by Powell.

So far as the Press – and most politicians – were concerned, the whole matter was buried by the landslide Labour victory of 31 March. But, quite apart from any general hints the episode may suggest about Anglo-American relations, the lack of confidence between Heath and Powell was to be demonstrated more dramatically later. For the moment, the important thing was the return of Harold Wilson to Downing Street with a majority of 100. 'Harold's got his century,' observed his Press Secretary, Joe Haines.

Galling though it was to be so thoroughly trounced, the Conservative Party showed no propensity to turn on Edward Heath. The previous year, indeed, a number of senior figures had questioned the wisdom of too quickly adopting the new system of choosing a Leader, especially when it became known that Home would not be a candidate. They reasoned in this way: an early general election was certain; Wilson was bound to win such a contest; better, therefore, to let Alec soldier on through another defeat (which he was perfectly willing to do) and then make a fresh start. If, the argument went on, a new man went down at the polls then he would start what might be a longish period of opposition already marked as a failure. Of course it was true that anything might happen, and that a collapse of sterling, say, might bring Home back as Prime Minister, but that would be no bad thing. After all, he had proved unexpectedly competent in his year of office and a surprisingly good campaigner. In any event the principal thing was not to have the new man start out with the brand of a loser on him.

These doubts and qualms and reservations were swept aside by the sentiment of the great majority of Conservative MPs. There were two principal reasons for this. The first was a slowly but steadily growing disgust, retrospective but real, with Macmillan's chicanery of 1963. Macleod's and Powell's refusal to serve, and Macleod's review of Randolph Churchill's book, both played their part in the creation of this feeling. That it was a real and genuine feeling no one could doubt. It was perfectly clear that the old system of choosing a Leader was now forever discredited, and the general view that nothing like the emergence of Home should ever happen again was a strong one. Moreover, though the bulk of MPs had come to have a high regard for Home, there remained a feeling that the legitimacy of his leadership was tainted. The modern Tory party simply had to find another way.

The second reason for making a change in 1965 was Harold Wilson. The Conservatives were, and for a long time remained, mesmerized by Wilson. Many hated him; all feared him. He had burst upon the scene after Hugh Gaitskell's untimely death and, with great energy and skill, carved out for himself a new image in British politics, that of the classless technocrat who was going to apply to the ailing British economy (to use his most famous phrase) 'the white heat of modern technology'. He had – just to rub irritants into a Conservative sore – a ready and sometimes devastating wit and he was adept at political manoeuvre. It is commonly the case that parties defeated at a general election tend somewhat to adopt the colouration of the victors, like certain kinds of lizard in dominant landscapes. This tendency in the Conservative Party was very marked after the defeat of October 1964. The theme song, as the late George Hutchinson once put it in conversation was, 'We must get ourselves a Wilson'. One was to hand in Edward Heath.

Of course, Heath lacked the style of Wilson. But he seemed relatively classless, and he had an enduring interest in – and far greater knowledge than Wilson of – this alien and difficult modern and technocratic world with which the Tories had to come to terms. All this, of course, seen from the perspective of the 1980s, seems the greatest nonsense. Wilson was not even an efficient technocrat; he was merely a great Party Leader in the old style.[26] Heath's lifestyle – with his yacht, his grand piano and his cultivated musical tastes – was far from the gritty image that, in their trauma, the Tories thought they needed. None the less, the general impression was what counted. Reginald Maudling, George Hutchinson used to say, lost any prospect of the leadership when, on seeing a photographer approaching his table at the Imperial Hotel in Blackpool in 1963, he quickly hid his large cigar under the table. Unfortunately, the photographer caught the action. Maudling's instinct was, none the less, sound. His bonhomie seemed out of tune with the times in 1965, whatever the opinion polls said. And Peter Walker, who was Heath's campaign manager in the 1965 leadership contest, was not slow to remind MPs that, in a remarkable act of prevision, Sir William Haley, the then editor of *The Times*, had in 1963, in a striking leader, advised the party to skip a generation and plump for Heath. His was the only newspaper so to do.

Thus, in a curious way, Heath's authority was enhanced after 31 March 1966. He could not be blamed for defeat. He had made a deep impression with his final TV broadcast. The slate was wiped clean. The political war had entered an entirely new phase.

On 6 April Powell rose to address the City of London Young Conservatives. His point of departure was that the party should now accept that it was in for a long period of opposition. That was fairly obvious to the Press, but it was not fashionable to articulate it as thoroughly and clearly as he did. The scholar as well as the ideologue in Powell actually seemed to relish this prospect. As he had said after the 1964 general election,[27] a break in government could be a very good thing, and offered the opportunity to think matters out anew. He listed four main areas of policy where, he thought, the intelligent youth of the Party could make their greatest contribution to the re-examination of Party policy. The first was trade union law; the second was nationalized industries 'in their entirety' and particularly the prospect of denationalization; the third was taxation, and particularly the way governments used their power to tax to discriminate as between different sections of the community; and the fourth was immigration and overseas aid, where means must be found to cut both drastically. Characteristically, however – and to Heath offensively – there was a particular Powell punch in the address. Heath had tried, before and during the campaign, to suggest that Wilson's eloquence was waffle, and that the approach to the nation's problems which he, Heath, favoured, one of taking decisive action rather than talking about it, was the right one. This view was encapsulated in the election slogan 'Action not Words'. Powell turned it on its head:

> The levers of power have been removed from our reach, or even our remote control . . . 'Words not Action' describes with precision the role of the Conservative Party as this new phase opens in its and the nation's political life . . . some of our words will be harsh, fierce, destructive words, aimed in defiance and contempt at men and policies we detest . . . we have liberty to question and to propose without fearing the

jealous scrutiny for pedantic consistency to which the words of a party in office or on the brink of it are forever of necessity obnoxious.

That – and especially the implied gibe against the manifesto slogan – was bad enough. However, on 10 April, while Heath was abroad, Powell issued a public statement condemning the decision of the government to use the Royal Navy to blockade the African port of Beira thus, in theory, cutting off oil supplies to rebel Rhodesia. Powell's principal argument was the realistic one, that the Beira patrol was irrelevant, since Rhodesia would continue to obtain (as she did for many years to come) all the oil she needed through South Africa. None the less he had put out his condemnation without even a vestige of consultation with the Deputy Leader, Reginald Maudling, in charge of the shop while Heath was away.

Powell, it seemed, had overstepped his final mark. Maudling's complaint to Heath was that Powell was – not for the first time – trying to make policy on his own, and without reference to either the Leader or the Deputy Leader (Maudling) of the Party. Powell has always said, with splendid academic consistency, that he was not making policy. He believed that Heath was aware of a much earlier statement by Harold Wilson that the Royal Navy would not in any circumstances be used to enforce sanctions off Beira. Since this statement was recorded in Hansard, Powell was merely drawing public attention to the fact that the Prime Minister was 'guilty of a recorded breach of promise'. Powell was perfectly correct. But to as casual and easy-going a man as Maudling, his statement could readily be seen as a breach of trust.

On Friday, 15 April Heath saw Powell at his chambers in Albany. Heath made it clear that he was anxious not to lose the services of this difficult colleague, but that the protests of other colleagues at his free-ranging incursions into their areas of responsibility were becoming clamant. What Heath wanted was for Powell to behave like everybody else – to speak mainly on his own subject of responsibility, to clear any planned utterance on grand policy with the Leader himself and, should he wish to enter the domain of another colleague, to consult that colleague first. On the interpretation of the last point great events were ultimately to turn. Heath took it, at the end of their conversation, to mean that Powell would *always* consult with the relevant Shadow colleague before making a speech outside his own area of responsibility. Powell took it that he was required to enter such consultation only when what he had to say might be judged controversial, as he had consulted Alec Douglas-Home before his speech on defence at the 1965 Party Conference. There was, as so often in such matters, room for different interpretations. The general view of the Press, however, particularly as put by the *Sunday Times* on 17 April, was that what Mr. Paul Foot[28] calls a 'genuine truce' had been arrived at. Mr. Foot is correct in saying that the silence on subjects outside his own which Powell for a time observed was 'relative', while Dr. Schoen[29] thinks it was well nigh absolute. On 30 April, for example, in Edinburgh, Powell attacked the civil service for its development of policy-making pretensions. For good measure he attacked businessmen who thought they could offer useful advice to politicians. On 6 May he told the Institute of Marketing in Wolverhampton that there was a frontal assault being made on free market principles by Ministers, and that it had to be resisted. To the London Young Conservatives at Wembley on 9 May he preached a sermon on the iniquities of governments which, through supposedly voluntary agreements, put pressure on different business groups, trying by bullying to force them into 'desisting from behaviour which is perfectly lawful'. On 20 May, at Gateshead, he made fun of the Chancellor's economic policy and particularly of the new Selective Employment Tax, arguing in particular that it was a tax which would restrict employment and yet a further indication of a vicious government attempt to control the economy. If the government really believed that SET would improve economic efficiency then 'we have made the greatest economic discovery of the ages. All we need to do is sit back and tax ourselves into prosperity.'

However, much though his colleagues could (and did) envy his pungency of expression, the range of his mind, and the capacity he possessed to excite attention (less, at this stage, from the Press than from his audiences), it could not be said that, in the weeks following the so-called 'Albany Compact' he strayed markedly from agreed policy lines. Nor did he neglect his own particular responsibilities. On 26 May at Claygate he delivered a withering attack on the Defence Review of 22 February. The thrust of the argument concerned the sale of British aircraft to Saudi Arabia and the proposed British purchase of F111A fighter-bomber aircraft from the United States. The argument is a highly technical one, and it is typical of Powell's assumption that he should treat all audiences with the same intellectual respect that he would treat, say, the House of Commons, or the Staff College, that he made it in a sleepy Surrey village. He exposed a vital contradiction between the projections made in the Defence White Paper and the Defence Review, argued that Britain was losing out over what were called 'offset payments' – that is setting the cost of an import against an export, with government, rather than private, funding – and concluded that Britain, if the F111A purchase went ahead (in the event it did not), would suffer grievously, both financially and strategically.

The logic was devastating and unanswerable, and shows Powell at his analytic best. The situation was this: the February Defence Review announced the proposed purchase of fifty F111A aircraft. The cost of these was to be offset by American purchases of British equipment and a permission to British firms to compete for US defence contracts without discrimination in favour of American firms. A fortnight later Fred (now Lord) Mulley, the Minister of State at the Ministry of Defence, announced that $400 million of the total cost of $725 million would not, in fact, be offset. This situation arose when Healey, in Washington on 18 February, showed Robert McNamara, the US Secretary of Defence, a proof of the British White Paper. McNamara told him bluntly that he had misunderstood the situation in imagining that the Americans would offset the whole cost of the F111A purchase. Healey, however, let the White Paper as it stood go to press, saying, after the election was over, that the sale of British Lightning fighter aircraft to Saudi Arabia would make up some or all of the cost of the F111As.

I describe this matter in some detail in order to demonstrate Powell's meticulous attention to his own job and his capacity for unveiling contradictions. One of his crucial pieces of evidence, for example, was his extraction from Mulley, by way of a Written Answer on 16 May, of some of the more recondite details of the bewildering exchanges between the British, the Americans and the Saudis. The salient political points, however, were two. First, the government had meekly accepted an American withdrawal from an offset agreement, but concealed the fact from Parliament by allowing the White Paper to go ahead even after Healey's conversations with McNamara. Second, the idea that the cost of the F111As could be made up by sales of Lightnings to Saudi Arabia was spurious. In the spine of the speech, however, lay the pith and marrow of Powell's distrust of the United States.

It was therefore particularly offensive to him that, during the following week, Heath should choose to discuss the 'Albany

Compact' in Washington. Powell believed that he had been playing by the rules of his conversation with Heath on 15 April. Heath held a Washington Press Conference on 3 June. A reporter asked him if Mr. Powell was now 'under wraps, and would he stay there?' Heath replied: 'Yes to both questions – at least he was when I left, and I think he has talked about nothing since but milk and the Co-ops.' Had such a remark been made in public in Britain it would have been bad enough. To make it abroad, and in the United States, was crass. However obliquely offensive to his colleagues many of Powell's speeches had been, he had never descended to the level of the crudely personal. His code of conduct often seemed arcane, and fully understood only by himself. His capacity to be prickly, and incapacity to be easy-going, were both marked. It is only fair to add, however, that Powell never saw his conversation with Heath on 15 April as imposing on either man a strict set of rules of behaviour. Heath, on the other hand, seems to have believed that he had persuaded a man of such independence and variety of mind as Powell to observe the same rigidly limited rules of discourse as were acceptable to others whom he had invited to join him on the Opposition front bench. While Heath's advisers have always referred to the 15 April meeting as producing a compact, Powell denies that their conversation ever produced anything so formalized. All that, in his belief, the discussion had produced was the 'friendly resolution of certain resentments against each other'.

It was fairly soon plain that Powell, at any rate, no longer felt himself under any particular obligation of restraint, though it was not until early 1967 that his willingness to dissent openly from generally agreed Party policy became blatant. To understand what he was attempting to do, however – not to mention the reaction of Heath to it – it is necessary briefly to mention a particular historical shibboleth (or, if one happens to support the Leader of the day, rule) of the Conservative Party. This states that the Leader, and the Leader alone, makes policy.[30] Heath, for all that as Prime Minister he was willing to tolerate dissent less and less, began with a more collegiate approach. He favoured lengthy discussion and what Iain Macleod called 'endless' reports. He was ever reluctant to take a sharply defined position, though he gave the impression (shown to be false when he came to power) that he would be adamantine in his resolve. As Leader of the Opposition, however, he was arrogant. There are many examples of these poles of character on offer between 1966 and 1970 but I will examine Heath's characteristics only in so far as they refer to Powell.

On 15 April Heath had concluded a truce with Powell, perhaps not least because he thought Powell an intellectual goad of value. It could be said that Heath had given Powell his 'marching orders', as the matter was put by the late Michael Wolff, one of Heath's closest advisers. That, at least, would explain the heavily humorous self-confidence of his remarks to journalists in Washington on 3 June. But, if he *was* confident that he had corralled Powell then, what could he have made of Powell's assault on the silliness of any government seeking to encourage industrial productivity by deliberate action other than that of freeing the markets – such being one of Heath's favourite themes – on 30 September 1966? What could he have made of a further assault, on 5 November, on businesses which co-operated with government in providing information (though under no legal obligation to do so) about their investment policies? Managerial co-operation between government and business was, after all, yet another of Heath's favourite themes. Indeed, for all that Powell and Heath started their relationship in 1965 from positions that were in many ways similar[31], the divergences between a managerial view of the nation (Heath's) and a philosophic one (Powell's) became evident almost day by day. Whereas Heath was striving, according to his lights, to devise a programme for an efficient Britain, Powell believed that, according to *his* lights, he was 'developing an assault on Wilsonian Socialism'. Given such markedly different approaches to the problems of the day, it is hardly surprising that, as Powell says, 'Speeches which, made by either of two men who understood one another, would have been inoffensive, were regarded as hostile.' The relationship between these two men – the political and professional relationship, that is, for they never had more than a vestigial personal relationship – was to have a profound and, in my judgement, very long lasting effect on the history of their Party and of their country, and its chemistry is therefore worthy of exploration. It may never be accurately or fully explored, and it certainly cannot be before the private papers and memoirs of all the participants are available to the students of a future generation. We can, however, be certain of one thing – that Powell regarded Heath's Washington statement as a licence to return to the freedom of speech he had enjoyed ('extracted' might be a better word) before he met Heath at Albany on 15 April 1966.

We can also ask a question before turning to the history of the period between June 1966 and April 1968, when Heath dismissed Powell from the Shadow Cabinet. The occasion of that dismissal –

Powell's speech to the West Midlands Area Conservative Political Centre on immigration – is well-known. The national furore over the speech is perhaps better remembered than any other in recent political history. We know, further, that both Edward Boyle and Quintin Hogg had made it clear to Heath that they could not serve in the Shadow Cabinet with a man who had made such a speech. These reactions, and the pressures they put on Heath, I will examine later.[32] It is sufficient to say now that they were considerable, and that a stronger man than Heath might well have bent in their face. But the question remains – why did he not dismiss Powell earlier for, on his own doctrine of Shadow Cabinet responsibility, he had ample reason to do so? The true answer can lie only somewhere within the recesses of his own personality.

From the middle of 1966 Powell knew that a sentence of dismissal from the Shadow Cabinet might fall upon him at any moment. Heath, however, declined to put his hand to the axe. This cannot have been because of any fear of a popular Powell appeal. True, he drew larger than the average audiences attracted by other Shadow Ministers, but that might have been because he gave his all to every performance. Certainly, his disquisitions on economic policy were not such as to cause fires to be lit on his behalf. For what they are worth the opinion poll records surveyed by Dr. Schoen[33] show no marked appreciation of support for Powell. And, as even the most bilious of witnesses against him – Mr. Paul Foot[34] – records, he did not seek to use against Heath the most emotive issue with which he could have identified himself, that of immigration.

In no ordinary sense of the word, however, could Powell be called a good colleague. His interpretation of his duty, exact and honourable as it was, was at least gnomic, if not even Jesuitical. Though there was nothing free nor easy in his relationship with his colleagues, there was nothing devious about it either. Powell was, quite simply, seized of a personal sense of mission and, aware as he was of a capacity to provoke and excite, used that capacity in every way that *he* saw as reasonable: if others could not understand his reasonableness, so much the worse for them. He could, when he wished, be attentive, kindly and sympathetic. He could be amusing. But everything was done in his own way, even if the doing of whatever he was about created misunderstanding. He was always, but more emphatically between the middle of 1966 and the beginning of 1968, a loner in Mr. Michael Foot's definition.[35] Everybody who approached him, however, got the full attention of his mind, and felt the full strength of his character. I find affecting, for example, an interview he gave in July 1966 to Miss Averell Wainwright and Miss Mary Morgan for the issue of 21 July of the Bolton School Girls' Division magazine. The young ladies asked him what, when he was their age (that is, a schoolboy) he wanted to be. He replied: 'I always wanted to be a poet.' They asked him what he thought of the women then in Parliament. He replied: 'The nice ones are very nice.' They asked him what he did of a Sunday and he told them, 'Number one, I worship, number two, I go out into the country with my family and, number three, I do any odd jobs my wife thinks I ought to do. I don't work on Sundays.'

There is, I think, a nice mixture of the metaphorical and the basic in that interview. But the most indicative of the replies is the one in which he states his poetic ambition. For Powell political action is invariably artistic in conception and execution. Action – and a speech is an action – may be hedged about by consideration of what colleagues and supporters may think, but in the same sense that a statement in verse may be hedged about by the metre the poet has chosen. Edward Heath's mind in so far as it was metaphorical, was musically inclined; Powell's music lay in words.

His intention, however, was to push his Party and his country towards new definitions of purpose and identity. Almost any one of his statements within his own field of responsibility between 1966 and 1968 would – especially given Heath's narrow definition of a Shadow Minister's role – have justified his summary exclusion from the ranks of those invited to occupy the Opposition front bench in the House of Commons.

On 30 October 1966, for example, he attacked not merely the fact, but the whole concept, of aid from developed to under-developed countries:

> In every period and place there are certain propositions which it is safe to propound without any need to justify them rationally. In our own time and country one of the subjects of which such propositions are made is 'aid'. Almost any statement in favour of 'aid', however patently grotesque, is safe from challenge.

Aid, Powell believed, was, more than anything else, a function of self-esteem, particularly for Britain. It was also a function of arrogance towards supposedly underdeveloped countries. So long as Britain was running a balance of payments deficit *and* an aid programme, she was borrowing from one group of countries to give or lend to another group of countries, a practice which could not make common sense. The object of aid was believed to be to enable the poverty-stricken nations of Asia and Africa to reach what Professor Thomas Balogh in *The Economics of Poverty*[36] called 'take-off point'. However, telling such countries what they ought to do was pure arrogance, for:

> . . . once upon a time the present government of our country too had a plan for 'growing' by 4% a year to 1970-1. Where is that plan now? In our own circumstances, with a refined documentation and highly developed administration, with decades of intensive study of our economy behind us, it remains an open question whether, and if so how, action by the state produces or assists economic 'growth'. Yet we happily talk about bringing India or Botswana or Peru to the point of economic 'take-off' by government-to-government transfer of a few hundred million pounds of resources.

The condition of success in foreign policy, Powell told a Conservative gathering at Whitby on 24 January 1967, 'is to recognize the truth about oneself'. This recognition was not at all palatable to Conservative audiences, bathed as they were in dreams of post-imperial glory. He enforced it on those who would listen to him, none the less. He seemed prepared, at every turn, to heap ridicule upon pretension, whoever it was being pretentious.

There were two specific assumptions in Conservative defence and foreign policy which Powell thought unfounded in reason. The first was the retention and supposed utility of overseas bases; the second the retention and supposed utility of the independent nuclear deterrent. As time passed he became more and more open in his opposition to both.

Thus, on 3 February 1967, in the *Spectator*, he reviewed Christopher Mayhew's book, *Britain's Role Tomorrow*. Mayhew[37] had been a junior Minister in the Foreign Office when Attlee was Prime Minister. He had been appointed Minister in charge of the Royal Navy under Harold Wilson and had resigned when the Wilson administration declined to provide what he regarded as adequate funding for a British military presence beyond – the phrase of the day was 'east of' Suez. Powell wrote:

The 'world role east of Suez' is a piece of humbug; the reality had resolved itself into the ability to operate either as an American satellite or on a scale so limited that it could not in the worst case demand more than a very small exertion of force. Equally a sham was the vaunt of the Minister of Defence that 'we intend to remain, and we shall remain, fully capable of carrying out *all the commitments that we have at the present time*.' Commitments – certainly the commitments for the most part highly imprecise and even implicit, which Britain has east of Suez – mean what you take them to mean, ranging from nothing to everything. For Britain 'the course of human affairs', combined with the government's decisions, had decided that the meaning would be near to the nothing end of the spectrum.

It could, of course, be said that, in less than two years – the period since his first speech as Shadow Secretary of State for Defence – Conservative opinion had moved Powell's way on the matter of military undertakings overseas. The same could not, however, be said of Tory belief in the necessity, and efficacy, of the nation's possession of her own nuclear weapon. To that belief Edward Heath was as devoted in 1967 as Alec Douglas-Home had been in the general election campaign of 1964. Powell, who had at the Party Conference of 1965 expressed his special pleasure at being made responsible for Tory defence policy and who, at Ripon on 8 July 1967 said that 'In no department of State is the responsibility of the present to the future more solemn,' took a different view. Reviewing Vice-Admiral Sir Arthur Hezlet's book *The Submarine and Seapower* in the *Sunday Times* on 23 April 1967 he wrote that the book would be welcomed 'by that growing number who are engaged in the assault upon the "nuclear hypothesis" '.

The nuclear hypothesis assumed that there could be no war in Western Europe that was not nuclear. In Powell's judgement, if the European powers went to war again, the likelihood was that their combat would be conventional. There was always, of course – and there still is – a continuing debate about the right disposition of the defence budget as between nuclear and non-nuclear arms and Powell had ever emphasized the importance of the non-nuclear. Precise calibration of financial estimates in such matters is never an easy business, but Powell was steadily moving to a position from which he regarded the independent nuclear deterrent by which so much store was set as irrelevant to any thoughts of further war. The argument was then, as it is now, an immensely complex one, a veritable thicket of logic in which every tree has a luxuriance of its own. There were, however – at least in the Conservative Party – two generally accepted beliefs. The first was that the advent of nuclear power had changed the future nature of war. The second was that, in such circumstances, the United Kingdom had to have her own nuclear weapon. Powell challenged both beliefs. Thus, in the *Journal of the Royal United Services Institute* of February 1968 he wrote:

> There appear to me to be the strongest grounds, both theo-
> retical and empirical, for regarding the nuclear veto as either
> wholly incredible or at any rate so far improbable as to make
> it necessary to be prepared to act on the assumption that it
> will not apply.

And, again, in the same article:

> Empirically, the fact is that during the last twenty years
> the nations, whether or not they possessed nuclear weapons,
> cannot be shown to have behaved otherwise than they would
> have done if the nuclear warhead had not existed.

However, much of what Powell was doing and saying between 1966 and 1968 was wrongly emphasized in commentary upon him. The tendency – as witnessed in a speech by Richard Crossman reported in *The Times* on 16 January 1967 – was to concentrate on his economic views, and his difference from Heath on matters economic. This 'Latter-day Savonarola', as Crossman called Powell, 'rampages round the country summoning congregations of the faithful to reject as heretics those Conservative leaders all of whom, in his view, have departed from the straight and narrow path of nineteenth century *laissez-faire*'. The devotion of time, energy and words to underlining the difference between Powell and the rest of the Shadow Cabinet – though that difference was a great deal less marked than appeared – was not unfair, and it was not wasted. But the fact of the matter was that Powell was steadily hardening his position on matters ultimately to have greater consequence for his future reputation and influence than economics. The defence speeches demonstrate an ever greater reliance on the principles of national identity; and that reliance was to be the fundament of the explosion of April 1968.

As I have already mentioned[38], Powell resisted early attempts by others – and, most notably, Cyril Osborne – to draw him into the growing, and festering, debate on coloured immigration. There were several reasons for this initial reluctance. So potentially sensitive a subject could best, he thought, be handled quietly. Then, he had the early conviction – in the first years of the 1960s – that R. A. Butler's 1962 Act limiting entry to the United Kingdom from the New Commonwealth (essentially, that is, the West Indies, India, and Pakistan) would be effective. There was also, into the 1960s, a residual feel for the United Kingdom as the mother country of an empire, her doors open to the subjects of the monarchy in whatever part of the globe. It is interesting to note, however, that in the August 1958 issue of *The National and English Review* Powell, recalling his 1938 arrival in Darwin on his way to take up his professorial appointment at Sydney, reflected on the wisdom of the Australian authorities in restricting Asian immigration to their continent, on the grounds of the incompatibility between a culture essentially English in its origins and one essentially Asiatic.

The fullest early statement on the problem of immigration was, however, given to his local paper, the Wolverhampton *Express and Star* in an article published on 10 October 1964. This article is of quite exceptional importance, both because it presages – even down to its detail – all of his later pronouncements on the same subject, and because it has been misrepresented. What has to be remembered, in the analysis that follows, is that from 1964 onwards Powell was speaking and writing on a great variety of subjects, on almost every one of which his views were at the very least controversial. Directly to criticize him as Mr. Paul Foot does[39] for not regularly addressing himself to the problem of immigration is to take one issue entirely out of context. Further, on the cover of Mr. Foot's 1969 Penguin volume, *The Rise of Enoch Powell*, there is emblazoned a single quotation from the article of 10 October 1964. It reads:

> I have set and always will set my face like flint against making any difference between one citizen of this country and another on the grounds of his origin.

Elsewhere, and, indeed, throughout his text – Mr. Foot argues that there is a serious and 'cynical' contradiction between this unequivocal statement of a policy of racial equality and Powell's later, and forcefully expressed, attacks on continued immigration and pleas for assisted repatriation.

Mr. Foot, however – like so many other writers on the subject – misses the significance to Powell of the word 'citizen'. From the very outset of his political career (in the Conservative Research Department) his overwhelming preoccupation was with national identity, of which citizenship is, necessarily, the foremost expression. Citizenship, to him as to most people (though not, naturally, to a self-declared Trotskyist such as Mr. Foot) involves duties as well as rights. Principal among the duties of an immigrant is assimilation to the *mores* and traditions of the host nation. So, in the *Express and Star* article:

> No doubt, like other groups, the [New Commonwealth] immigrants will often wish to retain for a long time some of their distinctive customs and beliefs; but the idea of them as an unassimilated element of our society, living apart in certain districts and following only certain occupations, is insupportable.

Elsewhere in the article Powell states for the first time two essential concerns which have, ever since, formed the staple of all his arguments on immigration and its attendant evils. These are numbers and concentration, meaning the concentration of immigrant communities in particular areas, especially urban areas. 'In 1963,' he wrote, 'the only complete calendar year since control came into force, there was a net admission of 50,000 coloured immigrants. Surely no one can imagine that, with a million already here, this country is capable of assimilating a further million coloured immigrants every twenty years.' The task of assimilation, he goes on to argue, would be all the more difficult because of concentration: 'It is the ten per cent and more of the considerable areas of population which present the real problem.' Everything essential to the Powell thesis on immigration – though its expression was to become more vivid, and the attention it attracted to have greater consequence, for himself as well as for others – was therefore stated in the 10 October 1964 article, just as it was implicit in his speech on the Royal Titles Bill.[40] It is nonsense, therefore, to argue, as Mr. Foot and other writers have done, that he opportunistically and unexpectedly took up the issue in 1967 and 1968, for want of a subject which would dramatize his differences with the rest of the Shadow Cabinet. Indeed, on 18 October 1964, in a review of the post electoral situation, he took advantage of a national platform – the columns of the *Sunday Telegraph* – to re-emphasize his views:

Immigration was, and is, an issue. In my constituency it has for years been question number one, into which discussion of every other political topic – housing, health, benefits, employment – promptly turns. It is not colour prejudice or racial intolerance to say that only if substantial further addition to our population is now prevented, will it be possible to assimilate the immigrants already here, which in turn is the only way to avoid the evils of a colour question.

Indeed, nearly four years before the Birmingham speech other politicians than Conservatives recognized Powell as a politician with a serious concern about levels of immigration; and shared his concern. After the general election of October 1964 Harold Wilson required two by-elections, one to return to the House his appointed Foreign Secretary, Patrick Gordon-Walker, who had lost his seat at Smethwick, and the other to bring into the House of Commons, as Minister for Industry, Frank Cousins, the General Secretary of the Transport and General Workers' Union. Cousins was to have an unhappy parliamentary career, but Wilson's intention was clear: he sought to repeat the brilliant manoeuvre of Churchill in bringing a previous General Secretary, Ernest Bevin, into Parliament and government in 1940. Gordon-Walker was chosen against the wishes of many local Party workers, who did not want to see their beloved MP, Theodore Sorensen (who was compensated by a peerage), removed against his and their will. Given the vestigial size of the government's majority and the ill-feeling which had been created in the constituency of Nuneaton – where Cousins was standing – the by-election was crucial for both major parties. Powell went north to support the Conservative candidate and George Thomas (later Speaker of the House of Commons and now Viscount Tonypandy) went north to support the Labour candidate, the two men travelling on the same train. They had a long conversation on immigration. Thomas told Powell that the new government did not intend to keep its manifesto promise to lift immigration controls, and might even make them more stringent. He suggested, in a fashion at once jocose and serious, that Powell and the Conservatives could steal Labour's thunder by making a major issue of immigration.

Upon his return to London Powell arranged a meeting with Maudling and the Conservative Chief Whip, Martin Redmayne. He expressed his own concern about immigration and advised his colleagues of what Thomas had told him. The three prepared a speech for Alec Douglas-Home, who was still Leader of the Party. With one exception, to which I will refer in a moment, nothing in Powell's 1968 speech at Birmingham varied from the speech delivered in February 1965 by Douglas-Home in London.

There was one, and only one, change in the content of Powell's policy on immigration after October 1964. It was followed in a speech in Birmingham on 21 November 1965 by an emphasis harder than hitherto on the desirability of voluntary repatriation of immigrants who found assimilation difficult. This harder emphasis was repeated during the 1966 general election campaign. The new development in recommended policy did not, however, appear until 1967 when, in an article in the *Sunday Express* of 9 July, he advocated the withdrawal of the existing automatic and unconditional right of immigrants already in Britain to bring in their dependents.

It can be questioned, however, whether this was a major change of substance to the policy enunciated in October 1964. The essence of his preoccupation (dominated as it was by his understanding of numbers and concentration) was the inability (on the part of the host culture) to absorb and the inability (on the part of the immigrant culture) to assimilate. It followed logically, then, that the immigrant communities could no longer be allowed to top up their numbers through the entry of dependents. After referring to the continuing net intake of 50,000 a year he goes on:

> The great majority of the immigrants now coming in are dependents, and most of these are women and children, who have all or most of their reproductive life before them. In other words, the race problem of the future is something we are still engaged in building up by this continued immigration. If the facts are as the government estimates,

he continued

> . . . there is surely no question about the net rate of intake at which we should be aiming. It is a maximum of *nil*. The natural increase of the million or more already within our shores will face us, and still more our children, with intractable problems enough. In the name of sanity and common sense we ought not avoidably to add to it.

What has to be remembered as part of the background to the

period between 1964 and 1967, however, is the fact that, though national debate about immigration and its consequences died down after the flurry of the 1964 general election, local concern increased sharply and MPs in affected areas (including, of course, Powell) found the subject constantly coming up at their constituency surgeries. Indeed, it was already beginning to become apparent in 1965 that local feeling in the Conservative Party was beginning to draw away from the feeling of the national leadership. It proved easy enough, at the annual Conference at Brighton that year, to ensure a peaceful passage for an anodyne resolution on immigration control. But, then, Tory Party Conferences are usually decorous and respectful affairs: it was not until the Brighton Conference of 1969 that anything approaching rebellion on the part of the assembled delegates posed anything like a threat to the leadership and that near rebellion was, in my own opinion, in large part provoked by a curiously casual and flippant response to the floor debate from the Shadow Home Secretary, Quintin Hogg.

By 1967, then, the signs were there – though, to be sure, they had to be looked for – that the problem of immigration could become an explosive one. From 1960 onwards, for example, the annual reports of Dr. J. F. Galloway, Wolverhampton's Medical Officer of Health, contained figures showing a high proportional occupancy of maternity beds in the area's hospitals by coloured mothers. It could be argued that, viewed in the most coldly rigorous statistical light, Dr. Galloway's figures were not exceptionally alarming – the very youth of immigrant mothers, and the fact that they often lived in areas sufficiently run down to discourage home confinements (a much more common practice in the sixties than today) – but the fact was that they were *felt* to be alarming. A potentially dangerous fissure was opening between the native inhabitants of the Midlands and the North and the political denizens of Whitehall and Westminster. The problems looming ahead were, though only to a trifling extent, recognized by the government which, having been elected in 1964 after giving undertakings to repeal the Butler Act of 1962, actually and progressively introduced further controls.

In two vital aspects, however, the political situation was altered in 1967. In June the Home Secretary, Roy (now Lord) Jenkins announced proposals for a Race Relations Bill which would outlaw discrimination on grounds of race in housing and unemployment. Though the legislation was objective in its language, in that it could be used by whites against coloured immigrants as well as *vice versa*, it was none the less clearly designed to counteract possible discrimination against the newcomers and was thus a response by Jenkins, wholly in accordance with his own political philosophy, to liberal expressions of worry in the face of rising dislike of the immigrant population. For the most part Conservatives were suspicious of, if not outrightly opposed to, such legislation, less because of the particular issue concerned than because of a broad and traditional dislike of laws regulating conduct between individuals.

The second change in the situation was brought about by the government of independent Kenya. It was Kenya, acting in her own interests as she saw them, who provided the catalyst for a political explosion in Britain. The merits of the two sides in what was to become a major dispute within both of the major Parties, but which was more poignant in Conservative ranks, are still discussed, and even debated with heat. But it is not difficult to understand the sequence of events.

In 1962, as we have seen, Conservative government legislation introduced power to control Commonwealth immigrants. The political hypocrisies prevailing at the time dictated, however, that the clear intention of the legislation should be to some extent clouded in opaque prose. The following year further legislation was introduced (following a constitutional conference) to provide independence for Kenya, which country, following the example originally set by India, promptly became a republic within the Commonwealth. The British offered, as one of their principal contributions to a peaceful and orderly transition to independence, to allow a two year period following the granting of independence for residents of the new country to decide whether they wanted to be Kenyan or remain 'Citizens of the UK and Colonies'.

It was, of course, clear that the white residents of Kenya were uppermost in the minds of those making this provision. Nobody – and least of all the new government in Nairobi – wanted to provoke the panic-stricken exodus of a community whose skills were held to be essential to the progress of the new nation. There was also, however, a substantial Asian population, long settled in Kenya, and there were also large Asian communities in Uganda and Tanzania. In 1964 the government headed by President Kenyatta declared its unease at the slow pace of Africanization of the economy. It was made clear that, whereas the small white population remained more or less welcome, the much larger Asian community (estimates as to its size varied between one and two hundred thousand) was increasingly regarded with hostility, a hostility not diminished by African memories of the fact that the Asians had not been notably enthusiastic in the struggle for independence. Sensitive to the situation, a very large number of Kenyan Asians (nobody can even now be sure how many) opted to remain UK and Colonies citizens after the interim period ended in 1965. Unlike the whites, of course, these Asians had no family or other roots in the United Kingdom. In 1967 the Kenyan government announced that, with a handful of exceptions, they were all to be expelled. The question immediately arose: did the Commonwealth Immigrants Act of 1962 confer on them a right to enter Britain?

The question did not admit of a genuinely straight answer, though there were some prepared to give one. Thus, in the *Spectator* on 23 February 1968 Iain Macleod argued that the Asians had been promised free entry. 'We did it,' he wrote, 'we meant to do it, and in any case we had no other alternative.' However, as Mr. Foot rightly points out,[41] the then responsible Minister, Duncan Sandys, 'prevaricated' when asked a specific question on this in the House on 28 November 1963. 'I would think,' he replied

> once they have acquired a Commonwealth citizenship and have given up their United Kingdom citizenship, they would be treated as citizens of the Commonwealth country to which they belong . . . but they may for a period still have United Kingdom citizenship before they opt for Commonwealth citizenship.

This reply, of course, begged the whole question of the rights of UK and Colonies citizens *vis-à-vis* entry to the United Kingdom, and there were many – like Macleod – ready to argue that virtually all of those expelled by Kenya had a right of entry. Matters were complicated by the fact that the Kenyans had always refused to tolerate any form of dual citizenship, so the many Asians who had failed to take up Kenyan citizenship were left only with some kind of British option. There was the further complication in 1967 that Duncan Sandys himself immediately took a leading role in the campaign to prevent an Asian influx from Kenya (and it should be added that the government was, at the time, striving might and main to persuade the government of Kenya not to be too precipitate in its programme of expulsions).

The niceties of interpreting the differences between the 1962 and 1963 Acts, were, however, lost upon a population increasingly troubled by the level of immigration, and not minded to welcome a sudden, and perhaps vast, increase in numbers. It was with them (and with Sandys) that Powell sided. On 18 October 1967, just after the Party Conference had opened at Brighton, he addressed an audience in Deal:

> When Kenya became independent in 1963 Parliament enacted that anybody who then became a citizen of Kenya automatically ceased to be a citizen of the United Kingdom and Colonies. It was, however, Kenya who defined her own citizens and they did so in such a way as to exclude hundreds of thousands of Asiatics and others who were residing there.

This was not quite an exact description of the situation. Kenya did insist that nobody within her borders could enjoy a dual citizenship: a choice had to be made between British and Kenyan. If the former choice was made the option of Kenyan citizenship was no longer available, and expulsion would therefore be the order of the day after the decision of 1967. Where serious difficulty was immediately seen to arise, however, was in the case of those who had taken up neither option by 1967. Kenya was set on expelling such people. Was the British option still legally available? Powell and his allies insisted that the clear intention of the 1962 Act, which intention was again and again repeated in the course of parliamentary debates in 1961, was to restrict right of entry to those born in the United Kingdom and to those holding a passport issued in the United Kingdom. A study of Hansard for the period bears out this argument, but inadequate drafting made it possible to claim in the late 1960s that the net was cast much wider. Powell believes that Colonial Office civil servants deliberately did not draw the attention of their political masters to the existence of the loophole. In any event, it was his case that the clear intention of the legislation should obtain when problems later arose with Kenya and Uganda. Further, even so far as the matter concerned those who had exercised the British option by 1965, could the United Kingdom cope with their numbers? Over and above all that, however, Powell was convinced that the effects of the 1962 legislation, of which an unknown number of Asians might take advantage, were unintended. Thus, at Deal:

It is quite monstrous that an unforeseen loophole in legislation

should be able to add another quarter of a million or so . . .
without any control or limit whatever.

From Deal onwards, it was clear (to employ a sporting metaphor) that the gloves were being peeled off and the bare knuckle
contest was about to begin. Following a speech at Bournemouth
on 19 November Powell took questions from his audience.
Unprompted by him, the matter of immigration was raised. He
replied forthrightly that drastic reduction in numbers had to be
the order of the day and that the unqualified right of dependents to immigrate had to be withdrawn.[42] On 8 December, at a
constituency meeting in Wolverhampton, he reiterated his dire
statistical predictions that current immigration policy would create in Britain a race relations problem of American dimensions
within some years. It is relevant to mention here – as Mr. Roth
stresses[43] – that Powell had paid his first visit to the United States
the previous month, and had been shocked by what he saw and
heard of the state of race relations in that country. Perhaps even
more to the point was the fact that Pamela Powell, who had been
anxious for her husband to undertake that trip, had worked in
New York shortly after the war, and formed a great affection
for that metropolis. She was horrified by the changes that the
passage of time had wrought in what she had always considered
to be a favourite, and a happy, city.

It is important also to remember, as 1967 drew to its close,
that Powell was not the only Conservative politician exercised
by the immigration problem, for Cyril Osborne and Duncan
Sandys, not to mention such less prominent figures as John
Cordle in Bournemouth and Harold Gurden in Birmingham
were all energetic in their advocacy of a policy of greater curbs.
Both front benches were coming under increasing pressure to
respond to an intensifying public mood of fear and reproach.
What the New Year brought, however, was not merely thunder,
but lightning.

The first hint of the new style in Powell's presentation of
the argument was to be found in a speech to his constituents
on 8 December. For the first time there was an injection of
a highly personal character into his oratory on this subject. In
what was clearly a reference to the criticism he and like-minded
politicians had been attracting, he assured his constituents that,
'No amount of misrepresentation, abuse or unpopularity is going
to prevent the Tory Party, my colleagues and myself from voicing
the dictates of common sense and reason.' Who was meant

by 'colleagues' is a moot question for, on the previous 15 November Quintin Hogg, the official front bench spokesman on Home Office Affairs, had sought to alleviate anxiety by – while stressing his Party's commitment to immigration control – playing down the long term significance of numbers.

It could be argued, of course, that the emerging difference between Hogg and Powell was essentially one of emphasis. But whatever may have been a matter of emphasis or style in the beginning was rapidly turning into a matter of substance. To put it simply Powell was becoming ever more concerned about precise numbers while Hogg (and, for that matter, the Cabinet, in which James Callaghan had just replaced Roy Jenkins as Home Secretary, Jenkins himself moving to the Treasury in place of Callaghan) simply did not regard precision as to numbers central. Powell saw that there was a serious possibility of conflict between himself and Hogg but within the borders of the latitude so far allowed him by Heath (whatever private irritation there was), he felt reasonably safe in pronouncing on immigration, particularly if he spoke on the subject as one which was generating great concern among his constituents and in his Midlands area.

This qualification must be borne in mind when considering the text of his speech at Walsall on 9 February 1968:

> There is a sense of hopelessness which comes over people who are trapped or imprisoned, when all their efforts to attract attention and assistance bring no response. This is the kind of feeling which you in Walsall and we in Wolverhampton are experiencing in the face of the continued flow of immigrants into our towns . . . The rest know little or nothing and, we may sometimes be tempted to feel, care little or nothing.

He went on to make the now familiar arguments about restricting numbers and restricting the existing rights of dependents. He adverted to the new problem of the Kenyan Asians. But it was in a passage that excited particular anger that he used, in what seemed to be sarcastic mimicry, a phrase made famous by Quintin Hogg. During the 1964 election campaign Hogg described voters who supported Labour as 'stark staring bonkers'. Powell referred to the fact that illegal immigrants who escaped immediate detection were almost invariably allowed to remain in Britain. While this laxity did not (it was thought) materially affect the numerical size of the immigration problem, it was, clearly, an offence against justice and common sense. He addressed it thus:

> Then there is the whole question of legality and verification.
> It is almost incredible that under our law a person who has
> made good his entry into this country unlawfully cannot be
> sent home when the malpractice comes to light. The people of
> other countries, Commonwealth countries no less than others,
> have no hesitation whatever in expelling those who break the
> law to cross their frontiers. They must think that, to use a
> famous phrase, we are 'stark, staring bonkers' to offer all
> illegal entrants a prize for breaking the law . . .

This speech unquestionably touched raw nerves. the *Sunday
Times*, in particular, assailed Powell in its following issue, arguing
that, 'His latest speech no doubt accurately represents Wolverhampton's fears of being swamped by immigrants. But its
unreliable statistical projections and its tones of lurid menace
are irresponsible.' For several years to come Powell's projections
became a matter for heated discussion, into which he himself
entered with vigour and which, indeed, have been the staple of
much of the writing about him which has since appeared. The
matter is discussed below[44] but is, in my judgement, of lesser
consequence than either Powell himself or his critics attributed
to it. The fact was that even on the lowest estimations the figures
justified concern, and the existence of concern in the public mind
was a political fact of high importance.

Powell had some open national support, most notably from the
Sunday Express and the *Daily Sketch*, and his post bag reflected
growing public appreciation of his views.[45] Iain Macleod and
Quintin Hogg were both, however, distressed by the tone of
the speech and said so at the Shadow Cabinet meeting the week
after its delivery. Powell endeavoured to defend himself, but
debate was curtailed by an intervention on the part of Heath. It
was to be on a rather different, though related, matter that the
next serious misunderstanding was to arise between Powell and
his closest colleagues.

On the government side, meanwhile, matters had also been
moving. 1967 was a wretched year for the Cabinet, culminating
as it did with the devaluation of sterling and the consequent
exchange of offices between Roy Jenkins and James Callaghan.
It is now known[46] that before Jenkins left the Home Office he
had discussed with the Leader of the House of Commons, Richard
Crossman, the possibility of finding time in the parliamentary programme for a Bill to restrict the immigration of Kenyan Asians,

should this be judged to be necessary. Confidential discussions had taken place with both the Kenyan and Indian governments to persuade the former to relax at least its rate of expulsion and the latter to offer succour to as many Asians from East Africa as possible. But President Kenyatta remained adamant and, although Mrs. Gandhi was willing to offer private professions of help, she was unwilling to make public statements of those professions, since to do such might encourage more expulsions.[47] It was deemed advisable by Jenkins at least to prepare legislative ground, given the rising anxiety of public opinion. There was, too, another consideration in his mind. His heart was set on the passage of his long-awaited Race Relations Bill. He had no illusion that it would be generally popular, and he was in doubt about what line the Conservative Opposition would take. It was clearly, therefore, as well to be prepared to administer a judicious dose of stick and carrot: a law limiting the Kenyan intake would demonstrate that the government was concerned about immigration, while a law regulating relations between the races would cosset liberal opinion (as well as redeeming a pledge in Labour's 1964 manifesto).

The situation which confronted Callaghan upon his arrival at the Home Office was not a pleasing one. Month by month the stream of immigrants from Kenya was rising. Thirteen thousand arrived in the first two months of 1968 and the rate at one stage approached 300 a day. Massive publicity attended the influx and contributed greatly to the anxieties not merely of the public, but of the government. Callaghan quotes himself as saying in Cabinet that, 'We shall remain subject to these risks of continuing tensions and stimulation of prejudice unless we amend the law so that the public in this country are confident that immigration is being effectively controlled. Only in such an atmosphere can good race relations be fostered.' His approach (based on the draft Bill prepared for Jenkins) was first, to undertake completely to fulfil the alleged commitment to the Asians but, second, to stagger the intake by issuing a limited number of vouchers each year over the years it would take to discharge the obligation. The Cabinet decided to bite the bullet and the necessary Bill was put through all its stages in the House of Commons and the House of Lords within seven days. It became law on 1 March 1968.

Mr. Foot in particular,[48] but other critics as well, attribute the government's action, and the haste with which it was implemented, almost solely to Powell. As I have shown, however, the matter had been in contemplation for some time, though I have little doubt that the rising tempo of debate, to which Powell had so greatly contributed from his October speech at Deal onwards, did make a great deal of difference to the speed of legislative movement.

The next item on the agenda was the Race Relations Bill. Initially undecided about the line it should take, the Shadow Cabinet eventually resolved to table a reasoned amendment, a procedure which, as has already been mentioned, would enable the Opposition to register disapproval without committing it to line by line criticism thereafter. Powell played an important part within the Shadow Cabinet in making this decision, and in the drafting of the amendment which was finally agreed at a full meeting on Thursday, 11 April.

The sequence and weight of events now assume the greatest importance in describing motivation and reaction. Powell had a long-standing commitment to address the Annual General Meeting of the West Midlands Area Conservative Political Centre on Saturday, 20 April, and it was known that his subject would be immigration. Heath had a commitment of shorter standing to contribute an article, dealing in the main with the same subject, to the *News of the World* for its issue of Sunday, 21 April. This article, drafted for him by his principal speechwriter, Michael Wolff, was typically subfusc and even banal; but it was an important exclusive for the paper none the less.

At the Shadow Cabinet meeting of 11 April there was discussion, not merely of the reasoned amendment to the Race Relations Bill (due for its Second Reading on Tuesday, 23 April) but of the whole subject of immigration and race relations. Memories of what was said, and impressions of how things were said, differ, but what is certain is that Powell left the meeting convinced that what he was going to say was wholly in line with party policy: he therefore felt no requirement to discuss it with Hogg. To anticipate events somewhat, it should be mentioned that, in response to Press inquiries, Conservative Central Office issued a statement on the evening of Saturday, 20 April confirming that the Birmingham speech was not out of line with policy and, indeed, in subsequent months Heath more than once confirmed this himself, by proposing measures wholly in line with those which Powell was urging.[49] In any event, as Powell later recorded, 'I travelled to my constituency with a light heart. At last the seriousness of the problem was being seized. At last there was unity on what needed to be done.'

One accusation of bad faith has, not infrequently, been made against Powell. That is that he did not, as is the common practice, deliver a copy of his speech to Conservative Central Office for distribution. But there is nothing to be made of this, for it was Powell's frequent practice when speaking in his own area to use the facilities of the Party's Area Office for distribution of texts. There is no evidence, further, to suggest that either Powell himself or the area officials had any expectation that he would create a greater effect than he normally did – that is, an effect of considerable appreciation for his efforts and his eloquence. What was evident before the meeting started (at 2.30 p.m.) however, was the existence of considerable Press and television interest. Local editors had for the most part seen the newsworthy potential of the advance text, and took care to cover the event. The audience, however, numbering eighty-five – the average for this kind of gathering – though they applauded their speaker warmly, was unaware that anything special had occurred when Powell, having finished his speech, left. Over the years I have spoken to a number of people who were present. Their opinion is unanimous that at 3.30 p.m. they had not noticed that anything remarkable had happened, though it is fair to add, as I have already mentioned,[50] that it frequently takes time for the significance of a political speech to sink in. Reading the text even at this distance in time, however, one can see how correct the journalistic instinct was.

The beginning was quiet enough, and almost academic:

> The supreme function of statesmanship is to provide against preventable evils. In seeking to do so, it encounters obstacles which are deeply rooted in human nature . . . Above all, people are disposed to mistake predicting troubles for causing troubles and even for desiring troubles . . . At all events, the discussion of future grave but, with effort now, avoidable evils is the most necessary occupation for the politician. Those who knowingly shirk it deserve, and not infrequently receive, the curses of those who come after.

Then he threw the first rhetorical hand grenade. He told of a conversation with a constituent who had professed a desire to emigrate, and would certainly encourage his children to do so because 'In this country in fifteen or twenty years' time the black man will have the whip hand over the white man.' Powell went on:

How dare I say such a horrible thing? How dare I stir up trouble by repeating such a conversation? The answer is that I do not have the right not to do so. Here is a decent, ordinary fellow Englishman, who in broad daylight in my own town says to me, his Member of Parliament, that this country will not be worth living in for his children. I simply do not have the right to shrug my shoulders and think about something else.

This passage marks an important shift in Powell's rhetorical manner. He had always spoken as though he embodied some important principle related to the national identity (indeed, the speech on the Royal Titles Bill was wholly based on that assumption) but the expression tended towards the abstract. Here in Birmingham there was an important shift of gear, as he assumed the role of mouthpiece for his constituents and his correspondents.

He then went on – this time using figures provided by the Registrar General – to project a coloured population of three and a half million by 1988, and to emphasize the significance of the fact that, rather than being uniformly spread, it would be concentrated in a few areas. He then stated the first principle of Conservative policy: to act 'by stopping, or virtually stopping, further inflow, and by promoting the maximum outflow'. He referred to the continuing high rate of immigration and introduced the first of several vivid metaphors which would make the speech ring around the nation:

Those whom the gods wish to destroy, they first make mad. We must be mad, literally mad, as a nation to be permitting the annual inflow of some 50,000 dependents, who are for the most part the material of the future growth of the immigrant descended population. It is like watching a nation busily engaged in heaping up its own funeral pyre.

Repeating that repatriation (which he called 're-emigration') was also a vital part of Conservative policy, he stressed its urgency and its importance:

It can be no part of any policy that existing families should be kept divided;[51] but there are two directions in which families can be reunited, and if our former and present immigration laws have brought about the division of families,

247

albeit voluntarily or semi-voluntarily, we ought to be prepared to arrange for them to be re-united in their countries of origin. In short, suspension of immigration and encouragement of re-emigration hang together, logically and humanely, as two aspects of the same approach.

Powell went on to the third plank of Conservative policy. In a passage usually ignored by his critics he asserted, in terms as ringing as any he had used before, the necessity of holding the belief of equality before the law. However, he combined this with an outright attack on the Race Relations Bill. It would, he believed, lead to a system of discrimination *in favour* of the immigrant communities. Moreover, it was designed to regulate private conduct. Both of these intentions were offensive, though he did not expect that to be understood by 'newspapers which year after year in the 1930s tried to blind this country to the rising peril which confronted it, or archbishops in palaces, faring delicately with the bedclothes pulled right up over their heads'. Such people

> have got it exactly and diametrically wrong. The discrimination and the deprivation, the sense of alarm and of resentment, lies not with the immigrant population but with those among whom they have come and are still coming. That is why to enact legislation of the kind before Parliament at this moment is to risk throwing a match on to gunpowder. The kindest thing that can be said about those who propose and support it is that they know not what they do.

After a review of one of his besetting preoccupations – the extra privilege Commonwealth citizens enjoyed over aliens in the matter of immigration and settlement – he passed on to integration. He had always, of course, argued the virtues of assimilation, provided the immigrant sedulously sought to assimilate himself to the habits, laws and traditions of the host country, to become, in effect, a coloured Briton. He introduced the theme, however, with his most explosive anecdote so far, the use of which alone would probably have been enough to ensure his dismissal from the Shadow Cabinet.

Among the many hundreds of letters he had received after his speech in Walsall, he said, one recounted the story of an elderly white woman who kept a lodging house in a street in Wolverhampton. Over a period the other properties in the street had been taken over by immigrants. Her white tenants gradually left and 'the quiet street became a place of noise and confusion.' She declined to let rooms in her house to immigrants, and declined, likewise, to sell it to aspiring immigrant landlords. Then he quoted a longer extract from the letter:

> The telephone is her lifeline. Her family pay the bill, and help her out as best they can. Immigrants have offered to buy her house – at a price which the prospective landlord would be able to recover from his tenants within weeks, or at most months. She is becoming afraid to go out. Windows are broken. She finds excreta pushed through her letterbox. When she goes to the shops, she is followed by children, charming, wide-grinning piccaninnies. They cannot speak English, but one word they know. 'Racialist,' they chant. When the new Race Relations Bill is passed, this woman is convinced she will go to prison. And is she so wrong? I begin to wonder.

Having thus dramatized the situation as his correspondent saw it, Powell went on to discuss integration:

> To be integrated into a population means to become for all practical purposes indistinguishable from its other members. Now, at all times, where there are marked physical differences, especially of colour, integration is difficult though, over a period, not impossible. There are among the Commonwealth immigrants who have come to live here in the last fifteen years or so, many thousands whose wish and purpose is to be integrated, and whose every thought and endeavour is bent in that direction. But to imagine that such a thing enters the heads of a great and growing majority of immigrants and their descendants is a ludicrous misconception, and a dangerous one to boot.

It was, he went on, the very concentration of immigrants in particular urban areas, a concentration which the more readily enabled them to remain separate from the host community, which created the danger and ensured the impossibility of integration. And he concluded, in the most famous passage from this famous speech:

> For these dangerous and divisive elements the legislation proposed in the Race Relations Bill is the very pabulum they

need to flourish. Here is the means of showing that the immigrant communities can organize to consolidate their members, to agitate and campaign against their fellow citizens, and to overawe and dominate the rest with the legal weapons which the ignorant and ill-informed have provided. As I look ahead, I am filled with foreboding. Like the Roman, I seem to see, 'the River Tiber foaming with much blood'. That tragic and intractable phenomenon which we watch with horror on the other side of the Atlantic but which there is interwoven with the history and existence of the States itself, is coming upon us here by our own volition and our own neglect. Indeed, it has all but come. In numerical terms, it will be of American proportions long before the end of the century. Only resolute and urgent action will avert it even now. Whether there will be the public will to demand and obtain that action, I do not know. All I know is that to see, and not to speak, would be the great betrayal.

The speech was headline news, and led practically every radio and television bulletin. As was their practice the Powells went to St. Peter's Church for Sunday morning service. When they emerged it was to face a large gathering of reporters and photographers, of whom Powell asked, 'Have I really caused such a furore?' He consented, however, to break his rule of no work on Sunday to speak to the BBC radio programme *The World this Weekend* and to Independent Television News. On the first programme he defended his right and, indeed, duty to speak 'about the deep fears, the resentments and anxieties for the future which I know exist'. Asked by ITN whether the speech had been cleared with Heath, he replied that there had been no necessity since 'It was a speech entirely on the lines he had set out.' The point could be made[52] that on the matter of dependents he was somewhat out of line; but in the main his defence of himself was just.

In London, Heath was telephoned by Gerald O'Brien, an official in the Press Office of Central Office who had good media contacts, one of whom had tipped him off that Powell was about to receive maximum coverage. This was followed by a steady stream of calls from the Press. He adopted the stonewalling tactics usual on these occasions, by insisting that he could make no comment until he had studied the full text (which O'Brien had informed him was not available at Smith Square). Of far greater importance, however, were calls from Edward Boyle, Quintin Hogg and others, who were outraged, principally because of the heightened language Powell had chosen to employ, but Hogg was particularly furious because Powell had crossed over into his own bailiwick. Both Boyle and Hogg made it clear that they could no longer serve in a Shadow Cabinet of which Powell was a member.

Heath telephoned his Chief Whip, William Whitelaw (now Viscount Whitelaw), in his constituency on the Scottish Borders. He was uncertain what to do and wanted to canvass opinion before making up his mind. The question was whether a split in the Party at its highest level (a thing which, as a former Chief Whip himself, he abhorred) was now avoidable. Certainly, he and Whitelaw agreed, he could not lose Boyle[53] and Hogg for the sake of Powell and, in any event, they both thought the speech offensive. Whitelaw agreed to leave immediately for London, so as to be available for consultation the following day. But by early evening Heath had made up his mind. The Powells having no telephone in their Wolverhampton home, he got in touch with Powell's agent, who fetched his Member to the telephone. In the course of a brief and curt conversation Powell was told that he had been dismissed from the Shadow Cabinet.

After a few hours' sleep Powell wrote to Heath objecting to the attempt 'to stigmatize my speech in Birmingham as racialist. You must surely realize it was nothing of the kind.' He praised (in a somewhat condescending way) some of Heath's qualities, but said that there was 'one cause of anxiety . . . the impression you often give of playing down and unsaying the policies and views which you hold and believe to be right for fear of clamour from some section of Press and public.' Then he went back to South Eaton Place to the largest post any British politician had ever received.[54]

He also came back to a generally execratory Press. An analysis by the Institute of Race Relations of forty-five local and national newspaper editorials showed that twenty-eight were unfavourable, ten mixed and only seven friendly. However, as Dr. Schoen points out[55], the two nationals which were well disposed, the *Daily Express* and the *News of the World* had a combined circulation of 11.3 million, more than the total circulation of the seven critical nationals. *The Times*, on Monday 22 April, was particularly savage. Under the heading 'An Evil Speech' the editor wrote:

The Birmingham speech was, of course, disgraceful . . . because it was racialist . . . The more closely one reads the text of Mr. Powell's speech, the more shameful it seems. The language, the innuendoes, the constant appeals to self-pity, the anecdotes, all combine to make a deliberate appeal to racial hatred. This is the first time that a serious British politician has appealed to racial hatred, in this direct way, in our postwar history.

The paper went further, providing on its features pages a large display of generally liberal reactions to the speech, beginning with Humphry Berkeley's comparison of Powell to the pre-war Fascist leader, Sir Oswald Mosley. This may have given somebody at Printing House Square what passed for a bright idea for, two days later, there appeared on the features pages a compendium under the headline 'MOSLEY SPEECHES RECALLED' which quoted the views of Fascist leaders from Mosley down and including the former leader of the National Front, then of the National Socialist Movement (and an ex-convict) all in praise of Powell. The statement of guilt by association quickly became a popular one with other papers of a liberal bent, and reporters were set to work to find material which cast doubt on the veracity of Powell's anecdotes and on the reliability of his statistics.[56]

Powell was bewildered, hurt and embittered by all this, and was to be even more so when, on arriving at the House of Commons on Tuesday he found himself shunned not merely by the Labour Members but by the great majority of Tories, and particularly all of the Shadow Cabinet, with the exception of Sir Alec Douglas-Home. The general opinion of the parliamentary Press was that, while he had undoubtedly picked up support since the leadership contest of 1965, following the speech he had at the very outside no more than fifty supporters.

There were, however, consolations. By the morning of Tuesday, 23 April the Powells and family friends were sorting out more than 45,000 letters at South Eaton Place: of these all but a few thousand were favourable, and included a round robin signed by all the Immigration Officers stationed at Heathrow airport. There were four more large sacks waiting for him at Westminster. This volume was not to fall for some time and, as Mrs. Spearman points out in her various studies of letters received by Powell, singularly few of them could be regarded as racialist or obnoxious. The spread was extraordinary; it covered all Party allegiances, all social classes and all economic sectors. On the afternoon of 23 April, moreover, a procession of dockers numbered in thousands marched to Westminster in his support.

There were a few unpleasant incidents – catcalls for the Labour MP Ian Mikardo and the booing of the Jamaican High Commissioner – but considering the evident explosiveness of the issue, and making comparisons with the verbal and physical violence of the hostile demonstrations that were to pursue Powell over the following years, the whole affair passed off with good humour and dignity. Moreover, four different opinion polls, Gallup, ORC, NOP and *Daily Express*, all recorded overwhelming public support for him. Gallup recorded 74%, ORC 82%, NOP 67% and the *Express* 79%. The corresponding opinion figures against were 15%, 12%, 19% and 17%. On the question of whether Heath had been right to dismiss him three of the same polls, in the same order, gave the figures for Heath as 20%, 18% and 25% and against him 69%, 73% and 61%. The *Daily Express* poll did not ask about the dismissal. Moreover, however the pollsters tried to break down the figures, whether by social class or in other ways, they came up with the same answer: Powell's support was uniformly spread throughout all sections of the community and all regions. Hounded by the Press and abandoned by his colleagues he might be; but he had become a national figure, with a huge following. In addition, he now had the clearest possible evidence that the politicians of both parties were seriously and even dangerously out of line with public opinion on the immigration issue. This seemed to him to justify even more the technique he had adopted both in Walsall and Birmingham, of allowing his correspondents and constituents to speak through him. He thus became a genuine tribune of the people. He was to speak at Eastbourne on 17 November, in just this sense, saying that a dangerous gap had opened 'between the overwhelming majority of the people throughout the country on the one side and, on the other side, a tiny minority with almost a monopoly hold upon the channels of communication, who seem determined not to know the facts and not to face the realities, who will resort to any device or extremity to blind both themselves and others'.

The most important thing about the April 1968 speech was not its content, still less its argument. Powell had said the same sort of thing before and others – albeit in a far less elegant and well-turned fashion – had delivered a similar message. The really important thing was the impact. Virtually overnight Powell was transformed from being an interesting – but perhaps marginal – political figure into being a cynosure of attention, whether admired, or hated.

The question any student must ask is: why was this so, why did it happen in this way? Powell had been controversial before. He had been brave before. He had defied both general opinion and the leadership of his party before. He had, in the seminal speech on Royal Titles, brandished his defiance of most conventional opinion. 1968, however, made a difference; and I think that the reason for this difference is simple to elucidate.

When Powell spoke in the House of Commons in March 1953 about Royal Titles, however great his passion and erudition, he was speaking to a confined audience. After April 1968 he was speaking – and being heard by – the nation as a whole.

I record the view that Powell was right on immigration, and that the extraordinary reaction to the Birmingham speech had almost nothing to do with its simple statement about numbers. While he was accused of being racist, he was merely talking about identity; and it was for identity that people feared. He was attacked by people who wanted to be polyglot, people who would pretend (and often believe) that there was no serious difference of race, nor culture, nor creed, between the inhabitants of these islands and those leaving the Empire's successor nations to their own devices, and moving across the world to England.

Powell's opponents lit their fires in two camps. In one camp it was said over the fires of debate that there should be a great amalgamation of cultures, that language mattered little, as did colour of skin. In the other camp, around another fire, while the polyglot thesis was not held it was maintained that the United Kingdom would not change simply because of a massive immigration of people of different colour and culture. This second camp consisted, in the main, of people already committed to the new alliance summarized in the putative accession of the United Kingdom to the European Community.

What Powell touched was not simply a nerve, but a whole series of nerves. There were the nerves of all those who had loved the old Empire. There were the nerves of those who hated that Empire and believed that its history was one of exploitation by white peoples of coloureds; and that the whites had a duty of reparation. There were the nerves of those who wanted to believe that there were really no differences between peoples. Events since 1968, however, have clearly demonstrated difference, and difference which is much less a matter of prejudice than a matter of belief. We see, in this decade, the proud assertion by immigrant communities of identity, and the making of provisions for them to state that identity: Powell was stating the right to a British

identity, one exclusive to the native inhabitants of these islands
– exclusive both historically and geographically.

The grand questions in Powell's mind were not of superiority
or inferiority, but of difference and identity. Identity has been
the great preoccupation of his public life. The reaction to the
1968 speech showed that it was a preoccupation of many others
as well, whether they loved him or reviled him. All this was to
be demonstrated again in the debate over British membership
of the European Economic Community.

For the moment, however, he did not return to the subject
of immigration, and was not infrequently criticized by Labour
MPs for declining to bring it up in the House of Commons. In
general, he resumed his life as it had been before entry into the
Shadow Cabinet, a melange of scholarship, journalism, reviewing
and public speaking. His support was sought by the twenty plus
Opposition MPs who were against British entry into the EEC
(led by the most intelligent and consistent of them, the late Neil
Marten). He politely declined, though he told them he shared
their views. His judgement was that he already had a series of
major campaigns going on, and he did not, for the moment, want
to add to their number. He was biding his time and enjoying the
nervousness which speculation about his intentions was arousing
in the ranks of the advocates of entry, for his scepticism was
widely known. In the event, he was not openly to declare his
opposition to British membership of the EEC until a speech at
Clacton on 21 March 1969.

This speculation was based on a question of very great importance for Powell's friends, rivals and enemies. It was this:
would he be able to translate his sudden and immense support gained through the immigration issue into other policies?
The signs were not propitious. The Gallup poll for July 1968
asked avowed Powell supporters whether or not they favoured
state intervention in the economy: 36% did. However, of all
respondents who wished Heath to move to the right 47% preferred Powell as Leader. The truth appears to be that a very
large part of the electorate had only the haziest knowledge
of where he stood on anything other than immigration. This
reflected the fact that, whereas over the years leading up to
April 1968 his reputation had been steadily growing, it had
remained an intellectual one. Now, in a series of speeches
in September, on economics and defence, he began to push
the arguments in various areas well beyond the limits of Party policy, particularly on denationalization and devolution for

Cummings

THE 'HAS-BEENS' CLUB

IMMIGRATION WARNINGS ABOUT RACIAL STRIFE

"What is utterly indefensible and unforgivable, Mr Powell, is that you're a politician who's actually been proved RIGHT ! "

Scotland and Wales, a topic suddenly fashionable with both front benches.

Then, in November, 'another subject found me'. This subject was, indeed, to remake his parliamentary reputation and gain for him and his partner, Michael Foot, their greatest House of Commons victory. The subject was the reform of the House of Lords.

Throughout the century Liberal and Labour governments had again and again been foiled by opposition to their measures in the Lords. Various steps had been taken to reduce their lordships' power and by 1968 they could no longer alter money bills and were restricted in their power to delay other government legislation to only nine months (a provision which came into effect in 1949). Substantial sections of the Labour Party desired the abolition of the Lords altogether, and it was partly in consciousness of this threat that Lord Carrington, on becoming Leader of the Opposition in the Upper House in October 1964, spelled out his policy to his supporters:[57]

> If the Labour leadership are reasonable, we let them get away with it. They know how far they can push us. Once we

256

start using our veto, we're damaging the object of a Second Chamber. If the House of Lords is to work, we must share forbearance and commonsense.

In other words, a Conservative Leader of the Lords, faced with a Labour government sustained by a Party already deeply suspicious of, when not actually hostile to, the institution, had to walk with particular delicacy. From time to time over the years various schemes for reforming the Lords had been canvassed. These largely arose because of widespread feelings, ranging from unease to outrage, at the seeming anomaly of a legislature largely hereditary in composition. All the schemes had foundered, however, partly because it was agreed that the Upper House performed an invaluable role in the technical scrutiny of legislation and its amendment, and partly because it was accepted that constitutional reform could and should not proceed without agreement between the Parties, and this was never forthcoming.

However, during the long Labour years of opposition the fertile brain of Richard Crossman[58] – by 1968 Leader of the House of Commons – had come up with a scheme for change. Crossman tried, as early as 1964, to interest Iain Macleod in his proposals, but to no avail. He found Carrington more receptive, and interparty talks proceeded in a desultory way until 1968. Wilson was more interested in the matter than Heath (not least because he constantly feared a Lords' rebellion on his policy of imposing sanctions on Rhodesia) but both Leaders gave Crossman and Carrington a fairly free hand.

The formula the two men and their assistants came up with was essentially one devised by Crossman. All existing peers – so it ran – would retain their seats, but not the right to vote. There would be created, in addition, about 230 peers who could vote. These would all receive salaries and would be appointed by the Prime Minister of the day who would, however, be required to make the appointments in exact reflection of Party strength in the House of Commons. Both front benches in the Commons considered this plan with a good deal of satisfaction, though Macleod warned his colleagues that the complacency with which they viewed the prospects of success might well prove to be unjustified. The situation in the Lords was, from the point of view of the would-be reformers, far less satisfactory; but the Lords could be overruled or, if the lengthy process of overruling them seemed too tedious, as many as eighty new peers could be created to give a reform majority in the Upper House, a scheme sharply reminiscent of Asquith's pre-First World War proposal to swamp the Lords with Liberal peers to ensure the passage of his financial legislation. On 19 November Richard Crossman rose in the House of Commons to introduce the Parliament (No. 2) Bill, embodying the fruits of all his thinking and negotiation.

He and his allies had, however, given insufficient consideration to several important facts. There was no enthusiasm for – or even interest in – the Bill in the country. Many Conservative backbenchers (not to mention Conservative peers) disliked it intensely, as being (though this was not yet a particularly closely thought out position, and did not become so until Powell intervened) an offence against the natural order of things. Conversely, it was not popular on the Labour back benches either. Labour abolitionists saw it as a piece of unsatisfactory tinkering; others regarded it as likely to accord to the Prime Minister of the day (not to mention the Leader of the Opposition) far too much power of patronage – this at a time when the seemingly steadily increasing power of the Prime Minister had become a source of considerable concern. The champion of the anti-patronage argument was the Galahad of the Labour left, Michael Foot.

Powell was not insensitive to the argument against patronage: during the Committee stage of the Bill, on 25 February 1969, in a discussion on the proposed remuneration of the proposed appointed peers, he advised the House that '. . . we are giving the government an entirely new kind of patronage, a patronage which enables them to influence the effective composition of a relatively small chamber so as to make it subservient to their will by that act of patronage and to exercise a patronage which confers on the recipient a substantial and secure income up to retirement age.' But his fundamental objection was deeper: he was determined to resist tampering with the constitution, which he regarded in an almost sacerdotal light. His conviction was that arguments for reforming the House of Lords were based on general political theories. To him, however, that House depended for its form on prescription – that is sanction by tradition and long usage. He found offensive the belief that prescription could be overturned by modern notions of propriety and usefulness.

The battle lines were drawn during the debate on the issue on 19-20 November 1968 when what Lord Carrington was later to call 'the unholy alliance' of Michael Foot and Enoch Powell was born. It is important to remember, however – particularly as one is inclined to read backwards from the later expressions of high regard of each man for the other – that their collaboration in the fight against the Parliament (No. 2) Bill was a collaboration at arms' length, most necessary liaison between the two groups of doughty fighters against the legislation being carried out by John Boyd-Carpenter (now Lord Boyd-Carpenter) on the Conservative side and Robert Sheldon from Labour. None the less, the two front benches simply did not appreciate for some time how dangerous, and ultimately debilitating, for their cause would be a combination of the two foremost parliamentary proceduralists of the day.

The rebels on both sides initially enjoyed one significant advantage, and laboured under the burden of one significant disadvantage.

The advantage lay in the use, or non-use, of certain aspects of parliamentary procedure. The Bill was a constitutional Bill: its Committee stage (the period during which proposed legislation is scrutinized clause by clause and line by line) would, therefore, be taken in Committee of the Whole House. (The examination of ordinary legislation is usually consigned to a Standing Committee, a group of members chosen to reflect party strength in the House as a whole.) This meant that every single member had a right to put his oar in at any given time. Further it is against traditional practice to guillotine – that is, to cut short by resolution the time available for debate on – a constitutional Bill. Crossman, as it happened, was quite prepared to guillotine the Parliament (No. 2) Bill, but the Conservative front bench would not support him on that and the government did not feel secure enough to put the matter to the touch. This meant, of course, that the dedicated and inexhaustible cohorts led by Foot and Powell – spending all day in the Chamber, ever on the *qui vive*, ready to challenge every comma, ears ever open for the slightest error or ambiguity, immensely more learned than their opponents – could, by prolonged debate, wreck the government's legislative programme. Moreover, Ministers and Opposition frontbenchers had other business to attend to: as the Committee stage ground on, the senior figures – and in particular Crossman and James Callaghan, as Home Secretary the Minister responsible for piloting the Bill through – were less and less in evidence. Partly in consequence the less interested – or uninterested – backbenchers absented themselves, and it was more than once necessary to cut short a debate (which would have to be continued the following day) for fear of lack of a majority. Determination and assiduity were powerful weapons in the hands of such rebels as these.

There was a peculiar irony in the tangle in which Crossman

found himself. It was he, as Leader of the House, who had introduced regular morning sittings. This, of course, gave yet more time to the opponents of his beloved Lords Reform Bill. However, because so many Members did not care to turn up in the mornings, the government found it impracticable to call votes before, at the earliest, 1 p.m. This further hampered their conduct of business.

The disadvantage to the opponents of the Bill lay, in the initial stages, in Powell himself. If, since his speech of 20 April, he had been regarded with dislike and anger by his fellow-Tories, he was regarded, in the main, with detestation on the Labour benches. A true flavour of that detestation was given by William Hamilton, the Labour Member for West Fife on 19 November. Powell had (as he was perfectly entitled to do) added his name to a wrecking amendment tabled by Hamilton, who confessed his embarrassment at this act, stating that his Labour support was the less because his supporters felt that the Opposition lobby would 'be soiled by the presence of the Rt. Hon. Member for Wolverhampton South-West'. The Speaker forced a partial and unsatisfactory withdrawal of this remark, but it was a genuine expression of feeling none the less.

In time, and first during the debates on the Bill, Powell was to win considerable regard, at the very least as a skilled parliamentarian, from the generality of Labour Members. But the hostility that grew like a rank flower from the April speech was never eradicated. In 1974, for example, the campaign for a 'no' vote in the referendum on whether the United Kingdom should remain a member of the Common Market was considerably weakened (as I personally discovered as one of the national organizers) by the refusal of prominent Labour members of the National Referendum Campaign Committee (the umbrella opposition organization chaired by Neil Marten) to appear on the same platforms as Powell or, for that matter, on the television broadcasts which the Committee made. It was, of course, the sheerest folly not to make the fullest use of an orator with far greater influence on the electorate than all the other members of the executive of the NRCC put together; but the Labour members – Michael Foot excepted – could not overcome their repugnance for him and his views on immigration.

The acquisition of a great parliamentary reputation is no easy business, and its characteristics are by no means easy to define. A Prime Minister, say, obviously has great parliamentary power. But that is in virtue of his office, not of his performance. The perfect example of this dichotomy is Edward Heath: for a brief period during his residence at No. 10 Downing Street he certainly dominated the House of Commons, but that was because of the power he held from the electorate, not because of parliamentary skills which, in any event, he possessed in no marked degree. Harold Wilson was adroit, and had a priceless ability to think quickly on his feet; but his reputation was a meretricious one: nobody thought of him as a true Parliament man.

Until November 1968 Powell had what might be called an academic parliamentary reputation. As a speaker he was greatly admired. His prodigious knowledge of the history and rules of the House of Commons was envied. And his deep love of the institution was respected. But his causes – such as opposition to the Royal Titles Bill – were judged esoteric and in any event their purpose, let alone his expression of that purpose, was beyond the understanding of most Members. That Powell (and, of course, Foot) could mount a brilliant constitutional action against the government's proposals for the Lords was not in doubt, but most of the government's (and the official Opposition's) business managers were satisfied that it would be a rearguard action. When Powell rose as fourth speaker on 19 November there were few outside the thin ranks lined up behind Powell and Foot who believed that parliamentary rhetoric and logical argument, however fine, could be translated into the kind of power required to stop a government with a majority of 100 and supported by the Opposition front bench, in its tracks.

'A shiver of apprehension,' Crossman later said, 'ran down my spine when Powell spoke.' As is common with him, Powell first reduced the whole argument to first principles. He took the hypothesis that reform of the Lords was necessary (a hypothesis that he did not himself accept). There were two ways to reform. The first was that under consideration – the creation of a nominated second chamber. The second was the superficially more plausible idea of an *elected* rather than a (mostly) hereditary second chamber. So far as the latter was concerned, 'However the mode of election was rigged, we could never escape from this dilemma: how can the same electorate be represented in two ways so that the two sets of representatives can conflict and disagree with one another?' He concluded that elected second chambers were appropriate and workable only in countries with federal constitutions (such as Australia and the United States). His full scorn, however, was turned on the proposal for a nominated House of Lords:

At one and the same time the proposals seek to secure a built-in government majority and also to make it possible for the Upper House to disagree with this House, vote against it, throw out the government's proposals and get away with that . . . Upon that inherent dilemma this scheme is bound to perish.

The Bill provided for some thirty cross-benchers, this being part of Crossman's attempt convincingly to assert that the changed House of Lords would have independence from government. Powell would have none of it:

Then there is the other grand absurdity of the cross-benchers, those thirty appointees, appointed on the basis that they are neither fish, fowl nor good red herring, upon the very basis that they have no strong views of principle on the way in which the country ought to be governed; upon the promise that they will fluctuate from case to case, from question to question, and not seek to decide in the light of any such general principles as bind us respectively together in this lower House.

Powell had once written a series of essays gathered together in volume form as *Great Parliamentary Occasions*. The Second Reading of the Parliament (No. 2) Bill would certainly merit a place in any such future collection, and Powell's contribution would be the centre of any literary consideration of the moment.[59] Pale and intense as always, body moving slightly from side to side, but using none of the dramatic gestures he employs on public platforms, his voice quiet, but carrying, an audience attending to every syllable in rapt silence, his was unquestionably the speech of the debate. Certainly, the government carried the day on 20 November, but their tally of 272, though sufficient, had ranged against it the substantial figure of 161 votes: this was enough to set alarm bells ringing.

None the less, the government pressed ahead, and the Committee stage of the Bill began on 12 February 1969. It is not necessary in this study to take the reader through all its stages, but a few salient points may be picked out.

The alliance between Conservative and Labour opponents of the Bill did not involve their supporting each others' amendments: thus, for example, on 12 February Powell himself devoted much time to criticizing Robert Sheldon's amendment to abolish the hereditary peerage. The tactics lay, rather, in each group knowing what the other was going to do, and being prepared to devote knowledge and time to discussing it. Their unity was evident principally when they joined together against the government as, for example, on 19 February, when they forced the Attorney General, Sir Elwyn Jones, into a lame explanation of why the principles of the Bill had not been included in its preamble – a procedure generally accepted as being an indispensable part of legislation laid before the House.

The tactical objective was, of course, to use up parliamentary time, so that the government would be forced to choose between this Bill and the rest of its programme. But, however pedantic the opposition to the Bill might often seem, it is fair to say that the objections of Powell and his allies on both sides of the House invariably went to the heart of some principle. I have already mentioned that Ministers were, because of pressure of other business, forced to exclude themselves from most of the Committee's procedures. Even this, however, Powell was able to turn to quick advantage. When, on a rare visit to the Committee James Callaghan denounced the opposition as 'frivolous', Powell had a ready riposte. He wondered whom the Home Secretary had in mind

> in referring to frivolous opposition. Those who have sat through this debate, as he has not, will be aware that the vast majority of speeches have been very far from frivolous and have gone to the heart of about the most serious matter – the constitution of Parliament – that the House could possibly debate.

It was increasingly becoming clear that the Bill was eating ferociously into government time. By April it had made only pitiful progress. At the Cabinet meeting of 15 April the reluctant decision was taken that it would have to be abandoned. On 17 April the Prime Minister rose in the House to confess defeat. As he gabbled his way through his text – necessary embarrassment, after all, to be got over as quickly as possible – Powell interrupted with the cry, 'Eat it slower.'

The cry of victory was eminently justified. But perhaps the most satisfying – if rueful – tribute was to come years later. In his memoirs[60] James Callaghan wrote:

> From opposite ends of the political spectrum Enoch Powell and

Michael Foot made brilliant mockery of the Bill's proposals, and by their tactics held up any serious progress for days at a time . . . I found myself the Minister responsible for the Bill, but any reluctant admiration I might have felt at the virtuosity of the Bill's opponents was soon smothered beneath increasing bafflement and frustration as we failed to make progress, and lumbered on against a stream of witty, logical and devastating oratory from its two principal, merciless opponents.

There is a footnote to the history of the Parliament (No. 2) Bill. Richard Crossman did not take defeat easily, and Peter Carrington was still anxious for reform. The talks between the two men continued, therefore, even after the *débâcle* of 17 April. One of the continual preoccupations of those times was, of course, the matter of sanctions against Rhodesia. The leadership of the Conservative Party, albeit with reluctance, consistently supported the government on the maintenance of sanctions, which had to be renewed each year by a resolution in both Houses. Carrington was finding it increasingly difficult to hold the line against peers sympathetic to the Rhodesian cause, and he was forced to temporize by promising that, after one more positive vote, the matter would be reconsidered. The Prime Minister used this flicker of disagreement as an excuse to break off talks on the Lords without, so Crossman tells us, consulting their begetter.[61]

The Crossman *Diaries* and the Callaghan memoirs record no more than the truth – and do so commendably – when they pay a tribute, however reluctant, to the victory of the numerically insignificant combined Labour and Conservative forces opposed to the scheme of reform of the House of Lords. A small body of determined gallants, led in effect (if not actually in name) by Powell and Foot had defeated the combined forces of a government with an unshakeably satisfactory majority, supported (if with varying enthusiasms) by the official Opposition, on a great constitutional issue. Memory of this humiliation, indeed, caused Callaghan, after he had become Prime Minister, to move with the greatest care on a constitutional issue of similar magnitude – the granting of devolution to Scotland and Wales.[62] That one, too, he got wrong.

It is tempting to speculate whether, had Powell still been in the Shadow Cabinet when its members were considering the *entente* on the Lords reached between Carrington and Crossman – if, in other words, he had not made the April speech, nor been dismissed for making it – he would have considered Conservative acceptance of the plan a matter for resignation. Even if one succumbs to the temptation (as I do now) it must be hedged by consideration of contingencies. Inside the Shadow Cabinet, Powell would have been a powerful advocate against the *entente*, and might have won his case. Had he not, however, I feel convinced that he would have resigned.

In any event, the conclusion of the battle over the Lords left Powell personally in an intriguing position. He had lanced the boil of universal Labour hatred of him, caused by the Birmingham speech. There remained – and remain to this day – many Labour politicians, in and out of Parliament, who both feared and hated him. But there were also many – and particularly those in the then higher reaches of that party – who had come to have real respect for him, and who were prepared to work with him. One striking instance of this I shall give later.[63]

His relations with his own party were similarly mixed, but the details have to be read backwards, as though seen in a mirror. Powell had no supporters in the upper reaches of the Conservative Party (or, at least none ready to declare themselves) but the rank and file were always at hand to offer him enthusiastic acclaim. It would be wrong to say that there was, here, a preference for Powell over Heath: rather, there was a desperate wish that the two men could get together and, specifically, that Heath should adopt Powell's policies on immigration. When Powell calculated his future actions, and considered any impact he might have on the nation's politics, however, he had to bear two things in mind.

The first was his own certainty that he would never hold office under Heath (who affirmed that that view was correct during the 1970 general election campaign), was, indeed, 'unlikely' to hold office again.[64] The second was the staggering popularity and support he continued to enjoy among the electorate at large. Under a democratic presidential system it is perfectly possible (and sometimes easy) for a politician beyond party to stand alone, and garner immense support. Under a parliamentary – and, perhaps, especially the British parliamentary – system it had hitherto been impossible for a rebel to stand by himself, and yet command widespread loyalty. Yet, National Opinion Polls found,[65] when they asked respondents in September 1968 to choose between Heath and Powell for Prime Minister, 41% were for Heath, but 37% for Powell. Asked the same question by the same firm in January 1969 it could be seen as an improvement for Heath: 49% were for him. But Powell still had 34%. Considering that

Heath, as Leader of the Opposition, was constantly in the public eye, and enjoyed the unquestioning allegiance of a major political Party, which allegiance was buttressed by that Party's expensive, efficiently organized and energetic bureaucracy, whereas Powell had only his wife, secretary and a handful of friends, his rating on the psephological seismometer must be considered astonishing.

Years before[66] Powell had said that he could not sustain too many rebellions. After Heath had dismissed him from the Shadow Cabinet, however, it was less necessary to choose between rebellions: timing, not subject, was all. Behind the question of timing lay the larger question of whether or not he could transmute the acclaim which his stand on immigration had won him into support for other, and less recognizable, policies to which he had given his heart. The great plough to which he now laid his hand was that of opposition to British membership of the European Economic Community.

For Powell the matter of membership became one not of power merely, but of identity. He explained his view with disarming frankness in the introductory notes to a collection of his speeches in 1971:[67]

> I was not an opponent of British membership of the European Economic Community in 1961-2. I was prepared to accept it, on the ground of trade, as the lesser evil, compared to being excluded. But we *were* excluded; and the events of the years that followed convinced me this judgement had been mistaken. Meanwhile it became indeed clear that the Community, if it survived at all, would be something quite different from a free trade area, and something to which Britain could not belong.

The point about identity needs to be taken a little further. Powell has consistently taken the view – even in the days when he was an enthusiastic advocate of empire – that the perennial British sin has been one of self-denigration. Thus, at Clacton, on 21 March 1969:

> To watch the British mopping up their daily ration of bad news, you might think that they not only liked it but throve on it. I believe this is only an outer covering of assumed indifference. I believe that underneath it there lies a sense of humiliation which has got deeper with the years. To begin no further back than 1956, there was the humiliation of the episode of Suez,

followed, as time went on, by the elimination of almost the last vestiges of our former presence from Africa and Asia. Then there was the humiliation of our serious and increasingly chronic deficit on the balance of payments from which we were always about to 'recover' but never did, and which rendered us persistent borrowers from other governments. Economically, there was the humiliation of finding ourselves equalled and surpassed in wealth by our neighbours and rivals. At home, there was even the humiliation of discovering that we could not define who we ourselves were, in time to avoid a grave and potentially tragic domestic conflict of a kind we never dreamt of. All these experiences and more have added up to a mood somewhere between dejection and desperation.

It had, for some time, been feared in Conservative circles that Powell would come out against British membership of the Common Market. The warning bell rang on 25 February 1970.

On 24 and 25 February 1970 the House of Commons debated the policy of the Wilson government on British membership of the EEC. Hugh Gaitskell, whom Wilson had succeeded, had passionately inveighed against the Macmillan idea of British membership of the Community. Wilson had continued in that tradition but, under the strains and stresses of a failing economy, an economy recalcitrant, it seemed, to the implementation of all the bright proposals which formed his argument for victory in 1964 and 1966, he yielded to the widely held belief that the United Kingdom could not survive in prosperity outside the Community. It is important to note – and future historians will have to note – the difference between Heath's and Wilson's approach to the scheme of Britain joining the EEC: Heath was – and is – an idealist on the subject, and favoured the ultimate creation of a politically united Western European state; Wilson, on the other hand, approached the conglomerate of the then six members cap in hand.

Powell attacked on both fronts, for he was as hostile to Heath's Eurocentric internationalism as he was to Wilson's craven pragmatism. This was the difficulty about his speech on 25 February, for he assailed both the Leader of the Opposition and the Prime Minister. He had scornful fun at the expense of the idea of the absolute necessity for the United Kingdom to ally herself with nations or organizations enjoying a higher growth rate than she: if that proposition was accepted then suit should be paid to Japan rather than to the EEC.

This, however, was skirmishing. The kernel of his objection to membership of the Community was loss of sovereignty. He was satisfied that he could win the argument on the grounds of supposed economic advantage. But, even were he to suppose he could lose on that ground, he had a higher purpose. It is expressed in two passages from the speech, one philosophical, one deadly, and the latter expressing with absolute clarity the fundamental nature of his political being. He had come to believe, he explained, that the EEC had much less to do with economics than with the creation of a new nation, success in the creation of which would ultimately ensure the extinction of his own country:

> Now, an electorate which sustains a true Parliament has to be an homogeneous electorate. By that I mean that every part of the electorate has consciously to say, 'We are part of the whole: we accept the verdict of the majority as expressed at the poll' and then, somewhat curiously as reflected in the composition of this House . . . The question posed to us is this: can we now, or in the next ten years, or in the foreseeable or immediate future, believe that the people of this country would regard themselves as so much part of an electorate comprising two hundred to two hundred and fifty million other electors that they would accept the majority view on taxation, on social policy, on development, on all matters which are crucial to our political life. I have to confess that I do not believe such an attitude of mind is foreseeable.

The deadly point arrived by way of historical analogy. Failing to understand – or, for that matter, be much interested in – the basic nature of Powell's nationalism, his political contemporaries had tended to think of him as a romantic (if they approved) or a Chauvinist (if they did not). There were those – again, for or against – who saw his nationalism as racial, those who saw it as cultural, and those who saw it as political. 'Enoch,' said one elderly Tory who sympathized with him on most issues, 'is an imperialist gone bad.' Powell sought to persuade the House to see what might have been when he said:

> In 1940 we were members of an alliance. Let us suppose that the forces raised from this Kingdom had been part of a political and military unit with a single political government and a single

command . . . does anyone suppose that the force which saved
this country would not have been thrown into the lost battle by
that political unit and swallowed up in defeat?

From the point of view of those who supported entry into
the EEC there was an obvious fallacy in this line of reasoning.
For if the EEC – or something like it – had existed in 1939, on
their reasoning, there would have been no war anyway. Indeed,
the genesis of the EEC, conceived in the brain of Jean Monnet,[68]
stated that the ideal of preventing military conflict in Western
Europe would best be served by the creation of a political and
economic alliance between like-minded democratic countries.
Powell did not, in my judgement, altogether do himself justice
in the 25 February speech by his use of the analogy from events
in 1939-40: his resistance to a continental entanglement of a permanent nature ran much deeper than the analogy suggested.

But, then, Powell was still a member of the Conservative
Party and, while anxious to convert that Party to his way of
thinking on an extensive series of issues, not anxious to bring
about a final breach between it and himself. The difficulty of his
position throughout 1969 was that, while affection and regard for
him among the public continued undiminished, his support in the
middle and higher reaches of his Party was divided as to issues.
Nicholas Ridley, for example, a friend and supporter on the whole
range of Powell's economic policies – and on immigration as well
– was deeply committed to the EEC. John Biffen, who had voted
(like Ridley) for Powell in the leadership election of 1965, was as
passionate as that gravely humorous man can be in his opposition
to membership of the Community, but much less energetic than
Powell in all matters of social and domestic policy, feeling, as
he once put it, 'really quite sympathetic to Roy Jenkins'. The
problem for Powell from April 1968 to June 1970 was that his
support among Conservative politicians was so fractured.

There were those who supported him with fervour on one issue,
and opposed him with equal fervour on another. He none the less
went his own way, and accepted support where he could respect
it. The major point about Tory politics during 1969, however, was
the increasingly vitriolic relations between himself and Edward
Heath. In January 1970 Powell made a speech at Scarborough
which, while deprecating the idea that the concentration of
central government subsidies on supposedly socially deprived
areas was wise, also contained the proposition that concentration on areas with a high immigrant population was particularly

ill-advised. On 19 January *The Times* reported Heath's reaction
to this speech: he described it as 'unChristian' and an example of
'man's inhumanity to man'. William Whitelaw, in his dutiful role
as Chief Whip, sought to effect an exchange of letters between the
two which would be at least polite. Powell, angry though he was
with what he saw as a deliberate misrepresentation of his views,
was perfectly willing to agree a formula; Heath was not. He told
the Parliamentary Lobby of journalists on 23 January that Powell
would never be a member of any government headed by himself.

Whitelaw's position was a very understandable one. Like every
other year since the triumph of 1966, 1970 looked like being bad
for the Wilson government. What would not do in Whitelaw's
judgement, would be for the Tory party to go into an election
campaign with Powell and Heath at odds. However, the fissure
had become an increasingly personal one. In principle – with
the single exception of membership of the European Economic
Community – there was not much to choose between the policies of the two men. Even on immigration, the subject on which
Heath found Powell's rhetoric distasteful, there was agreement
that provision should be made for assisted repatriation. Powell
had first brought it forward; it was enshrined in the Conservative manifesto. It remained the case that, whereas Powell was
prepared to stomach Heath, albeit on his own terms, Heath
could not stomach Powell.

As 1969 wore on the Conservatives grew more confident
that the many disasters of the Wilson government would see
them home. Heath's very earnestness was now an obvious virtue. But as the summer of 1970 arrived, things began to change.
The stewardship of Roy Jenkins as Chancellor of the Exchequer
promised good things. The Labour Party began to overhaul the
Tories in the opinion polls. A slight touch of chill entered into
Conservative hearts. Harold Wilson decided to go to the country.

It was a curious and, indeed, unique, campaign. The weather was of balm. The Prime Minister, soporifically confident,
declined to make set speeches and chatted his way through
interviews, occasions and meetings. The polls showed a mounting Labour lead, amounting to thirteen per cent in the middle of
the second week of the campaign. The sense of doom descended
at Conservative Central Office. On the morning of Thursday 11
June, Heath, slumped in his chair, and surrounded by anxious
supporters, servants and employees, was handed an advance
copy of a speech Powell was to deliver that evening. He glanced
through it. 'That's Powellism,' he said, 'there's nothing I can do

about it.' He tossed the transcript back on the table; it was the air of resignation with which he said it which convinced those in the room that he had almost abandoned any hope of electoral victory, and that he had given up nearly all hope he had of winning the soul of the Conservative Party from Powell. Of those present, whose job it was to advise him how to handle his day, one of their number provided the only moment of humour – a kind of gallows humour – when, after a long silence, he suggested that Heath sat rather than stood at his Press Conferences because 'Mr. Wilson standing looks even worse than you.' It is only fair to say that, within twenty-four hours, Heath had recovered his courage to the extent that he was willing to fight the battle, with all his energy, to its very end; and to rely on the possibility of victory. In these last days of the campaign he had two worries: that his vision of the future for the United Kingdom would be denied its implementation; and that Enoch Powell, as he and many other Tories feared, would cheat him of victory at the polls.

While, in spite of many inquiries from his Conservative friends, Powell would not immediately reveal his intentions, he had, in the meantime, made four significant speeches. Each one was a thorn in Heath's flesh. He spoke about economic policy in his constituency on 6 June, on immigration in the same place on 11 June, on the idea that there might be subversion of the nation's institutions in Birmingham on 13 June (a speech which Heath repudiated in rage, but the terms of which he was to repeat, himself, to the United Nations General Assembly later in the year) and in Tamworth on the Common Market on 15 June. The assumption everywhere in Conservative Central Office, and in the higher direction of the Conservative Party – and the assumption, it is fair to say,[69] of Heath himself was that Powell was set to scupper Heath's chance of an electoral victory which, anyway, was not very good. However, expressions by the leadership of its uncertainty about Powell's intentions – readily conveyed to the Press until the last moment – were not altogether justifiable. For, on 13 June – the last Saturday before the election – Powell, at his own request, met a representative of the Conservative Whips' Office in Birmingham. He announced that he had a 'shot loaded for firing'. He then intimated that he would support the election of a Conservative government before the campaign was over.

On 16 June Powell made his final election speech in his own constituency, on the eve of the poll. I have quoted a part of it at the head of this chapter. The concluding paragraph reads:

Listen, then; for there comes a time when it is too late to listen. On Thursday let none delude you that you are choosing between individuals, or that the questions you decide will come up again in the same form, the same circumstances, a few years ahead, should you dislike the outcome now. On Thursday your vote is about a Britain that, with all its faults and failings, is still free, and great because it is free. On Thursday your vote decides whether that freedom shall survive or not. You dare not entrust it to any government but a Conservative government.

On that Thursday a Conservative government was elected, with a plurality of forty-two over the Labour Party and of thirty-six in the whole House of Commons.

The sadness and the irony of the history of the Conservative Party in this period lies in the fact that Edward Heath owed his victory to a man whose views he had consistently rejected, but who enjoyed a national support that Heath himself was never to achieve.

7

The Nationalist
1970-1974

I knew therefore by the end of 1973 that unless some
incalculable change came over the Conservative Party
I must give my supporters timely warning that I should
not be defending my seat; and I had fixed upon May
of 1974 as the latest date by which in all reason
and fairness I must do so. In the event the matter
was struck out of my hand by the unforeseen event
of the Prime Minister suddenly dissolving Parliament
upon an issue, which, as I have explained, made it
in any case impossible for me to defend my seat as
a Conservative candidate. This left me with only one
question to answer, and that not a difficult one, namely,
whether to keep silence as I stepped out of public life or
whether, at this supposedly last moment of it, to exert
what authority and influence I still possessed in the
cause, which to me was supreme and all-embracing, of
national independence. I chose the latter, not imagining
that an unforeseeable and improbable outcome would
shortly bring me back to Parliament as a member of
a small independent party committed to opposition to
Britain's loss of independence by membership of the
European Community.

> – *J. Enoch Powell, to the South Kensington*
> *Young Conservatives, 30 September 1976.*

The quotation at the head of this chapter presages its conclusion – Powell's decision to vote for the Labour Party in

FRANKLIN

" SOMETHING'S ROCKING THE BOAT AGAIN, TED "

the general election of 1974 and to advise those of a like mind
and persuasion to do the same. Many did so.[1] The consummation of February 1974, however, the taking of his hat out of
the ring in his cherished constituency, and the throwing of it
into the maelstrom of a national political situation rendered
fevered by a deadly confrontation between the government
led by Edward Heath and the National Union of Mineworkers
led by Joe Gormley, was preceded by more than three years
of battle, on almost every imaginable front, between Powell
and the leadership of his party, the victory of which he had
so unequivocally advocated in the general election of June
1970.

Between the beautiful summer of 1970 and the pallid spring
of 1974 the political landscape of British politics changed in a
way that could scarcely have been foreseen. 'We were returned
to office,' Heath told the conference of his party in October
1970, 'to change the course of history of this nation – nothing

274

less.' He went on to lay down the agenda of economic policy as foreshadowed at Selsdon Park in 1969.[2]

Within two years that policy of what Heath called, in the 1970 speech, the 'quiet revolution' had been reversed; in three and a half years he was out of office. Powell, having fought for Heath's victory in 1970, fought for his defeat in 1974.

It has from time to time been suggested that Powell's final speech in the 1970 campaign was a cynical one, that he expected that, even without his advocacy, Heath would be returned to office, but with a slender majority, and with his moral authority much diminished. To take this view is to mistake the man, and, further, to read back from later events and conflicts in order to judge the events of 1970. It is particularly important, when studying somebody of so casuistical a bent of mind as Powell, to get motivation and the order of unfolding happenings correct.

In the summer of 1970 Powell was convinced that he was unlikely to hold office again; and certain that he would not do so as long as Edward Heath was Leader of the Conservative Party. This, essentially, was because of the furore created by his avid stand on immigration. On the other hand, he still considered himself to be a true and committed Tory. He was not, to be sure, willing to alter the terms in which he advocated particular policies in order to gain – or even to seek – favour. On the other hand, he was committed to a Party cause, that cause being a Conservative triumph under the banner of Heath, however little, in personal terms, that victory was likely to appeal to him.

Much that Heath had to offer was appealing. The Conservative manifesto, for one thing, included proposals for the voluntary but financially assisted repatriation of immigrants. It promised, further, the advocacy of a free enterprise economy, exactly along the lines Powell had been supporting for the whole of his political life. The general package, therefore, of wares on the Tory stall in June 1970 was agreeable to the Member for Wolverhampton South-West. It behove him, in consequence, to support the senior salesman of that package with every ounce of energy and authority he possessed. Certainly, had Powell wished to see Heath defeated, and perhaps secure the succession for himself (for the party was unlikely long to tolerate a man beaten in successive general elections) all he had to do was fall silent after his speech on the Common Market at Tamworth on 15 June 1970. A conspirator for power would not have gone on, the following day, to urge in

"That fellow Enoch's a fanatical believer! We heretics should burn him at the stake!"

such vehement terms the return of a Conservative government. But then, Powell, for all appearances to the contrary, has never been a conspirator.

The Tamworth speech is of particular interest for the way in which Powell stated his opposition to British membership of

the EEC without severing his links with the Conservative Party.
Thus:

> We are thinking, let us say, of the next general election but
> one. At that election, if the Economic Community survives
> and develops – presumably there is no point in this whole
> debate unless we assume that will happen – and if Britain
> is part of the Community, then my fellow candidates and I,
> even if we are candidates for the European and not the British
> Parliament, will have a very different tale to tell you. Prices
> (let us imagine) have been going up by five or six per cent a
> year, and you the electors are justifiably angry. You want to
> turn out of office those responsible for this, much as you are
> going to turn out the present Labour government this week.
> But we, my fellow candidates and I, will say to you: 'Sorry;
> these are the results of the policy followed by the European
> government, which controls the European currency. We have
> done, and we shall do, our best; but this is how the majority
> in the Community insist on having it.'

Later, when Powell launched in full blood his campaign against
British membership of the European Economic Community – and
particularly, when he advised those who agreed with him about
the EEC to vote Labour in February 1974 – it was suggested in
Tory circles that he had not made his position clear in 1970. The
fact of the matter, however, is that it was tenable – if only just
tenable – for him to remain a Conservative candidate in 1970
because Heath's commitment at that stage, endlessly reiterated
by him according to a formula drafted by Michael Wolff, was 'to
negotiate, no more and no less.' Even if, in retrospect, one judges
him to have been naïve, Powell was entitled to assume that the
party of which he was a member entered the June campaign with
its hands free, so far as membership of the EEC was concerned.

If Powell was naïve, then his was an honourable naïvety. Its
rhetorical expression was to be seen and heard and read many
times in the years following the general election of 1970. Few
who met Heath privately could doubt the strength, the fervour,
or the plain and simple faith of his belief both in the desirability and, even, the necessity, of the United Kingdom joining
the (apparently) burgeoning economic system. It is fair to say
that there were those who, still believing in the shibboleths of
the argument for membership of the Market during the 1960s,
entertained the notion that, once in, the United Kingdom would

lead the other Western powers as she had led their resistance movements between 1940 and the end of the war. Such people were foolish, for the Community of the Six was, year by year – and, it sometimes seemed, almost day by day – creating a structure which amounted to an institution which transcended national political interests. The idea that Britain, once in, would lead, was nonsense, and a patent nonsense. But it was, for such as George Brown, Foreign Secretary in a Labour government, and one of the most passionate and vocal advocates of the cause of entry, a belief, or a straw which they were only too willing to grasp. No doubt[3] there was also a conviction that what was desired would be. Once under the link chain fence, as it were, the superiority of British diplomatic method, the immense reservoir of skill acquired during the administration of (and the ordered withdrawal from the administration of) the largest empire the world had ever known, would certainly prevail in any argument about the future direction of a Western Europe now united.

These were certainly foolish, but they were not unworthy thoughts. As, again and again, Powell hammered home their folly,[4] a folly based on the assumption that membership of the EEC was something of a replacement for a lost empire, the tawdry nature of that assumption became clearer and clearer, and aroused a perfectly justifiable contempt on the part of the putative European economic partners. In his memoirs,[5] for example, Maurice Couve de Mürville, for long French Foreign Minister in governments headed by Charles de Gaulle, wrote in some exasperation of British assumptions. Miss Nora Beloff[6] – herself deeply and emotionally committed to the EEC – reported that Couve was against de Gaulle's policy of excluding Britain. Couve, in conversation,[7] denied this.

The time of euphoria for the Conservative Party lasted throughout the halcyon summer of 1970. There was, after all, much to celebrate: the grim and unfancied Tory outsider had beaten to the post the seemingly casually invincible Labour runner widely regarded as the most astute political manager in the kingdom. Moreover, following its defeat in June the Labour Party began – and it was evident that it had begun – its descent into the abyss of internal strife whither it has been falling ever since. There was to be a recovery – a, so to speak, scrambling back up the rocks of disaster – when Labour again held office between February 1974 and June 1979; but there was a provisional air about the third and fourth Wilson administrations, and the first – and only – one led by James Callaghan. No longer was it possible to proclaim as

278

Harold Wilson did in his heyday, that the Labour Party was 'the natural governing Party' in the country, a view which, flamboyantly expressed by an exultant politician, was, none the less, one supported by academically respected opinion.[8] For the moment it seemed unimaginable, when the new Prime Minister, Edward Heath, addressed his Party's conference in October 1970, that by 1974 the Conservative Party would be divided, unsure and neurotic.

Exultation is a natural corollary of electoral victory, especially so when the victory is an unexpected one. On the morrow of the Conservative victory Norman Collins – novelist of quality and repute, and the progenitor of commercial television in Britain – observed with a smile, 'The Queen's at Ascot, the Tories are back, and all is right with the world.' What he said reflected the satisfaction that order had been restored – against the odds – which was widely felt in business and Conservative circles. For the moment, Edward Heath could do no wrong. Indeed, as Jock Bruce-Gardyne[9] wrote, 'Mr. Heath would have been cheered to the echo when he addressed the final rally on the morning of 10 October if he had announced his intention to nationalize the means of production, distribution and exchange.'[10] Lord Bruce-Gardyne's somewhat cynical – and certainly world-weary – judgement had then, as it has now, a powerful validity in British politics, particularly in so far as the Conservative Party is concerned. There are elements in that Party, and they were to show themselves powerfully and increasingly during the life of the government headed by Edward Heath, deeply concerned with such impalpables as patriotism and justice, with ideals of conduct, and with a sense of right. But above all, the Party is concerned with winning general elections, and therefore holding office. Labour politicians, of course, also like to win: but the Labour Party has a far deeper fissure in its nature than has the Conservative, between those who want to hold office for the good they believe they can do the nation, and those who hold fast to what they see as a true doctrine of Socialism, within the borders of which the holding of office is suspect, unless the constitutional system of government is altered out of all recognition.[11]

How much deeper party divisions – divisions within as well as between parties – were to become was apparent to few in October 1970. But Lord Bruce-Gardyne, writing in March 1974, after the Heath government had been defeated at the polls, noted something particularly significant about the Conservative Party Conference of 1970:

Not only had they just won a general election: they had won a general election which, only four months before, most of them were expecting to lose.

The mood, Bruce-Gardyne says, was one of 'jubilation heightened by relief'. Neither jubilation nor relief could be relied upon to sustain a government through the dark and anxious hours certain to disturb the sleep and the composure of any British government elected in the decade that began in 1970. Conviction, and truly national support, was required for a government of innovation; and it eventually appeared that Edward Heath did not have the required conviction.

Powell had already observed[12] that willingness to revise apparently received opinions was necessary for Party survival; and that willingness openly to state and examine the problems of the country was essential if there were to be anything approaching renascence. If Heath wanted his revolution to be quiet, Powell was willing to be noisy about his. For the moment – in 1970 – however, few had a fixed view of his importance, or his power. There were many points of congruence between himself and the new government, and many points of difference. Asked by Arthur Butler in the *Daily Sketch* of 1 December 1970 what his role in the new Parliament would be, he replied:

> People who go around looking for a role are like people who keep looking at themselves in the looking glass. Once you start fitting yourself to a role or a type, then all is falsified. You start to act – to portray something which is not yourself.

He did not imagine that events, and Heath's conduct of government, would give him a role of power.

His position when Parliament re-assembled in the autumn of 1970 must be considered in relation to two questions. They are simply expressed. How much influence had he had on the outcome in June? And, how far would he take warfare – on a number of subjects, but on British membership of the Common Market in particular, with the Heath government?

In democratic politics, and particularly in British democratic politics, there are two kinds of authority. There is the authority of power: a Prime Minister whose party has been elected with a sufficient majority in the House of Commons need, for a year or two at least, concern himself or herself merely with quarrels

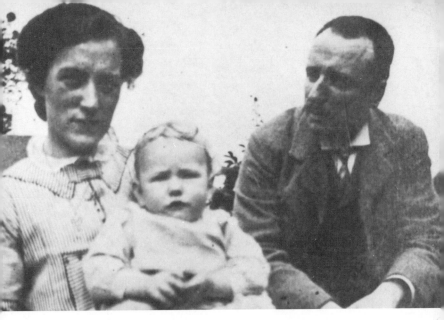

1 *Above* Powell, with his parents, in the garden of the house in Stechford, Birmingham, where he was born, in the spring of 1913.

2 *Below left* Powell, aged thirteen, at his books. He was probably the most assiduous – and brilliant – pupil of his generation at King Edward's School, Birmingham.

3 *Below right* Powell – in 1930 – as an undergraduate at Trinity College, Cambridge. He won all the major prizes in classical studies.

4 *Above left* Brigadier Powell, India Command, 1944. Having been the youngest professor in the Commonwealth, he became the youngest brigadier in the Army.

5 *Above right* The prospective Conservative candidate for Wolverhampton South-West in the spring of 1949.

6 *Below* December, 1951. Powell with his *fiancée*, Pamela Wilson.

7 Powell with his wife and children in the garden of their home in
Wolverhampton in 1961. Susan is on Mrs Powell's right, Jennifer on her
left.

8 *Above* Return to office. Having resigned from the Treasury with Peter Thorneycroft and Nigel Birch, Powell returned to the Macmillan government as Minister of Health in July, 1960, when this photograph was taken.

9 *Below* Powell, as Minister of Health, inspecting a mobile health education unit on 8 October 1962.

10 *Above left* Powell, arriving for a Cabinet meeting on 13 June 1963.
The meeting was called by Harold Macmillan principally to discuss the
accusations being levelled at John Profumo. It was, by all accounts, a
somewhat fraught occasion but, the following weekend, Powell came
out in support of the Prime Minister. The photograph was taken in the
courtyard of Admiralty House, where Macmillan was living while
structural repairs were being made to No. 10 Downing Street.

11 *Above right* The Opposition spokesman on defence, visiting British
troops in Germany in 1967.

12 *Above* Powell speaking to the Surrey Young Conservatives in February, 1971. This was his first major speech on immigration after the general election of 1970.

13 *Below* Campaigning, as an Ulster Unionist candidate, in Down South during the general election campaign of October, 1974.

14 *Right* Powell on Westminster Bridge in October 1974. He had just been returned to the House of Commons as Ulster Unionist member for Down South.

15 *Below* Powell, about to go on patrol with members of the Ulster Defence Regiment in Newry, Northern Ireland, in 1977.

16 Enoch and Pamela Powell, walking near their home in Ballynahinch, County Down, during the general election campaign of June, 1987.

within his Cabinet, brawls over public spending between the spending ministries and the Treasury, and the discontents of his or her backbenchers, usually assuaged by the cajoling or the bullying of whips whom he or she appoints. There are, of course, always rebels. The House of Commons would not be the House of Commons without such as care less for office than for statement. The fact of the matter, however, is that such rebels, against the office of the day and the government of the day alike, have normally been relegated to the sidelines, such is the force of Party in the Palace of Westminster. To challenge those leading a Party, especially if that Party is in government, requires, normally, either a wild egotism or a settled conviction.

The egotist can be denounced and – so far as Parliamentary politics are concerned – destroyed, by a determined Prime Minister, and an assiduous Party organization. In 1956, for example, Sir Harry Legge-Bourke declined further to receive the Conservative Whip because he disapproved of the policy of the government of his Party in the Middle East. Again, between 1964 and 1966, Desmond Donnelly and Woodrow Wyatt made it clear that they would vote against Labour's plans to nationalize the steel industry and, the parlous parliamentary situation of the government being what it was, the measure could not get through. Later, Lord Wilson nationalized steel. Mr. Donnelly, his political career ruined, committed suicide. And Woodrow Wyatt, eventually ennobled by Mrs. Thatcher, entered a pleasant retirement as Chairman of the Horse Racing Betting Levy Board, and a columnist in *The Times* and the *News of the World*. The causes of all three (and there are others) may be thought just: the effect of their defiance was null.

But there is another kind of authority in British democratic politics, an authority which can best be described as moral. It is an authority which has had effective exercise only twice this century, once by Winston Churchill, and once by Enoch Powell. Churchill's defiance of received opinion eventually led him to office with almost dictatorial power; but, before he gained that power, he was on the verge of being disowned by his constituency Party.[13] The fact that so many of his fellow countrymen saw the threat of German advance in the same way as he did initially availed him nought until, in May 1940, when he replaced Neville Chamberlain as Prime Minister, it availed him mightily.

Powell, likewise, when the 1970 Parliament assembled, had a moral authority akin to Churchill's, in that it was derived from the implacable evidence of support from the public for his views on nationality. He had, however, the disadvantage of a finicky conscience, which forbade him to intrigue within the Conservative Party against those who then led it. His brief in the closing months of 1970 was a watching one. He would support the Heath government to the extent that the government agreed with him, and opposed it without care of personal consequences when it did not.

In the 1970 Parliament Powell's hyper-activity, notable throughout his life, became as much a matter of political necessity as a function of personality. He had always been a most formidable parliamentary orator; by June 1970 he had established himself as by far and away the most powerful public speaker in politics, one likely as not to excite opposition, certainly, expressed in demonstrations and violence whenever he appeared on a public platform; but one also regularly generating massive explosions of enthusiasm, both for his ideas and for himself. This enthusiasm put down deep roots in the Conservative Party in the country but, in truth, it transcended party, as Mrs. Spearman's successive analyses of Powell's correspondence demonstrate.[14] On the other hand, he was scarcely advancing in the House of Commons – in the sense that advancement meant the building of a substantial cohort of support which would gain him access to votes. This cohort did not appear until the great battles over legislation to enter the EEC – and when it did appear it was to a large extent not personal. It was inevitable – as the late Neil Marten observed, with a generosity characteristic of him, but still remarkable in that he had been the leading Tory against the Market long before Powell entered the fray – that Powell would lead the Conservative opponents of membership: no one of their number approached his mastery of parliamentary procedure, nor could so readily hold an audience. For the moment, however, his standing in the House was the standing of an invariably interesting and provoking speaker, one who could empty the bars and the tea rooms when the television annunciators scattered all over the Palace of Westminster showed that he had risen to speak. But the strength of his influence was always open to question; and the battle over reform of the Lords had far from expunged the hatred of many Labour Members for him, a hatred stemming directly from his immigration speeches.

It is not entirely true to suggest, as Dr. Schoen does, that immediately after the election Powell became 'a political recluse'. He was active on a number of fronts and his characteristic unbounded energy was undiminished.

Among other works – and I select only three – were an erudite lecture for the BBC on 25 June, mainly on German and classical Greek, but also on other literature, and an immensely technical, detailed and scholarly review of Mr. Corelli Barnett's *Britain and her Army* for the Journal of the Royal United Services Institute. This last piece consisted of a reprise, but an intellectually deepened one, of his advocacy of a European continental military strategy for Britain which had caused difficulties for him during his time as Opposition spokesman on Defence, and thus had important political implications. Then, on 19 October, in *The Daily Telegraph*, he launched a broadside entitled 'UN: time to explode the myth' which was vitriolic in both tone and judgement. Opening with a characteristic sentence mocking hypocrisy – 'Denouncing something which purports to produce peace appears like preaching sin or praising evil' – he went on to savagery. 'The United Nations is, always has been, and always will be, an absurdity and a monstrosity, which no lapse of time and no application of ingenuity or effort can remedy.' In particular, he assailed as nonsense the idea that, fundamentally, UNO was a concourse of equals.[16] The UN, he believed, was, through some inexplicable delusion, determined to conceive of itself as a parliament of nations in which each member would have the same weight as any other. To Powell this conceit is a palpable absurdity, for it would make, say, Fiji the notional equal of the United States for:

If anything this basis has become more pronounced over the past twenty-five years during which no sooner has the tiniest group been recognized as a nation than it has been enrolled in the company of the elect. As between these entities the United Nations purports either to maintain what those ignorant of Latin imagine to be the *status quo*, or to regulate its alteration without the use of force: which must of necessity include the prospect of the use of force.

This article is vintage Powell, consisting as it does of a grimly humorous use of paradox to unveil the unconscious paradox of others. It is instructive to note, however, the fundamental difference between Powell's assault – made, as a matter of interest, from the point of view of a British nationalist who had then as he has had later a most profound respect for other nationalisms – on the United Nations and his assault on British membership of the EEC. The UN he regarded as an absurdity principally because its structure immediately unveiled pretensions which it could not fulfil. The EEC, on the other hand, he had come to regard as a serious threat, an organization which might well come to have the power to dominate, and issue orders to, some at least of its constituent elements, including the only one he personally cared about, the United Kingdom.

None of these speeches and writing could be considered the work of a political recluse. All, indeed, had political point. Around this time those who feared him encouraged a rumour – which Dr. Schoen believes – that Powell was deliberately absenting himself from Parliament. I discussed this rumour with Powell and he commented on it in a letter to me of 21 July 1988:

> With regard to the allegation of my 'non-attendance' in the House in the part of the 1970-71 session between the opening of Parliament and the summer recess 1970, I find that I took part in five divisions (8, 9, 13, 20 and 22 July) during that period and tabled six Parliamentary Questions for Written Answer. There were five other divisions on 15, 17 and 23 July, but these were divisions in which only a minority of government supporters voted. As you are aware, there is in the House of Commons no record of 'attendance'; but I think in the light of the above facts the notion of my 'non-attendance' should be regarded as unfounded.

However, when it became known that he would not be going to the Conservative Party Conference at Brighton in October 1970 the thought began to grow – in the higher reaches of the Conservative Party in particular – that, in the words of Sir Michael Fraser,[17] 'Enoch is planning to take his case to the people.' This view was more forcefully expressed in references, endlessly repeated, to Powell's supposed retreat to 'Wolverhampton-les-deux-eglises.'[18] This mood, diffuse and generalized though it was, might almost be said to amount to a prediction. As a prediction, it depicted fear. Powell's Wolverhampton base was more than secure. The swing to him in the general election had been 8.7%, or 3.6% more than the national average swing to the Tories. There was, thus, highly tangible evidence of the devotion of his followers in the constituency to him: if he wanted to retreat into a redoubt and await events he could hardly be dislodged, even given the best efforts of Conservative Central Office, which efforts, should they be made, might well prove to produce results the opposite of what was intended.

In some respects, indeed, it could be said that Powell was in a stronger position, albeit in a different kind of democracy, than that which Charles de Gaulle enjoyed before he returned to power in France in 1958. De Gaulle had dissolved the party which he had formed – *Rassemblement du Peuple Français* – and awaited events at Colombey. For a time he was almost forgotten or, if remembered, regarded as a monument. Powell had a loyal base, and a following that went well beyond that base. The comparison was infectious, however, and its fires were fuelled when, in the *Spectator* on 7 November 1970, Powell reviewed de Gaulle's *Mémoires d'Espoir* – the only volume of a planned triptych of post-war memoirs produced before his death – in terms almost of rapture:

> De Gaulle's ultimate assertion, however, was first, last and always the nation. In a Europe and a Western world which was trying to pretend the nation away, the replacement of the nation in the centre of politics and diplomacy worked like a spell. As de Gaulle expresses it in one passage: 'The action of a France which does not avoid or conceal the fact of being France arouses the attention of the Third World.' But it was not only the Third World. From Moscow to New York, from Bonn to Montreal, the other nations discovered that they were vulnerable to a head of state who asserted this simple but sovereign fact. It was, de Gaulle believed, what he was there to do: '*Moi suis-je là pour autre chose?*'

What, of course, lay behind this quite general worry about Powell's conduct was the grand question of what influence, if any, he had had on the outcome of the general election. There were, to be sure, ancillary modes of unease within the Conservative Party and, to some extent, within what are called the professional classes, particularly those concerned with expressing their own opinions and seeking to form those of others – commonly called 'the media'. There were fears that Heath's supposed radicalism would founder upon the rocks of entrenched opposition, principally that of the trade unions; and a general supposition that the genteel decline of Britain was inevitable, something which could be delayed, but not reversed. The fact, perhaps not fully digested, but certainly acutely felt, that during the campaign Powell had enjoyed so much newspaper coverage – twenty column inches in *The Times*, for example – was worrying for many, for the coverage was out of all proportion for a back bench member with no expectation of office.

Could it be said – this was the tricky problem requiring reso-lution both by Edward Heath's supporters and by what might be called conventional liberal opinion, which was so bitterly opposed to Powell's speeches on immigration – that the Conservatives owed their victory to the Member for Wolverhampton South-West? If such were the case then that moral authority which I have sought to define might accrue to him in greater measure than any ordinary rabble-rouser could be expected to enjoy. Then, assuming him to enjoy Gaullist ambitions, there might be a dangerous possibility of his realizing them, supposing the Heath government were to run into difficulties.

It is important in any study of Powell, and particularly when dealing with the stage of his career which began with the June 1970 election result, to seek to settle this matter. Two articles, by Nicholas Deakin and Jenny Bourne,[19] argued that his impact was only marginal and, even then, confined to the area surrounding his own constituency. Formidable though their argument might appear to be, however, the fact that Mr. Deakin and Miss Bourne had for long been identified with that school of thought which argued for more generous interpretation of the law on immigration and more concerted action by the state to elimi-nate grievances felt by the immigrant community,[20] encouraged scepticism as to their conclusions. Towards the end of 1971, to the gratification of those who wanted to believe in Powell's irrelevance, or near-irrelevance, there appeared the eighth in the prestigious series of studies of general elections emanating from Nuffield College, Oxford.[21] In accordance with the general format of these volumes it contained, in addition to an examina-tion of the period leading up to the election, and a bald narrative account of the campaign itself, various specialist studies, including a chapter entitled 'The results analyzed', by Michael Steed.[22] Mr. Steed's conclusion was, broadly speaking, the same as that of Mr. Deakin and Miss Bourne. Mr. Steed concluded that '. . . Powellite candidates fared exactly as their party did nationally – an average swing of 4.7%.' 'There is,' he went on, 'no way of using election statistics to test the theory that Powellism brought votes to the Conservative Party nationally, regardless of whether such recruits lived in an area affected by immigration or had a Powellite candidate.'

Mr. Steed's argument is disingenuous to say the least, as was later to be demonstrated by Dr. Schoen.[23] But it is important to appreciate the underlying thesis of the writers already quoted (and of countless other articles published around the same time). The thesis was that Heath would have enjoyed a substantial victory whatever Powell did. This was, very naturally, a view that Heath and his colleagues were only too willing to go along with, while for the so-called liberals on immigration and race it was a way of (apparently) pushing him to the margins of politics. It further enabled those making attacks on Powell whenever he spoke on controversial matters (and, of course, particularly on immigration) to give to their assaults a satisfactorily narrow focus. Powell, it could now readily be said or implied, was an inflammatory and embittered pro-Fascist. His followers were either to be found among the intellectual dregs of society, or among poor deluded folk disturbed by the pace of change (necessary and enlightened change, of course) in their lives: these would soon see the error of their ways, given an intensive programme of wise propaganda about race relations (the carrot) and the extension of such restrictions on conduct as were laid down in the race relations acts (the stick).

There were certain difficulties here. For one thing, as time went by, Powell's relentless presentation of statistics on immigration excited a growing conviction that he was right and his critics wrong, a conviction strengthened when the Runnymede Trust was reported in *The Times* on 10 March 1970 as saying that, in the opinion of its investigators, Powell was more right than wrong: the Trust was one of the most important, and one of the most prestigious, of the various organizations set up to work in the race relations field, and it had – to put the matter as mildly as possible – a reputation for scholarly objectivity enjoyed neither by the more senior Institute of Race Relations nor by the various other critics of the position so dramatically taken by Powell in the course of the Birmingham speech which led to his dismissal from the Shadow Cabinet.

If Powell's difficulty was to maintain his position of influence (if not power) against the sustained hostility, not merely of the leadership of the Conservative Party, but of most institutions concerned with immigration and race relations, and of much of the press, radio and television as well, his opponents were in a more difficult fix. Few could doubt that he had struck a chord in his argument about immigration. It was not so easy to decide on the accurate response to the chord. Was it to be said that there was no serious immigration problem, and that he had merely employed his unquestioned rhetorical talent to inflame the ignorant? Was it to be argued that successive measures regulating and governing the behaviour of the native (and mainly white) race towards those coming into Great Britain from former colonies would suffice to procure inter-racial harmony in the post-imperial age? Was it necessary, in other words, to seek to dragoon the majority of the population into a posture of hospitality which they found, at the very least, uncomfortable, in the service of larger, and more beneficial ideals? What the right policy was had to be determined through consideration of how much electoral support Powell commanded. This meant, in turn, making a judgement on the effect he had had on the general election result in June 1970. Every question regarding his standing between that month and February 1974 depended for its answer on an accurate assessment of the effect specifically of his speech of 16 June 1970 and, more generally, of his conduct from 1968 onwards.

That Edward Heath, savouring his victory, should deny any contribution of significance made to it by Powell was understandable. That individuals who dissented from Powell's view of the right way forward on immigration and race relations should seek likewise to denigrate his power with the voters was equally understandable. The Labour Party was, however, in something of a quandary. It was agreeable to attribute Heath's victory to the supposed racist effect of Powell, if only because it made confrontation with a new and supposedly reforming government easier. To go too far in that direction, however, would be to admit Powell's strength, and to admit the strength of appeal of the policies he was putting forward. This the Labour leadership was not prepared to do until February 1974; and Harold Wilson was prepared to do so then only in private.[24] The brute fact of the matter, however, was that the most sentient politicians, and a majority – if not a substantial one – of those who wrote or broadcast on political affairs realized that Powell had had a far greater effect on the outcome in June 1970 than was admitted publicly.

In their *Political Bulletin* for June/July 1970 the psephological firm National Opinion Polls produced a devastating resumé of their work. Forty-two per cent of a post-election sample took the view that Powell had had an influence on the campaign. Of that percentage thirty-seven per cent indicated that he was an influence in favour of their voting Conservative. Twenty-three per cent found themselves inclined in the opposite direction. Once, however, the general sample was broken down according to professed Party allegiance the figures acquired a different contour. Forty-seven per cent of avowed Conservatives said that Powell's campaign had made them more likely to turn out to support Heath on the day; six per cent said that he had had a contrary effect. However, while fifty-one per cent of those favouring the Labour cause told the pollsters that they had been strengthened in their conviction by Powell, eighteen per cent said they had voted Tory because of him; and twenty-two per cent avowed that they had considered doing so.

Now, both of the major British political Parties possess a certain bedrock of support. The size of each bedrock has been variously estimated, and their constituent elements relentlessly analyzed.[25] Social class has, more often than not, been adduced as a cause of electoral behaviour. The current performance of the national economy has, likewise, been given as a reason for voting behaviour. What both (indeed, all) parties fear, though, is abstention on the part of their natural constituency. The movement between Labour and Conservative is usually a small one; but abstentions can be significant – as they were, to the detriment of the Tory cause, in 1964, 1966, and, twice, in 1974. What we can clearly see from the NOP judgement (and there are similar judgements available from different sources) is that in June 1970 Powell was able substantially to make firm natural Conservative votes and, even more importantly, to attract about eighteen per cent of people who considered themselves natural Labour voters to the Conservative cause. Until 1983, when Mrs. Thatcher, buttressed by the popularity of her general economic programme (and particularly her restriction of the powers of trade unions and her extensive sale of council houses to their occupants), won a massive majority, no politician save Powell could be said to have had so distinct and personal an effect on the polling booth behaviour of the British voter. Certainly, the stark figures make it clear that Dr. Steed's attempt to show that Powell's influence was confined to constituencies near his own is untenable. The Powell effect was – for good or ill – far more widespread than that. And, while it is possible to argue that Heath might have come home victorious without Powell, it is impossible to gainsay the view that his majority would have been a great deal less comfortable than in fact it was. The mystery about British politics in the next (nearly) four years is how Heath managed to squander his capital. In that process, too, Powell was an influence.

He was an influence, however, very largely because he was perceived as a Tory. The fundamental fact was that Powell was perceived as expressing something innate in the identity of the Party to which he belonged, and perhaps expressing it more truly than did the elected leader of the Party. The American scholar, Dr. Donley T. Studlar,[26] enjoying the advantage of an outsider suffering no involvement with the intricacies of British politics, found himself

> led to the conclusion that Powell was the major influence in differentiating the party policies in the mind of the voters. Most of the electorate had heard of Powell, knew generally what his proposals on immigration were and were closer in their own positions to Powell than to the actual positions of the Labour and Conservative Parties. The events of the parliamentary campaign in 1970 worked to associate Powell's position with the Conservative Party, however much the Party may have baulked at the notion.

'This', Dr. Studlar concluded, 'is the first indication that a social issue could have the same effect on the British electorate as economic and class issues do.' It is, however, with no sense of disrespect to the work of Dr. Schoen and Dr. Studlar that I observe that such a conclusion could be drawn by the application of common sense. Those journalists who devoted so much space to Powell during the June campaign are less to be convicted of seeking colour and drama in a generally subfusc campaign than reflecting the evidence of their senses as they travelled around the country, evidence to the effect that, however hard it was at the time exactly to assess the impact and effect of Powell, that impact and that effect were palpable.

In spite of all this, however, events might have led to a different conclusion than that which was reached in February 1974, when Edward Heath fell at the polls, never to rise again. Developments during the years in which Heath had charge of the British government will long remain enigmatic to the historian. What happened, though, can be swiftly adumbrated. First, Heath, elected with a programme of economic reform not – at least in its general outline – very dissimilar to that advocated by Powell, reversed that policy in a matter of months, and conclusively repudiated it when he adopted an incomes policy in 1972. (In 1981, it is worth noting, one of the strongest considerations influencing Margaret Thatcher in her refusal to undertake a similar reversal was precisely the fact that reversal had led Heath to destruction.) Second, the Heath government embarked with determination on the Prime Minister's favourite and fundamental policy of securing British membership of the European Economic Community, but through Parliament alone, and without any further recourse to the views of the electorate. It was the energetic – and, in execution, ruthless – pursuit of this policy in this fashion which compelled Powell to act as he did in February 1974. It cannot be said, however, that Heath's advocacy of EEC membership secured his downfall: under the Labour government which succeeded his administration, after all, British voters called to a referendum on the matter opted to stay within the Community. They did so, however, in a defeatist rather than a supportive mood. The probability – it cannot amount to a certainty – however, is that combined with the reversal of so many policies laid down in the 1970 manifesto, the method of entry contributed to a feeling that the Heath government had very rapidly become aloof from the emotional concerns of those who had placed it in office. This feeling had an effect on the government's fate.

Third, though, and in many respects most important, was the Cabinet's decision to sanction a further substantial influx of immigrants, this time of people of Indian origin expelled from Uganda. To a great extent the Ugandan Asian controversy was a reprise of that concerning the Kenyan Asians discussed in the last chapter. It was not easy, however, for a government that had been elected at least in part because of a promise further to curb immigration, which was – supposedly at least – committed to encouraging repatriation, and which had introduced legislation (the 1971 Immigration Act) which went some way towards treating Commonwealth citizens as aliens, suddenly to announce that 50,000 Asians had a right of entry, which right would be fully respected, to the United Kingdom. It could plausibly be argued, indeed, that a Conservative government in 1972 was prepared to be more generous in its treatment of aspirant immigrants from East Africa than their Labour predecessors had been. Fifty thousand could not be taken to be an insignificant number and – as Powell wrote in *The Times* on 17 August 1972 – whatever historically based obligation there might be to ease the plight of men, women and children summarily to be expelled from the country in which they had spent their lives, it was not felt to be a burden that the United Kingdom should unilaterally assume, given the existing difficulties faced by British society in absorbing previous waves of immigrants. The Home Secretary, Mr. Robert Carr (now Lord Carr of Hadley) was, it is true, understood to have secured private assurances from the Indian government that, in an emergency, India would receive – if not actually welcome – substantial numbers of Ugandan Asians. Private assurances, however, were not enough; and there can be little doubt that, not for the first, nor for the last, time, the government was acting in defiance of the wishes of the public, and in accordance with canons of its own devising. Powell, naturally, had no choice but to take up cudgels on behalf of a populace which felt itself yet again betrayed. The hard fact of the matter, however, was that what was perceived as another *bouleversement* on Heath's part constituted an issue which might well have been designed to enhance the prominence he had enjoyed between 1968 and 1970, bewail the fact though many did.

Powell's stand against the new Ugandan immigration was therefore, together with his regular (but less frequent than supposed) speeches on the immigration question generally, highly important in keeping him in the forefront of public attention for the duration of the Heath government. His stand against British membership of the EEC, though it provided some memorable parliamentary setpieces, and though it struck important chords of agreement among the public, aroused fewer passions and (for all Powell's frequent expressions of confidence that the government could be beaten on the issue), given the likelihood (which proved to be actuality) that a substantial number of pro-Market Labour MPs would sustain the government in any serious difficulty, was always likely to fail, though there were some close calls.

It is less easy to assess the significance for Powell's prospects of retaining – and perhaps even increasing – his popularity and his influence of his increasingly savage assaults on the Cabinet's conduct of economic and industrial policy. The fact of the matter here was that, by the end of 1973, it was clear that Heath had reversed almost every single major policy on the management of the economy on which he had been elected. It was true that he had passed a complicated act for the reform of industrial relations; that he had secured passage for the European Communities Act; and that he had changed the face of local government, as well as making potentially significant administrative alterations to the central government structure in Whitehall. But these changes (each one of which was dear to the Prime Minister's heart, and each one of which he later looked back on with deep satisfaction) were either generally unknown – as in the case of Whitehall – or unpopular among large sections of the public. It could be argued, of course, that they were all radical measures, wholly in keeping with what amounted almost to a prime ministerial obsession with the machinery of government, and that they would take time to prove themselves. Even so they counted for little against the fact that industrial strife was rampant, that unemployment was over a million,'that inflation was out of control, and that the government seemed to have lost its way. The political situation was dangerously fluid, and it was just in such circumstances that Powell could expect to have maximum impact.

In many respects it was Powell's steadfast advocacy of economic policies which he had long propounded that offered the most intellectually intriguing aspect of his career between 1970 and 1974. This was because that advocacy related so closely to what was widely perceived as the most fundamental question about British politics at that time – the question of government competence. This question (like, as Powell argued, the question of the EEC) struck at the heart of what the British people thought about themselves.

The decade of the 1950s had, on the whole, been a good one economically, at least in so far as quotidian consumer interests were concerned. What was becoming increasingly recognized at the end of the period, however, was that the United Kingdom's performance relative to her competitors was nothing to be proud of. Increasingly discussion centred on whether the nation was entering a period of absolute decline, or one of relative decline which could be reversed by a determined government possessed of the right policies.[27] There was also a palpable, but less easily defined, feeling of unease abroad. That feeling fed, in the first years of the Sixties, on what was clearly seen to be the declining competence of the Macmillan government. There was the continuance of inflation; there were scandals; there was a general air of seediness about the leadership of a Party which had been in office since 1951. The Prime Minister seemed to have lost that sure and elegant touch he had displayed when leading the Conservatives out of the morass they were in after the Suez campaign and the resignation of Sir Anthony Eden. He seemed constantly on the verge of panic, as when he dismissed a third of the Cabinet in July 1962. Moreover, he seemed, to close colleagues as well as to political commentators and, as time went on, to the public, to have lost heart. For all the controversy that surrounded the choice of his successor, there was widespread relief – relief, even, on his behalf, and perhaps shared by him – when Macmillan laid down his burden in October 1963.

At the same time, after Hugh Gaitskell's death in 1962, the Labour Party was fortunate enough to find, in Harold Wilson, a leader of vigour and panache who could be said to have been made for his role. Quick on his intellectual feet, skilful in the House of Commons, at this stage of his career possessed of what amounted almost to genius in his handling of journalists, he was the ideal man to bring a tottering government to its knees, convince the people that the country was in a tragic mess, and bedazzle people with a glittering (today we would probably call it 'glitzy') rhetoric of movement, purpose and potential. Moreover, Wilson set himself very deliberately to, so to speak, de-socialize Socialism. The fear of left wing ideologists in the Labour Party, on which the Conservatives had hitherto successfully played, was almost expunged by his skill. Even so, it should never be forgotten that the electorate drew back from him at the last moment, and awarded him only a derisory majority in 1964, though handsome amends were made eighteen months later. The question was now, what would Wilson make of his opportunity; and there was a corollary for the Tories – could their new Leader organize the kind of recovery they had enjoyed between 1945 and 1951?

The events of the ten years following Wilson's 1964 victory were to be of immense consequence for the history of British politics. They were also to be of considerable consequence for Powell himself, as well as for Heath and for an unknown young woman of ambition, Margaret Thatcher. While it does not do to underestimate the deep-seated and long-continuing reasons for British failure and decline in those years, a few observations will serve to set the necessary context.

First, by 1964 the electorate had come to accept that the national situation was bad, and getting worse. A supposedly radical government was chosen to deal with affairs. The radicalism of the Wilson Cabinets, however, was much more apparent than real. The Prime Minister,[28] moreover, was obsessed, less with his programme than with cutting a figure on the national and international stages, and, above all, convincing the citizenry that Labour was competent to govern. Meanwhile, the Conservatives regrouped and returned fresh to the fray. In 1970 a new start was made under the leadership of what was then an extremely unfamiliar type, a self-proclaimed radical Conservative. Less than four years later, he fell from office amid industrial and political strife and a welter of recriminations. It is notable, in the case of both Wilson and Heath that trouble began very soon after taking office: Heath's great reversal of policy is usually dated to the so-called 'U turn' on prices and incomes in 1972; but the truth is that the rot had set in with the bailing out of the bankrupt Rolls-Royce company early in 1971, and confirmed in the mini-Budget in July of that year. It could even be argued that it began with the writing down of the Mersey Docks and Harbour Board capital in November 1970.

Whatever the truth of the matter, however – whatever precise dates and events we choose as the moments when Wilson or Heath began to flounder, the general picture of Britain between 1964 and 1974 – and even as far on as 1979 – was one of accelerating decline, confusion, nervousness, decay and fratricidal battle. It was during those years that the thesis began to be bruited abroad that Britain was ungovernable.

Heath's failure, though, had certain characteristics different from the failure of Wilson, and it is in its nature that we find the particular opportunity afforded to Powell. Heath's philosophy was above all that of a manager. With the single exception of EEC membership, no policy was sacrosanct to him. The reversals of 1971 and 1972, therefore, could be explained in simple and managerial terms: certain policies had been tried; they had not worked; so it became necessary to change them. All this, of course, was anathema to Powell, who held that the policies had not been properly tried. As the 1970 Parliament wore on, it was Powell who was increasingly seen as the man of consistency. All would have been well for the government had the new (or, rather, the revamped old) policies been seen to work. But they did not.

There were two further factors – other, that is, than the government's problems and his own eloquence – which greatly influenced events throughout the 1970 Parliament, and which conspired not merely to keep Powell in the public eye but secured for him a prominence and an influence such as no backbencher has enjoyed this century. The first concerned perception of him as the people's tribune, the man who stood for the rights – and for the fears and emotions – of the ordinary citizen who despaired of making his feelings effective against the decisions of high-handed government. It has often been remarked how paradoxical it seemed that so cerebral and almost pedantic a man could also possess the power to move a common audience. But, as has already been shown, Powell was never a populist in seeking to convince his hearers that he was one of them; and he never talked down to them either. People accepted the total genuineness of his concern for their feelings, and they were ready to believe in his effectiveness. Little of the cynicism which more and more of the electorate demonstrated towards other politicians rubbed off on him.

The second factor of importance which was advantageous for Powell was the sequence in which the three great controversies of the Heath years came up. For a short period after the June election it could be concluded (and was, in a highly satisfied way by his Conservative critics) that there was no longer any need for Powell, since the Heath government clearly planned to run the economy along lines he favoured, and gave the strong impression that they had grasped the nettle of immigration control. Membership of the EEC was a more problematic business since, according to the opinion polls, there were wild oscillations in the public view for and against. Powell's high minded approach to the subject – consisting as it did essentially of the assertion of national sovereignty in an almost abstract fashion – never lit quite the same fires as did his approach to immigration. It was not that he neglected the bread and butter matters, but he never succeeded in convincing the people that his was the only truth of the matter. He and his allies came nearest to success in the House of Commons, in a battle that was very largely above the heads of the citizenry.

All three of Powell's main issues were in play almost from the beginning of the new Parliament, but their potential impact shifted throughout its life. Though Powell continued to speak, as he had always done, on a wide range of subjects, his capacity, as a man virtually alone, to affect issues, varied according to the way the issues developed. In November 1970, for example, he was inveighing against the government for what it was already clear it intended to do about Rolls-Royce. This famous company had over-stretched itself on a new carbon fibre based engine, had promised to achieve what it could not achieve, and was about to go bankrupt: the new Conservative government, supposedly devoted to the free market, and counting among its number a Secretary of State for Industry who had publicly claimed that 'lame ducks' should go to the wall, decided to nationalize. In the same month Powell was on the attack against Maudling's new immigration bill, important amendments to which he was to achieve in the following year. And there was, of course, the EEC.

One of the things that sustained Powell throughout was an unforced conviction, born of Heath's (to him) incompetent and unprincipled conduct in opposition, that the business of the new reforming Cabinet would be botched, and that he would be proven to be right. He was fortunate, though, in the way that events broke. Throughout 1971 negotiations between the United Kingdom and the existing six members of the EEC continued. The issue was alive, and the public predominantly against membership. In January the following year the Treaty of Accession was signed. This then had to be put into British legislation, a process completed in July. Public opposition to entry had been fading, and the issue seemed to be closed. Almost immediately, however, President Amin of Uganda announced his intention to expel Asian residents of his country. Powell straight away opposed any scheme to allow them into Britain, and the government announced that they could come. At the Party Conference in October, in intriguing circumstances discussed below, Powell made an open challenge to the leadership. He was defeated but, as both I and David Wood of *The Times*[29] wrote at the time, his show of strength – 736 votes – was formidable. In January 1973, however, the government was in deep trouble with the economy, locked in serious conflict with various trade unions, and seemingly bent on reversing its manifesto policies. On the economic front throughout 1970 and 1971 Powell had largely been a sniper. Now he began what amounted to an artillery bombardment, and his rhetoric was regularly marked by an open savagery rarely before seen in his treatment of his erstwhile colleagues. Thus, in the House of Commons on 6 November 1972, when Heath announced a standstill on wages and prices, thereby entrenching the kind of incomes policy which he had always sworn to eschew, Powell was ready. He rose and asked:

> Does he know that it is fatal for any government, Party or person to seek to govern in direct opposition to the principles on which they are entrusted with the right to govern? In introducing a compulsory control on wages and prices in contravention of the deepest commitments of this Party, has he taken leave of his senses?

Such was the ferocity of the tone that Members immediately

concluded that the question was meant in a clinical, and not merely a political, sense. Asked later whether this was so Powell merely murmured, 'I can think of no other explanation.'

The bitterness in Powell's oratorical tones had been becoming more and more evident for some time, but nobody could doubt that the gloves were well and truly off from this moment. In the course of the next year Powell was to reach the decision – not to stand again as a Conservative candidate – which is described at the beginning of this chapter. At the same time, Heath and the government which he headed slipped more and more quickly down the slope to disaster. The interesting thing here, however, is that serious and even grim though Ministers could see the situation was, few of them (William Whitelaw was a wise exception) doubted that they could defeat Labour in an early general election, called in the midst of crisis. Though their opinion of their prospects was shared increasingly by the Press, the mood of those in the country who had supported them in 1970 was far less sanguine, or even friendly. There was, here, a curious mirror image to the state of the Labour Party in 1970, and almost to the end of the campaign of that year. Harold Wilson was insouciant, Ministers increasingly confident, and MPs almost euphoric – until they got back to the constituencies at the outset of the campaign and found the Party organization in tatters, while Party morale had reached depths almost of despair.

From 1970 to 1974 Powell conducted his life much as he had always done, with protracted and pertinacious industry, the scope of his interests and activities well beyond the reach of any other politician, the lectures, broadcasts, essays, reviews and speeches pouring out from him. None the less, the pattern was not quite as in earlier phases of his career. While after the April 1968 speech he had reached the realistic conclusion that he was unlikely to hold high office again, he could not but be sensible of the fact that many others did not think the same way. Were Heath, for example, to lose a second general election (after that of 1966) he would have to go, the Party would be in disarray, and many thousands of its members seeking the comfort of a charismatic leader. After 1970 the situation became increasingly different. His opposition to the government and the party establishment was so total – not only on the issues I have already mentioned, but on Northern Ireland, which I will discuss in the next chapter – that it seemed difficult to conceive of any substantial number of senior Conservatives who would either vote for him, or continue to work for him. Moreover, he took absolutely no steps to build up a coherent, substantial and organized group to follow behind his banner: indeed, he took pains to avoid giving the slightest grounds for suspicion that he would welcome the creation of such a group.

Numerous though they were, in any event, his followers were not of a mind with him – or with each other – on everything. His most significant ally in his own party during the battle against the EEC, Neil Marten, was a fervent supporter of the Commonwealth; he never concealed his unease with Powell's open derision for that detritus of Empire, nor his uncertainty about the consequences of Powell's stand on immigration. Nicholas Ridley, dismissed from the Heath government in April 1972, was a devoted adherent of Powell's economics, but a staunch advocate of the EEC. Many who supported him on immigration flinched from the ruthlessness of his economic policies, while, conversely, many who supported the economic policies disliked and even feared not merely his stand on immigration but the fashion in which it was expressed. In one way the essence of 'Powellism', which word had come increasingly into vogue, lay in the personality of the man himself and, so lacking in understanding of his inner motivation and likely future conduct were many of those who counted themselves admirers and followers, that even when, at Stockport in June 1973, he gave the broadest of hints that he might break with the Conservative Party and support Labour at a general election, they did not really believe him. (Harold Wilson immediately denounced the Stockport speech, and solemnly stated that he would never have any truck with Powell. He was later to change his mind.)[30]

None the less, there was a sense in which, in these years, Powell was becoming something of an institution. His speeches on immigration could still provoke the most vehement – and often violent – ire, but his magnetism and the protean character of his output was attracting more and more interest and attention (and even respect) in circles which had previously found him dangerous and abominable. *The Guardian*, for example, had been as ferocious as any of his critics following his dismissal from the Shadow Cabinet. The editorial staff of the paper had not yet reached the stage where it would regularly publish his articles. But, on 22 February 1971, he was interviewed for the paper by Hella Pick, than whom there could scarcely have been a journalist in Fleet Street more hostile to his views. Much of her space was devoted to an analysis of the evolution of his views on membership of the EEC, but there were two passages of great general interest to the student of Powell at this stage of his career. Miss Pick quoted against him accusations to the effect that he deliberately simplified profound subjects in order to appeal to a mass audience, and thereby inhibited rational discussion of them. He replied:

> But a nation is not a rational thing. There is no rational basis for nationhood. What a nation is, is what it feels itself to be, instinctively and emotionally. If the inhabitants of Scotland don't want to be a part of the United Kingdom, and if the inhabitants of the United Kingdom don't want to be part of a Super-Europe, it is no good telling them that this is a matter of feeling. What you belong to is a matter of feeling. Nor do I think that it is correct to describe the sense of belonging to one community and not to another as 'base'. If you called it 'fundamental' perhaps that would be more accurate.

Miss Pick then asked him about his own future, given his unpopularity with the party leadership:

> I can't say that it is my prime objective in life, for which I work day and night, to endear myself to anybody, front bench or back bench, top or bottom. What a strange way it would be to conduct one's political existence – trying to endear oneself. If there ever was a phase of political existence when the future depended on endearing oneself – inside or outside the whips' office – it is long behind us. Anyhow, even if I tried, I couldn't be sure I would succeed.

The prologue to what was to be seen in retrospect as the most bitter and conclusive battle in modern British political history – that between Powell and Heath – began in November 1970. The government was anxious, less to redeem its manifesto pledges on the subject of immigration, than to be seen or thought to do so. Here lay the essential difference between Powell and the Cabinet (and, for that matter, between Powell and all other governments from 1962, when the first legislation, introduced by R. A. Butler, was put before the House of Commons). No Home Secretary, and no Prime Minister, took the same positive view of the virtues of immigration control as did Powell. In each case control – effectively, limitation – of immigration was considered to be a necessary evil, a step or series of steps undertaken with regret, and only in response to expressed public anxiety. It was not that

Ministers in successive governments thought (though many commentators, and some in the soft centre or on the left of politics, did) that immigration was an unalloyed benefit. There was, it is true, a certain superficial humanity about attitudes – families should not be kept apart, it was said,[31] and dependents of those already here should be admitted and, further, the descendants of those who had built an empire based on the subjection of coloured peoples owed to *their* descendants a duty. None of this was very clearly thought out; but it is clear that no post-war Home Secretary approached the business of control with the relish which Powell would have displayed had he ever occupied that post. And there was a further inhibition: no Home Secretary was prepared too obviously, or too detectably, not to accord equal treatment to immigrants from the white Commonwealth and those from the so-called 'New', or coloured, Commonwealth. To Powell the Commonwealth was, as he was to state on innumerable occasions, 'humbug'.

Reginald Maudling, Heath's first Home Secretary, and Powell's old colleague from Research Department days, was the perfect executant of a minimalist policy. Maudling was a comfortable and, in essence, a lazy man. He had a quick and sometimes incisive mind, and he was given to somewhat vague philosophizing about the nature and purpose of politics, usually expressed in his annual letter to his constituents, faithfully reprinted in *The Times* each year. He was fond of easy living; he disliked passion; he was distrustful of controversy; he ever preferred the emollient way in dispute – though it is fair to say that on one issue during his tenure he came close to resignation on a point of principle. The German would-be revolutionary, Rudi Dutschke, had been admitted to Britain for medical treatment, following an incident in which he had been shot in the head. His treatment over, Dutschke applied to stay in order to pursue his studies in political science. There were a number of universities ready to receive him. A campaign of intensity was mounted on his behalf, the argument of which was based on the supposedly honourable and great British principle of hospitality to political refugees. Few in the Cabinet could see much reason to deny residence to Dutschke. Maudling told Heath that if he was not allowed to expel the man he would resign. His strength of feeling – and its expression – was unwonted and unexpected. It was also accepted. Dutschke was expelled to his native country, from whence he went to the University of Aarhus in Denmark, where he died.

No such determination attended the Immigration Bill which Maudling laid before the House. It had four essential provisions. It clouded, if it did not altogether eliminate, the distinction between aliens and Commonwealth immigrants. It laid down certain criteria, principal among them economic, for the admission of any immigrant. (Immigrants would be considered for residence only if they had been offered a specific job, or if they possessed qualities or qualifications which the Home Office judged useful and they would not, in the first instance, be granted a permanent right of residence. Nothing, however, was to be done to restrict the entry of the dependents of immigrants already here.) It provided, in the so-called 'patrial' clause, for an automatic right of entry for anybody with a parent or grandparent born in the United Kingdom. Finally, it seemed greatly to extend provision for repatriation.

In the course of his speech commending the Bill, Maudling took the opportunity to attack Powell for producing supposedly misleading statistics both on immigration and on the exponential growth of the coloured population. Powell vigorously defended his projections. This whole argument about figures was a matter of intense public concern at the time, the assumption of Powell's critics being that he had so grossly over-estimated the figures, through the use of faulty statistical methods, as to create single-handedly a race relations problem where there was none. But, to Powell, the question of numbers (not merely numbers coming in, but numbers produced by reproduction within the immigrant community) was always the essence of the matter. If Powell's statistical method could be shown to be grievously in error, then his general argument could be made to vanish. It would be sterile to go into great detail over this argument from the vantage point of the 1980s, for subsequent experience has demonstrated that, while Powell may have made the occasional error, the thrust of his argument was right. In particular, he was the only senior politician of the day to see that the Asian immigrant would retain the strongest ties with India and Pakistan, and that the Asian population pool would be constantly topped up through the system of arranged marriage. Thus, at Southall on 4 November 1971:

> It is by 'black power' that the headlines are caught, and under the shape of the negro that the consequences for Britain of immigration and what is miscalled 'race' are popularly depicted. Yet it is more truly when he looks into the eyes

of Asia that the Englishman comes face to face with those who will dispute with him possession of his native land.

'This,' said Maudling, happily, of his Bill, 'will draw Enoch's horns.' The widely held view that the Bill represented a massive concession to Powell was, certainly, an embarrassment, but one worth enduring. Maudling, moreover, was not displeased with the conflict with Powell over numbers, for this argument was becoming increasingly abstruse, and intellectual opinion was sharply divided upon it. It thus distracted attention both from the details of the Bill itself and from the intentions of the government in regard to its implementation – whether this would be vigorous or lax. The situation was such, therefore, that a number of Powell's friends and admirers thought that his best course would be to support the Bill, and claim credit for its introduction, a great deal of credit being undoubtedly due to him.

But this was not Powell's chosen strategy. He found the Bill defective in many respects (though he was not averse to saying that it would not have been tabled without his efforts). He was profoundly suspicious of the likely manner in which the repatriation clause would be administered. He did not, however, want immediately to take a bludgeon to it. His preferred instrument was the rapier, and fortunately such an instrument was to hand.

When a Bill receives a Second Reading in the House of Commons – that is to say, when its sponsors obtain a majority after a general debate on the principles embodied in it – a Standing Committee is appointed by the Committee of Selection to scrutinize it line by line. Such committees are designed to reflect the balance of the Parties in the House. But it is also the rule to appoint to any given committee members who have a special interest or competence in the subject under discussion. At the end of its deliberations the committee presents to the House any amendments a majority has found worthy; a Standing Committee thus acts basically in the same way as a committee of the whole House, procedure for which was described above.[32] When the amended Bill is reported to the House that body may, however, vote some or all of the amendments down. The House of Lords then examines, and may vote upon, the legislation. It was impossible, under the conventions, to deny Powell a place on the committee appointed to scrutinize the Immigrants Bill though, as he later said, Reginald Maudling would dearly love to have done so.

Committees, more readily than the whole House, tend to see the formation of cross-Party alliances. In the protracted sittings that followed the committal of the Immigrants Bill there was one curious alliance which amended the clause on patriality. At, essentially, the instigation of Powell a Conservative (Sir George Sinclair), and Liberal (David Steel) and sixteen Labour Members produced a majority against the government. Powell and Sinclair thought the patriality provision would allow more immigrants than was desirable; Steel and the Labour Members opposed it because they thought it drew a racialist line between citizens of the white and of the coloured Commonwealth. In the event, the government, embarrassed by an unlikely alliance, came up with the compromise on patriality which eventually found its place in the Act.

For Powell, though, repatriation was the crucial matter, since he had long concluded that it was not merely necessary to end intake, but to produce massive outflow, voluntary, certainly, but encouraged by the most generous financial provision. The government's view was different, and it was rounded out by an amendment to the Bill written in by the House of Lords, in its capacity as a revising chamber. First, a leaflet produced by the government made a point of underestimating the provision for repatriation. Second, the sums made available to assist it were derisory. Third, a means test was to be imposed on any immigrant wishing to return home, while Powell insisted that the facility should be available to anybody who asked. Fourth, as a result of the Lords' amendment, the authorities, before granting assistance for repatriation, had to be satisfied that the applicant was unsuitable to life in Britain. Fifth, and in many ways most devastating, the administration of the repatriation scheme was to be handed over to International Social Services of Great Britain, and not dealt with by the Home Office. ISS certainly did not have the administrative capacity to process any large number of applications. Their new found authority took the whole business out of the hands of government. And they could be – such was their intellectual bent – relied upon not to favour the principle of repatriation. Powell had been correct in his initial assumption that the new government would devote no great energy to encouraging the outward flow he felt to be essential. In the Southall speech just referred to he accused the government of having 'sabotaged' this, to him, critical aspect of the Act. On immigration, therefore, it was clear that there was to be no meeting of minds between

Powell and the Cabinet. The fissure, indeed, was widening, in spite of the fact that the government had come some of the way towards him.

The debate about immigration continued throughout the life of the government. But, although Powell spoke on the subject from time to time, it was the issue of Common Market membership which loomed most in his activity and public utterances.

In accordance with his desires and declared plans Heath, on being elected, immediately took up negotiations with the Six again. It is not, strictly speaking, proper to speak of new, or fresh, negotiations. When General de Gaulle had imposed his second veto on British entry, a veto responding to the application by the Wilson government, the Prime Minister of the day had declared that the application would remain on the table. Since then de Gaulle had retired, and his successor, Georges Pompidou, was of a much more sympathetic attitude of mind to the United Kingdom, particularly since he accepted Heath as a man of genuine devotion to the cause of a united Europe and who would, in consequence, be more malleable in negotiation. The negotiations were lengthy and technical, and it is not necessary to describe them here,[33] save to say that the crucial event in their progress was a summit meeting between Heath and Pompidou in Paris on 20-21 May 1971, at which the essence of top-level agreement was defined, and (from Heath's point of view) a favourable conclusion arrived at.

The battle against membership of the EEC Powell regarded then, and still regards, as the supreme contest of his career (though the parliamentary performance of which he is proudest is his speech on the Royal Titles Bill in 1953[34]). At almost every stage of the argument about immigration (or, as it increasingly became, the argument about high concentrations of coloured immigrant populations in various areas of the United Kingdom), he was advocating policies which he believed were practical to implement, and was convinced that the policies he opposed could be reversed. Although, to the end of his parliamentary career (and perhaps even now) he entertained the possibility either that the United Kingdom might withdraw from the Community, or that that top-heavy structure would collapse under its own weight of contradictions, he none the less regarded accession (formally concluded on 1 January 1973), once ratified by Act of Parliament, as representing a fundamental and unacceptable surrender of national sovereignty. From the moment, in July 1972, when the Treaty of Accession (sometimes called the Treaty of Brussels) was signed and was ratified by Parliament, his only hope could be that Labour would keep a solemn and unprecedented promise. This was that a Labour government would hold a referendum on continued membership (although, ironically, he did not approve of referenda), his hope being that this would issue in a negative vote. But, for all his public expressions of confidence that the Communities Bill would be defeated in Parliament, he knew that he faced an uphill struggle from the beginning.

It is one of the basic characteristics of Powell's speeches and writing that he invariably attempts, at some stage, to base his argument on first principles, and to define the very nature of his case. He was asked by Hella Pick, in the interview already quoted, how he came to oppose membership of the EEC, and gave a characteristically full answer:

I am prejudiced in favour of free trade and therefore of freer trade. Consequently I warmly approved of Mr. Maudling's effort to make a free trade area with the Rome Treaty countries and those of EFTA.[35] So when Harold Macmillan took the plunge in 1961 it seemed to me that on the whole this could be regarded as another essay in freer trade, that the political aspects weren't of practical importance, and that one could therefore concentrate on the fact that a net increase in freedom of trade would result from our entry. I wouldn't be sure that this attitude on my part was whole-hearted. A member of the government not of the Cabinet, who has his own department, does not commonly apply his mind fundamentally to the other things that the government is doing – I know one is not supposed to admit that: but it is a fact of life, and so it might as well be said – and I suppose that even then I had the odd twinge. (After all, my earliest defiance of the Whip had been when, in June 1950, I abstained from voting against the then Labour government for not joining the Iron and Steel Community.) However, that all finished at the beginning of 1963.

In British politics at the time there were considered to be two aspects of the argument about the EEC, the political and the economic. By the terms of the Treaty of Rome, what the original six nations founded was a European economic community. On the other hand, aspirations towards some form of political union were included in the rubrics of the treaty, and it is fair to say that a great number of those advocating entry looked forward to the creation of some kind of vested structure, perhaps eventually leading to the unitary state implicit in the Treaty of Rome. Few in Britain – and certainly no leading politician who was supportive of entry – cared to enter into the argument about political union, since it was assumed this would arouse the hostility of the electorate. Throughout the various campaigns, therefore, the voters were told, first, that the United Kingdom sought only to inquire whether acceptable terms of membership could be found and, second, that the issue was economic, and not political. In a speech in Co. Down, Northern Ireland, on 16 January 1971 Powell scoffed at both notions: he described the debate so far as being conducted on a 'trivial' level, and asserted that the position of the leadership in both major parties was essentially fraudulent. He set the proponents of membership a high challenge. They must prove, he said, that, 'If it is right . . . [it] must be plainly and supremely right . . .'

To Miss Pick he explained the essence of this argument. Negotiations, he argued, over the previous two years had been moving steadily in a political direction and had 'placed increasing emphasis on the Community as an embryonic political unit. Viewed in this light, the Community seemed to me to be something which Britain cannot join with full intent, even economically, let alone politically . . .' He then defined the argument over sovereignty as he saw it:

There is a fundamental difference between becoming part of a new sovereign entity with its own unitary policy, economic and political, and any of those voluntary or involuntary restrictions on freedom of action which all nations, like all individuals, accept. There is a common fallacy here. You cannot call a man unfree because he is a poor mathematician or has lost a leg; you can call a man unfree if he can be ordered or forced to do something against his will – if another's will is imposed on his. Similarly, no nation is free in the sense that it can do just what it likes, that its powers and resources are unbounded – that is true just as much of the United States as it is of Switzerland – and yet a nation which has not transferred to some other authority, for an indefinite period and in principle, the control over its sovereignty and policy, possesses a sovereignty which it would lose if such a transfer took place.

As time went by Powell more and more readily emphasized the

argument against EEC entry on grounds of sovereignty pure and simple. He was even prepared to concede that he would be against entry even if non-membership made Britain poorer, though he denied that such an eventuality was conceivable. It is important to understand, however, in advance of the parliamentary battle of 1972 what his tactics had been since he first came out against Market membership at Clacton in March 1969 and repeated in Wolverhampton a fortnight later. These tactics were political, in the ordinary sense that politicians manoeuvre for support – and seek to discredit their opponents – effectively or badly. To those who sought (and seek) to deride Powell for seeming changes of front on particular issues within a broad spectrum, it may merely be said that he never lost sight of the central issue (as it appeared to him) from Clacton onwards. He had no patience with the idea, strenuously propagated by Ministers, that the negotiations going on throughout 1971 were, in any ordinarily understood sense of the word, negotiations. It might have been that, had General de Gaulle won the referendum on which he had staked his future in 1969 and remained in power, Heath would have proceeded more cautiously, and taken pains not to risk a third rebuff. With the succession of Georges Pompidou, however – and particularly following Heath's meeting with the President in May 1971 – it was clear that the Six would not impose upon the United Kingdom terms which would be obviously humiliating, however disadvantageous they might be. The position being thus, it was also clear that Heath would accept whatever was going, given his belief, first, that entry was essential and, second, that, once in, Britain would be able to temper any initial disadvantage. With all this Powell would have no truck, and so his constant theme was to dismiss the relevance of the terms: Britain had a government determined to get in, at almost any cost. The prime cost would be her sovereignty.

His personal tactics from Clacton onwards have to be considered separately, though separating things normally considered personal from things normally considered public is, in the case of Powell, an unquestionably difficult business. The attempt, however, must be made.

As well as being a nationalist, Powell was a Tory in a fundamental and, indeed, a moral sense; he was also a member of the Conservative Party, and he cherished that membership very deeply. It constituted an allegiance, though certainly not an allegiance to any given Conservative leadership at any given time. If he had been as impetuous a man as some of his regretful admirers

Cummings

BRITAIN'S DE GAULLE.
C'EST MOI!

Wolverhampton
Les Deux Eglises
1

INFLATION
RAGES

RIOTS IN
PARLIAMENT
MOB
PICKETING

"I'm awaiting the call!"

concluded from time to time, there were a number of occasions before 1974 on which he would have broken with his Party – in fact, almost any time from 1968 onwards. If he had been as hungry and calculating a power-seeker as his enemies concluded (and feared) that he was, he could have taken advantage, both before and after the general election of 1970, of Heath's difficulties at least to give his blessing to avowedly Powellite candidates in by-elections. As it was, he clung on to his Party for as long as he considered it honestly possible to do so, for he was always a Party man.

To most people the description 'Party man' means either (pejoratively) a man who slavishly obeys the dictates of his Party bosses or (favourably) a man who is a good colleague to his fellows. Powell was never a good colleague in the ordinarily understood sense of the word, a sense best summarized in the word 'clubbable'. To Powell (and this may have been in part the result of the early influence on him of German idealism), 'Party' was more than an aggregation of individuals. There had to be a set of ideas or principles on which, in the main, the individuals agreed. On one thing or another, they could agree to differ, but if there was a difference between an individual and his Party on a matter (to him) of fundamental importance it was right that he should depart the ranks. Inevitably, it would be an unwilling, and a saddening, departure, but a man of good conscience would have to take his leave none the less. Powell would thoroughly agree with Iain Macleod, who hated being called a Conservative, and always preferred the ascription 'Tory' for, said Macleod, 'Conservative' meant being a member of a Party which might have different sets of policies at different times, but 'Tory' meant enduring fealty to an ideal. (Interpreting the philosophy of conservatism apart from Party, is, of course, another matter.)[36]

Certainly from early 1969, and possibly from an earlier date, Powell had to contemplate the possibility of being forced by his own conscience to leave the Party which he had joined immediately after the war. But there was no need to rush the matter, as long as there was a possibility that the Party would (in his view) either come to, or be forced by events to come to, its senses. For some time, he had two bulwarks against a decision to cut himself off. His first (which, it could fairly be said, he tended with an almost Jesuitical precision) was Heath's undertaking, expressed with simple force in the Conservative manifesto of 1970, that a government headed by him would be committed 'to negotiate – no more and no less' with the EEC. The second was Heath's further, and oft-repeated, promise not to enter the Community without 'the full-hearted consent of Parliament and people'. The first bulwark was swept away once Powell decided to argue that the negotiations were a mere sham.

The second bulwark lasted much longer. 'Consent' was one thing; 'full-hearted consent' was another. Powell had little time for referenda – indeed, as a politician who based his activities as much or more on an understanding of the history of his country as on anything else, he found the Labour proposal for a referendum on continued membership disagreeable, although he was to do his bit in the referendum campaign of 1975 – for he concluded, in general, that the will of the people could, and should, be expressed through Parliament. It was none the less of great importance, of course, to take the argument to the people, in the way he had taken the argument on immigration to the people. If he was successful there, constituency pressure could be exercised on Members of Parliament. Moreover, even if a narrow defeat was suffered in Parliament, there was the substantial argument that narrow victory could not be taken to represent 'full-hearted' consent.

Of course, Powell was not insensible to the advantage bestowed upon him by the fact that he was a Conservative Member of Parliament, and a Privy Councillor. He had a small personal following in the House of Commons, one much augmented when the issue was membership of the Community. In the Party in the country, however, his support was much greater, and among non-Conservatives still substantial. These were things (quite apart from his personal feelings) not lightly to be thrown away.

Moreover, there seemed, at the beginning of 1971, a distinct possibility that he could mobilize opinion on the EEC as he had mobilized it on immigration, for the polls showed from sixty to sixty-five per cent opposed to entry, with only between twenty and twenty-five per cent for entry. In March of the same year[37] Opinion Research Centre summarized its recent findings in this way. The people believed, said the pollsters, that:

There is a conspiracy on the part of politicians, media owners and big business to commit Britain to joining the Common Market before the public has had a chance to appraise the pros and cons or to know precisely what is happening. They are confronted with an unusual agreement between all three political parties that Britain should join, so normal political

311

allegiances give them no guidance. They tend to feel that they are fed only the information that is favourable to Britain's joining.

This was exactly the kind of situation made for Powell, one in which his parliamentary talents could be combined with his abilities as a public tribune. It was central, to make the obvious comparison to his campaign on immigration, to stress again and again the horrors and the dangers of politicians in Westminster ignoring the fears and feelings of the people. At the beginning of 1971 it seemed that they were doing the same over the EEC.

It was an important part of Powell's plan of action, while repeating his arguments about sovereignty, and dwelling from time to time on the more mundane disadvantages of entry – such as higher food prices – also to harry the government with the charge of dishonesty. The Conservatives had promised only to negotiate: in fact they planned to enter, come what may. The Conservatives had promised not to enter without full-hearted consent: they intended to avoid seeking it. To these two charges was added another. During the campaign – and there were intense and almost theological disputes on who was right on this question – Conservative Party managers had either promised, or at least let it be assumed, that any legislation presented to Parliament as a result of a successful application for membership would be put to the House of Commons on a free vote. That is to say, no pressure would be applied by the government whips to compel doubting or hostile Members to toe the official line. There can be little doubt that this promise, or half-promise, was a piece of deliberate obfuscation on the part of Conservative Party managers.

Every morning during the campaign of 1970, before the formal Press Conference, Heath and a large number of advisers – from his front bench, from Central Office and the Conservative Research Department, from the ranks of the public relations specialists advising him and from the National Union (the voluntary body charged with the organization of unpaid Party activists) – met in Smith Square. There were, of course, other, and more select meetings, between Heath and those closest to him. The object of the morning meetings, however, was to keep the campaign under close review; to alert the Leader to what difficult questions might come up at the Press Conference; to put the final touches to the major speech of the day, particularly with a view to seizing the attention of that night's news programmes and the following day's newspapers and, generally, to foresee difficulties and guard against them. The Common Market was not a central issue of discussion, but it did come up from time to time – as, indeed, it came up in informal questions around the country. A line was agreed (and subsequently transmitted to every Conservative candidate through the Questions of Policy Committee, which sat each morning in Old Queen Street under the chairmanship of Lord Carrington and with, as its secretary recalled for the duration, Powell's old friend David Clarke, of postwar CRD days) that the commitment solely to negotiate and the commitment to 'full-hearted consent' should be stressed, and that the implication that a free vote would be allowed should be given.

Now, as Powell, consummate parliamentarian that he was, fully realized, no government could hope to get complicated legislation of the kind envisaged through the House on a series of free votes. He and Michael Foot, after all, in the matter of the reform of the House of Lords,[38] had demonstrated that determined resistance could defeat even a policy agreed between both front benches. None the less, many among the public did not appreciate the fine distinctions involved and the two words 'free vote' had a pleasantly democratic ring. In these circumstances Powell (and his allies) were entitled to make all they could of the running against the securing of entry through recourse to Party authority, and they did so.

For most of 1971, since the negotiations were still continuing, the most Powell could do was to campaign in the country, and, indeed, in other countries. In what was regarded by many as a series of quixotic gestures, and by some of his supporters with dismay, because they thought of it as distracting his energies, he embarked on an anti-EEC campaign on the continent, speaking for the most part in the native language of the country in which he found himself. There was, of course, no other politician who could have even dreamed of mounting such a staggering display of oratorical fireworks, and there was a tendency to attack him for showing off, a tendency somewhat muted, however, by envy of, and sheer amazement at, the linguistic versatility he displayed, and which he displayed to advantage against two Party Leaders – Wilson and Heath – who, while claiming to be committed Europeans, and wont to descant on the glorious common civilization of the Western European powers, could scarcely manage a polite salutation in French, and pronounced such salutations atrociously.

313

In this series of speeches in the spring of 1971 Powell spoke in France, Italy, Germany and the Netherlands. For the most part the springboard of his argument was familiar, being based on his concept of British sovereignty, and his belief that the British people would decline to relinquish it. In Lyons on 12 February 1971, he dismissed the idea (and his audience in all probability agreed with his dismissal) that the EEC could be considered purely as a 'commercial' organization. But his purpose, he explained, was largely educational: he wanted to make British objections (objections supported by a considerable majority of the British people) 'intelligible in the context of British thought and history'. He reassured those listening that rejection of entry would – and should in his view – in no whit diminish the British military commitment to the continent, but he offered also the advice that, with the United Kingdom inside, the continental powers might find it difficult, if not impossible, to pursue effectively the goals envisaged in the Treaty of Rome.

In Frankfurt on 29 March the message was, broadly speaking, the same, but on this occasion he devoted some time to an analysis of the negotiations in progress: they avoided, he believed, the central question – yes or no – and concerned themselves only with the business of transition. He warned the Germans, in addition – and this was the first occasion on which he had spelt this out – what he and those of like mind would require in the way of British support for entry; a massive majority of Members of Parliament of both parties, and the demonstrable acquiesence of a substantial majority of the British people. At The Hague on 17 May the structure of the speech was the same, but much of the detail was designed to appeal specifically to Dutch interests.

They had to consider, he said, whether it was really in their interests to allow Britain in. In answer to a question, and knowing the difficulties the Netherlands was then facing in absorbing the detritus of their own Asian empire, he said that the only advantage in entry for the United Kingdom that he could see was that the British immigrant population could be spread throughout the enlarged EEC. (In the event, the continental powers took care to ensure that any such dispersion would be prohibited under the terms of the Treaty of Accession.)

There is no doubt that Powell enjoyed himself hugely on these forays. He has never been shy about displaying his polymathic powers, and there was glee in his voice and in his eyes when he recounted his experiences to friends and journalists, glee, particularly enhanced by the knowledge that no rival could have turned in so bravura a performance. The question, however, remained: was it worth the expenditure of his time and strength?

I raise the question because it was so often asked at the time. In truth, though, it is misconceived, and based on a misunderstanding of his personality. First, as I shall show in a moment, there was no perceptible diminution of effort at home. Second, it is important to consider the way in which Powell approaches any task or campaign. His method is fully to acquaint himself with his subject, form a view – or a policy – on it, and then to leave no stone unturned in his work to win the argument.

It was clearly an essential part of the argument, on this as on later European journeys, an essential part of his purpose to excite concern in continental breasts and minds about what the consequences of British entry would be, how it might well upset the hard-won balance of the existing structure. Obviously, Powell did not have the power of a de Gaulle, from personal authority to prevent entry. But he saw it as his duty to attempt what he could; and he was uniquely equipped to make that attempt. He had no illusions that his influence would be great, but the effort had to be made.

From the moment of his election, Heath was sanguine that, so far at least as the Six were concerned, his object could fairly readily be achieved; such anxiety as there was concerned the home front. It is important, however, to remember that, so far as this third bid was concerned, Heath was far, far better equipped to lead it than either Harold Macmillan or Harold Wilson had been. He, as Lord Privy Seal, had led the British team in the first abortive attempt. Asked to comment on his qualities Powell recalled a meeting of the Shadow Cabinet in 1967. Heath had returned from a visit to de Gaulle and reported to his colleagues. 'He produced,' Powell says, 'an ordered, structured précis which the most expert civil servant, having hours to prepare a draft, could not have matched. "Enoch," I said to myself, "you couldn't touch that." ' So far as the negotiations were concerned – and it is amply clear, as suggested earlier in this chapter and reiterated endlessly by Powell, that they were not serious negotiations in the sense that they might be allowed to fail – Heath had an early setback in personnel. His chosen negotiator was Anthony Barber. But the collapse and death of Iain Macleod shortly after making his first speech as Chancellor of the Exchequer enforced a Cabinet reshuffle. Barber went to the Exchequer and Geoffrey (now Lord) Rippon to Brussels to negotiate. In truth, though, it did not matter that the British negotiator betrayed no more than a moderate competence in the grasp of detail: the Prime Minister's grasp was sufficient for all. And, as George Hutchinson made clear in his highly sympathetic biography of Heath,[39] it had always been the Prime Minister's intention to accept all those provisions, not merely of the Treaty of Rome, but of subsequent Community edicts, which would involve turning the United Kingdom irrevocably away from her world trading posture and into a continental system bent on erecting walls around itself which would shut out free trade.

Heath's touch was less sure, however, when it came to the management of Party opinion, and particularly of Parliament. It was here that he was fortunate to have, for the presentation of the legislation, the deeply committed Solicitor-General, Sir Geoffrey Howe, and for parliamentary management the Leader of the House, William Whitelaw. The nexus of management could not have been better conceived: Whitelaw had been an outstanding Chief Whip in opposition, and on his elevation had been succeeded by his Deputy, Francis Pym. It was essentially with this small and cohesive team that Heath went into action in 1972.

As against Heath and the government Powell was, virtually, if not entirely, alone. There were, to be sure, both Conservative and Labour Members of Parliament ready and willing to oppose British membership of the EEC. Few of them, however, were willing to make open and public cause with Powell. Nor did he encourage any alliance that might form under his leadership. 'Gruff courtesy,' said one of those who did follow his lead during the tense debates in the first half of 1972, 'was the best he gave us.' The experience of the EEC debates underlined an important truth about Powell. If he cannot operate within the system of allegiance of a Party, he invariably operates alone. He does not take readily or, indeed, at all, to less formal groupings, or to the pressure group, or the caucus. Indeed, in answering questions after perhaps the most important speech of his life, in the Birmingham Bull Ring in February 1974, he said, 'You must understand. The essence of democracy is Party. A man who stands alone has only his own advocacy. And that is a very limited thing.'

There was another difficulty inherent in the situation as the life of the 1970 Parliament wore on. It, too, proceeded from Powell's nature, and from his willingness – indeed, determination – to speak out on all manner of subjects. The number of those who might plausibly be described as his followers was never great; and they were divided amongst themselves in that they had different reasons for being attached to him, as described earlier in the case of Nicholas Ridley and Neil Marten. The difficulties of these two men could be rendered manifold by reference to divisions of opinion within the ranks of other Conservatives critical of the progress of the Heath government and, increasingly, of the Prime Minister himself. Though all attempts to divide the lives of administrations into neat chronological segments must be suspect, it is not unfair to say that the government headed by Edward Heath had two distinct periods in its life. The first lasted from the general election of 1970 to April of 1972; the second from that month to the defeat of February 1974. It is perfectly true that the whole matter of accession to the Treaty of Rome cuts across this division of dates (the United Kingdom became a full member of the EEC in January 1973) but the fact of history is that it was the reversal of the free market (today we would call it monetarist) policy on which Heath was elected which produced a still-lasting conflict between himself and his Party. The ideological battle between those who favoured, or were prepared to favour, a state-controlled economic policy – buttressed, in particular, by an enforced incomes policy – and those who clung to the notion that the economy should be as near as possible untrammelled in its operation, was cast in relief by the departure of Nicholas Ridley and Frederick Corfield from the Department of Trade. While a number of other Ministers were either dismissed or shifted to new departments, these two, standard bearers of the 1970 policies, resigned. From April 1972 to the death of the government it was clear that advocacy of capitalistic notions would find little favour with Prime Minister or Cabinet. More, there developed within the ranks of those committed to the change of course advocated by the Prime Minister an unpleasant willingness to crush criticism, which willingness Dr. Butler and Mr. Kavanagh[40] note down as producing a general feeling in Conservative Party parliamentary ranks that business was not being conducted in the traditional fashion, and that dissent was likely to be the occasion of punishment, rather than something to be held in honest, if hostile, respect.

Where Powell stood out among other critics of the Heath government was both in the totality of his opposition to it (though he was prepared, albeit with an acid tongue, to welcome the floating of the pound in June 1972) and in the sheer elegance of his advocacy. It was, to be sure, a disadvantage to him that not all of those opposed to the government agreed with every jot and tittle of his alternative policy. But it was a singular advantage, not least in the business of gaining and holding public attention, that he could turn a phrase better than any other politician, and that he had a coherent and rounded view of everything within the purlieus of politics. While therefore, in his own mind the supreme constitutional issue between 1970 and 1974 was membership of the EEC, his views on immigration kept him well to the fore of public attention, and the travails of economic policy ensured a ready audience for his contrary prescriptions.

Again and again during these years Powell presented not merely criticism of individual policies, but a whole world view. The examples from his speeches could be multiplied *in extenso*, but twin themes emerged at an early stage, and may be noted particularly in a speech at Doncaster on 19 June 1971 and in London (at Painters' Hall) on 13 July. The first of the themes is demotic: it is his regular insistence that politicians must listen to the desires and opinions of the people they represent. The second theme is that of self-confident nationalism. This is, indeed, the centre of all his thinking and writing. Whether the subject matter be immigration, or the balance of payments, or membership of the EEC, he returns again and again to the desirability – the necessity – of national self-confidence. Given it, all problems are soluble. Without it, none is.

The brutal judgement the historian must make on the years of the Heath administration is that almost everything went wrong, except the great adventure of entry into the EEC, which Edward Heath himself might regard as a sufficient justification for his term of office: a less strong-minded and committed Prime Minister might well, as we shall shortly see, not have been able to put the necessary legislation through Parliament. From an early stage, however, other cherished policies ran into stormy weather. The trade unions revolted against the legislation restricting their powers (which legislation was later repealed by a Labour government). Industrial relations steadily advanced towards disruption as the months went by. Economic management was beset either by wrong judgement or outside events (such as the oil price crisis of 1973, occasioned by the Arab-Israeli war). On other matters, such as the reform of local government, the ending of free school milk (by the Secretary of State for Education, Margaret Thatcher) or the attempt to impose entry charges at museums or galleries, whatever the individual merit of these measures, the government managed to offend some section – and sometimes all – of the electorate. By the end of 1973, while Ministers might protest that they had got a number of things right (usually by changing tack, particularly on incomes policy), they did so *sotto voce*. There were no achievements to trumpet in the February 1974 general election campaign, and it was that fact which gave the election its peculiar character.

For the biographer of Powell, however, three main issues stand out – the EEC, immigration, and the management of the economy. Their importance, and the attention paid to arguments about them, ebbed and flowed; but they were all three ever-present, both in his own thoughts and utterances and in the wider field of parliamentary and public opinion. Heath's stated ambition – oddly emphatic for so normally staid, if determined, an orator – to change the course of the history of the country cannot be too often repeated. It was by the standard set by that ambition that he was more and more readily judged as the first years of a new decade wobbled to no very marked conclusion.

It is an irony that would have appealed to Gibbon that Powell brought Heath down[41] on what he considered to be only the second in importance of the three issues. He had said in Brussels that the only advantage he could see in British membership of the EEC was that immigration from the British Commonwealth could be spread all over the territory of the Community. There was a deliberate irony here, in that he had frequently referred to the propensity of immigrants to congregate in a limited number of areas in the United Kingdom. On 15 February 1971 he told Banstead Young Conservatives that, important as the issue of the EEC was, since it meant 'a gradual loss of our national identity', it was, on the scale of importance, less significant than immigration. The irony is that, while it was the subject that he considered the more important that gave Powell his power with the public, it was the subject that he considered of lesser (if only of slightly lesser) importance which forced the final, and deadly, breach with Heath. However, in relation to these issues, the matter of economic management may be considered somewhat like the backing in a tapestry on which raised figures pursue their conflicts. If the Heath government could make the economy work, then all of the dislikeable things they did would be forgiven them. It was, of course, the Powell thesis that, in virtue of their views (changing as these were) and philosophy, they could not make the economy work.

Entangled though the three subjects which dominated the

period 1970-74 were, we can only see them with clarity by taking them separately.

From Tamworth on it was clear that the running battle, likely to last most of the Parliament, between Powell and the leadership of his Party, would be on the Common Market. He could keep up pressure on immigration (as he did both on the Immigration Bill and on the Ugandan Asians) and on the economy. But the one certain thing from the first meeting between Edward Heath as Prime Minister and Georges Pompidou as President of France in May 1971 was that any agreement between the United Kingdom and the existing Community of six nations would require, to put it into effect, legislation and, thus, prolonged parliamentary scrutiny. Whatever else might command evanescent headlines, or constitute the elements of a continuous grumble of discontent, this was the issue which would have to be followed by debate in the House of Commons and, later, in the Lords.

Powell fought on both fronts (not to mention the salient he built on the continent in his speeches designed to convince continental audiences that the people of the United Kingdom did not share their intentions regarding the economic community). He sought to affect attitudes in Parliament by exciting pressure in the country; and he sought, once membership was tabled as putative legislation, by every artifice of industry and ingenuity to frustrate it, as he and Michael Foot had frustrated reform of the House of Lords.

It is a matter of record – and one worth recording – that there were 104 divisions (that is, votes for or against a clause or an amendment) on the European Communities Bill, providing for acceptance by the House of terms negotiated by the government. There are often good reasons for a Member not voting against a particular clause in a Bill which he opposes, and one can never, with full correctness, estimate opposition or support of a measure according to a count of votes. However, it is worth observing that Powell voted 81 times against the government (out of the 104 divisions). He was followed by John Biffen, with 78 votes in the same cause; Roger Moate with 71; and Neil Marten with 69. It should be remembered here that Marten, in the vein of those opposing membership of the EEC had, unlike Powell, serious problems with his constituency of Banbury. Banbury, in Oxfordshire, is an agricultural constituency, and many of its farmers supported with enthusiasm the idea of the United Kingdom joining the EEC, for, they believed, farmers would gain enormously from the operation of the Common Agricultural Policy, which is at the heart of the

Treaty of Rome. At the same time, what Powell called, in a speech to the London University Conservative Association on 11 February 1972, 'unparalleled exertions' were being made – quite in contrast to undertakings before and during the general election campaign of 1970 – to bend the will of Conservative MPs opposed to membership. Marten – like Roger Moate in Faversham and Richard (now Sir Richard) Body in Holland with Boston – had to look to their backs in their constituencies, as well as to their fronts in the House; and their attendance could not, therefore, be as consistent as that of the Member for Wolverhampton South-West, whose home base was secure. It is a matter of record that Neil Marten secured peace in Banbury only by offering to resign his seat, with the provision that he would then stand at a by-election as a Conservative Anti-EEC candidate.

The question the government was faced with immediately after the election of 1970 was how they should proceed with the business of securing parliamentary assent to a treaty of accession which they could feel reasonably sure they would obtain.[42] On 23 June 1971 the United Kingdom (with the Republic of Ireland and Denmark) agreed terms with the six founding members of the Community. The Cabinet agreed that the next step was to seek the approval of the House of Commons *in principle*, but without immediately tabling legislation. The government was anxious, however, not to rush this step: despite the confidence of their business managers in the House, some Ministers feared a Conservative rebellion (spearheaded, of course, by Powell) to the strength of which would be added the preponderant majority of the Parliamentary Labour Party, the leadership of which had by now, in the main, decided to blow cold on membership of the EEC, at least under the terms negotiated by Geoffrey Rippon.

Caution prevailed, and it was decided not to make a move in Parliament without first testing the water at the Conservative Party Conference. 'I do not believe,' Powell told that Conference:

this nation, which has maintained and defended its independence for a thousand years, will now submit to see it merged or lost, nor did I become a member of our sovereign Parliament in order to consent to that sovereignty being abated or transferred. Come what may I cannot and I will not.

A week later at Newport, Powell was to warn his Party and the government drawn from its ranks that it would be destroyed by its support of entry. At the Conference, though, his advocacy of nationalism and independence was to little avail: the motion supporting entry was carried by 2,474 to 324.

This result, and the evident inefficacy of Powell – the rebel they most feared – greatly heartened Ministers and they proceeded to lay before the House of Commons a motion favouring the principle of entry. This motion, on a free vote (though considerable pressure was exerted behind the scenes) was debated on 28 October.

As Powell knew perfectly well, the government was assured of a handsome majority on the free vote. Private exchanges secured an undertaking from Roy Jenkins, then the Deputy Leader of the Labour Party, and a substantial number of Labour marketeers that, come the day, they would support entry with their votes. Came the day sixty-nine of them did, and the government triumphed by 356 to 244. The only thing that could have embarrassed the Prime Minister seriously would have been a substantial Tory revolt, leaving him to depend on the Jenkins cohorts. In the event thirty-nine Conservatives voted against, with two abstaining.

Useful though this debate was as a propaganda exercise (Heath was later to claim that its result, taken together with the Party Conference vote, constituted the 'full-hearted consent' he was pledged to seek), it was clear to everybody that it was a sham battle, and that the real struggle would come only when legislation was tabled. The stark details of the price to be paid for membership might attract (and in the end did attract) far more opposition than the expression of a generalized aspiration. Moreover, it was uncertain how many of the sixty-nine Labour Members who had followed Roy Jenkins on 28 October would have the conviction or the courage to follow the same course throughout the grinding slog of Committee proceedings. It was on sustained warfare in Committee that Powell and his allies relied (as they had done on Lords' reform). Powell had been confident at Newham on 13 September that entry 'isn't going to happen'. On 17 September he spoke in Beckenham where the local Conservative Member, Philip Goodhart, had organized a referendum on the subject. In the course of his speech he suggested, for the first time (and anticipating the sustenance Heath would draw from the forthcoming votes at the Party Conference and in the House) that the Heath government should have another general election, it being 'unthinkable that a government should decide such an issue without the renewal of its own authority'.

Undismayed and unabashed by the two votes, Powell, on 15 January 1972, told the Liechtenstein Press Club that:

> The House of Commons is never at ease with general policies: it is most like itself when it turns its attention to the specific, the concrete and often the apparently trivial. The protracted debate of last year was no more than the overture; the real play or opera begins next week.

He continued with this line of argument, within and without Westminster during the Committee stage of the Bill, which had its second reading on 17 January 1972.

In truth, though, the battle was almost lost already. There were two major reasons why this was so. The first was the nature of the Bill and the government's attitude to the committee (which was of the whole House). The second was the stand taken by Roy Jenkins. Throughout the whole stormy period to July (when the Bill became law) the government, though there were some worrying moments, was confident that, in a crisis, Jenkins and at least some of his followers would come to their rescue. Accepting that his personal conviction necessitated such action in the event of danger, and observing with profound sadness the deepening hostility of his own party to the EEC, Jenkins resigned the Labour deputy leadership on 10 April.

Opponents of British entry into the EEC had assumed, first, that the Bill would be a monumental one (given the vast quantity of British law which required repeal or revision in consequence of the Treaty of Accession) and, second, that there would be opportunities for many amendments which would frustrate the government's purpose and make all other business difficult or impossible for a lengthy period. The parallel with the attack on Harold Wilson's attempt to reform the House of Lords was not exact for, on this occasion, most of the Labour Party could be counted on to side with the Conservative rebels. At first sight that might seem to make the government's task more difficult than Wilson's had been (given that the two front benches had reached agreement on the Lords) but in fact it was easier. This was because the Conservative Whips could (and did) make regular appeals to loyalty in the face of the Labour enemy; and because there would be regular whipping throughout. The government was to be often in trouble, but rarely in real danger.

To the consternation of those opposed to entry, the Bill

presented to the house by Sir Geoffrey Howe was of modest proportions. The first part dealt with the constitution and finance, the second with aspects of Community law, and the third with Britain's monetary obligations. The government had been as worried as its opponents were cheerful at the debilitating prospect of a massive piece of legislation. Howe was both delighted and astonished when his parliamentary draftsman, Sir John Sandilands, after a weekend's cogitation, told him, 'We can do it in twelve clauses.' The trick was simply to insert a clause giving over-riding authority to Community law where there was a conflict with British law. Then, in an unprecedented move, the government announced that it would accept no amendments whatsoever. In the course of the Bill's passage Ministers (and particularly Geoffrey Rippon) assured the House that the government (or any successor) would not be required to yield to the Community on any matter of major British interest. But this assurance was not quite the same thing as having a statement of ultimate British authority and sovereignty in cold, legislative print. Such a concession would, however, have been impossible, given the terms of the Treaty of Accession.

The first dangerous hurdle was the Second Reading. The sixty-eight who had voted with Jenkins for the most part melted away. Even though Powell and his allies had achieved the strength of forty-one in that same vote, however, the intense pressure of the Tory Whips made inroads on their numbers. Then, on the evening of the Second Reading vote, Heath announced that, if he were defeated, he would immediately seek a dissolution and a general election. Few doubted that he would, indeed, take this extreme course. But there were few who agreed with Powell that such a consummation would be desirable; the probability, after all, was that the government would lose an election called in such circumstances. No Conservative contemplates the fall of a Conservative government with anything approaching equanimity, so the pressure of self-interest as well as simple loyalty turned at least some of the disaffected. The vote was, nevertheless, a close thing, though the government Whips had felt confident enough to assure their Labour friends beforehand that their help would not be needed. In the event victory was won by the dangerously narrow margin of eight votes.

It was, however, the moment of maximum risk. Thereafter, though majorities were often slender, commitment on the part of the Prime Minister, and vigilance on the part of his Whips, made it certain that the Bill would get through, even though 'full-hearted consent' was evidently lacking. The original phrase, however, stated the requirement for the 'full-hearted consent of Parliament and people' and it was on this last word that Powell increasingly laid his emphasis. It justified, indeed, his insistence on the desirability of an election before the Rubicon was crossed but, more and more, he began to fear that the people would not speak, would not give him and his allies the commitment and support that he had received after his 1968 speech on immigration. Thus, at a meeting in his constituency at the end of January, he issued another of his warnings. If there was no general public outcry and if the Bill passed:

> Do not blame the whips; do not blame the patronage machine; do not blame the pressures, the threats, the promises, the bribes. It is the nation itself that will have judged itself. When it could have spoken, it will have stayed dumb; when it could have acted it remained idle.

Had there been such a massive upsurge of opinion against the EEC as had been seen over immigration, it is indeed probable that the government could not have seen its legislation through. One of the difficulties facing Powell, however, was that the general hostility to membership of the Community was both diffuse and half-hearted. It was true, also, that even during those brief periods when the polls showed a majority in favour of membership, follow-up questions indicated that large segments of the majority felt worry and even fear that, economically, the United Kingdom could not make it on her own: this was the result of the long years of economic and industrial decline. For the most part electors (and most MPs) saw the issue purely in economic terms: purists of either persuasion were few and far between. There was the further difficulty that most voters – and many politicians – freely confessed that they could not understand the technicalities of the debate, could not or did not dare to make their own calculation of benefit and loss. In such a climate, of course, apathy was the government's best friend, while prevailing uncertainty about what it was right to do made it all the easier for the Conservative leadership to cajole and browbeat (both in the constituencies and in Parliament) to an extent never before seen in British politics.

Still, Powell was prepared to fight every inch of the way. In Montgomeryshire on 4 March his theme was the unique relationship between the nation and the House of Commons, a relationship of a kind which existed nowhere in Europe: was it to be that that relationship would be destroyed by amalgamation with states whose systems of government were of very recent origin? At Willenhall on 8 April he addressed himself to the definition of 'full-hearted consent' in a sense highly critical of Heath. (He had already begun to abandon the convention, hitherto observed by him in the letter rather than the spirit, of eschewing personal attack.) On 1 July, addressing the Islington Conservative Association, he spoke of immigration and the EEC together. Since the continental countries had no intention of allowing coloured immigrants to Britain to cross the Channel for settlement, they were 'going to be spectators, not participators, in the tragedy of our cities'.

Nor did he relax his efforts in the House of Commons where divisions took place in which the government's majorities were tantalizingly narrow, but where victory ever remained elusive. In March, for example, Powell moved an amendment which would have provided that while existing EEC regulations would have authority in Britain, future regulations would not. It was defeated by 213 votes to 202. In the same month he argued that, should Heath succeed, he 'would go down in history bearing with him the indelible brand of broken faith and trust betrayed'. In April the Labour Opposition, hungering after a general election, moved to the half-way house of a referendum. Powell was no lover of referenda, but he and thirteen other Tories supported the motion, while fourteen others abstained. It was to no avail: due to Labour defections the government ran out with a majority of forty-nine. When the final vote, to pass the Bill into law, was held in July they got by with a majority of seventeen. For most people the battle was over. Edward Heath had triumphed. Once more, Enoch Powell was in a wilderness of his own devising.

It was now that Powell had to consider, not merely the future in general, but his own future. The tone of his speech to the Party Conference in October 1972, while in no way explicit, did express a profound disenchantment with Tory politics and led more than one observer to the conclusion that he might well one day leave the Party. However, the general conclusion was that if he did take that drastic step, it would be to found some sort of new Party, or organize a new force: those closest to him, however, knew that this would be a course of conduct quite out of character. Barring departure Powell thus – in the context of entry into the EEC, which formally took place on 1 January 1973 – had two prospects. He could work to re-convert the Party (a fairly forlorn hope) or he could anticipate the coming of a Labour government committed to a referendum: in Brussels in September 1972 he spoke with moderate approbation of the Labour Party. At Yarmouth a month later he foresaw eventual disaster for the Conservatives, for, 'No statesman, no government, no Party will survive if the essential compact with the people which is entered into as the price of office is wilfully or recklessly or deceitfully broken.'

Forlorn the hope of changing the Tory mind might be, but it was true that the gratification of Heath's dream, and the parliamentary victory he had enjoyed, did little for the prospects of his government. 1972 was to prove a troubled year. On 30 January the Parachute Regiment shot down thirteen Republicans in Londonderry. In February Lord Wilberforce recommended (and the Cabinet accepted) a settlement with the National Union of Miners which was not merely inflationary but which also whetted the appetite of the miners' leaders. On 30 March Heath felt forced to suspend Stormont (Northern Ireland's parliament, which had jurisdiction in internal affairs): direct rule from London was imposed, with William Whitelaw as Secretary of State responsible for the province. On 17 April the railway workers began a work to rule which lasted until 12 June. On 23 June the pound was floated. On 18 July the Home Secretary, Reginald Maudling, resigned because of allegations linking him to the crooked architect, John Poulson: Maudling's honourable reason was that he could not continue in a position where he was responsible for the police when he himself might come under their scrutiny; but he also refused the offer of an alternative post. Three days later the dockers went on strike, to remain out until 16 April. The general situation was not, therefore, a happy one for the government, particularly given the fact that the passage of the European Communities Act excited sullen resentment rather than the gratified enthusiasm the Prime Minister himself felt.

Then, on 4 August, General Amin began the expulsion of Uganda's Asians.

Powell was immediately in print in *The Times*.[43] The government made clear its belief that Britain had an obligation to 50,000 Ugandan British passport holders, and that it intended to fulfil that obligation. On 16 August Powell addressed a female audience in his constituency. His thesis was that there was no obligation and that control was clearly provided in the Commonwealth Immigrants Act of 1968. 'In order,' he said at Ramsgate on 12 September, to govern a people and to lead them, you must enter into their feelings and their fears, and they must know that you enter into them. At this moment hundreds of thousands of our fellow citizens here in Britain are living in perpetual dread; they dread for themselves, or they dread for their children, or they dread for both . . .

On 20 September, at Beaconsfield, he quoted an undertaking given by Heath to a correspondent in February 1970. Heath had said that, under a Conservative government, 'Future immigrants will only be allowed when they are needed for a specific job in a specific place for a specific time . . .' Powell took this to apply to the Ugandans, particularly given Heath's assurance, in the same letter, that the government would direct immigrants away from areas where the social services were over-stretched. 'Was Mr. Heath,' he asked regarding immigration policy,

misinformed before the election, or is he being misinformed now? It must be one or the other because the only other possibility is to assume deliberate, barefaced deception – and that I am not prepared to do.

The government's point, of course, was that the Ugandans were not, in the ordinary sense, immigrants – that is, citizens of another country coming to live in Britain. The Attorney General, Sir Peter Rawlinson, pronounced that the Ugandans enjoyed a right of entry; Powell declared that he had 'prostituted' his office; the Lord Chancellor, Lord Hailsham, rebuked Powell. Suddenly, the Member for Wolverhampton South-West whom so many had written off yet again the previous July, was back in the centre of things, and back in the headlines. And the Conservative Party Conference was approaching.

October and November saw a good deal of deft footwork on both sides. It should be said here that Conservative Central Office chooses – and not infrequently inspires – motions to be debated at the Conference; and that is the principal reason why they are, in general, anodyne. All the motions submitted, however, are printed in the official Conference handbook and one session is kept free for a so-called balloted motion. That is, representatives are invited to vote in order to select a subject and motion for debate. Their choice was overwhelmingly for immigration and the motion (which simply expressed support for immigration policy as laid down in the 1970 manifesto) was to be proposed by Harvey Proctor of the Hackney and Shoreditch Conservative Association. The leadership naturally expected Powell to speak. But he would have only five minutes, and he could be called well down the order. (It was agreed that it would be unwise not to call him, but at least this was a variation of the tactics of previous years, when the practice was to call Powell during the interval when the BBC had interrupted Conference coverage to broadcast *Play School*.)

The evening before the Conference the Party chairman, Lord Carrington, was due, as usual, to hold a Press Conference to acquaint journalists with Conference arrangements and deliver a general briefing. Just before this began Carrington received a note from Proctor. This said that he was waiving his right to propose the motion in favour of the President of his Association, one Enoch Powell. This little ploy, which would give Powell ten minutes and make him the centre of attention, had been hatched some time before. The press heard of it at almost the same moment as Carrington, and for some half hour had great fun at the expense of a highly embarrassed chairman.

The Party leadership knew – not least from their own correspondence – how strongly the bulk of their followers felt against them on the Ugandan issue. If they had any doubts the overwhelming wish expressed by the delegates to debate immigration would have disabused them. The difficulty they saw in conclave, however, was that if the motion, innocuous as it seemed, was passed on Powell's advocacy he would then be in a position to claim, throughout the country, that he had the support of the Party for his policy.

It was decided, therefore, to amend the motion, for they could not seek its defeat. David Hunt, the chairman of the Young Conservatives, was chosen to move an amendment endorsing in ringing terms the rights of the Ugandan Asians. Following all that the new Home Secretary, Robert (now Lord) Carr, would wind up with a speech the peroration of which would include a stinging attack on racialism, implicitly a rebuke of Powell. Party officials were asked to estimate what effect all this would have, and they confidently predicted a majority for the amended motion of about five to one.

On 12 October Powell rose and surprised everybody. Instead of being a clamant call to arms his speech was moderate, cogent and rather legalistic in tone. He rehearsed his argument that there had been no intention, at independence, to grant Ugandan holders of British passports preferential rights of entry and attacked the government – though, again, in moderate tones – for breaking its 1970 general election pledges both to curb immigration and encourage repatriation. He was warmly received and warmly applauded when he sat down (though there was some booing, mainly from Young Conservatives in the gallery). None the less, when he sat down to remain, impassive and unmoved, his arms crossed, for the rest of the debate, there was a sense of disappointment, both among his supporters and those (especially the press) who had expected fireworks. David Hunt's speech, which followed immediately, was more exciting, for Hunt was cheered to the echo by his own supporters, and booed to the echo by those who agreed with Powell. As planned, Carr's concluding speech was also quiet and reasoned until the peroration.

The result, however, though hailed as a triumph by Conservative Central Office, was privately greeted with some shock. The platform had won, but only with a two to one majority – 1,721 to 985 – not at all the sort of showing to be expected from an opponent of the platform at a Conservative Party Conference. Moreover, the results of a poll which I organized for the *Spectator*, and which appeared towards the end of the Conference, showed that 23% of delegates thought Powell had dominated the proceedings (as against 30% for Robert Carr and 8% for Edward Heath – though it has to be remembered that this poll was taken before Heath's own major speech). We also asked our respondents to state a preference for the leadership in the event that Heath, for any reason, should resign. Carr was preferred by 38%; Powell by 37%. He was back with a vengeance.

The Conference did not quite see the end of the dispute about the legalities of the Ugandan position. To date that dispute had been carried on between Powell (with various allies) and the Home Secretary, with the Law Officers taking a part from time to time. Back at Westminster after the conference season, however, Powell tabled a question for written answer on the question of whether undertakings had ever hitherto been given. The answer, on 23 October, was that none had. As Powell observed to the Oxford Monday Club on 18 November, 'If that statement had been deliberately drafted as a rebuttal of what Robert Carr told the Party Conference it could not have been drawn with more devastating precision.' Henceforward it was to be a regularly deployed part of his armoury.

The essential difference between the two sides was that, whereas the government accepted that the Ugandans presented a problem, but regarded it as a different problem from general immigration, Powell regarded the whole business as a seamless web. He had never, indeed, slackened his preoccupation with immigration. On 15 February 1971 he reviewed all the statistical arguments for the benefit of the Banstead Young Conservatives. His essential argument was that the Conservative Immigration Bill would have but little effect on inflow. What was particularly interesting about the speech, however, was the way he defined the essential character of the British nation, and traced his role in defence of it back to 1948:[44]

> Much of my own political life has been dedicated to exposing and confronting these consequences, from the time when the 1948 Act was still a Bill. But setting all that aside for the moment, the world of the 1970s is on any view so different from that of the 1940s, and this nation's place in it is so different, that the definition of 1948 is grotesquely inappropriate and a new one is urgently needed.

From now on the question of immigration was more consistently than ever before placed within a constitutional, historical and philosophical framework. By comparison with the speeches from 1972 onwards (though many passages in these continued his running commentary on immigration statistics) the famous speech of April 1968 in Birmingham seems almost homely. Thus, it would not be readily apparent to his simpler followers what this historical excursus at Banstead meant:

> British Nationality before 1948 was essentially feudal in philosophy. Its essence was allegiance to the Crown; its possessors were British subjects; and to be born 'within the allegiance', in the Dominions of the Crown, was its normal basis, though those so born could, in various ways, renounce that allegiance and others, not so born, could be admitted to allegiance at the Crown's pleasure. The world was divided into two: the Dominions of the Crown and the rest.

Powell's central argument was that the law of nationality – or of allegiance – should have been changed with the end of Empire. That it was not was due to the fact that post-war British politicians, while admitting constituent elements of the Empire to independence, wished to pretend that the newly created Commonwealth was a satisfactory substitute for

Empire, with the sovereign at its head. As part of this pretence, Commonwealth citizens were allowed, in principle, access to the motherland (though the newly independent nations did not reciprocate so far as native British were concerned). That right had, of course, been hemmed about by various restrictions, from the Butler Act of 1962 onwards. Powell believed, however, that until the root cause of definition was attacked, restrictions would avail little.

Powell had been an imperialist, in the common sense of that word. Unlike many of his ilk, however, he never became a Commonwealth man. Throughout his career he had treated the Commonwealth with deep suspicion at the very least, more usually with derision. An article in the *Illustrated London News* of May 1971 is one of his most comprehensive indictments of the whole Commonwealth ideal, and of attachment to it. It meant nothing to him that the Queen was still queen of some independent countries since, 'For each of them she is a different monarch and the recognition of herself and her heirs depends upon separate and independent decisions.' The independent countries which had once formed the Empire, he believed, 'have nothing, literally nothing, which is common to all and exclusive to others . . .'

For this reason the Commonwealth was a sham 'and must rank as one of the world's worst jokes . . . No more inappropriate and mocking name could be devised for this ghost or phantom of a vanished Empire.' If the whole business were no more than a poor joke that would not be so bad – except that Powell has always believed that humbug in politics is dangerous. The tragedy was that Britain, alone among the member nations, acted in the execution of her own policy as though the Commonwealth had a real existence, and as though membership imposed obligations. Of the other nations in the organization, he says, 'Their relations with one another are exactly those with other independent nations, which does not exclude, as with other independent nations, that they may have special relations with some and not with others.' But:

The United Kingdom, however, so far as within it lies, treats the phantom as real. All persons from any of these territories, whether citizens of that country or not, are treated inside the United Kingdom as indistinguishable from her own people: all, she still asserts in her quaint old-fashioned way, are 'British subjects' and as such entitled to vote and sit in Parliament.

Most important of all to him were the consequences that had flowed from this pathetic British practice:

> If the United Kingdom 20 years ago had treated the citizens of the rest of the Commonwealth as what they were and are – no different from the citizens of other independent countries – the result, far from increasing antagonism, would have been to prevent the creation of a problem (call it 'racial' or 'minority' or what you will) which provides endless matter for friction and hostility between Britain and other countries. The reason why Britain, and not France or Germany or Italy, is arraigned and denounced and badgered by a score of nations around the world is not because she washed her hands of former dependencies when they ceased to be dependent, but because she wanted to pretend that they all still belong to one and the same Commonwealth, and thus created undefined claims and presumptions which would always be disappointed. The moral is pointed with cruel humour when Commonwealth countries bully Britain with the threat of 'leaving the Commonwealth' or even 'expelling her from the Commonwealth'. Every country of the Commonwealth pursues, and is entitled to pursue, a commercial policy which it considers to be to its individual interest; yet the odium for limiting trade between itself and any other part of the Commonwealth attaches uniquely to Britain.

Powell, as I have had occasion to remark before, almost never speaks or writes, however short the compass or arcane the subject, without striving to state a general principle or truth, and without setting his matter within a large and general context. Even by his standards, however, this article is a remarkably cogent piece of work. It expresses his beliefs and states his case with a directness, cogency and comprehensiveness which no contemporary could achieve. It may be answerable; but none of the legions of his critics have ever answered it with statements of equivalent power and range. The article may, indeed, be taken as one of the seminal pronouncements of his philosophy.

The stream of speeches on immigration continued until the February 1974 general election; but it is unnecessary to study the individual texts in detail, since in the main they repeat the lineaments of a position already clearly established, and needed change only to take account of new releases of figures. There were, however, some sub-themes of the general argument which it is as well not to lose sight of. Thus, at Smethwick on 4 November 1971, he returned to an earlier point when he said, 'Our towns and cities are being taken over and transformed not by the Caribbean but by Asia.' He clearly still believed that there was a hope of drastic change in political attitudes to immigration, and he told an Oxford audience on 9 February 1972 that it was 'not always that a nation gets a second chance. Error becomes irreversible.' He harped again and again on the lamentable insufficiency of the government's provisions for assisted repatriation. He argued, following the Pakistani civil war, the war between India and Pakistan and the establishment of the new state of Bangla Desh, that Pakistani and Bangla Deshi citizens should lose their immigration privileges since Pakistan had withdrawn from the Commonwealth and Bangla Desh had not joined. (In the event the government decided to continue as though nothing had happened.)

The controversy over the Ugandan Asians began to fade towards the end of 1972. Powell believed that the controversy was in some ways a symbol of the growing alienation of the Conservative Party from the people, referring in Oxford on 18 November 1972 to 'the profound affront which was delivered to the elementary trust and confidence that ought to exist between government and people'. There was, however, one important consequence of the Party Conference of October. Immediately Parliament reconvened, the government, having proclaimed immense satisfaction throughout the year with its Immigration Act and the rules made under it, suddenly introduced a new set of rules. These further restricted the right of entry of Commonwealth citizens, and eased terms for the citizens of EEC countries. The same alliance came into being which had forced changes in the patriality rules.[45] Powell objected on the grounds that the rules for the Commonwealth were insufficiently restrictive, and was joined by other Tories who disliked the indication of liberality towards EEC citizens. On the other side of the House, however, Labour members objected to the apparent bias against the Commonwealth. In the event, six Conservatives went into the opposition lobby with Powell, but forty others abstained. The government was defeated by thirty-five votes, and had further to amend the rules. The revised rules restricted the automatic right of entry to those who had a grandfather born in the United Kingdom, stating that everybody else required a work permit. The objective of the government had been to use the rule to relax the law, while the objective of Powell and his allies was to enforce the strict application of the 1971 Act. Since these new restrictions, however, did not apply to the dependents of immigrants already in this country, it did not meet Powell's main point. None the less, it ensured that there could be no repetition of the Kenyan or Ugandan fiascos (though the Kenyan and Ugandan crises were in many respects very different from one another) and was seen as a considerable triumph for him.

It was obvious, from the beginning of 1973 onwards, that Powell, more thoroughly alienated than ever as he was from the leadership of his Party and most of its MPs, was restored to prominence in the eye of the public. Before the final act of the drama that was the 1970 Parliament is described, therefore, it is useful to try to make some estimate of his standing.[46] Gallup ran a poll immediately after the Party Conference and another in April 1973 asking respondents to estimate the value to their party of five politicians. Between the two dates everybody listed had declined in the public view. Douglas-Home went from 42% to 36%; Barber from 39% to 37%; Carr from 39% to 28%; and Heath from 36% to 34%. Powell held steady, at 41%.

In October 1972 Opinion Research Centre[47] decided to repeat a poll which they had done just after the 1970 general election. It was a poll solely about Powell and the most important question was whether the respondent thought the Tories would be better off with him as Leader and Prime Minister. In June 1970 19% of those questioned agreed. In October 1972 39% did so. There was also more anecdotal evidence. Over February and March 1973 Powell took part in three Sunday debates on BBC television under the chairmanship of Robin (now Sir Robin) Day. The subject was immigration and race relations, and the temperature of the debates was heated, even vitriolic, Mark (now Lord) Bonham-Carter comparing Powell to Eichmann. At the beginning of the third programme Day announced that the BBC had received some 5,000 letters and cards in response to the first two: 88% were for Powell.

The evidence, then, demonstrates a staggering consistency of achievement (and in some cases improvement of achievement) over a long period. That the Leader of a Party should go up or down in the public estimation a few points here or there, according as circumstances changed, would be no surprise. But the Leader of a Party (particularly one of the two major Parties) has an enormous organization behind him. He has an automatic access to newspapers, radio and television. Almost anything he does – even walking the dog – is news. If he is in power he and the Ministers he appoints will be regularly doing important things and thus staying in the public eye. If he is in opposition he has similar, if lesser, advantages. In opposition, moreover, he has a chance to shine, or at least make news, twice a week at Prime Minister's Question Time in the House of Commons.

Powell had no remotely comparable advantages. He had never sought to build an organization, nor even anything that might seriously be called a staff – though there were plenty of people willing to serve, and plenty of finance regularly offered. Certainly, he was a powerful speaker and writer, and a man of almost unlimited energy. But these characteristics would never have been enough to sustain him on his pinnacle. It had to be, therefore, that in much of what he said – and said with marked eloquence – he was successfully striking chords in the hearts and minds of the people. It was, of course, precisely in uneasy recognition of that fact that his critics and enemies feared him.

As at every moment since 1968 the question was, how to hold this position? He needed to command attention to get his various messages across. That meant that he not merely had to keep up his own high technical standards, but find new subjects or ways of elaborating on the old. He could continue, of course, speaking about immigration, and be sure of appreciative audiences. He could proceed with his programme of re-education on the Common Market; but to most people this was a dead issue.

Then circumstances came to his rescue yet again. I have already[48] observed that Heath gained nothing like the praise that he might have expected from manoeuvring Britain into the EEC. It certainly in no way began to compensate for the economic and industrial difficulties the government was meeting.

1972 was not by any stretch of the imagination a good year for the government in the domestic field.[49] The difficulty was that, for whatever reasons, Heath was presiding over what Iain Macleod had once called 'stagflation' – that is, a combination of industrial stagnation and monetary inflation. Heath had come to power with policies which, he believed, would stimulate industry while holding down inflation. The package consisted of tight money, control of the trade unions, and thereby a setting free of industry. He was against controls, and therefore repeatedly and emphatically eschewed the idea of governmental (by persuasion) or statutory (by legislation) control of incomes. Incomes control, so his thesis ran, involved an unacceptable bureaucracy and, in practice, would mean that, in any given national wage round, the highest awards would become the norm, irrespective of whether or not they produced higher productivity.

None of the pillars of the 1970 manifesto remained standing by the beginning of 1973. On 18 February 1972 the coal strike was settled at huge cost. On 29 March the National Industrial Relations court (set up under the trade union reform legislation) handed down its first fines. By 4 September the TUC had confirmed that it would expel any union which paid them. Meanwhile, the government had been pumping money into the economy in what was christened a 'dash for growth'. Rapidly rising inflation ineluctably followed and, on 26 September, the government, to the amazement and consternation of many of its followers, announced the adoption of an incomes policy, preferably through negotiation with the unions. By 6 November it was clear that no agreement with the unions could be reached and the government therefore announced a compulsory ninety day standstill in incomes and prices.

Not all of those conservatives who were appalled by these turns of events were keen supporters of the kind of free market economic policy adumbrated in the Conservative manifesto of 1970; and few as radical in their advocacy as Powell. What they all saw, however, was a government adrift, helpless in the face of circumstances, unable to enforce its laws, let alone its policies, incompetent and bullying by turns.

Worse was to come. In January the government made known the next step in control, announcing its intention of enforcing a policy of wage rises of 4% plus £1 per week. 'The country has twice before been through this cycle,' Powell proclaimed, 'and knows perfectly well how it inevitably ends in failure and ridicule. It is tragic that we have to go around again.' But he was the only Conservative to oppose the government in the vote: his colleagues were despondent and alarmed, but they were nowhere near the point of rebellion. Indeed, from the beginning of 1970 onwards the spectacle began to be visible – one often seen before – of a Tory Party in trouble rallying together. 'Somehow,' Powell said on 23 February, 'common purpose and understanding have to be regained and the chain of fatality broken which is leading to a catastrophe.' It was all to no avail. Ronald Butt might write, as he did in *The Times* on 1 March 1973, that what Powell had to say 'coincides with the instincts of many backbench MPs to a greater extent than at any other time since the party came to power.' Mr. Butt was unquestionably correct; but the bunker mentality which was beginning to prevail kept them from expressing their doubts, or support for the lone heavyweight critic in their ranks.

Nor was Powell willing to accept even the voluntary incomes policy that the government would have preferred. It would involve cajoling and arm twisting; he said in Wolverhampton on 13 June 1973, it

> has all the characteristics and consequences of government without law. It is arbitrary, it is capricious, it is uncertain, it is covert, it is unappealable. When we find that, with the best of intentions, we are being carried towards that goal, it is time to stop and think. Above all it is time for the individual to do so for, in the last resort, the defence of liberty under the law lies in his hands.

But the government proceeded on its way and, in April, further developed its incomes policy. By now, however, the shadow of another miners' strike was beginning to loom, and few imagined that the government's new resolutions would be proof against the miners if they struck. Later in the year the government's problems were compounded by the outbreak, on 6 October, of war in the Middle East. Oil rose dramatically in price and the NUM, as the producer of the main alternative source of energy, was in a stronger than ever position.

The situation in Britain throughout 1973 was one of constant crisis. On 16 June 1973 the *Economist* wrote of Powell, 'It is a rare Tory MP who doesn't have a Powell group of some real consequence in his local association. If any single man has the capacity to cause upheaval it is the member from South-West Wolverhampton.' Somewhat later, however, on 2 September, the same magazine noted that he had been unable to gain, and perhaps had lost, support in the Parliamentary Party. None the less, when a number of millionaires banded together in March to create a Powell organization he would have none of it, and turned a cold shoulder.

Yet again, the government was slowly starting to move his way. At the Party Conference that October he made a quiet speech on economic affairs, and pleaded for control of the money supply and a balanced budget. In return Anthony Barber publicly attacked him as having 'the moral conceit and all the intellectual arrogance of the fanatic'. Commentators have debated ever since whether it was Barber's intention to crush Powell by calling on the huge reserves of Tory loyalty to the leadership, or whether he had a guilty conscience arising from the fact that he intended to introduce (and did introduce, two months later) a Budget that moved the government some considerable way towards Powell. By then, however, it was a conversion without meaning. The miners were on the march.

The government had gone ahead with the creation of the apparatus of an incomes policy, notably the appointment of a Pay Board and a Prices Commission. On 8 October proposals for Phase Three of the policy were announced: a norm of 8-9% with certain special benefits on the side. Intensive efforts were made to persuade the miners to accept this – given, in any event, that their next round of pay negotiations was not due to begin until March. The National Coal Board immediately offered the full amount, without negotiation. On 8 November they proclaimed an overtime ban.

On 13 November the government declared a State of Emergency, which involved much curtailment of the use of electricity. The National Executive of the NUM was invited to No. 10 Downing Street for 28 November. There was in train a study of relativities (in pay and benefits) within the industry, and the Prime Minister offered certain concessions in this direction. The executive voted 18 to 5 against accepting the Prime Minister's offer.

For some weeks before this a number of Conservative officials began to press for an early election. The Cabinet was reshuffled and William Whitelaw was brought back from Northern Ireland to become Employment Secretary, a post in which he was expected to work miracles. On 13 December Heath announced a three day week to conserve energy.

By now election talk was in the public air, led by a front page story in *The Times* on 12 December. On the same day the rail unions began a go-slow. On 17 December the Chancellor announced the new, tighter economic programme referred to above. On 22 December everybody went home for Christmas, an unusually long holiday that year, since New Year's Day had become a Bank Holiday. Parliament was recalled early, and met on 9 January. On 5 January *The Times* speculated again about an early general election, and the following day the members of a Conservative Research Department seminar urged the case for one forcefully on Carrington, who got the same message at the Area Chairmen's dinner on 7 January. On 10 January, however, the 1922 Committee was reported as being just in favour of hanging on. Speculation was rife and it had to be said that, given the wretched state the country was in, the omens could have been worse. Private polls showed strong support for the government and NOP gave them a lead of 4% on 10 January. From this point on the principal advocate of an early dissolution in the Cabinet was Carrington; the principal opponent was Whitelaw. Everybody found Heath helplessly opaque and uncommunicative: we now know that he was suffering from a glandular illness which made him lethargic and dull.

On 29 October 1973 Powell launched a stinging attack on Heath, observing that, 'One cannot but entertain fears for the mental and emotional stability of a head of government to whom such language about incomes policy can appear rational.' On 15 January he issued a statement saying that an early general election would be 'an act of total immorality.' His reasoning here was that the only cause on which to go to the country would be in opposition to the miners. But anyone could see, he argued, that a re-elected Tory government would then settle with the miners on the miners' terms. (This is in fact what Heath was to offer during the campaign.) To seek a mandate for a policy which you have no intention of pursuing was, to Powell, the height of political sin.

About this time a handful of Powell's friends (which included Ridley and Biffen) began to get agitated about what he would do. They – unlike the generality – had noticed the importance of the speech he had made in Stockport the previous June. He had referred to Joseph Chamberlain, who had smashed the nineteenth century Liberal Party on the issue of Ireland, and he said that there were certain issues of transcendent importance:

> Independence, the freedom of a self-governing nation, is in my estimation the highest political good, for which any disadvantage, if need be, and any sacrifice, are a cheap price. It is worth living for; it is worth fighting for; and it is worth dying for.

In the course of the speech he made a favourable reference to the Labour Party, upon which Harold Wilson issued a statement saying that he would never work with Powell. This statement, as we shall see, in so far as it concerned his intentions or actions, was to be disproved.

Powell's friends had begun to fear that he would stand down, and his refusal to say either yes or no, while being evidently in a state of considerable stress, worried them all the more. The arguments which went on in that little group were fully as intense as those proceeding in the Cabinet.

On 9 January the TUC held out an olive branch: they would, they said, on the condition of the government accepting the NUM claim, encourage their members not to use it as a precedent for other wage claims (one of the besetting problems of administering an incomes policy). On 10 January the Prime Minister received the TUC Economic Committee. The atmosphere seemed cordial enough and Heath decided to resist Carrington's call for an election on 7 February. He had already reshuffled the Cabinet again, making Carrington the Secretary of State for Energy at the head of a new department.

It would be tedious and unnecessary to go over all the details of these fraught days: the salient one is that, after further talks, it was announced on 4 February that 81% of the miners had voted for strike action. Two days later, at a Press lunch, Jim Prior observed, 'The miners have had their ballot, perhaps we ought to have ours.' The following day it was announced from No. 10 that there would be a general election.

Within hours a letter was delivered to the home of George Wilkes, the Chairman of the Wolverhampton South-West Conservative Association. It was released to the Press at the same time. To most of the media it came as a bombshell. 'I consider,' Powell wrote,

it an act of gross irresponsibility that this general election has been called in the face of the current and impending industrial situation. The election will in any case be essentially fraudulent; for the object of those who have called it is to secure the electorate's approval for a position which the government itself knows to be untenable, in order to make it easier to abandon that position subsequently. It is unworthy of British politics and dangerous to Parliament itself for a government to try to steal success by telling the public one thing during an election and doing the opposite afterwards . . . I personally cannot ask electors to vote for policies which are directly opposite to those for which we all stood in 1970 and which I have myself consistently condemned. I shall not therefore be seeking re-election for Wolverhampton South-West.

In the succeeding days frantic attempts were made by members of his constituency executive to persuade him to retract: they might have known, after all their years of association with him, that that would be impossible. There was even an attempt to get a candidate to keep the seat warm pending his return. Rumours flew, including, among the more ridiculous, that he would stand against Heath in Sidcup. Powell himself retreated into total silence, refusing a number of lucrative offers to comment on the election, and even declining to write book reviews. After a few days interest in him died down. He was to remain in seclusion for thirteen days.

The final clash between Powell and Heath was now to hand. The intriguing thing about the general election campaign of February 1974 is, however, that both men were arguing on entirely different lines. For Heath domestic policy was all: he began the campaign on the slogan, 'Who governs Britain?' and, though he found that he could not sustain that theme for a full three weeks of electioneering, it remained at the heart of his case. The success, or otherwise, of his newly found incomes policy was the core of his message. He was not helped by two statements by people he readily imagined to be on his side.

On the afternoon of 18 February Mr. Derek Robinson, the Deputy Chairman of the Pay Board, told journalists that, after a study of relative pay levels, miners were, in comparison to other workers, underpaid. On 26 February Mr. Campbell Adamson, the Director-General of the Confederation of British Industry, stated that he would like to see the repeal of the Industrial Relations Act, largely because he thought that it had made sour relations between management and workers. Adamson's words marked the last statement in British politics of the assumption that the country could be governed only in collusion with the trade unions. Robinson's made plain the impossibility of efficiently ordaining levels of pay and prices from on high. Taken together the two views destroyed the logic of Heath's appeal to the country. The Prime Minister was flustered in his response at his morning Press conferences: his lack of authority was to prove fatal.

It was not, however, on grounds of domestic policy that Powell chose to intervene, for the last time with power and effect, in an election campaign. To him the major issue was still British membership of the EEC. Scornful he might be about Heath's attempts at an incomes policy; contemptuous he might be about the general direction of the government's economic policy; but what remained closest to his heart was the resignation of sovereignty which he saw as implicit in the Treaty of Brussels.

Harold Wilson and his closest advisers were fully aware of Powell's potential to damage Heath's cause. At the very beginning of the campaign Wilson's Press secretary, Joe Haines, and his senior policy adviser, Professor (now Lord) Donoghue were instructed by the Leader of the Opposition to find out what Powell's plans were. It seemed vital to Wilson, given the continued detestation of Powell in Labour ranks, that only those he most trusted would know that he fully intended to plan his own campaign schedule around that of Powell and that, while continually prepared in public to denounce the former Member for Wolverhampton South-West, he would privately work as closely as possible with his old adversary. The agent of collaboration was Andrew Alexander of the *Daily Mail*.[50]

Alexander was a long-standing admirer of Powell. He had been one of the most ferocious journalistic critics of Edward Heath. During the 1970 general election he had collaborated with Alan Watkins on a book entitled *The Making of the Prime Minister*, a work in somewhat pallid imitation of Theodore White's famous series on the making of American presidents. Alexander's contribution to this volume was redolent of admiration for Powell, full of scorn for Heath, and – written as most of it was during the campaign itself – expressive of the conviction that Heath would lose. Failure to predict accurately what the electorate would do did not, however, daunt Alexander, one of the most convinced and consistent political commentators of the day. By February 1974 he stood ready as the perfect liaison officer between Wilson's staff and Powell.

While it is hard to be certain in judgement on such matters, it is probably fair to say that Heath was seriously damaged in the minds of the voters by his failure to carry conviction on the fundamentals of his domestic policy. The theme of a strong government with a fresh mandate could not be sustained for three weeks. Various doubts, already mentioned, had been cast on the competence of the administration. Halfway through the campaign Heath made it reasonably clear that, if elected again, he would do exactly what Powell had predicted he would do – settle with the miners. The moral authority which he claimed in stating his message was thus vitiated from the outset.

It seemed clear, however, that Powell could enjoy his maximum impact on the election result not through learned economic discourses, but by finding a way to use the force of his personality in the truest and most effective way against the Prime Minister. For him there could be only one major issue on which he could deploy his eloquence and inspire to action the fervent personal loyalty which he commanded: that issue had to be continued membership of the EEC. Powell's decision to speak almost solely

'AND FOR MY NEXT TRICK I SHALL ATTEMPT TO MAKE HIM DISAPPEAR !'

on this issue suited Wilson, who had begun, following the instincts of his own Party, to blow cold on the Community. It is important to remember, however, that, contrary to the beliefs of a number of his Conservative critics of the time and later, Powell was never gulled by the notion that a Labour government would withdraw automatically from the EEC. What he saw was a stark contrast between a governing Party led by a Prime Minister who regarded membership as irrevocable and, moreover, the great cause of his public life, and an Opposition Party that would at least offer the people a choice of going on or coming out, a choice to be made by means of a referendum. Feeling and thinking as he did, there could be no doubt about how Powell would react.

From 7 February Powell had rejected all offers to write or speak in the campaign. The various offers to him, however, remained open. One of the main organizations pressing him to utter was entitled 'Get Britain Out', a direct successor to 'Keep Britain Out', which had fought against Heath on the matter of entry from 1970 onwards. On 20 February Powell announced that he had accepted an invitation to speak on a 'Get Britain Out' platform in the Bull Ring in Birmingham on the following Saturday. The Labour leadership quickly learned that he would advocate a vote for them. They also learned that he intended to devote more than one speech to the subject which he regarded as having over-riding importance.

It has been generally said[51] that Powell withheld his endorsement of Labour until a speech the following Monday – 25 February – at Shipley, when he proclaimed:

> I was born a Tory, am a Tory and shall die a Tory . . . I never yet heard that it was any part of the faith of a Tory to take the institutions and liberties, the laws and customs which his country has evolved over centuries and merge them with those of eight other nations into a new made artificial state and, what is more, to do so without the willing approbation and consent of the nation.

On the following day – Tuesday – the final blow was struck, when Powell told Thames Television that he had already, by postal vote, supported Labour in Wolverhampton:

> It would have been strange indeed if I had voted in any other way than the way in which I had advised the country to vote.

In fact, though, the advice to vote Labour had been delivered at Birmingham, but not in his prepared and pre-released text. His audience in the Bull Ring was massive. The hall was over-full, containing at least 2,000 people. With a very few exceptions, moreover, the crowd was supportive of its speaker, and no reporter who was present could doubt for a moment that the great bulk of those who heard Powell would vote as he advised. Such evidence is, of course, anecdotal, and I will later examine more broadly based evidence as to his effect on the electorate,[52] but it is not without consequence. In nearly a quarter of a century's political reporting I cannot recall a meeting of such fervour, a politician every turn in whose argument was raptly attended to, nor an impact so evidently profound. It was in recognition of this effect that Powell was accorded front page coverage by most newspapers for the following five days.

He said:

> This is the first and last election at which the British people
> will be given the opportunity to decide whether their country
> is to remain a democratic nation, governed by the will of its
> own electorate expressed in its own Parliament, or whether
> it will become one province of a new European superstate
> under institutions which know nothing of the political rights
> and liberties that we have so long taken for granted.

He referred to an undertaking given by Heath eighteen months
previously, in Paris, that the new EEC would constitute an
economic and monetary unit by 1980, and went on, with his
fundamental accusation of bad faith on the part of the Prime
Minister:

> The House of Commons was never given a hint that any such
> commitment was going to be undertaken, nor afterwards was
> it ever invited to debate or, still less, to approve it . . . Never
> was the "full-hearted consent of Parliament and people" more
> conspicuously non-existent than when Britain was hi-jacked
> into the EEC.

After the speech was delivered, Powell took questions. The
experience of watching him do so was a poignant one. When
one of a handful of those hostile to him shouted, 'Judas', he

swung round. His normally impassive countenance was wreathed in agony, as he found himself forced to sever for ever his connection with the Party he had seen, all those years previously, as the engine of the salvation of the nation and the empire. 'Judas,' he almost whispered to a completely silent gathering, 'was paid.' He paused and then said, almost reflectively, 'I am sacrificing my whole political career.' The hall erupted in applause.

He was asked whether he would (as many of his followers wished him to) stand as an independent candidate. 'There is here,' he replied,

> a profound and dangerous misconception. The elector votes not for a person but for a Party and not for a Party in the abstract but a Party majority in the House of Commons.

It followed that 'we have a clear national duty to decide . . . in the only way of which Parliamentary representation admits.' Pressed further by sometimes confused and sometimes almost appalled Conservatives about whether this really meant that they were being counselled to vote Labour, he replied that logic admitted of no other conclusion.

The final public opinion polls of the campaign reported on election day, 28 February. Marplan and Gallup gave the Conservatives a 2% lead. Louis Harris was even better: the government was, according to them, 5% in the lead, and ready to garner more than 40% of the national vote. At Conservative Central Office the general opinion was a little flat: the overwhelming majority for which the Prime Minister had asked was evidently not to be forthcoming. The likelihood seemed to be that Heath would be returned, but with a majority of between 40 and 50 or, roughly, what he had enjoyed before. With the exception of one or two pessimists at Party headquarters, however, and the journalistic exception of the *Spectator*, where I predicted a minority Labour government, there was little doubt that the government would be back.

The first signs of disaster came with the BBC exit polls on the evening of the 28th. These polls, based on questions asked of voters as they left their polling stations, have a high record of accuracy. It was clear by 11 p.m. that Heath was out. He strove vainly over the following weekend to retrieve fortune from disaster by forming an alliance with the Liberal Party, then led by Jeremy Thorpe. Even such an alliance, however, would not have enjoyed a Commons majority. The Tories had taken 297 seats, the Liberals 14. But Labour had won in 301 constituencies, and there were 23 members of smaller Parties, including the Ulster Unionists. Thorpe's followers would have no truck with a deal with Heath and so, on Monday morning, the Prime Minister who had entered with such high hopes and even higher determination less than four years previously, proffered his resignation to the Queen. A period of political instability was at hand. Heath was able to struggle on as Party Leader for another year. Few dispassionate commentators doubted, however, as he left Downing Street for the last time, that the knell had tolled for his career in high office. The question was: what had Powell contributed to this personally melancholy result?

8

The Ulsterman
1974-1979

I come before you tonight as an English Tory, a Conservative member for a constituency in Staffordshire, and one who, so far as I know, has no ties or connections either with Ulster or with any part of this island. I would have been astonished if someone, three years ago, had told me that my thoughts and energies would today be directed to the affairs of this Province, beyond almost any other political subject. Yet so it is – so much so that often, at the end of a parliamentary week, it strikes me as somehow incongruous that I do not return, like my Ulster Unionist colleagues, to a constituency in these six counties. What is it – I not merely can but should ask myself this question here in your presence – that has so created so unexpected and even paradoxical a link and sense of obligation?

The conflict of Northern Ireland is not about law and order; it is not about civil rights; it is not about peace and security; it is not about participation, community relations and all the rest of the newfangled claptrap expressions; it is not even about religion. It is about nationality; and unless it is understood to be about nationality, all discussion and contrivance and policy remain in the limbo of unreality and insincerity.

– *J. Enoch Powell, to the Belfast East Unionist Association,*
2 June 1972.

Two and a half years after this speech was delivered Powell was to gratify the emotion it stated, and perhaps the hope that it implied, when he returned to Westminster as the Unionist MP for Down South. For the remaining near thirteen years of his parliamentary career, until his defeat in the general election of June 1987, it was for a Co. Down constituency that he sat in the House of Commons.

Between February and August of 1974 (when he was adopted in Ulster) Powell continued to excite interest, speculation and hostility. The weight he carried in public and Party affairs, now that he was a mere private citizen, depended upon assessment of two things: whether and, if so, to what extent, his advocacy of the Labour cause influenced the general election result; and what, if any, hold he continued to have on the sentiment and support of the Conservative Party and the nation.

These questions I will shortly examine. But it would be useful, first, to sketch his activities between February and October, and then to give a brief account of his attitude to and relations with Northern Ireland before he became a Unionist Member.

He had more than once asserted that 'I will die a Tory.' It did not, to his mind, necessarily follow that he would remain – or, after February, become again – a Member of the Conservative Party. On 11 March 1974, in an article in *The Times*, he restated the reasons for his conduct over the previous weeks and months. In essence, this article was a justification of his view that Heath's prospectus had been fraudulent – in that he was seeking a new mandate on the basis of policies he had no intention of pursuing in office. 'If the public,' he wrote:

> really expects Parties to invert without shame or apology the principles on which they have gained power, and politicians to seek re-election on the opposite arguments to those on which they have spoken and voted in the last House, then obviously neither Parliament nor political Party can provide the electorate with the means to guide and judge the government or their country; for unless a broad correspondence is assumed and enforced between profession and performance, all links in the chain of democratic responsibility are snapped.

Then, in defence of himself:

> The consequent divorce of Party from policy reduces Party to faction. Support of a political Party becomes equivalent to

350

the support of a football team. This explains the paradoxical accusation of 'disloyalty' against anyone who invites the electorate to vote on policies, and the cries of angry or agonized astonishment at a Member of Parliament, personally elected upon a certain policy, who has maintained it by voice and vote in the House of Commons proclaiming it to be in his opinion (right or wrong) of over-riding importance, and who advises those electors who agree with him to vote accordingly when the first opportunity comes at a general election.

An outsider would think that that was a plain enough statement, that he had severed his links with the Conservative Party. Powell likes to be precise about the sequence of events which began with his letter to his constituency Chairman saying that he did not wish to be considered as a candidate in the forthcoming general election in Wolverhampton South-West in February 1974:

As it happened, I was no longer even a member of the Conservative Party in my constituency. I had chosen not to pay my subscription. In the period since 1968 a great many unsolicited gifts of money had been sent to me by people who supported my views on national policy. While I cannot now remember the total sum, it was certainly a matter of some thousands of pounds. All this I paid over to the Conservative Association in Wolverhampton South-West. I did not, therefore, feel obliged to pay a further subscription.

He goes on to say,

I never resigned from the Conservative Party, or anything else. Not being currently a member of my constituency Party, I ceased to be a member of the national Conservative Party when Parliament was dissolved. I had been for many years a member of the Carlton Club. [The Carlton is the main Conservative club in the country.] A number of my friends wanted to make it possible for me to remain a member of the Club. I found it necessary, however, to write to the Secretary and draw his attention to the Club's own rule book, in which it is ordained that nobody who is not a member of the Conservative Party can be a member of the Club. So, you see, strictly speaking, I never resigned from anything.

These intricacies are retailed by Powell with a pedantic gleam in

351

his eye. The difficulty, however, so far as the charting of moods and events was concerned was, first,that a number of Tories who considered themselves to be his ardent followers were not of the same mind as he was on the EEC, the principal issue on which he had advocated a Labour vote. They, like many others, were, by 1974, bitterly critical of Heath, and yearning for a change of direction – or, at least, a return to the policies of 1970. It is probable that they over-estimated their own numbers; but they were not insignificant. Such people simply could not believe that *their* Enoch was no longer available; had, simply, counted himself out. His enemies were of a mind with his followers on this: they pondered deeply on what sinister strategy Powell had now embraced, what devious plans he had made for bringing himself to power.

His followers derived some encouragement, indeed, from a speech Powell made on 18 May, which was not unreconciliatory in tone (but which a Heath supporter described as Powell 'offering magnanimously to forgive . . . [the Conservative Party]'[1]):

> I do not believe . . . that the great divisions which destroyed the unity of the Party have been dishonourable to those who took one side or the other. I do not believe that the progress of events has either consigned, or is in the course of consigning, to past history the matters themselves over which those great divisions occurred. If this is so, then I am sure that neither rancour nor pride ought to keep apart those who are no longer divided by disagreement over real issues.

The optimistic Powellites, however, mistook tone for substance. The 'real issues', to him, included above all the issue of membership of the EEC. As long as Heath was Leader that standard would never be abandoned. Thus, for all its relaxed, and even friendly, tone the speech in no way suggested that Powell was ready even to consider compromise on his major positions.

This did not, in the immediate aftermath of the election, prevent intrigue as well as speculation within Tory ranks. It should never be forgotten how parlous Heath's position was: the troops had rallied round (for the most part) for the February contest, but they were already dissatisfied with, and worried about, the man and his methods; he had now lost two out of three elections as Leader, and the Conservative Party does not love a loser; another general election could not be long delayed and, while the Labour Party viewed its prospect with some zest,

The Ulsterman

hoping to repeat the triumph of 1966, which had followed the close run thing of 1964, the Tories viewed the future with gloom. Against this background Heath intensified rather than changed his somewhat dictatorial style of Party management: his intentions, as well as his proper understanding of the danger he was in, were signalled by his appointment, on 4 April, of his trusted speechwriter, Michael Wolff as Director General of the Conservative Party, with complete control over Central Office. It was a move widely resented, and not only among Party professionals. Wolff, however amiable (and he was that), had no experience of administration and, besides, was deeply associated with defeat.

It could be argued plausibly that in some respects the Conservatives, if they had to lose in February, would have fared better had they been conclusively beaten. They could then have got rid of their Leader and restructured policy and organization afresh. As it was, the next few months constituted a period of anxiety and even turmoil. So far as Powell was concerned there were three strands of opinion. There were those who hated him, and derided him as a traitor for his Labour vote. There were those who adored him, and yearned for his return. And there was a not insignificant band in the middle who, lamenting the loss of his oratorical power and influence with the public, were prepared – so far as February was concerned – to let bygones be bygones, if only he could be persuaded to return. In no less than three constituencies – two of them winnable – strong moves were afoot to secure Powell's nomination as the Conservative candidate. Powell himself played no part in any of these manoeuvres, but made it clear to anybody who asked him that in the present circumstances, he could not conceivably stand as a Conservative candidate. He frequently remarked – and with increasing asperity – that he had made his position abundantly clear, and many times: as long as the Party held to support of EEC membership, he was not available.

Later, I will consider in more detail the evolution of the negotiations which led to his standing in Down South. For the moment, it is sufficient to note that his long-standing interest in and involvement with Ulster had intensified from 30 March 1972, when Heath suspended the activities of the Stormont Parliament in Belfast, imposed direct rule from London and installed William Whitelaw in the new position of Secretary of State for Northern Ireland. Involvement at this level continued after the February election.

353

For Powell the Ulster Unionist Party (in the shifting picture of Unionist politics it came to be known as the Official Ulster Unionists) which had, for most of the years during which Stormont survived, taken the Conservative Whip at Westminster had three singular advantages. He could not allow himself to stand as an independent;[2] only as a member of a Party. Here was a Party, albeit a small one. He was passionately involved in the Unionist cause, and gave to it his full energy, emotional and practical. And – in some ways best of all – the Unionists had steadfastly opposed the entry of the United Kingdom into the Common Market. It is true that their members did not have the same range of opposition to membership as had Powell. But they were at one with him on the matter of nationality. The fact that the Republic of Ireland had joined at the same time as Britain, while the Republic's constitution laid claim to sovereignty over Northern Ireland, seemed to them (as, indeed the Taoiseach – Prime Minister – Jack Lynch had once declared it would be) an ultimate threat to the Union.

For Powell, then, in the spring and summer of 1974, Unionism offered an acceptable, a satisfying, and, indeed, an honourable path down which to return to the House of Commons.

The Unionist view of Powell, however, was far less simple than his of Unionism. Certainly, it had been true that, since Partition in 1922 and the division of the island into the Free State (which was to become the Republic of Ireland) and a province that remained part of the United Kingdom, Unionist Members at Westminster had, until recent times, taken the Conservative Whip. But conflicting strands ran beneath this surface. Edward Carson, the greatest of Unionists, and the only one of their number to have had a major impact on Westminster politics, having failed to keep the whole of Ireland within the United Kingdom, accepted the creation of a separate province as the lesser of two evils. But Carson did not want a mini-parliament in Belfast:[3] he wanted what is now called integration with the mainland – he wanted his province to be treated in exactly the same way as any other part of the kingdom.[4]

By Powell's time, however, Ulster Unionists, greatly though they continued to revere Carson – the evocation of whose memory at any Unionist gathering is guaranteed to excite applause – had come to cherish their parliament, and when it was suspended in 1972 their anger knew few bounds. Ulster's allegiance, it began to be stated, was less to unity with the rest of the nation (such as Powell advocated and which was a vital part of his philosophy) than to the Crown directly. Moreover, there was a separateness between the political culture of Northern Ireland and that of England, similar to, if possibly stronger than, that which exists between the Scottish and the English. Powell was an Englishman, after all, and there were those who would call him a carpetbagger. It did not help his cause that, addressing the Ulster Unionist conference in Portrush in April, he took a rigidly Carsonian view of the argument – to an audience for the most part still mourning Stormont.

Powell was to make more speeches in Ulster over the next few months, which will be examined later. But, already, there was a growing movement among some Ulster politicians, particularly those who had had experience at Westminster, that Powell might well prove an invaluable addition to their ranks. This was not wholly a new idea: noticing the attention which he, unlike any other genuinely senior Conservative MP sympathetic to the Unionist cause, had paid to Northern Ireland over the years, some perhaps timid, but none the less genuine, suggestions had been made, even during the life of the Heath government, to the effect that, should a final breach arise between Powell and the Conservatives, a parliamentary haven might well be found for him in the province.

Broadly speaking these suggestions came from among those who could plausibly claim to be the survivors and heirs of the old Unionist Party which had dominated Stormont for the whole of its existence, but who had broken it apart when successive leaders, Terence (now Lord) O'Neill, Major James Chichester-Clarke (now Lord Moyola) and Brian Faulkner, had seemed to them to truckle too much to the wishes of London governments in respect of public affairs generally and reform of the institutions of the province in particular. Initially, Brian (later Lord) Faulkner was the spokesman of a new Unionism: a middle-class businessman, he seemed, in 1969 and 1970, to represent a tougher – and perhaps more intransigent – political tradition than did O'Neill and Chichester-Clarke. It was Faulkner, however, who succumbed, in 1972, to the blandishments of William Whitelaw, and agreed to head, with the support of Gerry Fitt, a provincial executive in which power was shared between some unionists and some Republican politicians. Those Unionists who rejected Faulkner were described as the 'Official' Unionist Party. For the purposes of opposition to the executive, these Unionists formed a working alliance with the Democratic Unionist Party headed by Dr. Ian Paisley, and Vanguard headed by William Craig. All three groups worked under the general title of the United Ulster Unionist Coalition. They had an agreed manifesto and each group undertook not to put up candidates against the others, either in elections to the Northern Ireland Assembly or to Parliament in Westminster. By March 1974 the Coalition held eleven of the twelve Ulster seats in the House of Commons, the twelfth being held by Gerry Fitt. Of the three Unionist leaders Paisley was, in many respects, the most formidable. He had built his political party on the fervent strength of his Free Presbyterian Church and he had demonstrated a capacity for exciting public fervour surpassing that of either William Craig of Vanguard or Harry West, the leader of the 'Official' Unionists.

Like his colleagues, however, Paisley appreciated the value of Powell's interest in the affairs of Ulster. Although now out of the House of Commons, Powell still had a genuine and substantial national following. He was a parliamentarian of exceptional brilliance, and could argue and manoeuvre in the House of Commons better than any of them. There was no danger that, at any stage, he would prevaricate or compromise on the essence of Ulster's cause. In a word, there was no tribune better fitted to carry that cause to the mainland and, at the very least, to secure a more equitable numerical representation for Northern Ireland in Parliament. Though Paisley was later to claim that he had always opposed the choice of Powell as a UUUC candidate, he was one of three men – Craig and West being the others – who called on Powell at his home in London on 4 April 1974. All four men knew that Captain Lawrence Orr intended, for family reasons, not to offer himself again as a candidate in Down South. Orr had suggested that Powell would be a suitable replacement and the Unionist deputation hoped to assure themselves of Powell's availability. The last word after this meeting was spoken by Paisley: 'We must have that mon (sic).'

On 30 August 1974 Powell was adopted as the 'Official' Ulster Unionist Party candidate in Down South, though he would, of course, campaign under the banner of the United Ulster Unionist Coalition. In a sense his adoption merely made formal a long-standing relationship. He had identified himself with the Unionist cause for a number of years. He had an excellent personal relationship with Orr and was to develop one with James Molyneaux, who succeeded Orr as leader of the Parliamentary Party and, in 1979, West as Leader of the Party. What was immediately clear, however, was that Powell had taken a further step away from the Conservative Party. Indeed, any reconciliation between him and the Party which he had joined at the outset of his political career was now inconceivable.

Michael Harrington, one of Powell's strongest journalistic admirers, spoke for many when, in the *Spectator* of 4 May 1974, he begged Powell not to take the action he took in September, arguing:

> No serious British politician would dream of making the Irish question the very centre of his political activity unless he held ministerial responsibility and certainly not in the company of people who are regarded by most British politicians as bloodthirsty extremists.

Not long after, however, the die was cast.

The question of how formidable an advocate Powell would be for Ulster depended on evidence and happenings that lay in the future. In making him one of their candidates, however, the Unionists based their judgement in part at least on the conviction that he had demonstrated his power by unseating Heath the previous February. Indeed, for some time to come, the conviction that he had done just that was an article of faith on the part of some, and an argument to be derided by others. It is important to try to settle the matter before the narrative proceeds.

For the February 1974, as for the June 1970, election the most thorough examination of the available psephological evidence is that provided by Dr. Schoen.[5] Again, for February 1974, as for June 1970, the most authoritative source (authoritative because of the volume in which it appeared, rather than because of the quality of the argument) for the view that Powell had little or no influence on the outcome is Dr. Michael Steed.[6] It is a very large claim, which I have already made,[7] on behalf of a man, to say that he both made and unmade a government. Quite apart from the issues involved – the subjects and policies which made Powell speak out as he did – the idea of an individual (particularly, as in February 1974, when he was not even a candidate) having such an influence is alien to the British experience as well as to the British mode of writing political history. Governments have been destroyed, and Parties ruined, throughout British history by clashes of principle or of personality.

However, when Joseph Chamberlain, in the nineteenth century, smashed, for the nonce, the Liberal Party of Gladstone, on the issue of Home Rule for the whole of Ireland, he had a phalanx of some eighty MPs behind him in the House of Commons, not to mention the ranks of the Unionist peers. When David Lloyd George, in 1915, brought down Herbert Asquith, his own Party Leader and Prime Minister, he enjoyed, not merely a substantial Liberal following, but the unequivocal backing of the Conservative Opposition under Andrew Bonar Law. When, the war being over, the Liberal Party destroyed the already slim prospects for its own survival through internecine feuding, Lloyd George and Asquith – the opposing gladiators – each enjoyed a following, and each regarded himself as the leader of a Party. Closer to our own times, when, in 1981, Shirley Williams, William Rodgers, David Owen and Roy Jenkins came together to form the Social Democrat Party, the existence of which undoubtedly contributed to the magnitude of Labour's defeat in the 1983 general election, they had, first each other, then a number of disaffected Labour MPs, then the Liberal Party, and then, finally, a substantial body of often hitherto apolitical opinion in the country behind them. Moreover, they formed a proper Party, a Party with an organization, a headquarters and a Leader. Their future seemed bright – or, at least, possible. That by 1987-8 the initial Alliance would have broken into three groups and suffered electoral destruction could hardly have been foreseen, even by those who were fully conscious of the risks involved in attempting to set up a fourth Party within the British political system.

What the allied Liberals and Social Democrats, in 1981, were offering their followers was not merely a philosophical vision, but a prospect – distant, perhaps, but real none the less – of power. Powell did not, either in 1970 or in 1974, consider himself to have followers in this sense. He merely used his reason and his emotion, and the benefit of a status which he himself described as 'fortuitously acquired', to offer counsel to his fellow countrymen. Every step he took he regarded not merely as right, but as inevitable. Inured, however, as British politicians and journalists alike are to thinking in Party terms, his actions were not merely inconceivable, but often incomprehensible.

I have already mentioned[8] Powell's frequent, and scarcely veiled, irritation that people did not accept the (to him) plain consequences of his utterances before 1974 – that he would not, and could not, stand as a Conservative Party candidate. The implication might be thought to be that those within the Conservative Party who could not see him breaking away – or, having broken away, thought he could be tempted back – were foolish. If so, I am of their number. In October 1973, Powell came to lunch at the *Spectator*. His hosts were the proprietor, H. D. F. Creighton, and myself. The conversation turned, at one point, to Roy Jenkins. A few days previously I had appeared on a television programme with Jenkins who had, in its course, uttered vehement disapproval of Powell. Our guest was amused to hear this, and observed, 'He may be afraid that I will jump party, and unravel the whole European policy.' Creighton asked him, in tones shocked as well as bemused, whether he meant he would leave the Conservative Party. Powell replied with a disquisition on the career of Joseph Chamberlain. When he had gone Creighton and I – who published his articles and generally supported his line – discussed him at some length. We quite simply found it impossible to think of him as outside the Party, however difficult his position might be within. There may have been some who thought differently, but I never met any of them.

Powell's position in February 1974 was very different from that in June 1970. On the earlier occasion he was a member – however shunned by its leadership – of a major Party. He had a loyal and efficient constituency organization behind him. He had a formidable national reputation. He could be thought of (whatever his private convictions on this matter) as somebody who would enjoy in the future substantial influence in the higher reaches of his Party; who might well hold office; who might possibly be Leader. When he rose to speak in the Birmingham Bull Ring on 23 February he was a private citizen, likely to remain so, and one who had resisted all attempts to form an organization around himself.

Moreover, in so far as public opinion poll evidence can be trusted, he had a great deal less support in 1974 than in 1970. However, that support was still one of substance. Three weeks before the general election MORI found that 15% of voters polled thought Powell the politician who best represented their views. Further – as Dr. Schoen points out[9] – a further MORI poll just after the election found that 56% of voters could – without being reminded – recall a Powell speech during its course. To repeat the point: no individual in the position in which Powell had found (or placed) himself has ever attained such recognition in modern British political history.

The obvious question about June 1970 was: did the speeches of Enoch Powell contribute in any marked way to a Conservative victory? The obvious question about 1974 was: did he contribute to a Labour victory? We must remember that we are dealing in margins. The British electoral system is not presidential: Powell was at neither stage running for office. In terms of votes cast, the system offers surprisingly large rewards for relatively small percentage majorities at the polls. A shift of 1% – or even less – can make the difference between defeat and victory. That Powell had such an effect in February 1974 is testified to by the fact that (again as MORI found after the election) no less than 49% of Labour candidates in marginal constituencies thought that Powell's intervention had helped them; only 2% claimed that he had done them damage.

It is now necessary to deal with Dr. Steed. It will be recalled[10] that, in his analysis of the 1970 campaign he, while noting the distinct pro-Tory swing in the West Midlands, denied that Powell played any significant part in creating it. In 1974 the same area saw a substantial swing to Labour. Again, according to Dr. Steed, this had nothing to do with Powell's advocacy of a Labour vote.

Now, it is perfectly reasonable to state – as Dr. Steed does – that a considerable number of former Labour voters in the West Midlands voted Tory in 1970, and returned to their natural allegiance in February 1974. He adduces, further, a great many sociological and cultural reasons for his conclusions. But the fact of the matter is that there was no significant difference between the West Midlands in 1970 and the West Midlands in 1974, save that Enoch Powell was urging the voter to act one way in the first year, and the opposite way in the second. Surely Dr. Steed cannot believe that the abnormally high (in comparison with the rest of the country) swing to the Tories in 1970, and the abnormally high swing to Labour in 1974, had nothing to do with Powell, given the fact that the only difference between the two occasions *was* the stand Powell took. Moreover, a week before Powell intervened in the February campaign a Marplan poll in Perry Barr, a Birmingham constituency, showed a 13% Conservative lead over Labour. Powell spoke. And on 28 February *The Daily Telegraph* reported the follow-up poll in the same constituency: Labour now enjoyed a lead of 2%.

It is important to be very precise about the context of any claim that Powell, in effect, brought down the Heath government. Had that government been generally successful in its economic and industrial policy, the general election would not have been held when it was. Whenever it came, however, Powell would have stood down and, provided that the government had continued to be successful, while he would probably still have spoken out for Labour, his influence would hardly have had significance.

As matters stood his voice was the only element in the complex electoral equation that can be shown to have had an effect all of its own, and independent of other variables, such as the undoubtedly damaging effect of Heath's appearance of shifting tactical ground on the miners during the campaign itself – but, then, that shift was forced upon him by necessity. He had been correctly warned that a single issue campaign could not be sustained over three weeks. And, as Powell had correctly divined, he was not seeking a mandate for tough action, but authority to concede.

It is this last point that makes the sequence of events leading to the dissolution, and the dissolution itself, inexplicable. So far as coal stocks were concerned the Heath government was certainly in a position far inferior to that of Margaret Thatcher in her final confrontation with the NUM in the 1980s. But, then, Mrs. Thatcher was worsted in one confrontation with the miners before she engaged them in a struggle to the death. Heath had, likewise, been beaten once in 1972; but he had not taken the precaution of building up reserve stocks of coal in anticipation of a second battle: that was careless and slovenly. In spite of all this Carrington, the new Secretary of State for Energy, had, in the days before the fatal appeal to the country, announced that he saw every prospect of moving quickly to a four day week and lifting many of the restrictions on the use of energy earlier imposed. Was there – thus simply can the question be put – a crisis requiring a fresh mandate, or was there not? That ambiguity at the heart of its case certainly damaged the government at the polls. In addition, it was easy to ask, with a degree of plausibility, why a government with a more than adequate majority needed to put the people to the trouble of voting again. It was on this fertile ground that Powell was able fruitfully to cast his seed of doubt, discontent and opposition.

A glance at the swing figures actually recorded on the day of the election is useful. The swing to Labour in the Black Country (Powell's home territory) between 1970 and 1974 was 7.5%. In Wolverhampton South-West, despite the fact that the candidate, Nicholas Budgen, who held the seat, was a known supporter of Powell on most matters, it was a staggering 17%. Indeed, the swing against the Tories was even greater than that bare statistical comparison suggests. Between 1970 and 1974 there had been a redistribution of constituency boundaries. The consequences of this for the old seat of Wolverhampton South-West had been the loss of a number of wards which traditionally went to the

Labour Party and the addition of a number which traditionally went to the Conservatives. Taking redistribution into account, the anti-Conservative swing between 1970 and 1974 was in the region of 30%. In constituencies around Wolverhampton the average swing to Labour was 10%. In urban seats generally – those where Powellism, as it had come to be called, might expect some influence – the average swing to Labour was between 2% and 3%. Most interestingly – and, I would argue, most significantly – the swing in the Black Country over three general elections (taking the 1966 election as a benchmark) corresponded exactly to Powell's recommendations. In 1966 the Conservatives gained 44% and Labour 56%. In 1970 the corresponding figures were 56% and 44% – an exact reversal. In 1974 the figures were again exactly reversed. Dr. Steed seems to believe that, by arguing that Powell helped to bring out in 1970 a Tory vote which stayed at home in 1974, he somehow diminishes the argument for Powell's direct influence. But the point of campaigning is to encourage those who support you and discourage those inclined to support your rivals. It seems unquestionable, as Harold Wilson saw when he concluded his secret and arm's-length alliance with Powell at the beginning of the campaign, that there was a considerable 'Powell effect'.

So far as Powell was concerned, the period from February to October (or at least until August, after when he knew he would be a Unionist candidate in Northern Ireland) was, active though he continued to be, a period in limbo. Lunching with him at that time I asked him whether he missed the House of Commons. 'I was sure I would, terribly,' he replied, 'but I find I don't. Sometimes I have to pinch myself to make sure I am not dreaming, and do miss it after all.' But, of course, he was aware, as he could hardly fail to be, of the moves afoot to bring him back to the House in a general election which everybody knew could not be long delayed. He could, therefore, afford to wait, and observe from the sidelines with a certain disdain the difficulties of the third administration headed by Harold Wilson and the desperate travails of an Opposition still under Edward Heath. Thus, for example, when, in a speech on 5 September, Sir Keith Joseph urged the abandonment of the policies on which the government had stood, that of a statutory incomes policy and the control of inflation through control of the money supply – the policy by now widely known as monetarism – Powell's observation was caustic:

I have heard of death-bed repentance, but it would perhaps be more appropriate to refer instead to post-mortem
repentance.

This was to be his essential view of his old Party for quite some
time to come. All, however – including Powell's own career –
was held in suspense between February and October of 1974.
The overall political context was one unfamiliar not only to all
the actors engaged in the central struggle, but to the electorate
as well. The fact of the matter was that the United Kingdom
had not had a minority government – and one, moreover, which,
unlike its successor under James Callaghan, declined to make any
arrangements of a regular nature with the smaller parties – for
forty-five years.

Harold Wilson's defiance both of events and of parliamentary
arithmetic recalled the days when he had lived dangerously as
Prime Minister between 1964 and 1966. In 1974, as a decade
earlier, his supporters – and the Prime Minister himself – hoped
that another appeal to the country, which could not be long
delayed, would produce a substantial plurality at Westminster.
But Wilson was enormously helped by the morally fractured state
of the Conservative Opposition; and he retained sufficient of his
old cunning to exploit the divisions among those on the benches
opposite him.

The first Conservative disaster came with the Queen's Speech,
the document encapsulating the legislative proposals for the
government during its immediate lifetime. The hardier spirits
amongst the Tories – notably Julian Amery – believed that
every effort should be made to vote the speech down. Were this
course followed (and it could, of course, be successful only with
the support of the smaller parties) there could be one of three
results.

First, the effort – which amounted to a vote of no confidence
in the government of the day (such a vote as brought down James
Callaghan in March 1979) might fail: Scottish Nationalists, Welsh
Nationalists and Liberals might not support the Tories, being, at
the very least, fearful of the calls on their coffers of the general
election that might ensue. The enterprise as envisaged by Amery
might, therefore, come to an embarrassing conclusion.

Second, there was another thought in the minds of such
Tories as Amery. It was known that, when Barbara Castle, as
Secretary of State for Employment had, in 1968, sought reform
of trade union law, and had been supported in her effort by

Wilson, discreet advice from Buckingham Palace had been made available to the Labour Party. In support of the Minister he had appointed, Wilson threatened the Parliamentary Labour Party with a dissolution of Parliament which, in all likelihood, would result in a Conservative victory at the ensuing general election. The Palace advised Labour that a Prime Minister did not have, under the constitution, an automatic right to the sovereign's consent to a dissolution; and that if, in 1967, Labour could come up with a more acceptable (to them) Leader, the government of the day could continue in office. In 1974, and drawing upon this rumoured precedent, some enthusiastic Conservatives believed that, should the House of Commons throw out the Speech from the Throne, the Queen might refuse a dissolution to Harold Wilson and, instead, accept whoever could command a majority in the House of Commons as her first minister. In other words, the charade of the weekend which followed the February general election would be repeated as a play, but with a happier conclusion. Anthony (now Lord) Barber was foremost among those close to Heath advocating this risky enterprise; William Whitelaw was foremost against it.

But, third, neither the Leader of the Conservative Party nor his shadow Cabinet could make up their minds. The electoral ears on which their appeal for support had fallen in the general election had been proven deaf. It might well be that Harold Wilson would welcome a chance to ask the Queen to dissolve Parliament, succeed in his request, and win a major victory, which would certainly spell the end of Edward Heath's career. It was, moreover – and everybody involved accepted this – difficult to imagine success with the voters for any straightforward appeal for power on behalf of the Conservative Party, given the uncertain trumpet which that Party had played in February. The result of all these conflicting judgments and instincts was that in the debate on the Queen's Speech the Shadow Cabinet decided not to oppose; some Tories did oppose, and some Tories abstained. At a party on the evening of the vote Harold Wilson chuckled. He had played his last game of poker with Edward Heath and, because of Heath's inability to make a decision, he had won.

Meanwhile, Enoch Powell stalked government and alternative governments. His conscience was clear. Whereas, in 1970, quite apart from the matter of the European Economic Community – over which, it will be remembered, the Conservative Party was committed only to negotiate – there was a sharp distinction between the policies advocated by Harold Wilson and those put

---

forward by Edward Heath, throughout 1974 there was no such hard and fast difference. It could even be argued, indeed, that Wilson's disavowal of state-controlled policies on incomes (for all that the second government which he headed, that elected in 1966, had adopted such policies) made his manifestos, both of February and of October 1974, more palatable to potentially dissident Tories than those propounded by Heath.

Moreover, if – again leaving the EEC aside – one was to apply to both Parties Powell's acid test of accountability, that laid down in his *Times* article of 11 March, of fidelity or not to the undertakings given to the electorate, the third Wilson administration came out of the record rather well. It was with an entirely justifiable pride that Wilson was able to say to the voters at the outset of the October campaign:

> On our first day, the Tuesday, I appointed the Cabinet. We met the TUC at once. Our first priority was to end the miners' strike. We did that on the Wednesday. The lights went on again. We brought the heating back. We did what we said we would – and we did it at roughly the same cost for settling the miners' dispute as the Tories had committed themselves to pay. On our fourth day in office, we imposed a total freeze on the rents of council houses . . . and consigned to the litter bin the rent notices due to take effect on 1 April . . . We also froze rents of private lettings . . . In that same first week in office – we were three days old – we agreed the terms of the most progressive and radical Queen's Speech since 1945 firmly based on our manifesto . . . And as we started to act in those first few days, so we have continued ever since.

It was Wilson's further boast that no fewer than thirty-eight of his Party's promises had been implemented by the time he appealed again to the electorate for a renewed, and conclusive, mandate. In spite of his high hopes, however, there was to be no return to the heady days of 1966: Labour came back in October with an overall majority, certainly; but it was a great deal less than overwhelming. The governing party won 319 seats to the 277 of the Conservatives. But there were also eleven representatives of the Scottish National Party, three from its Welsh equivalent, Plaid Cymru, thirteen Liberals, and twelve MPs from Northern Ireland, including, of course, Enoch Powell. Labour thus enjoyed a majority of three over all other parties combined;

this was exactly the same plurality as had been won in 1964. The next two years were to see that majority, through the attrition of by-elections, vanish. By 1979 a Labour government now led by James Callaghan survived only by collaborating with the Liberals and the Scottish Nationalists and being able, on most votes, to rely on the support of the Ulster Unionists.[11]

It was, therefore, as clear in October 1974 as it had been clear exactly ten years earlier, that the electorate was unwilling to entrust a Labour Prime Minister with a comfortable majority – something, indeed, only twice awarded to Labour in its history, in 1945 and 1966. On the other hand, there was, evidently, no desire to turn back to Edward Heath and the Conservatives either. The Tory campaign of October 1974 was almost excessively lacking in lustre. All the hard edges of the first week of the February campaign were smoothed away. The appeal was above all – and designed to be above all – emollient. Heath promised that, if elected, he would seek to form a 'national' government, one which had among its Ministers people of other, and of no, parties. He was never, unfortunately for him, able to make his definition of 'national' a concrete one. One or two obscure peers did, it is true, offer him their services. Lord Chalfont – formerly the defence correspondent of *The Times*, as Alun Gwynne-Jones, Minister for disarmament, then for Europe, and then for disarmament again, in the first of Harold Wilson's periods of residence at No. 10 Downing Street – was a man of parts and ability. On 22 September he announced his resignation from the Labour Party. Disenchanted as people such as Chalfont might be, however, their weight was not sufficient to bring voters flocking back to the Conservative banner. When, more than once, Heath was asked the crucial question – would he give up his Conservative leadership if (as seemed likely) he personally proved to be the main stumbling block to the formation of a 'national' government, he declined to give a direct answer. His advisers were of different minds on how he should respond to this question. Some thought that an offer of sacrifice would gain for him an otherwise unprocurable moral authority; others took the view that it would merely suggest that he was weak, and undecided about what he would do with power. The result of the October election was thus, while it represented an advance for Labour over the election of February, inconclusive.

It must also be noted that a number of the steps taken by the government between February and October were found, later, to be unwise, from the point of view of the national, as well as of the Party, interest. For the moment, however, weaknesses were veiled: the covers were not to be torn away until the winter of 1978, which preceded the decisive electoral triumph of Margaret Thatcher in May 1979. These weaknesses were important, not least to Powell, for they enabled him and his Unionist colleagues to extract from a Labour government concessions which no government, of either major Party, which enjoyed a secure parliamentary majority, would have granted. From October 1974 until the lost vote of confidence on 28 March 1979, which brought down the government headed by James Callaghan, Powell saw more clearly than any of his Ulster colleagues except James Molyneaux that the interests of Ulster were best served by a Westminster government with a precarious, or even non-existent, majority. At the end Powell was willing to advise his colleagues to support the government on one important condition. This was the concession by the Prime Minister to the desire of the Unionists for a gas pipeline from Scotland to Ulster. This concession was not forthcoming, and in consequence Powell was one of those casting his vote against Callaghan when, late on that spring night, the Thatcher era began.

Such future developments were, however, unimaginable in October 1974. That Edward Heath would be replaced as Leader of the Conservative Party was clear to everybody except Heath himself, and a few of his devoted acolytes.[12] It was expected that he would be replaced by some such obvious figure as William Whitelaw. No participant or observer doubted, however, that the life of the new Parliament would be an exciting one.

For Ulster Unionists the future was both tantalizing and dangerous. Conscious of their long history of alliance with the Conservative Party, they were none the less offended by that Party's abolition of the Stormont Parliament, and imposition upon them of an executive comprised of Nationalists as well as Unionists (which collapsed in May 1974 following a strike which was general throughout the province), uneasy at the prospect of negotiating with – perhaps even working with – a Labour government. In a political climate which was queasy for everyone, the Unionists were more confused than most.

The election had seen them make one considerable gain, but also seen them suffer a dislocating loss. Enoch Powell was returned in Down; but the Leader of the official party, Harry West, lost his parliamentary seat, though he remained for some time Leader of the Party in the province. The Ulsterman most likely to follow West in the House of Commons was that self-effacing and dignified figure, James Molyneaux. But, 'I wanted Enoch for Leader,' Molyneaux later told me:

> You see, he had much more experience than any of us, he knew much more about the way government – not just the House of Commons – worked. I thought he would be the right man for our cause. But, when we all got together to talk about it, they decided on me. I didn't look for the job. I didn't want it. I wasn't even sure I could do it. But I took it.

It had been something of a nervous jump for the main Unionist party to pick an Englishman, however fervent he was in his support of their fundamental case, for Down South. It was far too much to expect them, almost instantly, to choose an Englishman as their parliamentary leader. As it happened, Powell was perfectly happy to serve, and did not seek to lead.

It seemed to many unlikely that Powell, a man who, if not exactly loquacious, was given to lengthy and reasoned utterance and – to put it no higher – considered intolerant with colleagues, would get on well with Molyneaux. The new Ulster Leader was, after all, a man of few words, stern, if patient of demeanour, judged eliptical by those who liked him (and had the opportunity of seeing his wise and often hilarious humour in private) and dim by those who did not. However, what began as a necessary alliance ripened into friendship and comradeship. Powell and Molyneaux exactly complemented one another as to character. Powell could always provide the arguments, and the eloquence. Molyneaux could always provide the down to earth wisdom of an Ulster farmer. Powell had often said that he had always felt a kinship with the people of Ulster, and a deep regard for their place in the scheme of British political affairs. Molyneaux, however, *was* Ulster. Initially a farmer, and the son of a farmer, he came from the bedrock Protestant stock of the province. He was not of what might be called the Ulster aristocracy, like the first and second Lords Brookeborough, Terence O'Neill or James Chichester-Clarke. On the other hand, he was not of the pulpit-bashing class of Dr. Ian Paisley either. In a phrase, Molyneaux was the Leader most likely to bring the best out of Powell: he was immovable in his convictions, kindly in their implementation, and always ready to listen to argument.

Though it is fashionable, nowadays, to deride the importance of the Unionist Members in the Parliament that began its life in October 1974, the dispassionate historian cannot but testify to the fact that they had a considerable influence upon its proceedings; and that that influence stemmed from the relationship between Powell and Molyneaux.

In a sense, Powell and Ulster were made for each other. It is true that some of his Conservative critics, on hearing of his selection in Down South, saw him as adopting the refuge of a fanatic – such is the incomprehension of the province on the mainland. Others, even among his most fervent admirers, thought him wasted in Northern Ireland, lashing himself to the wagon of an insignificant or obscure cause, and cutting himself off from the mainstream of political life as conceived in Westminster. But there was a logic to his behaviour which rose above all such cynical or dismissive arguments.

Powell and the Unionists with whom he allied himself (arrangements with Paisley's Democratic Unionist Party were discarded at the strike which Paisley precipitated in 1977) shared a fundamental belief, one held to by no comparable homogeneous group in the rest of the kingdom. The shared belief was in the value of nationality. Nationality is not nationalism, which word might be taken to imply an aggressive, or exclusive, creed. Nationality, to him as to them, meant, in practical political terms, the preservation, as an independent entity, of the United Kingdom of Great Britain and Northern Ireland. To that end all else was subject. It followed, of course, that the party Powell now joined would, like himself, be against British membership of the EEC. Their concern might, at a glance, seem more narrow than his. Powell's concerns were founded on wide and deep reading, and even wider and deeper pondering. Theirs, for the most part, were concentrated on the threat the government in Dublin – and the relevant clause in the constitution of the Irish Republic – posed to their identity, given that, as a fellow-member of the EEC, the Republic might well be able to influence decisions made in London which bore upon the affairs of Ulster. The differences were, however, of less significance than the fact that Powell had chosen new allies. And he made a point, in the succeeding years, of speaking frequently to English audiences of Northern Ireland affairs, and, in Ulster, of matters principally of concern to inhabitants of the mainland. His whole career as an Ulster Member of Parliament can, indeed, be seen as an attempt to educate two parts of the population of a united kingdom in the affairs and concerns of each other.

His interest in, and devotion to, the province went back several years. William Craig once observed to me how surprised Unionist MPs at Westminster had been in the late 1960s (and particularly after the present series of troubles in the province began in 1969) that Powell regularly turned up for Home Office questions (Northern Ireland being the responsibility of the Home Secretary until the suspension of Stormont in March 1972) when Ulster was on the agenda. For most conservative MPs (and most Labour MPs, for that matter) the subject of Ulster was an arcane irrelevance until the 1970s. Just as it had always been considered bad form for English members to intervene at Scottish Question Time, or in the proceedings of the Scottish Grand Committee, so Welsh and Ulster affairs were generally considered to be the province of those sitting for Welsh and Northern Ireland seats. Powell was welcomed by the Unionists, however, both because of his reputation and his forensic power, and because he invariably took their hard line. None the less, until 1972 he remained something of a curiosity: Ulster was widely regarded as another of Enoch's eccentricities.

There was, of course, a sense in which Northern Ireland was a peripheral issue in the second general election of 1974, if only because the mainland perceptions (of politicians, journalists and public alike) made it so. There were few, either in politics or the Press, who were sympathetic to the Unionist cause who followed its travails with anything like the intensity of Powell, or his attention to its detail. In the newspapers only T. E. Utley, of *The Daily Telegraph*, who actually stood as a Unionist candidate, though in an unwinnable seat in February 1974, wrote with regularity and insight about Ulster. In the House of Commons the number who thought like Powell was pitifully small, principal among them being John (later Sir John) Biggs-Davison and Ian Gow, elected for the first time, subsequently to serve as Mrs. Thatcher's Parliamentary Private Secretary and to hold junior ministerial office under her – an office which he resigned upon the conclusion of the Anglo-Irish Agreement between London and Dublin in 1985. In the situation that prevailed between 1974 and 1976 (when, on 16 March Harold Wilson resigned, to be succeeded as Prime Minister by James Callaghan on 6 April) Powell was increasingly considered a marginal figure in mainland politics. This situation was to some extent remedied during the spring of 1977 when the Callaghan government, uncertain of being able to secure a majority in the House even for day to day business, but unwilling to call a general election,[13] entered into agreements of greater or lesser formality with the minority parties: Powell was obvious candidate for the role of the chief Unionist strategist, partly because of his experience and skill, but also because of his friendly relations with the Leader of the House, Michael Foot, through whose office all arrangements for government business were made.

Nor was it true, as has sometimes been suggested, that Powell became invisible during the October election. On one foray to the mainland he made another speech advocating a Labour vote. He was much in demand by the media, wrote a campaign column for *The Times* and featured regularly on the front page of that paper and *The Daily Telegraph*, and was interviewed *in extenso* by Jon Akass of *The Sun* and Jean Rook of the *Daily Express*. However, the observation made in the Nuffield study of that general election[14] was almost certainly a just one. 'But,' the authors concluded of Powell, 'the writing was all low-keyed . . . He just needed keeping an eye on in case, like the San Andreas fault in San Francisco, he caused an earthquake.'

Certainly, therefore, Powell had nothing like the impact in October 1974 that he had enjoyed in February, or back in 1970. But, then, he had matters other than national to concern him. During all his activities between his dismissal from the Shadow Cabinet in 1968 and his not standing in 1974 he had had the solid backing of a loyal and efficient local organization in Wolverhampton. However outrageous his conduct might appear to be to the leadership of the Conservative Party, however dearly they wished he would go away, he was safe in his fortress. Murmurs of discontent and dissatisfaction were few and far between, and never of any insignificance. His constituency executive and his party workers were not merely loyal: they were proud to have him. Whatever the seething in Smith Square, Wolverhampton South-West would stick by its man.

Down South was another matter altogether. Quite apart from the fact that, as the record of his years in Wolverhampton had shown, he was a candidate (and a member) of formidable dedication and energy, the new constituency was not one he could take for granted. For one thing, since it had only been decided in August that he would be the 'Official' Unionist (strictly speaking, the United Ulster Unionist) candidate, there had been little time for him to get acquainted with those who, all being well, would be his new constituents. Then, Down South was a great sprawl of a place: campaigning there was much more difficult than it had been in Wolverhampton. Next, there was the surviving suspicion of an English incomer, however distinguished, a suspicion if anything increased when Powell made it clear that, unlike his predecessors, he intended to canvass in Roman Catholic areas – always hitherto ignored as a lost cause – and, if elected, would seek to address their problems with the same commitment as he devoted to Protestants.

Finally, there were the serious fractures within the Unionist movement as a whole. The old and monolithic party which had survived since 1922 had begun to break up in the late 1960s, largely because of the determination of the Ulster Prime Minister, Terence O'Neill, to introduce long urged reforms. On the advice of Harold Wilson, O'Neill called an Ulster general election in February 1969 in order to procure a mandate: he failed, and very nearly lost his own seat to Ian Paisley and resigned shortly thereafter in favour of his cousin, Major James Chichester-Clarke. Brian Faulkner, probably the most technically competent Minister in the O'Neill government, and a fine speaker, felt slighted, and snubbed by the old Ulster landed gentry. The party rapidly ran out of control. Faulkner succeeded Chichester-Clarke in 1971, only to find his Parliament as well as his government abolished by Edward Heath the following year.

Having hitherto been regarded as a hard-line anti-reformer, Faulkner was none the less persuaded by William Whitelaw to co-operate with the Catholic Social Democratic and Labour Party (formed from the ashes of the old Nationalist Party) which was led by Gerry Fitt, the Westminster Member for West Belfast, in a power-sharing executive. Unionism was now split several ways: there were the so-called Officials, the Faulknerites, the followers of William Craig (also once an O'Neill Minister) in an organization called Vanguard, while coming up fast on the rails were the Democratic Unionists led by Ian Paisley. Just to add to the complexity of affairs there were also the small Alliance (Catholic and Protestant) Party and the even smaller Northern Ireland Labour Party.

Ultimately, whatever prospects Faulkner had were destroyed by the February 1974 general elections, where his candidates performed lamentably: in Down South, for example, there was no candidate supporting Faulkner and the votes were split between the anti-executive candidate with just over 52% of the vote while the SDLP garnered about 10% less. In May the executive (and the Assembly from which it was drawn) collapsed under the pressure of a two week general (mainly Protestant) strike.

Relations between Harry West, on the one hand, and Craig and Paisley on the other, were never easy. Craig's movement was eventually to vanish into electoral sands. West, defeated for Westminster in October 1974, remained as Leader of his Party until his humiliating defeat in the European Parliament elections in June 1979.

Although the three segments of Unionism united for the purposes of the February election (in which they parcelled out nominations between them, and won eleven of the twelve seats) their unity was fragile. By September relations were bad, and Paisley even talked of putting up a DUP candidate against Powell. In the event he did not, and Powell performed creditably. However, with the turnout higher than in 1970 by 6.6% he could capture only 50.8%, while his SDLP rival increased his share to 45.5%. Though he was to hold a seat until 1987, through three general elections and a by-election (forced by the *en masse* resignation of the Unionists in protest at the Anglo-Irish Agreement), Powell could never feel completely secure. However, there was always the constant threat of a Paisleyite intervention which hung over him for nearly thirteen years.

From the beginning of his serious involvement in Ulster politics Powell was suspicious of, and often openly hostile to, Paisley,[15] sometimes in coded, sometimes in direct language. He frequently, indeed, went further in his attacks than any Ulsterman dared. The difficulty Powell faced (and it was a difficulty shared by all of his allies) was that it was seldom easy to work out exactly where Paisley stood, or in what direction he was moving. He was a dangerous enemy for any politician to have, not merely because of his proven ability to whip Protestant voters into a frenzy but also because, for all his fire, fury and bluster, he was a shrewd and capable parliamentary politician.

Powell's line on the future for Ulster was clear, if not always expressed with the brutal frankness of which he was capable. He wanted Northern Ireland treated and administered in exactly the same way as every other part of the United Kingdom, no more and no less. The 'no less' qualification became important, and protected him from subsequent Unionist criticism. The Unionists in their great majority were, as we have seen, yearning to have Stormont back: complete administrative integration with the mainland was, to them, very much a second best option. So far as Powell was concerned, however, proposals made by both Labour

373

and Conservative front benches for some form of devolution of authority to Scotland and Wales gave him the advantage of a protective screen. He was, at bottom, against all devolution but – so his argument ran – if Scotland and Wales were to get their own assemblies, then Northern Ireland must have one too.

Paisley, by contrast, was never as clear as this. For the better part of his career he has claimed to stand for the Union – insisting, frequently, that he is its only true and uncompromising guardian. However, he has often spoken as though his real purpose was an independent Ulster, Protestant dominated. And, going about entirely on the other tack, he once gave an extraordinary interview, to Liam Hourican, then the Belfast editor of Radio Telefis Eireann, the national broadcasting organization of the Republic. Paisley, and a then colleague, Desmond Boal, had a long session with a number of journalists from Dublin[16] in the Europa Hotel in Belfast on 25 November 1971. The general session went on until three o'clock the following morning, and Paisley thereafter gave Hourican a long interview, which was broadcast with only minor editing on Sunday 27 November. Hourican asked Paisley how he would react should the Southern Irish government act to change their Constitution. (Several aspects of that Constitution are offensive to Northern Protestants, most particularly its claim to sovereignty in the North, its prohibition of divorce and its assertion of the supreme and unique position of the Roman Catholic Church in Irish affairs.) Paisley replied that reform would constitute 'an entirely different set of circumstances' and that 'that would be the greatest guarantee to Protestants that they really meant business'. To Henry Kelly of the Dublin *Irish Times* he was even more extravagant:

'If the people of the South,' he said, 'want the Protestants of the North to join them in a United Ireland, then they should scrap entirely the 1937 Constitution and ensure that the Roman Catholic hierarchy could no longer exercise an improper influence in politics. If this were done, then the Protestant people would take a different view – there would be an entirely different set of circumstances. We are not saying that the majority of the South should cease to be Roman Catholic. All we are saying is that they should ensure that rule from Dublin would not be rule from Maynooth.'[17]

From whichever extreme, therefore, it was possible plausibly to argue that the unionism of Paisley, unlike that of James Molyneaux or Enoch Powell, was conditional. On this occasion his own supporters were dismayed – distraught would not be too strong a word, and Paisley was forced to alter course as he had frequently done before, and was frequently to do again. It was the volatility of his policy that, from the beginning, offended Powell. It was Paisley whom Powell had in mind when in later years he spoke at Newcastle, County Down, on 23 June 1979:

> Another fact . . . which we see more clearly now than two months ago, is that there are those that set no value by the Parliamentary Union and have no fundamental loyalty toward it, but who by offering misleading perspectives and prospectuses have, like the false prophets of scripture, 'turned away much people', to whom they have come in sheep's clothing though 'within they are ravening wolves'. To their victims the Unionist Party has this to say: 'be not deceived: the only sheet anchor of Ulster is the Union, the whole Union and nothing but the Union. Those who pretend otherwise will turn you adrift . . .'

Paisley was thus not a pure Unionist, in the sense that Powell was. It could, indeed, be argued that Powell was the only pure Unionist in the province, with the possible exception of his friend James Molyneaux who, in addition to his good war record in the RAF Regiment, held down senior positions on a number of charitable and medical organizations and was Grand Master of the British Commonwealth Royal Black Institution, an organization with close affiliation to the mainstream Unionist movement. Molyneaux's shyness, and the gruffness which proceeds from it, together with the fact that he is a less than impressive public speaker, has caused critics to undervalue him as a politician. The fact that it was known that he had wanted Powell rather than himself to succeed West, coupled with the fact that the two men almost instantly developed an exceptionally close working relationship, caused Molyneaux to be dubbed 'Enoch's poodle', and one Unionist colleague insultingly to describe their relationship as 'Powell running Jim with his foot.' The truth is that Molyneaux has considerable gifts, among which an unbending will and an ability to see a clear way through the most complex legislation are but two. There is, moreover, one character trait he shares with Powell: unlike most politicians he finds no difficulty in standing alone on an issue. He is, further, actually less socially inclined than Powell, preferring when on duty at Westminster, but when no pressing parliamentary business required his attention, to retreat to his flat with a volume of historical biography.

The chemistry of the relationship between the two was to prove to be of importance. Molyneaux freely recognized Powell's great superiority to himself as a constitutional scholar and a parliamentary tactician. He did not resent it, and again and again profited from it. Powell, on the other hand, respected Molyneaux's down-to-earth solidity and integrity: he was unforcedly and unambiguously loyal to him in a way that he had never previously been to a leader or colleague. When Powell – as happened from time to time – aroused ire in Ulster by seeming to take the logic of Unionism too far, Molyneaux defended him. And when Molyneaux was in doubt about the best way to proceed on any issue in the House of Commons Powell was on hand to enlighten and inform him. There were two important points, however, on which their judgements differed. One was on whether or not to vote against the Callaghan government on 28 March 1979. James Callaghan lost that vote (and thus the ensuing election) by one vote. Powell was inclined to sustain him in office; Molyneaux wanted him out. Powell followed Molyneaux. Again, towards the end of 1986, Powell was against the Unionists resigning their seats to force by-elections in what amounted to a plebiscite on the Anglo-Irish Agreement. Molyneaux was for resignation, and his view prevailed. Powell, however, excused himself from the meeting at which Unionist members signed a common declaration resigning their seats, thus expressing that resignation must be a personal decision.

To return, now, to the campaign of October 1974, Powell expected something very much like the result which occurred – either the continuance of a minority Labour government, or a small Labour majority likely to be eroded through by-elections. Powell had a shrewd idea of Labour's appetite for office. For all that he had succeeded in getting through thirty-eight measures since October, Harold Wilson had lost twenty-nine important votes. It had been, from February onwards, tactically wise of him to refuse to do any deals with minority parties, over whose unwilling heads he held the threat of an unwanted (and in some cases feared) dissolution. If, however, the October result was much like that of February, different tactics would be imposed by circumstances upon Wilson. In particular, dissolution would no longer be an effective spectre: nobody would believe that the electorate would take kindly to yet a third call to the polls. In such circumstances Wilson (or a successor, though nobody thought

that the Prime Minister would go as early as he did) would have
to deal with the minorities. Each of the small parties had their
desires and their sticking points. The Liberals, besides wanting
to tone down the more left wing proposals and secure a prime
ministerial commitment to the EEC, wanted consideration of the
reform of the electoral system. Scottish and Welsh Nationalists
wanted devolution. Gerry Fitt of the SDLP strenuously objected
to an increase in the number of parliamentary seats in Ulster to
which Callaghan was to agree in 1977. Unionists wanted, above all,
the continuance of the Union and, indeed, its strengthening. To
this end they had their own shopping list, and Powell and
Molyneaux fully realized that, in the situation likely to follow
the election, every vote would count. They would have some
chance of getting their desires from a government desperate to
hold on to office: at the very least they could no longer be
treated as pariahs, as they frequently had been by a Labour Party
a substantial number of whose members were Unionists in a quite
different sense, wanting an all-Ireland government with its capital
in Dublin.

For some years Powell had been spelling out, again and
again, what he sought for Unionism, and what he would fight
for in the House of Commons. A convenient *locus classicus*
is, however provided in a speech to his potential constituents
at Banbridge on 25 September 1974. He began by telling, in
general terms, what he planned to do for those who supported
him, if he returned to the Commons:

> What I shall say there in their name will not differ greatly
> from what I have been saying, here and elsewhere, for these
> last five years as a constant colleague and companion of the tiny
> band of Ulster Unionists, who stood up and told the truth about
> Ulster and sealed it with their votes in defiance of majorities
> indifferent or hostile, and of all the pressures, open or covert,
> that the mechanism of politics can bring to bear. That little
> group was led and inspired by the previous Member for this
> constituency,[18] whose unbroken comradeship over a quarter
> of a century and spontaneous personal generosity at the end
> of it I acknowledge with gratitude. When the people in Ulster
> in time come to look back on these dark years of affliction
> their historians will record that Captain Orr's steadfast courage
> against overwhelming odds in the parliament of 1970/4 was
> the indispensable condition for Ulster's survival and victory.

377

He went on to make eight points which constituted his personal platform. None was new: he had made all of them in one form or another before, either in the province or on the mainland. But he clearly felt the need to put everything together in one comprehensive statement in his first public speech as the Official Unionist candidate.

The first necessity, he declared, was the absolute, continued, and continual assertion of the integrity of the United Kingdom as at present constituted. That was the rock upon which all else was founded. Second, it was vital to draw attention again and again to the way in which this central issue had been fudged over the years. This statement was to form the basis for more and more detailed allegations of conspiracy between London and Dublin (with Washington in close attendance) to break up the Union.

Powell's third, and in many respects most immediately practical point was to demand equal parliamentary representation for Ulster at Westminster. The size of the Northern Ireland population entitled it to more seats, for preference twenty in all, as opposed to the twelve at October 1974; but he would settle for eighteen. As long as Stormont had been in existence, Powell believed, and the Northern Irish had been represented there, the inadequacy of their representation in the Parliament of the United Kingdom could be overlooked. But Stormont was no more, and reform was thus required. The implication here was not particularly noticed at the time. It was that if Ulster was fully represented at Westminster, Stormont – or a replacement – would be unnecessary.

Talks had been proceeding, on and off, between successive London and Dublin governments on affairs in Ulster for some years. Powell's fourth point was an expression of outright and absolute opposition to any concession from London that in any way involved the Republic of Ireland in the administration of Northern Ireland. It followed – as his fifth point – that there must be no return to the system of power sharing which, ardently advocated in Dublin, had been the *raison d'être* of Brian Faulkner's short-lived and ill-starred executive.

Sixth, Powell was determined that normal policing should return to Ulster. The argument here was somewhat intricate, but it was important. The British Army had originally been brought in in substantial numbers by James Callaghan (when Home Secretary in the 1966 Wilson administration) because the Royal Ulster Constabulary had declared itself unable to cope with constant street violence. Powell had, of course, no objection to the use of the Armed Forces as the ultimate guardians of the security (and existence) of the state. What, however, had been insensibly happening over the years was that the Army had been increasingly used for ordinary police duties, such as routine street patrolling, the breaking up of minor affrays, the quotidian protection of the citizens. Nobody – least of all Powell – would pretend that the situation in Northern Ireland was normal in the sense that it was normal on the mainland. What he wanted, however, was a steady push towards normality, and a principal part of that push should, in his view, be a steady return of responsibility to the police. Incidentally, this had for long been the repeated request of military commanders in Ulster: they felt that energy which should be concentrated on serious terrorism had been dissipated through the assumption of a policing role.

Powell's seventh and eighth points concerned relations with the Republic of Ireland. Southern Irish politicians, some of them Ministers (in successive governments) had taken to popping up unexpectedly in Ulster (there being no serious control of the main border crossing points) in search, through the expressions of care for the Catholic community which such visits suggested, of cheap headlines and radio and television coverage in the Republic. Powell was utterly opposed to such 'unannounced, uninvited and unauthorized visits of inspection of this part of the UK without protest or remonstrance from Her Majesty's Government . . .'

His eighth and final point was in some respects the most contentious so far as relations between London and Dublin were concerned. It also reiterated, and applied to Ireland, certain general points of national policy which he had adumbrated and recommended in the immigration debate and, indeed, as far back as his speech on the Royal Titles legislation.

To put the matter briefly, constitutional, diplomatic and political relations between the United Kingdom and the Republic were (and remain) anomalous. The Republic was in every sense an independent and therefore (as Powell constantly repeated) a foreign nation. It was also neutral: it did not belong, unlike Britain, to the North Atlantic Treaty Organization. (From time to time, in a way that increasingly excited Powell's suspicions, Irish politicians hinted that they would take a favourable view of an invitation to join NATO in the event of the situation in Ulster being rectified to their satisfaction. This was a prize the United States was particularly keen to seize, because of the contribution Ireland could make to guarding the Atlantic Approaches.) In

spite of the various measures of control over immigration introduced in Britain since 1962, moreover, citizens of the Republic
could still pass freely into, and take up residence in the United
Kingdom, subject to control at points of entry. (In 1974 a
separate piece of legislation allowed the government of the
UK to issue exclusion orders against the inhabitants of any
part of Ireland.) Moreover, an Irish citizen, once he had
taken up residence in the United Kingdom, was free to vote
in elections there. A Briton in the Republic did not, when
Powell was speaking in 1974, enjoy the same voting rights
in the Republic, though these have since been extended. The
extension is, however, purely a gesture: in some English seats
Irish immigrants acting together can determine the result of a
parliamentary election. There is never a sufficient number of
Britons resident in the Republic to have any such effect.

Powell's solution to these anomalies was simple: the Republic
of Ireland should be treated as any other foreign country. Irish
citizens should be required to show their passports at points of
entry. They would have no automatic voting rights in the UK.
And, perhaps most important, they would be subjected to the
same immigration control as applied to citizens of Commonwealth countries: the Republic did not, of course, belong to the
Commonwealth.

Of all Powell's proposals, this last might seem to the objective
observer to be almost the least contentious. One might make
a comparison with Canada. Canada was a fellow member of
NATO and a fellow member of the Commonwealth and had an
intimately shared history with the United Kingdom. Her troops
had fought, not merely uncomplainingly but with enthusiasm, by
the side of Britain in two world wars. In the first of those wars
the British government, when introducing conscription, decided
it would not apply in Ireland, for fear of Nationalist resistance
(though it is fair to add that there were many volunteers from
what is now the Republic of Ireland, in both wars). In the second
world war, Ireland remained neutral. Canada, moreover, had the
same sovereign as the United Kingdom. Yet a Canadian found
considerably more difficulty in entering, and settling in, the
United Kingdom than did a citizen of the Republic. To Powell
all this seemed not merely anomalous, but monstrous.

Yet, of all the proposals on his list, this eighth was the
one that attracted least sympathy, and produced less movement, from Labour and Conservative alike. Indeed, more than
one Conservative Party Conference (and wherever there was

sympathy for the Unionists it was among the Tory rank and file) voted down proposals for passport control of Irish citizens. No British government would, quite simply, consider altering the comfortable state of relations which existed with Dublin. And particularly, when the present troubles began, it was feared to give offence in that capital by withdrawing privileges which had been in place for so long. For their part, the Irish did not seem to notice that the relationship regarding passage and immigration which they enjoyed was essentially one of charity, and thus offensive to their proud sense of their own dignity and independence. Powell, however, had no animosity for the Republic as such. On 18 September 1973 in Londonderry he said:

> I have no wish to see other than cordial relations between the United Kingdom and the Irish Republic, nor have I ever criticized the policies, the government or the citizens of that independent state; but of all the acts and attitudes of HMG which maintain and exacerbate the war in the Province, none is more significant nor characteristic than its anxiety to associate the Irish Government with the policies of the United Kingdom in Northern Ireland. I am prepared to credit the government with the innocence of incomprehension; but there are circumstances when innocence and incomprehension are deadlier than malice in their effect.

Incomprehension, as between Powell and the Heath government in particular, and to a lesser extent between him and Labour, on the subject of Ireland, there certainly was. Over and beyond incomprehension, however, lurked Powell's great fear, one that was to burgeon and intensify over the years: that it was the settled intention of any government which held office in Westminster to prepare the way for the abandonment of Northern Ireland, support for which policy was enthusiastically given by the Foreign Office and the Home Office, and prodding in which direction came regularly from the State Department of the United States. The lineaments of misunderstanding, and the shadow of conspiracy had a long history, and had been sketched before Powell returned to the House of Commons in October 1974.

For many years, of course, senior Conservatives seemed to have some difficulty in understanding Powell, whether they were being wilful or simply incapable. It was this difficulty he referred to in the 'Vote Tory' speech on 16 June 1970 when he said that, referring to his then parliamentary colleagues, it was, 'Not for them to repudiate attacks on me which were unfounded and which they knew to be unfounded.' The subject then was immigration. But, as the Party leadership moved closer to Powell's position on that subject, his opponents within the Party increasingly referred to the objectionable tone of his speeches, rather than to their substance. The intellectual chasm between him and them opened still wider over Northern Ireland, as one fascinating exchange from 1972 illustrates.

From the very beginning of his involvement in the affairs of the province, Powell had urged Unionists – of whatever stripe – to avoid violence and law-breaking, whatever the provocation. His repeated avowal of their rights, of course, was, as the reader will have already seen, ever vehement, and might, by the more mealy-mouthed, be regarded as strident.

On 20 June 1972 Powell made a speech in his constituency which repeated in his usual terms and his usual tone the claims of Ulster. The speech included a passage exhorting his audience always to keep within the limits of the law. A constituent of a junior Minister at the Ministry of Defence, Peter Kirk, wrote to his MP in general support of Powell. Kirk replied in a fashion hostile to Powell, and utterly unappreciative of the policy he had been expounding. Powell took up the story in Armagh on 28 July:

. . . I warned the loyal majority in clear and solemn terms, against taking the law into their own hands; and it was delivered before those actions of the UDA which we all remember.[19] By chance, it came to my attention that, behind my back, in a letter to a constituent, one of Her Majesty's defence Ministers, a Mr. Kirk, had described the speech as 'bordering on incitement to subversion'. I concluded that he could not have seen what I actually said, and I sent him the text. To my astonishment he not only persisted in his accusation but cited verbatim in support of it the following sentence: 'All the more doggedly, therefore' – this is what I said to the Unionists assembled at Banbridge – 'must you fortify and entrench yourselves behind the plain uncomplicated things for which you stand.' And what were those 'plain uncomplicated things'? I will read on: The answer is: loyalty to the United Kingdom of Great Britain and Northern Ireland; and union, meaning the union of all its parts, including this one.

Powell thus – and justly – inserted the wedge of suspicion of the government's candour, understanding and motives into the argument. He continued:

> So things have come to this pass, that when a Member of Parliament exhorts his fellow citizens in Northern Ireland to remain peaceably loyal to the union of the kingdom, his words appear to one of Her Majesty's Ministers for defence – for defence, mind you! not social services or technological research – to be 'bordering on incitement to subversion'. When such is the mentality which prevails about Northern Ireland in the ranks of the government itself, need Mr. Whitelaw be so surprised if his assurances ring less than credible?

The contradictions between the words and actions of government were Powell's essential theme. Ministers (and, for that matter, Shadow Ministers) had constantly assured the Unionist population that no change in their status would take place without their consent. Yet, almost every action taken in regard to Ulster (this is how Powell saw matters) threatened where it did not weaken that status. And some ministerial statements teetered over into the absurd. Again in the Armagh speech – one of the most comprehensive and important delivered during the life of the Heath administration – Powell quoted the Prime Minister's call to an audience of the Royal Commonwealth Society to the effect that 'the British Government and people have a right to ask the people of Northern Ireland to assert themselves against men of violence.' It *was* an absurd plea, and in scathing tones Powell said why this was so:

> One would scarcely credit that such an exhortation could be addressed to unarmed men and women by a government which is conspicuously failing to provide them with the basic security and physical protection, let alone enjoyment of their lawful rights in peace, which it is the obligation of the government to furnish. It is hard to say whether the lack of imagination or the lack of comprehension is the more dangerous: lack of imagination to realize how such language must strike the inhabitants of Belfast and Londonderry, Strabane or Portadown; or lack of comprehension to understand that the essential ingredient which is missing is that which the government themselves have removed – conviction that the cause of Northern Ireland as part of the United

383

Kingdom is the cause of the British Government and the British nation.

It was, however, more often William Whitelaw, the Secretary of State for Northern Ireland, rather than the Prime Minister, whom Powell had in his sights at this time. Two more different personalities could scarcely be imagined. Whitelaw was a rich squire. He had been a gallant soldier and the recipient of the Military Cross. He had gone into politics in 1945 almost solely because of the sense of social responsibility instilled in him by the dread task of writing letters of sympathy to the relatives of men who had died under his command, and his subsequent visits to those relatives. He had been Opposition Chief Whip for five years and thereafter Leader of the House of Commons. Both of these jobs – which he performed admirably – required considerable abilities as a conciliator, and the first required something of the bully as well. Whitelaw was not a man of ideas; he was no thinker; he was a man of instincts and attitudes. Every task in politics was to him a problem, and all problems could be solved by good will, by diplomacy, by concession. He was bluff, gregarious, humorous, charming and kindly. When he took over the new post of Secretary of State for Northern Ireland he threw a party for his staff and the junior Ministers. As was his way, this was a lavish affair. It was introduced by Whitelaw with a statement to the effect that the job they all faced was probably an impossible one, and that the only way to make it possible was to approach it with good cheer.

It seemed unlikely, therefore, that there would be many points of contact between Whitelaw and Powell – who had already given the Secretary of State a number of headaches when he had been Chief Whip.[20] It happened, moreover, that Whitelaw's character, and his approach to his task, was to lead him into serious trouble.

June and July of 1972 were trying months both for the people of Northern Ireland, and for the government. Rioting was on the increase and, though it usually had a Catholic source, the UDA were provoking violence as well. To the embarrassment of the government, it had to be admitted that the security forces tolerated certain 'no-go' areas – parts of the Catholic ghettos which were, in effect, controlled by the IRA, and that they had done this on instructions from London, the Secretary of State hoping that this tolerance would create a climate in which constructive negotiation would take place. On 21 June the IRA issued a statement to the effect that they were willing to suspend hostilities provided they received 'a public reciprocal response'. The following day Whitelaw gave such a response. In the week before Powell's Armagh speech, however, the Army entered the 'no-go' areas almost without opposition: pressure in Westminster lifted from the shoulders of the Secretary of State, who invited all concerned to submit to him their ideas on how the whole problem should be solved. In Armagh Powell was scathing:

> But let no one make the mistake of concluding that thereby the fatal contradiction of the British government's policy has been eliminated. Within twenty-four hours Mr. Whitelaw was heard inviting all and sundry to write to him with their ideas about how Northern Ireland should be governed – like a competition in *Tit-Bits* or *Home Chat* – and promising himself an interesting postbag. Within forty-eight hours his Minister of State, Mr. Paul Channon, was inviting Miss Devlin[21] to 'come forward with some constructive way in which we can achieve a political solution'.

The point was, of course, that Bernadette Devlin, having first come to political notice as an apolitical activist demonstrating for improved rights for Catholics in 1968 was, by 1972, a full-blown Republican. Powell's fundamental point was that the government could not at one and the same time give credible promises to preserve the Union and negotiate without preconditions with those determined upon its destruction:

> The reason why Mr. Whitelaw and the government are disbelieved is not that people think they are deliberately telling untruths or seeking to deceive. The reason is simply this: their actions and their behaviour contradict their words. It is not possible both to assure the people of Northern Ireland that their place in the United Kingdom will be maintained, and at the same time to have parleyed with the IRA, face to face, in the capital of the Kingdom; or at the same time to bask in the adulation of an Opposition whose leader Harold Wilson has been publicly complimented by the government for proposals designed to produce a united Ireland in the foreseeable future; or at the same time to proclaim the intention of finding a 'political solution' to which no avenue will be treated as barred and to which the agreement was sought of those who

are fundamentally committed against Ulster being part of the
United Kingdom . . .

The deadly phrase here – and it was a phrase found deadly
and describing a disgraceful action by many in the Conservative
Party and in the Press who were far from sympathetic to Powell
– was 'parleyed with the IRA'. The sequence of events was this.
First came the IRA declaration of a ceasefire and then Whitelaw's
public response to it. That response left the Secretary of State on
very thin ice, for the government had repeatedly declared that it
would never negotiate with terrorists: this repeated promise was
one of the reasons why Whitelaw had couched his appeal for ideas
in such general terms. A number of journalists – statements and
counter-statements notwithstanding – were suspicious at the ease
with which the security forces had taken the 'no-go' areas, and
began to argue that the ceasefire had been a ploy – such as was
tried on many times in future years when the IRA needed a rest
period, and to which British governments invariably responded
with a naïve welcome – and that much more than had been made
public had been conceded. On 8 July a reporter asserted on Radio
Eireann that the Secretary of State had himself negotiated with
the IRA. Whitelaw was pressed on this matter in an angry House
of Commons and replied, 'I have not had personal contact' with
the terrorists. In a speech in Ballymena on 30 September Powell
observed that '. . . no one could then know by how thin a margin that word "contact" separated uncandour from downright
untruth.' By 10 July Whitelaw was forced to confess that a '. . .
truce was discussed by me with somebody who is in the provisional wing of the IRA on 7 July'. Ministers have been forced to
resign for less. But Whitelaw survived, on the grounds of the thin
implication that whoever he had spoken to had not actually been
a gunman. None the less, the anger his confession excited was
such that the experiment was unlikely to be repeated. Returning
to his theme of the untrustworthiness of the government Powell
analyzed what had happened on 30 September:

Had he ever signed any document that purported to be,
or could be represented as, an agreement with the IRA?
Such was the show of indignation in Whitehall that everyone confidently expected the answer capital "N" No. But the
answer was not capital "N" No . . . Instead the answer was a
long, prevaricating admission, "I signed no truce or agreement
jointly with the IRA."

Whitelaw had told the House on 22 June that the IRA had announced an 'unconditional' ceasefire. In fact, it had emerged that the ceasefire was by no means unconditional: that it was conditional on a public response. Whitelaw was forced to confess that he had met an intermediary bearing a note from his IRA colleagues setting out terms, to which the Secretary of State had agreed. Powell's conclusion was devastating:

> The Secretary of State had agreed with the IRA through an intermediary written terms for a ceasefire. Not only this, but it had been done behind the back of Parliament, which was to be led to believe that the ceasefire was a unilateral and unconditional event. The true nature of the Secretary of State's dealings with the IRA was only forced into the open by disclosures which could not be rebutted. It remains to be added that the government has so far refused to disclose to Parliament the text of the terms. Why not, if there was nothing to hide? It must be the first time, for a long time, that the House of Commons has been refused the sight of a document by which the government had bound itself.

By the time Powell returned to Parliament in October 1974, after his brief absence, he had acquired an ineradicable distrust of any possible government on the subject of Northern Ireland. Both major Parties, it was true, asserted that the Union would continue as long as the majority of the people of the province wanted it to. (It should be mentioned, by the way, that various plebiscites on the Union, not to mention the Unionist vote in a number of constituencies in various elections, returned figures which proved that a very substantial number of Catholics supported the continuance of the Union, however quiet they might keep about their desires in public. So the issue of Ulster is not a simple Protestant-Catholic one.) He was also by now formidably well versed in all aspects of Ulster politics, and ready to do battle.

There was, however, one major national issue to be dealt with—and, in any event, it was to take some time before Powell and the Unionists would be in a position to exercise pressure on a government. The major issue was continued membership of the EEC.

The early swings and roundabouts of Labour Party policy on the EEC have already been described.[22] By the time of the

February 1974 general election, sectional opinion on the issue had not massively changed, save in that different sections of the two major Parties had hardened somewhat in their positions. With the departure of Powell the anti-Market Conservatives had been seriously weakened, but those who remained – MPs included the statesman of the movement, Neil Marten, and Richard Body, Teddy Taylor, Roger Moate and John Biffen – were as doughty as ever. The Party leadership was unchanged in its collective opinion. Heath, with a sort of scornful reluctance, accepted that there probably would be a referendum, and determined to fight for the cause of his life might and main. Broadly speaking, he could be reasonably certain of carrying the bulk of his Party with him, and would put the full resources of Central Office at the disposal of the pro-European campaign.

Harold Wilson was in a far more difficult position, one which is well described in the memoirs of James Callaghan.[23] The history of Labour policy on the subject was starred with confusion and division. When, for example, in April 1962 Harold Macmillan announced, in a speech in his old constituency of Stockton, that he intended to apply for British membership of the Community the then Labour leader, Hugh Gaitskell, reacted with immediate passion: he was, on patriotic grounds, totally and utterly opposed to membership. Now, Gaitskell had already fought two major battles with the membership of his Party and the trade unions (who command millions of votes at Labour Party conferences). One was over his commitment to keeping the British nuclear deterrent. The other was over his desire to strike a general commitment to nationalization out of the Party's constitution. He had been sustained throughout his battles by able and devoted acolytes, notably Roy Jenkins, Antony Crosland, Shirley Williams and William Rodgers (though these were then only junior figures). He was deeply distrusted by the Party at large, and by most trade union leaders. Suddenly, on the issue of the EEC, he found himself wholly in tune with the general membership, but sundered from his friends: all of those listed were passionate supporters of the European idea, except Crosland, and Crosland was agnostic, and remained so to the end of his life. The divisions of 1962 continued right up to the referendum, which was held on 5 June 1975, and to some extent even beyond: even when, in 1987, Neil Kinnock, as Leader, announced that, were he to become Prime Minister, he would work within the Community, he excited bitter criticism from sections of the Party – notably that symbolized by Tony Benn – though it has to be said that the influence of the left-wing anti-Marketeers had been weakening since Kinnock's replacement of Michael Foot after the disastrous general election of 1983.

In February 1974 the two key figures in the new Labour government, so far as the Market was concerned, were the Prime Minister, Wilson, and Callaghan, the new Foreign Secretary, who was destined to go on to hold the supreme office and thus become the only politician ever to have held all the major offices of state – Chancellor, Home Secretary, Foreign Secretary and Prime Minister. Gaitskell had died within a year of Macmillan's opening gambit, and Wilson had succeeded him (beating Callaghan, as well as George Brown, in the process). His attitude on the Community was less strident than that of Gaitskell and, with Callaghan, he tended to blow hot and cold. He treated the Macmillan effort to enter (the chief British negotiator being Edward Heath) with detailed suspicion, but did not oppose it in principle. Indeed, when it seemed that the 1972 Labour Conference was going to vote outright against membership he threatened to resign if such a vote was carried: that was enough to ward off the rebels. Indeed, earlier, in May 1967, Wilson had made his own application for membership.

Throughout the Heath negotiations, as we have seen,[24] Wilson continued his balancing act, and the Parliamentary Labour Party was several times split. Wilson maintained throughout, however that he was not *au fond* against membership, merely against what he said he believed to be the disastrously conciliatory terms being negotiated by Heath and Geoffrey Rippon. Upon his return to office in February 1974, therefore, Wilson found himself with two unbreakable commitments. He would put the result to a national referendum. This stance enabled him to avoid saying whether or not he would recommend continued membership. He and the Foreign Secretary would see what could be exacted from the other EEC members, and then decide. Meanwhile, during the negotiations, Ministers would be expected to keep silent on their own thoughts. On one occasion when Tony Benn broke with this order he was sharply rebuked: his disingenuous defence was that he had attacked membership in a letter to his constituents, and was therefore acting as an MP, not a Minister. In a curious way, however, his rebellion was to gain an ultimate success. For, when the referendum was held the following year, Wilson – who could not keep the government together otherwise – decided to suspend the doctrine of collective Cabinet responsibility, whereby Ministers are forbidden publicly to disagree with each other on policy. Everybody was allowed to go his or her own way during the referendum campaign.

For all his preoccupations with Northern Ireland, Powell watched the unfolding of these events with intense interest. Throughout 1974 it seemed that the situation was not unpromising. Labour divisions were deepening, and among those determined to campaign against membership at least two – Michael Foot (now Secretary of State for Employment, and in the government for the first time)[25] and Tony Benn – had strong followings among Party Members. Those equally ardent on the other side – like Roy Jenkins and Shirley Williams – were elitist figures, distrusted by the Labour rank and file. A referendum, moreover, on a national issue, would be an unprecedented issue for the British people. While the waters were uncharted, it seemed possible – certainly the anti-Marketeers in the Conservative Party, and the very few of a like disposition in the Press, thought this – that a single issue campaign would enable Powell's oratorical power, and the continued regard in which large sectors of the electorate continued to hold him, to be used to their best effect. The opinion polls, however, suggested that, albeit in a resigned rather than a positive mood, the electorate by a majority of about two to one favoured continued membership. The anti-Marketeers in all parties – and, of course, in the unions – accepted that they faced an uphill struggle. The pro-marketeers, on the other hand, were reasonably confident, but still nervous, and nervous particularly of Powell.

It is beyond cavil that a substantial number of votes were cast against the Conservatives in February 1974 on the understanding that a Labour government might well take Britain out of the EEC. This anti-Market thinking was not, in every mind, precise: it rested upon the general awareness of the fact that there was a great deal more anti-Market sentiment in the Labour than in the Conservative Party. However, in the mind of Powell the thinking was very precise. Powell encouraged anyone prepared to take his advice to vote Labour because the terms of the Labour manifesto were incompatible with the Treaty of Accession: if the Labour leadership held to its promises then either the United Kingdom would have to leave the EEC or the EEC would have to change out of all recognition. Indeed, in the first flush of enthusiasm after his return to office in February 1974, at a European Foreign Ministers' meeting, the Foreign Secretary took the trouble to read the relevant passages from his Party's manifesto out loud to his fellow Foreign Ministers. It was not immediately realized, for all their early bravado, that both Harold Wilson and James Callaghan were keen to avoid leading their country out of the Community. It is possible, therefore, to convict Powell of naïvety in assessing the intentions of two such consummately adroit and inconsistent politicians. The principal concern of both Prime Minister and Foreign Secretary was to gain time through re-negotiation before the unavoidable national referendum was called.

And, there was time. It was conceivable, it was thought or feared, according to individual disposition, that the other member countries would turn Britain down. In which case Callaghan and the Prime Minister might well come out against membership, and swing the result. What was considered most likely, however, was that France and Germany – particularly Valéry Giscard d'Estaing in place of the deceased Georges Pompidou, and Helmut Schmidt, German Chancellor in place of the disgraced Willy Brandt[26] – would cobble together a face-saving formula; and this is, indeed, what happened. On re-negotiation the Conservative leadership was torn. Committed though they were to keeping Britain in, it would require a great deal of gritting of teeth, when Callaghan had finished his job, to agree, as a means of gaining votes for the cause, to say that he had succeeded better than they had. On the other hand, to deride his efforts would be to play into the hands of the anti-Marketeers.

Once it became clear that Wilson fully intended to keep his referendum promise (there had been those so suspicious of his reputation as an unabashed tactician that they thought he might well renege on it)[27] various people and groups began to get themselves organized for the coming fray. Since plans began to be laid almost as soon as Labour took office, and ran parallel with the Callaghan negotiations, it will be convenient to describe them here – and the problems which attended their formation.

It was early agreed, on either side, that umbrella organizations would conduct the opposing campaigns, and it was here that opponents of membership ran into difficulties over Enoch Powell.

It was known from the outset that, when the government introduced legislation to provide for a referendum it would also allocate funds from the Treasury, but only to two organizations, one on either side: these sums were to be equal. The European Movement (reconstituted as Britain In Europe) became the recipient proponent of membership, while the hastily formed National Referendum Campaign Committee was to be allocated the opposition funds. In addition, exactly equivalent amounts of airtime were allocated for political broadcasts for each side. So far as government was concerned, therefore, an even-handed approach as between the two sides of the case prevailed. Neither umbrella organization was in any way inhibited from receiving extra funds, up to any amount, from outside supporters.

The Britain In Europe organization had a number of advantages. It enjoyed the unqualified support of the great majority in the Tory Party, and the whole of its leadership. While the Labour Party was split, none the less, the Prime Minister, the Foreign Secretary, and Ministers best known to, and best respected by, the general public were all in favour of staying in. Most of big business, further, was on the same side, and made lavish contributions. Finally a well-funded parallel campaign, financed by the EEC itself, was going on at the same time. This needs a word of explanation.

The EEC has always – and quite reasonably – funded what are called information campaigns in member countries. Apart from the fact that they naturally extol the virtues of the Community, these campaigns are required to be non-partisan. For example, when, after the 1979 general election campaign in Britain, the Conservative Party was in favour of staying in the Market and the Labour Party on the whole against, it would have been impermissible for the Community financially to support a Tory general election campaign. Thus, in 1975, the institutions of the Community could not mount a campaign for a 'yes' vote. But by what was claimed by Britain In Europe and by the EEC Commission to be, for them, a happy coincidence, a major educational and advertising programme – far more lavish than was common – ran throughout the United Kingdom at the same time as the referendum battle was going on. There were, further – and, it was said, naturally – many social contacts between those handling both campaigns, and even professional cross-overs. Angry though the anti-Marketeers were about all this expenditure on a scale so great that it might be called American, no impropriety could be readily proved, whatever might be suspected.

By comparison, the National Referendum Campaign Committee was in a woeful state. First, there was the problem of money. There were only (relatively) small individual contributions to add to government funds. Various trade unions chipped in, but not remotely to the extent of matching the resources of Britain In Europe. Further, although the BBC was required to provide broadcasting support of a technical nature (for the political broadcasts), a general suspicion of the Corporation's attitude impelled the Committee to find, not only (as would be quite normal) its own presenters and scriptwriters, but its own editor and producer.

Then there was the problem of the political composition of the Committee. On the other side while, say, Roy Jenkins and Edward Heath differed on a number of areas of policy, their differences were not so great that they could not readily be, for the moment buried. The NRCC had to combine people who differed fundamentally on almost everything except the EEC. The trade union leaders – Jack Jones of the Transport and General Workers in particular – were dominant: they provided cash, and they had organizations that could be put to use for the cause. They did not, it must be said fairly of them, use muscle against the Conservative minority, nor seek to advocate trade union Socialism under the guise of an anti-Market banner. Jones, even, to his eternal credit, proposed that Neil Marten should become Chairman of the Committee. But the fact remained that most Tory participants were on the right, and favoured the kind of economic policy Powell advocated; which Heath had advocated in 1970, and which Heath had abandoned in 1972. Moreover, while Jack Jones and Hugh Scanlon – and even Clive Jenkins – were national figures, the Tory element possessed no one who could be considered that, with two exceptions. The first (though not in order of importance) was Edward (now Sir Edward) du Cann, the Chairman of the Conservative 1922 Committee – the assembly of all Tory backbenchers. But du Cann declined to participate in the NRCC, and did not intervene publicly in the campaign until its closing days. As Neil Marten bitterly observed at the time, 'That's typical of Edward. Having been bloody useless for most of the time he takes a stand when it's too late to do any good.'

The second major national figure who could be called Tory was Powell. Here we (I say 'we' because I played some part in the campaign and was a member of the NRCC) ran into an immediate difficulty. No trade union leader, and no Labour opponent of membership, would appear on the same platform or TV programme as Powell. This was principally because of their memories of, and attitudes to, his April 1968 speech in Birmingham, and no amount of persuasion, however fervent, however often repeated, could persuade the non-Conservative section of the Committee to change its mind.

Powell took all this philosophically, and did make one TV programme in the anti-Marketeer series. But the fact of the matter remained that the majority on the NRCC thus deprived the campaign of its most potentially powerful asset. It was recognized from the start that his absence from the centre of things would be a grievous handicap, but agreed that he would mount his own speaking campaign under the auspices of the Get Britain Out Movement (the successor to the old Keep Britain Out Movement). He, as well as the NRCC, had to hit two targets, both close together. It was necessary to continue the battle that had been waged against Heath before entry, and demonstrate that the arguments made then were still valid. But it was equally important to demonstrate that Callaghan and Wilson had produced no improvement: the case for improvement was at the centre of the government's invitation to the electorate to give support to membership.

Callaghan's view of EEC membership as he began his two years as Foreign Secretary is expressed succinctly in his memoirs:[28]

> My basic view of the effect of Community membership on Britain's economic prospects had hardly shifted since I had been Chancellor ten years earlier. That is to say I shared neither the conviction of the pro-Marketeers that it would result in a vast improvement in our economic performance nor the deep despair of the anti-Marketeers that membership would ruin Britain. I continued to affirm publicly and privately, as I had done in the 1960s, that Britain's economic salvation depended on ourselves: whether we were in or out of the Community was marginal to the result.

Despite taking this attitude, Callaghan was fully aware of how deeply his Party was split, and how many of its members held views, one way or another, with a passion that he could never himself command on this or any other issue. His principal difficulty abroad, however, was to persuade the European powers that a re-negotiation of the terms agreed between them and a Conservative government was worth their while. Since he particularly hoped for sympathy from the West German Chancellor Willy Brandt, a man who was not merely a pillar of European Socialism, but an old and trusted friend of the Labour Party, he flew first to Bonn, in preparation for his first meeting, arranged for 1 April, of EEC Foreign Ministers. He found Brandt tired and lacking in interest and energy. Hans Apel, West Germany's Minister of Agriculture, was, by contrast, decided and direct. He told Callaghan that there could be no circumstances in which the terms of the Common Agricultural Policy – that fundament of the Treaty of Rome, which established the original European Economic Community – could be re-negotiated. After all, if the United Kingdom were to pay less than Heath had agreed she would pay to the common fund, then West Germany would have to pay more, since West Germany was the richest and most economically successful member of the club. Callaghan found a readier, and more encouraging, hearing from Helmut Schmidt, destined to be Chancellor in a matter of weeks. Schmidt was a more easy-going man; he had a genuine feeling for the British Labour Party, for Britain, and for the difficulties – not serious, perhaps, but not trifling either – which the Community would have, supposing Britain were to withdraw. Also, unlike others whom Callaghan met on this first foray into the treacherous and dangerous waters of European politics, he understood the Foreign Secretary's problems. He offered – and this was a dangerous and brave offer on his part – himself to address a Labour Party Conference, and by his speech to persuade the British that the EEC was for them.

There were many technicalities attending re-negotiation which occupied and preoccupied Callaghan and the Prime Minister over the months which preceded the referendum. Harold Wilson had a great feeling for the Commonwealth, and his followers in the country as well as in Parliament found themselves – to take but one example – to be the most ardent supporters of New Zealand sheep farmers whereas, hitherto, their Commonwealth preoccupations had been almost entirely with the concerns of the so-called 'New' Commonwealth, the countries of Africa and Asia. Michael Foot, indeed, at one meeting of the European Strategy Committee – which body was created by the Prime Minister, in accordance with a system of political tactics he had always found useful for exhausting opposition – bewailed the effect of British membership of the EEC upon India, and most particularly the fact that a protocol to the Treaty of Brussels ordained that New Commonwealth immigrants to Britain would not have an automatic right to entry into other EEC countries. For the moment, however, Labour campaigners against membership found that New Zealanders were more likely than Indians or Pakistanis to excite the sympathy of the British electorate: they, therefore, became the flavour of the day.

It is instructive, at this point, both historically and politically, on the basis of what evidence we have by way of memoirs, academic studies, and journalism[29] to note, not merely the attitudes, but the attitudes struck, by the various central players in the high game of European politics. No round picture can be given here, since this book is not about the general subject, but about Enoch Powell, necessary though it is to describe the context of his times. From first to last Powell's objection to British membership of the EEC was on a higher plane of principle than that of such as Harold Wilson and James Callaghan, both of whom, having no particularly strong feelings of their own one way or the other, possessed, none the less, of a vague instinct that being in was better than being out, sought to balance differing elements within their Party. Thus, Powell, at Doncaster, as early as 19 June 1971:

> For a long time the British have been asking one another "When and how are we going to get back our pride and our confidence in ourselves?" Perhaps the answer is beginning to appear and, as is often the case when questions of that sort are answered, at an unexpected moment and from an unexpected direction. It is too soon to be sure; but what cannot be denied is that something very big and very deep had been happening in the minds of the people of this country in recent months.

Powell went on to say that he believed that the British people had awoken. 'Untutored,' he said, 'uninvited, and indeed unwelcomed, they have insisted upon discerning the one, simple, overwhelming important question, to be ourselves or not to be ourselves.' Powell was wrong in thinking that, once asked, the British people would insist on their identity, and repudiate any alternative. But it was a grand – I would think a noble – wrongness. Most certainly, it aspired to a higher plane of human endeavour than did the to-ing and fro-ing of James Callaghan, seeking to persuade continental politicians already set in the ways of their Community, to help him in keeping his Party together.

Callaghan faced two further difficulties of a very practical nature, quite apart from those created by division within the Labour Party. The first was constituted by history. The original EEC grouping – that of six nations – had come together and signed the agreements which gave it its collective identity in 1957. In a series of speeches in the years immediately following the war Churchill himself, indeed, had suggested and given his blessing to such a formation, resting as it above all did upon a reconciliation between France and Germany (subsequently widened and deepened by the actions of Charles de Gaulle and Konrad

Adenauer). But Churchill himself scarcely contemplated that the United Kingdom would attach itself to any new continental conglomeration, and his successor, Anthony Eden, was actively hostile to any further entanglement (over and above, that is, the defence alliance of NATO) on the part of Britain in European affairs.[30] It followed that, even by Edward Heath's time, the basic structure of the EEC was set in aspic. Had Britain joined in the negotiations which led to the Treaty of Rome, it is at least arguable that she could have created a community – basically a free trade area[31] – without political or federalist potential. By the 1960s, however, it was a question of the extent to which Britain would adapt to rules already and ineradicably established. It was the fashion in which the Community developed which excited the opposition to membership – or continued membership – of Powell and the others who thought like him.

The second problem was more immediate. The Labour government formed in February 1974 was of a provisional character. Everybody, including those who were Ministers, saw to that. The business of governing the United Kingdom was in a constant state of uncertainty. That uncertainty was increased not only by Wilson's constant threat to seek a dissolution if he was defeated on any matter of substance in the House of Commons, but by another of his tactical ploys – the constant spreading of rumours to the effect that he would seek a proper mandate from the voters in June. All this was evident to continental leaders. They understood the Party pressure that the Foreign Secretary was under, however much or little they were prepared to yield to his demands. But Edward Heath, they knew, would from their point of view be a much more amenable proposition. Their temptation was, therefore, to wait and see whether the February verdict would in the near future be reversed. This inclination Callaghan found most difficult to quell, and he was under constant pressure – among other things deluged by memoranda from anti-Market members of the Cabinet – to show even interim results from the re-negotiation process.

However, matters went fairly steadily ahead. On 26 February 1975 the government produced a White Paper setting out its proposals for the referendum. On 11 March an EEC summit meeting in Dublin made certain limited – but, naturally, much trumpeted – concessions to Britain. On the same day the House of Commons voted in principle in favour of a referendum. On 18 March the Cabinet voted by a majority of sixteen to seven for accepting the deal agreed in Dublin, but also confirmed that Ministers opposed to continued membership would be free to speak, write and broadcast to their convictions. On 10 April, by a majority of 312 to 248, the Commons gave the referendum Bill (drafted by a committee under the chairmanship of the new Deputy Leader of the Labour Party, Edward Short (now Lord Glenamara), its Second Reading. On 26 April a specially convened Labour Party Conference recommended the electorate to vote 'No'. The poll was set for 5 June.

Despite all the indications seeming to favour the pro-European cause, there were a number of incalculable factors. The most important of these – seismic, as it turned out in later history to be – was the deposition of Edward Heath as Leader of the Conservative Party and his replacement, on 11 February, 1975, by Margaret Thatcher.[32] There was no sense in which the new Leader could be described as against continued membership of the Community; but there was no sense in which she could be described as enthusiastic about it either. Certainly, however, most of those closest to her were, to put the matter at its lowest, sceptical about the European adventure, while outright opponents of the Treaty of Brussels, having for years been cold-shouldered by those in control of the Conservative Party, suddenly found the word 'welcome' inscribed on the mat at the entrance to the new Leader's office.

In part this was a reflection, not of sympathy merely, but of reality. At the outset of the leadership campaign – in October 1974 – Mrs. Thatcher was a highly unfancied outsider. Many voted for her in the first ballot only in order to get Heath out. Since the rules – adopted by a committee under the chairmanship of Lord Home – allowed for fresh candidates to join the fray on the second ballot, it was hoped by many Tory backbenchers (who constituted the relevant electorate) that she would damage Heath sufficiently to enforce his retirement, whereupon a more likely candidate – William Whitelaw was the favoured choice – could come forward. The comprehensive nature of her defeat of Heath, however, made it impossible to take away from her the palm on which she had laid her fingers.

She inherited, though, a bitterly divided Party, one still scarcely able to contemplate, let along credit, the spectacle of two general election defeats in a row. Heath still had his admirers, and they were fervent. Even beyond their ranks, however, there were many Conservatives who doubted the wisdom of choosing the first female Leader of a Western political Party and who, furthermore, were convinced that the policies which she advocated (similar in many ways to those which Heath had espoused in 1970) would lead to further electoral disasters. Between Heath and his successor there was a palpable coldness: there was, even, an unedifying dispute about whether she had offered him a post in her Shadow Cabinet or not. A fundamental fact for her, however, was that in the first leadership battle every single anti-Market backbencher had voted for her. In truth, of course, they would have voted for anybody who was not Edward Heath. But, since she was uncertain of her own legitimacy,[33] and undecided how to build up her own support in the Party, she was grateful to those who had supported her when the going had been hard. It followed that, while she publicly supported staying in the Community, she was unwilling enthusiastically to espouse that cause. 'It's Ted's issue,' she said a week after her election, 'so, let him lead the Tory campaign to stay in.' Central Office was instructed to give Heath any help he needed.

It would be putting matters mildly, therefore, to say that the political climate was unsettled during the first half of 1975. Powell stayed, however, outside the main ring of conflict and argument. He had not yet quite won the confidence of his Northern Ireland colleagues: his lack of enthusiasm for a campaign to restore Stormont was known and disliked. In the opinion of Philip Goodhart, moreover,[34]

> In part, the volume of Conservative support for the Common Market was a result of the loss of confidence in Enoch Powell that followed his advice to vote Labour in the two general elections of 1974. By removing himself from the Conservative scene, Enoch Powell had dealt a body blow to anti-Common Market Conservatives up and down the country. His departure – and the consequent bewilderment of his followers – had made it easier for local Conservative Associations to take up the Common Market cause with enthusiasm. When Enoch Powell first urged his supporters to vote Labour, he made a substantial contribution towards the Labour victory that made a referendum possible – at the same time his defection made a 'Yes' victory more likely when the referendum came.

There is certainly something in Goodhart's judgement. But, as I have already argued,[35] it has ever been the case that Powell's admirers and followers have not fully understood the personal character of his passionate sense of logic and honour. Whatever the outcome of the February 1974 election was to be, he could not stand as a Conservative candidate. There was no tactical scheming behind his decision to stand down: he has always been an effective tactician, but principally within Parliament. The public man has invariably laid his logic and his passion on the line, and invited support for his arguments. He does, however, follow things through. In February he could not stand as a Tory. He saw no hope of an exit from the EEC were Heath to win. He therefore campaigned against Heath, and opened the window of opportunity. Had he been able to campaign *as a Conservative* in the weeks leading up to the referendum the pro-Market victory would have certainly been less substantial. But, had he not advocated a Labour vote twice, there would have been no referendum. The outcome of that referendum was, indeed, a crushing blow to him and those who thought like him. On 5 June 1975 67.7% of those who voted, voted to stay in the EEC. 17,378,581 supported membership: 8,470,073 were opposed.

Within the limits that were forced upon him – his lack of a Conservative base and the reluctance of Labour spokesmen to appear with him – Powell none the less fought a doughty personal campaign, earning from *The Times* on 4 June, one of the more enthusiastic accolades delivered in a survey of the main campaigners on either side. 'On the "No" side,' the paper wrote, 'Mr. Enoch Powell has argued in a most skilful and sympathetic way, putting his argument, particularly on television, with a combined clarity and courtesy which reminded one of the traditional standards of English politics.' Matters had indeed moved a long way since *The Times*'s coverage of his April 1968 speech on immigration in Birmingham.[36]

However, at least in the early stage of the campaign, Powell laboured under a further difficulty, the nature of which is indicated by the fact that his first major speech – at Bournemouth on 11 May – went unmentioned by the BBC. Despite the suspicions of anti-Marketeers at the time, this was not part of a conspiracy against him. The fact was that, like the other broadcasting organizations, the Corporation had had no experience of covering referenda: in an attempt to balance their coverage between the two competing sides, they therefore tended, at least at the beginning, to concentrate on the official spokesmen of the two main organizations.

In the Bournemouth speech Powell showed himself to be either unaware, or scornful, of the kind of argument that Philip Goodhart was later to make. In it he directly attacked the Conservative Party as a whole, whereas hitherto he had selected individual targets within it. It was his new conviction that the Conservative middle classes, fearful of economic and industrial disruption at home, supported the European cause because the Community was a capitalist-inclined amalgam. He raised the spectre of a Conservative Party which would no longer be able to rally a substantial section of the working class. 'As I watch,' he said, 'and listen to the voices that are raised to persuade electors to surrender their own birthright because they fear their fellow subjects, I think I discern ahead the shape of a Conservative Party that is the party of a class, and not of a nation – and thus doomed to extinction.' His succeeding five speeches were in similar vein.

His problem was that shared by probably all the main 'No' campaigners: he and they (with the single exception of the junior trade Minister, Dr. John Gilbert) simply could not espy victory, however carefully they gazed at the horizon of 5 June. There is some evidence, however, from a May NOP poll that Powell had some influence at the margins: seven per cent of voters said that his advocacy made them more likely to vote against. On the other hand, polling surveys conducted by MORI indicated that less than half of the electorate even knew where Powell stood on the EEC issue.

It may well have been a fatalistic sense that defeat was inevitable which produced a certain change in Powell's style, much remarked upon by many who saw him in action over May and June. In the three general elections in which he had fought, for one side or the other, since achieving genuine national prominence, each major speech, in spite of moving and lofty periods, had a certain bitter and furious rage about it. Of course his rage – at least in his own eyes and the eyes of his supporters – was justified, in 1970 by the treatment he had received from Tory colleagues, in the two 1974 elections by the circumstances which had forced him out of his Party. In 1975, however, lavish though he was with scorn against the Conservatives, there was almost a gentle, certainly a puckish, note about his demeanour. He did, it is true, warn the country in Birmingham on 2 June of approaching national 'moral breakdown' and argued that membership meant 'death, the abandonment of all prospects of national rebirth, the end of any possibility of resurgence'. But on television and in public debate (such as one held in the Oxford Union) he was almost excessively courteous to his opponents, even expressing agreement with Shirley Williams (on the effect of the EEC on food prices) in a *Panorama* programme.

It was puckishness, however, that led to his ending his campaign on 4 June with a speech in Heath's own constituency. He knew perfectly well that, next to Margaret Thatcher, he was the critic who could most readily get under Heath's skin, and the speech in Sidcup unquestionably did that. The new Powell had, however, already been seen in action at an NRCC Press conference the day before, when he woke up journalists already bored by a campaign that was, generally, either banal or unacceptably technical. His humour has always been somewhat donnish, and the dry air of slightly pained incredulity with which he begins the demolition of an opponent's case is part of its charm. He entertained the reporters with humorous quips and asides, moving them (which is no easy thing for a politician at a British Press conference) to laughter and even applause. He repeated his joke about death-bed repentance,[37] but freshened it up with an entertaining guying of his own apocalyptic oratorical manner. He was asked what he thought of Mrs. Thatcher, and was caustic in his commentary on the fact that she had sat without complaint in Heath's Cabinet for nearly four years, even though she now appeared ready to ditch its heritage. It is interesting here to emphasize that Powell is never a critic of changes of mind, and frequently dwells on his own. What he objects to in other politicians is a change of mind not followed by action. If – thus ran his case – the new Leader, and the man dubbed by the Press her John the Baptist, Keith Joseph, had believed in Heath's policies, they had been foolish; if they had – Joseph implied this while Margaret Thatcher simply ignored the Heath years – believed in government what they now claimed to believe in opposition, then they were dishonourable. It was clear, indeed, that his audience was more interested in what he might have to say about his old Party than they were with his reasons for a negative vote on the EEC, and Powell went along with the mood. The flavour of the occasion is perhaps best captured in a remark he made when he was being asked his opinion about Heath. He approached the subject with pseudo-bemused wonder, considering how a man with such promise had turned out so badly. (Harold Wilson had recently adopted a patronizing and pretended complimentary attitude to Heath, musing aloud on how the Tories could have treated him so badly: it was no secret that the two men could not stand one another.) Powell went on to say that he could not readily form a rounded judgement on Heath, since he had never been close enough to him. 'I would dearly have liked to be friends, but' – here came one of Powell's pregnant pauses, accompanied

by a regretful shrug – 'like everyone else, I found it impossible.'
It was the common opinion of the Pressmen there that Powell's
had been the only genuinely entertaining Press conference of the
campaign. But it was all for nothing.

Once the result was declared, a substantial number of those
who had campaigned for withdrawal accepted defeat with grace.
These included Tony Benn, though he has long since changed his
mind yet again, and now argues that a Labour government should
leave the EEC without any further popular consultation. Powell,
of course, had never cared for the referendum idea: he had gone
along with Neil Marten's original Labour-supported proposal simply because there was no imaginable tactical alternative for the
anti-Marketeers. After the referendum defeat, the great majority of Conservative or Tory-inclined of their persuasion gave up
the battle: Neil Marten, for example, had no difficulty in taking
office in the government Margaret Thatcher formed in 1979.

Within the Labour Party – and even more within the trade
union movement – resistance continued for very much longer.
It continues, indeed, at the time of writing. Most commentators
and politicians agreed, however, that, the referendum over, the
likelihood of a British government of either party actually withdrawing from the EEC was one of remote improbability. There
might, perhaps, have been a chance had Michael Foot won the
1983 general election; but there was scarcely anybody, even in
Foot's own entourage, who thought that, after the 1982 Falklands
war and with the economy at length starting to pick up, the
possibility of a Labour victory existed outside the territory of
fantasy.

Over the years, even Powell himself seemed to become rec-
onciled to the idea that British membership, short of some
cataclysmic event, was permanent. It has only been occasionally
that he has given any detailed consideration to the possibility of
exit, and he has been more inclined simply to lament, in often
plangent terms, what he considers to have been, in effect, the
loss of his country.

What the referendum result essentially did was to remove
Powell from the position, sometimes of power, sometimes of
real or potential influence, at the centre of British politics
which he had so long enjoyed, whether as a senior Tory or
as a freebooter. It is true that, with his Unionist colleagues,
he was central to maintaining a government in office between
1977 and 1979. But the price paid for their actions – important
as it was – related only to Ulster. Powell continued to command

media interest and attention: indeed, as he moved into old age, as many animosities of the 1960s and 1970s faded, as more and more of his views on economic policy in particular came to be adopted and the far-seeing wisdom of his earlier predictions and prescriptions came to be recognized, it might be said that he commanded a wider and more varied interest than ever before.

But he recognized himself that future effectiveness, if any, would relate solely to Ulster, and he was content with that since, as we have seen, the province had always commanded a major part of his interest and its cause had ever been regarded by him as one of the most vital in the affairs of the nation. One of his greatest anxieties, however, was to persuade Ulstermen to see their affairs, and their troubles, in a United Kingdom context and, more specifically, in a Westminster context. None of his fellow Unionists (of whatever persuasion or sect) in the House of Commons could be described as parliamentarians of distinction. Indeed, since Edward Carson there had been no Unionist of the first rank in the House. Until the imposition of direct rule by Edward Heath Unionists had, for the most part with tranquillity, followed the Conservative Whip. It was Powell's business from the start, but especially once the referendum was over, to make his new Party alive to the possibilities the then parliamentary balance held out to them. It was his own conviction, of course, that the situation could and should be exploited. But he also had a particular authority to expound tactics: one of the reasons for selecting him for Down South in the first place had been his renown as a parliamentarian.

To maximize influence, however, it was necessary to maximize unity. Thus, at Kilkeel on 5 July, 1975:

> With Her Majesty's government uneasily poised on a theoretical majority of nil, its first by-election lost and more such losses no doubt to come, 10 Unionist members in Parliament are a power to be reckoned with.

The trouble was that the ten, split between Paisleyites and others, could not always be relied upon to act together. If they did:

> The claims which Unionism has put forward in three elections in 15 months are claims which, if we stand to them and fight our corner with skill, prudence and tenacity, neither government nor Parliament can refuse, deriving as they do from the integral

status of Ulster which Parliament and government themselves have affirmed and re-affirmed.

Only one thing, he believed, could deny them success:

> That thing is division – diversity of councils – discordancy of voices, infirmity of tactics, uncertainty of strategy – the political ailments of a house divided that can't stand. Against this danger there is one defence. That is a single, acknowledged, unitary leadership, which will embrace alike the Privy Councillor in Parliament, the official at headquarters, the officer in the constituency association, and the loyal rank-and-file in the street, the village and the homestead, and will weld them together in one united and irresistible host.

The unity of which he dreamed was never to come about. From time to time the troops led by Ian Paisley and those led by James Molyneaux came together at Westminster. But often they diverged. The divergences were not on Ulster matters, but on others related to general government policy and on questions regarding the survival of the government. The essential part of Powell's plan – unity on *everything* and pressure on the government – was never more than partially achieved.

None the less, the environment in which they operated did offer opportunity – as it offered opportunity to the Liberals and the Nationalists, the two other substantial minority groupings. Indeed, so tight did the government's position sometimes become that its survival could depend on the voice of conscience of no more than one or two men. This was to be demonstrated most clearly on the last night of the life of the October 1974 Parliament – 29 March 1979 – when either Gerry Fitt (the Irish Nationalist) or Gwynfor Evans (the Welsh Nationalist) could have saved, but chose not to save the administration headed by James Callaghan.

The history of the October 1974 Parliament (the final phase of the Wilson-Callaghan years) can be divided into two parts. The first lasted from the election (through the replacement of Wilson by Callaghan in March 1976) to the government's survival on a conservative censure motion on 23 March 1977, a survival made possible by the aid of the Liberals and some aid from the Unionists. The second period ran from that date until the Conservative return to power in April 1979. The second was the period in which Powell and the Unionists were able to achieve their maximum influence.

The life of the Labour government elected in October 1974 was almost bound to be limited. Yet, for various almost accidental reasons, it enjoyed a life prolonged well beyond what might have been readily assumed to be its natural term. For one thing, the leadership of the Conservative Party by Edward Heath survived from his electoral defeat in February 1974 into the next year. His authority had certainly vanished by his second general election defeat of the year (and the third in all). He continued, however, to hold the support of many – probably a majority – of Party workers outside Westminster: for this reason – one, essentially, of survival – he sought to extend the franchise in any new leadership election beyond the ranks of Conservative MPs.[38] However, for so long as he survived, the Tory front bench scarcely dared launch an out and out attack on the Labour government. When Denis Healey introduced the 1974 Budget the Shadow Cabinet initially planned to vote against it. But their hearts failed them, and the Opposition ended with a humiliating split on whether or not to try to bring Harold Wilson down.

Then, when Margaret Thatcher replaced Edward Heath in February 1975, Opposition self-dissatisfaction continued. The new Leader was untried, and desperately inexperienced. She seemed to want to introduce policies which a large number of her followers believed had failed between 1970 and 1972. There was a feeling, further, that a mistake had been made; that she had been chosen not on her merits, but simply because she was not Heath. She herself had a great deal to learn, and was uncertain of the extent to which she could depend on the support of many of her colleagues. For all these reasons, it was not until 1977 that the Opposition was ready to mount a fundamental challenge – and such as, if successful, would cause a general election – to the Cabinet.

At the same time, and in spite of the many problems the government faced, the replacement of Harold Wilson by James Callaghan as Prime Minister on 5 April 1976 gave a certain new lease of life to Labour. Callaghan tells us[39] that he first heard of Wilson's intention to go from Harold Lever (now Lord Lever of Manchester) over the Christmas holiday of 1975. On the following 11 March the Prime Minister told his Foreign Secretary of his imminent departure: he announced this to a stunned Cabinet on 16 March. At the time, and largely because few politicians and journalists could see Harold Wilson readily yielding up the reins of power, there were rumours about Wilson's health, and even of scandal. There is, however, no serious reason to doubt his own statement that he had long before settled on the date for his retirement, and had early informed the Queen when it would be. His wife had always disliked high political life. He himself was tired of facing again problems he had so often faced before, but this time without a fresh mind.[40] He had achieved considerable satisfaction from his 1974 comeback, and there were no remaining hills of ambition which he aspired to climb. A little later, and after a friendly campaign, Callaghan succeeded him.

The new Prime Minister was a very different kind of man from his predecessor. He was older than Wilson, having been born on 27 March 1912, while Wilson arrived in the world almost exactly four years later. If he had ever had aspirations to the highest office in the land, he had more or less given them up. He had, indeed, been tempted while in Opposition after 1970, by the thought that he might leave politics to run the World Bank. (His wife's lack of enthusiasm for living abroad may have been the decisive factor in his rejecting that temptation.) He had never been a dramatically successful Minister, and had so mishandled Treasury affairs as to be forced to resign as Chancellor upon devaluation of the pound in 1967. Having arrived unexpectedly in No. 10 Downing Street, he set himself to enjoy the job. His bluff personality seemed, at least in the early days, to please voters. Unlike Harold Wilson he had nothing of the gambler in his make-up: it would not be for him to dash to the polls, as Wilson had so disastrously done in 1970. Indeed, he was to put off such a recourse when the signs seemed most favourable to him in the autumn of 1978, and had to be forced into an appeal to the country by vote of the House of Commons the following year. The liking for office and the caution – perhaps it would not be going too far to call it fear – which was instinctive to him made it certain that he would employ strategems of almost any kind to stay where he had found himself.

The personality of the new Prime Minister, the inexperience and uncertainty of the Opposition, and the presence in the House of a number of minority interests all gave Parliament in those days a very special, and exciting, flavour. Ineluctably, however, the Callaghan government lost its majority. By April 1976 a by-election had been lost. Two Scottish Labour Members had defected, because they thought that insufficiently speedy moves were being made to bring about a Scottish Assembly which would grant to Scotland a measure of self-government. And, finally, the Labour MP John Stonehouse, having faked his own death in Florida because of business problems, having been discovered in Australia and having returned to the House, refused the Labour Whip while awaiting trial. The government was in peril.

Now, devolution for Scotland – and, though to a lesser extent, for Wales – had been for some time common ground between the two major Parties. Ulster Unionists of all varieties watched the moves towards devolution on the mainland with intense interest. If Scotland and Wales were to have their own assemblies then, surely, Ulster could not be denied the return of Stormont? This would, of course, be a return of Stormont proper, that is to say an Assembly chosen by the majority of the electorate and not the kind of Assembly forced on the province, however briefly, by Edward Heath and William Whitelaw, one in which Catholics and Protestants should share power, whatever the proportions decreed by the electorate. Powell, of course, was hardly an ardent Stormont man, believing as he did that Ulster should be treated exactly as was every other part of the kingdom. He was not insensible, however, of the nostalgia with which the great majority of Ulster Protestants regarded what had been (at least in all domestic essence) their own Parliament. His basic position in the debates of 1976 and 1977 was that, if Scotland and Wales were to have their own assemblies, then Ulster should have hers. But that was a legalistic and tactical position. At Ballyhill, in Antrim on 26 July 1975 he argued, forcefully and directly, against the idea that it would be a good plan for the people of Northern Ireland to choose the government of Northern Ireland. This was

the most anti-Unionist proposition that could be devised. It is something that no Unionist can say and mean. Those who adopt it and repeat it, whether or not they know what they are doing, are repudiating the Union. Nobody asserts that it is for the people of Kent to decide how Kent shall be governed, or for the Cornish or the Northumbrians or the East Anglians to devise a constitution for Cornwall or Northumbria or East Anglia.

Of the idea that legislative devolution for Ulster would somehow ensure the Union he simply observed, 'Nothing, alas, could be less true.'

He drove the point home (with a certain technical qualification about the possible nature of devolution) at Ballynahinch on the following 19 December:

The United Ulster Unionists have shown themselves wise and farsighted in taking steps to entrench themselves and Ulster against any such danger. From first to last we have made it clear that we neither seek nor will accept devolution in Ulster except in a form and on terms which strengthen instead of weakening Ulster's membership of the UK and which plainly correspond with its status as an integral part of the Kingdom.

On the mainland, however, the devolution debate was moving on. Initially, the Wilson government, although its members foresaw lengthy, and perhaps punishing, debates on the subject ahead, had hoped to be able to rely upon a considerable measure of bipartisan support for the principle of devolved administration for Scotland and Wales. After all, Edward Heath had been an enthusiastic proponent, and none of his senior colleagues had dissented. Certain difficulties, it is true, presented themselves in the case of the Scottish Nationalists. The difficulty for the Nationalists was that they *were* nationalist: to them devolution was merely a step on the way to their ultimate goal. They were uncertain, therefore, on whether they should trade general support for the government's policies in return for early devolution, or whether they should remain aloof, supporting devolution certainly, but picking and choosing among other measures. It was important to the self-esteem of the Nationalists to act as though they had no particular preferences as between the two major (or, as they liked to call them, 'English') Parties. Aloofness was fortified by the happy conviction that the electoral base of the SNP was unshakeable, and likely to be strengthened by time. That this conviction was disastrously misplaced was not to become apparent until the general election of 1979.

What upset all devolutionist calculations was the election of Margaret Thatcher to the leadership of the Conservative Party. It was apparent from the very beginning to those who knew her best that she was set on scuppering the whole notion of devolution. But it was necessary to move cautiously. There were many staunch supporters of the putative Scottish Assembly in her Party, not least among those Scottish Conservatives who had seen their interests steadily decline since the general election of 1955 – the last in which they had won a majority of seats north of the border. To such politicians (and to many others) devolution was a concession necessary to prevent the ultimate breakup of the kingdom. It behoved the new Leader to proceed with care and this she did, never denouncing the principle of devolution, but putting forward endless technical objections to its implementation.

By February 1977 the required legislation was bogged down. Mrs. Thatcher had succeeded in uniting her own supporters. Confidential exchanges took place between her aides and a number of Labour backbenchers hostile to devolution. When the government moved a guillotine motion – to curtail discussion on the devolution Bill – they were defeated. On 17 March Mrs. Thatcher tabled a motion of censure, for debate on 23 March. A government defeat would inevitably result in a general election, which the Prime Minister was reasonably sure would result in a Labour defeat: he had only days to save the government which he headed.

Nor was the devolution defeat Callaghan's only problem. The government whips advised him that he faced another defeat on his public expenditure policy which, in its most important provision, would restrict public sector borrowing to an annual £8.7 billion. The Prime Minister faced – as he had done years previously, when, as Home Secretary, he sought to pilot reform of the House of Lords through the Commons – an alliance of opposites. The left wing of his parliamentary Party objected to the proposals as being excessively draconian. The Tories objected to them as being insufficient, though in the public expenditure vote the government managed to survive because, for various tactical reasons the official Opposition supported them. Since, however, the current public opinion polls showed an average Conservative lead of sixteen per cent,[41] Callaghan decided that he must avoid a general election at almost any cost.

From time to time over the previous few years plans for voting arrangements at least – and occasionally full coalition – between one or more of the minor Parties and the government of the day had been mooted. The most famous – or notorious – of these had been Edward Heath's attempt to entice Jeremy Thorpe into agreement in March 1974.[42] But from that date on there had been a number of stillborn efforts to bring Labour and the Liberals together. Early in 1977 the Liberal MP Cyril Smith had been particularly prominent in the advocacy of an arrangement between his Party and the government. Once the motion of no confidence had been tabled, however, the matter became urgent, and Callaghan was almost certainly right in his judgement that David Steel and the Liberals looked forward to an electoral contest almost as little as he did himself.

410

Callaghan decided to appoint mediators with the various minority interests. Merlyn Rees, a former Northern Ireland Secretary held in some esteem by the Catholic community in Ulster, was detailed to talk to Gerry Fitt of the Northern Ireland Social Democratic and Labour Party. For the Unionists the current Secretary of State, Roy Mason, and the Leader of the House of Commons, Michael Foot, were selected, while the Chairman of the Parliamentary Labour Party, Cledwyn Hughes (now Lord Cledwyn of Penhros) was sent to see David Steel. Much of Sunday 20 March, 1977 was taken up by personal conversations and telephone calls as Ministers strove against time to patch together a political life raft. By Monday the Prime Minister had some grounds for cautious optimism. David Steel had agreed to meet him on that day, in advance of a meeting of the Parliamentary Liberal Party on Tuesday. Foot and Mason, moreover, were able to report that the Ulster Unionist Leader, James Molyneaux, was also amenable to at least exploratory conversation. Molyneaux, however, would be bringing Powell with him.

It says a good deal for Callaghan's shrewdness that he had picked two negotiators with the Ulster Unionists. No Ulster Secretary has ever enjoyed the complete confidence of the Unionist community, but the man attracting the least suspicion, and even a good deal of regard, was Roy Mason. Foot and Powell, it was well known, had a high regard for one another, and Molyneaux and Powell had become exceptionally close. Hughes and Rees were similarly well chosen for their assignments. All in all, and given that there was little Callaghan would not yield to stay in office, the Prime Minister rarely in his long career so justified his reputation as a political manager as during those hectic days.

Negotiations and conversations of various kinds continued until the early hours of Wednesday morning, the day of the censure debate, and the Cabinet was hard put to it to reach agreement in time on the terms agreed with the Liberals and the Unionists. The exchanges between Callaghan and Steel need not concern us here, save to observe that Callaghan had agreed to regular policy consultations between Ministers and Liberal spokesmen on day to day policy; on direct elections to the European Assembly, members having hitherto been appointed; on the re-introduction of proposals for devolution; and on various other measures dear to Liberal hearts. The agreement was to last until the end of the current parliamentary session.

Molyneaux and Powell had a less strong hand to play than Steel. The Liberal Leader could guarantee the united presence of his followers in the government lobby. The Unionist duo, in their final discussions with Callaghan and Foot, could offer no larger prize than a handful of abstentions. The difficulty the two men faced – and were to continue to face for the next two years – was that, for all the disillusion of Unionists with their erstwhile Conservative friends, they remained deeply reluctant to sustain a Labour government. There were various reasons for this reluctance, but two are worth particular mention. The various Unionist parties had an instinctive feeling for Conservatism, and always hoped, whatever the evidence, that the Tories would return to their fold: this feeling was assiduously and skilfully cultivated by the Opposition spokesman on Ulster, Mrs. Thatcher's friend and former campaign manager, Airey Neave. Secondly, they knew how strongly sentiment in favour of a united Ireland ran within Labour ranks: indeed, Harold Wilson, while assuring the Northern Ireland majority that they would not be forced into the Republic, had none the less declared that the creation of a thirty-two county republic was an aim of Labour policy which could be achieved within fifteen years.[43] These considerations made it difficult for Powell and Molyneaux to persuade their colleagues that it would be advantageous to the province to act to preserve the Callaghan administration.

The Prime Minister did not see the preservation of the Union and the interests of Northern Ireland in quite the same high-minded and fervent way as Powell did. 'Whatever the state of United Kingdom politics,' he wrote later,[44] 'the first priority of Northern Ireland's Members is Northern Ireland.' In return for their support the two Unionists wanted, first, an undertaking from the government to use its best efforts to secure an increase in the number of Westminster seats in Ulster and, second, a return of local government to the area. Callaghan had little difficulty in acceding to the first request (which would be followed through by means of an all-party committee chaired by the Speaker of the House of Commons). As to the second, Callaghan now contends that he was willing to consider proposals, while giving fair warning that he would pay the closest attention to the wishes of the minority Roman Catholic community. Molyneaux and Powell, however, have no recollection of this qualification. Callaghan had not expected to meet opposition to his undertaking to consider the matter of local government from the Secretary of State for that province. On the day after the vote, however, Roy Mason, supported by his civil servants, imposed what amounted to a veto on the Prime Minister's second promise to Molyneaux and Powell. He was still willing to extend to them the same kind of consultative facilities he was to offer to the Liberals. But the Unionists had no desire to enter into over-close relations with the government.

Events were to show that future consultation, especially between Powell and Foot, was to serve the interests of both sides well, but the fragile nature of Northern Ireland politics prevented as formal an arrangement as that between the government and the Liberals. Callaghan now went ahead with a Cabinet meeting. He argued that there was no time for a full meeting of the Parliamentary Party and, in truth, he was greatly relieved by that fact. As it was, forty-eight Labour backbenchers signed a motion which, while stating their willingness to support the government on the issue of confidence, also expressed a refusal to be bound by the agreement on a day-to-day basis.

Callaghan was still not out of the woods. Both the Scottish and the Welsh Nationalists, enjoying the misplaced confidence they had in their own appeal, proved deaf to Labour temptation. On the Conservative side there was not only anger at what seemed to them to be an entirely unscrupulous bargain, but there was concern and division as well. Not all of Mrs. Thatcher's colleagues – and particularly not her Deputy Leader, William Whitelaw – were happy with her appetite for constant confrontation. Her Private Office, however, consulted a number of historians. The advice that they wanted to hear was that there were historical precedents for a government in so parlous a position (and which had already, whatever the vote, lost the confidence of Parliament) resigning. This, however, was an argument which it was impossible to place on a sound historical basis and, frustrated by the lack of enthusiasm of her colleagues for her tactics, Mrs. Thatcher fell back on her own redoubtable spirit. 'I will,' she said on Wednesday morning when caution was advised, 'go on banging on that door until it falls down.' It was two years before she got her wish.

The debate was a heated and ill-tempered affair. Many in the Labour Party were unhappy. In particular, the Tribune group of Labour backbenchers, eighty in number, bitterly resented the fact that David Steel and his Liberals were to enjoy ministerial access denied to them. The Unionists were under pressure from home, a pressure particularly expressed by Harry West, to seek nothing but devolution. The Scots (including the two members of the breakaway Scottish Labour Party) and the Welsh wanted an election. And the Conservatives, of course, were furious, seeing themselves as baulked by chicanery, and deprived of a general election they were confident of winning. When the vote was taken, however, the government survived comfortably. Three Ulster Unionists abstained. The two Irish Nationalist Members and the Liberals went placidly into the government lobby. The Callaghan administration lived on, thanks to a majority of twenty-four, 322. votes to 298. One consequence of the size of that majority was that, despite the Leader of the Opposition's determination to carry war into the government's camp on all possible occasions, many Conservatives found their doubts about attempts to carry motions of no confidence greatly strengthened. For Powell and his fellow-Unionists, however – as for the Liberals – a period of some stability was to hand, and opportunities to influence government readily available.

It has been necessary to go into such detail about the developing situation in Westminster in order to explain the general context in which the fight of Powell – and others – for the survival of Ulster as a part of the United Kingdom was carried on. But, of course, as first Wilson, and then, more grimly and more desperately, Callaghan, fought to stay in office, the internal struggle in Ulster continued. Something has already been said[45] about the tangled quarrels of the province. But this may be put as a general view in the following way.

Following the agitation over a supposed lack of civil rights which began in 1968, the old and governing Unionist Party began to break up. In part this was because of internal contradictions; in part it was because – with the re-emergence of the IRA in the wake of street agitation – successive British governments pressed upon Official Unionism (that is, the old governing party and its successors in direct line) changes in the way the province was run which they conceived to be necessary or inevitable and which, at any rate, they believed would appease agitation and terrorism. In particular, successive governments constantly insisted that some share in power had to be conceded to the Catholic minority, in an institutional form. This, in principle, Powell constantly resisted. While he was consistent, Paisley indulged in tactical prevarications, being a believer in the treatment of Ulster exactly in the same way as every other part of the United Kingdom was treated until 1976. One of the more extraordinary things about Paisley's changes of front is that he had little to say for a restoration of Stormont before 1976; and everything to say for devolution thereafterwards.

One of Paisley's more staggering reversals has already been

noted.[46] The DUP sometimes worked closely with, and sometimes denounced, the Official Unionists. This party – effectively, Ian Paisley's fief – had grown from the roots provided by his Free Presbyterian Church and there is ample evidence[47] that, from the early days of his successful campaign against Terence O'Neill, Paisley saw it as an instrument by which he could take over the leadership of the whole Unionist movement. The difficulty was that he has never been able to preserve his populist base save from a position of intransigence. There are many examples of his reversals of policy, invariably under the pressure of the evident concern of his followers. Thus, on 30 October 1971 he issued a warning that the suspension of Stormont and the imposition of direct rule was not likely to be long delayed. His criticism of direct rule, however, was feeble by his rhetorical standards, and it seemed likely that he was perfectly ready to negotiate with a British government, were such negotiation to be to his advantage. The rank and file of his party were unhappy with this and, immediately, Paisley began to attack the idea of integration with the United Kingdom and became clamant in his demands for a return to the Stormont system. Again, in November 1979, the new Conservative Secretary of State for Northern Ireland, Humphrey Atkins, suggested a constitutional conference on Ulster. Having heard that the Official Unionists, in the person of James Molyneaux, were not willing to participate, on the grounds that the constitution was not in question, Paisley immediately accepted Atkins' invitation. He prolonged talks until the following spring and, as abruptly, abandoned them.

Powell's difficulties with Paisley were greater than any difficulties he had with colleagues in his own Party; and they were greater than even those colleagues had with the Leader of the Democratic Unionists. In my judgement he failed at the beginning of his time in Ulster to appreciate what a committed tactician Paisley was. When he did see it, he was readier than any other Ulster politician to denounce it. Powell did not, perhaps, apply always nor sufficiently to Paisley his own acute perception of the man's performance in the House of Commons. Paisley had begun his Westminster career by treating the Chamber as he would a revivalist meeting. Within a very short space of time after his 1970 election he had – without forsaking his style – adjusted somewhat his manner to the demands of Westminster. 'He is a person,' said Powell, 'who is very responsive to atmosphere and environment and he quite quickly picked up the vibrations of the House of Commons and learned to handle it.'

That was shrewd. It was obviously necessary for Unionists of all stripes – other than the para-military organizations with which Paisley from time to time flirted – to come together as often as they could. At one time in the early 1970s there had been a third element in Unionist politics, the Vanguard movement, led by William Craig. Craig, having set out to be more determined, even, than Paisley, suddenly decided, in May 1975, to offer, to a Unionist movement all strands of which were, for the moment, together in the United Ulster Unionist Council, a proposal for coalition – what he called a 'voluntary coalition', meaning one not made under pressure from London, with the Social Democratic and Labour Party, the inheritors, under a clever Leader, John Hume, of the banner of the old Nationalist Party, led for many years by Eddie McAteer, in futile opposition to Unionism. McAteer had been content to complain gently, and draw his Stormont salary. Hume wanted to move matters along. Craig believed that Vanguard and the DUP were in complete agreement about what should be done. At the time an Ulster constitutional Convention – in which all parties were represented – was sitting. The United Ulster Unionist Council – West's party, Paisley's party and Craig's party – were supposed to be in agreement in their resistance to the nationalist pretensions of Hume's Social Democratic and Labour Party. Craig suggested to Paisley that, in spite of the fact that the groups in the Convention seemed to be totally opposed, an agreement could be made which would produce a coalition (with the SDLP) which would govern Ulster; that coalition would also be able to make what Craig called 'a gentleman's agreement' with the government of the Irish Republic. Paisley encouraged Craig in these proposals. However, in June 1975 all the members of the UUUC met. Those at the meeting included MPs who were not elected members of the Convention, most important among whom was Powell.

Powell spoke with power and effect against the Paisley-Craig alliance. A vote was taken. Craig found that he was in a minority of one. Paisley suddenly discovered or – as a cynical observer might suggest – decided that, since he could not win with Craig, he would be better off denouncing that unfortunate man.

The Vanguard movement passed into dissolution. But – and this was the dangerous side of the matter for scrupulous Unionists like James Molyneaux and Enoch Powell – many, perhaps most, of his erstwhile supporters went over to Paisley.

Powell thinks that the seepage of support from Vanguard to the DUP has been over-rated. So far as the House of Commons was concerned, one Vanguard Member, Robert Bradford, a clergyman, joined Molyneaux. Another, John Dunlop, remained an independent Member. Furthermore, Powell believes that the majority of Vanguard voters thereafter supported Molyneaux rather than Paisley. Those from Vanguard who subsequently committed themselves to Paisley were, in Powell's opinion, members of the Free Presbyterian Church.

For the next year, however, Paisley supported the cause of union; and Powell was generous – perhaps over-generous – in describing his part in the scheme of things. On 16 September 1976, at Banbridge, County Down, he said:

> The coalition in Parliament today thus consists, under the leadership of Jim Molyneaux, of six Ulster Unionists, Dr. Paisley as leader of the DUP, and John Dunlop[48] who acts – and I may respectfully add, most effectively – in all respects as a member of the coalition team. I take this opportunity to place on record, for the benefit of some, particularly on the mainland, who apparently like to imagine otherwise, that, notwithstanding all the other cares and responsibilities which he has had to shoulder, no one could have a more cordial and co-operative member of the team than Dr. Paisley. From no colleague have I personally received greater courtesy and friendliness.

Events forced him to change his mind. Before the February 1974 general election the government headed by Edward Heath had set up, under the aegis of William Whitelaw, but with the support of Brian Faulkner, the then Unionist leader, an executive for the governance of Northern Ireland in which Unionists and Nationalists shared power. The election proved that the executive commanded little confidence. It was destroyed by a strike in Ulster less than a year later. That strike was massive, ordered, certain and civilized. In the face of it, Brian Faulkner resigned.

It was, however, regarded by many as a Paisleyite triumph. It tempted Paisley to go somewhat further when, in 1977, being out of countenance with the policy of the government – and certainly encouraged by suggestions from civil servants in the Northern Ireland Office to luxuriate in his own power – he decided to call another strike in the hope, perhaps, of repeating the trick, but with no clear end in sight. Many honest Unionists feared his energy. They also feared his supporters. He had, more than once, threatened Powell that he would put up a DUP candidate in South Down and thus, by splitting the Unionist vote, deprive Powell of his seat.

None the less, without hesitation Powell took Paisley on, Paisley having suggested that strike supporters would be justified in – or, at least excused for culpability in – acts of intimidation during the new strike. Powell thought there would be economic penalties for the strike, and to no good end, but that this was less important than such willingness to break the law as had been suggested. This willingness

> attaches to the act of criminal responsibility perpetrated against this province by a small knot of men whose true support and influence has proved to be derisory. That price, that penalty, will have to be paid; and inevitably the brunt will fall on the innocent majority.

The 1977 strike collapsed. It would be going far too far to say that Powell had a significant influence on that collapse, though there is no doubt that he had some. He came to the people of Ulster as an Englishman, albeit a friendly one, and he set out to explain to them not merely what he would give them but what he expected of them. To his constituents on 19 April 1975 he put the matter geographically; but also with political point:

> Actively and conscientiously though I seek to serve the 95,000 electors scattered over South Down's 900 square miles, I feel on their behalf a burning resentment when I think that if they lived in a similar part of Wales or Scotland or even England, there would be two Parliamentary representatives instead of one to serve such a population and area.

It was not, as we have seen, possible for Powell and Molyneaux to achieve all that they had desired from their agreement with the Callaghan Cabinet. Nor did the two men want the kind of consultative alliance with the government which gave the Liberals such enjoyment and, even, pride. The principle of increased (or, more accurately, equal) representation for Northern Ireland at Westminster having been conceded, the next objective was the normalization of local government in the province, an aim which was readily represented by such as

Paisley as a demand for devolved government, along the lines of the old Stormont. By the middle of 1980 a great part of political opinion in Northern Ireland believed that there would be a new Stormont in the province with Paisley at its head. It will be necessary to return, in the next chapter, to the convoluted politics of the different Unionist groups in Ulster, since the positions in which they found themselves, in relation to each other as well as in relation to the government of the day in London, determined their potential during what, after 1979, was to become called the Thatcher era. It is worth emphasizing here, however, how much Paisley's conduct of policy over the whole of his political career, but perhaps especially from 1977 onwards, was at variance with his rhetorical image of an unbending political and religious patriarch. In Powell's judgement (and I believe him to be correct) the single most important constant in Paisleyism is the determination to protect and ferociously to guard Protestantism and, in particular, his variety of Protestantism. 'If Unionism,' said Powell, 'served that purpose, then he would be a Unionist. But, if other means could be found that would serve as well, or better, then the other means would be adopted.'

This may seem to be an extravagant, or wilful, judgement to make on a man who, at every opportunity, has sought to draw the mantle of Edward Carson around his shoulders. But his willingness to conceive, albeit in unlikely circumstances, of some kind of agreement with Dublin has already been noted.[49] In the early life of the first Thatcher administration, he went some way towards persuading Humphrey Atkins that he was a man the Secretary of State could work with. The true explanation of his vacillations – his advances towards compromise usually followed by swift retreats – lies in the fact that, so far as politics pure and simple were concerned, he saw himself from 1969 onwards as the replacement for traditional Unionism: any arrangements with such as Orr, West, Craig or Molyneaux were conceived of as expedients requiring only a brief allegiance: the goal was not merely devolved power for Ulster, but devolved power for Paisley. On the other hand, loyal as his cohorts in the Free Presbyterian Church and the Democratic Unionist Party might be to him, and readily though they might almost invariably accept his right to lay down the law to them, there were points beyond which they could not be pushed. In some respects, for all that he frequently destroyed lieutenants who showed talent or independence, for all that his hand lay heavily on every section of DUP and Free Presbyterian administration, he was to some extent a prisoner of the loyalty readily and fervently accorded him. Any doubt or uncertainty about what he was doing was a potential canker, for his whole style of leadership depended on unwavering constancy and confidence in him among his followers; and they wanted no truck with deals such as Paisley may, at any given moment, be willing to contemplate. It was the tension between what he might have done had he been really free, and what his own image required of him that made it so difficult for politicians such as Powell and Molyneaux to deal with him.

While more or less subtle battles were being fought out in the ranks of Ulster politicians, however, the agreement of 1977, encouraging though it was to Ministers, can be seen in retrospect as the beginning of the end for the Callaghan government. Certainly, under the Lib-Lab pact, as it was called, the minority Party believed itself to enjoy at least influence, if not power, and Liberal Members preened themselves at every opportunity on the fact that they now enjoyed regular contacts with Ministers. But the truth of the matter is that Callaghan's single concession to the Unionists was of far greater importance than anything offered in the way of cosy get-togethers with the Liberals. The Unionists got, and had implemented for the general election of 1983, the one really big prize they sought. That for which the Liberals yearned – a commitment to, or at least a serious investigation of, proportional representation – was neither proffered nor seriously considered. So far as economic policy and devolution for Scotland and Wales were concerned there is no evidence that any Liberal pressure forced Callaghan in any direction in which he did not want to go. The Liberals served their purpose until the beginning of the parliamentary session of 1978-9 at which point, expecting an imminent general election, they withdrew from the pact, to the undisguised relief of many Labour politicians.

The government foundered on two major issues, devolution and the conduct of economic policy. The Prime Minister kept his pledge to introduce legislation providing for referenda on the devolution question in England and Wales but, as a result of an amendment moved by the Labour MP George Cunningham, it was enacted that unless at least forty per cent of the *total* electorate of Scotland supported the creation of a Scottish Assembly, the Act would fall. He had a majority of fifteen, and, in due course, on 1 March 1979, the proponents of devolution failed to rally the required number. From that moment on the SNP, still confident of their own electoral appeal, were determined to bring down the government. Callaghan by now realized that that appeal was far weaker than the SNP imagined, and he was to describe them in the debate which ended his term as Prime Minister as turkeys voting for an early Christmas.

In the economic field it was Callaghan's determination from the beginning to curb inflation by means of an incomes policy to be run, if possible, by agreement with the trade unions but, if that agreement could not be obtained, imposed from above. The fact of the matter was, until the winter of 1978-9, that the Prime Minister believed he could talk down inflation by persuading businessmen and trade unionists alike to respond favourably to the agreeable side of his personality. He had not yet learned the lesson of the experience of two Prime Ministers – Harold Macmillan and Harold Wilson – who had, in their time, believed they enjoyed similar magic. It would be tedious, and unnecessary for the purposes of this book, to discuss the ups and downs of his efforts. The crucial thing was that in the famous (or notorious) winter of discontent large numbers of workers took industrial action against restrictive economic policies which, to some extent, had been forced on the government by the demands of the International Monetary Fund. Many of the strikes and incidents of industrial coercion were in particularly sensitive fields, and notably in hospitals. Such credit as the government had gained for some modest improvements in the economy and through the Prime Minister's public exercise of a certain bluff and avuncular charm quickly evaporated. The stage was set for an election.

The autumn of 1978 was probably the last moment when Callaghan was happy in his exalted office. He tells us[50] that many of his colleagues, and particularly the Chancellor of the Exchequer, Denis Healey, seeing a series of favourable opinion polls at that time, urged him to go to the country. He resisted them, privately explaining his preference for the following spring. He did not, however, act to dampen down public expectation, thinking it wise to keep the Opposition at full and expensive stretch, and in a state of uncertainty about his intentions. When at the TUC conference in September, however, he announced that there would not be an early resort to the polls his audience – and the country – was astonished. From then on his authority deteriorated.

So, to some extent at any rate, did his determination. Once the referenda were over he knew that the SNP would take an opportunity to turn him out. Michael Foot proposed a manoeuvre. The failure to achieve the required plurality in Scotland

" We've found him ! After all these years he's still alive ! "

required the Secretary of State to lay before Parliament an Order repealing the devolution legislation. Why not, suggested Foot, persuade the House to vote the order down, whereupon devolution could proceed. Ten years earlier Callaghan, when Home Secretary, had used a similar device to avoid implementing a revision of constituency boundaries recommended by the Boundaries' Commission on the grounds that it was thought to favour the Conservatives, but by 1979 he no longer had the heart for Machiavellian tactics. When the SNP tabled a motion of no confidence in the government, he left it to Foot to try to put together yet another life-saving majority.

Powell believes that Callaghan did not really want to win the vote. 'If ever,' he commented, 'I've seen a man who wanted out he was that man.' Whatever the result, it was certain to be close. Foot strained every nerve, and Merlyn Rees was again to be seen in earnest conversation with Gerry Fitt. Powell personally was inclined to come to the government's rescue, his unfalteringly logical position being that the Unionists would enjoy the best chance of making headway with a minority government in office. In the excitement of the moment, while many politicians had forgotten the matter, Powell's mind remained fixed on the possibility that the legislation ordaining an increase in the number of parliamentary seats for Ulster would not, in the event of an early general election, receive the Royal Assent. That had been a constant preoccupation of his from 1977 onwards. Due to the honourable behaviour of the Labour Whip with particular responsibility for government business, Walter Harrison, the required Bill went successfully through all its stages.

In the critical moment in 1979, however, Molyneaux and Powell required something in return for their votes. At the time discussion was proceeding on the provision of gas to Northern Ireland. One plan was to lay a pipeline from Dublin, a proposal which Powell believed to be impracticable (as events proved it was) and also politically undesirable. The other was to lay a line from the mainland, which the Unionists naturally supported. Callaghan, however, vetoed Foot's proposal to accede to their request, and another tranche of votes was lined up against the Prime Minister.

The debate was set for 28 March 1979. The House was crammed, and manoeuvring went on until almost the last moment. Foot told Gwynfor Evans, the single Welsh Nationalist, that means had been found to speed up the payment of funds to Welsh miners suffering from pneumoconiosis. Evans replied that his vote was still against the government. Strenuous and successful efforts were made to bring to London Frank Maguire, the Irish Nationalist Member for Fermanagh and South Tyrone, who rarely put in an appearance there and who was regarded as notoriously unreliable. He arrived with his wife, who went into the public gallery, while her husband was entertained by Labour Whips. The part of the debate which she heard included Gerry Fitt's denunciation of the government for increasing the number of seats in Ulster, to the advantage of Unionism. She immediately left, told her husband that he could not possibly support a government so evidently basically pro-Unionist, and the pair promptly departed for home. When the vote was announced at 10.18 p.m. it was seen that the motion of no confidence had been carried by one vote – 311 to 310. Of course, any number of things could have turned out differently during the day; but it is pleasing to those interested in the minutiae of history to think that Marie Maguire's decision to pay her first ever visit to the public gallery of the House of Commons resulted in the bringing down of a government.

This was the first time since 1924 that a government had lost a vote of confidence. Callaghan immediately sought a dissolution from the Queen. On 3 May Margaret Thatcher and the Conservatives returned to power with an overall majority in excess of forty. In Down South Enoch Powell, having won by a bare majority in October 1974, was returned with a majority in excess of 8,000. But the pivotal Unionist position at Westminster had been lost and Powell and his colleagues took their seats infected, naturally, by the same curiosity as everybody else about what the inexperienced woman at the head of the new government would bring.

9

The Philosopher
1979-

All political lives, unless they are cut off in midstream
at a happy juncture, end in failure, because that is the
nature of politics and of human affairs.
  – *J. Enoch Powell,* Joseph Chamberlain *(London, 1977).*

The victory of Mrs. Thatcher – which heralded three (to date)
reforming Parliaments in which she increasingly became the
dominant figure – was greeted by curiosity, certainly, but also
by a strange mixture of hope, cynicism, and trepidation.[1] The
hopefuls were those who believed that she might, through the
force of her ideas and character, begin the reversal of the nation's
long decline. The cynical (many of them among her colleagues)
believed that reversal was impossible and, moreover, that the
economic policies she proposed to implement had already been
tried under Edward Heath, and had been proven not to work.
Those who viewed her with trepidation were those in the centre
and the centre-left of politics: they feared that she would do
what she said she would, and what their reading of her character
suggested she would like to do, and that the consequence would
be that the liberal, social and political consensus that had been
building since the 1950s, and particularly the 1960s, would be
shattered. In the event, only the cynics were proved wrong.

The new Prime Minister's resilience, will and energy were,
indeed, to be the crucial elements in the years of change that
lay ahead. Without her, it seems fair to say, nothing like the
dramatic changes in the internal polity of the United Kingdom,
and the changes in the country's standing in the world, would have

occurred. But she also enjoyed very considerable good fortune.

For some time the left wing of the Labour Party had been waxing in strength, in part at least because of the perceived failure, from a Socialist point of view, of the Wilson and Callaghan governments.[2] The increasing march of the left towards dominance led to the departure from Labour of a substantial number of centrist MPs, councillors and party activists, led by four former senior Ministers, Roy Jenkins (newly returned from his post as President of the European Commission in Brussels), David Owen, Shirley Williams, and William Rodgers. The dissidents formed, on 26 March 1980, the Social Democrat Party, which promptly entered into an alliance with the Liberals which lasted until after the general election of 1987. This haemorrhage was of material advantage to the Conservatives in the difficult years ahead.

Mrs. Thatcher was determined to curb the power of the trade union movement. She was strongly advised against over-radical measures in this direction by a number of her colleagues, but especially by her first Secretary of State for Employment, James Prior, the argument here being, as on so many other matters, that the Heath government had tried to do this and had failed. However, aided by the steadily increasing unemployment which was in some large degree caused by her stringent economic measures, and by the general unpopularity of unions, she chipped steadily away at the unions over a number of years, reducing their power almost to vanishing point. There was a protracted, and often bloody, coal miners' strike from which she emerged victorious, thus greatly sharpening the national perception of her as the strong leader for which the nation had been waiting. The struggle with the unions brought an added bonus: Labour simply could not, and would not, free itself from its trade union entanglements. The unions had, after all, founded the Party. They financed the Party. They were constitutionally entrenched in the party at all levels. And when, shortly after the election of Michael Foot to replace James Callaghan as Leader, the Labour Party changed its method of choosing a leader, the unions were given a massive say. The unpopularity of the unions therefore necessarily rubbed off on Labour; and this was another plus for the Prime Minister.

Finally, there was the choice of Foot as successor to Callaghan in October 1980. The choice was seen then, and can be even more clearly seen now, as one dictated almost purely by internal Party settlement. Foot was an old Labour war-horse. He was almost universally beloved. And his wife wanted him to make an attempt on the top job. But he was a disastrous choice. He was inconceivable as a Prime Minister and most of his policies – particularly his advocacy of unilateral nuclear disarmament – were anathema to the public. Further, the massive Conservative plurality (of 142) in the general election of 1983 was to some extent the result of the victorious war fought for the Falkland Islands the previous year. Contrary to some opinion, I do not believe that the war was the essential cause of the Conservative triumph in 1983; but it undoubtedly contributed to the size of the majority.[3]

The new Prime Minister, therefore, had plenty on her side at the outset of what she herself called her 'great adventure'. She had a stable majority, and faced a divided Opposition. She had worked out carefully what she planned to do, and was possessed of almost incredible self-belief (as well as phenomenal energy) in doing it. And, as mentioned earlier, she had priceless good fortune on a number of occasions. It is related of Napoleon, on an occasion when the merits of a particularly gallant officer were being laid out before him with a view to securing the man's promotion, that the Emperor interrupted to say, 'Yes. But is he lucky?' A politician can, by intelligence, industry and determination only do so much: luck is indispensable as well. Margaret Thatcher, finally, showed herself, to the surprise of many, to possess another gift wholly unexpected in one of so little experience (she had, after all, held only one fairly junior Cabinet post). She quickly developed an adroitness in political tactics which has almost invariably served her well.

As she made her first dispositions in office there was, however, one gaping hole in her armoury. On 30 March 1979 the head of her Private Office, and Shadow Secretary of State for Northern Ireland, Airey Neave, had been murdered – a bomb attached to the underside of his car exploded on the ramp as he was driving out of the House of Commons car park – by the Irish National Liberation Army, a small body in competition with the IRA. Neave was closer to Mrs. Thatcher than any other man except her husband. She trusted implicitly in his judgement, and deeply valued his friendship. He had, towards the end of 1974, offered himself as her campaign manager in the leadership battle. This was the beginning of their deep alliance, though they had known one another for many years – since, indeed, she had been a junior barrister in his chambers. He was a superbly efficient and effective manager and when, the battle with Heath being over, it was clear that he could have any job he wanted in the Shadow administration, provided it kept him close to her, he specifically asked for the Northern Ireland portfolio, and agreed in addition to run the Private Office. The request for Northern Ireland surprised her (who knew little or nothing of Ulster) for she had expected him to request either Home Affairs or Defence. It emerged, however, that Neave had a long-standing and close interest in the province. On one occasion during the years in opposition a number of friends quizzed him on his personal ambitions should there, eventually, be a Thatcher government. He stated, roundly and simply, that he wanted nothing more than to be Secretary of State for Northern Ireland.

It is fruitless, now, to speculate what kind of Secretary of State Neave would have been, or what particular line of policy he would have adopted. Certainly, he cultivated a relationship amounting almost to personal friendship with Gerry Fitt, in consequence of which Fitt's eulogy in the House on the morrow of his death was one of the most deeply felt and obviously sincere. But Neave – who invariably played his cards very close to his chest – also went out of his way to cultivate the Unionists. I saw him most days of the week for four years, and he repeatedly declared during that time that it was a principal aim of his to bring forward the day when the Official Ulster Unionists would again take the Conservative Whip in the House of Commons. Neave was no day dreamer, and he fully realized how far the Conservative government would have to go back, not merely on so-called initiatives undertaken by Labour governments to bring about a settlement in the province, but on Tory initiatives as well. Neave was determined, and knew what he wanted. It cannot be denied that his murder came at a most convenient moment for those who wished to break the union between Great Britain and Northern Ireland.

His murder left a great gap. Much to the surprise of her entourage the Prime Minister chose in his stead Humphrey Atkins, a polished, suave and humorous man who had been Whip of one kind or another since 1967. In that year he had first joined the Whip's Office. He became Deputy Chief Whip in 1970 and Chief Whip in 1973, continuing in that post until the election victory of 1979. He had never held departmental responsibilities at any time in his career, and was thus quite unprepared for the sheer administrative rigours of the Northern Ireland Office. It may have been thought that, given his long service as a Whip, he would be able – like William Whitelaw before him – to bring to Ulster a talent for negotiation, compromise and consensus which the great majority of English politicians believed was the only way of achieving what was euphemistically called a settlement. In the event he proved to be a disastrous choice, a puppet in the hands of his civil servants, and quite incapable, with his essentially amiable disposition, of coming to grips with the tides of feeling that mounted so strongly in Northern Ireland. A similar judgement was made on him as was made on James Prior, who succeeded him in 1981. It was said that, by sending so inexperienced a Minister to Belfast, Mrs. Thatcher was signalling that Ulster was low on her list of priorities. Likewise, when Prior, up to that date Secretary of State for Employment and moving, for the Prime Minister's taste, far too slowly on trade union reform, was given the choice of taking Northern Ireland or leaving government altogether, it was justly and angrily felt that she was taking the opportunity of sending a potentially awkward colleague to the British equivalent of a Siberian power station.

The appointment of the evidently inadequate Atkins was not, however, the sole difficulty the Unionists faced in the new Parliament, significant though the evidence was that the Cabinet was not over-exercised about the province. As Powell had correctly foreseen would be the case, the Unionist Parties were sidelined in the new Parliament. As long as a minority government had held office, even though they had declined to enter into close day to day relations with that government along the lines of the Liberals, the Unionists had ministerial eyes constantly upon them. So difficult and even parlous a situation dictated that the government of the day had always closely to monitor the feelings, ambitions, and even prejudices of the minority parties. Access to Ministers was relatively easy, and Powell and Foot in particular enjoyed excellent personal relations. Moreover, the Prime Minister himself had once (as Home Secretary) been in overall charge of Ulster, and had even written a book on the subject.[4] He did not greatly differ from the consensus of English politicians in other parties to the effect that the only way forward was through some kind of political agreement between opposing political forces in the province – the never-ending dream of reconciliation between people with diametrically opposed objectives – and occasionally let himself fancy that one day there would be, by agreement, a united Ireland. But at least he knew something of the subject; he was interested in it; and, as an old-fashioned Labour man of conservative tendencies from whose lips the word 'Socialism' came with a certain difficulty, he had a good deal of sympathy with the forces trying to impose law and order: after all, he had been parliamentary spokesman for the Police Federation for many years.

Quite apart, therefore, from the tight parliamentary situation, there was a degree of mutual understanding and fellow feeling between Labour Ministers and the Unionists: it would be wrong to make too much of it; but it was there; and it could not readily be replaced, after Neave's death, by any kind of understanding with the new men. The best, for the moment, that Powell and Molyneaux could do (and this applied to Paisley as well) was to hold a watching brief, see what the new government would do, and act accordingly.

So far as Powell himself was concerned the biographer can only note, sadly, that he had entered the final phase of his distinguished parliamentary career. His intellect was undimmed. His energy was as fierce as ever. His appetite for work was as keen as ever it had been: later, for example, I will discuss an important new project he had embarked upon in 1975, a biography of the nineteenth century Liberal Unionist, Joseph Chamberlain. But, whereas from October 1974 to May 1979 his parliamentary and political skills had been of the greatest possible practical use to his colleagues, in a Parliament where the government of the day had a clear majority – one which it was massively to increase in the last Parliament in which he was to serve – these skills were of less moment. His final intimate contact with the great issues of the day came in 1982, during the Falklands War. The Prime Minister having indicated that she was willing to provide confidential information to, and take counsel from, senior representatives, and preferably the leaders, of the Opposition parties, Molyneaux nominated Powell in his own place. Michael Foot declined to take part in the exercise.

It must be remembered, of course, that from that moment in October 1974 when he returned to Westminster as a Unionist MP Powell regarded Ulster as the most important by far – and sometimes the only one – of his charges. He did not cease to comment, usually astringently, on all aspects of policy. Nor did he slacken his attacks on membership of the EEC, though his cause in that area looked increasingly forlorn. But the prosperity and integrity of Ulster was, in his judgement, as much affected by EEC membership as was that of the rest of the kingdom. Indeed, given his views on Unionism, he could be expected invariably to insist that the matter of membership was as consequential in Belfast as it was in London, and he frequently spoke on relations with the Community to Northern Irish audiences. None the less, in ever-increasing measure, Ulster dominated his thoughts.

Before he became formally a Unionist he had, as we have seen,[5] taken a close interest in the fortunes of the province in Parliament and, generally, followed the line Unionist members took in debate and vote, even telling Lawrence Orr on one occasion, 'You are my leader.' The same loyalty he gave to James Molyneaux, all the more unstintingly in that he had a high regard for Molyneaux, far higher than any he had ever had for West, whom he always privately distrusted. A former Tory Minister, a stern critic of Powell, observing his conduct towards Molyneaux, once bitterly observed, 'I wish he'd given that kind of devotion to his old party.' What this man missed, of course, was the fact that Molyneaux and Powell were in total and unforced agreement on the matters which most vitally concerned them. This agreement, moreover, was in place before Powell joined the Unionist Party. It was the product of months and years of discussion and common action. It was not something that had to be hammered out, with possible cavils and qualifications, after Powell was returned for Down South. The indispensable basis of mutual trust had been established before their formal parliamentary alliance came into being. Thus, in the years from Molyneaux's assumption of leadership there were, quite simply, no grounds of principle on which the two men could disagree; and where there were differences over tactics, Powell was content to follow Molyneaux though, of course, and wisely, Molyneaux depended a great deal on Powell's advice. He has made no secret of the fact that his sense of loss since Powell's defeat in South Down is considerable.

Of course, it was not merely Powell's total and unwavering commitment to the Union that made him attractive to Molyneaux and other like-minded colleagues. There was also, as Molyneaux never ceased to emphasize, his quality as a parliamentarian. Powell constantly used his repute in this regard to drive home, not merely to his colleagues, but to the electorate of Ulster, the necessity of always behaving as part of the United Kingdom. Above all, he feared the potential ghetto mentality in the province, and even its extension to Ulster Members of Parliament who, historically, had played little enough part in the discussion of great national issues. He spelt out, in crystal clear detail, the duties that would fall on Unionist Members in the 1979 Parliament in a speech in Rathfriland on 16 February 1979. They had, he said, to look forward not merely to the coming Parliament, but to the one after

that, when Ulster would have seventeen or eighteen members of whom thirteen or fourteen would be Unionists. He warned his audience that the influence they had enjoyed in the hung Parliament just dissolved might well not continue. Thus:

> It is only fair to the electors of Ulster to tell them that Ulster's influence and future depends on their returning to the next House of Commons from every Unionist-held constituency a single phalanx of united and dedicated members of one party.

This was an appeal for the rejection of Paisley and the DUP and the return of Unionists only from his own Party. But there was more to the argument than that:

> The Ulster electorate must also understand that the next Parliament will place more rigorous demands than any previous Parliament upon the Ulster Unionist Members, especially if, as I believe we can be and hope we shall be, the third party in the House of Commons. Absenteeism would be disastrous. There would be no room for half-timers. From Monday to Thursday inclusively, Whip or no Whip, the place of a member of the third party is in the House of Commons. All subjects of government have to be covered; committees have to be manned; a presence in every debate in the Chamber has to be maintained. Remember: there is no pairing. Pairing, which you read and hear about, is between the two main parties only. For others there is no pairing – only physical presence. When numbers are so small, ineffectives cannot be carried; everybody has to pull his weight. Whatever a Member needs to do personally in his constituency or elsewhere in the country must be done either on Fridays (not all Fridays, however) and Saturdays or else when Parliament is in recess.

It was a demanding programme, and not at all one to which Ulster Members had been traditionally accustomed. It was also, implicitly, another hit against Paisley, who was notorious for his often lengthy absences from the Chamber.

Before Powell Ulster Unionism, in whatever form, had been a parochial creed. The very existence of Stormont, quite apart from the social constitution of Ulster, had encouraged parochialism. And when Stormont was suspended in 1972 the Unionists,

433

perceiving the threat to their status within the United Kingdom, naturally concentrated all the energies they expended at Westminster on their own affairs. It was vital to the Powell philosophy that Ulstermen and their parliamentary representatives should behave as they wished to be perceived – as members of a society which, though it had its own and highly distinctive cultural character, was an integral part of the Kingdom, concerned fundamentally, of course, about their identity, but concerned also about all the affairs of the Kingdom. Powell was acutely aware of, and frequently referred to, the incomprehension and indifference with which so many on the mainland observed the affairs of the province, an incomprehension and indifference to which was often added a direct hostility, encouraged by violence and disruption, to British involvement across the sea. The point can be seen in what even to some of his supporters seemed a rather pedantic argument about the different futures facing Ulster (but, then, words have always been vital to Powell). In speaking on 19 April 1975 on the forthcoming elected Constitutional Convention he observed that it was said that integration was one of the options available. To use that word with that thought seemed to him 'absurd, and, more than absurd, dangerously misleading'. The argument was both simple and profound. Ulster was already, politically and constitutionally, an integral part of the United Kingdom. Therefore, her people could not choose integration as a future option. The problem was that she was not being treated as an integral part of the whole: that was what required remedy. Powell has, therefore, always urged those who support him on Northern Ireland never to use words which suggest that they regard integration as a future possibility. Integration in the fundamental sense they already have: what they must do is hold on to it, both by insisting on receiving exactly the same treatment as every other individual part of the Kingdom, and by defending themselves against the pretensions of the Republic of Ireland and the persistent tendency of governments in London to appease opponents of the Union and, even, to contemplate an eventually united Ireland.

Ulster Unionists had always objected – though not always very forcefully – to the existence of a Common Travel Area between the United Kingdom and the Republic.[6] They had other objections to the privileged status accorded to the Republic and its citizens, notably the right of those citizens to vote in British elections and the fact that Irish currency was legal tender in Ulster.[7] Until Powell came these were, however, complaints expressed in rather an inchoate fashion. In a speech at Whiteabbey on 6 January 1977 Powell expressed all the objections in a coherent historical and philosophical framework.

He reminded his audience of something which, over the years during which they had grown attached to Stormont, they had forgotten or, at least, buried in their collective memory. This was the fact that Ulster had not wanted its own Parliament in 1920. What had happened was that, when the coalition government led by Lloyd George had accepted the idea of independence for an Irish Free State, they had intended the new entity to be composed of all thirty-two counties of Ireland.[8] This the Unionists in Ulster fiercely resisted and so Lloyd George, unwilling to accept the continued integration with the mainland of the six counties of Ulster, gave the Unionists their own assembly. It was clear, however, said Powell, that those who wrote the speech delivered by King George V on the opening of Stormont in 1921 meant that institution to be merely a stepping stone on the way to a united Ireland. Thereafter, when British governments did not behave with complete indifference to the future of the province, they had in their minds' eyes a future date at which the whole island would be united. This is a view which he has held with ever increasing conviction as the years have gone by.

At Whiteabbey, having established his historical starting point, he went on again to emphasize two of his cardinal points – the danger of devolution and the importance of playing a full part at Westminster. Since the Social Democratic and Labour Party (the successor to the old Nationalist Party) wanted devolution, and since they were hostile to the Union, it followed that devolution was a step away from the Union. He stressed the importance of the role Ulster Members had played in the debate on Scottish and Welsh devolution 'and in particular the keynote struck by Jim Molyneaux on our behalf at the outset, which drew a respectful comment from all the principal participants afterwards'. The importance of the 'almost daily involvement in the national debate, both from the point of view of Ulster and that of the Kingdom as a whole' got, he believed, too little notice, because of 'insufficient and unjust news coverage'.

The objection to citizens of the Republic having an automatic right to vote in the United Kingdom was one easily understood (and, indeed, has from time to time been raised at Conservative Party Conferences by delegates who have no particular concern with Northern Ireland). The question of the currency, however, was more important to Powell than to many of the people of

Ulster, who were accustomed to regular visitations from the Republic by shoppers seeking bargains in Belfast and paying for them with Irish money.

Powell sought to deepen understanding of the dangers of a foreign country – and it was vital to his argument that the Republic should be treated as foreign in the same sense as France, say, was so treated – enjoying the privilege of having its currency freely circulating in the United Kingdom. At Newcastle, County Down on 16 March 1975 he drew his audience's attention to the fact that a British banknote contained a promise to pay: in other words, all currency issued by government was a compulsory loan raised from the public. It follows that:

> If a government can get its notes and coins accepted in another country, it imposes a forced loan for its own purposes upon that country's nationals.

At Ballynafeigh in Belfast on 4 February 1978 he returned to the topic. He began with a classical allusion. He recalled the Greek joke that the King of Persia had driven the Greeks out of Asia with 20,000 archers. These were not soldiers, but devices stamped on Persian coins. They were used in order to bribe, and thus to corrupt, the Greeks and their dependents in the area.

> What message then is conveyed by the fact that, by the consent and connivance of Her Majesty's Government, the money of a foreign state passes current in that one part of the United Kingdom to whose territory that foreign state lays claim? It says, with all the eloquence that dumb things can command, that whatever the assurances, the protestations and the guarantees, the government does regard Northern Ireland as not fully an integral part of the United Kingdom and does accept, albeit tacitly and by implication, that in respect of Northern Ireland – but in respect of Northern Ireland only – the Irish Republic is not quite a foreign state, that there is something somehow reasonable about its claim to possess this part of the island.

In the event the link between sterling and the punt was later to be severed. It was, of course, the feelings that lay behind this specific argument that gave vent to the fierce opposition of Powell and his allies to all forms of agreement over the conduct of public affairs in Northern Ireland between governments in Dublin and London, and particularly dramatically to the Anglo-Irish Agreement of 1985.

But Powell was not content to let his argument depend merely on contemporary problems and recent (that is to say, twentieth century) history. At Cockermouth on 19 January 1980 he took his case about the difference between Ulster and the rest of the island of Ireland much farther back, and expressed that case with a much wider set of references.

He began by attacking a superficially plausible assumption which, to this day, is widely held:

> The fact that Ireland is an island creates no presumption that its inhabitants should belong to one state, any more than the Scandinavian and Iberian peninsulas imply that Norway and Portugal should not be separate Estates or that the geographical unity of the British Isles implies that one state should comprise them.

But he went much further back in history:

> From the earliest times the north-east of the island of Ireland has been geographically and geologically separate from the rest, and its main links, ethnic and otherwise, have been with the mainland of Great Britain.

It is a central part of the Irish Nationalist thesis that the separateness of Ulster derives from the plantations of English and Scottish settlers in the seventeenth century. But:

> This situation is in no way due to, though it was continued and strengthened by, the plantation of the early seventeenth century, which in any case did not affect the two eastern counties of Ulster, was not applied to the county of Monaghan, and did not result in any very substantial movement of the existing population out of the six 'plantation' counties.

Moreover, as Powell points out in reply to the widespread belief that a modern united Ireland would represent, in some sense, a return to a pre-British past:

> The north-east of the island of Ireland has never at any time been under the same government as the rest, except as part

of the British state; and even under the medieval monarchs the earldoms of Ulster were often virtually separate.

Finally:

There are now two constitutional courses open. One is to equate the position of Ulster and its population fully with that of Wales and Scotland, by restoring local government with roughly the same functions as in Wales and Scotland. It is misleading to describe this course as 'integration' unless it is contended that Wales and Scotland are 'integrated' with England. The other is to attempt to repeat the Home Rule experiment of 1920-22. This would either reproduce all the problems of a permanent Unionist majority or involve an artificial arrangement to give the representatives of anti-Union opinion an influence or a veto unjustified by their electoral support. Such arrangements, which would oblige the anti-Union representatives to use their position in such a way as to achieve their political objectives, would be interpreted by the pro-Union majority as denoting the intention of the UK Parliament and Government to work towards their exclusion from the UK, and would provide the IRA and its supporters with crucial encouragement by presenting Britain as neutral at best and hostile at worst towards the right of Ulster by majority will to remain part of the United Kingdom.

The reference to the IRA summarizes a very important part of Powell's thinking about Ulster, and also about how all opponents of the Union should be dealt with. He castigated all attempts to negotiate or organize ceasefires with the IRA and its political wing, Sinn Fein, not merely because of the immorality and impropriety of such proceedings, but on practical grounds: every concession, in his view, merely gave hope to the enemy; and until the enemy was denied hope, bloodshed and disruption in the province could not be brought to an end.

The same principle applied *mutatis mutandis* to the SDLP and the Republican government in Dublin. The Social Democratic and Labour Party succeeded a Nationalist Party that, over the years of Stormont's existence, when it was in a permanent minority, had become moribund. The SDLP consisted in its leadership of young men of energy and intelligence brought into politics during the civil disturbances of 1968 and 1969. In the end – in the general election of 1983 – they came to disown

438

even that grand old warhorse of nationalism, Gerry Fitt, in the West Belfast constituency. It was the practice of the Leader of the SDLP, John Hume, in keeping with the modernist image he sought to cultivate, to stress the social and economic policies of his party. But it remained, none the less, a fundamentally Catholic and fundamentally Nationalist party. So far as its nationalism was concerned, therefore, Powell wanted to treat it in exactly the same way as he treated the IRA: it, too, must be denied hope, through an utter refusal to discuss any of its constitutional proposals.

Dublin, likewise, had to be denied hope. In Powell's judgement the ending of what might be called a most favoured nation treatment for the Republic would, however angry the government of that country might be, be a means of cutting the tap root of its hope one day to govern Northern Ireland. Powell knew, however, that he was unlikely to be able to persuade any Westminster government to go that far. He concentrated, therefore, first on improving the parliamentary representation of Ulster, and then on restoring the full functions of local government. Gerry Fitt's speech and vote against the Callaghan government in March 1979, following the decision to increase the number of Northern Ireland's parliamentary seats, was ample proof that nationalism would be frustrated by every step taken towards a greater identification between the province and the mainland.

It cannot be emphasized too often that, throughout all the years of his involvement in the affairs of Ulster – and especially when he served as a Member of Parliament for an Ulster constituency – Powell sought intellectually wholly to fuse the province and the mainland. The situation of Ulster as a unit of the United Kingdom varied during that period from hopeful to desperate, and his speeches and actions reflected that variation. His necessary concentration on the danger which Northern Ireland constantly faced did not mean, however, that he lost sight of his other major preoccupations: it was important, indeed, that he related them to Ulster, and Ulster to them.

Of the two major issues with which Powell was identified in the public mind (his economic policies did not seize the general imagination) membership of the EEC was more readily tied into discussion about the fate of Ulster than was immigration. Both issues, of course, were closely connected, to the decline in a sense of nationhood. 'A marked feature,' he told an audience in Dromore, County Down, on 25 January 1975, 'of contemporary British politics is the widespread loss of confidence in

Britain itself – the sheer disenchantment with being British'. The upsurge of Scottish and Welsh nationalism appeared to him to be the counterpart of that loss of confidence. Thus, following the travails of the Labour government which resulted in massive borrowing from the International Monetary Fund:

> This very week the Chancellor of the Exchequer came back like a conqueror from a series of international meetings and was almost feted in the House of Commons when he announced that as a result of his negotiations Her Majesty's Government would now be able to borrow a lot more money. Where on earth has our common sense gone to, let alone our sense of shame? There is no need whatever for Her Majesty's Government to borrow any money – repeat, any money – from the International Monetary Fund or from foreign governments or from anywhere else in the world.

The broad and general point was, however, invariably brought together with something specific. Thus, for example, on 10 December 1976, at Newcastle, County Down, he addressed himself to new legislation which would extend fishing limits from 12 to two hundred miles from the coast and proclaimed that 'it is my pride as well as my duty to do all in my power to protect' the fishing interests of the area. However, he warned those listening that one of the consequences of British membership of the EEC was a significant loss of control over fishing rights and methods. It was, thus, ever his practice and effort to put the philosophical and concrete arguments together. In Belfast on 4 February 1977 he expounded again the theme that Ulster's problems were the problems of the Kingdom, and *vice versa*. 'The contemporary crisis of the nation,' he averred, 'to which I referred, is the crisis of the nation's confidence in itself, or to be more precise still, a crisis of the nation's belief in its own existence.' The submission of the United Kingdom to the EEC, and to other foreign interests, was described in the most scornful terms:

> Our Ministers bring home huge loans from other countries much as though they were victorious generals returning with the spoils and captives of distant conquests and not riveting the fetters of subordination around British ankles. We endure with apparent equanimity this self-satisfaction of our rulers when an American or a Japanese deigns to say anything even mildly uncritical about Britain's prospects and performance; and the

smile of a German Chancellor – accompanied, of course, by a few more hundred million dollars by way of loan – is hailed as the highest accolade of distinction.

The vote of genuine, heartfelt and – on behalf of the nation – humiliated anger here is vintage Powell. Again and again he showed his anxiety to make the people of Ulster understand how significant the EEC was for their own most deeply felt concerns, telling, for example, his listeners at a meeting in Edenderry, Armagh on 12 September 1977 of the importance of elections to the European Parliament which, under the terms of the Lib-Lab agreement, were due shortly to be held. If British sovereignty was, as he believed, to be on the way to dissolution in a European entity then, as Britain began to disappear into the EEC, so Ulster would begin to disappear into the Irish Republic.

It was in 1983, however, that the significance for Ulster, and the conduct of the affairs of the province, of British membership of the EEC became sharply apparent, and to a wider audience than the fishermen who set out on their work from the shoreline beneath the Mountains of Mourne. In April of that year the European Parliament, in Powell's words, 'even against the objections and warning of the British Government' voted to investigate the political affairs of Northern Ireland. Here, in a most immediate and dramatic fashion, was the threat to sovereignty constituted by membership of the EEC expressed. On 28 May, in the constituency, Powell spelled out what the appointment of a Dane, Niels Haagerup, to examine and report on the affairs of Ulster, meant:

It was a sharp reminder of the consequences of Britain being part of the EEC. People's intelligence told them truly that continental Europe is no friend of Ulster as part of the United Kingdom. On the contrary, the EEC, having conferred upon the Republic of Ireland the title of 'Ireland', it is supposed to take as an absurd and evanescent anomaly the fact that this Province is, and intends by the majority will of its inhabitants to remain, a part of the United Kingdom, to which we belonged before most of the states of the Common Market had even come into existence.

He went on to describe various ways in which the authority of the EEC in Brussels was intruding on British authority, instancing the plight of hill farms, the matter of milk quotas and the transformation of the textile industry:

'The result of this is that Ulster has exchanged its old position on the Atlantic flank of Britain for that of a peripheral province of a Britain which has itself become peripheral in relation to the continental heartlands of the EEC. This is one of those changes which are none the less profound for being impossible to quantify. Yet there are thousands in this province who could testify from their daily experience to the truth of what I am describing, not least those who have occasion to transport and export Ulster's products to the continent.

What Powell was doing was not redefining his own ideas, but, by applying them to his new responsibilities, extending them. As he explained the wider world, its problems and threats, to Ulster, so he explained Ulster to the wider world. From February 1974 onwards there were many Conservatives who regarded him, as the Scots and Irish had once regarded Bonnie Prince Charlie, as a king over the water: there were even a few dreaming spirits who imagined that under the new regime of Margaret Thatcher, he could be tempted back into the fold. He was invited to speak, at Saltash in Cornwall, on 16 October 1982 to a meeting of the Conservative Political Centre. In particular, he was asked, they would like to hear why he could not be a Conservative again. The EEC, he explained in his speech, was the essence of his reason. He thought it would be 'a monstrous frivolity, a moral suicide, to offer political allegiance to a party committed to the principle that the country's laws ought to be made, its taxes imposed, and its causes judged by an external authority . . .' He then gave his English audience the specific example of Ulster:

Meantime, there is another raw nerve which mention of territorial sovereignty touches. As I watched from 1969 onwards the behaviour of Her Majesty's Government and the UK Parliament towards a province of the United Kingdom that had been made the object of terrorist attack from a neighbouring foreign state which claimed, and claims, that province as its territory, horror was succeeded by indignation. It became clear to me that government and Parliament were deliberately manoeuvring, or being manoeuvred, to sever from this nation a population whose only offence was to belong to it and to desire to continue to belong to it. The words, the actions, and the legislation of the Heath government will bear no other interpretation: it was the self-wrecking behaviour of a nation bent on renouncing simultaneously its political and its territorial identity. Thereby Ulster's cause became the cause of the United Kingdom.

However, for Unionists as for many others, the crucially intriguing question in 1979, and for some time thereafter (at least until the end of 1981) was concerned with the character and prospects of the new government and, of course, the character and prospects of the untried Prime Minister who headed it. This was, further, a matter of more than ordinary moment to Powell himself. In the period which followed the débâcle of February 1974 his utterances on the subject of his old party and its likely future had been increasingly caustic and bitter.[9] The deposition of Edward Heath from the leadership did not incline him to any more charitable view, and he never abandoned his accusation of dishonesty or stupidity – or both – against those emerging tribunes of the right, Margaret Thatcher and Keith Joseph. At a *Spectator* lunch towards the end of 1974 we canvassed him for his opinion about who was likely to prove victorious in the forthcoming contest for the post of Leader. He had little, if anything, to say that was friendly to any of the likely candidates. So far as Mrs. Thatcher was concerned, he was dismissive. No woman, he believed, could get the job; and he was, in general, disapproving of women being Members of the House of Commons at all. Aside from policy, though, what he had against the first female to contest the leadership of a major party were 'that dreadful, that dreadful voice, and those frightful hats'.

Time did not soften what has remained a deep distrust of the Prime Minister, a distrust which re-emerged in full strength when she signed the Anglo-Irish Agreement in 1985. As the years went by, however, he was occasionally inclined to give her the benefit of the doubt. On 21 July 1978, at Devizes he tied her, and reactions to her, into another nationalist analysis. James Callaghan had taunted his rival with her inability to say a good word for Britain. Powell took up the taunt:

He meant his remark as a quick and superficial taunt. Inadvertently, he happened to express what the great mass of the British people desperately feel: that there is no longer any Party that speaks for Britain, that speaks for them. If that complaint lies at the door of the Conservative Party rather than any other, it is only because in our parliamentary constitution, being less inhibited by the immediacies of government, is the more under obligation to express the wishes and fears of the people, and also because historically, though (alas!) no longer, the Conservative Party has seen itself as the Party of the nation.

There were also certain things about Mrs. Thatcher – the pugnacious instinct, for one, the willingness to go against the supposedly established verities of the post-war years, and an unforced if unintellectual (and, to Powell, simply unthought-out) patriotism – which did, from time to time strike a chord with him. At Devizes he referred to an occasion, six months previously, when she had, in a television interview, referred to the fear of British people that they would be 'swamped' by coloured immigration. The remark, which had been made without consulting any of her Shadow Cabinet colleagues and, particularly, without consulting the Shadow Home Secretary, William Whitelaw, had created a tremendous furore, and called down on her head the imprecations of immigrant leaders, churchmen, newspapers and many others. Powell, however, referred to a 'great surge of hope and relief which a single word . . . by the Conservative Leader evoked from one end of the country to the other'.

Even this note of approbation, if not outright praise, was, however, qualified. Apart from the public row that had followed the interview, Mrs. Thatcher had occasioned serious embarrassment to some of her senior colleagues: Whitelaw had only heard of it over dinner at White's. It should be said that throughout her early career since succeeding Heath she has often been inclined to make public views of hers for which she cannot find support among her colleagues. On this occasion she had nothing to say by way of elaboration, which caused Powell to remark, after six months had passed, that 'a chloroformed gag was immediately clapped over the Leader's mouth . . .' He was, perhaps, putting the matter a trifle strongly; but it is a fact that the remonstrances of Whitelaw, Peter Carrington and Ian Gilmour had a part to play in causing her to fall silent on immigration.

Mrs. Thatcher and Powell have never been friends – nor, in any real sense, colleagues, save in that they were members of the same party. None the less, any biographical study of either must take account of the other. There are several reasons for this. The first is a similarity of character and aspiration. The second is, at least in the field of economic policy, a similarity of preferred method. During the bitter travails in this area which the government suffered for nearly two years after it was elected, there were manifold pressures on the Prime Minister and on the Chancellor of the Exchequer, Sir Geoffrey Howe, to turn the policy clock back, as Edward Heath had done after a similar period of experiment in 1972. Powell was certainly among those who believed she would weaken; and when she did not he was prepared to give her credit. Then there was another, and perhaps more important, thing which connected the two careers. Most of those who brought about the intellectual revolution in Tory politics which presaged the Thatcher triumphs (particularly men and women at the Institute of Economic Affairs and the Centre for Policy Studies) were ardent admirers of Powell, and a number were his personal friends. These connections were of importance as she, starting virtually from scratch, and with little but instinct to guide her, set about the business of designing a new Conservative programme. There are many examples of the cross-fertilizing influence between the two. But I will mention one, which surfaced at the time of writing. In the *Sunday Telegraph* of 7 August 1988 Oliver Letwin, a former member of the Policy Unit at No. 10 Downing Street, wrote an article savagely critical of the way in which the EEC was developing. Not only was the article, in manner and subject, unambiguously what has come to be called Powellite, but Powell was openly quoted as its inspiration. Nobody who worked for or supported Edward Heath could possibly have written, or been allowed to write, such an article.

As he repeatedly said, however, there could never have been any question of an open *rapprochement* between the two: the issues of the EEC and Northern Ireland stood between them. On all the major subjects on which he spoke out, and which he regarded as matters of principle, Powell was totally immovable: the language of compromise, other than on purely tactical matters, had long ceased to be a part of his vocabulary. Some commentators, broadly speaking sympathetic to him, professed to find inconsistencies between different parts of the whole Powell package. Thus, in 1981 the Freedom Association – a libertarian body which has much in common with Powell – was in the triumphal closing stages of a legal action taken at the Court of Human Rights in Strasbourg. This issue was the so-called 'closed shop' under the rules of which trade union rights to exclude non-members from jobs were protected by law. Since the Thatcher administration, though determined to move to repeal this legislation eventually, was proceeding with great caution against union privileges, the Association took up

the cause of a group of workers who had suffered, and won.
Naturally, they assumed that Powell at least would be an ally
in so good a cause. But his stern logic overrode any sympathy
he might feel, as he told a Blackpool audience on 18 September
1981:

> A month or two ago the European Court of Human Rights
> handed down a judgement against the Crown in Parliament.
> It found that our law, as made by Parliament, is incompatible
> with the Court's interpretation of human rights. The point
> which was at issue does not matter. It matters not whether
> you or I approve or disapprove of what is called the 'closed
> shop'. What matters is that by our will we have submitted
> ourselves and our laws to the arbitrament of an external court
> – something that no nation can do and remain a nation. Thirty
> years ago, at the summit of our downward path, we allowed
> our representatives to enthrone 'human rights', interpreted by
> foreign lawyers, above the law of this land. Now we are paying
> the price in humiliation, when every Tom, Dick or Harry who
> is aggrieved at the judgements or administration or laws of
> Britain trots off to the continent to get an order in his favour
> over the head of the Queen and behind the back of Parliament.

On the crucial subject – that of Northern Ireland – however,
Powell could contemplate a Conservative government without
Neave with, at best, caution and suspicion. Powell has since
said that, while he believed still that Neave would have been
by far the best Secretary of State for Northern Ireland from
the Unionist point of view, 'having his heart and his head in
the right place', even he would none the less eventually have
crumbled under the pressures quickly exercised on the Thatcher
government. The early conduct of Atkins, however, was such that
even Powell, quick as he was to anger in Ulster's cause, and ready
though he was to believe in conspiracy, found himself somewhat
taken aback.

Only months after taking the Ulster Office the Secretary of
State announced his intention of holding tripartite talks in New
York on the future of the province, the three parties being the
United States, the United Kingdom and the Republic of Ireland.
As a result of the intervention of the Prime Minister this plan was
abandoned. But the very fact that the plan had been mooted at
all provided evidence, first, that Neave's legacy was under threat
and, second, that, as Powell had always believed, the government

of the United States had a powerful – and quite illegitimate – influence on the internal affairs of the United Kingdom. For the moment, however, Powell was content to welcome the abandonment of the tripartite talks plan, and even to build on it, which he did in a speech at Rathfriland on 7 September 1979:

> If it is wrong to discuss Ulster's future anywhere outside the United Kingdom, it must be equally wrong to discuss it inside the United Kingdom with foreign governments or their servants.

The target here was, obviously, the declared anti-Unionist interests of Dublin and the SDLP. Later, he was to add Paisley, more and more openly, to this grouping and, later still, to come upon staggering and incontrovertible evidence that important members of the Northern Ireland Office itself were working alongside the Americans and the Irish Republic for the dissolution of the Union.[10]

But, alongside these battles, which could readily be called direct battles against direct enemies, Powell had other work of argument. He had to raise the understanding of Ulster to precisely the nature of the threat which the Union faced; and he had not merely to raise the consciousness of those on the mainland with regard to Northern Ireland, but to persuade individuals and those who formed English opinion that the only logical way to see things was the way in which he himself saw them. There are many speeches and articles on these subjects, but one of the most fundamental texts was a speech to the Annual General Meeting of his constituency association on 26 September 1979. Only days earlier Lord Mountbatten together with his daughter and grandson, as well as a servant, had been murdered by an IRA bomb while they were sailing off the coast of the Republic, where Mountbatten had a holiday home. The murder excited international outrage and horror, not because it was any worse than countless other IRA bombings and shootings, but because Mountbatten was the Queen's cousin. Powell was quick to point out, however, that the most humble Ulsterman or woman who died at the hands of the terrorists had as noble a place in the scheme of things as did the Earl. Thus, when he had occasion to write to a constituent who had been so bereaved, he never failed to point out that whoever it was who had died 'had died not for Ulster, not for Ireland but for the United Kingdom

. . .' and had therefore died 'in as full and honoured a sense as those whose lives are given in war'.

But he had a target. On the occasion of the Mountbatten funerals the Archbishop of Canterbury had delivered a sermon. Dr. Runcie's theme was that the conditions which underlay violence in Ulster should be reformed, so as to limit and eventually end the temptation to violence. Powell had always been scornful of the argument that social or economic conditions in Northern Ireland had anything to do with anti-Unionist violence. He inquired about what conditions the Archbishop had in mind, knowing perfectly well that the archiepiscopal analysis – like most so-called English liberal analysis – referred to the supposed unfortunate position of the Catholics in Ulster, and embraced the old power-sharing idea involving as it did substantial concessions both to the Republic and to the SDLP. He announced, though, that Runcie knew exactly what the real problem was:

> There is no secret about it. They [the conditions] consist in the simple fact that Northern Ireland is part of the United Kingdom. This is what, in the view of the IRA, justifies and has always justified, any deed of blood perpetrated against British people, high or low, service or civilian: that, and nothing else. Let me repeat: it is the fact of the Union itself, and has nothing to do with such incidental and subordinate matters as the manner in which Northern Ireland as part of the Union is governed and administered.

He turned in a similar way on the Roman Catholic Bishop of Down and Connor, Dr. Cathal O'Daley, who had sermonized in a fashion similar to Runcie, and explained that what the Bishop had meant when in his sermon he advocated reform 'is that active steps are not being taken, as they were by the Heath administration in 1972 and 1973, of which the effect and the intent would visibly be to lead towards the ending of the Union.'

Over his years in Ulster Powell varied in his reaction to events from optimism to pessimism. This did not indicate any inconsistency in attitude or judgement, but, rather, a necessary adjustment of analysis according to events – particularly the shifts and turns of British government policy in relation to Ulster, the Republic and the United States. He believed, he told a constituency audience on 3 January 1980, that, on balance, the Union had been strengthened over the previous decade, not least because the atrocities of the IRA had alienated public opinion and compelled Parliament to take more care over Ulster.

None the less, at the time of his speaking, 'The Union between Great Britain and Northern Ireland is probably in greater danger than at any time since the disastrous actions of the Heath government in 1972 and 1973.'

He was referring to Atkins's latest move – yet another initiative – towards change in the governance of the province:

The government says that it wishes to introduce changes in the present arrangements for governing Ulster. Well and good. It goes on, however, to say that it wants the maximum political agreement among the parties to those changes. Whose agreement? Not Unionist agreement – of whatever brand. If the changes are to be such as will evidently maintain and strengthen the Union, Unionist agreement is to be had for the asking – indeed, without even the need to ask. No, the agreement which the government seeks, and which it has set up a conference in order to show the world that it seeks, is the agreement of the SDLP.

The 'veriest tyro' in Northern Ireland politics could see, Powell continued, that the SDLP could not contemplate any move which would help maintain or strengthen the Union 'without self-destruction'. John Hume would be kept to the straight and narrow path of nationalist rectitude by 'the fate of poor old Gerry Fitt . . .' who, having appeared to countenance an apparent shift in governmental policy towards Unionism, was instantly thrown out of the leadership.

In Donaghadee on 26 January 1980 Powell opened (or, rather, re-opened) his second front. He recalled an earlier speech in which he had made reference to 37,000 'fools' who, in the general election, had voted for James Kilfedder, an Independent Unionist. They had voted 'in a way that could have no practical result whatsoever except to divide Unionism and weaken and damage it in Parliament'. Paisley himself Powell compared – in perhaps the most deadly insult one Ulster politician could direct against another – to John Redmond, the leader of the Home Rule (in effect, Irish Nationalist) Party in the House of Commons before the First World War. Redmond had described his followers as men who had no respect or regard for the House of Commons. This was exactly Paisley's position: it followed that he was 'anti-Unionist'. Powell laid claim to the exclusive support of all honest Unionists for his own party:

> There is no other party in Ulster which is the party of the Union, no other party which puts first, before all other considerations, the Union and the maintenance of the Union and which sets its face against anything which might endanger or question or qualify the Union. Others insert the word "Unionist" in their descriptions, as the crow in the fable strutted around in borrowed feathers; but their profession of being Unionists will not survive an examination of their words and actions.

In the context of the whole of British politics it is difficult to recall now how vulnerable Mrs. Thatcher appeared, not perhaps during the first few months after her general election, but throughout 1980 and 1981. To be sure, she had certain things widely held to her credit. At the 1979 Commonwealth Prime Ministers' Conference in Lusaka she began the untangling of Britain's involvement with and responsibility for Rhodesia which was completed the following year with the emergence of the independent republic of Zimbabwe. Since the Rhodesian imbroglio had defeated a number of her predecessors of both parties, here was an achievement widely praised around the world. However, even so spectacular a success was not fully placed to her account: general – and quite inaccurate[11] – comment praised the Foreign Secretary, Lord Carrington, as the true architect of the Rhodesian settlement. At home she was beset by criticism. Her economic policies were widely derided. The sharp increases in unemployment which followed their introduction were generally deplored. She was the butt, not merely of public criticism, but of whispering campaigns against her by Cabinet colleagues, and by a number of Conservative backbenchers. Northern Ireland was at the front neither of her agenda nor of her mind. Her battles over the EEC budget – to which, she believed, the United Kingdom paid an inequitable amount – mattered much more to her, and brought her into direct conflict with the government of the Irish Republic. Those battles (in which she was eventually successful) were, however, so strenuous that, whatever her instincts, she did not care to tackle the government of the Republic on another issue.

The plain truth of the matter – as we shall shortly see – is that the Prime Minister's failure to put her hand to the Ulster issue left successive Secretaries of State – Atkins and James Prior – more or less in the position of semi-independent imperial governors. Since both men believed that the way forward in Ulster was through accommodation with the Republic and appeasement of the Nationalist minority in the province, they were found to be agreeable masters for the civil servants in the Northern Ireland Office. Throughout 1980, however, and even well into 1981, matters tended to hang fire, at least so far as public perception was concerned. The IRA continued its campaign of terror. Local elections were held – but local authority powers were not restored, though the Prime Minister was believed to favour their restoration. Plans were drafted in the Northern Ireland Office (in close collaboration with the Foreign Office) for a new Northern Ireland Assembly which would produce a new Northern Ireland power-sharing executive. It is very hard, looking back over the gradual shift in affairs, to gainsay Powell's reiterated accusation that there was, in Whitehall, a settled determination first to weaken and, ultimately, to break the Union, for all that Ministers were ever willing to repeat the undertaking that Northern Ireland would never be dragooned into the Republic – or into a federation with the Republic – against the wishes of the majority of its population. Powell's argument, however, was irrefutable. The logic of the situation in Ulster was that the SDLP wanted the dissolution of the Union and the creation of a United Ireland, however long that might take. It followed that there could be no concessions short of ending the Union which would satisfy – or could satisfy – John Hume.

Although the SDLP were recently engaged in exploratory conversation with Sinn Fein (the political party which represents the IRA) it would be wrong to conclude that the relationship between the two is either close or collusive. The IRA operates according to an interior logic of its own; and it wants, not simply to break the Union, but to take over the whole island. There is no reason to doubt, moreover, that Hume deplores the violence inflicted by the IRA. None the less, equally it cannot be denied that that violence is indispensable to his success. Wide swatches of English opinion support him in his contention that the Union is the cause of the violence. More and more concessions to Nationalist opinion (as represented, of course, by himself and the government in Dublin) are thought to be required if the tide of violence is to recede. And the concessions required necessarily involve the weakening of the Union. As Powell has always seen, anybody who is prepared to go down the road of concession to Hume and Dublin cannot have the preservation and strengthening of the Union as their first priority, and this is quite apart from the evidence that there is, in Whitehall, not merely a settled policy of appeasing anti-Unionist opinion, but a settled policy of ultimately ending Northern Ireland's constitutional link with Great Britain.

I have, throughout, referred in the singular to the 'government' of the Republic of Ireland though, during the period from the beginning of the present crisis of Ulster in 1968 four men – Jack Lynch, Charles Haughey, Liam Cosgrave and Garret Fitzgerald – have held the office of Taoiseach, or Prime Minister in that country. Lynch and Haughey have been Leaders of Fianna Fail, which has invariably governed alone; Cosgrave and Fitzgerald have headed Fine Gael, which has always governed in coalition with the third party of the state, the Labour Party. The reason I use the singular is that there has been absolutely no difference between the Ulster policy of any of them, or of either party. That is not to say that there have not been differences of emphasis or tactics. Dr. Fitzgerald, for example, sought a major reform of the Irish Constitution, particularly the repeal of the clause which bestows on the Roman Catholic church a pre-eminent position in Irish society.[12] Fitzgerald's idea was that, by making his country constitutionally and socially more palatable to Northern Protestants he would take a seven league step towards the ultimate goal of unity. It is also true – and a qualification which visiting English journalists often take to be the whole substance of policy in Dublin – that no Irish government would want to take over immediate responsibility for the North. Indeed, both Fitzgerald and Haughey (who alternated in office until Fitzgerald's retirement) have been willing to declare that they have no desire to see an early departure of the British Army from Ulster. But this should not be allowed to obscure their long-term aim, which is the takeover of the province in good time, and in good order. Every concession a government in Dublin appears to make to a government in London – most notably on the favourite topic of co-operation on security between security forces on either side of the border – is incidental to that fundamental ambition.

On 1 February 1980, in Antrim, Powell made an important point, frequently forgotten or misunderstood, about Northern Ireland. Noting the tendency of commentators to refer to 'the Protestant majority' and 'the Catholic minority' he observed that there were two minorities in the province. The first was religious, the Catholics. The second was political, those opposed to the

Union. So far as the religious minority was concerned there was no question but that they were as equal before the law as their co-religionists on the mainland and that 'Parliament would neither perpetrate nor permit any invasion or limitation of the rights of Roman Catholic citizens in this part of the kingdom . . .' But, contrary to general opinion, the religious and the nationalist minorities were not co-terminous. It is impossible to contradict him. Elections whether national or local, referenda, and even the constant drip of opinion polls, all regularly produce a Unionist plurality so substantial as to demonstrate that a considerable part of the religious minority in the province is steadfast in its support of the Union. This is yet another of those fundamental facts about Ulster which nationalists and English pro-nationalists alike find it difficult, if not impossible, to acknowledge.

One of Powell's constant fears, expressed again and again, throughout his time in Ulster, was that the Unionists of Northern Ireland simply would not understand the dangers of devolution in the context of relations with Dublin and the SDLP. It was possible, of course, to use the word 'devolution' as an ambiguous shorthand for Stormont, as Paisley constantly did or – again as Paisley constantly did – to represent the Unionist claim for a restoration of powers to local authorities as itself an implication that a return to Stormont would follow the restoration of those powers. At Eglinton on 24 April 1980 Powell sought to dispel any such notion. 'Devolution,' he said, 'is dead; and all the sentiment and affection which yet clusters around the Home Rule Constitution of 1920, known as Stormont, will not avail to work a resurrection.'

More than once he posed the matter in its starkest terms. If Ulster politicians wanted Stormont back in its old form, then they would have to give up their hopes, for such a restoration would be unacceptable at Westminster. On the other hand, if Westminster did agree to the re-creation of an Assembly with some sort of power in Belfast, then Ulster would have to accept that this could only be done at the price of conceding a power-sharing executive. The only way forward for Unionists was to work for, argue for and fight for a system under which the province was treated in every respect in the same way as every other part of the Kingdom. This was so moderate a request that it is remarkable – and certainly instructive – to reflect on the fact that so many of those English politicians and commentators who took an interest in the affairs of Ulster regarded him as one of the most unbending and even fanatical of Unionists. After all, if the case for political reform in Ulster was, however cloudily, based on a conviction that Catholics had to be protected from Protestants, then the application of the same rule of democracy and justice which obtained on the mainland was the clearest route towards meting out fairness to all.

Although there were certain shifts of gear during 1980 and the early part of 1981, Powell could see the steady drift of the policy of the Thatcher government back towards (so far as Ulster was concerned) the policies once espoused by Edward Heath and William Whitelaw. Most of the elements of what Powell was eventually to see as an efficiently co-ordinated conspiracy against Northern Ireland had already appeared in various of his speeches and writings, though he was not to have devastating and conclusive proof until middle and late 1981. All along there was a certain puzzlement about the conduct of the Prime Minister. Those who have studied her over the years know that there is nothing more certain than a direct challenge to bring out the steel in the character of Margaret Thatcher. Thus, when in 1980 Republican prisoners in the Maze prison in Ulster went on hunger strike she determined to let those of them die who had the determination to do so. The strike was particularly well designed to exercise pressure on the British government. It was a strike against the refusal of the government to allow the prisoners political privileges, and its insistence that they wore normal prison clothes. The strike was not embarked upon collectively, but individually, one by one. When one prisoner died another took his place.

On 3 January 1981 Powell, speaking in Downpatrick, said he would judge the government's good faith on its will to resist the demands for political status, and the quality of its refusal to be blackmailed by the hunger strikers. The outcome, he believed, would depend on the Prime Minister's willingness to resist the pressure she was undergoing, from the civil service, from Dublin, and from the United States, to produce some conciliatory formula – various were suggested – which would persuade the prisoners to give up. Violence stalked the streets, as Republican sympathizers with those in the Maze began a series of riots which resulted in a total loss of life of sixty-one. Churchmen, politicians of all colours except Unionist orange, and many commentators pleaded with Mrs. Thatcher, tried to cajole Mrs. Thatcher, threatened Mrs. Thatcher with more violence than either Ulster or the mainland had ever seen before. It was all to no avail. The Prime Minister stood still. Ten prisoners died. The hunger strike crumbled.

But, if her stand on this occasion was satisfactory to Powell, it was also more and more evident to him that she was increasingly willing to go along with policies which he feared and opposed. A summit meeting with Charles Haughey towards the end of 1980, for all that it produced nothing more concrete than had her various meetings with Fitzgerald when he was Taoiseach, was a patent indication that London was over-willing to consult with the Republic about the affairs of one of the provinces of the United Kingdom. More clearly than most Powell saw that meetings of this kind create a momentum of their own: neither party can go on holding them without, eventually, producing results and, indeed, dramatic results were produced (there were more marginal gains for the anti-Unionist cause along the way) by the summit which led to the Anglo-Irish Agreement of 1985.

On 26 September 1980 Powell told an audience in Bangor that he proposed to outline to them an operation 'mounted almost a year ago' against Ulster and the Union, the principal participants in which were senior members of the Foreign Office, the Northern Ireland Office, and the State Department of the United States. The Foreign Office, he observed, was an 'inveterate' enemy of Ulster as part of the United Kingdom. Further, 'In its purposes the Foreign Office has an important ally, whether dupe or collaborator, in the higher echelons of the Northern Ireland civil service and the Northern Ireland Office.' The combined view of these enemies of the Union, Powell said, was the desirability of creating a simulacrum of Stormont, elected on the basis of proportional representation, which would support (though not necessarily choose) an executive for the province which would bring together willing Unionists, and which would defer to the SDLP. If that objective could not be achieved, Powell said, an advisory Assembly would do nearly as well, not least because – as he said on another occasion – 'there are collaborators in every party,' and anybody serving in what amounted to a talking shop would enjoy a decent salary and generous expenses. Neither he nor James Molyneaux would, Powell went on, seek election to any such Assembly. But, he asked, could it be used by those who would attend, to undermine true Unionism?

It was some four months later – on 8 January 1981, and before hard as opposed to circumstantial evidence came his way – that Powell, with all the rhetorical power at his command, began to express his as yet partial view of the jigsaw of intent and policy which, when assembled, meant the destruction of the Union. He had long been suspicious of those bland assurances offered by English Ministers to the effect that the people of Northern Ireland could rely on not being pummelled or cajoled into the Republic against their wishes. He treated such assurances with scorn:

> That notion is not only false but positively harmful. The true guarantee of Ulster as an integral part of the United Kingdom is the same as the guarantee of Wales or Kent – namely that they are represented in the Parliament of the United Kingdom.

From this position he has never budged. In the speech which I have just quoted, however, there is a sense of dawning understanding. There has never been a point in Powell's life, as scholar, soldier or politician, when he has not sought to relate the problem of the day to a judgement on fundamentals. He appears, often, to be intellectually arrogant. His manner has frequently been abrupt. But, then, he is different. It took a Cavalier, and not a calculating spirit to enter, yet again, into battle with Ian Paisley when Paisley had already tried to warn Powell off – with the threat of a Paisleyite candidate in Down South. Powell had been warned that he should not go out of his way to offend Paisley. It was dangerous. It might well be counter-productive. Even James Molyneaux was concerned. Willingness to fight rather than to compromise being embedded in Powell's nature, he again asked all those who believed in the Union to vote for his party, and against Paisley in the Ulster local elections of May 1981, 'because the DUP is the chosen instrument of those who want Ulster out of the Union.'

But Powell was unrelenting, and unrepentant, as he had been all his life. Referring to the plot he had discerned to break asunder the Union he said, in the speech just quoted:

> A leading role in the whole business has been played by the Democratic Unionist Party, and its leader, Ian Paisley, who was deeply involved in the scheme to assure the Province and the world, in tones somewhat above a whisper, that the new show should have been in operation by now – exactly what Ministers and officials in the Northern Ireland Office were counting upon. It is not the first of the Reverend Doctor's predictions to go amiss. It was also not the first, nor the last, occasion on which he was to reveal himself as the most resourceful, inveterate, and powerful enemy of the Union.

Paisley was stung; and it may be that he was stung by a guilty conscience. Since his whole experience of political activity had been one of brute populist power, and since he pretended to be a theologian – on the basis of a rather bad book[13] – he was affronted by an English Protestant Unionist who knew the texts better than he did. Having thought he could bring Molyneaux and Powell to his heel, and having believed that Powell could be the instrument of his ambition, Paisley came to the view that it would be worth the loss of a Unionist seat if Enoch Powell could be beaten when a general election came. The English intruder became Paisley's target, as many others had been in the past.

But evidence came to Powell's hand. 'I regret,' he says, 'that I did not see it all earlier. I now think that the turning point was 1979 and that it came with Airey Neave's murder. But I did not see the thing as a whole until 1981. For me, therefore, 1981 was a critical year. What is more, it was a year in which I fully realized that my involvement with Ulster was not merely something about a province, however important in itself, but something central to the whole business of foreign policy, and directly related to the pattern of Western alliances.'

In the spring of 1981 a research student at Keele University, Geoffrey Sloane, made contact with a senior official in the Northern Ireland Office, Clive Abbott. Abbott gave two interviews to Sloane – the second on 11 November 1981. Reading the texts now, one is staggered by the combination of arrogance and foolishness which Abbott displays. The arrogance lies in his contempt for elected politicians, and especially for Margaret Thatcher, the foolishness in his willingness to be so open with an interviewer. To appreciate fully the strength of Powell's argument that there was a conspiracy against the Union, it is necessary to quote the two interviews *in extenso*. They make chilling reading for any believer in democracy.

In Washington there is what is called an *ad hoc* committee on Northern Ireland. While it has no formal official standing, it numbers among its most prominent members Senator Edward Kennedy and Senator Daniel Patrick Moynihan. While the committee purports to be concerned principally with justice in Ulster, it is unashamedly opposed to the Union, in favour of a united Ireland under a Dublin government. It has close connections with whatever party is in power in the Republic of Ireland where, of course, the Kennedy name enjoys to this day a powerful attraction. It is also closely connected – as Abbott told

Sloane – with Noraid, the IRA's principal fund-raising organization in the United States, and with the Irish National Caucus, another American organization concerned with propagating the Irish Republican cause in the United States.

Abbott, having explained all this to Sloane, was asked about relations between London and Dublin before Mrs. Thatcher won the general election of 1979, and whether her arrival in office – the policy of Airey Neave fresh in her mind – made any difference. Abbott's reply was brutally direct:

> Before the Conservative Party came to power in 1979 it had promised that local government functions would be returned to local councils. We had to tell them it was just not on . . . we couldn't break certain undertakings we have given to the Irish government over the constitutional future of Northern Ireland.

But, Sloane asked, did not the granting of a further five parliamentary seats to Northern Ireland represent a strengthening of the Union or, as he put it 'a move towards integration'? 'Firstly,' Abbott replied,

> the Unionists will not get all the five seats. We would see that this does not happen by gerrymandering the boundaries[14] . . . I look forward to seeing John Hume, who is a personal friend, establishing a power base in the House of Commons as well as in the European Parliament . . . As I have said before, a devolved government with power returning to local authorities is not on. But an assembly which controlled such things as housing, through our already established NIHE,[15] given preliminary powers which would be extended progressively is a possibility. But any such developments would have to involve close consultation with the Irish government.

The point having been established that the government of the Republic had, in the view of the Northern Ireland Office, a constitutional role to play in a part of the United Kingdom, Sloane moved on to ask about relations with the United States on the subject of Ulster. Abbott, having observed that the 1921 Treaty (which settled the partition of Ireland and thus defined Northern Ireland as a province of the United Kingdom) 'was a squalid deal in which Northern Ireland should never have existed', replied that 'In any final settlement we have to realize that the United States will be given a discreet role to play especially in the financial field. Generally the two bureaucratic machines of the State Department and the Foreign Office work closely together.'

Sloane immediately quoted the Unionist argument that it was the settled policy of the Foreign Office to undermine their cause. Again, the reply was revealing:

> This type of statement has come mainly from Powell and is considered cranky by the Foreign Office.

Reading that opening sentence most people would, I fancy, expect a rebuttal of Powell's case to follow. Not so:

> In the end I think there will be a confederal Ireland, one could call it an honourable draw, in which a package would be put together whereby Protestant rights would be guaranteed. There would be some re-alignment with the Commonwealth and the Irish Republic and a defence agreement would also be made. There is less certainty than there has been in the past about the strategic irrelevance of Southern Ireland . . . The Americans would sleep easier in their beds if the Irish Republic were a member of NATO. The Irish Republic will not enter into any defence agreement until the issue of partition is resolved.

Two things were thus established in the person of Abbott, clearly the spokesman for an entrenched and long established policy. The first was the necessary involvement of the government of the Irish Republic in the internal affairs of the United Kingdom. The second was the acceptance of an American interest in those internal affairs.

From the imposition of direct rule and the suspension of Stormont by Edward Heath in 1972 the public case of the British government in favour of the creation of a power-sharing executive was that only such a body would give confidence and security to the Roman Catholic population of Northern Ireland. It was again and again clearly stated by successive governments and successive Secretaries of State that there was no intention of undermining the Union against the wishes of the majority in Ulster. In the persuasive mouth of William Whitelaw this formulation – justice for Catholics, but no threat to the Union – was very widely accepted on the mainland. The Unionists, however, consistently argued that the executive – and any successor body of a similar kind – would be merely a staging post towards the breaking of the Union. Likewise, successive British governments have consistently denied that their policy in Ulster is in any way influenced by the activities of the IRA. Abbott answered Sloane, in their second conversation, on both these points; Sloane asked if violence had influenced policy and Abbott replied:

> That is a perfectly reasonable assumption to make. The opportunity that direct rule gave us in 1972 was the opportunity to establish a power-sharing devolved government. If this can be established then the aspiration of half a million Catholics could be taken into consideration. Once this is established it is a half-way point to recognizing the interest of the Republic in Northern Ireland's future in a constitutional sense.

A little later Abbott gave Sloane a summary of the history of events over nearly a decade. In this summary he betrayed with appalling frankness the contempt civil servants felt for elected politicians:

> The Heath government in March 1973 acknowledged the Irish Dimension.[16] Rees helped to keep up momentum in the first three to four months of his office. After the fall of the power-sharing government we had to rethink it all. Roy Mason stopped all political movement. All the emphasis was on security co-operation and nothing else. Anglo-Irish relations were not very good. On the security side the IRA came near to total defeat. Thatcher, when she first came to power, wanted to continue this emphasis on security co-operation only, and she wanted to bring to fruition the Neave idea of a return to local government. In the past two and a half years it has come to be recognized by Number Ten that the Republic must have some sort of say in the constitutional position of Northern Ireland. One should not get too excited over Fitzgerald's proposals to change articles 2 and 3 of the Irish Constitution. It will be very hard to get them changed in terms of domestic rule. But it is a way of holding a pistol to HMG's head and putting pressure on it for further movement.

At the Dublin summit in December 1980, Abbott went on, the politicians merely wanted to make a show: the policy was already decided but, 'Thatcher wanted a lot of gold braid in front. Howe and a few other Ministers didn't really know why they were there, he and the others were just told to shut up and smile.'

Towards the conclusion of this second conversation Abbott gave his sketch for the future:

It is a mistake for Fitzgerald to see constitutional change as any precursor for a United Ireland. In any final settlement for the island of Ireland the entire Irish situation will have to be re-written. There will also be a considerable degree of autonomy in any future federal Ireland, although it will be a lopsided federation with one twenty-six county unit and one six county unit. But a political settlement for the island will have to be fudged and there are a number of ways this can be done: (1) a new Federal Republic which would come into existence would join NATO; if partition is removed then the Dublin government have said that this will be no problem. (2) Alongside this the Commonwealth can be brought into practice. It is in effect a loose federation of English-speaking states, and we can play up the Crown or play it down depending on who we are talking to. We can say to the Unionists: look, the Queen is head of the Commonwealth, and let them fly their flags on certain days and keep them happy. Then we can say to the Republic that India is a Republic with a President and yet a member of the Commonwealth.

In general, but particularly in this last quotation, there is evidence in Abbott of a third characteristic, in addition to arrogance and foolishness. The third ingredient is political ignorance. There is no sense in which the Commonwealth is a federation. There can be few Unionists who could be bought off by the frippery of which he gives details. And successive generations of the people of the Republic of Ireland have known that India is a republic within the Commonwealth: they have never been persuaded of the desirability of following her example.

In September 1981 Mrs. Thatcher decided to move against her critics in the Cabinet. Ian Gilmour, spokesman for the Foreign Office in the House of Commons; Mark Carlisle, Secretary of State for Education; and Christopher Soames, Leader of the House of Lords, were dismissed. Humphrey Atkins took Gilmour's place and Prior was offered the choice of Northern Ireland or dismissal. He chose Northern Ireland, after some well-advertised hesitation. It fell to him, therefore, to reply to constant, if selective, Unionist probing on the Abbott interviews.

It took him until June 1982, during the Committee Stage of yet another Northern Ireland Bill to create yet another Assembly, flatly to state that nothing Abbott had said represented the policy of Her Majesty's Government. Yet Abbott was not disciplined, but promoted. In November 1985 Mrs. Thatcher signed with Charles Haughey the Anglo-Irish Agreement which established on a formal basis the right of the government of the Republic of Ireland to have a specific say both in the constitutional argument about Northern Ireland and in the day to day running of the province. To this end the government of the Republic set up an office in Belfast, those employed there being charged with monitoring the activities of the British government and its servants within a province of the United Kingdom. If not in the precise way that he and his colleagues wanted, the first steps in Clive Abbott's grand plan were taken.

The Abbott material was, clearly, grist to Powell's mill. But it did not surprise him. There had been an earlier occasion when an officer of the Conservative Research Department in charge of Irish affairs, Alastair Cooke, had, in a briefing note issued during the general election campaign of 1979, stated clearly that, assuming a Conservative victory, Ulster policy would continue exactly as it had done during the Labour years: Neave was, of course, dead by the time this note appeared. However, while it could be argued against Powell between 1972 and 1981 that a great deal of the evidence he had for his belief that there was a steady and deliberate progression towards the dissolution of the Union was circumstantial – and in some, perhaps a large, part fuelled by an anti-American prejudice – this could not be said in the face of the Abbott transcripts and – perhaps even more importantly – in the face of the continued vacillations of a Prime Minister renowned for courage and determination in pursuit of the objectives she had set herself. Powell saw the danger in which Ulster stood; and he saw that any devolved central Assembly in Ulster (as opposed to the restoration of authority to local councils) would be the first step towards ending the Union.

On 6 November 1981 the Taoiseach and the Prime Minister met. Their meeting fuelled the hopes of Republicans, and depressed those of Unionists. In Coleraine on 12 December, Powell summarized his whole case. There was an aim, he said, of transforming totally the relationship between the two islands:

The central feature of that transformation is to be the creation

462

of an all-Ireland state, and the great prize to crown the achievement is to be the entry of that state into NATO, thus filling the gravest of all gaps in the American strategy for Europe and the Atlantic. The key which opens the door is to be an Anglo-Irish institution in which Ulster is to be represented as a third and distinct element and thus drawn progressively into economic and political relations with the Irish Republic. In all this the essential prerequisite is to have in existence an Ulster representative institution.

From 1979 to the end of 1981 was thus a period of intense fluctuation in the politics of Northern Ireland. From the Unionist point of view cautious hope at one moment became depression the next. Throughout it all Powell kept up his constant barrage of speeches, interviews and articles. Nor, despite the intensity of his preoccupation with the affairs of his constituency, did he neglect any of the other causes – like opposition to the EEC and immigration – that he had set his mark upon. The spring of 1982, however, brought a vast and unexpected new challenge: on 2 April Argentina invaded, and proclaimed the annexation of, the Falkland Islands.

This is not the place for a detailed account of the Falklands War and, in any event, a brilliant one exists already.[17] What was to become the war for the Falklands, however, was of inestimable importance to the fate of the Thatcher government, and of great significance to the Ulster Unionist cause.

There is no doubt that the Argentinians, having overcome a necessarily token resistance in Port Stanley, did not expect the United Kingdom to offer more than complaining bluster in the way of resistance: they had, after all, been encouraged by the Foreign Office for years to believe that Britain wanted to hand over that territory they called the Malvinas, if only a decent way could be found. Both the Prime Minister and Lord Carrington, the Foreign Secretary, were culpable in failing to make clear that the British insistence on the right of the islanders to determine their own future was serious. It was also the case that the Foreign Office was seriously derelict in their duty in failing to recognize the signs which warned of imminent invasion.[18]

The Prime Minister was in a particularly vulnerable position. It was obviously necessary to recall Parliament – at the moment adjourned for the Easter recess – and so Lords and Commons met, for the first time since the Suez war of 1956, on a Saturday. The mood of rage was almost universal. Both

Houses were full to overflowing. There were not many who were altogether sure what should be done; but they were sure that something decisive should be done. Moreover, since 1979 the Prime Minister had been portrayed by her admirers as a Leader of particular decisiveness, and she had, very evidently, enjoyed that role. The soubriquet 'Iron Lady', first bestowed upon her years earlier by Marjorie Proops in the *Daily Mirror* and later taken up by a Soviet military magazine, was one she relished, and repeated in speeches from time to time. Yet, here was the government of which she was chief convicted of unreadiness at best and incompetence at worst.

The Secretary of State for Defence, John Nott, made a wretchedly bad impression when opening the government's case. It was Powell, though, who posed the deadly question. He observed that Mrs. Thatcher enjoyed her soubriquet, and then coldly observed that the coming weeks would show 'of what metal she is made'.

She was not at her rhetorical best in her reply. But that mattered far less than the substance of what she had to say. 'A large task force,' she announced, 'will sail as soon as preparations are complete.' On 5 April the first part of the task force – a carrier group – set sail from Portsmouth. For the next twenty days uncertainty continued as a confusing number of efforts were made – most notably by the American Secretary of State, Alexander Haig – to settle the affair diplomatically. Many of the members of the armed services on their 7,000 mile journey believed that they would never be called upon to fight, that, in the end, they would prove to be a pawn in the negotiations. On 25 April, however, the force recaptured South Georgia. After many travails and alarms the Argentinian army, on 14 June, surrendered at Port Stanley. The Prime Minister's reputation had never been higher, and has probably never been higher since.

The importance of the war has since been the subject of endless discussion, but, in general political terms, it is fair to say that victory was taken by most of the world to be the most significant – as it was certainly the most dramatic – event in the restoration of national pride and in the restoration of the United Kingdom to a position of dignity in the eyes of other nations. Ulster Unionists, naturally, shared in the general mood of national rejoicing; but victory at Port Stanley had a particular import for them. 'If,' as Powell succinctly put it, 'you fight for the Falklands – as it was certainly right that we should – how much more should you fight for Ulster?'

The war over and won, Mrs. Thatcher was in a formidable national position. Although Michael Foot had originally supported the sending of the task force he – and other Labour leaders, notably Denis Healey and Neil Kinnock – had seemed to prevaricate during the campaign. Her unalloyed and unqualified support for British troops in the South Atlantic had gained her enormous credit with the public who, in any event, found it difficult to see Foot as a Prime Minister. The Conservatives also enjoyed the spectacle of a satisfactorily divided Opposition. The Liberal Party and the new SDP had come together in the Alliance and, Conservative Central Office strategists agreed, were more likely to damage Labour than the Tories. The economy, moreover, was showing signs of recovery. Home ownership and share ownership had both increased considerably. As 1982 drew to a close the principal political question centred around the date of the next general election. The so-called 'Falklands factor', the Prime Minister's advisers agreed, was of necessity a wasting asset, and it should be employed while there was still time. As ever cautious, Mrs. Thatcher for some time resisted their blandishments. In May 1983, however, she decided to take the plunge, and a general election was called for 9 June.

Powell was in immediate danger in the new marginal constituency of South Down. For one thing Paisley had decided to field a candidate against him. The Unionist vote would, therefore, be split. For another, and by a sad irony, his very success in the Unionist cause was likely to tell against him.

It is fair to say that Ulster owed to Powell more than to any other individual politician the fact that the province's representation at Westminster was to be increased to seventeen seats. One of the necessary consequences of this increase, however, was a re-distribution of constituency boundaries. What remained of the old Down South now became South Down. The old electorate was reduced from 97,000 to 69,000, and the areas Powell lost were predominantly Unionist. There were many among his friends who were convinced he could not hold the seat. It seemed to those who most strongly hoped for his survival that he should seek some sort of perhaps unspoken accommodation with Paisley. Powell, though, would have none of it. He maintained his stern insistence that only his and Molyneaux's party represented true Unionism and, on 6 June at Dromore said:

Each day since nominations closed has seen a growth in

confidence amongst my supporters and friends that this constituency is going to be held for the Union. There are, I think, two reasons for this visible and continuing process. One is the discovery that the efforts which, with the assistance of my Association, I have made during the last nine years on behalf of the constituents of all religions and all political persuasions have not been unnoted or fruitless.

The second reason was that he believed that it was understood that he represented the true Unionist faith. The supporters of Paisley were busy in their denigration of the Englishman who presumed to represent a truer view of Unionism than did Paisley himself. Powell, later in the speech from which I have just quoted, replied with force and dignity:

The division of Unionism, which the enemies of the Union in high places in Britain and abroad have created and fermented in the last one or two decades, was always an unnatural and a dangerous thing; and the people themselves have known and felt it to be so. Now, by a strange dispensation, South Down leads the way towards a better future. In so many people the threat to divide and defeat us has evoked a deeper instinct for that unity which is native to Unionism. In abstaining during this campaign from anything that might stifle or repress that instinct I have, as in so much else, been following the instinct of Jim Molyneaux[19] who, under a storm of misrepresentation and abuse has continued to work patiently and quietly to heal the divisions in Unionism and resisted every temptation to repay evil with evil.

When the result was declared Powell – who had predicted to his wife that he would have a majority of 500 – was the victor by 550 votes. On 17 June, in a speech which infuriated Paisley, he extended a magnanimous hand to those who had voted DUP:

I believe that I made it clear, by word and by silence, in my election campaign that I aspired to represent not only all electors within the South Down constituency but, more particularly, all sorts of Unionist electors. The 3,743 who voted for a certain other candidate undoubtedly felt, however mistakenly, that when they cast their vote they were voting for the Union and against an all-Ireland state. They are essentially on our side of the great divide, and mere differences of emphasis and tradition ought not to be allowed to divide or distract us. For my own part, it will be my object in the next three years or so, to the extent that lies in my power, to ensure that those 3,743 votes are added to the Unionist majority. I will go more than half way to meet them.

What stung Paisley was not merely the fact that he had failed to topple Powell. It was also the simple and understated assumption of the speech of 17 June in Saintfield that 3,743 voters who had supported his chosen candidate would have to be won over to a truer Unionism than he represented.

None the less, the fact that Mrs. Thatcher had come home to victory with a majority of 144 gave her unchallenged authority in national policy. On 2 October 1983 the Labour Party, after an immensely cumbersome leadership election which involved Labour Members of Parliament, constituency parties and the trade unions, put up against her the wholly untried Neil Kinnock. The overwhelming Conservative victory gave a signal to the Labour Party to embark on further internecine strife. The age-old questions a beaten Party in a democracy asks itself (and which the Conservative Party had asked itself in 1964, 1966, and twice in 1974) were asked again. These questions are two. The first is: did we fail to get our message over to the voters because of some failure in presentation? The second is: do our policies make it impossible to be elected, and should we not try to imitate the victors? There is, however, a great, a third, and a never answered question. It is this: have we got the whole scheme of things – notably the aspirations and the beliefs of the electorate – wrong? When a major political Party begins to lose faith in itself it is headed for electoral perdition. Thus, on 10 June 1983 Margaret Thatcher was triumphant; the Labour Party riven.

In 1983, as in 1979, the result of a general election left Powell and the Unionists bereft of any lever of power. In a curious way, however, this left Powell more free than he had ever been before to deploy his intellect over the whole field of national and international politics. The centrality of Ulster to the affairs of the Kingdom, the evidence he had seen to the effect that what happened in the province was a matter of concern, of interest, and of pressure to the government of the United States, gave him a conviction that his geographically (in relation to international politics) tiny constituency was a simulacrum of national interest, and of all the political problems that had beset him since he had returned from India at the end of the war. There is in the man a combination of many characteristics, but most notably a combination of subtlety and brutality of intellect. The subtlety lies in his willing ability to tease out the essence of a problem; the brutality in the bludgeon of the mind which he takes to those who cannot meet him on his own fierce grounds of passionate belief and intellectual efficiency. He has, throughout his career, frightened many fellow politicians. Yet 'I am amazed, and a little affronted when young men come up to me in the House of Commons and call me "Sir" or "Mr. Powell".' A Junior Minister in the Heath administration once came into a bar in the House of Commons and told me, with perfect confidence, 'Enoch has gone mad.' I sought his evidence. 'He was tearing up strips of paper all the way back from New York.' As it happens, Powell regularly tears up strips of paper, to make notes of telephone conversations, judgements on books he is reviewing, or inquiries to himself about whatever engages his mind. It is an academic habit, foreign, of course, to that young Minister. The anecdote may seem slight; but it is revealing. Powell is easy to understand for ordinary people. He is easy to understand by people with a similar academic background. In the middle he attracts either acolytes or those horrified by his abuse of the conventions they live by.

None of this meant that Powell fought any less fiercely than he had ever done for Ulster. But the scope of his argument had, in many respects, broadened. He has ever been prepared, when considering a particular political issue, to offer a judgement on its wider importance. He did this long before he was a politician, as when he offered his view on the relevance of Thucydides[20] and German scholarship after the First World War to the political history of Western Europe in the 1930s. Throughout his political career he has, however, never lost sight of the relationship between the particular and the general.

His views on what he considers to be the great issues of his time are already well known to the reader of this book. But it is important to mention that he never neglects, nor loses sight of, anything he has taken up, because everything that seizes his interest comes out of the whole of his mind, and not simply out of a part of it. Thus we find him, throughout the 1980s, continuing to speak powerfully on immigration and on the relationship – such as it is – between the United Kingdom and the European Community. But we find him also, because this has been the necessary political condition of his party, given Mrs. Thatcher's invariably substantial majorities, intellectually energetic, emotionally committed, unbreakably willing to reason, but not, any longer, central to the important business of making and breaking governments. When, as the Privy Councillor nominated by James Molyneaux, he was briefed on the progress of the war for the Falklands he was, for what was probably – though not certainly – the last time, listened to by those who were in government. As always, and out of his nature, he showed that he had that quality of *gravitas* so esteemed by the classical scholars whom he had admired and studied.

The Parliament of 1983-87 did, however, present certain problems, if not puzzles, to this foremost intellectual champion of the Union. A Northern Ireland Assembly was in existence, though it had only a consultative role. Not least because of Powell's influence, all Unionists withdrew from it on 21 November 1983. It was later dissolved. The conduct of the Prime Minister was inexplicable, except by reference to Powell's judgement on the forces in action against the Union. James Prior was succeeded by Douglas Hurd as Secretary of State for Northern Ireland. Hurd was, after a year, succeeded by Tom King. In November 1984 the Prime Minister had met Garret Fitzgerald at Chequers. To the dismay of the Taoiseach, Mrs. Thatcher, at her post-summit Press Conference, ruled out any role for the Republic of Ireland in the affairs of Ulster. 'Out, out, out,' she said of all the proposals emanating from Dublin. Powell was pleased, as he told an audience at Warrenpoint on 13 November, because he thought her remarks brought to an end the year in year out sapping of the foundations of the Union. He thought it was time to move on:

> I will not remain at the level of generalities. The process has to begin somewhere sometime. For all its claims to represent the principles of democracy I see no prospect that the Labour Party will make a start. If it is to be the Conservative Party that ends direct rule by breaking off the long intrigue of which direct rule was the instrument, then it is through the Conservative Party that those Ulster electors who, in Britain, would be supporters and members of the Conservative Party, must find a way to participate in the politics of their country, a country not a stepmother, but a true mother to Ulster.

This was the highest point of Powell's estimation of Margaret Thatcher. As always in his political life he was prepared to take assurances at their face value, just as his own assurances could be taken. It is almost certainly true to say that he felt happier in his cause when he made this speech at Warrenpoint, and more convinced that it might succeed, than at any earlier time. Indeed, Mrs. Thatcher's abrupt manner at her Press conference echoed a speech of his own at Ballynahinch on 26 May 1984. He was discussing yet another IRA murder, and considered particularly the fact that the territory of the Republic of Ireland, contrary to all political assurances offered, continued to be a haven for the IRA. He concluded:

> We have a message, too, for the USA and the EEC. It is shorter even than that message to the Irish Republic which has contained the security policy which will give protection to all the citizens of Northern Ireland, especially those living close to the border.[21] It consists of two words: 'Get lost'.

The relief which Powell felt after Chequers was to be short-lived. He had, by this time, developed a full, considered, and coherent view of international relations. Herbert Butterfield, that greatest of English historians, once said that a scholar's prejudices may lead him as close to the truth as may his reading of archives. From his earliest acquaintance with them in North Africa, Powell had not cared for Americans. When he was Shadow spokesman on defence under Edward Heath he had demonstrated a suspicion of the usefulness of nuclear weapons – the usefulness of Britain's independent deterrent. The prejudice led him to look at evidence others did not care to contemplate. As always, however, from the beginning of his life he proceeded from a fundamental sense of nation. It amused him, therefore, to be able, at Killyleagh on 2 June 1983, in a speech opposing the siting of American cruise missiles in Britain, to quote a speech by George Washington in his aid. Washington said that 'the nation which indulges towards another a habitual hatred or a habitual fondness is to some degree a slave. It is a slave to its animosity or to its affection, either of which is sufficient to lead it astray from its duty and its interest.' Thus,

> These are words which fit quite startlingly in the case of Britain. We have been led astray from our duty and interest and in some degree enslaved by habitual fondness towards the United States, and habitual hatred towards Russia, in which we have been taught to indulge. A perception that this has been so

lies at the heart of the present unease and it is one that owes nothing to the demonstrations at Greenham Common nor to the machinations of those who are on Michael Heseltine's list of the left.[22]

The extraordinary thing about Powell's intellectual development is the way in which it has continued, from roots that are clear and obvious, but which have the capacity to throw out new branches. There is no doubt that he is a man out of his time, but only in the sense in which André Malraux said of Charles de Gaulle, 'He is a man of the day before yesterday, and of the day after tomorrow.' Even now, as Powell approaches his eightieth year, the flow of articles and essays – not to mention speeches – shows not the slightest sign of slowing down, let alone drying up; and each piece of argument while its origins are clear invariably shows an exciting – and disturbing – capacity to challenge all received notions.

From 1984, however, the political career – in the electoral sense – was moving to its close. Powell was happy with the Prime Minister's statement of relations between the United Kingdom and the Republic of Ireland. But he was to be disabused a year later when the Anglo-Irish Agreement was signed. 'Treachery,' hissed a despairing Powell when she appeared to defend that document before the House of Commons. A number of Parliamentary reporters lamented the demise of a great Conservative statesman, imagining, in their foolish way, that the Agreement represented no more than a sensible arrangement between two countries which would contribute to an easement of terrorism. It has not, of course, contributed to any such easement. As with every other arrangement made between London and Dublin, it has procured an increase in the level of terrorism. The justification of Powell's appellation, however, did not lie in that measurement. It lay, rather, in the blatant contradiction between what Mrs. Thatcher said in 1984 and what she did in 1985. The Union had been thrown into danger only twelve months after it had seemed to be on the brink of preservation.

For the moment Paisley and Molyneaux came together. Against the advice of Powell all Unionist Members of Parliament resigned their seats. By-elections were called. The object of the Unionist operation was to demonstrate the support of the people of Ulster for their cause, and the opposition of those same people to the Agreement. It was, at best, a mixed success for, on 23 January 1986, when all the by-elections were held, the Unionists lost Newry to the SDLP. Powell, campaigning as assiduously as ever in atrocious weather, but this time without a DUP opponent, held South Down with a majority of 1,800. I saw him just before he set out for his campaign, when he predicted that his majority would be 'somewhere around 1,800'. A day before the poll I sent him a telemessage of good wishes. I mentioned the Red Hand of Ulster, the traditional symbol of the province, and quoted the Emperor Constantine, *in hoc signo vinceres*. A few days later I received a letter of thanks which was quintessential Powell. He thanked me for my message but added, 'I do not quite see why you put my victory in the subjunctive.'

Again under the influence of Paisley the returned Unionists were under pressure to boycott the House of Commons. This was a ploy certain to be ineffective, to the relief of the government. It was, however, warmly supported by Paisley's friends in the Northern Ireland Office, for it would leave their Secretary of State free of criticism from those who knew best what was actually happening in Ulster. Powell, however, declined to observe the boycott. So far as the political balance of power was concerned, however, neither boycott nor attendance mattered very much. 1986 moved on through the launch of the Channel Tunnel project and the violence attending a strike of printers at Times Newspapers to a Budget on 17 March 1987 which saw a reduction in income tax. On 11 May 1987 Mrs. Thatcher secured a dissolution of Parliament. Powell fought his usual resolute campaign in South Down. This time, however, more electors voted and he was defeated by 731 votes on a turnout seven per cent up on that of 1983.

Once Powell saw the turn-out figures he was convinced that he had been defeated. His principal hope of survival had been that the nationalist vote would be disastrously split between Sinn Fein and the SDLP. During the campaign, however, it became clear that the Sinn Fein candidate, in common with her colleague, Gerry Adams in West Belfast, would not, if elected, take his seat in the House of Commons. The Catholic vote, therefore, went in its great majority to the SDLP. In a conversation with Powell a few days before the poll a Catholic voter explained, with polite regret, why he would cast his vote for Mr. McGrady. 'It's been a long time since 1920, sir,' he said, 'and we really want to send one of our own to Westminster.' By 'one of our own', he did not mean a nationalist but a Catholic.

After the declaration the three candidates each spoke in the kind of tones judged appropriate on such occasions. The victor was greeted with polite applause; Powell in complete and respect-ful silence. This was greatly to his surprise, since both he and his wife had expected hostile demonstrations of triumph at his final defeat. The proceedings concluded after half an hour. Powell's agent asked him if he proposed to leave by the front door, or would prefer to depart quietly by the rear exit. Powell asked what the man thought he would do and began to walk towards the front door. Outside, there was a crowd of some hundred, most of them supporters of the victor. That honourable man came forward to shake Powell's hand and to promise him that he would care for the constituency with the same assiduity as his distinguished pre-decessor. Another in the crowd was Seamus Mallon, the Deputy Leader of the SDLP. 'I could not,' said Powell, 'have imagined that I could be so surprised.' Mallon, too, advanced to shake the hand of the defeated candidate and, with complete sincerity, to wish him well for the future.

On 31 October 1974 Jamie Camplin, editorial director of the publishing company, Thames and Hudson, wrote to Powell suggesting that he should write a short book – of about 25,000 words – in a renowned series which his company produced. The format was clear: the text would be an essay; the illustrations adorning it lavish. The series being biographical, Camplin wanted this modern Tory heretic to write about Disraeli, the – in the for-mulation of Harold Macmillan[23] – 'brilliant, dandified Jew', who rose to command the Conservative Party, and to leave a legacy which can, to the time of writing, be intoned in support of the idea that the Conservative Party has traditionally, indeed historically, believed in the systematic intervention of the government of the day for the cure of social ills. Powell on Disraeli would, indeed, have been a fascinating subject. The full truth about the brilliant, dandified Jew, however, is to be found elsewhere, and in a most copiously scholarly form.[24]

On 1 November 1974 Powell replied to Camplin, and arranged a meeting. 'I told him that I found Disraeli tedious,' Powell says; and the correspondence bears this judgement out. There was, however, one politician, a man who was beginning his rise from municipal to national prominence at a time when the sun of Disraeli's charm was setting, about whom Powell wanted to write a biographical essay. By the time the book was finished Powell had come to dislike Joseph Chamberlain. But the fact of the matter remains that, on 12 December 1974, Camplin wrote to Powell agreeing to the proposition that the Disraeli book should be a Chamberlain book. Camplin agreed, moreover, that Powell could have 35,000 as opposed to 25,000 words in which to state his judgement on Joseph Chamberlain, a man who, like Powell, came from Birmingham, who was more dandified than Disraeli – invariably appearing with a monocle in his right eye and an orchid in his buttonhole – and who broke apart two major political parties – the nineteenth century Liberals and the twentieth century Conservatives – because of his belief in two causes. These were union with Ireland, and economic protection within the British Empire.

Chamberlain was the subject of a massive, and uncompleted, biography by J. L. Garvin, perhaps the greatest editor the *Observer* newspaper has ever employed. Garvin's work was continued, in a quite different style, and a more flamboyant manner, by Julian Amery, a conservative Member of Parliament to this day, who earned some distinction as a Minister in the Heath government. Garvin and Amery had at their disposal the enormous Chamberlain archive which, now deposited in the library of the University of Birmingham, describes, in so far as these things can, not merely the life and career of Joseph, but those of his sons, Austen and Neville. Austen was the only Leader of the Conservative Party in the twentieth century not to become Prime Minister, while Neville enjoyed the doubtful distinction of being joint author – with Adolf Hitler – of the Munich agreement of 1938.

The closing years of Joseph Chamberlain's life[25] were devoted to trying to persuade the Conservative Party to abandon its advocacy of free trade among nations and adopt, instead, a system of Imperial Preference, in accordance with which the United Kingdom, the Dominions and the Colonies would form a single economic group, aligned economically against the rest of the world. Chamberlain urged this policy, not merely on his party, but upon his sons even after a stroke had deprived him almost entirely of speech and even, from time to time, of sense. It was understandable, therefore, that, moved by the simple drama of a man's determination in a cause in his dying months, Garvin, followed by Amery, placed the emphasis of their long story on the first decade of this century.

Powell, in 1974, saw the emphasis as lying elsewhere. '. . . I have,' he wrote, 'deliberately shifted the point of balance by placing in the centre the pivotal year 1886 . . .' On 26 March 1886 Gladstone told the Cabinet which he headed that he intended to introduce a measure of what was called Home Rule for the whole of Ireland. Chamberlain asked four questions of the Prime Minister, all designed to elicit precisely how much power and authority would, under the proposals, be devolved – it is not excessive to use this twentieth century word – to an administration in Dublin. 'Gladstone,' Powell wrote, 'for once, did not refine or prevaricate.' In sum, his plan would mean an Ireland independent of the Crown in every area except defence and foreign policy. 'Then,' said Chamberlain, 'I resign.' It was not until a century later that a Cabinet minister – in 1986 Michael Heseltine – again took leave of his office in the course of a Cabinet meeting. The crucial issue, the outcome of argument about which led to the death of the Liberal Party, was Ireland. It can readily be seen, therefore, how Powell, writing in 1974, interpreted Chamberlain's decision in a different way from that of his official biographers.

But, then, it is in Powell's nature constantly to sift evidence and to re-interpret experience. 'What,' a mutual friend said to me shortly after the 1987 general election, 'is Enoch going to do in retirement?' Having overcome amazement at the thought, I replied, 'Enoch will never retire.' Certainly, the flow of considered essays has increased rather than diminished with the absence of parliamentary responsibilities. He remains in fighting trim. He remains entirely *sui generis*, and ever active. I remember calling upon him one morning when he was writing. The lean figure who opened the door was in his usual three piece suit with his tie neatly in place, 'Do you ever,' I asked him, 'dress casually when you are slaving away at your desk?' He looked perplexed. 'But I am dressed casually,' he replied. There was a moment's pause. Then he pointed down to his feet, adorned by red leather slippers. 'These,' he said, 'are my writing slippers.' He was wounded, and deeply wounded, by his defeat in 1987 but, with that quirky humour which is his own, and that immense dedication to work which has been with him since childhood, he picked himself up and went on.

It will be a long time – since he still excites so much controversy in so many quarters – before the Conservative Party realizes what is owed to him. I quoted, earlier, an article by Oliver Letwin.[26] It is no more than indicative. Letwin was not born when Enoch Powell had completed the second of his lives. Margaret Thatcher was a humble backbencher when he was laying down laws about the right conduct of economic policy which she has since followed, and greatly to her advantage and to the advantage of the nation. Every threat to the nation he has foreseen. When his warnings have been heeded, the nation has benefited. When they have been ignored, the nation has suffered. This most austere of men has nevertheless proved again and again his ability to speak directly to, and arouse in the hearts of, people less well-educated, less disciplined, less articulate, less fervent than himself a sense of passion which no other politician since Churchill has been able to arouse. He chose to sever his links with the Conservative Party. Since he did so the Party has richly enjoyed the fruits of his intellectual heritage. The younger generation of Conservatives readily acknowledge their debt: it is more than time that their elders did so as well, and as freely. I have no doubt whatsoever that, a generation from now, historians will puzzle over the fact – sad as it is, and certainly tragic – that a political Party was so foolish as to lose him.

But, then, the reason why they lost – perhaps, given what he has left in terms of the mind, a better word would be mislaid – him was that, for what may turn out to be only a brief time in its history, the Conservative Party lost its sense of nationhood; and without an understanding of nationhood there can be no real understanding of Enoch Powell. Forever and forever again, in all of his lives, the pulse of nationhood beats strongly and truly. As he now embarks on a series of brilliant essays on the future of the balance of power in Europe; as he foresees the time when the United States will have withdrawn from these islands and the adjacent continent; as he ponders the significance of the changes consequent upon the alteration of the domestic and foreign policy of the People's Republic of China, as he predicts the demise of the European Common Market, we are required to ask ourselves one question. It is this: he has been right so often: might he not be right again?

And, of course, there are other things he has to do. Pamela Powell likes detective stories. Having a drink with the Powells one evening she and I exchanged a few remarks on the *genre*. Mrs. Powell said to her husband, 'You ought to write a detective story.' 'But,' he replied, 'I am writing a detective story.' The story in question involves a major reinterpretation of·the New Testament: for the purposes of his work Powell, in late middle age, set himself to learn Hebrew. As with the biographical essay on Chamberlain, as with his finest speeches, as with his best essays, everything Powell does begins with a massive amount of research, and then depends on the single insight that makes sense of the research material. It is, and has been so often, only when he has broken the ground that successors can make sense of the details.

Again, though, we have always to come back to the sense of nation. This brings us, necessarily, back to the last great cause of his public life, the cause of the Union. Those younger Conservatives who have benefited so much, most obviously in terms of economic policy but, more generally, in terms of high thinking and moral quality in politics, would do well to ponder a speech made in Birmingham on 18 October 1986. Powell reviewed the history of the Union as it is covered in the last two chapters of this book. He came to the conclusion that the policies of successive British governments had been perfidious, and over subservient to the policies of the United States. And he ended thus:

The charge which the Prime Minister, the Foreign Secretary and (if he has been let into the secret) the Defence Secretary face is not that they have assented to what they believed the national interest required. The charge is that they have deliberately withheld what they were about from the knowledge and judgement of the British people. I am one of those who believe that if in 1982 we had not reversed by force of arms in the South Atlantic the course deemed by the Foreign Office to be in the national interest, the world would have spat in our faces. The immorality being committed in our name against Northern Ireland is far greater. So will be our shame if we do not reverse it.

Look upon him. Learn from him. You will not see his like again.

Notes

PREFACE

1. See David Butler and Michael Pinto-Duschinsky, *The British General Election of 1970* (London, 1971) and David Butler and Denis Kavanagh, *The British General Election of February 1974* (London, 1974). The appendices entitled 'The results analysed' in both volumes were contributed by Michael Steed.

2. R. W. Johnson and Douglas Schoen, ' "The Powell Effect": or how one man can win', in *New Society*, 22 July 1978. See also Douglas Schoen, *Enoch Powell and the Powellites*, (London, 1978).

CHAPTER ONE

1. In John Wood (ed) *Powell and the 1970 General Election* (London, 1970) pp. 50ff.
2. 4 October 1969.
3. Powell has often been accused (most notably and thoroughly by Paul Foot in *The Rise of Enoch Powell* (London, 1969)) of cynically and suddenly taking up the issue of immigration in the Birmingham speech. Usually, he defends himself by referring back to the Walsall speech three months earlier. When, in 1986, I showed him the 1966 speech from his own archive he shook his head over it. 'I had completely forgotten it,' he said. 'It shows what a wretched memory I have. But it may also show that the issue had sunk so much into me that I did not regard reference to it as anything other than commonplace.'
4. For a full discussion, see below, Chapter Four.

5. In an interview with the BBC.

6. Throughout this book I will give references for remarks or statements made by Powell. Many of these will be to books, newspaper articles, or broadcasts. If I give simply a date (in the main for speeches) I will be quoting from his archive of press advances. An unadorned quotation, such as the one to which this note is appended, comes from a conversation between him and me.

7. See Jock (now Lord) Bruce-Gardyne, *Whatever Happened to the Quiet Revolution?* (London, 1973).

8. Hansard, 25 May 1973.

9. See below, Chapter Seven, p. 341ff.

10. See Chapter Seven.

11. Alvide Lees-Milne, *The Englishman's Room* (London, 1986).

12. *The Daily Record*, 19 October 1948.

13. For the economy of the Powell household see below, Chapter Two.

14. 14 July 1978.

15. Enoch Powell, *Freedom and Reality* (London, 1976).

16. John Wood (ed) *op. cit.*, p. 106.

17. *Sunday Times*, 17 July 1983.

18. See, for example, Humphry Berkeley, *The Odyssey of Enoch: a Political Memoir* (London 1977).

19. At the time I was political editor of the *Spectator*. There was a massive increase in the number of letters we received, and nearly all of them supported Powell.

20. Berkeley, *op. cit.*, p. 88.

21. See above, Preface, p. 3.

22. See below, Chapter Five.

23. *Ibid.*

24. The debate about what exactly Macmillan did about the succession to himself was, for a time, intense. It is now generally accepted that he ensured the defeat of R.A. Butler and the emergence of Alec Douglas-Home by rigging the figures. Iain Macleod first made the accusation in the *Spectator* on 17 January 1964, in the course of a review of Randolph Churchill's book *The Fight for the Tory Leadership*. Powell's review – which was even more savage than Macleod's and which argued that Macmillan lied to the Queen – appeared in the same paper on 11 October 1972. The fullest summary of the argument can be found in Anthony Howard, *RAB: The Life of R. A. Butler* (London, 1987) pp. 295ff. It is to be expected that in the second volume of his official biography of Macmillan, Mr Alastair Horne will provide much more information than is now available.

25. He has succeeded.

26. See note 3 above.
27. Robert Rhodes James, *Ambitions and Realities* (London, 1976).
28. This is discussed fully in Chapter Five.
29. See Andrew Roth, *Enoch Powell: Tory Tribune* (London, 1970) pp. 214ff.
30. Another man had died between the first assaults and the debate.
31. To a lunch at the *Spectator* in 1976.
32. Later Lord Rhyl, and now deceased. Birch was a flamboyant and fascinating character who was prevented by poor health and a naturally acerbic temper from political advancement. He awaits his biographer.
33. Berkeley, *op. cit.*, pp. 12-13.
34. *Ibid.*

CHAPTER TWO

1. *First Poems* (Oxford, 1937).
2. Doojen Napal *Enoch Powell* (Wolverhampton, privately printed 1975) vol. 1, pp. 46ff.
3. Albert Powell was, of course, too old actually to fight in the First World War, but he had served as a Volunteer in the Royal Warwickshire Regiment, into the ranks of which his son later followed him.
4. This astonished Welshmen. Many years later, however, Powell did a radio interview for BBC Wales and, though I am informed that his delivery was somewhat stilted, he nonetheless made a deep impression on his listeners.
5. The influence of Methodism on the history of British politics has often been noted but never thoroughly explored. It is indicated by the fact that Harold Wilson and Margaret Thatcher were both brought up as Methodists.
6. See Michael Foot, *Loyalists and Loners* (London, 1986) pp. 185ff. See also below, Chapter Six.
7. *National and English Review*, December 1959.
8. *The Times*, 8 August 1960.
9. See Patrick Cosgrave, *Margaret Thatcher: Prime Minister* (London, 1979).
10. Doojen Napal, *op. cit.*, *loc. cit.*
11. *The Sunday Times*, 17 August 1983.
12. Powell is currently at work on a major book concerning the evolution of the New Testament. This is discussed below in Chapter Eight.

13. There is a comparison here with Margaret Thatcher who, against the wishes of her teachers, left school a year early to go to University.

14. Howard Pedraza, *Winston Churchill and Enoch Powell* (London, 1986) p. 81.

15. 'Myself when Young', Summer, 1974.

16. See above, Chapter One.

17. *The Times*, 27 September 1962.

18. Powell was noted, as an undergraduate, both for dining in Hall only on the minimum number of occasions laid down by regulations, and for regularly 'sporting his oak' – that is to say, closing the outer door of his college rooms, an indication that visitors were unwelcome.

19. At Cambridge, a distinction is drawn between tutors and supervisors. Although a tutor will normally discuss academic work with a pupil, he is essentially charged with supervising moral welfare. The academic work is carried on under the direction of a supervisor.

20. Housman was one of the most famous, and feared, classical scholars of his day. His principal work as an editor was on the hitherto obscure Roman poet, Manilius. He reached a far wider public, however, with his famous collection of plangent poetry, *A Shropshire Lad*, a volume which had some important influence on Powell's own verse.

21. *The Times*, 27 September 1962.

22. *Ibid*.

23. Powell remains to this day an intensive reader of classical texts, though the fashion for the rigidity with which these matters were treated in his youth has passed.

24. Andrew Roth, *op. cit.*, p. 184.

25. Richard Bentley was a famous classical scholar of the eighteenth century, and Master of Peterhouse and later Trinity, Cambridge.

26. Housman's lecture, given in 1934, like all his criticism, included slashing attacks on fellow writers. However, there was more romanticism in this lecture than is generally to be found in his prose.

27. See Robert Graves, *Poetic Craft and Principle* (London, 1967).

28. See Yvor Winters, *In Defense of Reason* (Chicago, 1943).

29. *Ibid*, p. 79.

30. Babette Deutsch, *Poetry Handbook* (London, 1958).

31. Richard Porson was a notoriously bibulous but brilliant classical scholar of the seventeenth century. Various illuminating references to him are to be found in an outstanding book by Mr. Warren Derry, *Dr. Parr: A Portrait of the Whig Dr. Johnson* (Oxford, 1966).

32. Andrew Roth, *op. cit.*, p. 24.

33. On Paul Maas see below p. 57.
34. Proceedings of the Classical Association, May 1936.
35. Herbert Butterfield, *The Whig Interpretation of History* (Cambridge, 1936).
36. Herbert Butterfield, *The Englishman and his History*, (Cambridge, 1936).
37. See above pp. 44ff.
38. Historiography, as developed to its present sophisticated state by Herbert Butterfield, is the history of the writing of history. Butterfield worked for many years on a favourite idea of his, *viz.*, that, by the systematic study of the way earlier generations approached evidence, we could learn to avoid many of the pitfalls dug by sympathy and prejudice. His major work on the subject is *Man on his Past* (ed. 1969).
39. Winston S. Churchill, *My Early Life* (1930) Chapter IX.
40. Professor William J. Woodhouse, whom Powell succeeded, was also a Cambridge man and a Craven Scholar.
41. *English and National Review*, August 1958.
42. *The Daily Telegraph*, 27 May 1966.
43. The History Department in University College, Dublin, runs a course in which, over two successive years, selected students study intensively the contemporary documents of two different historical periods. In their examinations they are asked one question, which requires the imitation of a document from their period. There follow three days of intensive grilling, during which each pupil is subjected to the attacks of his peers and of three academic assessors. From my own experience I would suggest it is as intensive as anything Professor Powell thought up.
44. Andrew Roth, *op. cit.*, pp. 27ff.
45. He resigned the Durham chair when he decided to go into politics. He has never done any teaching since he was on military service. See below, Chapter Three.
46. The other occasion of shame was in 1975, when the British electorate decided, at a referendum, to maintain membership of the EEC.

CHAPTER THREE

1. See above, p. 38.
2. Ronald Lewin, *Ultra goes to War: The Secret Story* (London, 1978).
3. Richard Cave, *A Bodyguard of Lies* (London, 1984).
4. Andrew Roth, in his book, states the generally held view that

Powell had thought to join the Royal Warwicks because his father had served in that regiment. We now know that the manoeuvres that Powell made to join that regiment were carried out in a different way.

5. Sir David Hunt was later British High Commissioner in Lagos during the Nigerian Civil War.

6. Andrew Roth, *op. cit.*, p. 33.

7. See Michael I. Handel (ed.), *Clausewitz and Modern Strategy* (London, 1986).

8. *The Sunday Telegraph*, 17 July 1966.

9. See below, pp. 79ff.

10. It is worth noting, however, that Winston Churchill held very firmly to the view that the German attack on Russia meant that the Allies would eventually win the war.

11. See Martin Gilbert, *Winston S. Churchill, Vol. VI: Finest Hour* (London, 1983) Part Four.

12. See Patrick Cosgrave, *Churchill At War: Alone*, (London, 1971) p. 29.

13. See Martin Gilbert, *op. cit., loc. cit.*

14. See below pp. 77ff.

15. See Ronald Lewin, *op. cit.*, p. 267.

16. Ronald Lewin, *op. cit., loc. cit.*

17. See pp. 43ff.

18. See Desmond Young, *Rommel: Desert Fox* (London, 1952). A highly successful film, starring James Mason, and based on Brigadier Young's book, later further increased Rommel's reputation in the United Kingdom.

19. See Brian Bond, *Liddell Hart: A Study of his Military Thought* (London, 1976).

20. Powell was convinced from the very beginning that the American effort in Vietnam was doomed to failure. So many articles and speeches cover his judgement on this subject that it seems unnecessary to make specific reference to them.

21. See an article by Powell, 'Europe's Transatlantic Colony' in *Interplay* (March, 1968).

22. See Martin Gilbert, *op. cit., loc. cit.*

23. See Martin Gilbert, *op. cit., loc. cit.*

24. The phrase, 'a Bismarckian peace' was coined by Sir Arthur Nicolson (later Lord Carnock) who was Permanent Under Secretary at the Foreign Office during the First World War. It referred to the fact that after the crushing German victory in the war with France of 1870, Bismarck sought to impose moderation on German policy in order to avoid creating a state of permanent enmity with

France. See Harold Nicolson, *Sir Arthur Nicolson, Bart., First Lord Carnock. A Study in the Old Diplomacy* (London, 1930).

25. Michael Strachan, 'Educating the Professor', *Blackwood's Magazine* (February, 1952). Strachan's article originally appeared under his initials only.

26. He celebrated his thirty-first birthday on the day he and his companion set out.

27. Although he has never mastered the motor car to the satisfaction of his passengers, Powell nevertheless acquired considerable technical skills in other areas, notably becoming a singularly competent carpenter.

28. Strachan and Powell, despite the surreal comedy of their journey, became lifelong friends.

29. R. S. Surtees was a famous nineteenth-century foxhunter and his works are regarded by those who hunt as of an almost biblical stature.

30. I have already mentioned that, while at Cambridge, Powell had sought to volunteer for the Ethiopian Army after Mussolini's pre-war invasion of that country. See above, p. 50. Orde Wingate first made his reputation early in the war by fighting in Ethiopia. He later formed a military force dubbed 'The Chindits' to fight behind Japanese lines in Burma, where he was killed.

31. See *The Auk* (London, 1965). Parkinson was a brilliant young military historian who died in his thirties and is much lamented by all students of the period.

32. Chief of the Imperial General Staff, Sir Alan Brooke (later Lord Alanbrooke).

33. Lord Moran, *Winston Churchill: the Struggle for Survival 1940-1965* (London, 1966).

34. Even at home Powell dresses with great formality, his only concession to casualness being what he calls 'my writing shoes', a pair of red leather slippers.

35. Philip Mason, *A Shaft of Sunlight* (London, 1978), p. 197.

36. *Ibid.* p. 196.

37. Kingsway is one of the main thoroughfares in New Delhi.

38. *Op. cit.* vol. I, p. 156.

39. R. A. Butler, whom Powell strained every nerve to make Leader of the Conservative Party, in his youth in India, also became devoted to Muslim politics and culture. See his autobiography *The Art of the Possible* (London, 1971).

40. *Interplay*, March, 1952.

41. There are many references, but one of the most striking is to be found in the *Spectator*, 15 March 1973.

42. Again, there is such a variety of writing on the subject that it seems otiose to select from its number.
43. See Kenneth Rose, *Curzon in India* (London, 1985).
44. See below, Chapter Five.
45. Compromise *for* principle is not unknown to him. See below Chapter Seven and the discussion on the EEC.
46. In the *Spectator*, 5 September 1972. The books were my own *Churchill at War: Alone* and *Churchill* by Henry Pelling.
47. *Op. cit.*, p. 198.
48. 'Europe's Transatlantic Colony', *Interplay* (March, 1968).
49. In the *Spectator*, 13 September 1968.
50. There is a full discussion of the Committee in Philip Mason's *A Shaft of Sunlight*.
51. See above, p. 57.

CHAPTER FOUR

1. See Angus Maude and Enoch Powell, *Biography of a Nation* (London, 1955).
2. See Anthony Howard, *op. cit.*, Chapter Eleven.
3. See Patrick Cosgrave, *R. A. Butler: An English Life* (London, 1981), Chapter Five.
4. See Arnold Beichman, *The Conservative Research Department*, (New York, 1971).
5. I have called the Conservative Research Department CRD for brevity. It should be underlined, however, that in Powell's day the practice of calling it 'The Research Department of Conservative Central Office' was entirely wrong. The CRD was, as I have pointed out, housed separately from organizational Party headquarters in Victoria St., and had its own Chairman who was not the Chairman of the Party. It was not until the advent of Margaret Thatcher that, the lease on the CRD headquarters in Old Queen Street having expired, the Department was transferred to Smith Square. There was also the problem that Mrs Thatcher distrusted what she saw as the left-wing bias of Old Queen Street, and besides, had set up her own think-tank in the Centre for Policy Studies. At the time of writing the CRD is a shadow of its former self. It has lost almost all of the influence it once had on policy-making and is confined almost entirely to propaganda functions.
6. Lord Woolton, *Memoirs* (London, 1959).
7. I trust the reader will forgive a personal anecdote here. Twenty-three years after the events just described I joined the Conservative

Research Department. I was introduced to Nos. 24/32 by Charles Bellairs, a long-serving (and, indeed, still-serving) member of the Party, and my section chief. I was to share a room with the late Rosemary Marten and Christopher Patten (at the time of writing Minister for Overseas Development). Rosemary, Charles told me, sat at Iain Macleod's old desk and Christopher at Reginald Maudling's. I was to have that once graced by Enoch Powell. My first job was to analyse Powell's speeches and attitude on immigration.

8. See below, pp. 105ff.

9. In the library of No. 10 Downing Street there is a collection of books donated by Ministers of the Crown, past and present. It is a convention that any minister who writes a book contributes a copy to this collection. Macleod's book was entitled *How to Win at Bridge*. On the fly-leaf he wrote 'This is the only book in this place that is certain to profit its reader.'

10. See Anthony Seldon, *Churchill's Indian Summer: The Conservative Government 1951–55* London, 1981), pp. 5ff.

11. Patrick Cosgrave, *op. cit., loc. cit.*

12. See Anthony Seldon, *op. cit.* p. 215.

13. See Kevin Jefferys, 'British Politics and Social Policy during the Second World War' in *The Historical Journal*, vol. 30, No. 1 (1987).

14. See Janet P. Morgan, *The House of Lords and the Labour Government, 1964-1970* (Oxford 1975). Dr. Morgan's monograph is the outstanding work on this subject, and it will be many years before it is bettered.

15. J. Enoch Powell with Keith Wallis, *A History of the House of Lords in the Middle Ages* (London, 1968) p. ix.

16. *Ibid.*

17. For a concise consideration of this, see Humphry Berkeley, *op. cit.*, p. 52.

18. It is important to understand that when he refers to the 'Indian Empire' he means what is today India, Pakistan and Bangla Desh.

19. See below, Chapter Six.

20. See below, Chapter Six, p. 231ff.

21. See Chapter Nine.

22. See below, p. 147.

23. *Biography of a Nation*, pp. 7-8.

24. The same cast of thinking can be demonstrated in later controversies in which Powell was involved. I will mention Rhodesia and Ulster. Being satisfied that a majority of Rhodesians did not want to preserve allegiance to the Crown, Powell was happy to let the colony go. In Ulster, on the other hand, a majority did maintain allegiance to the Crown, and he thus fought might and main to

retain the province as an integral part of the United Kingdom.

25. T. E. Utley, *op. cit.*, and Andrew Roth, *op. cit.* I myself heard R. A. Butler, while Master of Trinity, more than once repeat the tale.

26. See Denis Judd, *Radical Joe: A Life of Joseph Chamberlain* (London, 1977), Chapter Six. When a government – even one enjoying a large majority – acts in a controversial manner, however, the Whips find it ever more difficult to resist pressure groups. Indeed, it may be said that a large majority even encourages rebellion, for MPs can hope to oppose particular measures without imperilling the life of the government they support. This has been the experience of the Conservative governments of 1983 and 1987.

27. Powell was supported by a former Research Department colleague, Cuthbert Alport, now Lord Alport, who was subsequently to resign the Conservative Whip in the House of Lords in protest against the activities of the government headed by Mrs Thatcher.

28. In 1961, Cuthbert Alport left the House of Commons to become High Commissioner to the Federation of Rhodesia and Nyasaland.

29. Now Lord Maude of Stratford-on-Avon.

30. Now Lord Carr of Hadley.

31. See below, Chapter Six.

32. Michael Foot, *op. cit.*, pp. 185ff.

33. See above, Chapter Three, p. 86.

34. See above, Chapter One.

35. The most acute critical examination of Powell's theology is in Humphry Berkeley, *op. cit.*

36. It is a central contention of Machiavelli in *The Prince* that religion should be fostered as a means of preserving public order.

37. Quoted in Humphry Berkeley, *op. cit.*, p. 29.

38. However, like Humphry Berkeley, I do not think that the accusation, in so far as it concerns public conduct, can be made to hold up.

39. Over the years Powell has not lost his interest in the architecture and history of churches, quite apart from their religious significance for him. His summer holiday in 1988 was spent visiting the great Carolingian cathedral at Aachen. 'I suddenly realized,' he said, 'that I was approaching my eightieth year and had never seen the place where Charlemagne reigned. I decided immediately to repair the omission.'

40. See below, Chapter Nine.

41. This anecdote was told to me by Macleod.

42. In spite of differences of opinion over the matter of the Suez Canal Treaty, Powell remained on cordial terms with Eden until the end of the latter's life.

43. Moran, *op. cit.*, p. 478.

44. See The Master of Lauderdale (now the Earl of Lauderdale), *The Expanding Commonwealth* (London, 1955).
45. Humphry Berkeley, *op. cit.*, p. 46. See also Powell's speech to the Royal Society of St. George quoted above on p. 1.
46. Now Lord Deedes.

CHAPTER FIVE

1. It is useful to remember that Powell declined a post at the Welsh Office during the life of the last Churchill government. He was believed to be holding out for an economic posting. Housing was not exactly that; but it was near enough.
2. *Medicine and Health*, p. 2.
3. Anthony Howard, *op. cit.*, p. 218.
4. It is always interesting to remember how brief Macmillan's tenure of the various high offices he held was, before he became Prime Minister.
5. Apart from committees of a party, formed to examine a subject of interest to like minds, there are two kinds of Commons committee. Standing Committees are appointed to scrutinize particular bills. Select Committees exist to examine subjects (as it might be, defence or agriculture). Both are chosen, broadly speaking, to reflect the balance of the parties in the House, though a given MP might be considered if he had special expertise in a given subject. The Committee of the Whole House is employed mainly (though not invariably) when a highly controversial or constitutional Bill is under discussion. Any and every Member may attend and contribute. The Committee meets in the Chamber and also goes through the legislation line by line. These Committees, as we shall see in Chapter Six, can be incredibly time-consuming and destructive of other government business. They can also witness defeats of the government of the day, for there is often a great deal of cross-party voting.
6. Now Baroness Brooke of Ystradfellte.
7. See below pp. 148ff.
8. This debate continues even today.
9. See Moshe Dayan, *Story of My Life* (London, 1976), pp. 251ff.
10. Anthony Nutting – who at one time had heroworshipped Eden – never returned to office and, indeed, under pressure from his constituency, left politics. The late Sir Edward Boyle was brought back into government by Macmillan. Subsequently, he served in the Heath Shadow Cabinet before retiring from politics to become Vice

Chancellor of Leeds University.

11. A villa at Sèvres.

12. Dayan, *op. cit.*, p. 180.

13. Reginald Maudling, *Memoirs* (London, 1978), p. 64.

14. Quoted in Anthony Howard, *op. cit.*, p. 241.

15. Eden's health had been uncertain for a long time before the Suez War, and he had several times taken sick leave during the life of the 1951 Churchill government. The strain of Suez finally broke him. But there was no sense in which the announcement of January 7 was a cover-up.

16. See Lord (R.A.) Butler, *The Art of Memory* (London, 1982) p. 96.

17. See Kevin Jefferys, *art. cit.*

18. Lord Thorneycroft later became Margaret Thatcher's first Chairman of the Conservative Party, though he declined a seat in the Cabinet in 1979, even by means of a sinecure.

19. Later Lord Rhyl

20. See below, pp. 184ff.

21. Macmillan, in the face of much criticism, appointed, later, Lord Home of the Hirsel as Foreign Secretary, a post Butler long coveted. He was to receive it from Home in 1963. Home's seniority was, in the same year, a distinct advantage to him when Macmillan manoeuvred him into No. 10.

22. See a review of Randolph Churchill, *The Fight for the Tory Leadership* (London, 1964) in Iain Macleod's *Spectator* article of 17 January 1964. The text of this piece – one of the finest political polemics of our time – can be found in George Hutchinson, *The Last Edwardian at No. 10: an Impression of Harold Macmillan* (London, 1980) pp. 123ff.

23. See Harold Macmillan, *Riding the Storm* (London, 1969) pp. 356–7.

24. In conversation with the author.

25. 12 February 1958.

26. Roth, *op. cit.*, p. 202.

27. See above, pp. 24–6.

28. *The Listener*, 9 and 16 October 1958.

29. One of the great subjects of contention between church and kings in the Middle Ages was the insistence by the church that clergy, of whatever crime accused, should be tried only in ecclesiastical courts.

30. See above, Chapter One.

31. Herbert Butterfield, *Man on his Past* (ed. 1955, Cambridge) pp. 1–32.

32. See below, Chapter Six

33. See Paul Foot, *The Rise of Enoch Powell* (London, 1969), p. 35.

The quotation is from an interview Powell gave to Foot.

34. See J. Enoch Powell, *Saving in a Free Society* (London, 1960). See, also, by the same author, *Income tax at four shillings and threepence in the pound* (London, 1970).

35. J. Enoch Powell, *Medicine and Politics*, (London, 1966, 2nd ed. 1976), p. 7.

36. *Ibid., loc. cit.*

37. See above, p. 15.

38. Powell is, however, invariably courteous towards smokers. When I began work on this book an ashtray was set out on my table but he suggested that I should do the smoking in the garden. I did not do so. I – a heavy smoker – have never smoked in his company except on social occasions.

39. See George Hutchinson, *op. cit.*, pp. 83–4. Hutchinson wrote what Macmillan wanted to say, with greater style than the Prime Minister could command. However, to the end of his days, he remained sceptical about the United Kingdom being a member of the EEC.

40. Nigel Fisher, *op. cit.*, pp. 276ff.

41. J. Enoch Powell, *Medicine and Politics*, pp. 6–7.

42. John Profumo made ample amends for his sins – such as they were – and, supported by his wife, Valerie, devoted himself to charitable work. Miss Keeler contracted an unsuccessful marriage, and wrote her memoirs over and over again. Major Ivanov was recalled and, judged mentally unstable by his masters was sent to a hospital in Siberia. Nothing is known of his subsequent life, if there has been one.

43. Anthony Howard, *op. cit.*, p. 298.

44. A member of either House of Parliament may say in the Chamber whatever he wishes about somebody not a member of either House. He cannot be prosecuted for anything he says in the Chamber.

45. See Howard, *op. cit.*, p. 297.

46. See above, pp. 149ff.

47. For a summary see Anthony Seldon, *op. cit.*, pp. xiff.

48. Nigel Birch (Lord Rhyl) told me, just before his death, that he had embarked on this journalistic adventure.

49. There was, at that time, a veritable plethora of books and articles on the supposed decadence, not merely of the government headed by Harold Macmillan, but of the Conservative Party in general. It is worth recalling, however, that Macleod (*loc. cit.*) believed that the interests of the country would be best served by Macmillan continuing as Prime Minister; and was prepared to accept Macmillan's assurance that he believed Profumo was telling the truth when he told his ministerial colleagues that he had had no involvement with

Miss Keeler.

50. Kenneth Young, *Home: A Biography* (London, 1978), p. 159.

51. The question of how the succession to the leadership of the Conservative Party was decided in 1963 is one of the most perenially fascinating in modern politics. My own view is set out in my *R.A. Butler: An English Life* (*op. cit.*).

52. Iain Macleod wrote, in the *Spectator* already referred to, 'The truth is that at all times, from the first day of his premiership to the last, Macmillan was determined that Butler, although incomparably the best qualified of the contenders, should not succeed him.'

53. Anthony Howard, *op. cit.*, p. 302.

54. *Ibid*. p. 312.

55. It seems that Macmillan proffered advice to the Queen on his successor while, though incapacitated, he was still Prime Minister. Even if, as has been suggested, Her Majesty asked for that advice it was, given the conventions of the constitution, improper for him to give it until his resignation was in her hands.

56. R. A. Butler, *The Art of the Possible* (London, ed. 1980) p. 46.

57. See Anthony Howard, *op. cit.*, p. 312. See also Susan Barnes *Behind the Image* (London, 1974). The Powell quotation comes from a BBC 2 documentary – one in a series called 'Reputations' – broadcast on 13 July 1983.

58. It is useful to recall the stark arithmetic of the views of Members of the Cabinet. Five members of the Cabinet met for lunch on the 18th: none of these were for Home. Their number did not include Butler himself, Hailsham, Powell nor Boyle. (Apart from himself, there were two other Cabinet Members for Home.) This left six Members. Even in the unlikely event that none of these six were for Butler, it is still impossible to claim – as Macmillan did to Her Majesty – that the preponderance of Cabinet opinion was for Home. See Patrick Cosgrave, *op. cit.*, p. 140.

CHAPTER SIX

1. There is nothing theoretically wrong about a peer becoming Prime Minister, and even staying in the Upper House. However, in 1923 Lord Curzon was rejected for the post of first minister, at least partly because he sat in the Lords. In 1940 Neville Chamberlain would certainly have preferred Lord Halifax, rather than Winston Churchill, to succeed him: Halifax declined on the grounds that, as a peer, he would not have day to day supervision of the Chamber on which the fate of government depended – the House of Commons.

Home could – though only in theory – have stayed in the House of Lords and been Prime Minister. The practical point that Macleod and Powell both made, that it was absurd to suppose that the Conservative Party had to have recourse to the House of Lords to find a leader, had, and has, great force. Whatever may be said in praise of Lord Home (and there is a great deal to be said in that vein) he was not outstanding when compared to his colleagues in the Commons.

2. See Michael Foot, *op. cit.*, pp. 186–7.
3. *Op. cit., loc cit.*
4. See above, p. 10.
5. Humphry Berkeley, *op. cit.*, p. 3.
6. See below, pp. 235ff.
7. Nor did Edward Boyle and Aubrey Jones. Their views were, in any event, antipathetic to the views of those who wanted further controls on immigration.
8. See Humphry Berkeley, *Crossing the Floor* (London, 1968). Berkeley lost his seat in the 1966 general election. He resigned his membership of the Conservative Party because he believed that Edward Heath was too inclined to give way to the supporters of stringent immigration control.
9. The government headed by Edward Heath eventually did float the pound. The essence of the idea of floating is that the government should not seek to determine by *fiat* the value of the currency in relation to other currencies though, of course, the Chancellor of the Exchequer can influence it through the interest rate, and the Bank of England can do the same by the purchase or sale of sterling. Until 1972, however, it was generally assumed that government should have total control of currency values, else the national economy would collapse. However, when the pound was floated, as Powell observed, 'The world did not end.' At the time of writing the pound is still floating, and the government is still determined not to join the currency regime of the European Monetary System.
10. Between 1964 and 1966 Harold Wilson was prevented from nationalizing steel because two Labour backbenchers, Woodrow Wyatt and Desmond Donnelly, joined the opposition parties in order to prevent the measure. In the 1966 Parliament, however, steel was nationalized. In the 1983 Parliament the industry, after many travails in the years between, was denationalized or, as the fashionable word goes, privatized.
11. Now Lord Harris of High Cross.
12. *Medicine and Politics*, pp. 6–7.
13. See above, Chapter Five.

14. See above, Chapter Five.

15. Aneurin Bevan was, for many years, the stormy petrel of the Labour Party and regarded by Labour leaders in the same way as Edward Heath regarded Powell. He had, however, a powerful effect on Labour policy and is regarded as the founding father of the National Health Service. The most recent biography is John Cambell, *Bevan* (London, 1987).

16. The Conservative Party is a curious mixture of ruthlessness and sentiment. It is far less tolerant of unsuccessful leaders than is the Labour Party. Nonetheless, its members proclaim loyalty as a quintessential virtue. They also need to feel that their leaders like them. When, in 1975, Heath was challenged for the leadership by Margaret Thatcher there was an insufficient residue of affection for him to draw upon.

17. See above, pp. 12-13.

18. James (now Lord) Prior was one of Heath's two Parliamentary Private Secretaries in opposition between 1965 and 1970. After the election victory of 1970 he was – though he had no ministerial experience – made Secretary of State for Agriculture. He subsequently served as Secretary of State for Employment and as Secretary of State for Northern Ireland. He is now chairman of GEC.

19. The disquisition about his youth in Kent was, and is, one of Heath's favourite party pieces. That he repeats it often, however, is no reason to question its sincerity. For myself, I am quite convinced that the origins of Heath's belief in British adherence to the EEC lie in those brooding moments; and they are none the worse for that. No doubt Heath's forthcoming memoirs will further enlighten us.

20. See above, p. 197.

21. The others present at the meeting were Heath's closest adviser Michael Wolff; Douglas Hurd, his political secretary (and now Home Secretary); Brian Reading, his economic adviser; Edward Rayner, his press adviser; and myself, representing the Conservative Research Department.

22. See Jock Bruce-Gardyne, *op. cit.*, Chapter 1.

23. In the run-up to the 1964 general election campaign, and in deference to the unilateralists in the Labour Party, Harold Wilson undertook to abandon the independent British nuclear deterrent, but to add it to a putative Atlantic Nuclear Force. In office, however, he preserved the deterrent.

24. The Archbishop had been detained, at the discretion of the government, in the Seychelles.

25. Powell first visited the United States in November 1967.

26. See Bernard Donoughue, *op. cit.*, pp. 38ff. It is widely held that Wilson was the most effective Leader of the Opposition in modern times.

27. See above, pp. 134ff.

28. See also Paul Foot, *op. cit.*, pp. 95ff.

29. Douglas Schoen, *op. cit.*, pp. 19ff.

30. The classical statement of this view of Conservative Party organization is to be found in R. T. McKenzie, *British Political Parties* (London, ed. 1967). Robert McKenzie was one of the most sagacious commentators on British politics. His great work first appeared in 1963 and was changed and refined, as a consequence of criticism and debate, through many subsequent editions. Most students of politics now regard it as the best guide to party politics in Britain.

31. See above pp. 209ff.

32. See below, pp. 260ff.

33. *Op. cit., loc. cit.*

34. *Op. cit., passim.* While Mr Foot's book is consistently and deliberately hostile to Powell, it is, however, worth recording something which Mr Foot himself acknowledges: that Powell, while knowing Mr Foot's political attitude and intentions, nonetheless afforded him information for his work.

35. Michael Foot, *op. cit., loc. cit.*

36. (London, 1968) pp. 30ff. See also Robert Z. Aliber, *The International Money Game* (London, 1973).

37. Now Lord Mayhew. Lord Mayhew left the Labour Party to join the Liberal Party in 1974. He is now a senior spokesman for the Social Liberal and Democratic Party.

38. See above, pp. 169ff.

39. Paul Foot, *op. cit.*, pp. 43ff.

40. See above, Chapter Two.

41. Paul Foot, *op. cit.*, pp. 129ff.

42. It is a matter of some debate whether the dependents of immigrants already in this country should be allowed an unqualified right to join them. From April 1968, at the very latest, Powell took the view that the right of entry of dependents had to be curtailed.

43. Andrew Roth, *op. cit.*, pp. 327ff.

44. See Chapter Nine.

45. See, in particular, Diana Spearman, 'Enoch Powell's Election Letters', in John Wood (ed), *Powell and the 1970 Election* (London, 1970), pp. 19ff.

46. See James Callaghan, *op. cit.*, pp. 393–4.

47. Private information.

48. Paul Foot, *op. cit.*, p. 111.
49. See below, Chapter Seven.
50. See above, pp. 8ff.
51. It is an essential part of Powell's thesis about immigration that it should not be possible for an immigrant, of either sex, to claim an unqualified right to acquire a spouse from overseas. While this, obviously, applies particularly to Asian immigrants, he says, 'I would apply it to Canadians, Australians and others as well.' The fact of the matter, of course, is that, while large numbers of Indians and Pakistanis want to come to live in the United Kingdom, very few Canadians and Australians do.
52. See Douglas Schoen, *op. cit.*, p. 33.
53. Sir Edward Boyle was, subsequently, to resign politics altogether for an academic life as Vice Chancellor of Leeds University.
54. See Diana Spearman, *New Society*, 27 June 1968.
55. *Op. cit.*, pp. 36–7.
56. Since 1968 there has been great debate, in newspapers and academic journals – as well as more popular magazines – on the statistics of the immigration problem. However, I think it fair to say that, at the time of writing, most commentators believe that immigration is of the numerical proportions which Powell suggested in 1968, and is suggesting still. There can be honourable disputation about whether this is a good or a bad thing, but there can be no serious argument about proportions.
57. See Janet Morgan (ed.), Richard Crossman, *The Diaries of a Cabinet Minister*, Vol. II (London, 1976), p. 523 and, also, Vol. III (London, 1977), p. 223.
58. See James Callaghan, *op. cit.*, pp. 502ff.
59. The Second Reading of the Parliament (No. 2) Bill was the first occasion on which I saw Powell perform in the House of Commons. I was reporting the occasion for Radio Telefis Eireann and saw the force of his oratory. The genesis of this book may well lie in that moment.
60. James Callaghan, *op. cit.*, pp. 502–3.
61. Janet Morgan, *op. cit., loc. cit.*
62. James Callaghan *op. cit., loc cit.*
63. See below, pp. 540ff. See also Bernard Donoughue, *op. cit.*, pp. 40–1. Professor Bernard (now Lord) Donoughue worked as senior policy advisor both to Lord Wilson and to Lord Callaghan.
64. See above, p. 250ff.
65. NOP Bulletin, September 1968 and January 1969.
66. See above, Chapter Four.
67. The first senior Conservative opponent of the entry of the United

Kingdom into the Common Market was the late Sir Neil Marten. However, he gladly relinquished the leadership of the Opposition to the legislation required for ratifying the Treaty of Brussels to Powell, a more formidable parliamentarian. Marten later served as Minister of Overseas Development in the first government headed by Margaret Thatcher.

68. Monnet is called, by those who approved of his ideology, 'The Father of Europe'. His idea for a United States of Europe was formed during the Second World War, which he spent safely in the United States of America.

69. In the second week of the general election campaign most polls predicted a crushing defeat for Heath. At an early morning briefing at Conservative Central Office (at which I was present on behalf of the CRD) Heath seemed distinctly depressed about his prospects. It says a great deal for the man that he shrugged off his depression and fought back so stoutly during the rest of the campaign.

CHAPTER SEVEN

1. The present author among them.

2. It is worth remembering that there was considerable agreement between Powell and Heath on economic policy in the year before the 1970 general election. The Shadow Cabinet seminar at the Selsdon Park Hotel in the Spring of 1970 laid out the essence of an economic policy which Heath was to abandon during the course of 1972. It also gave birth to one of Harold Wilson's most celebrated quips: he described Heath as 'Selsdon Man' and briefed the press to the effect that he meant Neanderthal man.

3. David Butler and Donald Stokes, *op. cit., ed. cit.*

4. Jock Bruce Gardyne, *op. cit.*, pp. 5–6.

5. It is a sad commentary on British insularity that the memoirs of this most distinguished of French Foreign Ministers have never found an English publisher.

6. Nora Beloff, *The General Says No* (London, 1966).

7. And at press conferences.

8. See David Butler and Donald Stokes, *op. cit., ed. cit, passim.*

9. Jock Bruce-Gardyne, *op. cit., loc. cit.*

10. The phrase comes directly from Clause Four of the Constitution of the Labour Party.

11. After their defeat in the 1970 general election the pressures on the Labour Party to become more ideologically socialist increased

greatly. These pressures increased even more after the Conservative victory of 1979. At the time of writing the direction of the Party is unclear. The most articulate case for believing that constitutional reform is required for the success of a socialist policy is made in Tony Benn, *Arguments for Socialism* (London, 1980).

12. See above, pp. 198ff.
13. See Martin Gilbert, *op. cit.*, Vol. V. pp. 1013ff.
14. See above, p. 252ff.
15. See below, Chapter Eight.
16. He did not, however, mention the Security Council of the United Nations. In the Security Council there are both permanent and rotating members. The United States, the United Kingdom, the USSR, France and China are the permanent members of the Council. Other members of the Council come on a regulated rotation from the General Assembly. This does not, however, wholly invalidate the Powell thesis. At the end of the Second World War the major victorious powers were not willing wholly to accept an absolute equality between nations large and small. It is nonetheless the case that such equality lies behind the theory of the organization.
17. Now Lord Fraser of Kilmorack.
18. General de Gaulle's private home was at Colombey-les-Deux-Eglises. For many years, with the exception of a monthly visit to Paris, he lived there in the confident expectation that he would, one day, be recalled to power, as indeed he was in 1958.
19. 'The Minorities and the General Election', in *Race Today* (July 1970) and 'Powell, the Minorities and the 1970 General Election' in *Political Quarterly* (October-December 1970).
20. Nicholas Deakin is also the author of an earlier study which reflects the liberal thinking on race relations in British politics. It is *Colour and the British Electorate 1964* (London, 1965).
21. See David Butler and Michael Pinto-Duschinsky *The British General Election of 1970* (London, 1971).
22. Mr Steed was subsequently a founder member of the SDP and an Alliance candidate in the general election of 1987.
23. *Op. cit.*, pp. 55ff.
24. See Bernard Donoughue, *op. cit.*, *loc. cit.*
25. The most careful and considered analysis of these questions can be found in Peter Jenkins, *op. cit.*, pp. 79ff.
26. See, for a discussion of and references to, Dr Studlar's views, Douglas Schoen, *op. cit.*, pp. 58ff.
27. See Peter Jenkins, *op. cit.*, pp. 50ff.
28. See Robert Rhodes James, *op. cit.*, p. 7ff.

29. I recall David Wood, one of the most distinguished political correspondents of the time, as saying how utterly surprised he was that Powell had made such a showing.
30. See below, p. 342ff.
31. See Reginald Maudling, *op. cit., loc. cit.*
32. See above, Chapter Six.
33. The most detailed account is available in Uwe Kitzinger, *op. cit.*
34. See above, Chapter Two.
35. Successive British governments declined, after the war, to join the nascent European Economic Community. As, however, the economic strength of the Community became apparent – and in particular, Franco-German amity took hold – it was felt that a rival organization should be founded. This was the European Free Trade Association. It was distinguished from the EEC by the fact that it had no political pretensions, and was based solely on the ideal of free trade. EFTA still exists. Its membership consists of those Western European countries which either declined to join the EEC or were prevented from doing so. The terms of the Russian withdrawal from the territory it had occupied in Austria during the 1950s precluded Austria from joining the EEC. The principal members of EFTA are Norway, Sweden, Switzerland and Austria.
36. See Michael Oakeshott, *On Being Conservative* (Cambridge, 1975).
37. See Uwe Kitzinger, op. cit., pp. 354–8.
38. See above, Chapter Six.
39. *Edward Heath: A Personal and Political Biography* (London, 1970) pp. 90ff.
40. See below, pp. 363ff.
41. The argument for British membership of the EEC, which, in all fairness ought to be considered, is best expressed in Uwe Kitzinger, *op. cit., passim.*
42. See above, pp. 280ff. One thing, however, which concerned the government was what tactics the Opposition would adopt. While Heath could depend on a substantial tranche of Labour support, Wilson's view of membership was very different from that of Heath: the Prime Minister regarded accession to the EEC as a matter of principle, Harold Wilson regarded the whole issue as simply one of party political manoeuvre.
43. See above, pp. 271ff.
44. See above, Chapter Four.
45. See above, pp. 300ff.
46. See *Gallup Poll Index* of October 1972 and April 1973.
47. See reports in *The Sunday Times*, 21 June 1972 and *The Times*, 16 October 1972.

48. See above, pp. 324ff.
49. It was later to be held by many of Heath's supporters, as well as by political commentators, that, had the government been more successful in its handling of domestic economic issues, the Prime Minister would have been able to gain greater popular consent for his policy of membership of the EEC. It seems fair to say that the British electorate accepted accession to the Community with a somewhat sullen air and the belief that there was no alternative. Certainly, there was no widespread enthusiasm for a policy so close to Heath's heart, and he was not a man with the rhetorical gifts to arouse the enthusiasm which he needed.
50. See Bernard Donoughue, *op. cit.*, p. 100.
51. See, for example, David Butler and Dennis Kavanagh *The British General Election of February 1974* (London, 1975), pp. 103ff.
52. See below, p. 357ff.

CHAPTER EIGHT

1. See David Butler and Dennis Kavanagh, *The British General Election of October 1974* (London, 1975) p. 46.
2. See above, pp. 341ff.
3. Carson has been strangely neglected, from the point of view of biography, by modern historians, though his force and power in the history of the politics of Ulster is fully recognised by most historians. To the wider public he is probably principally remembered as the prosecutor of Oscar Wilde. In my own opinion the best biography is Montgomery Hyde, *Edward Carson* (London 1968).
4. The creation of the Northern Ireland Parliament in Stormont was the result of a strange combination of determination, muddle and calculation. The initial hope of British government was to create a united Ireland which would be called a Free State. Such a state would be limited in independence so far as foreign policy and defence were concerned. The stout resistance of Carson and the (Protestant) majority in six of the counties of Ulster prevented David Lloyd George from achieving this ambition. It was therefore decided to establish a parliament whose jurisdiction would be limited to the domestic affairs of the six counties of Northern Ireland. It was hoped in London that such a body would join with the government established in Dublin in a Boundary Commission which would discuss the precise territorial delimitation between the two semi-independent states. In due course, as might have been foreseen, the Free State – that is, the twenty-six counties governed

from Dublin – declared itself to be a Republic. What is now the Republic of Ireland was, of course, neutral during the Second World War. The Northern Ireland Parliament survived until the imposition of direct rule from London by the Heath government in 1972.

5. *Op. cit.*, pp. 128ff.
6. See David Butler and Dennis Kavanagh, *The British General Election of October 1974* (London, 1975), pp. 330ff.
7. See above, pp. 270ff. and pp. 341ff.
8. See above. p. 273.
9. *Op. cit.*, p. 139.
10. See David Butler and Dennis Kavanagh, *The British General Election of 1970*, pp. 386ff.
11. See James Callaghan, *op. cit.*, pp. 451ff.
12. See my *Margaret Thatcher: A Tory and Her Party* (London, 1978) Chapter Two.
13. See James Callaghan, *op. cit., loc. cit.*
14. See David Butler and Dennis Kavanagh, *The British General Election of October 1974* (London, 1975), p. 178.
15. See Ed Moloney and Andy Pollak, *Paisley* (Dublin, 1986). This book is the first full account of Paisley from his origins in the Free Presbyterian Church to his later career as a politician. It is invaluable for the account it gives – immensely detailed – of this volcanic, powerful and complex man.
16. Ed Moloney and Andy Pollak, *op. cit.*, pp. 326ff.
17. Maynooth College was initially founded in the nineteenth century as a seminary for Roman Catholic priests. It became, further, the centre of the development of Catholic doctrine so far as it applied to politics, and its graduates were instrumental in inserting into the Constitution of the Republic of Ireland the clause which ordained and secured the predominant position of the Catholic Church in the affairs of the Republic. It thus, naturally, became, to the Unionist community of Northern Ireland, a symbol of much that they feared and detested. Over the years, however, Maynooth has become less exclusively preoccupied with ecclesiastical politics, and it is now a constituent college of the National University of Ireland.
18. Captain Lawrence Orr.
19. The Ulster Defence Association is the largest of the Protestant organizations in the province possessing a para-military wing.
20. See above, Chapter Six.
21. See Bernadette Devlin, *The Price of my Soul*, (London, 1969) *passim*.
22. See above, pp. 343ff.

23. See James Callaghan, *op. cit.*, pp. 297ff.

24. See above, pp. 313ff.

25. The policy of the government headed by Harold Wilson which was elected in 1966 was supportive of the American war effort in Vietnam. Michael Foot was perhaps the most trenchant of Labour critics of that policy. In an attempt to silence him the Prime Minister offered him the post of Home Secretary, which he turned down. By 1974, of course, the bone of contention between them had been removed and, besides, Wilson was prepared to give Foot a free hand in the reform of trade union law. His measures resulted in the greatest extension of trade union privilege ever known in the United Kingdom.

26. West German counter-intelligence unveiled a Russian spy in Brandt's private office, and the subsequent investigation concluded that the Chancellor had been woefully lax on security matters.

27. See Joe Haines, *op. cit.*, pp. 157ff.

28. See James Callaghan, *op. cit.*, p. 305.

29. The amount of literature which has been published on these negotiations is enormous. I have, however, relied mainly on Bernard Donoughue, *op. cit.*, pp. 126ff and James Callaghan, *op. cit.*, pp. 294ff.

30. Most historians would agree that the decision to seek entry to the EEC marked a dramatic reversal of centuries of British policy, which had always been based on the twin principles of command of the seas and division between the continental European powers. However, after the war, there were many in the United Kingdom who took the same view of the necessity for unity as did the French and the Germans. That is to say, unity, or a measure thereof, was regarded as indispensable to the averting of further conflict on the scale of 1914–18 and 1939–45.

31. See Uwe Kitzinger, *op. cit.*, Chapter 1. EFTA, of course, was an attempt by the United Kingdom to create the kind of free trade area most acceptable to British opinion and to British economic policy based on the United Kingdom's position as a worldwide trader. The fundamental view that the creation of EFTA represented can, at the time of writing, be seen in Margaret Thatcher's opposition to many of the integrationist measures favoured by the Western European nations.

32. It is easy to forget, now that she has won three successive general elections, how much scepticism there was in Conservative ranks about Margaret Thatcher's potential when she became Leader. See my *Thatcher: The First Term* (London 1985) Chapter 1.

33. *Ibid.* Chapter 3.

34. Philip Goodhart, *op. cit.*, p. 125.
35. See above, p. 351.
36. See above, pp. 251ff.
37. The theme of repentance was very much on Powell's mind at this time. It became a refrain in his conversation and in a number of radio and television interviews.
38. See my *Thatcher: A Tory and Her Party* (London, 1978) pp. 55ff. From 1965 onwards the Tory Leader has been chosen exclusively by MPs in the House of Commons. This, of course, represented a dramatic change from the previous method of choice by the Party grandees. Between October 1974 and April 1975 Heath believed, rightly or wrongly, that the Party in the country was more favourable to him than the Party in the Commons. He therefore desired to widen the number of those with a say in the election of Leader. But Tory MPs, having only a decade previously won the right to select their Leader, were in no mood to yield to his wishes.
39. See James Callaghan, *op. cit.*, pp. 386ff.
40. See Bernard Donoughue, *op. cit.*, pp. 86–87.
41. For the details see James Callaghan, *op. cit.*, pp. 451ff.
42. The attempt to form an alliance between the outgoing government and the Liberals under Jeremy Thorpe was doomed to failure from the start. Even together the two Parties could not produce a majority government. Moreover, the rank and file of the Liberal Party were utterly opposed to any agreement with Heath. Finally, the press and the nation generally felt that the Labour Party had won a moral victory and were therefore entitled, as the Party with most MPs, to form a government. It is instructive to compare Heath's conduct after the February election with his conduct in regard to the Conservative leadership after the October election. In both cases he manifested a dogged stubbornness, and seemed unable to grasp that authority was passing from him.
43. See above, pp. 379ff.
44. See James Callaghan, *op. cit.*, p. 454.
45. See also Ed Moloney and Andy Pollak, *op. cit.*, pp. 319ff.
46. See also *ibid.* pp. 326–7.
47. Initially, Paisley regarded himself – and called himself – an Independent Unionist. The crux of the matter was, of course, his determination to break the stranglehold which traditional upper-class Unionism had enjoyed on the politics of the province. Once Captain Terence O'Neill opened 'negotiations' with the Dublin government headed by Sean Lemass in 1965, thus arousing deep fears and suspicions in the Protestant community, Paisley's way was clear to build a power base of his own.

503

48. John Dunlop was unwilling, at this stage, formally to join James Molyneaux. However, to all intents and purposes, he was a loyal supporter of Molyneaux.
49. See Ed Moloney and Andy Pollak, op. cit., pp. 326–7.
50. See James Callaghan, *op. cit.*, pp. 529ff.

CHAPTER NINE

1. See my *Thatcher: The First Term* (London, 1985), pp. 24–5.
2. See Peter Jenkins, *op. cit.*, pp. 50ff.
3. See my *Thatcher: The First Term* (London, 1985), pp. 211ff.
4. *A House Divided* (London, 1973), *passim*.
5. See above, pp. 349–50.
6. It has frequently been a subject of irritation to Conservative Party conferences that historically not only has there been a Common Travel Area but that citizens of the Republic who migrate to the main island have been allowed to vote in British elections. However, this irritation has never been strong enough to persuade a Conservative government to change the law in either of these regards. In 1982 the Irish parliament – The Dail – passed legislation allowing British citizens living in the Republic to vote in the Republic's elections. This establishment of reciprocity, however, was no more than a gesture, for, while the Southern Irish population in the United Kingdom is substantial, the British population in the Republic is minute.
7. This is no longer the case since successive Irish governments have detached the Irish punt from its former exact equivalence of value with the pound sterling.
8. There have been many good books on this subject. One of the best is Ronan Fanning, *Independent Ireland* (Dublin, 1983).
9. See below, pp. 451ff.
10. See Garrett FitzGerald, *Towards a New Ireland* (London, 1972).
11. See my *Carrington: A Life and a Policy* (London, 1985) pp. 13 and 113.
12. Although Ian Paisley has, from time to time, vacillated on relations with Dublin, he has for the most part sternly opposed any intimate relations between Ulster and the Republic and, in general, used the Roman Catholic clause in the Republic's constitution as his principal reason for articulating the fear that a united Ireland would be inimical to the Protestant interest. Of his fourteen books perhaps the most emphatic on this subject is *Messages From the Prison Cell* (Belfast, 1969). Paisley has several times been imprisoned for

offences against public order.

13. See Ian Paisley, *An Exposition of the Epistle to the Romans* (Belfast, 1968). Paisley's pretentions in the direction of theological exegesis can also be found in a collection of transcripts of tape recordings, *This Is My Life* (Belfast, 1979).

14. Gerrymandering – the drawing of boundaries to give one section of the population an unfair electoral advantage – was practised by Unionist governments at Stormont to ensure that the Protestant community gained more seats in the Northern Ireland parliament than their numbers justified. It was universally regarded over the years by mainland politicians who took an interest in the matter to be corrupt and it ended after the introduction of direct rule in 1972. It is more than a little ironic, therefore, to find Clive Abbott commending the technique as a means of ensuring that a British government could get its way in forcing on the majority population of Northern Ireland a policy unpalatable to them.

15. Northern Ireland Housing Executive.

16. *The Irish Dimension* was the title of a White Paper published by the Heath Government in 1973 under the aegis of the then Northern Ireland Secretary, William Whitelaw (now Viscount Whitelaw). It represented the first move towards involving the government of the Republic of Ireland in the governance of Northern Ireland. For this reason it raised to fever pitch the anger and anxiety of the Unionist community first excited by the imposition of direct rule in the previous year.

17. See Max Hastings and Simon Jenkins, *The Battle for the Falklands* (London, 1983). Mr Hastings travelled with the Task Force to the South Atlantic while Mr Jenkins observed political developments in London. No praise is too high for the thoroughness and insight of their work and for the speed with which they completed it. Compliments are likewise due to their publishers, Michael Joseph, for getting the book out so quickly.

18. See my *Carrington: A Life and a Policy* (London, 1985), pp. 16ff.

19. At various times Ian Paisley has subjected James Molyneaux to vicious campaigns of denigration, though willing to work with him when it suited his purposes. Molyneaux has never shown other than dignity in response to these attacks, and Paisley has never been able to shake Molyneaux's hold on his Party.

20. See above pp. 53–4.

21. From time to time since the present troubles of Northern Ireland began in 1968 proposals have been made by some Unionists properly to close the border between Northern Ireland and what amounts to a foreign country, the Republic. At present there is free

movement between the two parts of the island without any passport checks and only sporadic security scrutiny. These proposals have invariably been resisted both by the Northern Ireland Office and by the Ministry of Defence on the grounds of their supposed impracticality. It is my own view that, though closing the border would be expensive, it would be perfectly practical.

22. During the resurgence of the Campaign for Nuclear Disarmament in the early 1980s the then Secretary of State for Defence, Michael Heseltine, as part of a high profile propaganda campaign, produced a list of leading CND figures who, he claimed, were deliberately, and because of their left-wing and Eastern European affiliations, acting in a manner prejudicial to the national security. Various threats were made to sue Heseltine for libel, but none materialised.

23. See Harold Macmillan, *The Past Masters* (London, 1974), pp. 8ff. Macmillan's book consists of a series of short reflections on past political leaders. The point he was making about the Conservative Party was that in time of trouble it was always perfectly willing to turn to unusual and unexpected Leaders for rescue. He compares the emergence of Margaret Thatcher with that of Disraeli.

24. The definitive biography is Robert Blake (now Lord Blake) *Disraeli* (London, 1966).

25. See Denis Judd, *Radical Joe* (London, 1977) pp. 238ff.

26. See the *Sunday Telegraph*, 10 October 1988.

Index

Issues with which Powell has been concerned appear under their own headings; major events and speeches in his life appear under his name.

Index

Index

Index

Index

Smith, Cyril 410
Smith, D.J.D. 40
Smith, Geoffrey 3, 20
Smith, Ian 215
Soames, Christopher 461
Social Democrat Party 358, 426, 465
Social Democratic and Labour Party
   (SDLP) 372, 373, 416, 435, 438, 447,
   448, 449, 451, 453, 455, 472, 473
social services 119, 158
Social Services: needs and means (Powell
   and Macleod) 119
socialism 108, 110, 165, 227, 279, 294, 393,
   394, 429
Sorensen, Theodore 235
South Africa 223
South Atlantic 465, 477
South Down 2, 126, 371, 418, 465, 466,
   467, 472 *see also* Down South
South Eaton Place 143, 162, 187, 251
South Georgia 62, 464
South Korea 107
Soviet Union *see* Russia
Speakership of House of Commons 200
Spearman, Mrs 252, 282
Spectator, The 5, 21, 85, 121, 191, 192,
   206, 213, 230, 239, 285, 330, 347, 357,
   359, 443
'stagflation' 336
Stalin, Joseph 75
State of Emergency 339
Statist, The 199
Steed, Dr Michael 3, 286-7, 289, 357, 360
steel 200, 213, 281
Steel, David 304, 410, 411-2, 413
sterling 149, 150, 156, 213, 218
Stirling, Patrick 105
Stock Exchange Gazette, The 166
Stonehouse, John 407-8
Stormont Parliament 327, 353, 354, 355,
   367, 370, 373, 378, 399, 408, 414, 415,
   417, 419, 433, 435, 438, 453, 455, 459
Strachan, Lt-Col Michael 68, 77-81, 82,
   84, 98, 123
strikes 155, 327, 337, 338, 341, 365, 367,
   418, 421, 472
Studlar, Dr Donley T. 290
Submarine and Seapower, The
   (Hezlet) 231
Suez Canal 131, 140, 147
Suez Canal Base 113, 131, 147
Suez Canal Company 147
Suez Canal Zone 21, 62, 89, 117, 127, 130
Suez Group 113, 117, 130, 131, 148
Suez War (1956) 131, 135, 140, 142, 145,
   146-9, 150, 152, 156, 182, 266, 293, 463
Sunday Express 236, 243

Sunday Sun, The 106
Sunday Telegraph 234-5, 445
Sunday Times 16, 49, 197, 224, 231,
   243
Swinton College Journal 202
Sybil or The Two Nations (Disraeli) 117
Sydney University 46, 50, 54, 55-6, 57, 61,
   63, 70, 121, 233

Tanzania 238
Tati, Jacques 4
taxation 153-4, 156, 157, 177, 222, 472
Taylor, Teddy 388
Territorial Army 212. 216
Thames Television 345
Thatcher, Margaret (née Roberts) 11, 205,
   214, 281, 291, 294, 370, 402, 403, 419,
   442, 443, 457, 458, 460, 476;
   declines pay increase 15; and Falklands
   War 62, 463, 464; health and welfare
   provision 119; triumphs in May 1979 145,
   367, 423, 425; and think tanks 201;
   economic programme 289; and NUM
   361; leadership campaign 398-9; replaces
   Heath 406; and devolution 409-10;
   appetite for confrontation 413; nature of
   leadership 425-6; and trade unions 426,
   429; good fortune 426, 427; and loss of
   Neave 427-8; appointment of Atkins to
   Northern Ireland Office 428, 429; and
   immigration 444; failure to tackle Ulster
   issue 450-1; and Maze hunger strikers
   454-5; dismisses members of Cabinet
   461; signs Anglo-Irish Agreement 462;
   as 'Iron Lady' 464; general election
   (1983) 465, 467; rules out role for Irish
   Republic in Ulster 469; dissolves
   parliament (1987) 472
Thesiger, Wilfred 35
Thorneycroft, Peter 26, 151, 153, 154, 156-
   9, 164, 165, 166, 169, 170, 203, 204
Thorpe, Jeremy 178, 347, 348, 410
Thucydides 41, 49, 51, 53, 54, 56, 59, 468
Time and Tide 121, 126
Times, The 3, 123, 179, 182, 232, 251-2,
   270, 286, 287, 291, 297, 301, 327, 337,
   339, 350, 365, 371, 400
Tinkler, R.M. 58
Tonypandy, Viscount 235
Tory Reform Group 151
town and country planning 100
trade unions 32, 194, 199, 212-3, 214, 222,
   289, 297, 336, 337, 342, 363, 388, 392,
   393, 421, 426, 429, 445
Trades Union Congress 337, 340-1, 365,
   421
transport 125, 192, 196, 197, 198, 200

All Pan books are available at your local bookshop or newsagent, or can be ordered direct from the publisher. Indicate the number of copies required and fill in the form below.

Send to: **CS Department, Pan Books Ltd., P.O. Box 40, Basingstoke, Hants. RG21 2YT.**

or phone: 0256 469551 (Ansaphone), quoting title, author and Credit Card number.

Please enclose a remittance* to the value of the cover price plus: 60p for the first book plus 30p per copy for each additional book ordered to a maximum charge of £2.40 to cover postage and packing.

*Payment may be made in sterling by UK personal cheque, postal order, sterling draft or international money order, made payable to Pan Books Ltd

Alternatively by Barclaycard/Access:

Card No.

Signature:

Applicable only in the UK and Republic of Ireland.

While every effort is made to keep prices low, it is sometimes necessary to increase prices at short notice. Pan Books reserve the right to show on covers and charge new retail prices which may differ from those advertised in the text or elsewhere.

NAME AND ADDRESS IN BLOCK LETTERS PLEASE:

....

Name————————————————————————————

Address————————————————————————————

————————————————————————————

————————————————————————————

————————————————————————————

3/87